Supply Market Intelligence

Series on Resource Management

Titles in the Series

Supply Market Intelligence

A Managerial Handbook for Building Sourcing Strategies

Robert Handfield

Auerbach Publications
Taylor & Francis Group
Boca Raton   New York

Published in 2006 by
Auerbach Publications
Taylor & Francis Group
6000 Broken Sound Parkway NW, Suite 300
Boca Raton, FL 33487-2742

© 2006 by Taylor & Francis Group, LLC
Auerbach is an imprint of Taylor & Francis Group

No claim to original U.S. Government works
Printed in the United States of America on acid-free paper
10 9 8 7 6 5 4 3 2 1

International Standard Book Number-10: 0-8493-2789-X (Hardcover)
International Standard Book Number-13: 978-0-8493-2789-6 (Hardcover)
Library of Congress Card Number 2005053553

Library of Congress Cataloging-in-Publication Data

Handfield, Robert B.
    Supply market intelligence : a managerial handbook for building sourcing strategies / Robert Handfield.
        p. cm.
    Includes bibliographical references and index.
    ISBN 0-8493-2789-X (alk. paper)
    1. Business logistics. 2. Business intelligence. I. Title.

HD38.5+
658.7'22--dc22   2005053553

Taylor & Francis Group
is the Academic Division of T&F Informa plc.

Visit the Taylor & Francis Web site at
http://www.taylorandfrancis.com

and the Auerbach Publications Web site at
http://www.auerbach-publications.com

Dedication

To Sandi, Simone, and Luc

Contents

Appendices

Preface

This book is intended for supply-chain executives who struggle to deal with the challenges of an uncertain supply market environment and who are tired of being whipped around by unexpected changes in customer requirements and commodity prices. Conversations with executives in several industries, but particularly those at Suncor Energy and others in the Supply Chain Resource Consortium, led me to believe that there is a better way. It will require an integrated approach to supply management that is based on solid market intelligence. These elements are not created through a simple vision; they require a lot of hard work and a focused approach backed by solid leadership. This book is an attempt to chart that course for those who seek to make the journey to supply-chain maturity.

Preface

Acknowledgments

Research is the product of many different people who work together to create new knowledge. The fact that my name is on the front of this book reflects very little about my personal contributions but rather is a statement of the fact that I was the one able to record the great work of many, many individuals who provided the raw material for this discussion. All of the research that led to the publication of this book was based on conversations and interviews with multiple individuals at different organizations in several industries: pharmaceutical, energy, electronics, third-party logistics, automotive, construction, and others. As such, it would be very difficult to cite all of the different sources that went into the thinking behind this book. However, certain individuals stand out as particularly notable contributors. The Suncor team coalesced many of the concepts that our team began working on in a series of workshops held in early 2004 in Calgary, Alberta. The people involved at these workshops included Doug Kent, Dave Minshall, Dave Balsom, Dave Redekop, Rod Haig. Tom Powers, Curtiss Riggsbee, Chris Laroque, Bill Somerville, Floyd Olson, Bryan Jackson, Rick Speers, and Glenn Smith, as well as Conrad Greer from IBM and Al Toews for Project Plato, Inc. Barb Piwek from Suncor is a truly brilliant individual, who has the insight into what it really takes to create a supply intelligence network and who has the vision to establish the processes required to create and maintain the model. The two individuals who kept everything moving, who later deployed the major process-mapping exercises in strategic sourcing, as well as continued to bombard me with input, feedback, and discussion were Kevin McCormack, chief executive officer of Supply Chain Redesign, and Wolfgang Steininger of Percipio Consulting. The work of these people was critical to this research. The efforts made by others on our team, including Vel Dhinagaravel, Mitch Javidi, Arun Gupta, Shovan Chandra, Cenk Ayabasacan, Jennifer Blackhurst, and Leslie Simmons, were instrumental to supporting the work. Many other executives at other companies associated with the Supply Chain Resource Consortium also provided input in creating the knowledge, through interaction with our faculty and students at North Carolina State University, including Sonoco, Duke Energy, Progress Energy, ChevronTexaco, Shell, Bechtel, IBM, GlaxoSmithKline, Milliken, Caterpillar, Bank of America, John Deere, General Motors, American Airlines, Menlo Worldwide, and Halliburton. The Supply Chain Resource Consortium team, especially Steve Edwards, Sandy Newville, and Susan Clark, helped to maintain the ongoing support for the infrastructure required for this type of research initiative. (Steve was the first one who mentioned to me that a book on market intelligence was really needed.) Thanks also go to Ross Harvison from Lyondell, Ron Zimmer from ConocoPhillips, and Paul Hicks from 17th Floor. Phil Priest from GSK was a particularly supportive individual for our team and provided ongoing input that helped us maintain our level of excitement. Vel Dhinagaravel from Supply Chain Redesign was a loyal student and a fantastic visionary. Danny Hughes and his team from Englehard were "true believers" in the value of supply market intelligence. Karen Weinstein, Sherry Zhao, Mike Kelly, and the team at Boston Scientific were instrumental in shaping my thoughts on applying a supply market risk framework. Kelly Wright was a fantastic editor, and this book reflects her careful reading and editing that helped make it a reasonably cohesive unit. Others who deserve recognition include Vince Messimer from Shell; Bob Monczka from CAPS: Center for Strategic Supply Research; Larry Giunipero from Florida State University; Dan Krause from Arizona State University; Jennifer Blackhurst from North Carolina State University; Don Holmm from Transalta; Sam Straight, Executive-in-Residence at North Carolina State University; Dick Alagna, Debra Elkins, and Datta Kulkarni from General Motors; Dave Nelson and Jon Stegner from Delphi; Bob Kee from Bank of America; Samir Hakooz; and, of course, my family during the writing process. Thanks to all of the others I forgot to mention. You can take your shots when you see me next ...

Chapter 1

Introduction

1.1 Chapter Outline

- What is supply market intelligence?
- Moving supply management from the tactical to strategic approach
- The profit-leverage effect of supply management
- How mature is your supply management function?
- Translating corporate objectives into supply management goals
- Bringing goals and objectives together — the strategic sourcing process
- A word on business and market intelligence (MI)
- Summary and book outline

In the Tom Cruise film *Minority Report*, the Department of Crime Prevention collected data in various fashions about crimes and murders that were going to happen. They pieced this together and then sent a special squad of experts to capture the villain before the crime had been committed. I think supply management is going to be a bit like that. We'll put together pieces of the jigsaw puzzle to determine what sort of people are needed in a special squad — suppliers or vendors — to plan a solution before it is needed or as a challenge actually arises.

— A senior supply management executive

1.2 What Is Supply Market Intelligence?

The senior executive's comment in this opening chapter provides insights into a critical need that is lacking in many organizations' competitive tool set today: the need for better decision making and strategy execution in the supply management function. During the 1980s and 1990s (and even today), many companies focused their attention on strategic sourcing, which in many cases involves simply reducing one's supply base, squeezing cost reductions out of suppliers through intense negotiations (or even worse, through reverse auctions), signing a contract, and leaving an internal customer to manage an already strained relationship with the selected supplier.

Although cost reduction may be achieved, this approach to strategic sourcing has several limitations. First, this method is a one-time "hit" rather than a planned endeavor to leverage spending opportunities from diverse business units (especially prevalent after a merger). Second, the savings may not continue and, in fact, may discourage a supplier from offering additional improvements in quality, technology, or cost savings in the future. As one executive noted, "The greatest savings take place after the ink has dried, but it requires a collaborative approach to savings and a whole different set of processes." Third, the strategic sourcing process described in the preceding text often takes place in a vacuum, without a thorough assessment of internal customer requirements, changes in the business environment, and events or changes in the supply market.

The notion of business and supply intelligence is not new. Indeed, no one knows better the importance of intelligence than the Central Intelligence Agency. White House experts have posited that the events of 9/11 could have been avoided if there had been more field agents on the ground identifying trends, discussions, and triggers that might have clued in authorities to the possibility of the disastrous events that took place that day.

In other cases, business intelligence and market intelligence (MI) are available with key people, but are not well disseminated to the users. There is tremendous value in sharing across a whole company proprietary insights into competitors, customers, products, supply market conditions, mergers, research, etc. As Lowell Bryan, an expert in this area, notes, "An individual's knowledge is self-contained, always available. But in companies, including small ones, it can be hard to exploit the valuable knowledge in the heads of even a few hundred employees, particularly if they are scattered in different directions."[1] It is even more difficult to collect information across a supply-chain network when the individuals are not located within the confines of the organization. Bryan notes that the typical approaches used to disseminate knowledge involve (a) big investments in document management services, (b) pushing knowledge to workers

---

[1] Bryan, L.L., Making a market in knowledge, *The McKinsey Quarterly*, No 3, 2004.

using large Web sites, or (c) letting organizational units solve their knowledge problems in a decentralized manner by allowing clusters of workers to share information using whatever technology solutions they prefer. Unfortunately, all three of these approaches have major downsides that make them ineffective.

Even organizations that succeed in developing supply market intelligence systems face a strategic sourcing problem: getting decision makers to apply the knowledge and use it in an effective manner. For example, in a recent book, *Secrets — the Pentagon Papers* by Daniel Ellsberg, the author noted that knowledge accrued through field agents in Vietnam was not applied in a suitable manner. Field agents were well aware of the unrest in Vietnam through discussions with villagers in hamlets, ARVN (Army of Republic of Vietnam) units, and bureaucrats. These agents knew early on that increasing the forces in Vietnam was not the solution, and that the war was in effect unwinnable. The author also demonstrates evidence that senior White House officials, including Lyndon B. Johnson, were made aware of this information through detailed reports and meetings but failed to apply the knowledge to revert to other strategies, including negotiations with Hanoi. The same rationale applies to businesses; even though the information is available, there is no guarantee that executives and managers will put it to good use.

These challenges form the basis of our effort to write a book that can assist managers in developing a supply market intelligence network and teach them to apply the collected information to successful strategic sourcing processes. This book is intended to help supply managers and company executives in any industrial section (whether it be in services, manufacturing, logistics and distribution, or others) transition from a processing approach to company spending decisions to a strategic approach. This strategic approach is largely grounded in MI and encompasses spending decisions that are both traditional and novel to the purchasing function.

The book provides a step-by-step model for a strategic, MI-based sourcing project. Although some sourcing strategy projects are initiated as a triage mechanism to reactively treat an identified spending problem, the model outlined in this book is predicated upon a sourcing strategy project that is implemented proactively as a means to develop a sustainable competitive advantage.

1.3 Moving Supply Management from the Tactical to Strategic Approach

Supply management organizations are consistently being challenged to build superior supply chains to increase competitive advantage. As supply-chain management (SCM) has matured into a recognized competency for competitive advantage, the need for supply management to contribute to competitiveness has quickly become recognized. Why? As users require greater customization of product and service offerings, the ability to do so will be a key element in the value proposition offered by the procurement function in building a stronger supply chain. How will supply management add to this competency?

In the future, there will be a greater need for integrating data systems, standardizing parts, and creating joint ventures in the procurement area. Strategic relationships will be essential to achieving these goals. Developing long-term partnerships with suppliers and maintaining those relationships will be a key value added, as teaming between buyers and suppliers will provide the opportunity to reap the fruits of a larger pie.

1.3.1 The Importance of Strategic Relationships

Developing and managing relationships is not second nature to all. In fact, MBA programs, including those of North Carolina State University, Florida State University, and others, have begun offering relationship management classes. During the courses, students go through a simulation requiring them to assess potential supplier or customer groups (made up of other students), select the partner, negotiate an agreement, and write a contract. Then, the relationship is "tested" through a one-year simulated supply and demand scenario, in which different events cause supply-chain disruptions. Students must then find creative ways of managing the tension of the relationship and thus deal with the potential conflicts that inevitably arise.

As we move further into the 21st century, supply managers will be asked to seek out new technologies and new suppliers more often and to think outside the box while continuing to ensure quality products and services. Supply managers will be required to work more strategically when evaluating suppliers and making the selection decision and will be forced to concentrate more on suppliers' strengths and capabilities and long-term quality output rather than pure yield results for upcoming quarters. Establishing solid, productive working relationships between extended business units of a corporation and their suppliers will be the driving force for accomplishing all strategic relationship goals.

The following comments from a series of roundtables in 2003[2] reflect the fact that managers feel a need to embrace strategic supply management in part by understanding the key strengths that suppliers can offer and by integrating efforts across functions within their organizations:

---

[2] Handfield, R.B. and Giunipero, L., Purchasing Education and Training II, Center for Advanced Purchasing Studies, February 2004.

■ One of the differentiating factors for us and a key to our future success is the way that we are working with those suppliers that we consider to be key suppliers — to bring them closer into the overall operation of the company, bring them much closer into the design process to leverage their resources for our design and execution of our solutions. Everyone understands what's been done to get to that target cost. If it comes down to beating up the suppliers — but still working with them to reduce cost so that we can hit target cost, they are much more amenable, because it's not just coming at them with the idea that "You need to reduce costs because we need to have it lower." They understand that we have done everything that we can and they need to look, ideally, within their supply chain. It's not a matter of taking costs out of them, but really helping them to reduce our cost so that it is a win–win for both.

■ We have to learn how to manage risk — and the only way to do that is by learning to write better contracts. We have contracts out there that are putting our organization in a very difficult situation in terms of risk — we need to think strategically and manage that risk by writing better contracts.

■ Right now supply management is just a purchasing function. There is a separate organization for logistics and a separate organization for planning. So we are not really linked together. That is another issue that prevents us from getting our product to market quickly. We are trying to get more finance people into our organization. Currently we do not have expertise to do accurate cost modeling, so we are guesstimating costs without a true understanding of the repercussions.

■ We have gone through an enormous centralization within supply chain, into one central supply-chain organization, bringing together resources that were separate within engineering and, perhaps even more significantly, all the manufacturing resources within the company.

1.3.2 Strategic Cost Reduction

In addition to strategic relationships, corporations will continue to view cost reduction as a means to maintain the bottom line and reach ever-changing company goals. A recent study of senior executives showed that not only is cost reduction important today, but looking forward, it will continue to be a major trend through the year 2010.[3] Finding ways in

---

[3] Giunipero and Handfield, CAPS Study, 2004.

both the domestic and international arenas to secure key materials at a cost that provides the company advantages in pricing, time, and delivery will become the standard by which purchasing will operate.

In today's economy, the driving force behind global competition can be summarized in a single equation:

$$Value = (quality + technology + service + cycle\ time)/price$$

Although supply management has a major impact on all of the variables in the numerator of this equation, many supply management executives are focused on the denominator, price, and its primary driver, cost. A major responsibility of purchasing is to ensure that the price paid for an item is fair and reasonable. The price paid for products and services will have a direct impact on the end customer's perception of value provided by the organization, a potential competitive advantage in the marketplace. By delivering value through continued progress in reducing costs and thereby improving profit margins and return on assets (ROA) for enterprises, purchasing is truly becoming a force of its own within the executive boardroom.

Evaluation of a supplier's cost to provide a product or service versus the actual purchase price paid is an ongoing challenge within all industries. In many situations, the need to control costs requires a focus on the costs associated with producing an item or service versus simply analyzing the price paid. Cost identification can lead to more innovative agreements on final pricing. In some cases, however, purchasing officers may not need to spend much effort understanding costs and should focus instead on whether the price is fair, given competitive market conditions.

Companies are looking more and more to their purchasing departments (sometimes called *procurement departments*) to help them achieve their competitive-advantage objectives, specifically in terms of their sourcing function — that is, the function of locating and buying products and services on behalf of the manufacturing (production) departments and production-support departments. Historically, this process has assumed somewhat of an administrative processing stance. Lately, though, people are recognizing that sourcing, well grounded in MI, is the real basis for strategic competitive advantage.

As noted earlier, MI refers to the knowledge that is possessed by the most talented employees, as well as the subject matter experts within an industry who have direct access to events that may impact supply strategy. These experts are unlikely to exchange their knowledge without a fair return for their time and energy expended putting it into a form in which it can be exchanged. The knowledge must also be filtered, codified, and expressed in a form that allows decision makers to understand the experts' thinking, without the parties necessarily having to talk to one another. Once the knowledge is exchanged, it must be integrated into the strategic sourcing process effectively, carried through to manage the ongoing relationship that exists with key suppliers into the future, and updated as appropriate.

This book is designed to walk you through a journey to supply chain maturity. This journey will develop a strategic sourcing, and relationship management process that is founded on an effective business intelligence and MI knowledge network.

1.3.3 Life-Cycle Stages

In the future, another focus of outsourcing manufacturing and acquiring companies will be to build greater competencies as a method of alleviating high financial risk.

Understanding what it means to manage a supply-chain relationship will be about more than just bringing parts in. It will be about codevelopment, resource sharing, and leveraging relationships.

Achieving the level of cost reductions required to maintain a competitive position will require more cooperation between firms to establish joint cost reduction strategies. Strategic cost management approaches will vary according to the stage of the product life cycle. Various approaches are appropriate at different product life-cycle stages. In the initial concept and development stage, purchasing will often be proactive in establishing cost targets. Target costing or target pricing is a technique developed originally in Japanese organizations in the 1980s to combat inflation of the yen against other currencies. Target pricing, quality function deployment, and technology sharing are all effective approaches to cost reduction at this stage.

As a product or service enters the design and launch stages, supplier integration, standardization, value engineering, and design for manufacturing can improve the opportunity to use standard parts and techniques, leverage volumes, and create opportunities for cost savings. During the product or service launch, purchasing will adopt more traditional cost reduction approaches, including competitive bidding, negotiation, value analysis, volume leveraging, service contracts focusing on savings, and linking longer-term pricing to extended contracts. As a product reaches its end of life, purchasing cannot ignore the potential value of environmental initiatives to remanufacture, recycle, or refurbish products that are becoming obsolete. For example, print cartridge manufacturers such as Xerox and Hewlett-Packard have developed innovative technologies that allow customers to recycle laser toner cartridges, which are subsequently refurbished and used again, eliminating landfill costs.

The major benefits of cost reduction efforts occur when purchasing is involved early in the new product development (NPD) cycle or service development cycle. When sourcing decisions are made early in the product life cycle, the full effects of a sourcing decision over the product's life can be considered. When purchasing becomes involved only later in the product development cycle, efforts to reduce costs have a minimal impact because the major decisions regarding types of materials, labor rates, and choice of suppliers have already been made. As noted by several executives:

> In the past, we allowed engineering to determine the specifications, the materials, and the supplier. In fact, the supplier had already produced the first prototype! That's when they decided to call in purchasing to develop the contract. How much leverage do you have in convincing the supplier to reduce costs when the supplier already knows they are guaranteed the business, and they have already sunk money into a fixed design and tooling for the product?
>
> We can no longer support all the resources necessary to design and implement solutions, and so we need the expertise of this key group of suppliers. Bringing them into the design process early enough so they can see the parameters of a particular piece of equipment and understand what the cost issues are, what our target pricing is and what we have to do to get that target cost can free up a great deal of creative energy from the suppliers in terms of contributing to solutions that can reduce costs.

Depending on a product's position in the portfolio matrix, a strategic focus in terms of price versus cost may be required. In general, low-value generics in a competitive market with many potential suppliers should emphasize total delivered price. There is no need to spend time conducting a detailed cost analysis for low-value items that do not produce significant returns. Greater returns can be obtained by having users order these products or services directly through supplier catalogs, procurement cards, or other E-procurement technologies. Commodities are high value products or services that also have a competitive market situation, for example, computers. These types of products and services can be sourced through traditional bidding approaches that require price analysis using market forces to "do the work" and identify a competitive price. With greater standardization being introduced in many industries, products once considered "critical" are being moved into the "commodities" quadrant, allowing further leveraging opportunities to accrue. An executive from a high tech procurement:

> There's going to be even more consortiums put together of different organizations to determine what their needs are at specific parts, for widgets or digits in an effort to get the suppliers to bid on that particular product for all of them. Even as an internal situation, we've got so many different business processes and process flow maps built for material delivery — same material, different site, different process.
>
> A product simplification task force pushes divisions to use standardized parts, even if that means a redesign. For example, a new low-end server was redesigned to accommodate the rear panel where cords connect used in PCs instead of the specialized part used in its predecessor. Eliminating the customized part saves $50 per unit on these servers — and we sell 22,500 of these machines in a year. We made a hundred such moves across the company. In the process, we have reduced inventories by a third, slashed suppliers by half, and pinched pennies at every turn. The big prize now — and the really hard work — comes from transforming the entire end-to-end operation. You cannot hope to thrive in the IT industry if you are a high-cost, slow-moving company. Supply chain is one of the new competitive battlegrounds. We are committed to being the most efficient and productive player in our industry.

Reducing costs is always an area of intense interest. Faced with global competition, companies are constantly searching for ways to reduce costs and pass the savings on to customers while preserving their profit margins and maintaining a return to shareholders. Companies often begin addressing costs by reducing their workforce. This option was used extensively during the 1980s and 1990s when many larger organizations eliminated millions of jobs in the course of corporate downsizing. To some extent, downsizing has reached its limits. Managers and workers today are required to perform more tasks and have greater responsibility with fewer resources and less time. The probability of obtaining significant cost savings through further downsizing is questionable.

Another way to reduce costs is through process reengineering. Any process contains a certain amount of non-value-added activity estimated to be as high as 80 to 90 percent of total process-cycle time. Companies such as Hewlett-Packard, Toyota, Ford, Nortel Networks, and Motorola have mapped their processes, identified significant non-value-added activities, and developed ways of reducing the time required to complete these processes.

Driving supply-chain innovation in organizations is no simple task, but in today's harsh economic environment, it may mean a company's very survival. As Charles Darwin noted, those who survive are not the smartest nor the strongest but those who are best able to adapt to change. Can your company be among the fittest and adapt? Engaging in a well-formed strategic sourcing process is a necessary step.

1.4 The Profit-Leverage Effect of Supply Management

One of the biggest opportunities for improving financial performance is by reducing the cost of goods in the supply chain. How much would you guess the average company spends on such goods and services? In manufacturing, the figure is astonishingly high: the average manufacturer spends approximately 56 cents out of every dollar of revenue on managing purchased goods and services, often in the form of inventory located in warehouses, in transit, or even on location at customer sites. In retailing, wholesaling, and high-tech industries the figure often is even higher. "Our inventory is worth its weight in gold," says one IBM manager. "Its value depletes at an average rate of three to five percent per month."

Consider the following financial information of a major retailer in the home improvement sector: pretax profit margin is 5.8 percent ($168,253/$2,915,664). This means that every dollar of sales generates a little less than 6 cents in pretax profit. Furthermore, the ROA is 2.7 percent ($168,253/$6,344,651). What strategic initiatives can help improve these figures?

Now consider another fact: every dollar saved in purchased materials increases pretax profit by a dollar. Therefore, this organization would have to generate $17 in sales to realize the same improvement to the bottom line as cutting $1 from its purchased merchandise costs. This profit-leverage effect is particularly important for low-margin businesses, such as retailing. Also note that in addition to affecting profits, cutting merchandise costs also reduces the amount of money tied up in inventory and therefore, produces a higher ROA. To illustrate these points, let us see what would happen if managers were able to cut merchandise costs by just 3 percent.

Pretax profits would increase 37 percent, and the new pretax profit margin for the company would be 7.9 percent ($231,143/$2,915,664). In comparison, marketing would have to increase sales by $1.1 billion ($62,890/5.8 percent) to have the same impact as a 3 percent reduction in merchandise costs. In addition, the new ROA would be 3.7 percent

($231,143/$6,281,761) — a full percentage point higher than the previous figure.

1.4.1 Share the Wealth — and the Cost

What will make this happen? SCM.

How difficult would it be to reduce the cost of goods by three percent? Using the strategies described in this book, it would be a lot easier than you think. Many opportunities exist to achieve dramatic cost savings far greater than the three percent figure used in the example cited — but such initiatives require vision and hard work. The greatest challenge, by far, involves getting associates in different parts of the supply chain to work together, led by the supply management function. That is because many organizations still operate in a functional-cost-center manner in which managers are rewarded for improving performance only within their own internal group.

To mitigate this risk and help drive change, some organizations have begun to develop internal supply management "consulting" groups. At Glaxo Wellcome (now GlaxoSmithKline), the supply management team included the CIO, chief procurement officer, and senior executives from the legal, manufacturing, and R&D functional groups. Although the procurement function operated as a cost center, the CEO specifically directed the group to work in a cross-functional manner to promote joint cost savings projects. The purchasing budget was allocated to drive strategic initiatives such as leveraging the company's overall purchasing volume, reducing its base of suppliers, and issuing procurement cards to capture spending data. But the savings generated by the team remained within each functional group.

Shell Oil takes a different tack; it views SCM as a cost center that operates in a consulting mode for the entire organization. The group is supported by a percentage of the savings it generates across the company, with the remainder of the savings being shared by the various functions or business units that buy into the plan. These cost savings may go toward the strategic business unit (SBU) or functional cost reduction goals set by the corporate executive team. The success of such programs has led senior management to establish an ongoing set of goals for cost savings in the supply chain on an annual basis.

An effective supply management strategy can make a big difference in organizational performance. In effect, supply management leads to:

- Improved quality, productivity, and profitability
- Reduced price/cost and improved total value from best-in-class suppliers

- Accelerated supplier technology and new product contributions ahead of competitors
- Reduced time to market and ability to meet introduction dates
- Exploiting of global sourcing opportunities and recognizing geo-political risks
- Ensuring alignment with supply markets and emerging environmental concerns

Before engaging in a major cost reduction effort, however, there is one more step required: beginning to identify your current supply management resources and capabilities. It is a good idea to understand the current "as-is" picture of your supply management processes before undertaking any major changes. Painting a picture of this relative level of maturity is a critical step in gauging how far you have to go in terms of new resources and requirements, and whether you can commit to the goals established with your CFO.

1.5 How Mature Is Your Supply Management Function?

The biggest and best enterprises already know the value of SCM. Amazon.com lives and dies by its effective supply chain; if flaws in the system slowed ordering and delivery, customers would click and shop somewhere else. The new model of SCM includes three major pillars: managing relationships, managing supply-chain material flows, and managing information. Despite all the hoopla about E-commerce, research from the Supply Chain Resource Consortium at North Carolina State University indicates that sourcing and physical distribution form the real building blocks of the next generation of supply chains. Business-technology leaders can significantly contribute to the strategic goals of their organizations by taking a hard look at the business processes that underlie the supply chain, targeting cost-saving opportunities, identifying IT solutions, and proposing investment returns that can be realistically achieved.

1.5.1 Supply-Chain Maturity

Think of the process of mapping your supply chain and business processes as a medical checkup for your bottom line. Just as a doctor studies critical measures (pulse, temperature, and blood pressure), interviews the patient to review symptoms, and identifies the location of aches and pains, managers must begin with a complete assessment of the company's physical and information flows. Before determining the system's requirements to "fix" things, you will need to determine the status of such critical supply-chain metrics as inventory levels, cycle times, customer complaints, and quality rejects. Many executives have done this successfully by figuratively stapling themselves to a customer order and interviewing all the participants they encounter along the way through the system.

In almost every project on which we have worked, this type of analysis has identified significant opportunities for improved communication among downstream customers, internal business functions, and upstream suppliers. In most cases, the lack of communication stems from a single root cause: a lack of alignment among business requirements, supplier and customer contacts, and information systems. Before embarking on an expensive supply-chain system implementation, technology executives need to clearly delineate how the system will help close these gaps.

A clear business case for improving supply-chain performance begins by assigning costs to the impact of poor communication. The diagnosis must be justified using hard metrics as well as qualitative symptoms and must include a treatment plan. Specifically, it must be established how new information systems can result in reduced inventory, improved product development cycle times, reduced material costs, reduced transaction costs, and improved customer satisfaction. At a recent supply-chain meeting at a major automotive company, one manager reported, "A senior executive stood up to share his solution to a problem we were experiencing. When he was unable to provide data to back up his solution, he was asked to come back when he had some data to share with the group!" Without translating supply-chain solutions for reducing inventory and improving cycle times into financial terms, such as economic value added, managers stand little chance of convincing senior management to invest.

Many companies today are deploying a myriad of procurement strategies, including:

■ Applying reverse auctions to all commodities
■ Applying strategic alliances with all commodities
■ Outsourcing key business processes
■ Leveraging and supply base reduction

Not all of these strategies have been successful. In fact, there is perhaps some confusion regarding how to proceed and which strategies are appropriate at what times. Clearly, there is a need to understand what makes sense, given the relative maturity of an organization's supply management processes. The reality is that many organizations are very inexperienced at SCM, and as with any technological innovation, they need to learn how to apply the new technologies and strategies.

Performance Measure	Companies with Mature Processes	Companies with Immature Processes
Profitability	13.7%	5.7%
COGS as a % of total revenue	60.7%	65.2%
Year-to-date change in COGS	-4.8%	3.0%

Figure 1.1   Performance for mature and immature companies.

Recent research[4] conducted by The Performance Measurement Group, LLC, concluded that discrete manufacturers whose supply-chain processes have a high level of maturity show 40 percent more profitability than other manufacturers in the same industry segment. Product innovation, channel management, and other factors certainly contribute to this profitability, but SCM seems to be a key factor for this improvement.

The research evaluated companies' maturity level in operations and technology and how this maturity impacted supply-chain performance. The study also explored the correlation between an organization's supply-chain maturity and its financial results. Supply-chain data from 70 companies from an original pool of over 125 were used for this study. These companies represented a range of geographic, size, and industry segments. Completeness of submission was also important in company selection. Most of the companies had a global reach and had revenue levels from $250 million to more than $1 billion.

The study results show that companies with mature processes performed better than their counterparts with less mature processes in all key areas of SCM: flexibility, responsiveness, delivery, and cost. Specifically, key metrics such as forecast accuracy and delivery performance were approximately 10 percent better in respondents with more mature processes. Further, they enjoyed a 10 to 25 percent savings in inventory-carrying costs, materials acquisition costs, and order management costs (see Figure 1.1). For example, a consumer goods company with mature processes delivered products close to one week faster, met customer requirements nearly 100 percent, and had 20 percent lower supply-chain costs. In summary, average supply-chain costs represented 9 percent of revenue for companies with mature practices, as compared with 10.7 percent for companies without mature practices.

---

[4]   http://www.prtm.com/pressreleases/2003/06.04.asp.

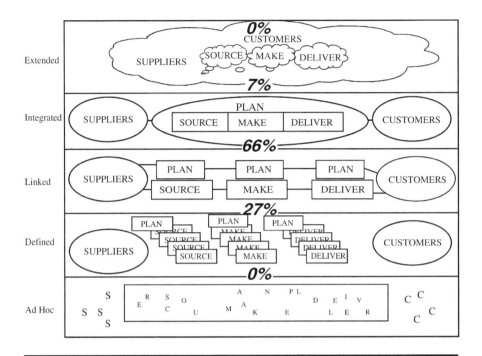

Figure 1.2   Distribution of companies at stages of supply chain maturity.

Supply Chain Redesign, LLC has obtained similar results.[5] Figure 1.2 provides a summary of the maturity levels of almost 500 medium-to-large companies, and Figure 1.3 contains a summary of some financial results for these companies. Both these large studies demonstrate that organizations that have a mature supply process perform better than others.

The Supply-Chain Maturity Model developed by Supply Chain Redesign is a theoretical and practical model based on accumulated knowledge, documented research, in-depth interviews, and observation of best practices across global organizations. It is an assessment tool that was developed to assist an organization to determine its level of maturity in various business process areas. The tool covers more than 120 distinct business processes. An organization uses this assessment tool to derive quantitative scores from qualitative information on business processes. This tool also helps to identify areas of opportunities on which companies can spend their time and efforts to improve overall business performance. An overview appears on the chart in Figure 1.4.

It is important to note that "Rome was not built in a day." Organizations typically proceed through an evolution of basic processes in supply

---

[5] Supply Chain Redesign, LLC, Raleigh, NC, 2005. www.supplychainredesign.com

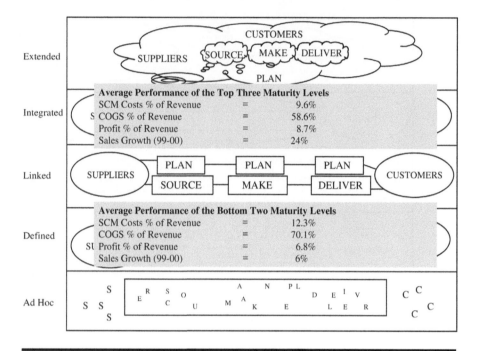

Figure 1.3   Benefits associated with improved supply chain maturity.

I - Basic Beginnings	II - Moderate Development	III - Limited Integration	IV- Integrated Supply Chains
■ Quality/cost teams ■ Longer-term contracts ■ Volume leveraging ■ Inventory and transport measurement	■ Adhoc supplier/ customer alliances ■ Cross-functional teams ■ Supplier/ Customer base optimization ■ Cross-location international teams	■ Global sourcing/ distribution ■ Define dalliances ■ Supplier development ■ Total cost of ownership ■ Parts/service standardization ■ Pull/demand flow inventory systems	■ Global supply chains with external customer focus ■ Comprehensive information visibility ■ Full service suppliers ■ Supplier Integration ■ Insourcing/ outsourcing to maximize core competencies

Figure 1.4   Stages of supply-chain strategy evolution.

management (see Figure 1.4), beginning with quality and cost teams and then moving toward cross-locational international teams and supplier reductions (as well as focusing business on key customer accounts). In later stages, global sourcing and distribution systems provide full visibility to materials throughout the supply chain, cost is managed on a systemwide basis, supplier capabilities are improved through joint efforts, and customers and suppliers are integrated into NPD efforts. Organizations may also consider which activities are not "core" to their business and decide to outsource those activities for which they are not world class.

The question of how far your organization has progressed in this maturity grid is not as important as understanding the relative baseline of where you need to go. Moreover, companies need to measure the maturity of their supply management function to set strategic priorities for training, education, and organizational development. Unless you have a baseline set of metrics, it is difficult to know where to go. One way to do this is through the assessment of the relative maturity of your company's procurement chain processes. These can vary substantially across a wide variety of business processes that are fundamentally defined for "design, plan, source, make, deliver, and sell." Through painstaking research and interviews with executives, a research team has developed a very detailed approach to measuring and defining the relative maturity of these processes, ranging from Ad Hoc to Defined, Linked, Integrated, and Extended. Each of these elements is measured at the business process level as a strategic process, a team-based process, or an operational (day-to-day) process. This model can be accessed at the following Web site: http://supplychainredesign.com.

We do not intend to go through all of the different elements of SCM shown in the full Capability Maturity Model. However, we will focus on some of the core processes associated with strategic sourcing and supply management in this book. One of our modules addresses the question of whether or not there is a process in place to manage supplier scorecards and activities such as identifying potential new suppliers, adding suppliers to preferred status, rationalizing the supply base, and developing effective sourcing strategies (shown in Figure 1.5). It is one thing to say, "Yes, we are doing that," and quite another to measure one's processes against the maturity grid shown in Figure 1.5 and Figure 1.6.

This is but a single example; there are many more. This book will provide the framework for increasing the maturity of your supply management function through the development of effective sourcing strategies.

Most companies are probably skewed toward the mid- to lower-levels of maturity, simply because it is so difficult to make significant progress. Based on our research, we have found that it normally takes organizations eight to ten years to move from left to right across all elements of the SCM maturity grid. This hypothesis can certainly be challenged. However,

	Design	Source	Make/Mfg	Market/Sell	Deliver	Service
Strategic	Customer/Supplier design collaboration	Supply base rationalization and allocations	Rationalize manufacturing/distribution network	Promotion strategy rationalization	Negotiate contracts or outsourcing partnerships	Establish Service Level Expectations and Agreements (SLAs)
	Product line/mix rationalization	Supplier Management	Capacity rationalization	Select/Rationalize sales channels	Logistics Partners planning	Select inventory stocking points
	New product requirements analysis	In/Outsourcing rationalization	Long-term expansion	Market Analysis	Rationalize Delivery Suppliers Selection	Service facilities rationalization
	DFx	Indirect materials strategy	MRO strategy	Marketing spend	Reverse Supply Chain planning	Rationalizes spares network
	Phase In/Phase Out	Supplier Selection and Contract Negotiation	Order management	Partner Products		
	Technology Roadmap			Branding		

Supplier Management – Managing supplier scorecards and activities such as identifying potential new suppliers, adding supplier stop referred vendor lists, deleting suppliers from preferred vendor list, barring suppliers, collaborating with suppliers during design process, etc. to improve the procurement processes.

1	Adhoc	• No organized process. Maverick buying is rampant. Suppliers are chosen on an As-Needed basis with possibly individual experiences or management directive weighing heavily on supplier selection.
2	Defined	• Tracks and documents supplier scorecards. • Has a policy for determining strategic sourcing, including when to add/delete suppliers from preferred supplier lists. • Uses measures such as total number of suppliers, supplier spend, % of suppliers involved in collaboration, % of supplier involved in design, etc.
3	Managed	• Measures are in place for determining optimal supplier spend, number of suppliers, etc. • Cross-functional teams are in place to create measures. • Externally, the organization is tracking suppliers to develop their score cards, understand supplier direction and its relationship to the organization's direction, improved parts, suppliers, and business processes.
4	Leveraged	• Cross-functional teams review optimal rationalization measures for alignment with organization strategy and strategic sourcing plans. • Sourcing processes incorporate rationalization. • Measures are documented, accessible, created by cross-functional teams and focused on supporting company strategy. • Externally, suppliers are evaluated based on measured performance. • Externally, the organization provides feedback and takes necessary actions.
5	Optimized	• Suppliers and customers join cross-functional teams to determine optimal rationalization. • Suppliers are empowered to work with each other to resolve potential problems including disaster recovery, capacity or delivery problems. • Information sharing about relevant criteria, such as capacity and demand forecasting, facilitates cross-enterprise decision-making. • All members of the supply chain scan for new technologies and processes to help with supplier assessment, communication or potential supplier identification.

Figure 1.5 Measuring supplier management maturity.

1	Adhoc	• No organized process. Maverick buying is rampant. Suppliers are chosen on an As-Needed basis with possibly individual experiences or management directive weighing heavily on supplier selection.
2	Defined	• Tracks and documents supplier scorecards. • Has a policy for determining strategic sourcing, including when to add/delete suppliers from preferred supplier lists. • Uses measures such as total number of suppliers, supplier spend, % of suppliers involved in collaboration, % of supplier involved in design, etc.
3	Managed	• Measures are in place for determining optimal supplier spend, number of suppliers, etc. • Cross-functional teams are in place to create measures. • Externally, the organization is tracking suppliers to develop their scorecards, understand supplier direction and its relationship to the organization's direction, improved parts, suppliers, and business processes.
4	Leveraged	• Cross-functional teams review optimal rationalization measures for alignment with organization strategy and strategic sourcing plans. • Sourcing processes incorporate rationalization. • Measures are documented, accessible, created by cross-functional teams and focused on supporting company strategy. • Externally, suppliers are evaluated based on measured performance. • Externally, the organization provides feedback and takes necessary actions.
5	Optimized	• Suppliers and customers join cross-functional teams to determine optimal rationalization. • Suppliers are empowered to work with each other to resolve potential problems including disaster recovery, capacity or delivery problems. • Information sharing about relevant criteria, such as capacity and demand forecasting, facilitates cross-enterprise decision-making. • All members of the supply chain scan for new technologies and processes to help with supplier assessment, communication or potential supplier identification.

Figure 1.6   Supplier management maturity.

if you really take a hard look at your organization's processes, benchmarking internally as well as externally with other organizations, you will have the beginnings of a baseline set of metrics for understanding how to set a vision for the future.

Why does it take so long to move the needle? Change. People do not change easily, but the faster you can drive change into your organization, the quicker you can move your organization through supply management levels of maturity, and the quicker you can achieve higher returns than your competitors. Let us begin by discussing the starting point for creating sourcing strategies: the alignment of goals with corporate objectives.

1.6 Translating Corporate Objectives into Supply Management Goals

The need for supply management to develop processes that enhance an organization's competitive position through strategic sourcing is greater than ever. From this perspective, an effective sourcing process means more than simply promising maximum efficiency or lowest cost. Given the diversity of available strategies, an effective supply management process is one that fits the needs of the business and strives for consistency between the internal capabilities and the competitive advantage being sought, as defined in the overall business strategy. The term *strategic alignment* means that supply management activities are consistent with the nature of the business strategy and make a proactive contribution to marketing effectiveness.

The concept of supply management alignment with corporate strategy makes sense — but how does it happen? Before purchasing can align with corporate strategy, supply managers must be able to translate corporate objectives into supply management goals. Goals and objectives differ across four major dimensions:

1. *Time frame:* Objectives are independent of time or open-ended, whereas goals are temporal or time phased and intended to be superseded by subsequent goals. For example, when John F. Kennedy stated that the United States was going to send a man to the moon, this was clearly an objective. When he added that it would be done "by the end of the decade," the objective became a goal.

2. *Measurement:* Quantified objectives are often stated in relative terms (i.e., with respect to another entity or organization). Goals are much more specific, stated in terms of a particular result that will be accomplished by a specified date. The objective that "we will be the top automotive company in quality" is relative to other automotive companies. The goal that "we will reduce defects to 1000 ppm" is an absolute metric, which is a goal.

3. *Specificity:* Objectives are stated in broad, general terms, whereas goals are stated in terms of a particular result that will be accomplished by a specified date. For instance, the statement, "We will be the best in customer satisfaction," is a very broad statement that is an objective. The statement, "We will reduce warranty costs by three percent on part number 333 by the third quarter," is more specific.

4. *Focus:* Objectives are often stated in some relevant external environment. Goals are internally focused and imply how resources will be utilized in the future. For instance, the statement, "We will be regarded by the public as an environmentally conscious company," is externally focused; the statement, "We will invest ten percent of our revenues in new environment-friendly technology," is internally focused and states how resources will be used.

Notice that each of these examples couples an objective with a goal. This is an important part of the strategy development process. Executives often develop very broad, sweeping statements regarding where a company is headed, what the overall mission is, and where it will be in the future. However, it is up to managers to translate these broad objectives into actionable, realizable goals.

1.6.1 Integrative Strategy Development

The process of aligning purchasing goals with corporate objectives is especially important for purchasing and supply-chain managers. These managers often face some very broad directives from corporate management, for example, to reduce costs or to improve quality. The strategy development process takes place on four levels:

1. *Corporate strategies:* These strategies are concerned with (a) the definition of businesses in which the corporation wishes to participate and (b) the acquisition and allocation of resources to these business units.
2. *Business unit strategies:* These strategies are concerned with (a) the scope or boundaries of each business and the links with corporate strategy and (b) the basis on which the business unit will achieve and maintain a competitive advantage within an industry.
3. *Supply management strategies:* These strategies, which are part of a level of strategy development called *functional strategies,* specify how purchasing will (a) support the desired competitive business-level strategy and (b) complement other functional strategies (such as marketing and operations).
4. *Commodity strategies:* These strategies specify how a group tasked with developing the strategy for the specific commodity being purchased will achieve goals that in turn will support the purchasing-, business unit-, and finally, corporate-level strategies.

Companies that are successful in deploying supply management strategies do so because the strategy development process is integrative. This means that the strategy is drafted by (or has significant input from) those people responsible for implementation. Integrative supply-chain strategies occur when corporate strategic plans are effectively "cascaded" into specific purchasing and commodity goals through a series of iterative stages in a sales and operations plan. Corporate strategy evolves from corporate objectives, which effectively evolve from a corporate mission statement drafted by the chief executive officer (CEO), functional executives, and

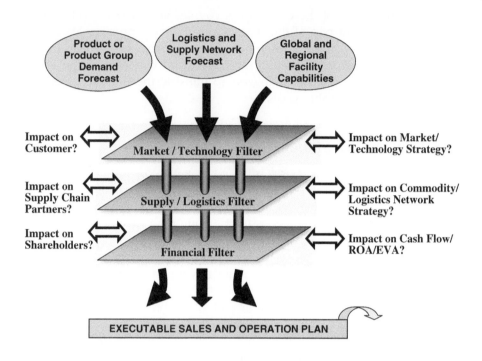

Figure 1.7   Annual sales and operations planning process.

the board of directors. The CEO, taking into consideration the organization's competitive strengths, business unit and functional capabilities, market objectives, competitive pressures, customer requirements, and macroeconomic trends, crafts corporate strategies. What distinguishes an integrative strategy development process is that business unit executives, as well as corporate purchasing executives, provide direct input during the development of corporate strategy.

A key feature of the strategy development process shown in Figure 1.7 and Figure 1.8 is the linkage, either directly or indirectly, between functional supply-chain strategy development and other functional specialties such as technology or R&D, finance, and marketing. Business unit objectives span multiple functions and provide clear directions so that all functional strategies (purchasing, marketing, operations, finance, and human resources) are aligned. This linkage recognizes the need to remove the barriers of cross-functional integration. A system that promotes integrative strategy development between functional specialties supports focusing limited corporate resources toward specific companywide objectives and performance goals.

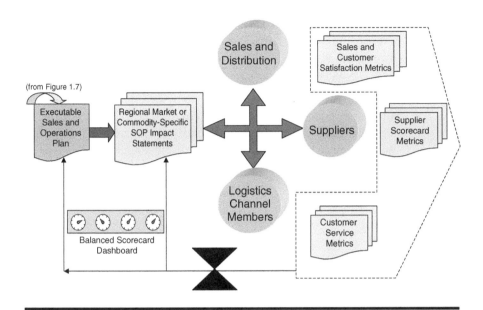

Figure 1.8 Ongoing quarterly reviews.

1.7 Bringing Goals and Objectives Together — the Strategic Sourcing Process

A major output of the strategy development process is a set of functional strategic objectives, including purchasing strategy objectives. As purchasing managers interact with other members within their business, as well as with corporate executives, a major set of strategic directives should begin to emerge. These strategic objectives may or may not provide details concerning how they are to be achieved. However, the process is not yet complete. Unless purchasing executives can effectively translate broad-level objectives into specific purchasing goals, these strategies will never be realized. Purchasing must couple each objective with a specific goal that it can measure and act upon. These specific goals become the initial step for a detailed commodity strategy formulation process. Remember: Objectives drive goals, whether at the highest levels of an organization or at the functional or department level. Examples of corporatewide purchasing goals associated with various purchasing objectives are shown in the following text:

Cost reduction objective

■ Be the low-cost producer within our industry. (Goal: Reduce material costs by 15 percent in one year.)

- Reduce the levels of inventory required to supply internal customers. (Goal: Reduce raw material inventory to 20 days' supply or less.)

Technology or NPD objective

- Outsource non-core-competency activities. (Goal: Qualify two new suppliers for all major services by end of the fiscal year.)
- Reduce product development time. (Goal: Develop a formal supplier integration process manual by the end of the fiscal year.)

Supply base reduction objective

- Reduce the number of suppliers used. (Goal: Reduce the total supply base by 30 percent over the next six months.)
- Joint-problem-solve with remaining suppliers. (Goal: Identify $300,000 in potential cost savings opportunities with two suppliers by year end.)

Supply assurance objective

- Assure uninterrupted supply from those suppliers best suited to filling specific needs. (Goal: Reduce cycle time on key parts to one week or less within six months.)

Quality objective

- Increase quality of services and products. (Goal: Reduce average defects by 200 ppm on all material receipts within one year.)

The next level of detail requires translating companywide purchasing goals into specific commodity-level goals. Although not always the case, companies often use commodity teams to develop purchasing strategies. Purchasing strategies often apply to commodities (general categories or families of purchased items). Examples of major commodity classifications across different industries include body side moldings (automotive), microprocessors (computer), steel (metalworking), cotton (apparel), wood (pulp and paper), petroleum products (chemicals), and office supplies (all industries). A commodity team is often composed of personnel from manufacturing, product design, process engineering, marketing, finance, and purchasing. The personnel involved should be familiar with the commodity being evaluated. For instance, if the team is tasked with purchasing computers, then users from information systems should be included. If the team purchases vehicles and vehicle parts, then it would be a good idea to include maintenance managers who are familiar with the characteristics of these commodities. In general, the more important the commodity, the more likely cross-functional members and user groups will be involved. Together, the commodity team will develop a commodity

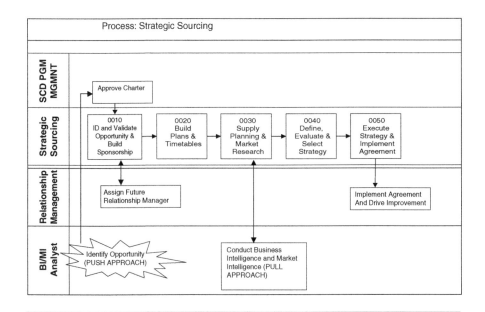

Figure 1.9 Strategic sourcing and supply market intelligence processes.

strategy that provides the specific details and outlines the actions to be followed in managing the commodity.

This book explains the major phases of developing an integrated supply management strategy that involves integrating the key elements of relationship management and supply market intelligence. As shown in Figure 1.9, this involves the steps of developing an MI network, developing a sourcing strategy, and establishing key individuals to manage the ongoing relationship with critical suppliers.

1.8 A Word on Business and Market Intelligence

Before engaging in any type of sourcing strategy, teams need to educate themselves about what is happening in the marketplace, as well as what their internal customer requirements are.

1.8.1 Step 1: Teaming, Plan Development, and Market Research

Companies are increasingly using a team approach to sourcing decision making by bringing together personnel from multiple functions who are familiar with the product to be purchased. Part of the first phase of the integrated supply management process is to identify the people who should be involved, as well as the key subject matter experts who may be part of the "extended team." It is also important to publish a project charter, define the scope of the project, and develop a work plan and communication plan. These steps help to define the purpose, boundaries, and goals of the process, identify the tasks involved, and provide a plan for communicating the results to the primary stakeholders.

Chapters 2 and 3 will address issues involved in teaming and plan development, suggest questions to be asked in determining user requirements, and introduce the steps in developing a market research plan. It will also introduce topics that should be addressed in a thorough market analysis.

1.8.2 Step 2: Strategic Analysis and Resource Commitment

The second step when developing a purchasing strategy is to fully understand the purchase requirement relative to the business unit objectives. This is typically achieved through a strategy segmentation tool known as *portfolio analysis*, the premise of which is to categorize every purchase or family of purchases into one of four categories. The results of this analysis can then be compared with the current purchasing strategy for the commodity group. Also involved in this step is a thorough supplier spend analysis to determine past expenditures for each commodity and supplier, as well as the total expenditures for the commodity as a percentage of the total.

Other tasks in this phase are to identify current and potential suppliers, determine any information technology requirements, and identify opportunities to leverage the commodity expenditures with similar commodities. A thorough discussion of the tasks involved in this step can be found in Chapters 4 through 6.

1.8.3 Step 3: Strategy Approval and Supplier Selection

The ultimate result of this step is to make supplier recommendations. Before this occurs, the commodity team should perform a supplier analysis, examining selected financial ratios, relative market power of suppliers, and strategies of the market leaders in the supplier industry. There should also be a determination of current and future volumes using forecasting techniques. Next, the team develops a profile of the sourcing strategy to be employed for the particular commodity group and reaches consensus on the strategy. The team then develops a supplier short list and views presentations from these suppliers. Finally, the suppliers are chosen that

best fit the commodity strategy to be employed, based on their performance in the supplier analysis. Chapter 7, Chapter 8, and Chapter 9 cover
issues related to strategy approval and supplier selection.

1.8.4 Step 4: Strategy Implementation and Contract Negotiation

After the sourcing strategy has been determined and suppliers have been
recommended, it is time to implement the strategy and negotiate the
contract. Effective implementation of the strategy includes establishing
tasks and timelines, assigning accountabilities and process ownership, and
ensuring adequate resources are made available to the process owners.
The strategy should also be communicated to all stakeholders, including
suppliers and internal customers, to obtain buy-in and participation.

Before entering into contract negotiations, the commodity team should
perform an analysis of market and pricing issues so that a fair price for
both parties can be agreed upon. This analysis attempts to define the
marketplace, including best price, average price, and the business unit's
price, and determines expected trends in pricing. In preparation for
negotiations, the buyer should develop a negotiation plan and an "ideal
contract." There should also be a contingency plan in case negotiations
with the recommended suppliers do not go as expected. Finally, the
negotiation is conducted, and a contract is signed. Chapter 9 discusses
these topics.

1.8.5 Step 5: Supplier Performance Measurement and Continuous Improvement

The strategic sourcing process does not end when a contract is signed
with a supplier. The buyer must continuously monitor the performance
of the sourcing strategy, as well as the supplier. The buying firm should
revisit the sourcing strategy at a predetermined interval to ensure that it
is achieving its stated objectives and may need to make modifications to the
strategy if it is not working as planned or if there are changes in the market.
The buying firm should also continuously monitor the performance of
suppliers based on predetermined and agreed-upon criteria such as quality,
delivery performance, and continuous cost improvement. And there should
be a plan in place to manage any conflicts that occur with suppliers.

As supply chains become more integrated, there has been an increasing
focus on supplier development. It is usually in the best interest of buyer
and supplier organizations to engage in supplier development to foster
mutual trust, achieve process efficiencies to bring about cost improvements,

and strengthen both firms' positions in the marketplace. Chapter 9 and Chapter 10 offer comprehensive insights.

1.9 Summary

In case you have not discovered it yet, developing an integrated supply strategy is a whole lot of work! The requirements to deploy a strategy that is effective and can capture competitive advantage rest on a critical element: people. As we noted in the opening of this chapter, supply management decisions will only succeed if they are (1) based on multiple insights from key people in the field, as well as critical secondary sources, and (2) communicated to decision makers in a form that is useful, resulting in actions that are directly tied to the insights gleaned from the information. To assist readers through achieving these objectives we have laid out the remainder of the book in the following fashion.

Function	Objective	Tactical Step	Chapter/ Appendix
Supply market intelligence	Supply market research	Opportunity identification and validation	2
		Project approval	2
		Establishing the team	3
	Plan strategy	Project plan	3
		As-is assessment	4
		Conduct research	5
	Facilitate decision making	Market forecasts	5
		External and market analyses	6
	Strategy and resource commitment	Detailed supplier evaluation and research	7
		Evaluate current and alternative strategies	8
		Understand contract formation	8

Strategic sourcing	Negotiate and select supplier	Develop relationship strategy	8
		Strategy position paper	8
		Develop requests for information (RFIs) and build negotiation strategy	9
		Negotiate	9
		Final supplier selection	9
		Form contracts	9
	Implement and promote compliance	Implement contracts	9
		Transition to relationship manager	10
Relationship management		Communicate expectations	10
	Improve supplier performance	Measure performance	10
		Resolve issues and develop supplier performance	10
Benchmarking processes	Set a vision for change	Build an organization for supply-chain excellence	11
		Benchmark supply chain processes	12, App. B, C, D, E

Chapter 11 discusses the creation of an organizational structure for SCM. A benchmarking framework is provided in Chapter 12 that will allow you to identify where your organization is in terms of supply management and supply intelligence maturity. Appendix A discusses the specific impact of managing global suppliers in China, an ever-increasing trend in today's global environment. Best practices and a set of case studies in Appendix B through Appendix D provide additional examples of strategic sourcing and supply market intelligence in action. Finally, a list of references and Web sites for additional research in supply markets is included in Appendix E.

Chapter 2

Intelligence and Opportunity

Function	Objective	Tactical Step	Chapter/ Appendix
Supply market intelligence	Supply market research	Opportunity identification and validation	2
		Project approval	2
		Establishing the team	3
		Project plan	3
		As-is assessment	4
		Supply market research	5
		Market forecasts	5
		External and market analyses	6
	Strategy and resource commitment	Detailed supplier evaluation and research	7
		Evaluate current and alternative strategies	8
		Understand contract formation	8

Function	Objective	Tactical Step	Chapter/ Appendix
Strategic sourcing	Negotiate and select supplier	Develop relationship strategy	8
		Strategy position paper	8
		Develop requests for information (RFIs) and build negotiation strategy	9
		Negotiate	9
		Final supplier selection	9
		Form contracts	9
	Implement and promote compliance	Implement contracts	9
		Transition to relationship manager	10
Relationship management		Communicate expectations	10
	Improve supplier performance	Measure performance	10
		Resolve issues and develop supplier performance	10
Benchmarking processes and driving continuous improvement		Build an organization for supply-chain excellence	11
		Benchmark performance and drive continuous improvement	12, App. B

2.1 Chapter Outline

- Business intelligence (BI) and supply market intelligence (SMI)
- The need for a dedicated BI/MI team
- The push approach to BI/MI
- Building a case for change: Identifying a trigger
- Have you spoken to your CFO about supply management recently?

■ What is an opportunity?
■ Detecting an opportunity
■ Types of opportunities
■ Acting on an opportunity
■ From opportunity to prospective project
■ Validate the opportunity and estimate the prize
■ The project proposal
■ Intelligence and opportunity checklist

> Opportunity is often difficult to recognize; we usually expect it to beckon us with beepers and billboards.
>
> **— Unknown**

> Opportunity is missed by most people because it is dressed in overalls and looks like work.
>
> **— Thomas Edison**

Getting traction to initiate change is the first and often the most difficult step in driving supply management initiatives. Randy Kesteron, founder of the Society for the Leadership of Change, notes that many organizations experience the symptoms of this disease but do not know the diagnosis. If they do know the diagnosis, they do not know how to effectively treat the problem. What is this common disease? It is a fracture in an organization's change initiatives — a broken supply management program. There is, however, an effective treatment for this disease. By engaging leaders at various levels to understand the strategic plan, the change tools, and the people skills necessary for bringing these two together, organizations can write the prescription that best treats this problem within their unique culture.

2.2 BI and SMI — A Massive Challenge for Enterprises in the Future

The current business climate has companies running leaner than ever. In supply management, people are being asked to do more with a smaller budget while still exceeding increasingly challenging cost and revenue goals. In particular, teams asked to develop strategic sourcing (SS) plans and derive increased efficiencies from their supply chains are faced with a task of the greatest scale and scope in the entire history of management decision making. Yet, with all the IT and analytic technology at an individual's disposal, one might argue that supply-chain knowledge workers can easily access critical data for improved decision making now, more than at any other time in history. The statistics, however, argue otherwise. Consider the following:[1]

- According to Gartner, in 2003 white-collar workers spent between 30 and 40 percent of their time managing documents, up from 20 percent in 1997.
- Merrill Lynch estimates that more than 85 percent of all business information exists in unstructured data, which is unaccounted for in the typical decision–support systems used by knowledge workers.
- According to market research from Outsell, Inc., office workers spend an average of 9.5 hr each week searching, gathering, and analyzing information. Moreover, nearly 60 percent of that time, or 5.5 hr a week, is spent on the Internet, at an average cost of $13,182 per worker per year.

These trends illustrate a costly and paradoxical problem facing businesses today: The explosion of unstructured information (contained in e-mails, call-center notes, newsgroups, presentations, Web pages, etc.) has created an environment in which the answer to almost any question can be found. Yet common reporting and analysis tools available to knowledge workers focus only on structured information (that might be housed in a data warehouse). This places the onus on end users in supply management to creatively search multiple internal and external repositories of information for SMI and BI, and then to collate this information and deduce the results to arrive at an answer.

This situation is shown in Figure 2.1. Typical forms of information that are required include not only internal BI elements such as demand and total company spend but also the current performance of internal business units, suppliers, internal finance budgets, quality reports, and other key pieces of data. This information is generally located in a variety of different databases that are dispersed widely across the company.

Even more difficult to obtain is the set of data required to develop supply market information (see Figure 2.2). This includes information on trends in diverse supply markets (found on Web sites and in analysts' reports), industry trends (perhaps available in various trade magazines and Web sites), pricing information on goods and commodities, financial status of specific suppliers, new technology trends, and details of mergers and acquisitions. It also includes information on the emergence of cutting-edge suppliers in diverse geographic locations, competitor strategies and

---

[1] Bassett, G., Searching without boundaries: the BI and enterprise search paradox, *DM Review*, September 2004, DMReview.com.

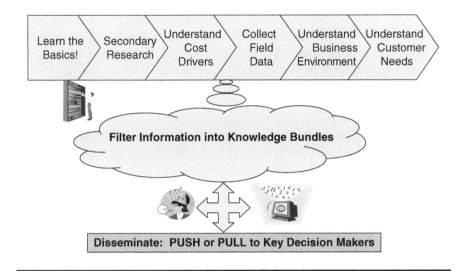

Figure 2.1   Process for building a market intelligence community.

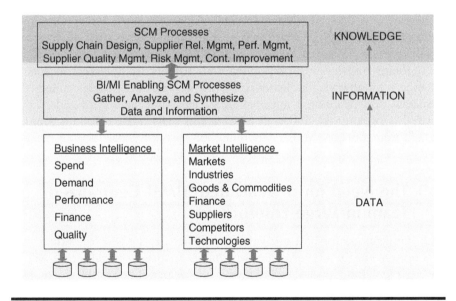

Figure 2.2   SCM enablers — data, information, and knowledge.

acquisition, technology shifts, and other forms of general and specific knowledge about industry events that have a direct impact on sourcing decisions. All this data is located in diverse and difficult-to-identify sources that must be continually scanned, read, filtered, and summarized into "packets of information." These information packets are synthesized and processed into templates that must be communicated effectively, efficiently, and in a timely manner to key decision makers involved in critical supply-chain management (SCM) processes. Only then can users apply this information to make more effective decisions.

The difficulty of capturing this information is being felt not only in the supply-chain field but also in just about every business function and every industry. To understand the magnitude of this problem, consider Table 2.1, from a recent Giga Research study, profiling the types of analytic users in a typical organization.[2] Of particular note is the right-hand column, which shows that all classes of users spend considerable amounts of time using decision-support tools and applications (BI solutions). The report highlights the fact that the vast majority of decision makers are information consumers, yet typical BI solutions are geared toward an information producer's requirement and focus on structured data alone.

All of these trends highlight the need for a new type of information retrieval that is designed for a supply manager — who is an information consumer — and which accounts for all of the potential information sources at an organization's disposal, be it a data warehouse, a document repository, or an Internet search engine. In the Giga study, Bassett notes, "What is needed is a solution that is information agnostic, yet is 'smart' enough to understand the ways in which real people ask questions (that often require some level of contextual interpretation)." Furthermore, the solution should incorporate traditional BI reporting and insight distribution concepts to provide a framework for clearly conveying and sharing insights culled from disparate and distributed information sources. Information providers who seize this opportunity and craft elegant and easy-to-use solutions stand to benefit tremendously in this continuing information explosion.

2.3 The Need for a Dedicated BI/MI Centralized Team in Large Enterprises

The implications for SMI are very clear. There is a need for a dedicated resource within every organization that is focused on gathering, sifting through, collating, and organizing data for the benefit of end users making decisions in supply management. The fact that few, if any, organizations have this function today is not a good reason not to proceed. Moreover, as argued earlier, given that an organization spends on average 40 to 60 percent of its cost of goods sold on external materials and services, it would make sense for these organizations to devote at least as much time

[2] Bassett, G., Searching without boundaries: the BI and enterprise search paradox, *DM Review,* September 2004, DMReview.com.

Table 2.1 Types of Analytic Users

Constituency	Percentage of All End Users	Percentage That Are Producers of Data/Analysis	Percentage That Are Consumers of Information	Decision Makers	Percentage of Work Time Allotted to BI Solutions
IT	2	98	2	No	15
Power user	5	84	16	No	42
Business user	25	18	82	Yes	12
Casual user	80	8	92	Yes	4
Extended enterprise user	38	3	97	Yes	2

Source: Bassett, G., Searching without boundaries: the BI and enterprise search paradox, *DM Review*, September 2004, DMReview.com.

to SMI as they do to consumer MI because supply and demand must be balanced in the supply-chain equation.

In general, companies in today's economy find that their primary source of competitive advantage lies in the unique proprietary knowledge they possess. Put simply, there is great value in sharing, across a whole company, proprietary insights into customers, competitors, products, production techniques, emerging technologies, and the like.[3] In practice, of course, companies find it far more difficult than individuals to take advantage of all this knowledge. An individual's knowledge is self-contained and is always available. But companies are discovering that it is increasingly difficult to exploit the valuable knowledge possessed by a few hundred employees, particularly if they are scattered in different locations. In large, diverse companies with complex global supply chains, the task expands to cover thousands of highly educated professionals and managers spread across a variety of specialties, locations, and countries.

Most companies have been reasonably proficient at distributing knowledge by using technology no more advanced than the telephone and fax machine. Most companies have tried one of the following three approaches to managing knowledge, with mixed success:[4]

1. "Build it and they will come" — Companies that make large investments in document management systems, shared servers, and other technology solutions believe this approach is enough to allow employees to access knowledge. The result, however, is failure. The sheer volume of documents at large companies today is overwhelming, and many of them are out of date, poorly written, or otherwise difficult to parse. Even a diligent search by a determined knowledge seeker will reveal only a handful of valuable, easy-to-access insights.

2. "Take it from the top" — Companies with large corporate staff try to push knowledge to users, often via intranets. The effort can be worthwhile when the idea is to push down best practices. However, the limitations of centrally led planning are exposed. Do people who write the documents know what knowledge seekers really want, or are they guessing? Are content producers the real experts? Do corporate staff even know who the experts are? In many cases, knowledge disseminated in this manner is not in the appropriate format and is not timely enough to be useful.

3. "Let a thousand Web sites bloom" — An approach that has been more successful is to let organizational units solve their own

[3] Bryan, L., Making a market in knowledge, *The McKinsey Quarterly*, No. 3, 2004.
[4] Ibid.

problems. This allows people working on a common set of knowledge problems and having common interests exchange ideas easily. The units, in turn, use the technology solutions they favor to develop small, specialized approaches to managing knowledge. However, this approach often produces mixed results. Often, there are expensive failures because of the parochial nature of the group. These approaches and technological tools have few common protocols or standards, and they provide a fraction of the benefits of exchanging knowledge on a companywide scale.

For companies to overcome these problems, Lowell Bryan[5] recommends several criteria be kept in mind. First, the company is the ultimate beneficiary of the effort to form and maintain a knowledge marketplace. As such, the company is responsible for rewarding authors to ensure that they are motivated to produce valuable knowledge. The trick is to provide incentives so that individuals who contribute their distinctive, valuable knowledge enjoy greater recognition and success than they would have experienced had they kept their knowledge to themselves. Thus, the company must create a culture in which employees are expected to contribute valuable codified knowledge. This requirement also means that companies must protect individual intellectual property rights. Those who develop and disseminate knowledge must be identified and credited as authors.

Dialogue is often the primary source of the knowledge exchanged in companies. However, experts in a large company may not have the time to both do their jobs as well as have discussions with persons interested in topics that have generated great interest. Therefore, a knowledge object must be made available to everyone, which means that knowledge objects may compete for attention at the level of quality and popularity. Experience shows that companies providing recognition to those who produce the highest-quality knowledge objects (as judged by experts and senior management) or the most popular ones (as measured by download volume) ensure that internal authors will be motivated to compete with others on both dimensions.

The challenge of creating an effective companywide knowledge market is daunting. It may take $20 million to $30 million in annual incremental spending to launch an initial prototype knowledge market in a large company. Most of this amount would go toward creating the knowledge services staff whose members would act as market facilitators. A cost–benefit analysis for this kind of expense would face the same subjective measurement problems that executives have with efforts to assess the impact of IT expenditures. But with U.S. companies spending trillions of

---

[5] Ibid.

dollars annually on the salaries of knowledge workers, not to mention the technology that supports them, anything that would boost their productivity by even one percent would justify the investment. In practical terms, taking the first step toward building a knowledge market requires the formation of an initial companywide market in at least one knowledge area. Our argument in this book is that SMI is a key focal area that would generate the greatest return on the investment.

2.3.1 Supply-Chain Design: The Major Consumer of BI and MI

In addition to the SS team discussed in this book, a major consumer of BI and MI is a team of people responsible for the program management of major supply-chain initiatives, which we will call the supply-chain design (SCD) team. Although this topic has been dealt with extensively in other texts, it is worthwhile to discuss it briefly.

SCD establishes the supply-chain network architecture and ensures that the components are aligned with corporate and supply-chain strategy, and that supply chains are as efficient and effective as required. The elements of SCD include:

- Annual review of supply-chain strategies and structures
- Prioritization of resources to those strategies and structures that are the most beneficial
- Annual supply-chain improvement program approved and resourced appropriately
- Project management methodologies used to implement supply-chain improvements
- Cross-functional team-sponsored improvement initiatives
- Supply-chain strategies that ensure delivery reliability, responsiveness, flexibility, and efficiency
- Forecast-based budgeting that is responsive to changes in the supply market
- Supply-chain performance benchmarked against the marketplace

As shown in Figure 2.3, SCD is, in effect, a program management activity that seeks to coordinate supply management strategies across multiple business units to ensure alignment between strategies, business unit objectives and functional business objectives. In the example shown in Figure 2.3, the maintenance and reliability group may seek to reduce their costs, improve productivity (wrench time), and reduce capital expenses associated with purchase of new equipment. The supply-chain team may be seeking to reduce contractors' prices for refurbishing equipment, reducing

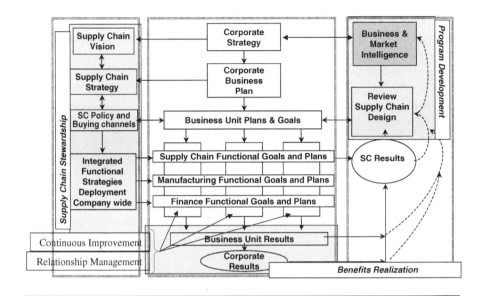

Figure 2.3   Supply-chain design.

inventories of spare parts and prices on new spare parts purchased, and improving on-time delivery of supplies. A particular business unit may simply be interested in maximizing revenue by running equipment for a high-demand product at full capacity with minimum planned maintenance activities.

Taken independently, the business-unit–level strategy, supply strategy, and maintenance strategy may not align effectively — and may imply independent decisions that may be at odds with one another. The cross-functional teams working on sourcing strategies for these efforts must work together to optimize the joint outcomes of the different strategies. The SCD group is ultimately responsible for gauging the outcome of these initiatives, rolling up results from all of the multiple initiatives underway across different business units and different sourcing teams, and reporting the findings to the corporate committee. This, in turn, may lead to a series of recommendations regarding redesign of existing supply channels, initiation of a new set of improvement projects, and sourcing teams that align with these elements and integrate key insights gleaned from the BI/MI group into the decisions that emerge.

Because of the need to coordinate internal business unit strategies, major supply-chain strategies, and different functional strategies, the BI/MI group has a core role in helping to shape corporate strategy, SCD, and supply-chain strategy. The BI/MI team serves as the major source of information regarding supply market trends, internal spending, technology trends, and other major issues that have a significant impact on the competitive outcomes. For this reason alone, every major corporation should be thinking about putting together a team of people who are dedicate their time to pursuing knowledge and information, and interpreting and disseminating it to key decision makers throughout the organization.

So, why do we not see more of these activities in organizations? For one thing, individuals who make good business market intelligence analysts are few and far between. These individuals must be proficient in market research, Internet searching, and data analysis and must also have excellent communication skills and solid business acumen — a rare combination. Unfortunately, most business analysts are very good at doing searches but may not be effective at summarizing data that is important to managers. Business managers often do not have the patience or research skills to engage in the type of "digging" that makes for a good BI analyst.

So, what would such a BI or SMI team look like, assuming that we could create such an entity? To begin with, we would need to understand the ebb and flow of information requirements of the organization. The objective of this process is to increase effectiveness, efficiencies, and risk management of other processes through improvement of intelligence accuracy, timeliness, and scope of BI and MI. The process would also be integrated with other key initiatives including SCD (the design of the supply-chain network) as well as SS. The BI/MI team would consistently gather data, analyze it, and synthesize information to provide knowledge to help improve business and process performances.

An important part of this mission is to establish an intelligence network of key subject matter experts (SMEs), both internally and across the extended enterprise, who would be consulted on a regular basis for updates. The network might consist of customers, suppliers, and external partners including research organizations, universities, contract researchers, consultants, and other entities. Eventually, this network would mature and grow into a "community of practice" to improve its own effectiveness and efficiencies and to better serve the entire company and improve business.

Within the context of the BI/MI function, knowledge can be provided either on request (pull) or proactively (push). The pull strategy requires that the BI/MI team gather data and analyze and synthesize information before the requestor (SCD or SS) actually requests knowledge (knowledge at your fingertips). In such cases, the BI/MI group may be contacted for specific information on assessing a new source of supply and identifying current market conditions on a very specific commodity group, and for detailed financial analyses of supplier health, current internal spending across multiple business units, or detailed information on pricing or cost trends. The push strategy, on the other hand, requires that the BI/MI team proactively inquire about and identify demand for knowledge and have the ability to provide it where needed. Both strategies, therefore, demand involvement of the BI/MI team not only in the early developmental stages of SCD and strategy but also during later processes.

This method consists of an "organize and analyze" process and an "establish and sustain" process. A critical success factor will be the introduction of an intelligence network consisting of the development of an intelligence portal or repository to store information and turn it into knowledge when demanded or as applicable.

An example is in order here. In the early stages of an SS effort, a cross-functional team may identify the need for MI related to a particular commodity, for example, steel. At this point in the process, the SS leader would contact the central BI/MI group and share with them their project timeline to establish the fact that the team will initiate its first meeting three months from that point and that they will need to identify key trends in pricing, market dynamics, mergers, supply conditions, etc., for steel at that particular time. Given this advance information, the BI/MI team can establish its own project plan to be able to deliver the information to the steel commodity team, thereby saving this group a lot of work in an area in which they are not particularly proficient. The BI/MI team does this type of research all the time and is, therefore, much more efficient and effective at collecting and disseminating information of this nature. This is a good example of a push application of BI/MI.

On the other hand, let us assume that the steel team developed a strategy six months ago and is now in a "sustain" mode. That is, they have established a relationship manager who is managing the current set of selected suppliers providing erected steel. Because steel is a critical commodity for this company, the BI/MI team has established a set of performance indicators designed to track the price of steel as well as market conditions. One day, a BI/MI analyst reviews her dashboard of metrics and notices a sharp spike in the price of erected steel. On further study and Internet searching, she is able to attribute the source of the spike to the recent announcement of a shutdown of a large steel mill in the Midwest that she discovers is also a major supplier of steel to the company's first-tier supplier.

The analyst immediately sends an e-mail or makes a phone call to the steel commodity team leader, who in turn contacts the key supplier to deploy contingency measures and quickly shift the burden of demand to a smaller, secondary supplier. The smaller supplier is glad to get the additional business as the commodity team has repeatedly told them (at the behest of the BI/MI analyst) that they are an important secondary source of steel for the company. In this manner, a major emergency is transformed into a minor glitch because of the proactive strategies initiated by the BI/MI analyst. The costs of establishing these types of data resources are small compared with the impact on operations that can be avoided through this investment. Let us investigate the requirements for a push and a pull BI or MI system separately.

2.4 The Push Approach to BI/MI

To effectively create BI and MI that enable SCM functions to become more effective and efficient, organizations need to develop a centralized group dedicated to the management of internal and external intelligence. This group is tasked with two major functions:

■ Advancement of financial analysis and business development expertise, i.e., BI
■ Development of market, industry, and supplier expertise, i.e., SMI or MI

The group's charter is to:

■ Enable timely access to relevant information and establish a structured approach to business, market, industry, and supplier analysis
■ Develop new skills, tools, and techniques to create knowledge
■ Design a structured approach to identifying new internal and external opportunities for SCM
■ Mitigate risk in other SCM processes

A combined and specialized BI/MI function enables the development of other core processes including the design of the supply chain and SS and relationship management (RM) strategies, which are discussed later in the book.

As shown in Figure 2.4, the BI/MI structure comprises three major phases:

1. *Monitor indicators and identify new opportunities* — continuous monitoring of predefined key SCM indicators to track patterns and identify new opportunities
2. *Validate and identify SCD opportunities* — involvement of the BI/MI lead in the early stages of program or initiative developments; effective and efficient data analysis, information synthesis, knowledge development, continuous internal improvements, and identification of new internal and external opportunities for SCM
3. *Execute approved SCD opportunities* — effective and efficient data analysis, information synthesis, knowledge development, continuous internal improvements, and identification of new internal and external opportunities for SCM

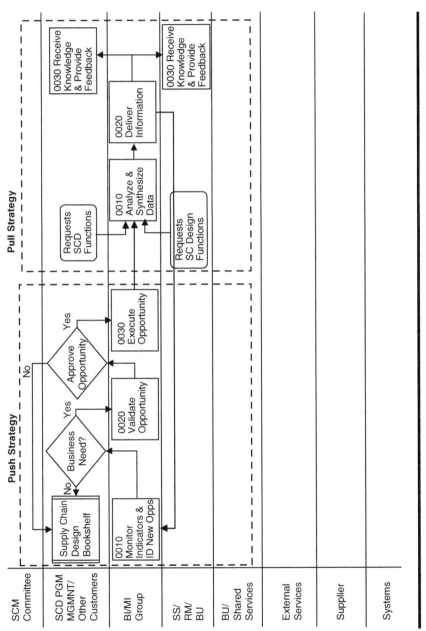

Figure 2.4   Business/market intelligence: overview of push and pull strategy.

The activities for this process are initiated and driven by the BI/MI team lead. The network of relationships between internal and external experts will build the foundation for an intelligence network. The processes associated with executing a push or pull BI/MI strategy are shown in Figure 2.5 through Figure 2.7 and are self-explanatory in terms of their scope. However, one of the biggest challenges associated with this process involves understanding how and where to look for information. How does one go about identifying the types of information required and where it can be found?

A useful approach at this stage is to establish a statement of work (SOW) document and a project plan for collecting information. A good example of an SOW is illustrated below:

SOW for Data Collection and Analysis in Push BI/MI Strategy

Assumptions: The team will be able to access data and information, technologies, techniques, and capable personnel. There will be predefined key indicators established through discussion with internal customers. The team will have the required experience, training and development, a retention strategy, and a big-picture approach, and will be focused on identifying key trends.

Purpose: Identify new opportunities.

Scope: Perform analysis of internal and external data and information using BI/MI technologies, techniques, and tools.

Internally: Business and financial analysis (e.g., analysis of spend-and-demand profile).

Externally: STEP (sociological, technological, economical, political) analysis, e.g., commodities, industries, labor costs, currencies, markets, costs and cost drivers, and competitors.

Responsibilities:

Lead: BI/MI team facilitates analysis by using BI/MI technologies, techniques, and tools.

Shared services: Provides input and participates if required.

External services: Provides input and participates if required.

Customer: Provides input and participates if required.

Supplier: Provides input and participates if required.

Systems, tools and examples: Financial, market, and business analysis tools, brainstorming, presentations by key speakers, interviews with key subject matter experts SMEs, corporate growth plans, ERP and legacy database analysis, scenario planning, what-if analysis, tracking tools and techniques, and trending technologies and techniques.

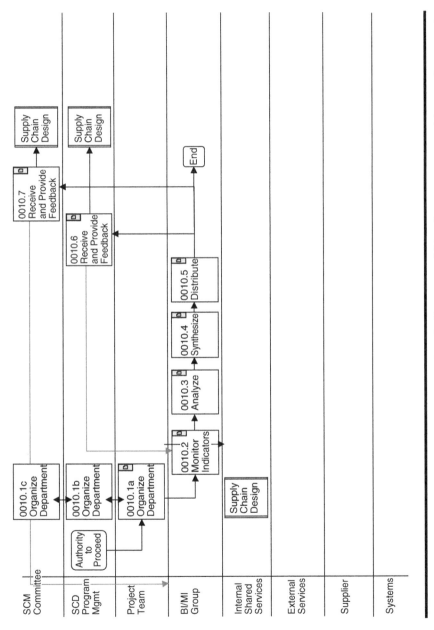

Figure 2.5   Business/market intelligence: monitor indicators and identify new opportunities (push strategy).

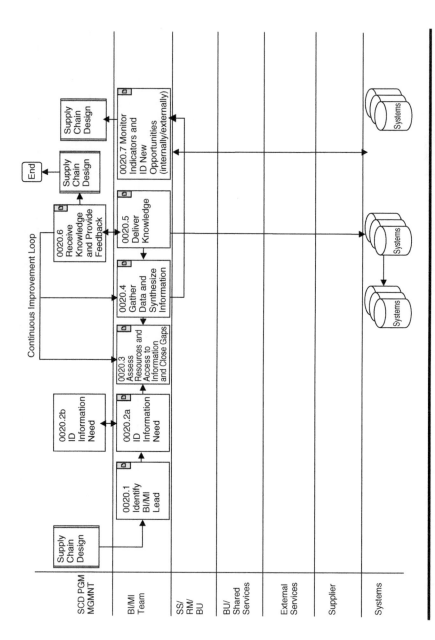

Figure 2.6 Business/market intelligence: validate and identify SCD opportunities (pull strategy).

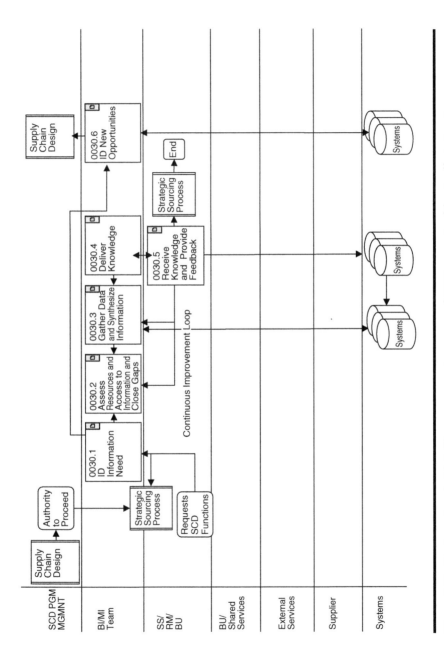

Figure 2.7 Business/market intelligence: execute approved SCD opportunities (pull strategy).

In this SOW, note that diverse approaches are used to collect the data, compact it into information bundles, and identify methods and technologies to disseminate it. Although this work can be done by an SS team, our research indicates that developing a thorough picture of the BI/MI environment can take up to six months or more. If an organization is focused on speed of execution of supply management strategies, it makes sense to improve processes as quickly as possible to deploy more sourcing strategies and deliver cost savings, value, and performance to the bottom line more quickly than competitors. It is this fundamental value proposition that merits establishing a dedicated BI/MI team with the acquired skills, knowledge, and training to effectively deliver knowledge and trends to the right people as and when required, using both push and pull strategies.

2.5 Building a Case for Change: Identifying a Trigger

Most companies, even those without a formal supply management program, experience the fractured change initiatives "disease" at some point. Even in environments in which the CEO does not encourage the use of SCM, the symptoms exist because employees use substandard techniques in an attempt to improve existing processes. These companies actually run a risk of suffering symptoms more severe than those with a formal plan.

So, what are the symptoms? They may vary with environment but are a good starting point for triggering discussions on how to address change. The symptoms could be

1. Separate change initiatives run independently of one another, often prompting infighting among the various camps; for example, purchasing and operations battle over projects and resources.
2. The supply-chain strategy is not aligned to the strategic plan; therefore, the change initiatives in the process are not relevant to the company's strategic action plans.
3. Employees complain that they want to be involved in strategy deployment and improvement initiatives, but because they do not understand the strategy, they do not feel that they are a part of the plans for change.
4. People complain that the CEO is not supportive of their initiatives.
5. Individuals are trained in the change tools but do not understand the soft (people) skills for getting others on board. They meet with resistance and cannot overcome employees' fear of change.

Are the following scenarios familiar?

■ Susan attended an SS training program, and she did quite well. She returned to work armed with a portfolio analysis tool and a solid understanding of the principles; however, her first project floundered because she did not have the skills necessary to establish a financial business case for the project that would satisfy the finance team with budget authority.
■ Bob was excited to be involved in the new SS initiative, but his group encountered difficulty in selecting a project. They complained in their meetings that they needed more direction from the top.
■ John, the new CEO of XYZ Company, sits in on a project review. As he listens to the reports, he realizes that the current improvement projects in supply management are not of strategic importance to the company and will have little, if any, impact on the bottom line.

There are many other signs of trouble that may appear.

2.6 Have You Spoken to Your CFO about Supply Management Recently?

These problems often arise because of the fact that many companies in the United States do not perform the task of strategic supply planning well. The result is often a limited focus on functional purchasing activities with minimal or no linkages to the corporate strategic plan. In some cases, the purchasing department's limited understanding or awareness of companywide strategies causes this. In other cases, purchasing has not been included in the strategy development process. Perhaps the greatest problem is that executive management fails to recognize the importance and contribution of the supply-base management and, therefore, has not focused on linking purchasing and corporate strategy. Without executive commitment to purchasing involvement in corporate strategy development, SS results are unlikely to be successful.

So, how do you initiate the process? Begin by getting your chief financial officer (CFO) on board. Why do you need the CFO? Because as you move forward with initiating supply management strategies, you will need to

1. Spend money on resources initially, including assessment of your current processes, data collection, market research, training, and people.

2. Validate the savings achieved by supply management and drive them to the bottom line.
3. Sustain the initiative by making presentations to senior executives who support the move toward integrating supply management function with other functional groups in the supply chain, including marketing, research and development, and accounting.

The individual who can ensure that all of this will happen is the CFO, so you need to begin by convincing this person that you need to work together.

A recent study[6] conducted by Accenture, Stanford, and INSEAD found that 89 percent of senior executives at leading companies viewed supply chains as being critical or very important to their company and industry, and 89 percent also agreed that investments in supply-chain capabilities have increased in the last three years. Further, the nine percent of companies identified as leaders in SCM were found to demonstrate significantly higher financial performance than the lagging companies. Some of the most important financial metrics impacted by SCM included cost reductions, enhancing revenue, and reducing working capital.

CFOs are especially interested in SCM. Driven by cost-cutting needs and general dissatisfaction with supply-chain performance, CFOs are adding SCM to the financial levers they already control. They see this activity as integral to meeting their strategic goals and view the supply chain as having a large or very important influence on their ability to achieve corporate objectives. Above all, CFOs consider reducing operating costs as a key goal of their supply chain, with improving customer service coming a close second. This suggests that CFOs are not just interested in financial rigor, but also appreciate the importance of customer RM to the future of their organizations.

According to a survey,[7] 34 percent of CFOs have assumed more of a leadership role in SCM, and 49 percent believe that they will be playing such a role in two years. And CFOs see themselves as suited to the task; they wield significant corporate power, yet have no ax to grind in a supply-chain sense because they are not bound by the traditional political and organizational ties that anchor this discipline within companies. CFOs can bring "a certain degree of coherence to what may be a fragmented reporting structure," said Gene Long, president of UPS Consulting. Because

---

[6] A Global Study of Supply Chain Leadership and Its Impact on Business Performance, Accenture and INSEAD, White paper, 2003.

[7] Developed jointly with Atlanta-based UPS Consulting, the survey titled "CFOs and the Supply Chain" was carried out by CFO Research Services. Reported in "Paying Attention" Chief financial officers get involved in managing more supply chains Traffic World, 09-02-03.

they are already charged with managing cash and capital allocations, in a supply-chain sense they "probably are in a critical position to be able to manage the trade-offs that should be made," he added. Also, he said that CFOs are adept at quantifying value, which is something from which SCM can benefit. In many cases this is already happening — 20 percent of respondents said that senior supply-chain professionals already reported to the CFO, and the survey indicates that this trend will become more widespread, enabling financial executives to take a more proactive role.

Historically, CFOs may have been involved in supply-chain decisions, "but not on a level where decision making is quick and decisive," said Long. Moreover, the survey shows that CFOs regard improving supply-chain performance as crucial to the future of their companies. Seventy-six percent see reducing logistics and distribution costs as important, and 75 percent see increasing the number of "perfect orders" as important. (*Perfect orders* are those delivered to the right customer in the right quantity at the right time.) At the same time, they are not naive about the obstacles to major change. For example, individuals such as plant managers and purchasing managers are often unwilling to relinquish power as part of efforts to centralize decision making. Also, respondents acknowledged that breaking long-established ties with trading partners was not easy.

What does this mean for supply managers? Clearly, you need to get CFOs on your side and approach them about working together to link financial metrics with supply management strategies. Doing so can improve your prospects for career development and allow you to drive home the benefits and validate the savings. Also, you need to create a "win–win" scenario: CFOs can learn from supply-chain professionals as well. With continued pressure on these individuals to cut costs, it is unlikely that this interest in working together will disappear anytime soon.

Once you have gotten the CFO's attention, how do you get started? The first step is to establish some tangible cost reduction goals for supply management that you believe are reasonable and can be achieved within the next six months.

2.6.1 Making the Business Case Argument for Supply Management

In the manufacturing sector, more than 50 percent of operating budgets — in fact, about $0.56 on the dollar — goes to outsourced goods and services. Developing sourcing strategies can help reduce this figure. Better yet, every dollar saved in purchased materials increases the company's pretax profit by a dollar.

Lucent Technologies crafted a more strategic spend analysis that was synergistically linked to production and new product development (NPD)

Table 2.2 Case Study: Lowe's Home Improvement

Lowe's pretax profit margin equates to 5.8 percent, so that for each dollar in sales, nearly 6 cents is line-itemed for pretax profit. Their ROA (return on assets) was 2.7 percent. To improve their bottom line, Lowe's could run with either increasing sales or optimizing costs as their primary profit driver or strategy. Because every dollar saved in purchased materials increases pretax profit by a dollar, Lowe's would have to generate about $17 in sales to make the same improvement to the bottom line. To impact the bottom line through increased sales, they would need to bring in an extra $17 in extra sales revenues, which could also be achieved through saving $1 in supply costs — keep in mind, that this is in terms of total cost and not just in purchase price tags. Nevertheless, this profit leverage effect is extremely significant, especially for low-margin businesses such as retail. Also, total costing is less fickle and is dependant upon the health of the current economy. If Lowe's relied on increasing sales (either by a price hike or by trying to reach out for a larger, or more frequent, customer base) for their competitive strategy, it would work better in times of economic expansion and would not be effective in times of recession or depression. Of course, the same could be said about the purchase price of the products that your company buys. But remember, we are talking about supply in terms of total costs, of which purchase price is but one factor. Note that by optimizing or reducing total costs, you not only increase profits but also reduce the amount of money tied up in inventory, which would result in a higher ROA.

activities. In the first year of its implementation, they saved fifteen percent on component costs. This was a significant increase from their previous year's nine percent cost savings. Read the case study in Table 2.2 for another perspective.

2.7 What Is an Opportunity?

Every project begins with an *opportunity*. An opportunity, as used in this book, is a reasonable possibility of adding more value to a specific procurement activity. Therefore, a prospective *value* — which comes in three flavors: time, money, and quality — really drives a prospective opportunity for a sourcing initiative. Because of this, a manifested opportunity is sometimes described as the *win*, or the *prize*. It is interesting to note that these values mirror other business fundamentals: constraints and competitive advantages. These value drivers can be described as the driver triumvirate (see Table 2.3). Every initiative struggles with the distribution of resources among these inherently competing constraints. Similarly, every competitive advantage reflects these components. In the supply management arena, the value that drives an opportunity must be such that it

Table 2.3   The Value Driver Triumvirate

Time
Money
Quality

Table 2.4   Linkage Sourcing Contribution to Value

Constraint	Objective	Net Benefit
Money	Cost reduction	Lower supplier prices Leveraging of supplier capabilities Exploiting supplier ideas for cost savings
Time	Time efficiency	Quicker time to market Lower inventory Improved throughput Improved responsiveness
Quality	Quality enhancement	Lower warranty costs Improved operational efficiencies Lower maintenance costs Improved customer satisfaction Increased revenues

translates to the company's bottom line, whether directly or indirectly, to effectively fuel the opportunity.

Time, as it relates to sourcing, can offer direct or indirect benefits to the corporate bottom line, depending on the particular circumstances. It connotes speed-to-market strategies. These strategies could pertain to life-cycling in the product design stage or to inventory or shipping and receiving operations.

Money-based value drivers are most representative of purchasing's historical reason for being: to reduce the company's costs. This value driver is critical for boosting company profit margins, implementing lowered product pricing as a competitive-advantage strategy, or ideally, both. When used as part of a competitive strategy, this driver indirectly benefits the company's bottom line. Normally, though, its intended function is more straightforward and directly impacts the company's bottom line.

The final driver in the value triumvirate is quality. This is usually intertwined with a competitive-advantage strategy and represents another indirect impact on the company's bottom line.

Many opportunities that become sourcing projects contain some combination of these value drivers, but tend to be predominantly driven by one of them (see Table 2.4).

Besides assessing value, opportunities can also be qualitatively characterized in other respects. Opportunity's scope can be broad (for example,

Table 2.5 Opportunity Detection Triggers

Trigger Type	Trigger Subtype	Examples
Reactive	Troubleshooting triggers	Unplanned plant shutdowns Abnormally high volume of customer complaints
Proactive	Maintenance triggers	SKU analysis or leveraging Technology (every five years)
	Best practice triggers	Centralizing spend-data IT systems Migrating to a data mart system Recruiting strategic sourcing managers Establishing a maintenance project schedule
	Special-needs triggers	Mergers New product development (NPD)

to find ways to reduce customer complaints) or relatively narrow (for example, to come up with leveraging solutions for a commodity). Some opportunities are predominantly product driven (as in the leveraging example); others are more process driven (for example, devising expedited speed-to-market strategies).

2.8 Detecting an Opportunity

Opportunities can be detected in any number of ways and from anywhere within the organization, but they tend to be detected in response to specific and tangible red flags, or triggers. Triggers can be either proactive or reactive, as shown in Table 2.5. One trigger can be framed in terms of reactively solving a problem; that is, it has a problem-resolution or troubleshooting focus. Any unexpected supply disruptions, such as a project cost overrun or an unanticipated plant shutdown, can be included in this category. A sourcing strategy is important for better preparation should similar circumstances occur again in the future.

Another trigger might aim to make what is acceptable better, and so reflect a proactive quality, having a competitive-advantage focus. Relevant scenarios that come to mind include NPD initiatives and the attempted combination of two merging organizations' purchasing IT systems.

Proactive triggers can be further subdivided into the following functional categories: maintenance, best practice, and special needs. Maintenance-oriented opportunities are critical for keeping ahead of the game on known problem areas. It is similar to getting the oil changed in your

Table 2.6   Maturity Model Tip

If you have trouble presenting opportunities appropriately, the maturity model might help you in preparing a business case argument for initiating best practice sourcing projects. The maturity model is a tool I devised for my consulting work. It is a form that is specifically designed for assessing the strategic capabilities, or the relative maturity, of a company's sourcing operations. You can download maturity model questions from my Web site at http://www.supplychainredesign.com/.

car. You skip the maintenance for a while without any discernible impact to your car's performance. But after some time, the car's performance will be handicapped. Best practice implies dutifully performing the 30,000- and 60,000-mi checkups that enable top performance. Special needs apply to specific, irregular situations that demand attention, which is similar to getting the car ready for a camping trip by making sure the tire pressure is optimum and attaching the minicarrier for loading up all your camping gear.

An opportunity can be fairly elusive, and may be merely a gut feeling that some better remedy surely exists and should be pursued. Or an opportunity could spring from part of someone's overall knowledge (giving meaning to the phrase "knowledge capital"). This scenario can be illustrated by a site-level purchasing manager's general recognition that best practice sourcing strategies have outpaced the company's actual practices. For more, see the tip in Table 2.6.

Opportunities can be first perceived at any level by anyone on the organizational chart. A senior executive, a department manager at a given site, or a staffer — any of these people could be the first to detect an opportunity. An executive might discern opportunities after reviewing internal status reports. The company's year-end organizationwide spend analysis offers a likely example: A CFO or a chief procurement officer reviews the data and discovers six commodities, say, with unexpectedly high levels of spend, indicating cost hemorrhaging. Or a production operator or customer service representative in order fulfillment might be the first to identify a problem or a solution when an opportunity exists. The operator and representative may not think of it in terms of opportunity or even of sourcing, or SCM, but they are aware that it exists.

2.8.1   Consult with Key Suppliers

Many companies also consult with key suppliers to identify opportunities. This is particularly true in the case of new products and new technologies in which a supplier may be an expert. Outside suppliers provide materials

None	"White Box"	"Gray Box"	"Black Box"
No supplier involvement. Supplier "makes to print."	Informal supplier integration. Buyer "consults" with supplier on buyer's design.	Formalized supplier integration. Joint development activity between buyer and supplier.	Design is primarily supplier driven, based on buyer's performance specifications.

Increasing Supplier Responsibility

Figure 2.8   Supplier integration.

and services that contribute to a major part of the cost of many new products. In addition, suppliers may provide innovative or new products or process technologies that are critical to the development effort. The supplier may have better information or greater expertise regarding these technologies than the buying-company design personnel. Supplier input or their active involvement may be sought at any point in the development process (see Figure 2.8).

Although the concept and design engineering phases of NPD incur a relatively small portion of the total product development costs, these two activities commit, or "lock in," as much as 80 percent of the total cost of the product. Decisions made early in the design process have a significant impact on the resulting product quality, cycle time, and cost. As the development process continues, it becomes increasingly difficult and costly to make design changes. It is crucial, then, for firms to gather as much product, process, and technical expertise as possible early in the development process. In addition, companies whose development plans are well aligned with those of their key suppliers can shorten overall development time.

2.8.2 Develop Preliminary Demand Profile

Discussions with marketing to identify future product-planning scenarios can be another important source of opportunities. Opportunities may arise in answering the following questions. What technologies will become important? What regions are forecast to generate the highest sales? Which parts of the business are growing and which are shrinking? Through open discussions with marketing, a sense of the growth opportunities and potential for savings can be identified.

Executive team decisions may also be underway regarding outsourcing of current or future process technologies. For example, many pharmaceutical companies are looking at outsourcing manufacturing to third-party suppliers or, in other cases, outsourcing clinical and preclinical trials to providers such as Cardinal Health and others. Senior executives formalize the insourcing or outsourcing technology strategy and communicate it to the concerned divisions, that are then responsible for establishing current and future new-product requirements. The process of cascading the decision to the next organizational decision-making level is achieved through a variety of means.

2.9 Types of Opportunities

In the past, supply transactions were conducted as a reactive, administrative processing task. Now, senior executives are looking at the supply management function with fresh eyes, accurately viewing it more in terms of its strategic possibilities of helping the company achieve its competitive-advantage objectives in the marketplace.

2.9.1 Company-Level Opportunities

The company's enhanced focus on supply management is in response to two challenges that are staring them in the face: customer demand and globalization. Cost reduction opportunities can be identified in both areas.

2.9.2 Customer Demand

Customer demand (that is, the customers' expectations about a product's quality, price, and delivery speed), spurred by Internet access, which enables customers to efficiently compare products and suppliers, has become highly sophisticated. This evolution in customer demand has fundamentally transformed the commercial landscape from a cozy seller's market to a tough buyer's market. A few of the potential opportunity areas include

■ NPD
■ Product line additions and extensions

- Customer service
- Distribution channels
- Shipping methods and expectation

In sum, not only are customers now more demanding, but their choice of companies (all of whom are trying to woo the customer) has been thrown wide open. By identifying clear opportunities, you can answer that call.

2.9.3 Department-Level Opportunities

Transforming the supply management function from a quasi-administrative role into a strategic force will require much more than an expanded content knowledge base or a few select project initiatives, such as cost audits or delivery speed solutions. At its pinnacle, the transformation will fundamentally alter the meaning of "business as usual," not only within the supply management departments but also across the entire company, and beyond.

As a matter of strategy, most supply managers will identify the need to centralize the supplier base and proportionately reduce the number of suppliers that they use. Supplier identification, tracking, and evaluation will be key in this move. Just as centralizing the supplier base is a crucial supply strategy, so too is centralizing all of the company's internal-supply–relevant members and actions, with the supply management departments (purchasing, inventory, and logistics) at the leadership helm. In the end this will effectively reallocate the decision-making power from the production and production-support managers to the supply managers. To be fully effective, this reallocation will entail nothing short of a major restructuring endeavor. Currently, most supply-chain organizations are structured as functional silos, commonly in the form of distinct cost centers, in which managers are rewarded only for those improvements transacted within their own group domain.

From a production and a production-support–manager perspective, this restructuring presents two readily foreseeable tensions: a parting of ways with some suppliers and a surrender of some supply-related decision-making authority. The transformation will necessitate deft RM skills (and may require training development in this area) to successfully navigate this tightrope-balancing act.

2.10 Acting on an Opportunity

As we all know, detecting an opportunity alone is not enough. Once a supply management opportunity is uncovered, it must be acted upon.

Employees should be encouraged to express their thoughts on sourcing problems and solutions, as discussed earlier in the chapter. Once detected opportunities have been captured from all corners of the company, management ought to be ready with a strategy in place to target selected ideas.

2.11 From Opportunity to Prospective Project

Let us say we have a specific opportunity that has been identified. Who should be our point of contact? And what should we say?

Some opportunities do not need full-blown projects; they can be considered and implemented much more directly. But we are interested in the opportunities that have very high returns and do warrant project follow-through. A proposed opportunity that evolves into an actual project faces, and passes, three functional levels of review within the screening process. First, the preliminary merit review takes place at the point of opportunity detection if it happens to be below the senior executive level. Opportunity ideas detected at the departmental level should be funneled to the company's SS group or BI/MI team.

Second, merit verification review, which is always centralized, is transacted at the headquarters. The review may be conducted by a sourcing council (more on this subject later) or the CPO. The reviewing entity will assess the proposal pitch on its merits: how big the "prize" is and what the opportunity is likely to offer. A sufficient prize might be a 5 percent cost reduction.

From there, the last step in the screening process is a feasibility review. As a general guideline, these review processes should ensure specific quantity or quality levels that will be achieved should the project move forward. Absolute precision is, of course, not the goal. A running record of declined or tabled opportunities should be filed and archived for future reference.

The executives who authorize the project, the *project co-sponsors*, are the CPO and CFO, or a sourcing council. The project sponsor should formalize the project by documenting it in a project proposal packet.

2.11.1 SS Managers

A number of companies have adopted the best practice strategy of recruiting for new positions. These positions tend to go by the title "sourcing strategy managers" and make up a separate group within the purchasing department at the corporate level: the sourcing strategy group. These managers are usually recruited externally and have expertise in advanced sourcing strategies, with a proven track record of successfully creating and deploying sourcing strategies at other companies that both reduced costs and added value to supply opportunities. They are the "prize fighters" in SS. This group reports to the CPO. Their home base is likely to be at corporate headquarters, but most of the time they will not be found there because they are extremely mobile, with perhaps 85 percent of their time spent on the road. They are the project specialists; the CPO assigns them each one project to which to provide consulting services. Often, a company might have four or five sourcing projects going on at any given time (therefore, normally around five SS managers are recruited). If this has not yet taken place at your company, then it in itself may serve as a worthwhile SS project.

The external hires should have a wide range of abilities including communication, project management, leadership, sales, finance, negotiation, contracting, engineering, and database skills. Perhaps one of the most important traits, sales ability, does not mean proficiency in selling products, but a track record of selling concepts and strategies to company executives and staff in other departments, as well as suppliers. These managers should have extensive experience in achieving cooperative buy-ins at multiple levels. These sourcing strategy managers do not specialize by product line or commodity; they are process specialists, perpetually moving from one sourcing project to another.

In communicating a chosen opportunity idea up the ladder to an executive team, a sourcing strategy manager will describe the opportunity, the trigger argument, any ideas for potential solutions, and any supporting data that might be available at this level. This might involve a bit of preliminary research to further quantify and substantiate the opportunity's prize. For instance, it might be useful to look at what other companies have done in similar circumstances for a particular project pitch to craft some benchmarking analyses. Even gathering competitive product prices can be helpful. In drawing up the proposal's business case argument, the proffered prize should be made as specific and attainable as possible.

2.12 Validate the Opportunity and Estimate the Prize

Once it is clear that an opportunity exists, the next job is to convince the CFO and other decision makers to draw the same conclusion. This may involve a series of actions, including, but not limited to, the following:

■ Work with IT to collect high-level spend data across business units.
■ Estimate the number of suppliers currently used, identify groups of similar purchases, and prioritize different business expenditures based on the monetary size of each spend.

- Identify price trends in the marketplace and key cost drivers.
- Visit sites currently purchasing the commodity or service and interview key SMEs to understand the rationale in using current suppliers, key business needs, major areas of opportunity or dissatisfaction with current suppliers, and capabilities of current suppliers.
- Estimate potential savings based on input. Generally speaking, for commodities that have never been through an SS process, five percent cost savings is a realizable goal.
- Summarize potential savings through analysis of data spend and consider risks and barriers.

Using all of this collected data, develop a short white paper, budget, and presentation to summarize the opportunity. The white paper will serve as a project proposal.

2.13 The Project Proposal

The project start-up materials should include the statement of charter (SOC), the project budget created by corporate finance (payroll allocation and travel), and any ancillary documents. For example, if a project is commodity specific and aimed at reducing costs, then ancillary documents should probably include an extract of the commodity-relevant data from the global spend analysis. Note that in terms of best practice, all sourcing projects should describe the opportunity in a holistic manner. All documents should be signed by the CFO.

2.13.1 Statement of Charter

The first order of business is for the project sponsor to draw up an SOC. An SOC is a document that defines the project by describing its scope and overarching goals, identifies the time and expertise requirements, and formalizes the executive-level project authorization. An SOC tends to be fairly uncomplicated, but should generally frame the project in terms of its identified opportunity, its target prize, and its wrap-up date. In a way, the SOC is similar to a customer apparel order that identifies the product number, size, and color specifications. The SOC is the project's specification sheet.

2.13.2 Department Members

The target team composition will vary, depending on the particular type of sourcing strategy project involved. An SS project will always involve one or more client departments. The client department is the one (or one of a few) that is most directly impacted by the sourcing opportunity, the one at which the project's activities are directed. This could be a production department (e.g., packaging), a production-support department (e.g., facilities management), or a business-support or operations department (e.g., human resources).

An opportunity might involve additional client departments, which serve a more ad hoc role in the sourcing project. A general opportunity to cut costs across the company or a specific opportunity to expedite speed-to-market processes would not only involve the production department as the primary client department but would also implicate, say, the logistics department as a functional partner in the overall strategic opportunity.

For example, a sourcing project aimed at optimizing payroll costs would identify the HR department as its primary internal client, but would also involve subset departments such as logistics to assess whether outsourcing this function would be a cost benefit for the company. As this example suggests, these projects can affect many facets of the organization in uncomfortable ways: a logistics manager might not appreciate even considering an outsourcing strategy, which would substantially alter his or her role within the company. When these situations arise, tread lightly; team members need to be sensitive to the vulnerable positions of all employees.

Some departments will participate in the project as standing members through their team member representative, providing start-to-end project support. Others will function as a supporting cast comprising both standing and ad hoc members. Standing-member departments routinely include purchasing and finance. Typical ad hoc members on a sourcing project may include the IT and marketing departments.

2.13.3 The Project Timeline

Generally, a sourcing project runs for about six months to a year. The milestone breakdown tends to run as shown in Table 2.7.

Table 2.7 Project Scheduling Breakdown

Milestone Stage	Typical Time Frame (Months)
Data collection[a]	2–4
Market research	2–4
Supplier evaluations	1–2
Contract negotiations	1–3

[a] Tracking local spend data, reviewing goods or services specifications, and grassroots interviewing.

Table 2.8   Web Sites with Free Downloads for Project Management Templates

ganthead.com
techrepublic.com
4pm.com
tenstep.com
pmi.org

Sample: An SOC for a Quality-Improvement Sourcing Strategy Project

One of the nice things about modern technology is all the free stuff you can get. Project management files, such as SOC templates, can be discovered through a simple Google search. A *template* is a file that serves as a blueprint, standardizing appearance and content elements. It is always a good idea when dealing with a recurring or redundant document, such as an SOC, to begin with a template. Templates remove some of the guesswork and help writers determine initial content. Templates can also benefit reviewers such as sourcing council members, helping them to immediately know where to track down specific information. Some Web sites that offer free project management template downloads are listed in Table 2.8.

And keep in mind that you or a form designer can always modify the template to fit your purposes. A sample SOC is shown in Table 2.9.

2.13.4 Supporting Documents

The SOC is a standard item in preparing a business case argument for initiating a project, but it should not stand alone. The purchasing manager may choose supporting documentation that best meets the particular circumstances, and these may include the merit verification review, notes from the sourcing council, or preliminary market research information.

2.13.5 Sourcing Councils

A key part of enabling a company's supply strategy is the approval of a corporate supply-chain council (sometimes called a corporate committee) to support the supply-chain redesign effort. These groups essentially serve as steering committees for sourcing projects. They provide idea generation,

Table 2.9 A Sample SOC

Statement of Charter: Packaging Cost Reductions

Primary Opportunity Type

☐ Cost reduction   ☐ Speed to market   ☐ Quality improvement

Note: Problems and solutions pertaining to an unchecked opportunity type that were encountered during the project's duration should also be documented and submitted to the project sponsor for consideration.

Project Objective
To ascertain the current spend for all products packaged in corrugated boxes companywide,[a] to research market conditions (e.g., customer demand, competitor's solutions, and regulatory influence) for outer packaging, and to develop strategies for reducing box container costs by five percent.

Department Members
> Standing members
>> Client department (final packaging)
>> Purchasing
>> Finance
> Ad Hoc Members
>> IT[b]
>> Marketing

Scheduling
> Project milestones

As-is analysis:	1 month
Market research:	2 months
Supplier evaluation:	1.5 month
Contract negotiations:	1.5 months
Expected total project duration:	6 months

> Project start: January 2005
> Project end: June 2005

Project Authorization

_____   _____

Tom Cruise, CPO   Whoopi Goldberg, CFO

---

[a] This encompasses all of the company's sites, including sites located in other countries.

[b] The information technology department, alternatively called information systems, or IS for short.

approvals, technical assistance, funding, and oversight functions. These councils handle both of the reviews — the merit verification and the feasibility — in the project review and approval process. Companies that have employed a supply-chain council include FedEx, General Motors, Honda, and Toyota.

A sourcing council is also highlighted as a critical element of leading-edge organizational SCM design in recent survey by Robert Trent. Trent[8] found that firms perceiving their current organizational design as promoting the achievement of procurement and supply objectives are more likely to stress certain design characteristics and features, and these features are affected to some degree by organizational size.

Sourcing councils commonly comprise the senior vice presidents (VPs), CFO, CIO, COO, CPO, and other relevant parties. Each member should be a strong representative, but the CFO always has ultimate veto power based on the financial feasibility of a project. Additionally, the council should include VPs of key product lines and from various work sites as decision makers and implementers, as necessary. If the company has multiple key product lines, they may consider time-limited appointments, perhaps two-year terms. The senior executive VPs, who would serve the council as standing members, may randomly appoint product VPs. Moreover, if the current members of the council do not have specific functional expertise regarding a potential project, then the council could include relevant ad hoc members to provide that input. SS managers may not attend sourcing council meetings; the CPO (often their reporting supervisor) can serve as their messenger.

The council members should review the agenda and project pitches before each meeting so that they are prepared for discussions on canceling, tabling, or moving forward with each opportunity. They may conduct additional research before meetings to ensure smooth and intelligent discussions. Depending on the size of the company and number of proposals, this group may decide to meet quarterly or as needed to review project proposals and active project status updates.

2.13.6 Presenting to the Supply-Chain Council

Regular meetings with the committee will be required to approve supply strategy mandates and decisions that have a major impact on operations, business requirements, and functional strategy. The committee should also participate in critical SCM sessions that impact corporate policy and strategy. An important lesson learned from benchmarking other companies

---

[8] Trent, R., *Procurement and Supply Management Organizational Design Survey*, Lehigh University, 2002.

Table 2.10 Effective Organizational Designs

- Regular strategy or performance review presentations by the CPO to the president or CEO

- Formal procurement and supply strategy coordination and review sessions between business units or divisions

- Physical collocation between procurement personnel and key internal customers (such as operations)

- Cross-functional or self-managed teams that manage some or all of the procurement and supply process

- Regular strategy or performance review presentations by the CPO to the Board of Directors

- New product or process development teams that formally include procurement and supply representatives

- An executive position responsible for coordinating and integrating key supply-chain activities from supplier through customer

- Formal strategy coordination and review sessions between functional groups (engineering, procurement, operations, etc.)

- A shared services model and structure that coordinates common activities or processes across business units or locations

- Physical collocation between procurement and marketing personnel

is that executive support from operational units is fundamental to the successful deployment of supply-chain strategies. The features in Table 2.10 characterize the most effective organizational designs that promote the achievement of procurement and supply objectives.

2.13.7 Feasibility Review

The sourcing council generally conducts a feasibility review. If the company does not have a sourcing council, then the CFO would perform this task alone. The feasibility review is intended to assess the project pitch in terms of the company's resource capability. The main factor here is financial: Does the company have the monetary means to see the project through to completion? Scheduling is another pivotal issue. Proposals may be tabled for reconsideration as the project calendar allows. For instance, the current political climate within the company might make a high-quality project idea impracticable at the moment.

Let us consider this scenario: six project ideas pass the merit review in all respects except funding, which exists only for three or four of the ideas. So, how do you pick and choose? How do you prioritize? At this point, three guidelines can be especially useful.

First, some projects are driven by nonnegotiable external factors (e.g., by regulatory mandate). These should always get top priority.

Second, projects that present the biggest — and quickest — prize that has been quantitatively verified as realistically feasible should be selected next. Here, the focus is "business-as-usual" purchasing cost reductions. You are looking for ways to cut costs quickly and a high probability of prize realization.

Third, project ideas for functional-level sourcing strategies should be evaluated in terms of their compatibility with the corporate-level strategy plan, which is spearheaded by the CEO and reviewed and set annually. So, for instance, if the corporate strategy contains a goal to reduce corporate costs by 15 percent, then cost reduction projects should be prioritized over quality-improvement or speed-to-market opportunities. This highlights a key SS operational policy, namely, to truly link corporate-level strategies with functional-level strategies. Moreover, this link should be bidirectional. Corporate strategies should not only be routinely considered in pursuing functional sourcing strategies, but also be considered when developing the corporate strategy plan.

Some of the key elements that should be covered with a corporate sourcing council include the following:

- What is the spend area?
- How much do we spend?
- What is the total market spend?
- Who are the main suppliers in the market?
- Who are our main suppliers?
- What are the opportunities to reduce costs through leveraging, bidding, relationship building, or other strategies?
- What are the resource requirements to achieve this goal?
- Who are the key functional representatives from operations, business units, IT, or other areas that will be required to serve on the team?
- How much time will be required of these representatives?

■ What is the project plan for completion of the sourcing strategy?

During a presentation, be prepared to answer questions with backup slides if necessary. At the end of the presentation, summarize specific action items to use if the decision is to proceed. If the project is not approved, summarize reasons why it was not approved and file for future reference, noting specific items that were overlooked or otherwise not strongly supported that may have resulted in nonapproval.

If a project gets a green light, then the CPO should get the ball rolling in terms of coordinating the project's start-up. He or she will initiate the SOC for the project, notify the target department participants, and assemble the project team. The CPO should identify an appropriate project sponsor at the executive level, send appropriate materials including the SOC, and wait for corporate buy-in. More information about reporting structures is presented in Table 2.11.

Getting buy-in into this initiative is one of the most challenging and important steps in leading change for a supply management effort. Once the project manager has executive support, he or she now has to be able to deliver the benefit (or prize) that has been promised. This can be a double-edged sword — be careful not to promise too much, but promise enough to indicate that the project is worth pursuing. If you can exceed expectations on the promised benefits, you will look like a hero!

However, it is not time to rest on your laurels. The real work is about to begin, so roll up your sleeves!

2.14 Intelligence and Opportunity Checklist

■ Understand BI/MI and the push approach.
■ Speak to CFO. Understand corporate objectives to ensure they are reflected in the project objective.
■ Consult with business units and key suppliers to identify SS opportunities.
■ Validate opportunity exists by quantifying potential savings.
■ Develop project charter, budget, and presentation summarizing the opportunity.
■ Review with senior management or sourcing council.
■ Obtain go or no-go decision.

2.15 Results

■ Action plan
■ Next steps

Table 2.11   Reporting Structures

The Challenge

Historically, there has been an empirical disconnect between senior purchasing managers and senior executives in U.S. companies. Executives have not perceived SCM as a reckoning force for the company's overall financial metrics. Consequently, executives have not been consulting purchasing managers in developing corporate strategies. Meanwhile, purchasing managers have not been very sensitive to the corporate-level strategic plan. This arrangement makes for two unrelated supply strategy plans: one at the corporate level, and the other at the purchasing level. This disconnect severely limits purchasing's strategy initiatives because it makes accessing prerequisite resources and organizationwide buy-ins virtually impossible. It also handicaps the company's supply-based competitive-advantage strategies. If companies want to retain their competitive advantage in the 21st century marketplace, they must start by exploiting the mutually rewarding resources at the executive and purchasing levels.

Fortunately, this is starting to happen. Senior executives are recognizing the strategic value that SCM initiatives can contribute to the company's overall financial objectives, from reducing costs to enhancing revenues. Some of the supply-specific objectives at the executive level include reducing costs in operations, logistics, and distribution. Another top supply-chain priority at the executive level is improving customer satisfaction performance, measured in terms of perfect orders (that is, orders that are delivered to the right customer, in the right quality and quantity, and at the right time). Note that the executive focus on customer satisfaction is greater now than in times past; this suggests that executives are realizing that customer RM should join financial management as a critical driver of future corporate success and can no longer be minimized.

Since 2000, the majority of leading companies have put their money where their proverbial mouths are by increasing supply-chain budgets, primarily to expand supply-chain capabilities. But they are wisely not stopping there. Without additional resource support, more money will not deliver in the long term. Companies have begun to realize that an ongoing and strategic executive–purchasing relationship is warranted. The executive position that most logically lends itself to this particular strategic relationship is the CFO because his or her objectives, in terms of financial returns, are the most closely linked to purchasing. A number of CFOs have consequently become much more involved, at a practical level, with purchasing operations; this trend is anticipated to grow significantly in the coming years.

Table 2.11   Reporting Structures (continued)

The Goal

Some companies have progressed as far as prioritizing this strategic relationship in their reporting structure by having senior purchasing managers report directly to the CFO. Granted, the purchasing manager has been going to the CFO with various requests for years now without a direct link such as the revised reporting structure. But because of the traditional disconnect between these two offices, these endeavors were fraught with lengthy proceedings and justifications. A direct CFO–purchasing manager relationship will expedite decision-making processes; it will inject greater "decisiveness" into the decision-making outputs. Therefore, this updated reporting structure, which systemically links these two offices together, should be the objective for every supply-chain organization.

This CFO–purchasing tie empowers purchasing managers in multiple ways. The purchasing manager can more efficaciously secure start-up funding from the CFO for SCM project initiatives. The purchasing manager can ask the CFO to be a liaison to the executive committee. For instance, the CFO could deliver strategy recommendations and supporting data to the boardroom on behalf of the purchasing manager. The CFO could also advocate on behalf of the purchasing manager to other senior executives the critical need for incorporating strategies from the purchasing department's functional plan into the corporate strategic plan. The CFO is also the purchasing manager's gateway for invitations into the executive boardroom to present in-person business case arguments for major changes, such as seamlessly linking all of the company's disparate internal supply elements into a single, synergistic supply management function.

But the CFO's involvement should not be limited to the "go to" channel for money and executive backing. Why stop there when the CFO can be used for so much more? The CFO can also help the purchasing manager in more substantive ways by sharing knowledge and technical assistance. The purchasing manager can consult the CFO regarding decisions involving cash management and capital allocations. Tapping into the CFO's knowledge base is particularly advantageous for some of the newer competitive challenges posed by the contemporary market environment that purchasing managers face. Two main examples are globalization and large-scale outsourcing. The CFO can also help the purchasing manager in transitioning from simply quantifying costs to quantifying value. And more benefits will probably be revealed as more and more CFO–purchasing manager links are established and developed.

Table 2.11   Reporting Structures (continued)

There are many ways in which the CFO can support the purchasing manager, who, in turn, will be better able to support the company's capacity to compete in the marketplace. This is so simple and so critical. If this link is not currently present in your company, start paving the way for it. If you are a CFO, invite your senior purchasing manager out for lunch. If you are a senior purchasing manager, invite your CFO out for lunch. If some executives remain stubbornly resistant, then for the financial health of the company, the other executives need to start planning for replacements by offering attractive early-retirement incentives and by scouting for candidates who are familiar with supply management needs and opportunities and who are comfortable doing what it takes to support this function. (Note that this personnel replenishment criterion applies to VPs and supply-relevant department managers as well.) One way or another, this restructuring in general and the executive support in particular must be accomplished.

Career Benefit

This strategic relationship benefits the company, but it is also not bad for the purchasing manager. This revised reporting structure can effectively advance career opportunities for purchasing staff.

Chapter 3

Establishing the Team

Function	Objective	Tactical Step	Chapter/ Appendix
Supply market intelligence	Supply market research	Opportunity identification and validation	2
		Project approval	2
		Establishing the team	3
		Project plan	3
		As-is assessment	4
		Supply market research	5
		Market forecasts	5
		External and market analyses	6
	Strategy and resource commitment	Detailed supplier evaluation and research	7
		Evaluate current and alternative strategies	8
		Understand contract formation	8

Function	Objective	Tactical Step	Chapter/ Appendix
Strategic sourcing	Negotiate and select supplier	Develop relationship strategy	8
		Strategy position paper	8
		Develop requests for information (RFIs) and build negotiation strategy	9
		Negotiate	9
		Final supplier selection	9
		Form contracts	9
	Implement and promote compliance	Implement contracts	9
		Transition to relationship manager	10
Relationship management		Communicate expectations	10
	Improve supplier performance	Measure performance	10
		Resolve issues and develop supplier performance	10
Benchmarking processes and driving continuous improvement		Build an organization for supply-chain excellence	11
		Benchmark performance and drive continuous improvement	12, App. B

3.1 Chapter Outline

- Getting the project started
- The CPO and the project budget
- The project coordinator
- Issuing the project charter
- Assessing requirements
- Identifying skills needed

- Recruiting a relationship manager (RM)
- Cross-functional teams
- Kickoff meeting
- Distributing tasks
- Checklist

The global procurement organization will need a much higher level of expertise and understanding of purchasing goals and the ability to operate at a strategic level.

Leadership is a bigger picture. It requires someone who has a vision and can see the whole picture. I think about it as a boat. You can either be looking at where you've been on the back end of the boat to see what you've done or be looking forward and saying, "Yes, we haven't done it before, but what's possible? What could we do?"

Usually when you've got good communication skills, there's the attribute of leadership, and an attribute of courage: being able to draft a presentation, give a presentation, talk to the correct audience, have confidence in yourself, think on your feet. Just the whole gamut. Talking one on one to people and speaking to executive-level management and maybe folks on the factory floor, there is a whole spectrum that really pulls in a lot of different attributes. And so if you can find someone with good communication skills in those areas, you tend to find your good leaders.

**— Comments from an executive focus group
on strategic sourcing skills for the future[1]**

All of these executives are experiencing intense pressure to improve the performance of their firms and are fully expecting this level of pressure to increase even more in the years ahead. Many firms are responding to this pressure by creating organizational structures that promote cross-functional and cross-organizational communication, coordination, and collaboration. In support of this effort, cross-functional sourcing teams have become increasingly important as firms pursue supply management strategies.

Cross-functional sourcing teams consist of personnel from different functions and, increasingly, suppliers, brought together to achieve purchasing or supply-chain–related activities. This includes specific tasks such as product design or supplier selection, or broader responsibilities such as reducing purchased-item cost or improving quality.

---

[1] Handfield and Giunipero, CAPS Study, 2004.

When executed properly, the cross-functional sourcing team approach can bring together the knowledge and resources required for responding to new sourcing demands, something that rigid organizational structures are often incapable of doing. However, a famous researcher by the name of Likert noted 40 years ago that groups and teams can accomplish much that is good, or they can do great harm. There is nothing inherently good or bad, or weak or strong about teams, regardless of where an organization uses them.

In this chapter, we cover one of the most important elements of deployment associated with supply strategy: forming the team. We will go through the steps associated with establishing and developing the team, developing a project charter, and establishing the project plan.

3.2 Getting the Project Started

The project is approved; now what? Things start moving in two directions. In the previous chapter, we noted that several high-level opportunities were identified, generally through a "push" strategy from the business intelligence team. These opportunities were validated as feasible, and a statement of charter was developed. At this point, the senior supply management executives (generally, a chief procurement officer [CPO] or vice president of supply management) will designate team leaders for the different strategic sourcing opportunities. As noted previously, this activity is one of the key steps in the program component of supply-chain design. This chapter discusses both of these functions and provides a picture of how the sourcing project should get started.

So, you have been charged with creating a sourcing strategy for a commodity or service that your firm needs to purchase. Where do you begin? It is best to have a plan of attack, a process that is logical, can be replicated in the future, and most importantly, produces the information necessary to drive value for internal customers of the selected commodity or service. In the first step in the sourcing process, the team is formed, a plan for the entire process is developed and communicated, and the market research strategy is devised.

3.3 The CPO and the Project Budget

If the project gets the green light, the CPO will establish a project budget. The project budget will often be relatively simple, including payroll for the various project team members and, perhaps, some incidentals such as travel expenses. It should also describe who will pay for the project (that is, which departments or cost centers) and how. Ideally, the project budget should be broken down into project milestones: as-is statistics, market research, supplier evaluation, and supplier contracts. A one-week turnaround for this type of budget is normally manageable. One of the biggest challenges facing a CPO is freeing up resources from non-supply-management departments to participate in the team. This may require a formal commitment from the senior executive from that department, as the business unit may be reluctant to fully allocate that individual's time to the initiative.

The company should have a system in place in which various departments' budgets are not only charged but also rewarded with some of the resulting wealth. Allowing space in the budget for awarding individual members and their departments real incentives is a good way to motivate them to creatively and strategically pursue sourcing solutions and ensure they have a vested interest in the success of the project.

3.4 The Project Coordinator

The job title for the person who fulfills the role of leading the project team will vary, depending on the company's setup. So, instead, we'll use a functional title, project coordinator, to describe this role. If the company has strategic sourcing managers, then the CPO may assign one of them to the project. If not, the CPO may function as the project coordinator.

The project coordinator may be chosen from corporate headquarters or any of the sites with potential involvement in the project. The project coordinator may come from purchasing, IT, finance, or marketing. Because the traditional focus on price-based negotiation will be disappearing, quality project coordinators should have business backgrounds and the capability to understand the entire supply-chain process, internal and external requirements, effective management of merger activities requiring supply base integration, and exploitation of supplier technologies.

3.5 Issuing a Project Charter

Once a sourcing requirement and project coordinator have been identified, it is important to issue a project charter. This is an official announcement that a new project has begun. The project charter can be issued before or after the cross-functional sourcing team has been formed, and in fact, it can be used to garner interest from potential participants in the process. The purpose of a project charter is to demonstrate management support for the project and its manager. It establishes *referent authority*, i.e., the use of another highly respected person's authority, and is usually signed by the project sponsor or customer. In this case, the project sponsor might be the VP of Purchasing or Chief Purchasing Officer. The audience of the project charter is anyone who might be involved in the project. The minimum content of the charter should be the name and purpose of the project, the name of the project manager, and a statement of support from the issuer (i.e., the project sponsor).

The project coordinator should contact managers from each department (relevant to the project), inform them of the approved project, and ask them to consider potential team member recruits. The team for a sourcing project should reflect a cross-functional setup. A cross-functional team (CFT) will be created by the project coordinator or a business unit executive vice president. A CFT is formed in response to a very specific business need and is chartered to deliver very specific business outcomes that they are held accountable for delivering, as well as for ongoing management of the integrated process. In most cases, a CFT that includes supply management is composed of several other functional representatives as well. Many SCM groups are still not comfortable with this situation as it creates a fundamental tension because a functional representative may, in some cases, be asked to suboptimize their functional outcomes to optimize the overall business objectives. (For example, a team may not get the best price from a supplier, but decide to choose a supplier that provides the best delivery reliability.) The challenge of the team is to ensure not only that all functional requirements are addressed, but that consensus is reached on maximizing the overall desired business objective.

There are several roles at the SCM functional level that oversee all of the CFTs. A *CFT member* refers to an SCM professional who sits on the team and works with the team members toward achieving the stated business objective. These individuals are not in a position to aggregate for other CFTs and so need to work with them on constraints.

Functional aggregators (FAs) are associates who specialize in buying the same material or service across multiple business units and are generally assigned to manage the spend for a specific commodity or service across multiple business units. These individuals are tasked with resolving conflicts that may arise between CFTs and the supplier, and make decisions related to allocation of aggregate spend. The functional aggregator steps in when conflicts arise in CFTs related to allocation of spend across business units to more than one supplier. The FA also works to manage constraints that may arise in delegating spending to suppliers. A relationship manager (RM) would be the equivalent of a functional aggregator, or alternatively, it could be the buyer who manages the CFT. As shown in Figure 3.1, the aggregator must consider volume requirements, supplier capacity constraints, and operational business unit requirements to optimize sourcing decisions across business units.

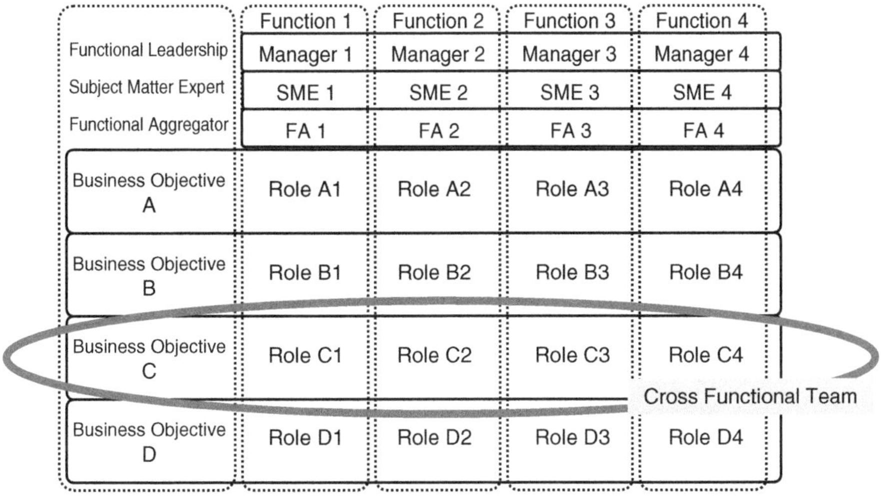

	Function 1	Function 2	Function 3	Function 4
Functional Leadership	Manager 1	Manager 2	Manager 3	Manager 4
Subject Matter Expert	SME 1	SME 2	SME 3	SME 4
Functional Aggregator	FA 1	FA 2	FA 3	FA 4
Business Objective A	Role A1	Role A2	Role A3	Role A4
Business Objective B	Role B1	Role B2	Role B3	Role B4
Business Objective C	Role C1	Role C2	Role C3	Role C4
Business Objective D	Role D1	Role D2	Role D3	Role D4

Cross Functional Team

Figure 3.1   Generic matrixed organization.

Buyers for a given commodity may play the role of the functional aggregator for a particular commodity group, whereas planners, schedulers, and coordinators may be a part of the CFT that is focused on the business objective of improving production efficiency.

In cases when major conflicts arise, the VP of SCM may need to intervene in establishing guidelines for aggregation. This can occur when conflicts arise between two business units, and the VP and his representatives need to make a decision to ensure the optimal supply solution.

Subject matter experts (SMEs) are knowledgeable about specific aspects of a functional element that may run across multiple lines of business. They are knowledgeable enough to facilitate and to drive improvement. They may also be aware of developments in the field, in terms of identifying "blue sky" technologies and emerging facts and trends, and can serve as resident experts in a particular process or line of business. As opposed to FAs who are involved in day-to-day activities, people will go to SMEs to ask questions and better understand key issues such as scheduling, surplus materials, policy and procurement issues, and multiple other areas that are critical to your line of business. SMEs could be located in a particular business unit, because they know the most about a specific area, but could also be located elsewhere. CFTs will rely heavily on SMEs for advice on specific issues and may call on them to review their decisions on a regular basis to ensure that they are optimal.

These roles may be very difficult for your team to understand and engage in. Training should focus on role-playing, situational assessments, and scenarios in which tough decisions need to be made. By putting people into situations in which they are forced to encounter these environments, openly discuss them, and identify how the decision will impact the greater good of the corporation, successful change for cross-functional teaming efforts can occur.

Every project is going to require standard representation from purchasing, finance, and the client department (the department that the project is most intended to benefit). Note that some projects will deal with issues, e.g., commodity-specific, which affect multiple departments. In these cases, someone from each of the affected departments should be appointed to the project team. Ad hoc members can include representatives from IT and marketing.

To find out which sites or departments are relevant to a given project, global spend analysis might help. As E-procurement technologies are implemented, the need for transaction-focused planners and buyers will diminish. Instead, supply managers will be asked to lead category management teams that are responsible for conducting supply market research, project management, goal setting, and execution of a category or commodity strategy. An increasing number of category teams are focused on nontraditional services categories including information technology, professional services, travel, document management, facilities management, payroll, human resources, accounts payable, and many other areas that are candidates for outsourcing.

3.5.1 Commodity Teams

Some companies use commodity (aka category) teams to develop purchasing strategies. Commodities are general categories or families of purchased items. Examples of major commodity classifications across different industries include body side moldings (automotive), microprocessors (computer), steel (metalworking), cotton (apparel), wood (pulp and paper), petroleum products (chemicals), and office supplies (all industries).

A category team could be composed of personnel from manufacturing, product design, process engineering, marketing, finance, and purchasing. The personnel involved should be familiar with the commodity being evaluated. For instance, if the team is tasked with purchasing computers, then members from information systems should be included. If the team purchases vehicles and vehicle parts, then it would be a good idea to include maintenance managers, who are familiar with the characteristics of these commodities. In general, the more important the commodity, the more likely that cross-functional members and user groups will be involved. Together, the commodity team will develop a commodity strategy that provides the specific details and outlines the actions to follow in managing the commodity. Strong skills in team building and leadership, decision making, influencing internal users and suppliers, and compromising in reaching a team consensus are, therefore, important to be found in individuals who will succeed in these roles.

3.6 Assess Current and Future Environmental Requirements

Before establishing the requirements for developing a commodity program, executives need to link this effort to the current and future business requirements as well as the environmental changes that organization is likely to face in the next decade. For example, if the current focus on cost reduction is unlikely to subside in the next decade, key skills in this area will be in high demand. In addition, purchasing, as a strategic value-added function, will be important, especially with an increased focus on collaborative relationships with suppliers and external and internal customers.

There is a tough question that executives must ask themselves at this juncture: "Is our current workforce in supply management prepared to deal with this set of conditions and requirements?" Unless an organization has a training program that emphasizes these elements and is universally adopted into the requirements for supply management career development, the answer in most cases will be "no."

An important tool that can assist organizations in establishing current and future environmental challenges and the need for training requirements is the Hoshin plan, which identifies key supply management performance metrics for the future. As identified earlier, strategic relationship management with suppliers, strategic cost reductions, integrated systems, and greater focus on total cost were the top four elements identified as trends. An example of a supply-chain management Hoshin plan that is aligned with these trends is shown in Figure 3.2. Each of the goals is matched with a key performance indicator to establish performance objectives in terms of the customer, internal associates, and shareholder value.

3.7 Identify Skills Required

Key purchasing environmental elements are identified and goals are established through a Hoshin plan or similar strategic planning tool. Once this takes place, senior management should work with a high-level team representing human resources, operations, finance, information systems, marketing, and strategy to identify key skills that are vital to developing and executing a successful project. Input from internal customer groups

Management VISION		To be recognized as World Class for Supply Chain Management throughout the Industry.
Supply Chain Management VISION		Create a sustainable competitive advantage by implementing innovative supply chain processes, working as a team, and improving business processes.
GOALS		
CUSTOMER ➡	1.1	Drive suppliers to world-class performance in cost, quality, and technology in support of world-class customer satisfaction.
Provider of Choice	1.2	Support the corporate commitment to our multi-cultural and global customers.
X % Customer/Business Partner Satisfaction	1.3	Develop and implement innovative end to end supply chain processes with internal customers to achieve a competitive advantage through team-based integrative sourcing strategies.
ASSOCIATE ➡	2.1	Create a performance driven culture, which attracts, retains, and rewards associates to drive growth.
Employer of Choice	2.2	Provide the support and tools that Associates need to excel.
90% Associate Satisfaction	2.3	Enable Associates to achieve professional growth balanced with personal goals.
	2.4	Reflect the diversity of the communities and customers we serve in our work force.
SHAREHOLDER ➡	3.1	Focus SCM expertise and business acumen to create value for shareholders through increased profitability and shareholder return.
Investment of Choice	3.2	Leveraging Six Sigma methodologies reduces cost of goods sold, improves quality levels, and achieves annual productivity improvements to grow market share.
Double digit year over year productivity	3.3	Reduce risk of supply shortages, satisfying regulatory requirements, and minimize exposure to legal risks.
	3.4	Integrate global business unit supply chain functions and leverage opportunities to grow global market share.

Figure 3.2   Example of a generic Hoshin plan.

is critical because the types of individuals who have the skills to perform on the team may be few and far between. In the longer term, training programs must be developed with the idea of aligning training to corporate strategy heading into the future.

The use of cross-functional input into purchasing training cycles is likely to increase, as indicated by 67 percent of respondents who said they would have such councils in place by 2010. The purpose of these councils will be to determine the direction and priority of programs, provide targets, help develop course content, determine training requirements by position, evaluate training, approve budgets, and review instruction methods. More organizations are also assigning to high-level directors the responsibility for training and results.

The task of creating a team to work on a particular strategic sourcing team requires that you identify how the trends identified in the purchasing environment translate into organizational requirements, strategic sourcing team structure, and leadership roles for future sourcing initiatives that will

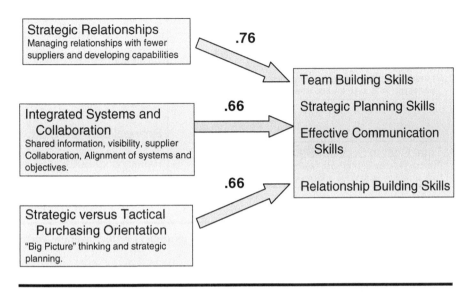

Figure 3.3   Strategic trends and skills. (Numbers reflect average correlation between training and skills.)

span these different areas. This makes it even more important to obtain internal customer input. One company we met with has identified a need to increasingly centralize the sourcing of marketing campaigns and information systems development over the next two years. Integration of key representatives from marketing, desktop technology, systems development, and other internal customers would greatly increase the probability that the skills required would in fact meet the needs of these internal customers.

Figure 3.3 through Figure 3.7 illustrate some of the crucial skills identified in a recent study of ours that align with each of the major trends identified in the focus groups. Evidence of the link between trends and skills in the form of a correlation between the elements is also shown in these figures. For example, the trend of increased strategic relationships with fewer suppliers and increased internal integration and collaboration will require employees with a high skill level in team activities, strategic planning, effective communication, and relationship management.

Several elements are notable from this analysis. First, team building, strategic planning, effective communication, and relationship management are critical for success in managing almost every one of the purchasing trends identified in the study. This provides additional support for prior studies that have also identified the demise of the traditional "buyer" who was relegated to managing purchase orders. With the increasing application of E-procurement to these tactical elements, purchasing will be called upon to deliver greater value in terms of supply market intelligence, cost

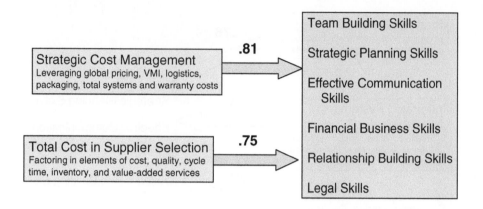

Figure 3.4 Cost management trends and skills. (Numbers reflect average correlation between training and skills.)

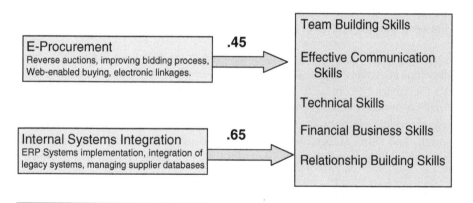

Figure 3.5 Systems trends and skills. (Numbers reflect average correlation between training and skills.)

management, creative problem solving, and management of internal and external customer requirements.

The role of the supply manager itself is also changing to focus on improving integration across internal functions and through to the customer, and deeper penetration across multiple tiers of the supply base. As such, supply managers must have a broader range of knowledge spanning the end-to-end supply chain, changes in market and business conditions, supply market trends, and customer requirements. Financial acumen, negotiation skills, supplier evaluation skills, Internet literacy, and strategic thinking are all important skills for supply-chain managers today and in the future.

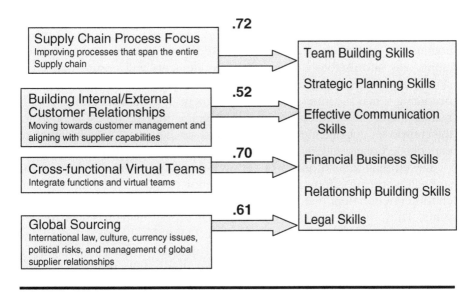

Figure 3.6 Relationship management trends and skills. (Numbers reflect average correlation between training and skills.)

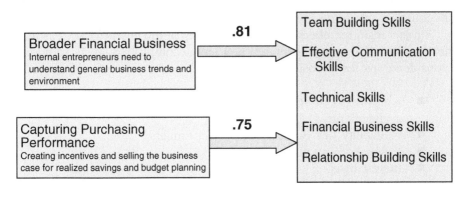

Figure 3.7 General business trends and skills. (Numbers reflect average correlation between training and skills.)

The top purchasing trends identified in our study[2] are forcing senior executives in supply management to review the current skill sets that exist in their purchasing function management and to reevaluate the need for additional training and development of key personnel. Executives are increasingly realizing that the systems in place today are not going to

---

[2] Handfield and Giunipero, CAPS Study, 2004.

succeed without considerable change. At the same time, companies are also realizing that the skills of their purchasing function are becoming a prized commodity and a core competency. Additional investment to develop employees and establish career path requirements will ensure that these skilled individuals are retained within the company for the future. This is becoming a major cornerstone for deployment of solid strategies in supply management. Although some internal programs may be robust enough for this purpose, outsourcing of training and of personnel development to experienced organizations can lower cost and increase efficiency.

Developing a solid group of supply managers responsible for leading strategic sourcing efforts requires that senior executives identify the purchasing environment that their organization will encounter in the next ten years. They should consider the skills that supply managers will require to manage elements of this environment. Once these criteria have been identified, executive management should delegate a team to establish a focused plan for acquiring or developing these skills through focused training, recruiting of new talent, and linkages to career planning and development for the global workforce in supply management. This task can follow many of the requirements for a focused sourcing strategy, which involve identifying potential providers, executing an insourcing and outsourcing analysis, identifying total costs, evaluating suppliers and bids, negotiating, awarding the contract, and managing and tracking results.

Project team members should share many of the characteristics as their leaders and supply managers, just at a less accomplished level. Additional considerations for choosing the team include:

■ Logistics (work space accommodations, separate work site travel arrangements)
■ Availability (for duration of project timeline)
■ Personality and work style
■ Interest level

3.8 Recruiting an RM

At this stage in the process, we have also noted that it is an opportune time to recruit a relationship manager (RM) who will eventually "own" the supplier relationship. This individual should be recruited from the primary operations or business unit that is responsible for the greatest amount of spend with the key commodity. The RM will review optimal rationalization measures for alignment with organization strategy and strategic sourcing plans. Initially, the RM is recruiting as an active member of the strategic sourcing team and interacts with strategic sourcing processes to incorporate suggestions and ensure that the business unit needs are being met.

Later, the RM measures are documented, made accessible, and managed in a cross-functional manner to ensure that the relationship continues to align with company strategy. Suppliers will be formally evaluated based on measured performance, necessary actions will be taken, and progress will be reported to the RM. Suppliers also participate in RM teams on a regular basis. The RM will develop strategy to manage relationships and categorize different kinds of relationships (tier one, tier two, tier three), describe communications and monitor responsibilities for each category and each relationship, and recommend additional suppliers to align with processes.

3.9 Cross-Functional Teams

There are a number of benefits to using cross-functional commodity teams in the development of purchasing strategies, particularly if the approach receives the proper amount of support and energy, and teams meet their performance objectives. These benefits include

- *Reduced time to complete tasks*: CFTs can overcome functional silos that contribute to duplication of effort between groups and eliminate the need for individual sign-off by each group because agreements will be made together. A team approach also allows tasks to be split among team members so that they can be performed concurrently.
- *Increased innovation*: Everyone is familiar with the old saying "Two minds are better than one." A CFT brings together people from diverse backgrounds who can offer creative ideas and solutions to the sourcing decision at hand. It is important that the proper environment is created to foster innovation, which means that teams should be subject to lower levels of formal rules and procedures and informal organizational structures.
- *Joint ownership of decisions*: CFT interaction exposes the various parties in the sourcing decision to each other's concerns, requirements, and limitations. This leads to solutions that diverse departments can support. Buy-in is established, which makes implementation of the decision easier.
- *Enhanced communication between functions or organizations*: Creation of CFTs brings team members in direct contact with one another, facilitating the open and timely exchange of information.
- *Realization of synergies*: The total group effort is greater than the expected sum of the parts. A CFT approach brings together individuals with different perspectives and expertise, allowing the

group to perform better on a task compared with individuals or departments acting alone. The synergistic effect of team interaction generates new and creative ways to approach a problem or task.

■ *Better identification and resolution of problems*: A CFT with diverse knowledge and skills can more often quickly identify causes of problems, which may help minimize or prevent the total impact of the problem. Teams should assume joint ownership of the problem and its solution.

Although the use of cross-functional commodity teams can have many benefits, there are also potential drawbacks to the approach. These include:

■ *Team process loss*: Process loss occurs when a team does not solve its task in the best or most efficient manner or members do not invest the energy to create a successful outcome. This is the opposite of synergy in that the total group effort is less than the expected sum of the individual parts.

■ *Negative effects on individual members*: CFT membership can have a negative effect if individuals are pressured to conform to a decision or position that they do not support (i.e., peer pressure). And some people just do not perform well in a group setting. It is important to take into consideration the personalities and work styles of the people selected for the team to ensure that the group will be able to work together well.

■ *Poor team decisions*: Unfortunately, CFTs can arrive at bad decisions. Teams can become subject to groupthink, the tendency of an otherwise rational group to arrive at a bad decision despite the availability of information contraindicating its being the best solution. To help prevent this, a process should be in place to ensure that all relevant information and alternative courses of action are considered.

3.9.1 Relevant Members of Commodity Teams

Once personnel requirements for a sourcing project team have been identified, the project coordinator should confirm that all relevant sites and departments are included in the search. A simple e-mail as in Table 3.1 should enable the coordinator to cover all bases.

Some of the relevant functions that should be included on a commodity team are described in the following subsections.

Table 3.1   E-Mail Form for Identifying Relevant Sites and Departments

Hello — We are planning/proposing to initiate an X sourcing project in the near future, and we would like your help in identifying the sites and departments that we need to include. Please respond to the questions below by 5 pm EST on mm/dd/yy. Thanks for your help. Do any of the departments at your site use X commodity/service/process? Yes No If "yes," then please list the following identifying information below (if more than three departments would apply, then please note those as well): Site name: Department 1 Department name: Department 1 Manager's name: Department 1 Manager's e-mail: Department 2 Department name: Department 2 Manager's name: Department 2 Manager's e-mail: Department 3 Department name: Department 3 Manager's name: Department 3 Manager's e-mail:

3.9.1.1 Client Department

The department manager for each relevant site would ideally be a team member; this is usually the person who is going to be able to navigate the transition from project planning to postproject operational implementation for their group. Some managers might be resistant to project recruitment efforts, as the time investments are sizable. An employee may be requested to participate two to three days a week for six or more months, a commitment that interferes with current job responsibilities. This is another reason why project sponsorship at the senior executive level is so important; it would be easy for target departments to shrug off significant project participation otherwise. Note that if the project involves new product development (NPD), the NPD team would function as the client department, whether or not it reflects an actual department or group within the organizational chart.

3.9.1.2 Purchasing

The purchasing team member should be a buyer or manager at each site. This member will provide expertise on all things relating to supply-chain management, leading the benchmarking effort to understand trends in the supply market as well as savings potential based on internal and external industry analysis. Among other functions, this person is critical in evaluating supplier capabilities.

3.9.1.3 Operations

The sales and operations plan (S&OP) identifies the level of production and sales for a six-month to one-year period. The components and services needed to implement this plan must be sourced. These could include materials, software, travel services, information technology, or outsourced labor. Many firms are now "colocating" purchasing personnel directly at operating locations to increase response time to the department's needs. A representative from operations can offer input into this process.

3.9.1.4 Quality Assurance

As firms externally source a larger percentage of finished product requirements, purchasing and quality assurance must work together closely to ensure that suppliers perform as expected. Joint projects involving these two groups include supplier quality training, process capability studies, and corrective action planning. This linkage has become so important that some firms have placed the responsibility for supplier quality management directly with purchasing.

3.9.1.5 Engineering

The need to develop quality products in less time has drawn purchasing and engineering closer over time, yet, the relationship between the two departments can still be challenging. Engineers and buyers can develop open communication by working together on product development or supplier selection teams. The key to a successful relationship between purchasing and engineering is open and direct communication, which, in turn, should lead to increased teamwork and trust. The engineering department needs the most technically and financially capable supplier who is also capable of meeting quality and delivery targets. A supplier's production capabilities, active involvement early in the design process, and creative thinking are important to the success of engineering projects.

3.9.1.6 Accounting and Finance

Another critical element in establishing the credibility of the project is to get someone from finance on your team to validate the numbers. Participation from this department can also assist with calculating handling and material rework costs resulting from poor supplier performance or adjusting capital expenditures. A good finance person should be able to estimate inventory costs and establish cost savings through reduced complexity, decreased material handling, less obsolescence, and improved customer service. Finance is likely to be able to contribute ideas for all types of opportunities (cost savings, speed to market, and quality improvement), but they do so from a monetary perspective. Finance plays a key role in validating the potential for cost savings, or revenue gains, as various strategies are presented and brainstormed. This team member will be instrumental in crafting the business case that establishes the need for a supply-chain strategy.

3.9.1.7 Information Technology

Information technology (IT; alternately called information systems or IS) members will play a critical role in mining databases to identify current spending. Even if the project is geared at speed-to-market or quality improvement ends, assessing local spend is a fixed first step in any sourcing project. In addition, they will need to map out and identify current legacy systems that are in use across the organization in the areas of accounts payable, E-procurement, enterprise systems, and other electronic and manual requisition systems. The IT member may also need to establish a Web portal for collecting data from external supplier sources in the event that the chart of accounts cannot be effectively mined to query and download supplier spend data. This is a good assignment for junior-level IT staff, often a database administrator or data processing specialist. They would mainly be responsible for pulling the spend data for the project team but could remain as on-call technology consultants for the duration of the project.

3.9.1.8 Marketing and Sales

This is a critical partner during the market research phase of the project. This team member, guided by the team's direction, will run reports to gather the requisite market research data, present an encapsulated version of their findings (accompanied by handouts of the written reports), and work with the team to delineate target strategies founded on the market intelligence. Marketing also develops sales forecasts that convert into production plans.

3.9.1.9 Legal

The team will require counsel on specific elements of contracts. Issues that may arise include patent ownership terms in new product development, intellectual property, product liability claims, antitrust, long-term contracts containing escape clauses, and other legal issues. E-commerce also raises many legal issues that require consultation with the legal department.

3.9.1.10 Environmental Management, Health, and Safety

The team is responsible for ensuring that chosen suppliers are employing safe methods of transportation and are complying with Occupational Safety and Health Administration (OSHA) standards and safety regulations. A safety representative's insights on this process are helpful.

3.10 Kickoff Meeting

Once your team has been recruited, the final step is to set a date for an initial project meeting. This meeting is intended primarily as a meet-and-greet session. The only work focus is taking care of project management matters: identifying project tools and allocating functional responsibilities.

Both the team members and the managers from the participating departments should be invited. If the project spans multiple sites, then the project coordinator should set up a teleconference or videoconference (e.g., WebEx) so that all the teams at each site can be involved at one meeting.

What happens if people do not show up for the first meeting? This, believe it or not, is not an uncommon event. It generally indicates a formal lack of interest on the part of the business unit or functional area these individuals represent. Their lack of participation is equivalent to shouting, "I don't believe this is worth my time." At this point, the project coordinator should bring this situation to senior management's attention to ascertain that the project is, in fact, a priority for the group. In certain cases, a different individual may be asked to participate and represent this business function.

A sample kickoff meeting agenda follows:

- Do verbal introductions: Project manager, senior executives, site and team members. (Individual contact information is provided via e-mail.)
- Define expectations.
  - Outline the preliminary project plan and objective.
  - Identify the amount of time required to be part of the team.
  - Identify conflicts.
  - Ensure team members know that they will be responsible for carrying back the message to their functional unit in supporting the strategy.
  - Identify a potential RM, if not already assigned, to own the relationship once strategy is complete.
- Define responsibilities (assign tasks).
  - Do we fully consider CFT planning issues?
  - Is executive management practicing "subtle control" over our teams?
  - Do we recognize and reward team member participation and team performance?
  - Is our team effectively establishing performance goals?
  - Will key suppliers and customers be part of the team process?
  - Does our team have the ability to self-diagnose the quality of its interaction and performance?
  - Write a statement of work (SOW).
  - Create a communications plan.
  - Create a work plan.
  - Develop a market research plan.
- Appoint team leaders (see Table 3.2) and secretary.
  - Define reporting structure.
- Create timeline.

Table 3.2 Team Leader Job Description

The team leader is responsible for making sure the project stays within budget and on schedule. If problems arise, the team leader communicates directly with the project coordinator (the strategic sourcing manager or the CPO). The team leader will allocate tasks and keep tabs on progress. The leader should keep meetings focused and be able to mediate any personal frictions that might arise. Quality communication and speaking skills are a requirement. The team leader should be a quick learner and smart with follow-through activities.

3.10.1 Writing an SOW

An important document that the team should draft immediately is the statement of work (SOW), which lists the goals, constraints, and success criteria for the sourcing project. It also includes a statement of the project scope. It is a good idea to include the sourcing team in the development of the SOW, to create buy-in and ensure joint ownership from all concerned parties. The minimum content of the SOW should be

- *Purpose statement*: The purpose statement answers the question "Why are we doing this project?" If there is a business case or cost–benefit analysis, these should be referenced in the SOW.
- *Scope statement*: The scope statement describes the major activities of the project and defines what the project will and will not do.
- *Deliverables*: This section describes what tangible items the team will deliver throughout the project. This may include milestone reports, e-mail summaries, or other paperwork created by the team.
- *Cost and schedule estimates*: This section establishes a budget and a deadline for the project. It also addresses the reasoning behind the size of the budget and how the deadline was determined, as well as the reliability of the estimates and how flexible they might be.
- *Objectives*: The objectives of the project should be specific and contain measurable criteria that gauge the success of the sourcing process.
- *Stakeholders*: This section identifies anyone who will influence the project, particularly the project manager, project team, sponsor, management, and customers.
- *Chain of command*: The chain of command establishes who reports to whom on this project. It is very important when dealing with cross-functional project teams because the reporting structure will be different from the hierarchy within functional areas.

The SOW is directed solely at stakeholders from within the same legal entity. This document should not be circulated to current or potential suppliers, although you may want to communicate the project charter to suppliers via a supplier newsletter or other means to solicit interest in this sourcing opportunity.

3.10.2 Creating a Communication Plan

The final housekeeping task to be completed is to draw up a communication plan. The communication plan is a written strategy for getting the right information to the right people at the right time and should answer two questions:

- Who needs information?
- What information is needed?

Those who need information might include the project sponsor, functional management, customers, the project team, and the project manager. Information that needs to be communicated includes authorizations, approval process steps, status changes, progress reports, and problem logs. The plan should also define how communication will take place among team members. Informal communication should also be encouraged and nurtured.

Although not necessarily critical in a sourcing decision, it can be a good idea to have in place an escalation procedure, which indicates what level of management should be informed if there are variances from the project budget or schedule. One way to ensure that problems are communicated to upper management in a timely manner is to schedule regular progress meetings. This also makes certain that problems are addressed sooner rather than later so that the project does not get too far behind schedule.

3.10.3 Creating a Work Plan

It is useful to create a work plan that breaks down the sourcing process into manageable tasks. One method is to build a work breakdown structure (WBS) using software such as Microsoft Project, which breaks down the project into summary tasks made up of work packages that represent individual tasks. Besides generating manageable chunks of work, the WBS also provides a detailed picture of the project scope. It generates a product that can be used to monitor progress, creates cost and schedule estimates, and aids in team building by illustrating to team members how they fit into the process. Team members can also be asked to participate in designing the WBS to create a sense of joint ownership.

The first step in building the WBS is to list all the major deliverables or tasks from the scope statement in the SOW. The next step is to name all the tasks that are required to complete or produce each of these high-level tasks or major deliverables. These intermediate-level tasks are called *summary tasks* and are made up of a collection of even lower-tier tasks, called *work packages*. In addition, each summary task and work package should be named as an activity that produces a product, using an action verb and a strong noun, to avoid creating open-ended tasks and activities that never get completed. The final step is to organize the work packages in a way that is meaningful according to the situation. For instance, work packages may be organized based on the steps laid out in this handbook, or they may be organized according to the team members responsible for carrying out the task.

3.10.4 Developing a Market Research Plan

At several points throughout the strategic sourcing process, it will be necessary to gather data to make the most informed sourcing decision possible. Just as there is an overall project plan, there should also be a market research plan. The market research plan should include broad specifications of how the problem will be addressed, a break down of the problem into salient issues and manageable pieces, and a broad and detailed definition of the information needed to address the problem.

There are three general categories of research: exploratory, descriptive, and causal.[3] Exploratory research is used to gain insight into the general nature of a problem, which can suggest solutions to the problem or lead to new ideas. Descriptive research is designed to provide a summary of some aspect of the environment or ascertain magnitudes when hypotheses are tentative and speculative in nature. Causal research tests the cause-and-effect relationships between two variables and is based on very specific hypotheses. Most research related to developing sourcing strategies involves descriptive research, but causal research may come into play when examining the factors that drive pricing. Exploratory research is least likely to be relevant.

Research data collection methods can use either primary or secondary data. Primary data is collected to address a specific research objective,[4] and can produce both qualitative and quantitative results. Primary data collection methods include observational studies, focus-group studies, surveys, behavioral studies, and experiments. Secondary data sources are already available, but have been collected for a purpose other than the current research objective.[5] These can also be qualitative and quantitative in nature. Primary data is usually more accurate and relevant than secondary data because it was collected for the researcher's specific goals and tends to be more current. However, primary data is often more expensive and time-consuming to obtain. The choice of primary versus secondary data should be influenced by the results of the portfolio analysis of the various commodity groups (portfolio analysis is covered in Chapter 8).

---

[3] Aaker, Kumar, and Day, *Marketing Research*, New York: John Wiley & Sons, 1998, p. 73.

[4] Ibid, p. 78.

[5] Ibid, p. 77.

Good supply market research is scientific yet creative (not that these are mutually exclusive). It uses multiple methods of research, including those that yield both primary and secondary, and quantitative and qualitative data. Good research also realizes the interdependence of models and data. It acknowledges the cost and value of information. It maintains a healthy skepticism, and above all, it is ethical in nature.

3.10.4.1 Collecting the Information[6]

Information on the market and potential suppliers can and should be gleaned from different sources. The data collection process will be hard work, and access to the information may not be easy. It may involve performing personal, telephone, mail, or electronic interviewing, particularly when identifying potential suppliers.

3.10.4.2 Preparing and Analyzing the Data

Once you have collected all this data, what do you do with it? The data preparation phase involves the data processing steps necessary to get the data ready for analysis. It is the step that enables researchers to derive meaning from the data. It includes the editing, coding, transcription, and verification of data in preparation for statistical analysis.

3.10.4.3 Preparing and Presenting the Data

The final step in the process is preparing and presenting the results of research and analysis. The final report should address the specific research questions identified in the problem definition. It should describe the research approach and sources used and provide details on the data collection process and data analysis, including the major findings, conclusions, and recommendations. The findings are communicated to the commodity team both in a written report and an electronic presentation.

3.11 Distributing Tasks

A general breakdown of the project team's tasks should be reviewed at the first work meeting. First, an as-is assessment of the project's particular issue will be conducted. Second, gathering intelligence capabilities via market research data collection and analysis will provide a microlevel

---

[6] Monczka, Trent, and Handfield, *Purchasing and Supply Chain Management,* 3rd edition, Cincinnati, OH: South-Western College Publishing, 2004.

perspective of the problem. Third, evaluating current and alternate suppliers and recommended performance metrics will add substance to the proposed strategy. Next, synthesizing data culled from the previous three stages will illuminate prospective and appropriate suppliers. This initiates the decision-making phase of the project. After determining target suppliers, negotiating, contract planning, and implementation follow. Finally, the team's sourcing strategy proposal is submitted to the sourcing council or to the CPO and the CFO for final review and approval.

Tasks from the WBS should be divided among the team members. Strive for an equitable distribution of the workload; if one task is meatier than another, then allot more time or people to it. Remind the task leaders that they are responsible for the outcome of that task — even if they delegate downward.

At this point, it is a good idea to do a check and obtain management approval. You have made a lot of progress and have identified a plan, and it is always a good idea to ensure alignment with the corporate strategy and the business. A last-minute check can make certain that things have not changed from the time you began the effort. From a risk management perspective, an approval also ensures that there are no unforeseen consequences of which you need to be aware as a result of the team plan. An approval can be as simple as a brief discussion with the CPO, a teleconference, or short presentation. Once you get the go-ahead, it is now time to set the plan in motion — the next step of the process.

3.12 Checklist

- Work with finance on project budget.
- Present to supply-chain council for approval.
- Introduce a project charter.
- Assess required skill sets for team members.
- Establish communications across relevant departments and recruit a CFT.
- Host kickoff meeting to introduce project, define expectations and responsibilities, and write SOW, communications plan, work plan, and market research plan.
- Assign tasks.
- Find management approval checkpoint.

3.13 Results

Established team and preliminary project plan
Tasks to be completed and ownership

Project plan with key milestones and completion schedule
Information to be collected and ownership of tasks
Sources of information
Resource estimates
Time-phased schedule
Major milestones identified and tied to deliverables of project charter
Management approval to proceed

Chapter 4

As-Is Assessment (Creating Internal Business Intelligence)

Function	Objective	Tactical Step	Chapter/ Appendix
Supply market intelligence	Supply market research	Opportunity identification and validation	2
		Project approval	2
		Establishing the team	3
		Project plan	3
		As-is assessment	4
		Supply market research	5
		Market forecasts	5
		External and market analyses	6
	Strategy and resource commitment	Detailed supplier evaluation and research	7
		Evaluate current and alternative strategies	8
		Understand contract formation	8

Function	Objective	Tactical Step	Chapter/ Appendix
Strategic sourcing	Negotiate and select supplier	Develop relationship strategy	8
		Strategy position paper	8
		Develop requests for information (RFIs) and build negotiation strategy	9
		Negotiate	9
		Final supplier selection	9
		Form contracts	9
	Implement and promote compliance	Implement contracts	9
		Transition to relationship manager	10
Relationship management		Communicate expectations	10
	Improve supplier performance	Measure performance	10
		Resolve issues and develop supplier performance	10
Benchmarking processes and driving continuous improvement		Build an organization for supply-chain excellence	11
		Benchmark performance and drive continuous improvement	12, App. B

4.1 Chapter Outline

- Getting started: defining user requirements
- Internal analysis
- Identifying historical cost and volume trends
- Segmenting spend by user, type, and supplier
- Data warehouses
- Creating a spend analysis report

- Project cost and demand requirements
- Analyzing data
- Reviewing paperwork
- Performing cost audit

What is interesting about self-analysis is that it leads nowhere — it is an art form in itself.

— Anita Brookner

Before a strategic sourcing team jumps into a major analysis of external suppliers or any other action for that matter, there is a need to identify the current internal situation. Before any type of new strategic change initiative can begin, it is critical to understand the current status within your organization. In the words of a senior vice president of supply-chain management at a major Fortune 500 company, "I come from the 'old school' of thinking: get the basics right first before you launch into any project!"

As the team maps out the project, it is critical to allocate time to understand the current spend patterns, user requirements, sourcing processes, and technology requirements for the category. Understanding the status quo gives you an idea of the opportunities for improvement, as well as the challenges and roadblocks that might lie ahead in driving change. Start with the customer. In this case, customer refers to the "internal customer," or the internal user group that is ultimately paying for the product or service for which your team is managing the supply base. One of the most important steps when developing a sourcing strategy is to understand the needs of the end users of the goods to be purchased. These customer or user requirements will guide your team's direction into the initial supply market research activities.

In addition, a thorough spend analysis should be conducted using a dedicated business intelligence (BI) team if possible. This is often the most challenging portion of the work, because it may involve sifting through multiple databases, legacy systems, and data warehouses to bring together an accurate picture of where the money is being spent, with whom, and by whom. Because of the time required to develop this information, the team may think about getting the BI function involved early in the project charter portion, so that the internal BI analysis can be reported on a timely basis and does not hold up the entire project. An external team is always a good idea, as having information system specialists who know where and how to look for the data is critical to success. Most of the time, people assigned to a strategic sourcing team are not considered data-cleansing experts.

4.2 Getting Started: Defining User Requirements

The internal user group may be a business unit, a function, or even an entire division that ultimately defines the need for the sourced product or service. To understand their needs, the project team must solicit firsthand input from people in various functional areas of the company who use or influence the use of the commodity goods in question. So, what information needs to be collected from users?

The following series of questions can be a starting point for collecting comprehensive data on users' needs and other issues associated with the purchase decision:

- What are the product specifications? How is the product used? Does it have any proprietary advantages?
- What is the target cost or price to be paid? What is the current cost or price per unit, and what is the overall budget? Do the users or the company have any cost reduction goals in mind?
- Are there specific delivery requirements (daily, weekly, or monthly intervals)? What are the costs of different delivery options versus the carrying cost of warehousing the goods?
- What are the volume requirements (material requirement forecasts based on marketing projections)?
- What are the service expectations from the supplier? Should the supplier be involved in product design?
- What performance or design quality standards need to be met?
- What is the importance to the end user application? Is it a component part or one used indirectly in the production of the end product?
- Are there specific packaging requirements for storage (space and breakage considerations)?
- Are there specific transportation requirements?
- Are there any viable substitutes for the commodity that could reduce cost or increase quality?
- Is there any opportunity for standardization?
- Is volume ramp-up or ramp-down anticipated?
- Are there expected design changes in the foreseeable future?
- What is the likelihood of vertical integration?

The information gained from answers to these questions can form the basis for a questionnaire that can be designed for various users to rank the most important criteria in the purchasing decision. Input should not be confined to members of the commodity team. It is important to go to the scene of the action. In addition to surveys or other indirect methods, visit the plant floor or engineering lab to experience the design or production process firsthand, and talk to the people directly involved. Go back to your notes from the project team recruitment process; it is likely you were pointed in the direction of some resident experts, who can now assist you with collecting information. Understanding the specific objectives is important here. A buyer's needs and objectives may include:

- Price or cost reduction
- Improved quality performance
- Improved delivery performance
- Improved technology
- Increased levels of customer or service support
- Higher degree of supplier responsiveness

For example, one of the sourcing strategy teams we interviewed in the past was examining user requirements for fuel additives. After extensive meetings, the team was able to derive the following strategic objectives for the commodity, based on meetings with internal users:

- Reduce fuel additives' annual spend by ten percent by the end of the year.
- Review the current fuel additives usage in all business units involved and develop a corporatewide spend profile for fuel additives.
- Have a clear price or cost structure for fuel additives that allows the enterprise to monitor and benchmark prices with the market.
- Justify the number of fuel additive providers.
- Develop infrastructure for supplier services to enhance technical research and support.
- Develop and implement continuous-improvement process with selected suppliers.
- Ensure that manufacturers and suppliers satisfy sustainable supply-chain management policies.
- Reduce total cost of materials and services to lower the cost per barrel across the organization.

4.3 Internal Analysis

As user requirements are understood, the team will move into preparing an as-is assessment of the current supply-sourcing policies. This phase of BI gathering tracks actual spend for use by the strategic sourcing team. The as-is assessment is threefold. First, a local spend analysis is performed for the specific commodity or service. Second, the contract terms and specifications for the commodity or service are reviewed and compared with historical outputs. Third, user input is obtained.

4.3.1 The Local Spend Analysis

The purpose of a local spend analysis is to identify and track all of the company's costs (or spend) on inbound goods and services that are used to develop outbound goods and services. The spend analysis is broken down into specific expense categories. Each expense category could correspond to either a commodity or a service, depending on the particular subject matter focus of the sourcing project. The spend is broken down by user, type, and supplier (in that order), resulting in a useful database file. This task can be performed in-house with a spend analysis software program or can be outsourced.

One of the most difficult parts of understanding user requirements is in examining nontraditional spend areas such as services and utilities. Many of these items are considered "sacred ground" as users have always had the authority to decide where to purchase these services. However, the fact that nontraditional purchasing spans areas that have been considered the domain of other functions for many years simply means that the input of these stakeholders is more important than ever. Involvement helps ensure that ownership of the resulting decisions can be established within the user group. This is a key requirement for a successful deployment of any supply management strategy.

In assessing the different types of nontraditional purchases made by the organization, not all forms will be classified as *strategic*. Moreover, there may exist certain types of purchases that are best made by internal clients, as they are relatively standard, and the client uses sound purchasing practices in awarding the business. In deciding which types of commodity groups or service groups to address, the team should target those purchases that exceed an agreed-upon baseline level and offer the non-value-added reductions with the potential for significant cost savings or competitive advantage.

Analyzing all purchases can be tricky. In some organizations, an internal client department, such as finance or information systems, initiates the involvement of purchasing in sourcing decisions. Organizations may also initiate purchasing involvement via some form of control system. For instance, an internal audit of payments and matching purchasing orders may reveal a significant amount of "backdoor buying," which bypasses the formal purchasing process.

A comprehensive spend analysis across all strategic business units and functions will include all forms of spending within the cost of goods sold.

Although most organizations have a good handle on their major commodity spends, capturing spending in nontraditional purchase volumes may be difficult. Some organizations in the process of implementing enterprise resource planning (ERP) systems (such as SAP, Oracle, and Baan) are already being forced to identify these levels of spending. These systems will aid in standardizing databases and can help automate the process of analyzing all purchasing data. However, before these systems can be used, a consistent understanding across all of an organization's operating units is required to introduce value-added purchasing in nontraditional areas. A key activity at this stage should be to look for commonalities of activities and materials among user sites or subunits to identify opportunities for leveraging. This may require a commodity-classification–coding scheme and an internal-organization–coding scheme to aggregate the information.

Some of the different approaches identified by companies we interviewed at this stage are as follows:

- Through our accounting systems we can identify, measure, and monitor large volumes of procurement spend based on general ledger account code, supplier, customer, and dollar volumes. We identify this spend with various representatives of each strategic business unit (SBU) and determine if purchasing can provide a value add to the current process. Additionally, this allows us to identify where the large spend is occurring and perhaps combine it with other areas within the corporation for greater discounts.
- We use a bill payment database to identify areas to which we may potentially bring value. In addition, we have identified, through company publications, areas that were being outsourced, and we pursued those contract opportunities.
- We have a summary database that shows our expenditures by supplier, commodity, and business unit. We use that summary database to evaluate areas of spend in which commercial procurement might be able to provide improvement in total cost. We also keep abreast of changes in the business world to identify areas in which recent legal or policy changes may allow us to leverage our business. Examples include deregulation of electricity and natural gas.
- The process followed to gather information on potential nontraditional areas was to review annual accounts payable data for each location including corporate offices. Several databases were reviewed, and suppliers from whom and areas in which purchases exceeded $100,000 were targeted. Accounts payable data, which included location, supplier ranking by total expenditure, supplier name, and annual expenditure, were sent to a nontraditional supply

management representative at each location. The following information was requested: estimated expenditure, type of purchase (nontraditional, production [direct], or nonproduction [indirect]), commodity, department authorizing the expenditure, whether subject to an agreement (divisional, regional, national, or global), and expiration date of agreement.

Be careful! Doing a spend analysis can in some cases mean diving into a black hole. In about 80 percent of the companies we interviewed, an initial venture into spending analysis proved to be a data nightmare. For example, many companies found that their spend analyses were tracked using Excel spreadsheets. At one company, this was the case across the entire organization (see Table 4.1).[1]

Table 4.1   Corixa Case Study

Corixa is a nine-year-old biotech firm working on autoimmunotherapeutics for treating and preventing cancer and autoimmune and infectious diseases by understanding and directing the immune system. "We've always been good about not having a lot of different people making purchases," says Corixa's purchasing manager Kris Kepperler. "There's never been a dollar cutoff below which a person outside of purchasing could buy and expense something." But just because purchasing has always handled spending for the company doesn't mean it has always had a good handle on what it's spending.
In the days before Corixa got access to e-procurement and supplier enablement technology, the company's researchers and other employees would requisition items using an Excel template that "looked like a requisition form." Requisitioners would fill out the spreadsheets (the rule was one requisition per supplier), save them on their desktops and then e-mail them to the purchasing department for processing. Once they had created requisitions, researchers or other employees would then store the spreadsheets on their computers, Kepperler says, resending the originals to purchasing when they needed to reorder items. "Of course, if a product or a part number changed, it never changed on the spreadsheet, which meant we would have to repeat the same corrections over and over," Kepperler recalls.

[1] Adapted from *Purchasing*, Corixa betters buy process with hosted e-procurement, June 19, 2003, pp. 36C2–36C4.

Table 4.1   Corixa Case Study (continued)

The bigger problem, however, was that all the data about how Corixa was spending its dollars was scattered around the company on computers of individual employees. There was no way to understand what we were spending in the aggregate," Kepperler says. "It would take me two full days just to prepare our purchasing performance reports." Fast-forward a few years to when electronic sourcing and procurement burst onto the scene. "Many of our suppliers started to offer ordering capabilities through Web storefronts," Kepperler says. "We took advantage of those, but a company our size could never afford a big enterprise E-procurement system.
Corixa then learned of a company called SciQuest, headquartered in Research Triangle Park, North Carolina, which offered a technology to funnel purchases through a single system so that companies such as Corixa could better understand what they were buying. Corixa saw Sciquest as a way of automating their purchasing process without paying huge sums. Today, SciQuest enables and aggregates suppliers' electronic catalogs and other content and also handles punch-out integrations to suppliers' Web storefronts where needed. Corixa's researchers can search and place orders for such things as lab supplies — Corixa's biggest spend category — and computers, maintenance, and office supplies.
When Corixa negotiates contract pricing with particular suppliers, Kepperler says, suppliers are responsible for loading relevant data into the SciQuest system. If buys are either small or rare enough to obviate the need for catalogs, Kepperler can load suppliers and their products into the SciQuest system in person, making them available through the commercial search tool. Researchers love the new tool. Kepperler notes that "SciQuest is where our researchers find what they want and route requisitions to purchasing which then approves and pushes orders out — through SciQuest — to suppliers." An indication of success is that SciQuest usership is now in excess of 99 percent on all orders. Aside from fact finding, requisitioning products is now much easier for end users. They have actually grown to liking its use, despite some grumbling initially.

As you collect data, total the annual spend for each commodity or service. If any hidden separate costs (warehousing or transportation) are relevant, tack those on to the total amount, too.

4.4 Identifying Historical Cost and Volume Trends

As you collect information on local spend, begin identifying any cost and volume trends that become apparent in the data. These trends may appear in multiple ways: by user, department, geography, season, etc. The as-is picture will continue to map itself as you study the value chain of each commodity or service. Most organizations have no idea what lies beyond their tier-one suppliers, yet the information can often be produced relatively easily during the data collection process.

A knowledgeable analyst who understands how to mine information on the Web can offer a great deal of assistance in more obscure cases. For example, consider this announcement: "This week, company XYZ announced that they would begin producing gyrochips for the U.S. company who produces brakes for automotive companies such as Ford and General Motors. XYZ noted that demand for the chips was growing and that they would need to expand their production facilities significantly to meet the growing need for gyrochips."

This short snippet of information provides several key pieces of information: (1) demand is growing, (2) gyrochips may be in short supply, and (3) there is a three-tier supply chain here. To get at this information, an analyst would need text-data–mining tools to be able to convert time snapshots into information bundles, assess their relevance, and begin to develop a database to create the value chain network. These networks are constantly changing, so they need to be updated on a regular basis. Word-of-mouth data from buyers and suppliers can also be captured and input into the database to assist in mapping the value chain; see tip in Table 4.2.

The real skill of supply-chain intelligence lies in configuring the information and diagramming it to build a model to mine and detect historical trend information. There are lots of supply-chain models to optimize a network, but they all assume that the network is given and is populated with plenty of good data. What is needed is a dynamic network to capture inventory levels, the structure of the network, and an understanding of the disruption and propagation of new networks. You also want to understand the network overlays of different major supply-chain partners, as well as the other industry elements, that may interface with the network.

Table 4.2 Using a Web Analyst: Tip

When using a Web analyst to map supply chains in China, the challenges increase. Chinese has many dialects, but fortunately, all public information is in the same language, Mandarin. When mining data on Chinese networks, there is no need of a higher-end translation, but there is a need to identify people, places, nouns, and simple relationships. Again, a good analyst can capture information from the Web and put the map together.

4.5 Segmenting Spend by User, Type, and Supplier

An important part of understanding the as-is supply situation involves defining category priorities and delving into the data. To make sense of the data, a coding structure is needed to "clean" the data and understand the different elements.

An example of a typical scenario that might be faced by a senior executive attempting to gain control of the unit's spend is shown in Table 4.3.

Table 4.3   Example Scenario

The CEO has asked me to develop an action plan to improve inventory accuracy, reduce staff numbers where feasible, and ensure that customer service levels for tier-one customer orders will consistently average 99 percent for the next three years. I am really under the gun here, and let me tell you why.

I joined the company 18 months ago and was told to reduce costs and make the supply chain more efficient. The first thing I did was expand our manufacturing facility to meet growth objectives. The new facility was sized to accommodate significant expansion. Additional floor space was added to enable the redesign of workflows to streamline order processing and deliver substantial productivity improvements. We have cut inventory and are moving to a just-in-time production pull system.

Second, I set about trying to reduce the size of our supply base. I collected our spend data, which was in many different legacy systems, and had an analyst spend three months cleaning the data, sorting it, etc. We discovered a lot of problems in the data. For example, IBM was listed in three different fields as International Business Machines, I.B.M., and IBM. We are now trying to rationalize our supply base, to leverage our spend volumes and get quantity discounts. So far, we are finding this difficult, because everyone wants to use his or her preferred supplier.

Third, I am trying to establish a forum for sales and operations planning, to allow everyone to be working off the same forecast. Right now, we have a marketing forecast that our planner and schedulers do not believe is real, so we have had shortages. We have a lot of overtime because of poor capacity planning, and some SKUs have far too much inventory (six months worth), whereas others are stocking out and making some of our best customers furious with us. To make matters worse, we are projecting growth in the area of 100 to 300 percent in the next five years. If we cannot manage our current orders, what will happen when we double or triple in size?!

Clearly, with so many priorities, this individual's hands are full. However, a top priority in this case would be to understand current spending and clean the data to develop a clear picture of the opportunities. This is a foundation for supply-base optimization and reduction.

The following is a checklist for segmenting data:

- Working with IT, collect high-level spend data across business units.
- Estimate number of suppliers currently used.
- Identify groups of similar purchases by user, type, and supplier.
- Prioritize different expenditures based on the monetary size of each spend.
- Establish common coding structures by supplier and by stock keeping unit (SKU) or statement of work (SOW).
- Group similar commodities and services into common codes.
- Apply North American Industry Classification (NAIC) coding structures when possible to facilitate ongoing research and linkages to pricing indices and market analysis (see Appendix D in this book for more details).

4.6 Data Warehouses

Most companies are overloaded with volumes and volumes of data from their internal and external information systems. Managers find it difficult to make sense out of all the data they have, and this puts them at a competitive disadvantage. Data warehousing is one way of handling this "information overload." It must be deployed in conjunction with an organizational master data process redesign that often accompanies a major ERP implementation effort.

A data warehouse is a huge relational or multidimensional database (sometimes with terabytes of disk storage), which stores volumes of historical data for the company. If this data is organized departmentwise or functionwise, it is termed a *data mart*. Data warehousing, on the other hand, has many different meanings to different people but can be simply defined as a process that involves the physical separation of an organization's production operations (day-to-day tasks) from its decision-support operations (long-term tasks).

Data warehousing involves the tasks of extracting, converting, and standardizing an organization's operational data from ERP and legacy systems and loading the data into a central archive, the data warehouse. ERP systems comprise integrated multimodule, companywide software systems with the objective of integrating key processes such as order entry, manufacturing, procurement, accounts payable, payroll, and human resources. The goal of ERP is to facilitate information sharing and improve

Table 4.4   Assessing Database Functionality

What are the tasks, both actual and ideal, that the database's users want it to do for them?
What types of data elements (that is, *fields*) are currently in the database?

communications across the organization. Examples of various ERP systems are SAP, Oracle, PeopleSoft, Baan, and J.D. Edwards. Legacy systems are large software systems that perform crucial work for and are vital to the organization. These systems are generally large, hard to understand, hard to maintain, and difficult to modify. To assess database functionality, ask the questions listed in Table 4.4.

The primary data warehousing tasks include:

- Modeling data for the warehouse, based on the company's information needs
- Extracting data from the operational databases
- Cleansing data (such as eliminating negative inventory quantities or standardizing field or attributed titles)
- Transforming data into the warehouse model
- Loading data into the data warehouse database

4.6.1 Company's Existing Data Warehouse

It is generally prudent to involve the IT, supply management, project management, and finance departments in developing a data warehouse that provides significant benefits to the company as a whole and to employees as individuals. Existing ERP and legacy systems should be taken into account when designing a new system in which information regarding spend with suppliers can be stored in one common place. Details such as which suppliers are paid, price, quantity purchased, etc. will be easily accessible. This data warehouse can enhance the ability to manage suppliers and also reduce the administrative time required to collect information.

4.6.2 Data Warehouse Structure

The information in the data warehouse should be structured into four major security levels:

- *Spend analysis level:* Information displayed is at the enterprise level.
- *Business unit level:* Displays information for the entire business unit.

- *Plant level:* Information displayed is restricted to a particular plant.
- *Month-to-date spend review level:* Displays detailed information regarding the current accounting period.

The key parameters by which the data can be filtered to generate reports for the different levels should be decided by business requirements. An example follows:

1. Date parameters, which determine the date range of the information being requested are:
   a. Year — indicates the year for which data report is required
   b. Beginning period — indicates the starting month to gather information, given in numeric form (1 = January, 2 = February, etc.)
   c. Ending period — indicates the ending month to gather information
2. Business operation, which shows how the company's business units and plants are structured:
   a. Segment — could be consumer, industrial, or corporate
   b. Segment manager — vice president responsible for the operating group
   c. Operating group — groups that are associated with the manager
   d. Business unit — business units that are associated with the operating group
   e. Plant — individual plant that is associated with the business unit
3. Supplier classification, which is a four-digit alphanumeric value that is assigned to each supplier based on the type of product or service provided. A supplier may provide multiple products or services to the company, but the classification code is based on the highest percentage of spend in a particular commodity:
   a. Level 1 — the first character of the code refers to an overall category such as direct, indirect, capital expenditure, nonsourceable, or uncategorized
   b. Level 2 — the second character defines the supplier's product or service
   c. Level 3 — the third character further defines the supplier's product or service
   d. Level 4 — the fourth character further refines the information defined at level 3
4. Purchasing order (PO) and sourcing information:
   a. PO origin — indicates how the POs were created or in which the applications (e.g., ERP) they were created
   b. Sourcing agent — personnel responsible for the management of a commodity or group of commodities

5. Commodity; classification codes assigned to groups such as items or products:
   a. Division — allows user to see details of a commodity, based on how his division has labeled that commodity
   b. Supply — maps all division commodity codes to a common numbering scheme; allows the user to retrieve information across all divisions, based on a single commodity value
6. Supplier inquiry, which provides the capability to inquire by supplier identification number or by supplier name and wild card combination:
   a. Supplier number — vendor number assigned to the supplier by PeopleSoft or other software in use by the company
   b. Headquarter parent number — associates individual suppliers to their major U.S. company
   c. Global parent number — associates individual suppliers to their major global company

4.6.3 Supply Management Data Warehouse Reports

The user should be able to fill in the parameters mentioned earlier, as per his or her requirement, and generate any of the following reports:

1. Supplier spend analysis — total spend by supplier for a selected segment, business unit, or plant for a specific period
2. Spend analysis by segment and unit — total spend by business unit within the business segment
3. Top 50 suppliers by segment — top 50 suppliers based on total spend for a specific period for a particular segment
4. Supplier spend detail — information that includes PO, receipts, and vouchers.
5. Supplier classification review — listing of the supply management's coding structure for commodities and suppliers

4.6.4 Need for Commodity Classification

Although creating a data warehouse will be invaluable to the sourcing process, it will be challenging to tie all purchasing systems into the warehouse and to ensure all products are identified by only one code. These problems can cause variance while cross-referencing product data. As communication about miscoded products increases among members of the supply chain, the chances for error further increase. Therefore, as the product moves through the supply chain, it would be much more efficient for all parties to reference the product by the same code; hence, the need for a common commodity classification code.

For more on commodity classification, see Appendix D.

4.6.5 The Data Breakdown

4.6.5.1 By User

You have already identified who the users are and how the data warehousing works. Now it is time to find out how much each user (by site and department) spends on the particular commodity or service.

4.6.5.2 By Type

Complete an SKU analysis to identify spend by type of commodity. You will refer to an SOW analysis when looking at a service.

The data for this analysis, if not centralized, might be housed in a materials resource planning (MRP) or bill of materials (BOM) database for commodities, or SOW for service vendors. SKU analysis can be one of the biggest challenges in the project if information is not organized properly. The company's engineering department often creates SKU codes without guidelines for consistency, creating a new SKU for every product order.

A couple of examples: One company routinely bought safety gloves for various production and lab tasks. After doing an SKU listing report, they found that across the company a total of 100 different varieties of safety gloves were being bought, a number that struck the project team immediately as being unreasonably high. After speaking with the employees who use the gloves, the team deduced that all requirements could be met with just five different types of gloves. Similarly, another company looked at their product packaging: corrugated boxes in a variety of shapes and sizes. There were a total of 16 types of boxes being used, but after some research, the project team found that they could make do with just three different sizes. A "perfect fit" was not necessary for each product as previously thought.

One thing to keep in mind regarding the SKU analysis: do not strive for perfection here. It is not worth it. Go instead with the "good enough" guideline of 80–20 accuracy (the Pareto principle). For instance, with the glove example, perhaps the reduction could have been even greater, say down to three gloves, if the team had persisted in their inspection. But go with the kaizen approach here: fast and big results (as much as possible) as a means of accomplishing incremental change. SKU reduction is a common value-building opportunity part of any commodity-based project.

Such dramatic savings may not be found while looking at services, but control methods to prevent excessive variability in terms of suppliers or database listings may be beneficial. If applicable, place similar commodities and services into category groups. In some cases, spend reflects a mixed good and service combination. If the product could be attained without the service factor, then categorize it as a commodity. But if the primary driver for the vendor is based on their skill or knowledge, then classify it as a service.

4.6.5.3 By Supplier

If noncentralized, supplier data is likely to be located in the site's accounts payable database system. Watch for suppliers listed in different formats: e.g., IBM, International Business Machines, and I.B.M. Corp. Standardize consistency when possible; this in itself is a value-build opportunity. One easy way to address the latter problem is to create standardized list-box options in the database that do not allow for user-level additions.

4.7 Creating a Spend Analysis Report, Including Unit-Cost Analysis

Once the data on total spend is aggregated, the project team performs a strategic analysis of spend patterns in nontraditional areas. (Remember, the team may include key stakeholders from different groups, who can help in identifying major areas of nontraditional spending that have potential for savings through purchasing involvement.) It is important to note that this stage of the process involves considerable research on the part of purchasing and other functions to identify these areas. Commodity or service groups should be "Paretoed" according to two major categories: (1) volume or potential return and (2) ease of attaining cost reductions or objectives. The deliverable at this stage is a portfolio of nontraditional purchases, with the objective of targeting those purchases that have a high potential for immediate savings (in the form of leveraging, headcount reduction, simplification, etc.) and also have a high probability of success.

4.7.1 The Spend Analysis Report

After each data category has been extracted, make a cumulative plot graph for visual analysis. The graph should chart the annual costs compared with their strategic value (if X occurs). Also run query reports for written summaries. When the data is prepared, ship E-files out to all of the site team members and the project coordinator. When the project coordinator arrives at the site, the IT member should make a presentation of the findings to the full team.

The IT team member should make hard and soft copies of the presentation and spend data and give them to the site team members. The team administrators at each site should send the data to the project coordinator (the strategic sourcing manager or chief procurement officer [CPO]).

4.8 Project Cost and Demand Requirements

Understanding the projected spend and the future site-level agreements is critical for current and future project planning. There is simply no substitute for calling a meeting with the key user groups to go through a detailed discussion on the following:

- Importance of the item to the using firm
- How and where the item is used in the firm
- Prices paid for the item
- Item specifications
- Quality requirements
- Delivery requirements and scheduling information
- Packaging requirements
- Transportation requirements
- Substitution opportunities
- Standardization opportunities
- Volume requirements
- Expected design changes
- Likelihood of integration
- Others

Forecasts for the product or service may include the following:

- Projected lead-time requirements
- Current and future volume requirements
- Current and future delivery window requirements
- Seasonality considerations
- Future trends
- Changing quality requirements
- Emerging technologies to consider
- Value-added services that may become available in the near term and future
- Potential mergers and acquisitions in the industry
- Emergence of new global sources
- Financial forecasts for key suppliers

4.9 Analyzing Data

4.9.1 Analyzing the Spend Data

Market risk is quantified on a case-by-case basis, depending on the company's particular situation. Common considerations, though, include product specifications, technological capabilities, regulatory affairs, and supply availability. For instance, a commodity could be comparatively pricey but at the same time be a necessary component to a company's hot product that requires custom production by a highly specialized process. Alternatively, a technology may be so cutting-edge that it is still patented, but using it gives the company a strong competitive edge in its key product.

4.9.2 Reviewing Paperwork

In addition to collecting information from people, some documents must also be perused at this stage, including the SOW for services or the BOM product and engineering specifications for commodities. The main purpose of reviewing these documents is to serve as a quality control measure; sometimes, after using something for a while, we begin to overlook performance in areas such as delivery or promised features and benefits. When it comes to these "spec" documents, the team should invite someone from engineering to serve as a consultant.

4.10 Performing Cost Audit

An audit of the company or department cost accounting database comes next. When assessing a database, regardless of type, a primary goal is to ensure that the information tracked by the database is entirely based upon users' input about specifications. Therefore, it is a good practice to first clarify its usage objectives. What is the database intended to do for the department? To find out, simply survey its users. You can do this either electronically or in person, but either way, try to get a solid sampling pool of input. You can also ask them how well the database delivers the intended objectives and whether there is any additional related functionality that they think would be beneficial, which you could pass along to IT for review.

Compare this input with the database itself. Using the general ledger view in which costs are always recorded, identify each of the company's (or department's) SBU cost centers. Then, consider the types of information being tracked. How closely and intuitively does this information correlate to the stated usage objectives? Is it complete, reflecting all of the necessary fields, or are certain types of useful information currently lacking? Are any of the fields or other data no longer needed? If so, should they be deleted?

This is the last step in performing the local spend analysis and will set the project team well on its way to implementing a successful new sourcing strategy.

4.11 Grassroots Interviewing

The final stage of the as-is assessment is to focus on identifying the users' (internal or external) requirements for the particular sourced commodity or service and its communication systems. This activity, instead of interfacing with database files, is done using the old-fashioned in-person interviewing approach. In our high-tech world, sometimes the most effective methods are the least tech-dependent. Purchasing managers can learn about a specific opportunity or even discover what kinds of opportunities currently exist simply by talking to the people in other departments.

To get things started, the standing team members should seek broad-level input from the client department team member, exploring the perceived strengths and weaknesses of the given commodity or service. This inquiry should include queries such as: What are the usage objectives for the commodity or service? How about its communication systems? (Note: Do not jump to the conclusion that your communications system needs to be changed or upgraded. Technology can be a terrific expeditor, but not always.) Are there any quality or efficiency problems? Is there anything your department does that works especially well? Do you have any thoughts on how it could be improved upon? Ask the same questions of the team member's employees for a broader scope of input.

To mine these built-in information sources, the purchasing manager should take advantage of both formal and informal communication channels. For example, formal communication mechanisms could include a predrafted questionnaire survey (from simple to complex) for managers and staffers to complete. Informal channels can help establish and build relationships, for example, soliciting feedback from employees or other internal customers about critical issues that may have been overlooked in the survey or other discussions. Informal communication channels are often opened up when managers have developed a level of trust with their employees.

By the end of the as-is assessment period, your project team will have amassed a significant amount of data. You will have a clear understanding of user needs as they relate to each sourced product or service. You will be able to cite historical cost and volume trends and segment spend by category and to project some future requirements based on the data warehouse that has been created or updated. Finally, you will have created a report, the as-is assessment, detailing your conclusions, that will launch the external market intelligence effort.

4.12 Checklist

- Define user requirements.
- Perform local spend analysis.
- Identify cost and volume trends.
- Segment spend by user, type, and supplier.
- Create spend analysis report.
- Project cost and demand requirements.
- Analyze data.
- Review paperwork.
- Perform cost audit.

4.13 Results

- Understanding of user needs
- Proper data warehousing
- As-is assessment

Chapter 5

Developing Business Intelligence and Market Intelligence

Function	Objective	Tactical Step	Chapter/ Appendix
Supply market intelligence	Supply market research	Opportunity identification and validation	2
		Project approval	2
		Establishing the team	3
		Project plan	3
		As-is assessment	4
		Supply market research	5
		Market forecasts	5
		External and market analyses	6
	Strategy and resource commitment	Detailed supplier evaluation and research	7
		Evaluate current and alternative strategies	8
		Understand contract formation	8

Function	Objective	Tactical Step	Chapter/ Appendix
Strategic sourcing	Negotiate and select supplier	Develop relationship strategy	8
		Strategy position paper	8
		Develop requests for information (RFIs) and build negotiation strategy	9
		Negotiate	9
		Final supplier selection	9
		Form contracts	9
	Implement and promote compliance	Implement contracts	9
		Transition to relationship manager	10
Relationship management		Communicate expectations	10
	Improve supplier performance	Measure performance	10
		Resolve issues and develop supplier performance	10
Benchmarking processes and driving continuous improvement		Build an organization for supply-chain excellence	11
		Benchmark performance and drive continuous improvement	12, App. B

5.1 Chapter Outline

- The sales and operations plan
- The three laws of forecasting accuracy
- Market forecasts
- Forecasting uses
- Forecasting types
- Characteristics of a solid forecasting system
- Six steps of forecasting
- Sales and operations implementation

Prediction is very difficult, especially if it's about the future.

— Niels Bohr, Nobel laureate in physics

Some things are so unexpected that no one is prepared for them.

— Leo Rosten in *Rome Wasn't Burned in a Day*

An unsophisticated forecaster uses statistics as a drunken man uses lampposts — for support rather than for illumination.

— After Andrew Lang

To expect the unexpected shows a thoroughly modern intellect.

— Oscar Wilde

It is far better to foresee even without certainty than not to foresee at all.

— Henri Poincaré in *The Foundations of Science*

The competitive environment we face today is characterized by increased globalization, low-cost labor in China and the Far East, and resulting increased price pressure in every industry. In a recent study of global supply-chain trends,[1] the primary trend that every manager identified was increasing cost pressure. This pressure is driving companies to adopt a new approach to competitive strategy that involves adopting an end-to-end supply-chain perspective of process improvement. A senior vice president at a global logistics meeting I attended at a large pharmaceutical company echoed these findings. When he was asked for the three things that he felt were important for the next year, he said, "Results, results, and results!"

At several of the companies I visited in the past year (including American Airlines, Shell Oil, Chevron Texaco, Milliken, and GlaxoSmithKline), every manager I spoke with was seeking to "cast the net" farther and extend approaches that were working well in procurement or logistics across a broader spectrum. The commonality of this theme in these different industries was notable. In every case, managers were seeking to find ways to move beyond simple cost reduction to value creation for the end customer to contribute to increasing market share, revenue, and profits.

The scope of this book focuses on improving value through improved management of the supply function. This is best accomplished when the

---

[1] Handfield, R. and Giunipero, L., Purchasing and Education Training Requirements, Center for Advanced Purchasing Studies, 2004.

supply management function adopts a supply-chain perspective and identifies how best it can play a role in creating value for the entire business. Nowhere is this more important than in the development of an internal business intelligence unit that not only captures the needs of internal customers, but also integrates the needs of external customers into planning and decision making. As such, this chapter focuses on one major aspect of this role — understanding the nature of demand for supply market inputs and services, and how best to meet this demand.

5.2 The Sales and Operating Plan

One of the most common elements enabling companies to lower cost and deliver results is a well-defined sales and operations plan (SOP). The SOP represents a fundamental element of supply-chain strategy. In the estimation of an academic with whom we have been working in this area, Dr. Kevin McCormack, 80 percent of the companies he has encountered do not have a formal SOP process that is rigorously followed. This is rather frightening when you consider that the plan is the only element that links the execution of major strategies in marketing, finance, human resources, operations, logistics, purchasing, accounting, and IT. A well-developed SOP should also be the basis for establishing budgets, forecasts, inventory goals, recruiting, and training, not to mention fixed-asset utilization and capacity planning. Very simply, a SOP is a process to

1. Establish agreement on upcoming demand or resource requirements that balance needs of business and customers.
2. Identify exceptions and take appropriate action for remediation.
3. Review what-if results of plan deployment and adjust accordingly.

It is a collaborative process for planning and decision making between core business functions. The SOP is also a critical element in the internal business intelligence unit's list of value-adding functions. By establishing trends and understanding the changing nature of demand in the supply chain, it can play a pivotal role in shaping supply strategies that deliver value to the end customer. So why is it not done well in most companies?

In many cases, the process was established years ago and subsequently fell into neglect. The SOP is not a major technology breakthrough or management fad — it is, in its simplest form, a structured methodology for agreeing on future demands, noting resources required to meet that demand, and identifying possible problems that need to be targeted and resolved. As shown in Figure 5.1, a formal SOP planning process forces members of involved functions to sit down across the table and admit

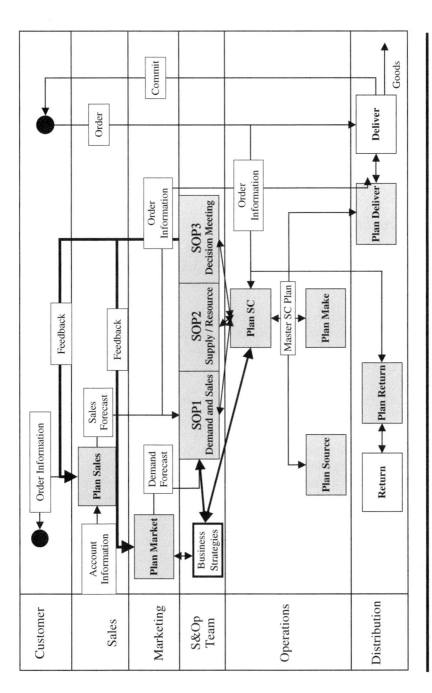

Figure 5.1 Basic supply and demand planning process with SOP.

that there may be problems with the plan. It also forces them to make changes that can accommodate elements that are simply not executable given current resources and market environments. It will not result in a plan that will make everyone happy; it will, however, result in a plan that is executable and realistic.

5.3 The Three Laws of Forecasting Accuracy

How useful a given forecast is as a decision-support tool varies according to the quality of individual inputs of the forecasting process. In particular, there are three laws to be aware of from the get-go.

5.3.1 Timeliness of Source Data

To a certain extent, forecasting, by its nature, resembles a guessing game. Predictions of future trends are inferred from historical data. At the same time, the indicators that the historical data represent (such as product prices and features) do not stand still, thoughtfully waiting for forecast analysts to track and analyze them before they change. Change will always clock at a faster pace than forecasts. Consequently, forecasts are fated to be fallible and imperfect, and this explains the need for error margins. This inherent struggle gives us the first law of forecasting accuracy:

> Law 1. Forecasts are intrinsically imperfect.

Given that forecasts are intrinsically imperfect, the primary focus then becomes, just how imperfect are they? This can be a crucial inquiry. If a manager makes large-impact decisions based on a forecast that is riddled with inaccuracies, it could wipe out a year's worth of profits. Although the first law of forecasting accuracy is a constant, it is qualified by two scope-based variables: the forecast's duration and the topic's breadth. The next two laws address these issues.

5.3.2 Timeline for the Forecast

The length of the forecast's outlook is one objective indicator of its level of reliability. It is a whole lot easier, for example, to predict events and behaviors over the next two weeks than it is to predict them over the next two years. Similarly, two-year forecasts are much more manageable than twenty-year forecasts. This brings us to the second law of forecasting accuracy:

Law 2. Shorter-range forecasts are more accurate than longer-range ones.

5.3.3 The Forecast's Scale

When creating a particular type of forecast, the analyst needs to decide whether to study the functional topic as a whole category or to break it down into its various subcategories (technically referred to as the forecast's *unit of analysis*). For example, beer manufacturers can opt to forecast customer demand of U.S. beer consumption by total gallons or by volume (kegs or six packs), packaging (aluminum can or bottle), and feature (regular or light). If forecasting for total-gallon consumption levels, then the forecast is described as in the *aggregate*; if broken down into subcategories, then it is described as *per stock keeping unit (SKU)*. Because aggregate forecasts require less detail-level itemizing, they are more manageable and controllable than per-unit forecasts. The SKU forecasts, having various points of entry, also have an increased chance for error. This leads us to the third and final law of forecasting accuracy:

Law 3. Aggregate product forecasts are more accurate than unit product forecasts.

Table 5.1 discusses some of the forecasting problems in the grocery industry. Having said that, note that per-unit forecasts are not unimportant. In fact (unfortunately), they are more important than aggregate forecasts. Knowing how many total gallons to produce has limited usefulness: if the consumer wants a keg of light beer, but the company had elected to sell its light beer only in six-pack volumes, then the company experiences a lost opportunity in the form of a missed sale that goes to a competitor.

Table 5.1   Case Study: Per-Unit Forecast Error Rates in the Grocery Industry

The grocery industry continuously forecasts product demand based on inventory-tracking measures that rely on scanning inbound and outbound product flows. Yet, in any given grocery store on any given weekend for any given product, there is a 15 percent chance that the product will be out of stock; all in all, a dispiriting outcome, especially given all the work put into the initial forecasts. The specific problem faced by the grocery industry (and they are certainly not alone) is that even if their per-unit forecasts are reasonably accurate, they still fall short as a decision-support tool because they do not account for per-store demand levels. So, a product will gather dust at one store location while losing multiple sales opportunities at another store location.

Missed opportunities are par for the course. But, in today's world of commerce, there are only so many lost-opportunity hits that a company can take without it starting to hurt. See Figure 5.1 for an overview of the supply and demand planning process.

5.4 Market Forecasts

Market forecasts are written reports that attempt to challenge the existing assumed market requirements used in the SOP; this may span economic, demographic, and technological factors. *Forecasting* is the process of researching and analyzing market trends. Generally performed by a forecasting analyst group housed in the company's marketing department and reviewed and distributed by the finance department, forecasts are designed to help guide managers in their various planning functions, essentially fulfilling a decision-support role.

Plot graphs are useful for visually identifying trend patterns. The goal of time-series analysis is to discover nonrandom patterns, for example, a steady increase or decrease in a control variable such as demand. (Any time-series model will include a certain amount of inexplicable and random erratic behavior. These fluctuations are the reason for having inventory buffer levels.) A positive trend shows an increase and a negative trend shows a decrease. For example, DVD movie sales have a positive trend, but VHS movie sales have a negative trend.

A forecast analyst might be called upon to assess the number of people who will order Chicken McNuggets at a given McDonald's location during the lunch rush on a given day. To answer this question, the analyst would need to consider the potential variables in Table 5.2.

5.5 Forecasting Uses

Once the SOP and forecast are established, a set of impact statements should be prepared that communicate in clear and certain terms the effect of this plan on demand, capacity, transportation requirements, supply market requirements, and customer priorities (see Figure 5.2). These statements should be shared not only with relevant internal functions (sales and distribution) but also with critical suppliers and logistics channel partners.

As the year progresses, critical customer metrics, supplier scorecard metrics, and sales and customer satisfaction metrics should be tracked and reviewed quarterly in a "balanced scorecard" dashboard. This ensures that overall performance does not suffer due to an inappropriate strategy

Table 5.2   Forecast Conditions and Variables

Condition Type	Variable
Time conditions	Time of day
	Day of the week
	Seasonal time of the year
Economic conditions	Current competitive positioning
	Store location
	Competitor near store locations
	Dietary habits of local population
Business conditions	Recent advertising promotions
	Recent health inspection grades
Weather conditions	Weather forecasts

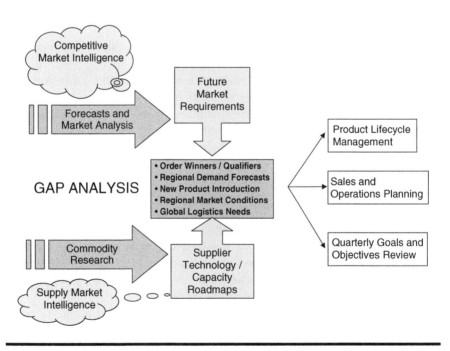

Figure 5.2   Informed decisions require effective data collection mechanisms.

conflicting with other elements in the integrated strategy. This assessment will identify what is working now (the drivers) and what is not working (the barriers). In any supply chain, there are some forces working for you

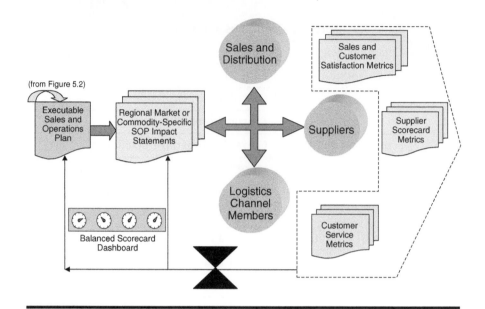

Figure 5.3   Ongoing quarterly reviews.

and others working against you. What do you notice about the nature of the gap that has to be closed?

Forecasts can help supply managers identify what kinds of component materials or service offerings are needed, in what quantity, and at what time. They can also help inventory managers plan for replenishment, HR managers plan for recruiting, and logistics managers plan transportation allocation and scheduling. Forecasts help production department managers plan their production schedules. Even postproduction managers use forecasts. Marketing managers, for instance, refer to them when fashioning product lines and their price ranges, and advertising campaigns and budgets. Sales staff can use forecast data to plan promotions and to help build value and goodwill at the reseller–customer level. Customer service managers can turn to forecasts as the baseline in assessing the status of customer orders; and all managers can look to forecasts to help determine staffing and recruitment needs. Quarterly reviews, as shown in Figure 5.3, can ensure that planning continues on track.

Forecasts also provide a benchmark against which to measure supplier performance in cost, quality, and delivery. Supplier performance metrics are simply a tool to align customer requirements, internal SOP plans, and the supply base to ensure communication, identify potential problems, and drive improvement toward a specific set of goals. Achieving this requires that the necessary resources are included in annual budgets. See Table 5.3 for an example.

Table 5.3   Case Study: Forecasting Reseller–Customer Sales Trends

Kellogg's is one company that uses its forecasting function as a means of adding value for their retail customers. They not only forecast data as it pertains to themselves, but also forecast their product sales data at the customer level, which the sales force can use with customers to jointly develop a promotional plan to drive the accounts' sales. This benefits both Kellogg's and their customers alike.

5.5.1 Forecasting-Outlook Ranges

Forecasts span three time horizons, depending on how far into the future they will predict. Short-range forecasts are used to predict trends up to one year out and reflect mostly quantitative data. They provide the foundation for decision-based items such as component quantity ordering requirements, inventory replenishment or buffers, and production and delivery schedules. Midrange forecasts support operational decisions and also investment-based decisions — albeit fairly short-term investments, which can be fully implemented within one to three years. Planning applications include two-year aggregate production and budget plans, equipment purchases, facility or trucking-fleet expansions, employee hiring, or joint company–supplier projects. Long-range forecasts try to anticipate what might transpire three to five years down the road and are more qualitative. These tend to focus on significant capital expense planning decisions.

5.6 Forecasting Types

Forecasts can be developed for a variety of functional topics, as highlighted in the following text:

1. Customer demand (or simply demand)
2. Price (including international exchange rates)
3. Competitor (identification and competitive ranking)
4. Capacity (resources including technology advancements)
5. Supply resources
6. Regulatory

Demand forecasts are primarily associated with internal business intelligence systems, that is, understanding what the internal business units will require for the product or service specified. The other elements involve external and supply market intelligence and will be covered in Chapter 6. Although each type of forecast is important for any given company, their individual significance will vary from company to company. Note also that some forecast types (e.g., demand, supply, and regulatory) will be ongoing, whereas others might be on a more periodic (competitor and price) or as-needed (e.g., capacity) basis. This chapter uses the demand forecast as its main reference point because it is ongoing and is also often the foundation of many of the other forecast types.

5.6.1 Demand Forecasts

Demand forecasts predict how many customers will order a particular product or service during a fixed period, such as the following year. This type of forecast pertains to a product's current and projected demand, inventory or human resources available (as well as planned inventory holdings for the end of the year), and typical lead times for deliveries from suppliers. This information is often captured on a "single sheet of music" shown in Table 5.4. This template shows the basis for the different inputs required to capture inventory status, planned demand, and pro-duction schedules for the year in a production environment. (A similar planning format can be used for services using HR man hour units but with no inventory.)

Note that the process of developing a forecast can be difficult because everyone has different agendas. Finance is typically driven purely by sales revenue forecasts and may not have insights into the stock keeping unit (SKU) level sales required to generate revenue. Typically, finance will also be pushing for severe inventory reductions, to increase the return on assets ratios. Marketing will often have sales targets for their regions that they must meet, and may drive promotions or, worse yet, push sales that are not required by customers into their warehouses to meet these targets. Production managers are often driven by cost targets for their facilities, which can be improved through large batch runs with minimal setups. These targets may or may not be aligned with customer-demand or inventory planning levels. The challenge of the SOP process is to take these inputs and, through a process of consensus, arrive at a single executable forecast on which everyone can agree. This is the forecast that should then be shared with suppliers and used in planning commodity strategies. See Table 5.4 for an example of a sales and operations planning worksheet.

The impact of a poorly developed forecast on the success of a supply management strategy is shown in this table. Note that overforecasting will result in too much product, especially when a formal commitment is made to a supplier based on leveraging a given volume. Costs incurred may include excessive inventory and holding costs, transshipment costs, obso-lescence, reduced margin, and a major conflict with the supplier and loss of goodwill if the negotiated contract falls short of the forecasts. On the other hand, underforecasting can result in higher expediting costs, greater prices due to spot buys, lost sales, lost companion product sales, and further forecasting errors. In either case, the situation is not good.

Table 5.4 Sales and Operations Planning Worksheet

Sales and Operations Planning Worksheet

Family: **Pharmacol**							S&OP Meeting Date:	9/19/2003
Year: 2003			Units of Measure:	Mlbs.				
Key Targets:	Perfect Order **90%**	FG Inv.: **60 DOS**	Line Utilization: **85%**	OT: **15%**				

	Beg.	J	F	M	A	M	J	J	A	S	O	N	D	Total
Inventory Position Using FM Forecast														
FM's Forecast		8000	6000	6667	8000	12000	13333	13333	16000	17333	17333	18667	20000	156667
MM Forecast (11/1/04)		6,667	5,000	5,556	6,667	10,000	11,111	12,222	13,333	14,444	14,444	15,556	16,667	131667
Difference		1333	1000	1111	1333	2000	2222	1111	2667	2889	2889	3111	3333	25000
SM's Production Plan	Beginning			12325				48450			32300			93075
Inventory (FM Forecast)	32220	24220	18220	23878	15878	3878	-9455	25662	9662	-7672	7295	-11372	-31372	142145
DOS	90	68	51	67	44	11	-26	72	27	-21	20	-32	928	24
Target Inventory (DOS)	30	30	30	30	30	30	30	30	30	30	30	30	30	30
Inventory Position Using MM Forecast														
MM Forecast (11/1/04)		6,667	5,000	5,556	6,667	10,000	11,111	12,222	13,333	14,444	14,444	15,556	16,667	131667
SM's Production Plan				12325				48450					32300	93075
Inventory (MM Forecast)		25553	20553	27322	20656	10656	-455	35772	22439	7995	-6450	-22005	-6372	71253
DOS		71	57	76	58	30	-1	100	63	22	-18	-61	-18	32
Target Inventory (DOS)		30	30	30	30	30	30	30	30	30	30	30	30	30
TO COMPLETE IN NEGOTIATIONS:														
Negotiated Inventory	Assume Monthly Dema	10740	Daily = 358 Cases											
Negotiated Forecast (WITH MM)														
Negotiated Prod Plan (WITH SM)													32220	
Forecast Inventory														
DOS														90
Target Inventory (DOS)														30

Forecast Inventory = Beginning Inventory - Forecast + Production

Note: This scenario assumes that the finance manager (FM), market manager (MM), and supply manager (SM) must reach a consensus on production, sales, and inventory planning. Typically the consensus development is coordinated by an SOP or "demand" manager.

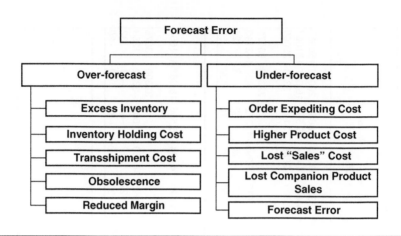

Figure 5.4   Forecasting errors and impacts.

Demand data is further complicated by *seasonality*: a pattern of demand fluctuations that recurs at regular intervals. Perhaps the most extreme example of seasonality is sales of toys, electronics, and other consumer goods, which peak during the Christmas season (and plummet shortly thereafter, when the bills start streaming in). But other examples abound; for instance, apple sales are highest in the fall, when apples are at their best. Fishing gear and boat sales are strong in summer but weaker in winter. Hospital ER demand peaks during Christmas and flu season.

Manufacturing companies rely on demand forecasts to determine how much of the product to make and, therefore, how many components to keep stocked in the inventory, and how much advance ordering time is needed for component parts. Service companies (that is, distributors and resellers) use demand forecasts to plan their human resources activities, including hiring, scheduling, and compensation. The demand forecast can be used to establish capacity planning for their workforce and drive thinking on the number of shifts, and it may also translate into computer and automation equipment purchases as required.

The process of generating timely and accurate demand forecasts is critical as an input into the SOP, as well as the firm's long-range forecasting process and sourcing strategies. As such, it is an activity that must be scheduled regularly, and enough time should be devoted to the process.

5.7   Characteristics of a Solid Forecasting System

5.7.1   What Types of Data Do We Need?

Sometimes, with data collection initiatives, the operating instinct is similar to "all you can eat" buffets: grab as much as you possibly can. Although data collection processes definitely do tend to be large scale and comprehensive, they should still maintain a targeted focus.

There are several other best practices regarding forecasting that firms should consider:

- *Establish an owner for the forecasting process:* A single individual should be assigned the task of developing and coordinating inputs for the forecast. If there is no owner, it is not likely to get done.
- *Document the forecasting process:* Be sure to document the sources of inputs into the forecast, the assumptions made during the process by each function, how it was resolved, and the consensus reached. This is important for several reasons. First, you can always go back and review the assumptions when the situation changes and revise the forecast accordingly. Second, it establishes accountability for information that was used in developing the forecast and identifies how to improve the process the following year. Third, it allows for a postmortem the following year when the forecasting process occurs again.
- *Analyze the variability of demand for your products and services:* This means questioning the assumptions behind the forecast. Different products and services may have different seasonal patterns, different demand drivers, etc. As such, it makes sense to forecast at the product level, group SKUs into products, and then produce the forecasts. Understand what is driving the variability, and drive its root cause.
- *Conduct this process on a regular (scheduled) basis:* The forecasting process should occur at least once a year and should follow a defined process similar to the one shown in Figure 5.5. If it is followed, then a truly executable SOP will result.
- *Develop a forecast for each product:* Each product may be subject to competitive forces and have different supply inputs; therefore, each product will require a separate forecast.
- *Develop a forecast for each customer:* Use the information collected in the field that can help drive the critical elements. This can lead to understanding why demand is changing (or not).
- *Update the forecast weekly:* Once an annual forecast is generated, a weekly update should be used with a rolling ten-week horizon. This horizon should be shared with key suppliers, as well as internal parties, to better allow them to plan capacity, scheduling, production, etc.
- *Develop a credible and believable forecast:* If a forecast is not credible, people will throw it out with the bathwater. This is often the case when finance and marketing build an overly optimistic forecast and production cuts it in half because they do not believe

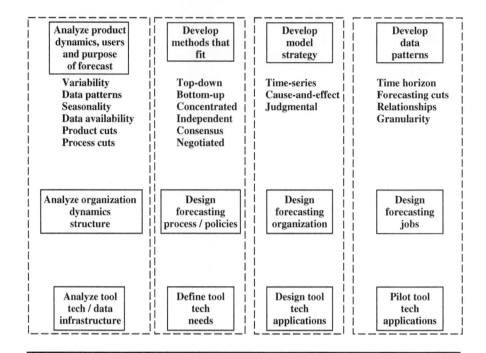

Figure 5.5   Building a best practice forecasting process.

it. Marketing may be building a forecast based on their quotas, not on the actual requirements. To a varied and business-literate audience that is new to forecasting, note that not only does the source data need to be summarized and the analytical findings discussed, but the accuracy also needs to be demonstrated and supported. The forecast needs to address the oft-silent but persistent question in the mind of every manager: Why should I believe you? Note that this element, and this question in particular, eclipses all of the others.

■ *Establish information systems to support the forecasting process:* A system to support the forecasting process through automatic updating will ensure that the forecast is kept up to date and that the updated information is communicated to the right people.

The particular forecasting model used should be relatively low maintenance. It should satisfy the four "easy" criteria:

■ *Easy for which to get source data:* The data should be available; that is, it should be currently obtainable (e.g., through existing databases).
■ *Easy to compute:* The database's query capabilities should be sufficiently powerful and the interface should be intuitive to operate.

■ *Easy to validate:* It is important that at least some previous data be available for validating the forecast. This criterion is further subdivided into two: First, the relevant conditions should not have changed so much that what happened in the past cannot be used to predict the future. Second, the validation needs to be such that it is credible to its ultimate users (managers).

■ *Easy to distribute:* We are living in a paperless world. Electronic copies, as well as paper (hard) copies, are great for distribution objectives.

Building a best practice forecasting process, as shown in Figure 5.5, begins by analyzing product dynamics, users, and how the forecast will be used. At this point, factors to consider are variability in the data, patterns, seasonality, and other elements. In addition, various tools should be employed to identify the requirements. Next, with the help of a top-down forecasting process, an independent consensus of what the forecasted demand will look like can be developed. Next, a process owner must be assigned, and a forecasting organization developed. The specific application tools should be decided. Next, the actual jobs for individuals should be created around each forecast, with specific roles assigned. The forecasting tool should be piloted to ensure it works, before it is applied in real life. Additional expert representation from the marketing (both forecast analysts and account managers) and sales (order fulfillment and customer service for customer complaints) departments should be recruited. In cases when a dedicated business intelligence unit exists, generating this type of demand forecast becomes a regularly scheduled activity that is integrated into the quarterly task of the team.

5.8 Six Steps of Forecasting

To determine which method produces the highest-quality forecast, we need to follow the forecasting process shown in Figure 5.6. Following the steps in this process will produce a forecast of the highest quality.

5.8.1 Step 1: Calculate Forecast Accuracy and Generate Baseline Forecasts

5.8.1.1 Collect the Data

To generate a baseline forecast, where do you look for the data? There are two basic types of data that should be collected: *source data* and *double-check data*. Each type is discussed more fully in Table 5.5.

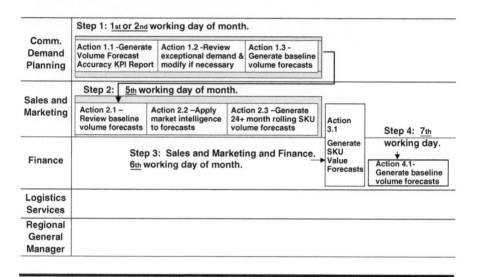

Figure 5.6 Six steps of forecasting.

Table 5.5 Types of Data

Data Category	Data Type	Data Collection Method
Source	Forecast data elements	Database import
Double-check	Current and past variables comparison	Internet research In-person manager interviews Delphi group assessments
	If applicable: previous forecast's accuracy level	Internet research In-person manager interviews Delphi group assessments

5.8.1.2 Collect Source Data

The term *source data* refers to all of the data elements to be analyzed in the forecast; it is the forecast's subject matter. Collect the source data from available sources, typically from databases or ERP systems. Use a hybrid approach to data collection: first, the breakdown approach, supplemented later with the buildup approach.

5.8.1.3 Collect Double-Check Data for Accuracy

After assembling the source data, collect data to validate the source data. This means collecting double-check data on the source data. This data, based on previous on-point forecasts (if any) and supplemented with

Internet and interview research, is used to refine the qualitative parameters of the source data. First, find out if the relevant market conditions have stayed the same or changed since the last on-point forecast. Second, if other on-point forecasts were previously performed, determine how reliable their results proved to be.

Some basic questions can be used to help determine current, as opposed to previous, market conditions. Assess the level of competition; is it comparable to the levels indicated in the previous forecast, or has there been a significant change? Gauge the general health of the economy; is it growing or in a recession? How is the economy's current condition likely to impact the target product's sales? Do not assume that all products do poorly in an anemic economy. Discount product lines, for example, tend to thrive in this environment. How do competing products compare in terms of the competitive strategy triumvirate of price, quality, and speed to market? Consider also the technology capabilities, in terms of both what the company currently has and what is available on the market, keeping in mind that the technology sector is extremely fluid and new-generation technologies are being released all the time.

Both types of information can be obtained by some combination of the following means: consulting reliable Internet Web sites; interviewing target managers in sales, marketing, and engineering; and assembling a Delphi group (a group of targeted people representing cross-functional expertise). Plugging into a variety of functional perspectives is an effective double-check measure in the data collection effort. Often, data variables agreed upon by consensus in this group setting are likely to ensure the effectiveness of the data inputs, which would improve the reliability of the data outputs as well.

In these double-check information elements, hard numbers are not always necessary; rather, what is needed is high-level feedback regarding the dependability and current applicability of the source data (culled from previous on-point forecast data).

5.8.2 Step 2: Apply Market Intelligence to 24+ Month Rolling Volume Forecasts with Sales and Marketing

Forecasts can be analyzed and assessed using buildup analysis and breakdown analysis.

5.8.2.1 Buildup Analysis

Buildup analysis essentially employs a two-tier, bottom-up approach. First, it analyzes data on a per-unit scale. Then these results are combined and totaled, either by division or companywide, to produce an aggregate forecast. For example, Proctor & Gamble might forecast demand for its individual soap product lines — Ivory, Dove, and Irish Spring — and then tally them all to get a number for total soap demand.

5.8.2.2 Breakdown Analysis

In this approach, aggregate forecasts provide the starting point and are further broken down into per-product forecasts. A product's overall demand data across a specific region is analyzed first. Analysts then break the data down further by splitting it into product-unit (SKU-level) forecasts, based on historical trends. For example, Proctor & Gamble might develop aggregate-level forecasts for soap for global regions: United States, Canada, Mexico, Latin America, Europe, Asia, and the Pacific Rim, and then split the global forecasts into per-product forecasts (for instance, quantifying the demand levels for Ivory in Mexico). This approach is useful when a region's demand levels for the product are quite stable or uniform.

5.8.2.3 Brainstorming Model (Delphi Studies)

Brainstorming has proved to be an effective approach for creatively tackling problems and proactively seeking solutions. This approach is grounded in gleaning information and ideas, stream-of-consciousness style, from a comprehensive assortment of people in a team setting. Sometimes called Delphi studies, this approach to forecasting is founded on comprehensive input, by recruiting expert representation from the various relevant supply-chain members. Sales and marketing should definitely be included in this approach.

At one major software firm I visited, the following approach was used. The sales team was asked for their sales quota, what they had booked to date, what they could book for the remainder of the year, and what the resulting gap was. Next, they were asked to develop a list of the top three customer prospects that they had for the coming year. Finally, they were asked to share with the group the size of these prospects and the probability of booking them, as well as the concerns that were preventing these customers from agreeing to the sale. This then resulted in a structured action plan for each sales associate and also generated a much more realistic forecast; when it was learned, for example, that the customer's budget had been cut and that the likelihood of the forecast coming to fruition was unlikely. The forecast was revised downward.

5.8.2.4 Demographic Studies

The underlying focus of this form of long-range forecast is on consumers and their likes and dislikes; therefore, it applies to forecasts that assess future customer demand. The consumers are categorized by demographic classifications such as income, gender, race, age, and geographic location. Analysts study the demographic data to identify future demand trends, and to help them predict demand levels in various demographic markets. By looking at demographic data, analysts can discover, for example, that U.S. consumers care more about how much a beverage costs and how convenient it is for them to buy, whereas Japanese consumers care more about how the beverage is packaged. Moreover, analysts could learn about trends in niche markets (which can then be applied to mass-customization decisions), such as beverage preferences among Japanese-Americans or any other specific demographic niche.

5.8.2.5 Test-Marketing Initiatives

These initiatives are primarily used in conjunction with new product development, prior to initiating full production. Similar to demographic studies, this method functions to identify long-range customer demand. However, test marketing differs from demographic studies in two respects. First, the data that test marketing collects comes directly from a representative sampling of the target customer market, or at least key supply intermediaries, as opposed to using secondhand data, usually compiled initially by and acquired from market research firms. Second, the demand data that is collected from test marketing is specific to the particular product prototype, whereas demographic data is much more generic, running along general product classification lines; it is not company specific, let alone product specific, as is test marketing. The company can then make design modifications or, if the response is especially discouraging, scrap the product entirely, based on the preliminary feedback. Automobile manufacturers test-market their prototypes among select dealerships and at car shows. The software industry also relies heavily on test marketing (or beta testing) by distributing advance copies to key customers and resellers.

5.8.3 Step 3: Generate 24+ Month Rolling SKU P&L Value Forecasts

Using this input and identifying trends can generate a 24+ month rolling forecast by SKU, which also shows the estimated profits and losses by SKU of products associated with this forecast.

If using a cross-functional team, distribute the plot charts of the past few (maybe two to ten) on-point forecasts. Ask the team to review the plot charts, with an eye toward spotting any cumulative trends over the

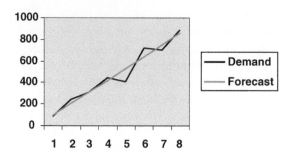

Figure 5.7   Plot chart example.

years covered by the prior forecast periods. For example, food industry analysts could have referred to prior forecast data, dating back to, say, 1980, to spot the trends of growing sales for high-protein and vegetarian foods and of shrinking sales for carbohydrate foods, such as bread and pasta. If a trend is spotted, then dig deeper to try to find the underlying reason for it. One specific type of trend to look for is seasonal fluctuations. For example, sales of high-protein foods might be higher in winter than in summer, and the converse might be true for vegetarian food sales.

Use a plot chart to visually quantify the data for analysis. Record the data on a plot chart, putting *time* on the *x*-axis and the forecast variable (*demand*, for example) on the *y*-axis. An example is shown in Figure 5.7.

Some of the methods that can be used to generate a 24-month forecast include linear regression, exponential smoothing, and other algorithms. These will not be covered in detail in this chapter.

5.8.3.1 Seasonal Indices

For products with large seasonal variation, a seasonal factor can be calculated and used to weight the forecast up or down according to the season.

5.8.4 Step 4: Perform Financial Gap Analysis

Once the 24-month forecast is generated, it should be shared with finance and translated into financial planning numbers. Finance may not like the looks of the forecast at this point, but this forecast provides the most realistic approach yet as to what is really happening. At this point, the review will identify the volume and value forecasts against the plan, resolve the gaps with an associated risk analysis, hold the actual SOP meeting (at which the forecast is finally agreed upon), and submit the net forecast requirements to the SCM group, which is then passed on to the suppliers.

Substantial inaccuracies in a given forecast can disrupt any managerial function, but even slight inaccuracies can be detrimental to supply management functions. The importance of obtaining a consensus at the SOP meeting is particularly important. When certain conditions come together, the *bullwhip effect* (described in the following text) can occur — similar to a chemical experiment gone wrong. Things can go haywire very quickly, leading, for instance, to ineffectual production and transportation schedules, bloated or deficient inventory levels, and misguided capacity plans.

The bullwhip effect is the consequence of a particular mix of contributing factors. One, a forecast is released that anticipates increased demand levels for a specific product. Two, supply managers from various departments make ordering and scheduling decisions, independent of one another (as is common practice among nonsynergistic organizations), based on the forecast. Three, the forecast's demand predictions end up being off, even a little bit, either high or low, leaving the provided-for resource allocations correspondingly high or low.

These conditions combine to create one or two domino effects. The first domino effect that is sure to occur under these conditions is that the off-target resource allocations are unnecessarily multiplied due to the fact that managers pursue misaligned responses to the forecast. The consequences of the exponential off-target resource provisions from the first (and constant) domino effect are made worse by the second potential (but realistically probable) domino effect: the cumulative off-target resource provisions emanating from multiple forecasts over a period of time. The bullwhip effect describes the exponential factor in off-target resource provisions at either level. An example is shown in Table 5.6.

Even if the demand was only mildly inflated, the bullwhip effect can easily occur. For instance, a stockpiling of resources at the various supply departments, sometimes at as many as ten different locations along the supply chain, can drive a bullwhip effect. Cumulatively, this stockpiling can cause a glut that can remain unabsorbed for a full quarter or longer.

It is worth noting that the bullwhip effect is actually a symptom of the dreaded functional silos that this book aims to help put an end to. If the various supply managers habitually powwowed to review demand forecasts and then developed a coordinated resource ordering and scheduling plan, then the resulting stockpile would be significantly streamlined, isolated primarily in one or two departments that would have provided a centralized resource point for the supply-chain, companywide. The net dollar impact of the bullwhip effect? Thirty billion in today's economy is a ballpark estimate — all mostly avoidable.

Table 5.6   Real-Life Example: The Bullwhip Effect at Proctor & Gamble

When the demand forecasts are changeably over- and underestimated over time, the resulting resource-provision responses tend to resemble a lie detector test: sharp upward and downward strokes or an erratic yo-yo effect: up and down, down and up, and so on. Proctor & Gamble experienced the bullwhip effect with one of their most popular products, Pampers diapers. After a while, purchasing managers observed these fluctuations in demand levels, and began looking into the matter. They deduced that the consumers (babies and toddlers) and the buyers (their parents) were unlikely sources of the demand fluctuations. So, they started looking at the demand levels higher up the supply ladder: the distributors and the retailers. They found that demand levels were fairly stable among retailers, thereby confirming their presumption that the demand fluctuations were not occurring at the consumer level. Among distributors, they did find more fluctuations in demand levels. They continued backtracking the supply-chain timeline, to their own internal sourcing activities, predicated on inaccurate demand forecasts.

Source: "The Bullwhip Effect in Supply Chains," in *Sloan Management Review,* Spring 1997, by Lee L. Hau, V. Padmanabhan, and Seungjin Whang.

5.8.5 Steps 5 and 6: Approve Team-Based Forecast at Commercial Review Meeting

An overview of steps 5 and 6 is provided in Figure 5.8. The commercial review SOP meeting is a high-level, systematic technique for a company to balance aggregated demand with production and supply capabilities. The SOP meeting occurs monthly and ensures that the business plan matches the company's overall strategic plan, both in units and in dollars. In essence, by periodically reviewing sales and operations data, it gives a company greater forward visibility allowing it to make the necessary adjustments needed to meet or exceed customer expectations. The proper use of SOP leads to an effectively managed supply-chain operation. Some benefits of SOP include:

- Higher customer service
- Better-managed inventories
- More stable production rates, less overtime — leading to higher productivity
- Enhanced teamwork among middle management and executive groups
- Greater accountability regarding actual performance to plan
- Forward visibility and fewer surprises
- Ability to make changes quickly
- More proactive decision making[2]

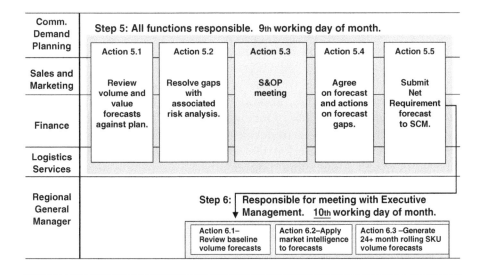

Figure 5.8   Six steps of forecasting (steps 5 and 6).

Wallace describes a five-step generic SOP process that can be adapted to multiple situations:

- Sales and forecast reporting
- Demand planning
- Supply planning
- Pre-SOP meeting
- Executive SOP meeting

Although Wallace gives a detailed description of each step, we will cover some salient aspects here. The sales and forecast reporting step provides updated data to the demand planning step, based on the previous month's sales and new market information. In demand planning, sales and marketing update the demand forecast over a preestablished, rolling time horizon. Note that the purpose here is to develop an unfettered picture of potential demand, regardless of supply constraints. In supply planning, production takes a first cut at determining whether it can, or even should, meet the updated demand forecast. The pre-SOP meeting brings the sales and marketing and production sides together to review any changes or gaps between demand and supply, and to develop an updated business plan on which all sides can agree. Finally, the executive meeting is used to inform top management about the updated plan, and to iron out any disagreements that require a decision at the executive level.

---

[2] Wallace, T.F., *Sales and Operations Planning — The How-To-Handbook.*

Note that SOP does not just comprise a set of meetings; it can require significant changes in the way the various functional areas plan and coordinate with one another. Implementation must occur through a carefully thought-out plan agreed on by all relevant parties. SOP implementation normally takes eight to nine months and begins with a common understanding of what it is, how it works, what it will cost, and how it will impact the bottom line. Once the decision to implement SOP has been made, the next step is to develop an SOP policy document, establish product families, and develop the supporting data reports and spreadsheets. Included in the supporting reports should be a system to continually monitor and improve the SOP process. Many companies are successfully using sales and operations planning by focusing on best practices within the industry.

A typical agenda for this type of meeting is shown in the following text.

When: Last week of fiscal month
Attendees:
> Vice president, global supply-chain operations
> Director, global supply-chain operations (facilitator)
> Manager, global market allocations
> Manager, production planning and inventory control — facility A
> Manager, production planning and inventory control — facility B, etc.
> Vice president, worldwide sales and marketing
> Manager, sales forecast and market support
> Vice president, manufacturing — facility A, B, etc.
> Senior vice president and site head — facility A
> Senior vice president and site head — facility B, etc.

Inputs: Updated ship schedule, regional inventory levels, and list of issues needing to be resolved. Key performance indicators updated within the SOP executive dashboard.

Outputs: Approved and mutually agreed-upon ship schedule for facilities A, B, etc. Meeting minutes and opportunities for improvements (constructive critiques from each attendee) to be distributed to all involved parties.

Agenda:
1. Review executive dashboard.
   a. Address red-light issues.
2. Review consensus forecast and unresolved-issues list.
   a. No issues? Approve.
   b. Address issues list and make executive decision. Approve.
3. Compare consensus forecast with business plan.
4. Recap decisions made.
5. Critique current month's planning process and recommend improvements.

5.9 Sales and Operations Implementation — Best Practices

There are several key questions to review, pertaining to the characteristics of a successful SOP implementation:[3]

- *Who are the people/functions that have to be involved?* One important point to note here is continued executive sponsorship. If the president or general manager or other appropriate executive is not available, it may appear that the SOP process is not being given the importance it deserves.
- *Who is accountable for what?* One of the most important characteristics of an SOP project is that people are held accountable for the information they present.
- *What are the product groups to be reviewed and in what detail?*
- *Are all system requirements in place to obtain the necessary data regarding the product groups that have been identified?*
- *Are actual results available in a clear and concise format, and are these results or metrics available upon demand?* When considering the metrics needed to estimate performance, a company should always be able to compare a projected plan against what actually happened. In doing this, these metrics should be "fit for use" meaning they should measure what is needed as per the SOP and be available when needed throughout the month.
- *Are the SOP calendar and agenda established?* This is very important and should be published to all parties. This is necessary to ensure that everyone is prepared on time with the appropriate data.
- *Is the SOP meeting a working session?* The key to the success of this monthly cycle is that the executive team makes important long-term decisions during the review. This means that the meeting should be interactive with a lot of involvement by all parties.
- *Is an action register maintained as a result of the SOP?* This success factor ties in with the fact that the *SOP* should be a working session. Key decisions should be made, and where resolution is not immediately available, actions should be taken that can be executed before the next review.

Along with understanding the factors, which can make a company's SOP successful, there should be an awareness of common mistakes that

---

[3] http://www.jeboyer.com/s&op.html.

hinder the expected results. Some of these mistakes are the result of not following the guidelines for success highlighted earlier. These include[4]

- *Having the wrong people involved.* This will result in indecisiveness, lack of support, and potentially, multiple plans (which is the problem SOP tries to solve).
- *Unavailable data.*
- *Adding too much detail in the SOP.* Most of the minutiae should be handled during pre-SOP meetings and in day-to-day activities.
- *No feedback or feedback that is not in a meaningful or easy-to-understand format.*
- *Time of the month when SOP occurs.* Many professionals will argue that the SOP is too often tied to financial closings when, in theory, it should occur at the beginning of the month. This should be soon enough to make adjustments and is close enough to the previous month's results.
- *People do not have a clear understanding of when things are to be done.* In other words, there is no established calendar.

5.9.1 Linking the Forecast to the Strategic Plan[5]

David Tabor, in *Parallax View*,[5] describes the strategic planning process for forecasting as a focused activity that should be done on a regular basis. The strategic planning process should not produce a big document; i.e., it should create a concise model of how the company will fit into its market, its economic "ecosystem." The document should consist of about ten slides, including one for the action plan of each major functional area of the company.

This is not to say that the strategic plan should be lightweight. Your executive team will need to work together for at least a couple of days, they will engage in vigorous arguments, and there may be a measure of politics. This style of strategic planning is not about exploring giant economic trends or Michael Porter–style competitive analysis. It is about setting coherent goals and milestones for all parts of the company, and setting criteria and metrics so that progress can be estimated on a quarterly basis. Tabor recommends that the best way to formulate a strategic plan is as a dynamic process, with iterations and midcourse corrections on a regular basis. Details change too fast to use only an annual cycle. Following is an outline of the process:

---

[4] http://www.jeboyer.com/sandop.html.
[5] Tabor, D., Strategic planning, *Parallax View*, Vol. 2, No. 8, http://www. chainlinkresearch.com/parallaxview/V2_08/home.htm.

1. Set aside a couple of days at the beginning of each quarter for a series of strategic planning meetings. The meetings should be off-site, but near to your corporate headquarters so that staffers can come in quickly if needed.

2. Prior to the meeting, all major VPs will have been given a home-work assignment: to describe what they think the world will look like in 18 months. This "environmental forecast" should cover their area of expertise (e.g., new technologies for the CTO and new labor regulations for the head of HR). The forecast should be in the form of bulleted lists and simple charts, limited to four pages per department. To the degree possible, leave out the immediate crises and fire drills (e.g., shareholder lawsuit!) unless they are going to be an ongoing part of your world. These domain forecasts should be circulated to all participants for reading in advance so that everyone starts with common information.

3. The first part of your executive meeting will be devoted to creating a consolidated environmental forecast across the whole company. This is surprisingly hard, as there will be contradictory trends and healthy disagreements about assumptions. Do not short-circuit the debates. Masking fundamental differences in the meeting will lead to a faulty strategy.

4. Next, describe the "whole product" that will be the marketplace leader 18 months from now. Hopefully, this will be your product (or service), but if your company is not in a position to deliver the "killer" product, you still need to know what it will look like in the market. The goal here is to understand what the product will offer customers. This should be described in a single slide.

5. Now you need to decide whether that killer product is yours or somebody else's. Following the dictum of Jack Welch, you really have to be number one (the leader) or number 2 (the strong challenger) in a market, or not pursue the chosen market at all. Again, this is an area of healthy argument — be brutally honest. CEOs: reward realism, not overconfidence and toadying, because the most important discovery you can make is that you have an unachievable goal.

6. Next, fully describe what is expected to be your company's flagship product 18 months from now. You need to describe the whole product as it is experienced by customers, including your services, the products and services provided by your channel, and the related products provided by your partners. This should be described in a single slide, probably an annotated diagram.

7. Describe what each department needs to be doing now to deliver that product or service, in terms of milestones, deliverables, and

metrics that can be reviewed. You will discover some areas to which you just cannot get there from here; the required investment is too high, the architecture just will not go that far, and the market will not accept you without more references. As you discover these concerns, keep track of them and go through steps 5 and 6 until the "impossibilities" are resolved. Again, realism is all important here.

8. The big issues usually show up in engineering/manufacturing or sales/operations, although they will sometimes be masked as finance (not enough money) or marketing (not enough leads). Make sure you focus on problems and root causes, not symptoms or surface issues. Sometimes, you will identify the requirement "to OEM" a product or merge or make fundamental changes to your channel. These big changes need to be confirmed to the executive-only version of the plan.

9. At the end of the process, you will have a brief action plan. Although it is high level, it should be coherent across all departments and easy to understand. The plan needs to be published internally (via an intranet site), and each department's goals should be set around meeting these strategic objectives, as well as the short-term deliverables for the quarter (e.g., product delivery and revenues). The departmental goals should also be published via your intranet.

10. At the end of each quarter, score each department's progress on the strategic goals as well as on the tactical ones required to satisfy shareholders. If there are significant shortfalls, the affected VP needs to troubleshoot the problem and factor it into the plans for the next quarter's strategic cycle. Avoid the temptation to blame the affected department; think of the shortfall as a symptom and lack of companywide coordination as the real problem to be solved.

Despite the SOP publications and resources available, many companies are not utilizing their capabilities to the fullest. A survey of 246 manufacturing professionals by the Oliver Wight consulting firm found the following statistics.[6] Some positive results include

■ Seventy-six percent of the respondents have an SOP process in place, with 77 percent of those having had it in place for over one year.

[6] Making Business Processes Work, *The Wight Line Online Newsletter*, Issue 1, 2000.

- Of the companies that are not currently using an SOP process, 37 percent are planning on implementation within a year of the survey.
- Fifty-three percent of the respondents indicated that this process had reduced the need for executive meetings.

Some of the more negative aspects of the survey include

- Only 27 percent of those who have implemented SOP considered the process effective. This is partly due to the fact that most respondents used SOP with new product initiatives, whereas only 30 percent used it for other programs and initiatives.
- Only 50 percent of the companies surveyed took advantage of a formal demand and supply planning meeting as part of their SOP planning process.

In summary, this survey has shown that there is a positive trend toward seeing the need for SOP; however, companies should become more educated as to the full capacity and technique required for successful implementation.

5.10 Conclusion

Creating and identifying internal and external customer-demand requirements is a prerequisite for building a solid supply management strategy. This chapter has emphasized that forecasting and SOP are critical planning elements that must be adhered to religiously and are a never-ending task. The need to identify changes in business requirements is one of the most difficult elements of a supply management team's efforts, as these serve as inputs for sourcing strategies, contractual negotiations, relationship management, and performance management. Too often, this step is overlooked in the planning function. The need to develop a dedicated forecasting team and establish a rigorous sales and operations planning process is fundamental to success for SCM performance improvements.

5.11 Checklist

- Collect data.
- Check assumptions.
- Identify trends.
- Select forecasting methods.
- Calculate error rate.

- Select forecasting models.
- Analyze data.

5.12 Results

- Accurate forecast data for use in strategic sourcing and sales and operations plans
- Fully deployed SOP process with key stakeholder input and buy-in

Chapter 6

Supply Market Intelligence

Function	Objective	Tactical Step	Chapter/ Appendix
Supply market intelligence	Supply market research	Opportunity identification and validation	2
		Project approval	2
		Establishing the team	3
		Project plan	3
		As-is assessment	4
		Supply market research	5
		Market forecasts	5
		Supply market intelligence	6
	Strategy and resource commitment	Detailed supplier evaluation and research	7
		Evaluate current and alternative strategies	8
		Understand contract formation	8

Function	Objective	Tactical Step	Chapter/ Appendix
Strategic sourcing	Negotiate and select supplier	Develop relationship strategy	8
		Strategy position paper	8
		Develop requests for information (RFIs) and build negotiation strategy	9
		Negotiate	9
		Final supplier selection	9
		Form contracts	9
	Implement and promote compliance	Implement contracts	9
		Transition to relationship manager	10
Relationship management		Communicate expectations	10
	Improve supplier performance	Measure performance	10
		Resolve issues and develop supplier performance	10
Benchmarking processes and driving continuous improvement		Build an organization for supply-chain excellence	11
		Benchmark performance and drive continuous improvement	12, App. B

6.1 Chapter Outline

- Integrating market intelligence with risk assessment
- Types of forecasts
- Assessing global logistics risk
- Tying together the elements of risk
- Eighteen best practices for supply risk management
- Checklist

You don't need intelligence to have luck, but you do need luck to have intelligence.

— Jewish proverb

Intelligence is like a river. The deeper it is, the less noise it makes.

— Unknown

6.2 Introduction

As we noted in Chapter 2, there are a number of approaches used to collect business intelligence and supplier intelligence data, compact it into information bundles, and identify and disseminate it. Although this work can be done by an individual strategic sourcing team, my research indicates that a sourcing team may need up to six months or more to develop a thorough picture of the business intelligence (BI)/market intelligence (MI) environment. If an organization is focused on speed of execution of supply management strategies, it makes sense to improve processes as quickly as possible to deploy more sourcing strategies and deliver cost savings, value, and performance to the bottom line ahead of competitors. It is this fundamental value proposition that merits establishing a dedicated BI/MI team with the acquired skills, knowledge, and training to effectively deliver information to the right people on teams as and when required, using both a push and pull supply market intelligence strategy.

6.3 Integrating Market Intelligence with Risk Assessment

Earlier in the book, we noted that BI/MI is critical in assessing opportunities that may result in a supply-chain design team developing a charter for a strategic sourcing team. However, an integral part of the charter for a BI/MI team is to also assess supply-chain risk. In fact, assessing risk is a major deliverable for the BI/MI team whether a push or a pull approach is being used. Moreover, assessing risk is a way of determining how to tie together the different types of data that can be identified in the supply chain. As shown in Figure 6.1, a formal process is required to develop a formalized assessment of risks, identify the potential impacts, and develop a set of contingency plans to mitigate risks.

The types of risk that are present in the supply market can impact many areas of the company. Market intelligence and risk assessments are

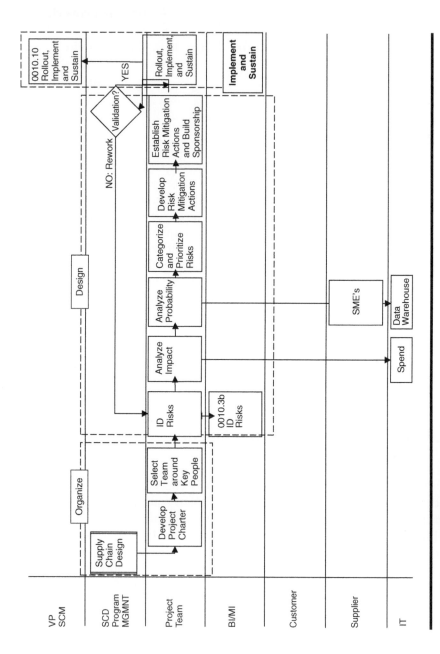

Figure 6.1 Supply risk management.

used by various functional and business units in the organization, not just SCM. Some of the major elements of market and business intelligence include the following:

1. Customer demand (or *demand*) for the supply input
2. Price (including international exchange rates)
3. Competitor (identification and competitive ranking)
4. Capacity (resources, including technological advancements)
5. Technology forecasts
6. Supply resources
7. Regulatory
8. Supply-chain risk

Chapter 5 focused on developing demand forecasts as a method of assessing internal business intelligence opportunities. This chapter will focus more on developing external supply market intelligence, as it pertains to the preceding areas.

6.4 Types of Forecasts

6.4.1 Price Forecasts

These forecasts predict short- and long-term prices for component materials and services that the company needs to make their product and get it to their customers. Prices are often driven by supply and demand, as well as strategic inputs such as technology capabilities, information sharing, and operational streamlining. Price forecasts assist a company in laying out their buying strategies. For commodities that are expected to have rising prices, the purchasing department may stockpile the commodity (buy it in larger-than-normal quantities and store the excess commodity in inventory for future use) to save money. Common stockpiling strategies are *forward buying* and *hedging*, which involves buying more than required for the next month, and perhaps for the next year. Conversely, if prices are expected to fall, buyers could utilize the *hand-to-mouth buying* strategy: buying fewer quantities than usual until the prices go down. The purchasing manager's index (see Table 6.1) can be a helpful tool.

An interesting approach is to look at the producer price index (PPI) and consider the different forces shaping supply and demand. For example, consider the PPI for plastic in the following scenario.

A buyer is looking for pricing irrationalities within a family of plastic shields. Any unusual pricing might require further analysis and negotiation

Table 6.1 Purchasing Manager's Index

The PMI is a leading index for tracking fluctuations in U.S. total purchasing expenditures. Published by the Institute for Supply Management (ISM), it documents month-by-month purchasing spend. NAPM polls U.S. purchasing managers on a monthly basis, querying them as to their total purchasing expenditures for the month. The numbers are entered into the PMI-tracking database. ISM analysts then compare the current month's numbers with the previous month's numbers for each respondent company. The numbers are totaled, and the status for the overall purchasing spend is ascertained as a percentage change: increased, decreased, or same. The data is then rated and published on a scale from 1 to 100. Basically, anything under 50 is indicative of decreased total purchasing spend; anything over 50 shows increased total purchasing spend.

The total purchasing spend is important, because it is a strong indicator of the overall health of the economy. The PMI, therefore, is a critical tool for forecasting projects, particularly for short- and midrange forecasts.

ISM publishes their results in book and Web formats, which are available on a subscription basis. They also publish other indices and periodicals that are helpful, such as *Purchasing Today*, a monthly magazine. Learn more by visiting them online at www.ism.org.

with suppliers. The buyer is performing this analysis by reviewing pricing data between 1999 and 2003. Volumes for each of the part numbers have been similar, so any price differences are not the result of material volume discounts.

Design changes occurred for parts 4 and 5 during 1999 and 2000. In Table 6.2, the prices are given per unit and the figures in parentheses denote the total amount of plastic in the components.

The buyer has also collected other data to help with the analysis. He has tracked the PPI index for plastic between 1994 and 2003 and has developed the labor index based on PPI data for 1999–2003. Finally, he has developed an estimate of the cost breakdown (Table 6.3) for the component, based on discussions with an engineer who reverse engineered the component.

At this point, he compared increases in PPI with increases in pricing attributed to the higher costs of plastic and labor put forward by the suppliers. Several pricing irrationalities requiring further analysis and negotiation with the supplier were identified.

As shown in Table 6.4, there were clear surcharges in pricing during 1999–2000, as well as in 2002–2003, that would require additional investigation.

Table 6.2 PPI Example: Plastic Shield Price Analysis

	Per-Unit Price ($)				
	Part Number				
Year	1	2	3	4	5
2003	$4.95	$5.02	$4.89	$5.99	$6.50
2002	$2.75	$3.45	$2.75	$3.55	$3.65
2001	$2.85	$3.75	$3.02	$3.88	$4.02
2000	$2.99	$3.98	$3.01	$3.87 (1.60 lb)[a]	$3.99 (1.63 lb)[a]
1999	$2.25 (1.95 lb)[a]	$2.47 (1.85 lb)[a]	$2.23 (1.90 lb)[a]	$2.89 (1.85 lb)[a]	$3.09 (1.95 lb)[a]

[a] Numbers in parentheses denote the total amount of plastic in the components.

6.4.1.1 Example of Effective Supply Planning — Suncor Energy

A good example of price-hedging strategies (using supply-market intelligence) that were effective at one company involved steel. One of the key success stories at Suncor Energy, a bitumen-mining operation in the tar sands projects in northern Alberta, has been in steel, a typical leverage item (with lots of suppliers available to provide the material). In developing a sourcing strategy, Suncor Energy did a global search and ended up selecting a local supplier, Wayward Steel, based on alignment of culture. They were excited about a long-term contract approach and were willing to work overtime during emergencies despite a strong Ironworkers' Union on site. The union realized that they had to meet this major customer's needs. Even though Wayward had many other customers, their preferred relationship with Suncor allowed them to meet the demand on short notice to grow their business and profit. Further, though several union renegotiation contracts followed, there was no increase in steel prices, owing to productivity improvements. On the last project, there was not a single engineering change overrun. The key here is that the group worked as a team.

A win–win point is that the major cost of steel is not in its price, but in the total cost of ownership of erection, measured in working hours per ton. At Suncor's major project construction sites, the cost per ton was about 50 hr per ton prior to the relationship with Wayward, with the industry average about 48 hr per ton. Using the new relationship approach, Suncor achieved an improvement to 21 hrs per ton. They are paying the

Table 6.3 Cost Breakdown

Year	Jan	Dec	Annual
1994	130.8	152.6	137.7
1995	156.9	147.8	159
1996	146.1	154.2	149.6
1997	154.1	150.3	153.9
1998	150.4	129.2	139.2
1999	130.1	159.1	142.8
2000	158.3	162.9	164.3
2001	165.6	146.3	159.9
2002	142.7	153.9	148.9
2003	157.8	164.8	167.7
2004	168.6(P)	(P)	(P)

Note: P = preliminary; series id = PCU325211325211; industry = plastics material and resins manufacturing; product = plastics material and resins manufacturing; and base date = 8012.

Laminated Plastic Price Index Element	Cost by Percentage	At Year Ending	
Direct materials	45	2003	159.3(P)
Direct labor	15	2002	159.1
Manufacturing burden	25	2001	158.1
G&A	8	2000	151.7
Profit	7	1999	150.4
Selling price	100	1989 (base year)	100

Note: P = preliminary.

Year	Labor-Monthly-Statistics-Based Hourly Earnings Index
2003	162.3
2002	157.8
2001	153.4

Table 6.3   Cost Breakdown (continued)

2000	147.9
1999	142.5
1989 (base year)	100

Source: Data extracted April 8, 2004.

same price as before but erecting it at half the cost! This translates to a savings of $2500 per ton on erection over their project.

How did Suncor achieve these savings? One of the biggest drivers reducing working hours per ton is having the steel available and delivered to the project site when required. Late deliveries occur due to capacity problems at the steel mill. Companies such as Wayward are experts in market intelligence and can inform customers when to order steel to best capture the lowest cost of ownership. Wayward can book the steel mill run capacity ahead of time and have the materials even when competitors cannot (who then must get them on allocation). To do so does not require a detailed specification. Suncor, when notified by Wayward that steel prices may be rising, can take a rough quantity off the project plan and then develop and share a forecast with these suppliers. Suncor can allocate work based on quality and price, and the business will grow based on improved performance. On Suncor's project Millenium, there were savings of $350K on a single order, when chrome pipe pricing varied from $700 per foot with 23 weeks lead time to $1600 per foot with 16 weeks lead time — and ordering early drove the savings.

Working with suppliers can identify the good, the bad, and the ugly in terms of long lead items and dollars, and minimize engineering surprises. Early timelines and relatively clean materials requisitions can allow suppliers to book fabrication windows, resulting in substantial savings. Early involvement of fabricators can minimize construction surprises. And avoidance of bid processes for every job saves time and money for everyone. In effect, fabrication and construction drive the process, with materials supply and engineering reporting to them. Block flow diagrams and process flow diagrams can provide early warning to suppliers, and chosen supply-chain partners become an integral part of this process.

6.4.2 Competitor Forecasts

Any forecast should also consider competitors' actions and attempt to identify what their needs for products or services will be. This can be challenging, but can be achieved with good market intelligence. Many of the principles of supply-market intelligence apply here as well — speaking

Table 6.4   Surcharges

Material Percentage Price Increases (45 Percent)

	1	2	3	4	5	Percentage PPI Material Change
1999–2000	14.80	27.51	15.74	15.26	13.11	15.06
2000–2001	−2.11	−2.60	0.15	0.12	0.34	−2.68
2001–2002	−1.58	−3.60	−4.02	−3.83	−4.14	−6.88
2002–2003	36.00	20.48	35.02	30.93	35.14	12.63
Material % Volume Changes						

Labor Percentage Increases (15 Percent)

	1	2	3	4	5	Percentage PPI Labor Change
1999–2000	4.93	9.17	5.25	5.09	4.37	3.79
2000–2001	−0.70	−0.87	0.05	0.04	0.11	3.72
2001–2002	−0.53	−1.20	−1.34	−1.28	−1.38	2.87
2002–2003	12.00	6.83	11.67	10.31	11.71	2.85

Material Volume Percentage Changes[a]

			4	5
1999–2000			−12.70	−16.41

	1	2	3	4	5
1999	2.25	2.47	2.23	2.89	3.09
2000	2.42	2.65	2.39	2.94	3.09
2001	2.40	2.63	2.38	2.92	3.07
2002	2.34	2.56	2.31	2.84	2.99
2003	2.48	2.72	2.46	3.01	3.17

[a] "Should-be" price in dollars (based on 1999 pricing, ppi changes, and design changes).

with key subject matter experts, going to trade conferences and speaking to other people in the network, and speaking to customers about their planned requirements. Of course, one of the biggest challenges is separating true and fictional forecasts. Consider the case of Cisco Corporation in Table 6.5.

6.4.3 Capacity Forecasts

Capacity refers to key resource capabilities, broken down by all of the various types of relevant issues: human resources, warehouse space, transportation, machine time, or inventory. The objective of a capacity forecast is to quantify capacity requirements, as broken down by differing hypothetical demand levels. Companies use the capacity forecast data in developing their operating budgets. They also refer to it to assess whether more human resources will be needed and, if so, whether to address the need by offering overtime incentives to current employees, or to instead hire new employees. These forecasts are also important for gauging whether more equipment or warehouse space will need to be purchased.

These forecasts are usually done in conjunction with demand forecasts, and use that projected demand as their point of reference.

6.4.4 Supply Forecasts

Supply forecasts collect data on all factors that can potentially influence the supply chain. This includes data on the suppliers in the market — on a global scale, now —who can supply the components needed to make the product. It includes the competitors who supply customers with a competing product. It also includes data on competing technologies and the ability of competitors to seize market share. A big consideration is global competitiveness, particularly if the company is currently or planning soon to be buying commodities and selling their finished products globally, which has become an instrumental competitive strategy.

Supply market capacity is a difficult element on which to gather intelligence, but understanding the subject is instrumental to making sound sourcing decisions. Once again, establishing a network of subject matter experts is critical, especially suppliers who can provide information on changing market conditions. Consider the example of the market environment for electronic components, as described by an electronics distributor representative from Converge.

Traditionally, original equipment manufacturers (OEMs) such as IBM, Nortel Networks, and Cisco work directly with component manufacturers and new product development (NPD) departments to develop a bill of

Table 6.5 Cisco Vignette

In the summer of 2000, with its order book overflowing but its assembly lines sputtering from lack of parts, Cisco Systems decided to crank up its supply line. It committed to buying components months before they were needed and lent the manufacturers who build most of its Internet switching gear $600 million interest free to buy parts on Cisco's behalf. As it turned out, Cisco made a bad bet.

On Monday, April 16, 2001, with both its sales and the value of its surplus components shrinking, Cisco said it would write off $2.5 billion of its bloated inventory. People were in shock. Cisco was the darling of Wall Street and had enjoyed unprecedented growth and an associated rise in its stock value. CEO John Chambers said his company was the victim of a sudden, unanticipated economic chill. As recently as November, Cisco's orders were growing at a 70 percent annual clip. However, some claim that Chambers and other Cisco executives ignored or misread crucial warning signs that their sales forecasts were too ambitious. They overestimated Cisco's backlog because of misleading information supplied by Cisco's internal order network and continued to expand aggressively even after business slowed at some Cisco divisions. In April 2001, they laid off more than 8500 people after hiring more than 5000 between November and March. Alex Mendez, an ex-Cisco executive who left in November to become a venture capitalist, claims that "Cisco always had a bit of trouble finding the brakes."

Like other high-tech companies, Cisco was caught unawares by the one–two punch of the broader slowdown and the retrenchment in the telecommunications sector. When Cisco's 600 top executives met for their annual retreat in May 2000, they planned on increasing revenue by 60 percent. One cloud loomed on the horizon: components for some products, particularly switches used in corporate computer networks, were in critically short supply and customers had to wait as long as fifteen weeks for delivery, compared with the normal one to three weeks. To help the situation, Chambers and top aides devised a twofold strategy to revitalize Cisco's supply chains: help contract manufacturers accumulate parts and commit to buying specific quantities of components from key suppliers.

Contract manufacturers worried that this strategy involved setting overly aggressive expansion plans. For example, Solectron had warned Cisco that they appeared to be ordering more parts than needed. In October 2000, sales in the telecommunications industry grew less than ten percent from the previous quarter. At this time, at least two Cisco suppliers began warning the company that shipments were slowing or not meeting forecasts. By November, Chambers says orders were "comfortably" more than 70 percent ahead. Further, he emphasized that the latest downturn was an opportunity for Cisco to break away from rivals such as Nortel and Lucent Technologies. By December, however, he had changed his tune. On December 15, Chambers gathered his top executives and asked, "What happens if we're off by a billion or a billion and a half in quarterly sales?"

Table 6.5 Cisco Vignette (continued)

Things got worse; sales to telecommunications carriers fell 40 percent in the January quarter. The speed of the sales decline was surprising. The root cause was then determined: facing two- and three-month waits for popular Cisco products, some customers had been double- and triple-ordering, once from Cisco and then again from Cisco distributors. Once the product was shipped, customers canceled the duplicate orders. All of a sudden, their backlog vanished into thin air. Mr. Volpi, a Cisco executive, claims that without the misleading information "we might have seen better and made better decisions." Chambers noted that "We will always err on the side of meeting customer expectations. The day we stop taking risks as a company is the day I would sell the stock." An expensive gamble indeed: even after its write-off, Cisco reported inventories of $1.6 billion, up 33 percent from July 2000.

Source: Adapted from *The Wall Street Journal*, Behind Cisco's Woes Are Some Wounds of Its Own Making, by Scott Thurm, p. A1, April 18, 2001.

materials (BOM) for a new product. The BOM is sent to contract manufacturers such as Solectron, Jabil, SCI, and Flextronics for quotes. The contract manufacturers then partition the BOM into direct components such as memory and chips, and request quotes from component manufacturers such as TI, Motorola, Intel, and AMD. The contract manufacturer may also receive quotes from franchised distributors such as Arrow and Avnet. The quote package will then be sent back to the OEM, who will review it and award the business.

For the purposes of this example, let us assume that Solectron is the selected contract manufacturer. Solectron may assign 14 buyers to manage the product, with each buyer responsible for certain component commodity families. Note that global contracts for these commodity families may have been negotiated through Solectron's global commodity management teams, but the buyers manage releases and inventory levels. The buyer may place the order with the component manufacturer or a franchised distributor.

The relationship between component manufacturers, franchised distributors, and third parties (often called independents, nonfranchised, or brokers), such as Converge, is complex. Buyers will often go first to the component manufacturers to purchase a part of the requirements, and then they may go to franchised distributors. Franchise distributors work closely with the component manufacturer to stock parts as buffers; they account for the additional 12 to 18 percent inventory-carrying charge through markups to the contract manufacturer. They also bear the risk of obsolescence costs in the event of an economic downturn. In a sense, they are an extension of the component manufacturer's sales force, and many distributors have hired engineers to work with the sales force at OEMs to get direct components designed into new OEM products. They are in turn compensated via a debit program.

For example, if Texas Instruments sells a component for $2.00 to an OEM, the franchise distributor will sell the same part for $2.50. However, if the franchise distributor was responsible for a "design win" (i.e., through engineering working with sales in the OEM's NPD process) that gets the component designed into the product, the franchise distributor will receive a $0.50 debit from the direct manufacturer for every component they sell.

Going back to our example, the Solectron buyer who wants 10,000 components may get a partial order of 5,000 from a component manufacturer and 3,000 from a franchised distributor, and still require 2,000 units. In such cases, an independent such as Converge will act as a "market maker" to complete this requirement. At its headquarters in Peabody, Massachusetts, Converge has a triangular trading floor with 350 dedicated customer sales representatives. They also have a "pit" of commodity managers who monitor global commodity conditions and pricing. Prices are presented via a trading board over the pit throughout the day. The Solectron buyer contacts the Converge sales representative, who then e-mails the sales floor requesting 2,000 components. Each salesperson will contact his or her databases of customer components to check for available inventory or even stock in the pipeline that is not destined for a particular location. At this point, the negotiations begin. Through interactions with customer representatives, franchised distributors, and component manufacturers, Converge will leverage its core relationships worldwide to create markets. They will negotiate to obtain the best pricing as well as help to dispose of inventory for customers when needed. Converge relies on its core relationships to obtain required parts.

With the economic downturns and expansions, these types of supply market dynamics are critical to understand. Converge works with key customers to help them manage excess inventories. As shown in Figure 6.2, supply exceeded demand in 2001, whereas only a few months earlier, supply shortages were common. Herein lies one of the real challenges of creating effective supply market intelligence processes: organizations must be able to go from accelerating their operations to putting on the brakes in an instant, without accelerating excessive expediting charges, obsolescence charges, or inventory-carrying costs.

6.4.5 Technology Forecasts

Many firms I have visited with indicate that the costs associated with retooling, engineering changes, and process redesign resulting from major design changes were often crippling. The uncertainties of market demands

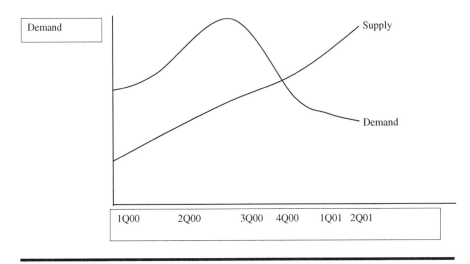

Figure 6.2   Supply and demand in the high-tech component industry. (Source: Interview conducted by Robert Handfield with Spence Huffstetler, *Converge,* May 2001.)

make the benefits of early supplier involvement in developing new technologies even more questionable. There is a risk associated with committing to an outsourcing decision too early in the NPD process. Interviews with managers revealed that a major risk associated with early supplier involvement in design was the potential for choosing the wrong supplier. One firm mentioned that on a previous project, they had chosen a supplier who was unable to meet the new product deadline, even though they assured the buying company that doing so was feasible. Consequently, the firm missed its window of opportunity, and the company was shut out of the market. In these environments, the need for supply market intelligence on competing technology solutions is more critical than ever.

Even when a known, clearly identified market for the innovation exists, the design of the product itself is sometimes in such flux that manufacturing or suppliers cannot identify, develop, or purchase the appropriate production equipment. In this situation, an unknown product form negatively affects the viability of the parallel approach. Predevelopment activities such as preliminary market study and technical assessment are important to successfully bring new products into the market quickly. This involves a close integration of marketing, design, and manufacturing to carry out customer tests of the prototype or sample. Whereas close and frequent interaction between marketing and manufacturing is critical to this approach, high levels of uncertainty often compromise benefits in environments of discontinuous innovation. Because marketing's knowledge about the market is often poorer under these conditions than in products associated with more incremental innovations and the customer may not yet perceive a need for the product, such interactions may be less useful.

Before embarking on the NPD process and committing themselves to a particular design platform, project managers are well advised to thoroughly investigate technology options both inside and outside the firm by working closely with supply management. A common argument against involving supply management personnel in this process is that they are typically averse to anything new and different. Traditionally, this is because purchasing's goals and performance metrics focus on low costs, which are generally at odds with any type of new process. Managers in radical development projects confirm this problem. For instance, the lead designer involved in one project had this to say about his interactions with manufacturing when he proposed design changes: "The manufacturing manager will give me a list of things that I absolutely do not want to do in this order: (1) you are offending God, (2) you are offending the saints, and (3) you are offending the pope. And in this kind of decreasing order, you figure out what you might be able to do."

Other interviews with managers revealed how discontinuous innovations similarly affect sourcing decisions. The result of the increased risk associated with uncertain technologies in the insourcing or outsourcing decision frequently requires that managers wait patiently for the technology to stabilize. By putting such technologies on the shelf, the potential for making the right technological decision increases. The need for careful, serial market analysis was made evident in discussions with a large Japanese computer components manufacturer. Once a year, the company goes to an industry consortium with other leading companies to identify future technology road maps, standardized configurations, and forecasted technology trends. The company also has face-to-face meetings with its major customers to identify their future software requirements. By delaying product development decisions until after these meetings take place, the product development manager is able to identify critical future technological requirements that enable the firm to develop a breakthrough product that fills a market need. This is particularly important in the computer industry, in which hardware requirements are often unable to keep up with changes in software requirements.

The project manager in another firm struggled to develop a project at the more discontinuous end of the spectrum. In summarizing this process, he noted that in the early stages of their project, "All we could prove to a typical manufacturing engineer was that we don't know enough to be wasting his time." There was little point in speeding up the project's development, because the product requirements were unknown.

Much that has been written about this parallel approach has to do with activities at specific development stages. However, at early stages of these more discontinuous innovations, much less can be pinned down with regard to specifics of the product and process attributes. Further, even if one could make an educated guess, the penalties associated with committing manufacturing too early are often significant.

A perfect example of this situation arose in discussions with an engineer at a U.S. electronics manufacturer that was attempting to develop a new programmable automation system requiring specialized components at different stages in the system. In mapping out the technology, the engineer identified "green dots" (well-known technologies), "amber dots" (unstable technologies), and "red dots" (emerging technologies with many defects). Even though the planned system contained many red dots, salespeople were overzealously promoting it to their customers prior to its development! The engineer immediately contacted the salespeople and admonished them for announcing the innovation before the technology had become available.

In the next project stage, he consulted with several university research centers on the best methods for developing the red dot technologies, including the possibility of outsourcing. The researchers convinced him that the technology could be developed, but that it should be done internally to maximize the probability of success. The firm purchased the equipment for developing the products later that year. It took another year of careful process design experiments to stabilize the technology; during this time, the engineer emphasized that to perfect the technology, a certain "peace of mind" was required to complete the design of experiments. To create this environment, an actual "cage" was built around the equipment to avoid its being integrated into existing production processes. The engineer described this process as follows:

> To bring in the product, the process technology has to be developed in a closed environment. Concurrent engineering doesn't work for such breakthrough technology — you simply can't rush it! This approach really worked for us. By the time the actual product design was developed according to the technology road map, we were able to "wheel in" the process technology in time to meet the market window.

A large Japanese computer manufacturer noted that in the case of basic research at the laboratory stage, informal meetings with key suppliers are very common (with no formal contract in place). Information sharing occurs in the form of joint meetings with suppliers, beginning with their top management, to gain commitment. The firm approaches a supplier's top managers and asks them if they are willing to work on development for a future product. This is a trust-based approach with a noticeable lack of formal contracts. For such basic technologies, the R&D group is primarily involved in approaching and evaluating suppliers. Suppliers are asked to share ideas on the technology in the hope of integrating an external core level of expertise with an internal level of expertise. The idea is that the synergies achieved will result in a radical new product. In such meetings, R&D leads the discussion; purchasing personnel may not even be involved.

At this stage, nondisclosure agreements are not used for technology sharing. One manager noted, "We do not want to get locked into letting a supplier develop a promising technology, particularly if we are working on a technology internally." Discussions are primarily of a technical nature, and often focus primarily on the supplier's technological capabilities and expertise. Once R&D determines that the supplier is capable, purchasing and legal personnel may help develop a nondisclosure agreement.

6.4.6 Political and Economic Country Forecasts

Political and economic assessments of supply-chain risk are critical, especially instabilities in regions that the company sells to or buys from. An example of the effect of the general political landscape on supply planning is from the aftermath of the second war in Iraq. A number of oil mines became inoperable, affecting international supply. Any company that buys oil for use in their product or to resell it will be affected. America's embargo restrictions on Iraq have been lifted, but political turmoil in Venezuela, Russia, Nigeria, and other key oil-producing regions continues to make the supply of oil a major variable in many supply-planning processes.

There is a need for a dedicated market intelligence group that can provide a level of risk assessment for major suppliers located in different parts of the globe. In one of the companies we interviewed, executives were evaluating the addition of manufacturing capacity in their footwear supply chain, as they were expecting to increase sales in global markets (Asia, Eastern Europe, and Latin America) significantly over the next six months. The challenge was to understand strategies revolving around developing a portfolio of suppliers to optimize the company's financial position and its capabilities. Specifically, executives were developing a methodology to consider the balance of risks and rewards (government, political climate, exchange rates, industry-specific issues regarding labor, etc.) in maintaining a global portfolio of suppliers in low-cost–country sourcing. What things might be considered relative to location that could help the organization from a supply-chain perspective? For example, are there benefits to sourcing locally, given the size of the growing Chinese market for the footwear manufacturers? As part of this process, a more rigorous risk evaluation approach was considered to assist executives with developing strategic decisions in this important area of competition. Although the company does not produce more than three percent of products without a customer order, there is an expectation that as demand grows, responsiveness would become a critical element of this strategy.

The company developed a risk profile of each country or region for their current supply locations, added other locations to be considered, and used a risk portfolio approach to find the optimal network risk profile. In addition, validation of theoretical and true capacity at different locations was established, with estimates of potential for capacity expansion at each site determined. The key inputs for developing a capacity risk strategy included collecting information on each country's:

- Existing supplier locations — theoretical, proven, and potential capacity, as well as quality and cost
- Potential supplier locations — availability of qualified sources for manufacturing footwear
- Tax environment related to goods located in or moving through the country
- Labor-cost trends of existing locations relative to the considered locations
- Infrastructure
  - Roads, with some effort on air and ocean
- Number of national holidays
- Cost of land
- Price of fuel
- Unemployment
- Labor stability
- Propensity for work stoppages
- Holiday conventions
- Manufacturing and distribution costs
  - Per pallet
  - Per square meter
- Population
- Healthcare spend
- Political stability
- Other (major) distribution centers in the country
- Natural disaster propensity
- Technology infrastructure assessment
- Crime/theft assessment
- Employment legislation
- Strictness of consultation rules
- Other issues as appropriate

Data on each of these elements was captured by analysts using a variety of data input sources available on the Web and in other locations, including:

- U.S. State Department
- Asian, Latin American, and East European trade associations
- World Bank
- Supply Chain Resource Consortium data sources
- Corporate Asian Distribution Reports
- Standard & Poor's country profiles
- Logistics contacts — Menlo, Ryder, Schenker, Eagle, Exel, etc.
- CIA intelligence reports
- Department of Commerce reports
- Local news agencies
- Other entities

The analysts developed risk profiles for the specific supply-chain configurations under consideration. This was achieved by creating a risk algorithm that incorporated all of the data into an overall risk score by weighting individual measures based on probability of outcome and severity of impact. The outcome was a maturity grid with definitions associated with different levels of maturity. The grid had five levels — very unsuitable (score: 1) to very suitable (score: 5). Source data for each rating was documented in each case. Based on primary research, this maturity grid was developed and populated with characteristics and definitions corresponding to each level for each parameter. An example for one parametered geographical region is shown in Figure 6.3.

Specific research on each considered location enables the scoring on this grid. The positioning also leads to the allotment of a score (1–5) for this parameter to the location. This type of subjective evaluation required an analysis based on insights from interviews, secondary and primary research, and evaluation of news updates.

As we can see from the fictional example in Figure 6.4, the score for Poland on the parameter "labor" is 3.25. This evaluation is based on development of a score derived from a number of different subjective evaluations. Although not a precise measure, it provides a guideline for establishing a baseline by which to make global sourcing decisions, allowing a comparison of Poland with other areas of the world.

Based on this framework, a prototype implementation system for future scenario analysis was developed, and scenario analysis was carried out. Using input from executives, several probable scenarios for allocating capacity in the next six years were defined and assessed. Each scenario was run through the risk profile, identifying the high-risk elements associated with each strategy.

Labor	Labor Climate	Very unhospitable for mfg.		Somewhat hospitable for mfg.		Very hospitable for mfg.
		*Extremely difficult to lay-off employees *Very high union membership *Scarce availability of qualified employees *Large number of work stoppages in the last year	→(arrow)	*Average amount of flexibility in hiring and firing employees *Moderate union membership *Qualified employees are available in some occupations and are unavailable in some others *Moderate number of work stoppages in the last year	→(arrow)	*Very good amount of flexibility in hiring and firing employees *Very low union membership *High availability of skilled labor *Negligible number of work stoppages in the last year
	Unemployment	>20%	15-20%	10-15%	5-10%	0-5%

Figure 6.3 Example maturity grid.

Labor		Very unhospitable for DC's		Somewhat hospitable for mfg.		Very hospitable for DC's
Labor Climate		*Extremely difficult to lay-off employees *Very high union membership *Scarce availability of qualified employees *Large number of work stoppages in the last year		*Average amount of flexibility in hiring and firing employees *Moderate union membership *Qualified employees are available in some occupations and are unavailable in some others *Moderate number of work stoppages in the last year	Poland	*Very good amount of flexibility in hiring and firing employees *Very low union membership *High availability of skilled labor *Negligible number of work stoppages in the last year
Unemployment	>20%		15-20%	10-15%	5-10%	0-5%

Figure 6.4   Maturity grid: country scores. (Example only—not actual information.)

6.4.7 Regulatory Policy Forecasts

A globalizing firm has to manage a number of regulatory bodies around the world, not just those of the home country. Firms may find themselves interacting with up to 50 or 60 such agencies worldwide. The best example is the pharmaceutical industry, which has one of the most complex regulatory networks in the world. The FDA is the toughest drug-regulating agency in the world. This poses some difficulties, as well as opportunities, for American firms. If a drug survives the FDA approval process, firms can probably expect approval anywhere in the world. The FDA will not accept another country's approval and has the most scrutinizing drug policies across the globe. For instance, some pharmaceutical companies will not come into the United States because the standards are too strict. However, that does not mean they cannot earn a profit in another, less stringent country. Since 1996, the FDA has approved fewer and fewer products each year. It is getting more and more difficult to develop a product with a high market value. Put another way, the simpler diseases have been conquered.

The approval process is just the tip of the iceberg. After approval comes the issue of how to gain access to patients around the world. This issue has major cost implications. Along with proving efficacy, firms must show that the product adds value to society (for instance, Pfizer's portrayal of Viagra as having a positive social impact). The U.S. market is a free market. However, most European nations are social-democratic countries with government-run healthcare systems requiring individual price negotiation. If a price cannot be agreed upon, patients will not be reimbursed by their healthcare system. Pharmaceutical companies must deal directly with governments to win approval for sales of their products.

It is also important to understand and forecast changes in other laws around the world, particularly when it comes to patents and intellectual property. As suppliers become increasingly integrated in new product development, intellectual property agreements are becoming the norm. The U.S. Constitution provides the framework for the intellectual property legal system, including patent and copyright law, as we know it today, through Article 1, Section 8, Clause 8, which says that "Congress shall have the Power ... To promote the Progress of Science and useful Arts, by securing for limited Times to Authors and Inventors the exclusive Right to their respective Writings and Discoveries."[1] There are three kinds of intellectual property in the United States: (1) patents, (2) copyrights, and (3) trade secrets. Patent law has been established in several federal patent statutes including the Patent Act of 1790, 35 USC. Section 1, and companion laws. Copyright law is founded in the federal statutes, particularly in the

---

[1] Kintner, E.W. and Lahr, J.L., *An Intellectual Property Law Primer*, New York: Macmillan, 1975, p. 6.

Copyright Act of 1976. Federal patent and copyright laws overrule any contradictory state statutes. By contrast, trade secret law is grounded in common law and is intended to protect unique ideas that would not otherwise have legal protection under patent and copyright law. Because common law varies by state, there is some variance in actual statutes. However, most states have created laws that are very similar. In its most basic form, a patent is an agreement between the inventor and the federal government. Successful patentees in the United States are now entitled to exclusive rights (to make, use, or sell) an invention for the life of the patent 20 years from the filing date with the U.S. Patent Office.

Note that in some countries such as China and India, copyrights and patents may not be recognized at all. In recent years, because of the entry of these countries into the World Trade Organization, both China and India recognize copyrights (at least on paper), but piracy remains a constant problem.

A firm must protect itself from inadvertent patent infringement whenever it purchases a product from a supplier. This can best be done by including a patent indemnification clause in all purchasing documents. This clause should consist of three parts:

1. An indemnification, which seeks the supplier's assurances that the goods being contracted for do not infringe on any other party's patents.
2. The right to require the supplier itself to defend any patent infringement suit.
3. The right to have the purchaser's own attorneys involved in defense of any lawsuit concerning patent infringement.

6.4.7.1 Regulations Affecting Global Purchasing

Many laws — U.S., foreign, and international — affect global commerce. The following briefly summarizes some of the laws that can affect a purchaser's international business dealings.[2] A proactive supply intelligence group should investigate the relative impact of and changes in these laws as they pertain to the dynamic and changing supply market environment:

Foreign Corrupt Practices Act — This law prohibits payments (such as bribes) that might benefit a foreign official personally. Although usually pertaining to sellers, purchasers should understand this law's provisions so they can recognize situations addressed by the act.

---

[2] Martin J., Cabarra, J.D., and Ernest Gabbard, J.D., What's on the books: other laws affecting purchasing and supply, *The Purchasing and Supply Yearbook*, Ed., John A. Woods, New York: McGraw-Hill, 2000, pp. 332–339.

Antiboycott legislation — Various laws address doing business with countries that support the boycott of one nation against another. Examples include the boycott of Israel by Arab countries and the boycott of Taiwan by mainland China. These laws require reporting of any request to participate in a boycott, which purchasers often fail to do.

Export Administration Act — Various laws and regulations govern, and sometimes even restrict, the export of goods, information, and services. Purchasers may not perceive that they are engaged in exporting. However, the law views certain types of drawings, specifications, and prototypes forwarded to a foreign entity as restricted exports of technology. Purchasers are urged to seek the advice of an expert when questions arise in this area.

Customs laws — This body of law addresses the importation of goods into the United States. Customs brokers who are familiar with customs laws can be quite valuable in understanding the rules and regulations governing importation.

Foreign laws — In addition to the U.S. laws that apply to foreign transactions, the laws and regulations of other countries involved in a business transaction may also apply. These laws will likely address contract law, export control, currency control, and criminal law. Some transactions could be illegal if structured in a certain manner.

International laws — Other laws may apply to business transactions that are not part of any specific country's laws and regulations. Maritime laws are a good example of international laws that affect international commerce. Several international documents are also pertinent to international transactions. These include the United Nations Convention on Contracts for International Sale of Goods (CISG) and International Contracting Terms (INCOTERMS).

Country-of-origin labeling — The World Commercial Organization has only just begun to identify and harmonize global regulations regarding labeling products with their country of origin. However, this is a long way from being deployed. In the interim, there is a complex and confusing set of laws specific to every country regarding the country-of-origin documentation required on shipment to another country. This needs to be carefully monitored, or a decision support tool such as one developed for a major pharmaceutical company.

6.5 Assessing Global Logistics Risk

It is particularly important for supply market intelligence groups to be aware of intelligence as it relates to doing business in different countries, as well as the impact of major disruptions on the business. With the movement toward global sourcing to China, India, and Eastern Europe, many companies are now recognizing the increased level of supply-chain risk that exists in these worldwide distribution channels. Global sourcing affords many benefits in the form of lower price and expanded market access, but senior executives should recognize that more frequent and larger-scale product and service flow disruptions are potential risks of this strategy. A major disruption in the supply chain can shut down a company and have dire consequences for profitability.

This has been felt most drastically in the last few years, including after 9/11, the war in Iraq, the West Coast port stoppage, and even through events such as the legislation capping hours on truck drivers. Other unexpected events can include natural disasters or poor communication of customer requirements, resulting in errors and back orders, part shortages, poor material quality, and a negative impact on the company brand. These disruptions can be costly, result in significant supply-chain delays, and in some cases, bring distribution and production to a screeching halt. Further, the impacts of these disruptions may be amplified in lean or time-sensitive environments and may cause disturbances throughout the supply chain.

One of the major impacts of 9/11 has been on the environment for doing business in different countries, as well as the movement of materials between countries. A thorough discussion of doing business in China appears in Appendix A. Supply market intelligence teams must keep their finger on the pulse of global trade, country-specific events, and logistics regulations that can impact their supply management environment. Some of the major risks and threats that should be identified are discussed in the following subsections.

6.5.1 Antiterrorism Laws

More and more companies are focusing on global regulations such as Customs–Trade Partnership Against Terrorism (C–TPAT) and Partners in Protection (PIP). These are joint government business initiatives to build cooperative relationships, with a goal of strengthening the overall supply chain and border security. Benefits provided to logistics partners include:

- Reduced inspections and faster clearances
- Prerequisite for other programs
  - Monthly duty payments/Fast/ISA
- Being viewed as supporting homeland security
- Key for being ranked low risk
- Status verification interface (SVI)

Table 6.6   Requirements for C-TPAT

Procedural security	Does your company have procedures in place to protect against unmanifested material being introduced into the supply chain?
Physical security	Are all buildings constructed in such a way that they deter unlawful entry and protect against outside intrusion?
Access control	Is unauthorized access to facilities and conveyances prohibited?
Personnel security	Does your company conduct employment screening, background checks, etc.?
Education and awareness	Does your company have a security awareness program provided to employees, including the recognition of internal conspiracies, maintaining cargo integrity, etc.?
Manifest procedures	Are the manifests complete, legible, accurate, and submitted in a timely manner to Customs?
Conveyance security	Is your company's conveyance integrity maintained to protect against the introduction of unauthorized items?

Most of these agreements require doing the following:

■ Conduct a comprehensive self-assessment of supply-chain security.
■ Sign and return the agreement to participate.
■ Complete the supply-chain security profile and return to customs within 60 days.
■ Develop and implement an enhanced security program.
■ Communicate security guidelines to other companies in the supply chain and assist them in developing a security program.
■ Process applications in 60 days.
■ Validation within three years.

The requirements for C-TPAT are shown in Table 6.6.

The reality in terms of forecasts for these elements is that they are only going to get stronger. Customs security concerns are permanent, but there are also discussions around radio frequency identification (RFID), "smart seals," and smart box technology on containers. In addition, increased inspection of imports has begun and security concerns will be a focal point of customer as well as trade compliance. There is also discussion of instituting industry-specific security standards, and coordinating with other agencies such as the Department of Transportation and the FDA.

The issue is that the global and U.S. logistics infrastructure is stressed, and there are no signals that significant relief will come in 2005. In fact, indicators show it will get worse before it gets better. Santa is going to pass right by companies that did not prepare this year as shelves dry up and inventory gets stuck in transit. All companies should begin preparations now for the next few years.

6.5.2 Logistics Vulnerabilities[3]

Companies are scrambling to thwart the delays, skyrocketing lead times, and soaring costs resulting from logistics problems. Getting products to store shelves has never been harder. Companies are dealing with dramatically increased ocean traffic and severely congested ports; deficient U.S. capacity for transporting goods by rail and truck caused by new hours-of-service rules, driver shortages, and rising fuel prices; and heightened security regulations and trade rules that further complicate the situation. Let's face it: Santa has never had to deal with the rigor of the new cross-border declaration laws! Companies have scrambled to circumvent the problem but not without cost.

Consider these cases:

■ A consumer durables company made changes to its distribution network to more strategically locate the inventory of its fastest-moving products so that it could create continuous loops with the same carrier and vehicles, thereby having more access to critical capacity. Because a few of its carriers failed to deliver on preagreed commitments for capacity, the company scrambled to make alternative arrangements to secure coverage — at much higher rates. It marks the first year the company will not be able to hold or lower its logistics costs. This is the kind of event that costs holiday bonuses.

■ A toy manufacturer, with 60 percent of its annual sales coming in the holiday season, had to divert freight coming from Asia to Oakland and Seattle–Tacoma instead of Long Beach because of a backup of up to ten additional days in the Long Beach harbor, with 20 to 30 ships sitting offshore waiting to be unloaded. The

---

[3] Aimi, G., Cecere, L., and Souza, J., Stressed supply lines threaten Christmas this year and years to come, *AMR Research*, November 18, 2004, http://www.amrresearch.com/Content/view.asp?pmillid=17766.

company then had to shift some of its truckload traffic to rail because it could not secure capacity. The result: order cancellations because the company could not deliver on time. The next Tickle Me Elmo may very well still be sitting in the Long Beach harbor come Christmas morning.

■ Dell recently said it would build a new production facility in Greensboro, North Carolina to better serve its U.S. East Coast business and consumer customers. Because Dell specializes in custom orders, inexpensive but slow shipping methods often don't work. Locating a production facility closer to customers can keep shipping costs under control, allowing them to address custom demand more readily. People may still be getting Dells, thanks to planning and acknowledgement of logistical drawbacks.

Significant increases in directional trade volume are stressing the global logistics infrastructure and capacity on many levels. This imposes a constraint on the just-in-time supply chains we have built over the past decade. Although companies may understand how to plan for the longer lead times (often two to three times longer), the increase in lead-time variability (25 to 75 percent greater) has a hugely unpredictable effect on perfect order performance, customer service, and required inventories.

Across the modes, ports, and travel lanes, providers are reporting staggering increases in volume. Certain economic events signal continued growth and promise to further stress the infrastructure. Here is what is happening in each area:

■ *Ocean:* A Japanese container line reports that revenue will grow 43 percent from 2003. A European container line reports a 14 percent increase in volume from 2003. Another carrier reports volume is up 12 percent and rates are up 10 percent on average from 2003. Panama Canal traffic is 6.7 percent higher than last year. The World Trade Organization expects container shipping to increase by another 60 percent over the next four years.

■ *Air:* Lufthansa and American Airlines report air cargo volume is up 10 percent and 12 percent, respectively, from 2003, reinforcing claims that manufacturers have made increased use of expedited service. Frankfurt reports a 14.5 percent increase in air cargo traffic from last year, setting a record high.

■ *Surface:* The Morgan Stanley Truckload Index (dry-van only) shows U.S. truckload demand versus supply ratio is now 10:1, double the ratio of 2003. The driver shortage and the new rules regarding hours of service are clearly having an impact. The Energy Information Administration reports average diesel fuel prices of $2.13

per gallon, up 65.1 percent from the same period last year. The Surface Transportation Board reports that rail speeds have decreased 20 percent in the past two years because of congestion and rail infrastructure problems.

■ *Trade Policy:* The U.S. International Trade Commission reports that dramatic changes are expected beginning in 2005, when worldwide apparel and textile quotas will be completely phased out. This is expected to accelerate the shift of apparel manufacturing to low-cost and efficient producers in China and India.

The end result is that with such growth, demand for capacity will continue to exceed supply in the short term, which in turn will push prices up and limit the ability to trade. See Table 6.7 for an example of a company taking risk seriously.

The laws governing supply management are complex and varied. Other laws address environmental and labor issues. This overview simply points out that today's purchaser must be aware of the laws and regulations governing domestic and international purchasing. A purchaser is urged to discuss with legal counsel any questions that arise during the performance of job responsibilities. Ignorance of the law is not a valid defense.

6.6 Tying Together the Elements of Risk

Based on recent research that involved detailed interviews with senior supply-chain executives, a research team[4] from the Supply Chain Resource Consortium developed a list of 18 different best practices that companies could explore to enhance supply-chain operational resiliency and risk management. These options were classified by matching them up with the organizational functions that would typically implement or own the specific supply-chain risk management capability. Figure 6.5 shows the four key organizational areas that already have some supply-chain risk management capabilities and responsibilities. Note that the risk management matrix in Figure 6.5 divides risk management responsibility by internal operations or external supply base interface on the horizontal axis, and current or future business on the vertical axis.

Although these groups often already have risk management processes in place, supply-chain risk management is a core competency for these four groups. There must be regular cross-functional, multidirectional information sharing and feedback regarding interdependent risk management

---

[4] A "To Do" List to Improve Supply Chain Risk Capabilities, Debra Elkins, Robert Handfield, Jennifer Blackhurst, and Chris Craighead, *Supply Chain Management Review*, January 2005.

Table 6.7   GlaxoSmithKline Takes Supply-Chain Risk Seriously

To protect GSK's supply chain from the threat of terrorism, the company voluntarily applied to become part of a U.S. Customs program called C-TPAT (Customs and Trade Partnership against Terrorism). This program, which was created in response to the September 11, 2001, attacks in New York City, was designed to heighten the security of trade channels against acts of terrorism.

GSK was recently informed that its supply chain has been approved and validated. Four best practice examples were derived from GSK and are being used as examples for other U.S. companies of what a secure supply chain should look like.

"The world around us has changed and continues to change dramatically. As such we have to move to new business processes that allow us to conduct our business securely and efficiently," says GMS president David Pullman. "A great example is the way we have embraced C-TPAT, taking a leadership position and helping to shape the procedures and policy around this. Not only is this a good way to execute our business, it is also good for the company's reputation."

To get validation, GSK had to prepare a comprehensive security profile, which covered many areas of the business, including physical security, personnel security, access controls, and data security. This profile was presented to the U.S. Customs and Border Protection validation team, which did walk-throughs of many of the security processes.

As a result of the C-TPAT validation, GSK will be subject to fewer inspections of imports, which equates to fewer delays and less money lost. The C-TPAT ways of working are being embedded into the GSK corporate ways of working, guaranteeing that the company will always be up to standard when it comes to supply-chain security.

Becoming C-TPAT validated was a joint effort between Global Logistics in GMS and Consumer Healthcare. The project leads were Mike Melia, Director of Cross-Border Compliance, GMS; Rob Montague, Director, Global Distribution, GMS, and Bill Ramos, Director, International Supply and Brand Protection in Consumer Healthcare

Source: C-TPAT in *eNetworker*, the GMS online magazine, September 9, 2004.

responsibilities. For example, if the real-time supply base management group is observing a type of risk event repeatedly disrupting material flow at suppliers located in a particular country, they can feed the information to the strategic sourcing group to make sure that the risk event is explicitly considered in future business sourcing decisions. Similarly, the enterprise risk management or strategic supply-chain design group can pass down information to the real-time supply-chain operations group on elements

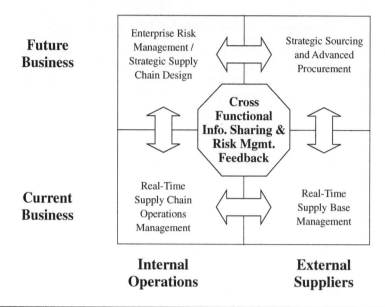

Figure 6.5   Organizational functions with supply-chain risk management capabilities and responsibilities.

such as material flow hedging strategies or contingency plans evaluated for most effective response to key port disruptions. In addition, the two strategic future business groups and the two current business operations groups must interact to coordinate decisions made and actions undertaken for more effective risk management with the strategic-level handling proactive risk management and the operational-level handling reactive risk management functions.

6.7 Eighteen Best Practices for Supply-Chain Risk Management Strategic Sourcing

The following best practices are ideas that companies can adopt to enhance the strategic sourcing process. (Companies should incorporate the recommendations of the BI/MI group as they pertain to the specific commodity group being analyzed and establish contingency measures incorporated in the finalization of contracts for material or service supply.)

1. Screen and monitor (regularly) current and potential suppliers with respect to potential supply-chain risks through self-assessment templates or internally developed risk-scoring methods (which can include risk metrics on quality, financial condition of supplier, technology leadership, price competitiveness, location-risk exposure,

shipping modes and routes exposure, etc.) to identify high likelihood or high severity of potential disruptors for use in the RFQ evaluation process. Note that the ongoing monitoring of current and potential suppliers naturally includes maintaining a database of suppliers and tracking assessment results or risk scores over time.

2. Require critical suppliers to produce a detailed plan of disruption awareness and identify supply-chain risk management capabilities that can be executed if disruptions occur in the supplier's own supply base network. The supplier's business continuity plan should be reviewed as part of the bid evaluation process. The strategic sourcing group can work with the chosen suppliers to improve those plans if necessary as part of the bid acceptance contracting process.

3. Include expected costs of disruptions and operational problem resolution in the total cost equation derived through the strategic sourcing decision process.

4. Require suppliers to be prepared to provide timely information and visibility of material flows that can be electronically shared with your enterprise.

Relationship management deals with ongoing day-to-day interaction with existing suppliers as well as the transport of material from these sources to domestic warehouses and points of use. Modifications include the following:

5. Conduct weekly teleconferences with critical suppliers to identify current issues that may disrupt daily operations and tactics to reduce them. Option 1, i.e., screening and monitoring of suppliers, can provide input into the teleconferences and a method to track effectiveness of tactics implementation.

6. Seek security enhancements that comply with new initiatives in C-TPAT, Container Security Initiative, and others.

7. Test and implement technologies (e.g., RFID) to track containers in distribution channels to enhance global pipeline inventory visibility.

8. Conduct a detailed disruption incident report and analysis following a major disruption event, using root cause or failure mode and effects analysis (FMEA) to learn from and prevent recurrence of similar events.

9. Create "exception" event detection and early warning systems to discover critical logistics events that exceed normal planning parameters on an exception basis, which can trigger managerial action to mitigate the impact of the disruption.

10. Gather supply-chain intelligence and monitor critical supply base locations to allow real-time sense and response maneuvers against material flow disruptions.

Real-time operations management includes all processes from the point of delivery by the supplier and the banks or buffers of inventory held at warehouses, manufacturing locations, and distribution centers. Notice that we have deliberately separated internal operations management from external supply base management to differentiate internal and external risks. Options to improve resiliency include the following:

11. Improve visibility of inventory buffers in domestic distribution channels at a component level, to assist real-time contingency planning and mitigation execution.
12. Classify buffered material for different levels of criticality to ensure appropriate inventory positioning (safety stock) to mitigate risk of disruptions.
13. Train and educate key employees and groups to improve real-time decision-making capabilities, and equip managers and associates with plans and processes for managing disruptions if and when they occur.
14. Develop real-time supply-chain reconfiguration decision support to enable evaluation and execution of contingency plans in response to disruption discovery.

Enterprise risk management/strategic supply-chain design includes systemwide issues pertaining to disruptions, including systemwide supply-chain redesign issues.

15. Develop predictive analysis systems, incorporating intelligent search agents and dynamic risk indexes at major nodes in the supply chain to identify potential problems (including likelihood of occurrence and potential impact if the disruption occurs).
16. Construct damage control plans for likely disruption scenarios by modeling supply-chain events and using scenario-envisioning tools.
17. Utilize supply-chain redesign tools and models to understand cost tradeoffs between strategies such as increased inventory, premium freight, parts substitutability, or manufacturing process flexibility.
18. Enhance systemwide visibility and supply-chain intelligence in the form of improved databases collecting daily or hourly snapshots of demand, inventory, and capacity levels at key nodes in the supply chain, including ports and shipping locations.

Table 6.8 Best Practices Survey

Subjective Rating	Points Assigned
We do not perform this activity	0
We perform this activity, yet significantly below the needed level	1
We perform this activity, yet below the needed level	2
We perform this activity, yet slightly below the needed level	3
We perform this activity at the needed level	4

6.7.1 How Can Companies Prioritize the Best Practices for Adoption and Integration into Business Processes?

Clearly, some of these actions can be taken with a minimum level of investment and should yield immediate benefits. Other elements will require additional effort and business case justification for the significant investments to be deployed (e.g., visibility systems). Companies may want to use the best practices list as a starting point to determine a priority order of supply-chain risk management elements to strategically pursue for adoption and integration. At a minimum, organizations need to develop a focused long-term plan for building supply-chain resiliency and responsiveness, which identifies the short-term actions that can be deployed with a minimum of investment, while establishing a road map for deploying intensive project team resources, business intelligence systems, and improved supply-chain infrastructure.

A second possible use of the 18 best practices is to develop a survey to measure current awareness and internal business knowledge of supply-chain risk management capabilities and responsibilities across a company. For example, for each of the best practices, the survey participants (company employees) can be asked to rate the company's risk management capabilities on a 5-point scale as defined in Table 6.8.

Survey data can then be analyzed to identify strengths and weaknesses as perceived by the survey participants in the different supply-chain risk management capabilities and best practices. The priority list for short-term action and longer-term action can then be developed based on the survey benchmark of the company's own internal assessment of supply-chain risk management capabilities.

To our knowledge, few companies (if any) have achieved all of these supply-chain risk management best practices in their purchasing and supply-chain organizations. However, there is definitely a new awareness and recognition among global companies of the need to develop better risk management capabilities and responsibilities in their procurement and supply-chain operations.

6.8 Conclusion

The way organizations view supply chains as contributors to success of their businesses has changed dramatically in the last years. Until recently, organizations focused on improving marketing, product differentiation, and the exploration of new ways of distribution such as the Internet, E-commerce, E-business, and E-marketplaces. Our interviews with senior supply-chain executives from Fortune 500 companies suggest that supply market intelligence is a capability that few companies today have fully deployed, yet it is a critical need for effective decision making in the global manufacturing environment.

The most common problem experienced by manufacturers is *supply-chain fragmentation:* the inability to link common processes and decisions across multiple nodes of the supply chain. This is being driven by the increased movement toward sourcing in China, as well as the price pressure to reduce costs. Other common problems include a lack of global project resources, an inability to create effective mechanisms for collaboration and business intelligence, and increasing global competition driving pressure to reduce prices to customers while facing conditions of rapidly increasing raw material prices. So what is interesting about these results? Manufacturers recognize that immediate corporatewide action is necessary to avoid failure in achieving stated financial and market goals. However, many manufacturing executives we spoke with were at a loss as to what could be done.

Additional analysis by our research team suggests that companies have entered a new zone that requires innovative new solutions. Supply market intelligence can help enable companies to be more nimble and have access to solutions that provide more visibility to global supply-chain trends, and facilitate interaction between global supply-chain partners. However, these capabilities will require not only new business intelligence technologies, but also new business processes to enable the application of this intelligence to reduce risk and establish contingency plans. Companies that are best able to deploy these elements in the shortest time will have a significant advantage over those that are not.

6.9 Checklist

- ▪ Understand risk assessment by using different types of forecasts.
- ▪ Assess global elements to risk.
- ▪ Adopt best practices for risk assessment as part of the strategic sourcing process.

Chapter 7

Supplier Evaluation

Function	Objective	Tactical Step	Chapter/ Appendix
Supply market intelligence	Supply market research	Opportunity identification and validation	2
		Project approval	2
		Establishing the team	3
		Project plan	3
		As-is assessment	4
		Supply market research	5
		Market forecasts	5
		External and market analyses	6
	Strategy and resource commitment	Detailed supplier evaluation and research	7
		Evaluate current and alternative strategies	8
		Understand contract formation	8

Function	Objective	Tactical Step	Chapter/ Appendix
Strategic sourcing	Negotiate and select supplier	Develop relationship strategy	8
		Strategy position paper	8
		Develop requests for information (RFIs) and build negotiation strategy	9
		Negotiate	9
		Final supplier selection	9
		Form contracts	9
	Implement and promote compliance	Implement contracts	9
		Transition to relationship manager	10
Relationship management		Communicate expectations	10
	Improve supplier performance	Measure performance	10
		Resolve issues and develop supplier performance	10
Benchmarking processes and driving continuous improvement		Build an organization for supply-chain excellence	11
		Benchmark performance and drive continuous improvement	12, App. B

7.1 Chapter Outline

- Identifying key supplier evaluation criteria
- Identifying potential suppliers
- Organizing data
- Financial analysis
- Total cost/value chain assessment
- Supplier evaluation
- Checklist

Though a good motive cannot sanction a bad action, a bad motive will always vitiate a good action. In common and trivial matters, we may act without motives, but in momentous ones, the most careful deliberation is wisdom.

— W. M. L. Jay

Suppliers are like fish in the ocean. We, the buyers, are the fishermen. The key challenge facing us is how to put out the right bait, so that we can pull up the right suppliers at the right time and get them to help us develop our products. There are several problems associated with fishing: How do we know we are using the right bait? How do we know the right kinds of fish are in the water? Most important, when we catch a fish, how do we know whether it is the right fish and whether we should keep it or throw it back in the water? Finally, how do we know the fish will follow through with its commitments if we decide to keep it?

— Senior supply management executive, IBM

Chapter 6 identified the primary processes associated with "pushing" business intelligence (BI) and supply market intelligence (SMI) to sourcing teams, managers, supply-chain design program managers, and other key consumers of information. This information may be utilized to modify or alter their sourcing strategies, change the criteria for suppliers, modify their project charters, initiate an entirely new sourcing team, or take other appropriate actions. This chapter deals with the "pull" requirement for MI and BI, that is, the situation in which a strategic sourcing team approaches the BI/MI function prior to initiating a major sourcing project and identifies the need for intelligence related to a specific set of suppliers for a particular commodity. This typically occurs once the internal demand requirements and external business trends and issues have been identified and a thorough spend analysis has profiled the current spending across the company. The opportunity for cost savings has been discovered. Now the team must evaluate all of the current suppliers and weigh the benefits of using alternative suppliers. The BI/MI team can play an integral role in ensuring this takes place in a structured manner.

Figure 7.1 is a high-level overview of the process to be followed when identifying and evaluating suppliers for a given supplier strategy. It forms the basis for the discussion in this chapter.

7.2 Identifying Key Supplier Evaluation Criteria

Based on the internal BI elements and the discussion about demand forecasts, a set of key requirements is developed by the team. The sourcing

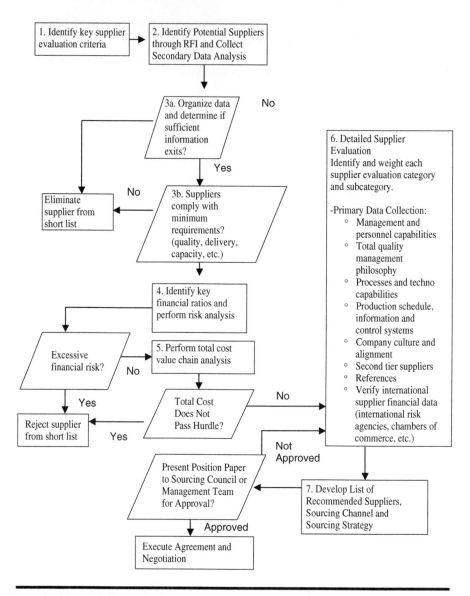

Figure 7.1 High-level overview of supplier evaluation process.

team should "understand the requirements that are important to that purchase" and should evaluate "the various supplier performance areas."[1] These areas include management and employee capabilities, cost, quality performance, technological capabilities, environmental compliance, financial

---

[1] R. Monczka, R. Trent, and R. Handfield, *Purchasing and Supply Chain Management,* 3rd edition, Cincinnati, OH: Southwestern College Publishing, 2004, p. 208.

stability, production scheduling and control systems, and the potential for the development of a long-term relationship.[2] The performance areas of interest identified will serve as a framework around which the supplier evaluation and selection survey will be structured later in the process.

A critical input that determines the criteria for evaluating suppliers is a specification for the product or service. Material requirements might include equipment, components, raw materials, subassemblies, or even completely finished products. On the other hand, examples of service requirements include the need for computer programmers, hazardous waste handlers, transportation carriers, or maintenance service providers. Users (also called internal customers) identify a need for material or service requirements and communicate this need to purchasing. The most common method of informing purchasing of material needs is through a purchase requisition. Users may also transmit their needs by phone, by word of mouth, or through a computer.

Sometimes a service is required. For instance, marketing may want to purchase an advertising campaign, R&D may need a clinical trial, or human resources may need to print a brochure. In this case, the user will complete a statement of work (SOW) that specifies the work that is to be completed, when it is needed, and what type of service provider is required.

A standard purchase requisition or SOW is used most often for routine, noncomplex items, which are increasingly being transmitted through online requisitioning systems linking users with purchasing. An online requisition system is an internal system designed primarily to save time by efficient communication and tracking of material requests. These systems should be used only if the transaction requires purchasing involvement. A corporate procurement card may enable a user to purchase an item directly from a supplier; in this case, requisitions forwarded to purchasing are unnecessary.

Wide differences exist across organizations in the quality and use of electronic purchase requisition systems. A system that requires users to submit needs to purchasing electronically is similar to e-mail. This type of system provides little added value apart from speeding the request to purchasing. On the other hand, another system studied was so complex that users were afraid to use it. They bypassed online requisitioning and relied instead on the phone or intracompany mail. For routine, off-the-shelf items, a requisition may contain all of the information that purchasing requires. However, for technically complex or nonstandard items, purchasing may require additional information or specifications with the requisition. Examples of such specifications are grade of material, method of manufacture, and detailed measurements and tolerances.

---

[2] Ibid., pp. 215–221.

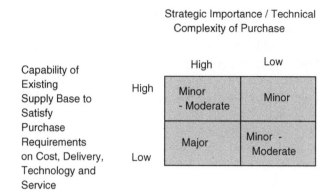

Figure 7.2   Information search — suppliers.

7.3 Identifying Potential Supply Sources through RFIs and Secondary Market Research

Commodity teams rely on various sources of information when identifying potential sources of supply. The degree to which a buyer must search for information about suppliers is a function of several variables. Figure 7.2 summarizes the intensity of an information search under various conditions.

Quadrants I and IV generally require a minor-to-moderate information search, whereas quadrant III requires a major search. In quadrant I, existing suppliers have the ability to satisfy a strategic or nonroutine purchase requirement. In this situation, a buyer may pursue additional information to verify that he or she has considered the best possible sources of supply. Because the buyer has information about a current supplier or suppliers with the required capabilities, the information search will probably not be as intensive as that in quadrant III. In quadrant IV, the purchase requirement is routine or less strategic, but the buyer has no current access to suppliers capable of satisfying the purchase requirement. Given the nature of the purchase in this quadrant, the search requirements will be lower compared with those in quadrant III but greater than those in quadrant II. The following subsections discuss various sources of information used in the evaluation of potential suppliers of new purchase requirements.

7.3.1 Current Suppliers

A major source of information comes from current or existing suppliers. Buyers often look to existing suppliers to satisfy a new purchase requirement. The advantage of this approach is that the purchaser does not have to add and maintain an additional supplier. Moreover, the buyer can do business with an already familiar supplier, which may help save the time and resources required to evaluate a new supplier's capabilities. On the negative side, using existing suppliers may not always be the best long-term approach, although it may be easier and quicker. A purchasing manager may never know if better suppliers are available without information on other sources. For this reason, most organizations continuously seek new sources of supply and are expanding this search to include suppliers from around the world.

Selecting an existing supplier for a new purchase requirement may be an attractive option if a list of preferred suppliers is maintained. Being designated as a preferred supplier means that he or she consistently satisfies the performance and service standards defined by the buyer. A preferred-supplier status conveys immediate information about the supplier's overall performance and competency. However, the buyer must still determine if a preferred supplier is capable of providing a particular purchase requirement.

7.3.2 Sales Representatives

All purchasers receive sales and marketing information from supplier sales representatives. These contacts can be a valuable source of information. Even if an immediate need does not exist for a supplier's services, the buyer can file the information for future reference. A visit to a purchasing manager's office would probably reveal a set of cabinets or drawers that contain sales and marketing information.

7.3.3 Information Databases

Some companies maintain databases of suppliers capable of supporting an industry or product line. National Cash Register (NCR), for example, has compiled and maintains data on about 30,000 companies serving the computer industry. The company searches trade journals and financial newspapers for information about potential suppliers. This database serves as a source of information for NCR buyers at the plant level. Furthermore, purchasing sends a newsletter on market developments twice a month to buyers, engineers, and management at NCR plants worldwide. The company also mails a quarterly overview to plants detailing supplier strengths, weaknesses, and technological capabilities. The use of automated databases can quickly identify suppliers potentially qualified to support a requirement.

Maintaining a supplier database is particularly important in industries in which technology changes rapidly. The database may contain information on current products, the supplier's future technology road map, process capability ratios, and past performance.[3] Database users may quickly determine whether existing suppliers are capable of producing or supplying a given part or service requirement. It is important that supplier databases be updated on a regular basis.

7.3.4 Experience

Purchasing personnel may have gained knowledge about potential suppliers from experience. A buyer may have worked within an industry over many years and is familiar with the suppliers, sometimes including international suppliers. One argument against rotating buyers too frequently between product lines or types of purchases is that a buyer may lose the expertise built up over the years. Because few purchasing organizations have put forth the effort to develop an intelligence database about suppliers, a buyer's experience and knowledge about a supplier market becomes valuable.

7.3.5 Trade Journals

Most major industries have a group or council that publishes a trade journal or magazine that routinely contains articles about different companies. These articles often focus on a company's technical or innovative development of a material, component, product, process, or service. Suppliers also use trade journals to advertise their products or services. These advertisements target a specific audience and can provide information about sources of supply. Most buyers follow (or should follow) trade journals closely.

7.3.6 Trade Directories

Almost all industries publish directories of companies that produce items or provide services within that industry. Such directories can be a valuable source of initial information for a buyer who is not familiar with an industry or its suppliers.

---

[3] Handfield, R. and Pannesi, R., Managing component life cycles in dynamic technological environments, *International Journal of Purchasing and Materials Management*, 20–27, Spring 1994.

7.3.7 Global Suppliers

Do not forget to explore global supplier options. This is an area that has yet to be fully exploited by many U.S. companies and, as such, poses both risks and rewards. (A detailed process to evaluate global suppliers in China is provided in Appendix A). To find out about global suppliers, turn to the U.S. Department of Commerce; you can get world trade reports and commodity- and company-specific reports. *Trade Directories of the World* (Croner Publications) and *Fortune 1000 Foreign Companies* (Dun & Bradstreet) also give information about global suppliers. If you are interested in a few specific countries, contact the consulates of those countries in Washington, D.C.

7.3.8 Industrial Trade Shows

Trade shows may be an efficient way to gain exposure to a large number of suppliers at one time. Associations such as the Chemical Manufacturers Association, American Society of Automotive Suppliers, or Sematech, which represents the semiconductor industry, often coordinate shows. Buyers attending trade shows can gather information about potential suppliers while also evaluating the latest technological developments. Many contacts between industrial buyers and sellers occur at trade shows.

7.3.9 Second-Party or Indirect Information

This source of information includes a wide range of contacts that are not directly part of the purchaser's organization. For example, a buyer can gather information that might be valuable, such as knowledge about a noncompetitor, from other suppliers. Another second-party information source includes other buyers. Attendees at meetings of the Institute for Supply Management (ISM) can develop informal networks that provide information about potential supply sources. Other professional groups include the American Production and Inventory Control Society, the Council for Logistics Management, the American Manufacturing Engineering Association, and the American Society for Quality Control.

Some purchasers give public recognition to their quality-certified suppliers. Recognition may come in the form of a newspaper advertisement that highlights the achievement of superior suppliers. Delta Airlines periodically expresses appreciation and recognition of its best suppliers in full-page advertisements in the *Wall Street Journal*. In the advertisement, Delta lists each supplier by name and explains why he or she is being recognized. Because of Delta's approach to recognizing its best suppliers, a buyer gains visibility to a group of blue-chip suppliers. Examples of other major corporations with supplier certification programs are Chrysler (Pentastar Award), Xerox, GM (Targets for Excellence), Ford (Q1 Award), Eastman Kodak (Quality First Supplier Award), and Cummins Engine (Preferred Quality Supplier Program).

7.3.10 Internal Sources

Many larger companies divide business lines into units, each with a separate purchasing operation. The sharing of such information can occur across units through informal meetings, strategy development sessions, purchasing newsletters, or the development of a comprehensive database containing information about potential supply sources. Internal sources, even those from diverse business units (BUs), can provide a great deal of information about potential supply sources.

7.3.11 Internet Searches

The Internet has powerful search engines capable of providing reams of information. Buyers are increasingly using the Internet to locate potential sources that might qualify for further evaluation. Sellers are increasingly using the Internet as a key part of their direct marketing efforts.

7.3.12 Requests for Information

Another alternative is to develop an RFI. This is a broader document that may contain several fields for the supplier to complete, and may include the size of the supplier, key markets, key customer references, capacity, cost structure, number of employees, union membership, requests for product samples and brochures, and other information. Interested suppliers will generally provide this information in the form of a customized package with a letter expressing interest in pursuing further discussions for additional business.

7.4 Organizing Data and Determining If Sufficient Information Exists

After collecting information about potential supply sources, the sourcing team must begin to sift through and consolidate the information. This can be a huge task, depending on the number of suppliers and the information obtained. Generally speaking, a matrix profiling a supplier should be created, which identifies as many of the following key variables as possible to enable decision making:

- Annual sales volume
- Supplier size: number of employees and number, locations, and size of plants and distribution centers
- Major customers of the supplier
- Sustainability and environmental record
- Market share information
- Organizational ownership
- Capacity utilization situation within the industry: total capacity and utilization rate
- Capacity utilization situation within the firm: total capacity, capacity utilization rate, and expected increases or decreases in capacity
- Order-backlog situation
- Pricing history
- Cost structure and trends
- Length of buying firm's relationship with the supplier
- Type and level of competition existing: price, quality, delivery, or supply availability
- Primary product uses; secondary product uses
- Future market supply and trends
- Cost structure and trends for the past, present, and future
- Technology trends
- Regulatory analysis

Once the data is organized, the team can begin the process of eliminating the suppliers who are not capable of meeting the buyer's needs or do not make a good fit. Eliminating these suppliers and creating a short list is the next step. Purchasers often perform a first-cut, or preliminary, evaluation of potential suppliers to narrow the list before conducting an in-depth formal evaluation.[4] This may take the form of a very-high-level financial risk analysis, a review of historic records of suppliers that have been used in the past, or distribution of additional RFIs, all of which reduce the number of contenders by identifying suppliers that are clearly not interested in the business.[5] They may not meet the criteria in terms of capacity, quality, or other critical metrics. To limit the number of suppliers under consideration, the team should also meet and discuss

---

[4] R. Monczka, R. Trent, and R. Handfield, *Purchasing and Supply Chain Management,* 3rd edition, Cincinnati, OH: Southwestern College Publishing, 2004, p. 212.
[5] Ibid., p. 212.

each supplier's cost, location, and product samples provided. This can occur through additional requests for quotes or additional interviews with key subject matter experts identified in the BI unit. Finally, the sourcing team will develop a short list of potential suppliers that should be approached for a detailed discussion and evaluation.

7.5 Detailed Financial Analysis

It is important to remember at this stage that the team must continue to chip away at the short list until the right mix of potential suppliers who require evaluation is identified. Also, every supplier must pass a detailed evaluation of financial health conducted by the sourcing team.

Assessment of a potential supplier's financial condition almost always occurs during the initial evaluation process. Some purchasers view the financial assessment as a screening process or preliminary condition that the supplier must pass before a detailed evaluation can begin. An organization may use a financial rating service to help analyze a supplier's financial condition. If the supplier is a publicly held company, other financial documents will be readily available. Because buyers rely on fewer suppliers today to support their purchase requirements, it is important to reduce risk by selecting financially sound suppliers who are expected to remain in business in the long term.

Selecting a supplier in poor financial condition presents a number of risks. First, there is the obvious risk that the supplier will go out of business. This event can present serious problems if other sources of supply are not readily available. Second, such suppliers may not have the resources to invest in plant, equipment, or research that may be necessary for longer-term technological or other performance improvements. Third, the supplier may become too financially dependent on the purchaser. This can be constraining if the need arises to switch suppliers (the buyer may feel an obligation to the supplier). A final risk is that financial weakness is usually an indication of underlying problems. A buyer must understand why a supplier is financially weak. Is the weakness a result of poor quality or delivery performance? Is it a result of wasteful spending by management? Has the supplier assumed too much debt?

Circumstances may exist that support the selection of a supplier in a weaker financial condition. A supplier may be developing, but has not yet marketed, a leading-edge technology that can provide a market advantage to the purchaser. Gaining access to new product and process technology before competitors is one indication of purchasing effectiveness. Also, a supplier may be in a weaker financial condition because of uncontrollable or nonrepeating circumstances.

If the supplier is a publicly traded company, specific financial ratios can be obtained from a variety of Web sites providing detailed financial ratios and industry averages for comparison. Among publicly traded companies, the Securities Exchange Commission (SEC) also polices this information. This is fortunate for us because we can find all reports free of charge and for all public companies in one convenient spot: www.sec.gov/edgarhp.htm. If you are looking at a few select companies, check out their Web sites, which usually offer "investor relations" links that provide the same information, but perhaps in broader form. If you are interested in a private company, check out Dun & Bradstreet at www.dnb.com.

Dun & Bradstreet also provides a number of formula-based approaches that allow buyers not having detailed knowledge of the financial background of suppliers to obtain an overall assessment of their financial health. Many of these ratios can also be calculated using income statements and balance sheets. Some common ratios used to assess supplier financial health appear in Table 7.1. Some of the Web sites available to obtain such information include the following:

- Yahoo! Financial section (http://www.biz.yahoo.com)
- Morningstar (http://www.morningstar.net)
- Marketwatch (http://www.marketwatch.com)
- 411Stocks (http://www.411stocks.com)
- The Street (http://www.thestreet.com)
- Dun & Bradstreet (http://www.dnb.com)

Not all sourcing teams will have the expertise to conduct a detailed financial analysis. Increasingly, teams are relying on their treasury personnel to assist in evaluating financial ratios because they can provide quick and valuable insights into a supplier's financial health. These teams can identify red flags that may signify potential financial difficulty. If at any point the sourcing team has reason to believe that the supplier is facing a financial crisis of some sort, the supplier should be consulted for an explanation before any immediate action is taken.

The items in Table 7.1 are a good set of indicators for evaluating the supplier.

7.6 Total Cost/Value Chain Assessment

Total cost of ownership (TCO) requires a purchaser to identify and measure costs beyond the standard unit price, transportation, and tooling when evaluating purchase proposals or supplier performance. Formally,

Table 7.1 Interpreting Key Financial Ratios

Ratio	Interpretation
Liquidity ratios	
Current ratio = current assets/current liabilities	Should be over 1.0, but look at the industry average; high — may mean poor asset management
Quick ratio[a] = (cash + receivables)/current liabilities	Should be at least 0.8 if supplier sells on credit; low — may mean cash flow problems; high — may mean poor asset management
Activity ratios	
Inventory turnover = costs of goods sold/inventory	Compare with the industry average; low — problems with slow inventory, which may hurt cash flow
Fixed-asset turnover = sales/fixed assets	Compare with the industry average; too low — may mean supplier is not using fixed assets efficiently or effectively
Total asset turnover = sales/total assets	Compare with the industry average; too low — may mean supplier is not using fixed assets efficiently or effectively
Days sales outstanding = (receivables × 365)/sales	Compare with the industry average; or 45–50 — if company sells on net 30; too high — hurts cash flow; too low — may mean credit policies to customers are too restrictive
Profitability ratios	
Net profit margin = profit after taxes/sales	Represents after tax return; compare with the industry average
Return on assets = profit after taxes/total assets	Compare with the industry average; represents the return the company earns on everything it owns
Return on equity = profit after taxes/equity	The higher the better; the return on shareholders' investment in the business
Debt ratios	
Debt to equity = total liabilities/equity	Compare with the industry average; over 3 — means highly leveraged
Current debt to equity = current liabilities/equity	Over 1 — is risky unless the industry average is over 1; when the ratio is high, the supplier may be unable to pay lenders

Table 7.1   Interpreting Key Financial Ratios (continued)

Interest coverage = (Pretax Inc. + Int. Exp.)/Int. Exp.	Should be over 3, the higher the better; low — may mean supplier as difficulty paying creditors

[a] Cash includes marketable securities.

TCO is defined as the present value of all costs associated with a product, service, or capital equipment that are incurred over its expected life.

Most large firms base purchase decisions and evaluate suppliers on cost elements beyond unit price, transportation, and tooling. Research indicates, however, that companies differ widely on what cost components to include in a total cost analysis.

Typically these costs can be broken down into four broad categories:[6]

- *Purchase price* — This is the amount paid to the supplier for the product, service, or capital equipment.
- *Acquisition costs* — This includes all costs associated with bringing the product, service, or capital equipment to the customer's location. Examples of acquisition costs are sourcing, administration, freight, and taxes.
- *Usage costs* — In the case of a product, this includes all costs associated with converting the purchased part or material into finished product and supporting it through its usable life, in the case of a service, all costs associated with the performance of the service that are not included in the purchase price, and in the case of capital equipment, all costs associated with operating the equipment through its life. Examples of usage costs are inventory, conversion, scrap, warranty, installation, training, downtime, and opportunity costs.
- *End-of-life costs* — The includes all costs incurred when a product, service, or capital equipment reaches the end of its usable life, net of amounts received from the sale of remaining product or the equipment (salvage value); examples of end-of-life costs are obsolescence, disposal, cleanup, and project termination costs.

---

[6] This section is based on an article written by Sanjit Menezes, vice president of the Anklesaria Group, Del Mar, California, *Purchasing Today,* January 2001, pp. 28–32.

Consider the following when building a TCO model:

- Building a TCO can be a costly and time-intensive activity. Use it for evaluating larger purchases.
- Make sure to obtain senior management buy-in before embarking on a full-fledged TCO. It will make data gathering much easier, especially if several people from different parts of the organization have to be interviewed.
- Work in a team. This will greatly reduce the time required for data collection activities, which can be distributed among team members.
- Focus on the big costs first. Spending extended periods of time quantifying small cost elements will only delay the decision, which in most cases will not be impacted by them.
- Make sure to obtain a realistic estimate of the life cycle. A life cycle that is too short or too long could result in a wrong decision.
- Whether evaluating a purchase option or making an outsourcing decision, a TCO model (see Table 7.2) will ensure that the right decision is made, at least from a cost perspective.

Table 7.2   Example of a TCO Model

Cost Elements	Cost Measures
Purchase price (step 1)	
Equipment (step 2)	Supplier quote: $1,200 per PC (steps 3 and 4)
Software license A	Supplier quote: $300 per PC
Software license B	Supplier quote: $100 per PC
Software license C	Supplier quote: $50 per PC
Acquisition cost	
Sourcing	2 FTE @ $85K and $170K for 2 months
Administration	1 PO @ $150, 12 invoices @ $40 each
Usage costs	
Installation	$700 per PC (PC move, install, network)
Equipment support	$120 per month per PC — supplier quote
Network support	$100 per month — supplier quote
Warranty	$120 per PC for a 3-year warranty
Opportunity cost – lost productivity	Downtime 15 hr per PC per year @ $30 per hr

Table 7.2   Example of a TCO Model (continued)

End-of-life costs	
Salvage value	$36 per PC

Note: Supply manager Joe Smith was considering the purchase of 1000 desktop PCs for his organization. The life cycle was three years, and the organization's cost of capital was 12 percent. He calculated the TCO for one of the purchase options as shown in the table. Using these elements, the TCO for each of these decisions was calculated as shown in the following table.

Cost Elements	Present	Year 1 (Step 5)	Year 2	Year 3
Purchase price				
Equipment	$120,000			
Software license A	$300,000			
Software license B	$100,000			
Software license C	$50,000			
Acquisition cost				
Sourcing	$42,500			
Administration	$150	$480	$480	$480
Usage costs				
Opportunity cost — lost productivity		$450,000	$450,000	$450,000
Installation	$700,000			
Equipment support		$1,440,000	$1,440,000	$1,440,000
Network support		$1,200,000	$1,200,000	$1,200,000
Warranty	$120,000			
End-of-life costs				
Salvage value				($36,000)
Total	$2,512,650	$3,090,480	$3,090,480	$3,054,480
Present values @ 12%	$2,512,650	$2,759,799	$2,463,113 (step 6)	$2,174,790

Note: Based on this model, the supply manager should explore the possibilities of reducing service costs such as equipment support and network support; these appear to be highest and contribute most to costs. This is also typically the most profitable area for the supplier as services are often not audited.

Another approach that is useful at this stage in the process is to develop a "value chain mapping" that identifies the critical suppliers, the relationship of the focal buying firm with these suppliers, as well as the competitors both within and outside the industry for these products and services. This is a critical point; understanding the dynamics of a supply market requires that the broader picture of supply-chain relationships be understood within the context of this specific sourcing strategy. For example, one cross-functional team looking at fuel additives developed a description (shown in Table 7.3) of the current spend situation that drove them to reevaluate the entire market requirements for the products being purchased.

7.7 Performing a Detailed Supplier Evaluation through Supplier Visits

At this stage, the preliminary set of suppliers who have not met the team's requirements has been eliminated. Further discussion with suppliers is required if the team is to reach a definitive conclusion on the sourcing decision. The team will want to contact each of the suppliers and schedule visits to the suppliers' production facilities or sites to gather additional information. The following subsections discuss the key supplier evaluation criteria and detail those often used by a cross-functional team during supplier visits. The use of teams for supplier evaluation and selection is increasing, particularly among larger organizations that have the resources to commit to this approach. The advantage of the cross-functional selection team approach is that each team member contributes unique insights into the overall supplier evaluation. For instance, one team member may be an expert in quality, engineering capabilities, or manufacturing techniques and so is uniquely qualified to assess the supplier in this regard.

7.7.1 Key Supplier Evaluation Criteria

Purchasers usually evaluate potential suppliers across multiple categories using their own selection criteria with assigned weights. For example, requiring consistent delivery performance with short lead times to support a just-in-time production system may require emphasizing a supplier's scheduling and production systems. A high-technology buyer may emphasize a supplier's process and technological capabilities or research and development.

Most evaluations rate suppliers on three primary criteria: (1) cost or price, (2) quality, and (3) delivery. These three elements of performance are generally the most obvious and most critical areas that affect the

Table 7.3   Creating a Value Chain Based on Market Research

In the current supply chain for a company's fuel additives, the team identified marked differences among BU processes for sourcing fuel additives. BU 1 and BU 2 acquire fuel additives directly from manufacturers, but BU 3 deals with an additional major intermediary, XYZ, and consumes a very high quantity of the product. BU 3 purchases the supplies and services of the majority of the fuel additives from XYZ, and a very small portion is purchased from a different supplier, ABC. Both companies are located at places within 300 mi from BU 3, where they store, blend, and, ship their products from. Both ABC and XYZ acquire their manufactured materials before blending, mainly from major manufacturing companies. XYZ, though, relies heavily on its headquarters for raw materials and finished product to blend. They also purchase and rebrand finished additives from other suppliers.

As a result of market analysis, the major industry cost drivers were identified as:

Crude price (50 percent)
Raw materials including solvents (30 percent)
Supply-chain management costs like transport, freight and duties, inventory, distributor fees, and emergency charges (10 percent)
Utilities during the manufacturing process (10 percent)

The sourcing team realized that this value chain could be shortened to acquire fuel additives directly from the manufacturer, just as other BUs were currently doing. The major driver for going in this direction is the high premiums paid to the distributors for these commodity-type products. The prices paid for fuel additives include the cost of the fuel additive, plus the distributor profits and the service portion. Currently, there is no clear line separating these costs. By approaching the manufacturer, the company was able to negotiate directly for the costs of the commodities, and leverage on volumes and existing price agreements between these manufacturers and other BUs.

In the revised value chain model the manufacturer would supply the fuel additives directly to the company, and the services would be provided either by the manufacturer or by the distributor. This reduces the requirements for "cocktailing," which had a service and supply component associated with it. The company can now purchase pure fuel additives as commodities without the need of a third-party provider for the "cocktails." All BUs need to make sure that the technical support and the process servicing are provided if needed.

purchaser. For many items, purchasers will be concerned with only these three performance areas. But for critical items needing an in-depth analysis of the supplier's capabilities, a more detailed supplier evaluation study is required. An initial supplier evaluation will usually cover the following supplier performance categories to some extent:

- Supplier management capability
- Overall personnel capabilities
- Cost structure
- Total quality performance, systems, and philosophy
- Process and technological capability, including the supplier's design capability
- Environmental regulation compliance
- Financial capability and stability
- Production scheduling and control systems, including supplier delivery performance
- Information systems capability (e.g., EDI, bar coding, ERP, and CAD/CAM)
- Supplier purchasing strategies, policies, and techniques
- Longer-term relationship potential

7.7.2 Management Capability

It is important for a buyer to evaluate a supplier's management capability. After all, the management runs the business and makes the decisions that affect the future competitiveness of the supplier. There are a number of questions a buyer should ask when evaluating a supplier's management capability:

- Does executive management practice long-range planning?
- Has management committed itself to Total Quality Management (TQM) and continuous improvement?
- Is there a high degree of turnover among managers?
- What is the professional experience of the managers?
- Is there a vision about the future direction of the company?
- How many purchasing professionals are certified purchasing managers?
- What is the history of management–labor relations?
- Is management making the investments that are necessary to sustain and grow the business?
- Has management prepared the company to face future competitive challenges, including providing employee training and development?
- Does management understand the importance of strategic sourcing?

Many of these questions are difficult to answer with a simple "yes" or "no." It may be challenging to identify the true state of affairs during a brief visit or with a questionnaire. Nevertheless, asking these questions can help the purchasing manager develop a feel for the professional capabilities of the managers in the supplying organization. When interviewing the management at a supplier's facility, it is important to attempt to meet with as many people as possible to get a true picture of management's attitudes. During such interviews the team may often discover differing viewpoints on where the organization is truly headed in terms of management orientation.

7.7.3 Personnel Capabilities

This part of the supplier evaluation process requires an assessment of nonmanagement personnel. The benefit that a highly trained, stable, and motivated workforce can provide should not be underestimated, particularly during periods of labor shortages. A purchaser should evaluate these points:

- The degree to which employees support and are committed to quality and continuous improvement
- The overall skills and abilities of the workforce (especially with regard to education and training)
- The state of employee–management relations
- Workforce flexibility
- Employee morale
- Workforce turnover
- The opportunity and willingness of employees to contribute to improving a supplier's operation

A buyer should also gather information about the history of strikes and labor disputes. This can result in a general idea of how dedicated the supplier's employees are to producing products or services that meet or exceed the buyer's expectations.

7.7.4 Cost Structure

Evaluating a supplier's cost structure requires an in-depth understanding of a supplier's total costs, including direct labor costs, indirect labor costs, material costs, manufacturing or process operating costs, and general overhead costs. Understanding a supplier's cost structure helps a buyer determine how efficiently a supplier can produce an item. A cost analysis also helps identify potential areas of cost improvement.

Collecting this information can be a challenge during the initial evaluation process, as a supplier may not have a detailed understanding of its own costs. Many suppliers do not have a sophisticated cost accounting system and are unable to effectively assign overhead costs to products or processes. Furthermore, some suppliers view cost data as highly proprietary. A supplier may fear that the release of cost information will undermine its pricing strategy or that competitors will gain access to its cost data, which could provide insight into a supplier's competitive advantage.

As a result of these concerns, buyers will often develop reverse pricing models that provide approximate estimates of the supplier's cost structure during the initial supplier evaluation. Although these cost models are never completely accurate, they can be useful in obtaining more information and querying suppliers further on their cost structures. Once cost elements have been understood by both parties, a cost-based pricing approach can be used to derive mutual benefits. However, this requires a high level of mutual trust and commitment.

7.7.5 Total Quality Performance, Systems, and Philosophy

A major part of the evaluation process addresses a supplier's quality management processes, systems, and philosophy. Buyers not only evaluate the obvious topics associated with supplier quality (e.g., management commitment, statistical process control, and number of defects) but also evaluate safety, training and facilities, and equipment maintenance. For example, Alcoa defines its supplier quality requirements in four broad areas: management, quality measurement, safety, and training and facilities.

Many purchasers are adopting supplier quality evaluation systems that are based on the Malcolm Baldrige National Quality Award or ISO 9000 criteria. In 1987, President Ronald Reagan signed the Malcolm Baldrige National Quality Improvement Act, which established a national award to recognize quality improvement among manufacturing, service, and small businesses. Since then, the criteria, which have been revised, have become an operational definition of TQM. The wide distribution of the application guidelines has exposed many suppliers to the Baldrige definition of quality. Companies such as Honeywell, Motorola, Southwest Bell, Cummins Engine, and others are using modified versions of the Baldrige criteria for supplier quality measurement and evaluation.

7.7.6 Process and Technological Capability

Supplier evaluation teams often include a member from the engineering or technical staff to evaluate a supplier's process and technological capability. Process consists of the technology, design, methods, and equipment used to manufacture a product or deliver a service. A supplier's selection of a production process helps define its required technology, human resource skills, and capital equipment requirements.

The evaluation of a supplier's technical and process capability should also focus on future process and technical ability, which requires assessment of a supplier's capital equipment plans and strategy. In addition, a purchaser should evaluate the resources that a supplier is committing to its research and development effort. This information will indicate the emphasis that a supplier places on future process and technological improvement.

A purchaser may also assess a supplier's design capability. One way to reduce the time required to develop new products involves using qualified suppliers who are able to perform product design activities. Ford, for example, now requires almost all of its suppliers to have production and design capabilities. The company has transferred most of the design of its component and component system requirements to suppliers. The trend toward the increased use of supplier design capabilities makes this area an integral part of the supplier evaluation and selection process.

7.7.7 Environmental Regulation Compliance

The 1990s brought about a renewed awareness of the impact that industry has on the environment. Government regulations are increasingly harsh on polluters. The Clean Air Act of 1990, for example, imposes large fines on producers of ozone-depleting substances and foul-smelling gases, and the Clinton administration introduced laws regarding recycling content in industrial materials. Furthermore, purchasers do not want to be associated with known environmental polluters from a public relations or potential liability standpoint.

At Herman Miller, Inc., a manufacturer of office furniture, environmental concerns are integrated closely into the supplier evaluation and selection process. For instance, Herman Miller includes the supplier's packaging as an important evaluation criterion. Corrugated packaging is being used more often because it is easier to recycle. Standardized, reusable shipping containers are also favored over disposable ones; in fact, such containers can be used to support just-in-time deliveries. Labeling is also important. Herman Miller now requires its suppliers to label the chemical composition of its plastic items so that recyclers will know the exact content in the plastic found in the parts.

7.7.8 Financial Capability and Stability

Additional financial analysis beyond the secondary market analysis discussed in Section 7.4 may be merited at this stage if the sourcing team believes there are other indications of financial problems. For example, many Dunn & Bradstreet reports are not current. If the team suspects that there are financial problems, they may wish to speak to the suppliers' suppliers to determine their accounts payable information or request an independent financial audit from the supplier (an extreme measure).

7.7.9 Production Scheduling and Control Systems

Production scheduling includes those systems that release, schedule, and control a supplier's production process. Does the supplier use a material requirements planning (MRP) system to ensure the availability of required components? Does the supplier track material and production cycle time and compare this against a performance objective or standard? Does the supplier's production scheduling system support a purchaser's just-in-time requirements? How much lead time does the supplier's production scheduling and control system require? What is the supplier's on-time delivery performance history? The purpose behind evaluating the production scheduling and control system is to identify the degree of control the supplier has over its scheduling and production process. The benchmark for this element of evaluation is whether the supplier has a certified Class A MRP system.

As defined by Oliver Wight, a Class A MRP user:

> ... is one that uses MRP in a closed-loop mode. It has material requirements planning, capacity planning and control, shop-floor dispatching, and vendor scheduling systems in place and being used, and management uses the system to run the business. They participate in production planning. They sign off on the production plans. They constantly monitor performance on inventory record accuracy, routing accuracy, attainment of the master schedule, attainment of the capacity plans, etc. In a Class A company, the MRP system provides the game plan that sales, finance, manufacturing, purchasing, and engineering people all work to. They use the formal system.

Suppliers can formally claim to have a Class A production system once they have undergone a formal review of their system by a professional external reviewer who has verified that the requisite criteria are satisfied.

In some cases, companies who are considering sourcing high volumes of product with a supplier that has multiple facilities may also want to consider whether the supplier has any plans to implement an enterprise resource planning (ERP) system. ERP systems effectively provide a single information system linking accounting, operations, purchasing, logistics, finance, marketing, and sales. Such information systems provide a higher level of accuracy on cost tracking, delivery, and scheduling across multiple facilities.

7.7.10 E-Business Capability

The ability to communicate electronically between a buyer and seller is becoming a requirement for entering into a purchase contract. In the past, electronic data interchange (EDI) was considered a primary condition for doing business. However, more and more companies are moving to Web-based platforms for their transactions. Such systems are often referred to as business-to-business (B2B) electronic commerce. In early 2000, relatively few companies had implemented B2B electronic commerce platforms, but the rate of technology change in this area has been escalating rapidly. For instance, IBM stated that the majority of its purchases (by dollar spent) occurred via the Web. However, such statements assume that suppliers have the required ability to adapt to an E-commerce approach. In contrast to EDI, E-commerce requires a relatively low investment on the part of suppliers. Ford Motor Company has offered to provide their suppliers with a computer, modem, and Web software for as little as $5 a month and expects to significantly reduce its cost of transactions with suppliers as a result. Besides the efficiencies that B2B E-commerce provides, these systems support closer relationships and the exchange of all kinds of information.

The team should also evaluate other dimensions of the supplier's information technology. Does the supplier have computer-aided design (CAD) and computer-aided manufacturing (CAM) capability? Does the supplier have a Web-based supplier measurement system in place? Is bar coding used where appropriate? Can the supplier send advance shipping notices (ASNs) or accept payment by electronic funds transfer? Is the supplier able to communicate via e-mail? Are managers networked throughout the company? Evidence that the supplier is using these technologies can provide reasonable assurance that the supplier is staying current with new E-commerce capabilities.

7.7.11 Supplier Sourcing Strategies, Policies, and Maturity

Understanding the concept of a supplier's suppliers is a key part of integrated supply-chain management. Unfortunately, organizations do not have the resources or personnel to investigate all of the suppliers within their supply chain. However, there are ways to indirectly obtain information on the performance capabilities of tier-two and even tier-three suppliers. It is possible for a purchaser to develop an understanding of the purchasing approaches and techniques of suppliers three tiers below the primary buyer.

Assume that during the supplier selection process, a purchaser (level 0) evaluates the sourcing strategies, approaches, and techniques of its first-tier supplier (level 1). Through discussions with the purchasing department of the first-tier supplier, the purchaser can gain insight about its second-tier suppliers (level 2). If the supplier at level 1 (the purchaser's first-tier supplier) also evaluates the sourcing strategies, approaches, and techniques of its first-tier suppliers (level 2 suppliers to the purchaser), then this can provide information about third-tier suppliers (level 3). The original purchaser has an opportunity to gain information, with support from first-tier suppliers, about suppliers three tiers below.

Evaluating a potential supplier's sourcing strategies, policies, and techniques is one way to gain greater insight to and understanding of the supply chain. Because few purchasers understand their second- and third-tier suppliers, those that do can gain an important advantage over competitors. Integrating information systems across multiple tiers of suppliers can improve planning and forecasting, reduce lead time throughout the supply chain, reduce in-transit inventory, and significantly reduce costs. On the technology side, engineers can obtain advance information on new innovations being developed by second- and third-tier suppliers, thereby improving the design of their own products.

Chrysler, now part of DaimlerChrysler, has developed a concept it refers to as the extended enterprise. This process requires Chrysler to map its supply chain for its purchased materials all the way to raw materials. Part of the process requires Chrysler to enlighten suppliers far up the supply chain about how their products are used in Chrysler vehicles. This process also helps Chrysler understand its total supply chain.

7.7.12 Longer-Term Relationship Potential

Assessing a supplier's willingness to develop longer-term relationships that may evolve into alliances or partnerships is increasingly becoming part of the evaluation process. Robert Spekman (a supply-chain researcher) argues that approaches emphasizing supplier efficiency, quality, price, and delivery are sometimes incomplete. Although these performance areas are important, they do not necessarily cover the issues upon which to base a longer-term relationship or partnership. He presents a number of questions that a buyer should ask when evaluating the potential of a longer-term relationship:

- Has the supplier indicated a willingness or commitment to a longer-term or partnership arrangement?

- Is the supplier willing to commit resources that it cannot or will not use in other relationships?
- How early in the product design stage is the supplier willing or able to participate?
- What does the supplier bring to the relationship that is unique?
- Will the supplier immediately revert to a negotiated stance if a problem arises?
- Does the supplier have a genuine interest in joint problem solving?
- Is the supplier's senior management committed to the processes inherent in strategic relationships?
- Will there be free and open exchange of information across the two companies?
- How much future planning is the supplier willing to share?
- Is the need for confidential treatment of information taken seriously?
- What is the general level of comfort between the two parties?
- How well does the supplier know our industry and business?
- Will the supplier share cost data?
- Is the supplier willing to come to us first with innovations?
- Is the supplier willing to commit capacity exclusively to our needs?
- What will be the supplier's commitment to understanding our problems and concerns?
- Will we be special to the supplier or just another customer?

This is not a complete list of questions for evaluating the possibility of a longer-term relationship. However, this does provide a framework regarding the types of issues that are important. It is relatively straightforward to create a numerical scale to assess these issues as part of the supplier evaluation and selection process.

7.7.13 Developing an Initial Supplier Evaluation and Selection Survey

Supplier evaluations often follow a rigorous, structured approach through the use of a survey. An effective supplier survey should have certain characteristics. First, the survey should be comprehensive and include the performance categories considered important to the evaluation and selection process.

Second, the survey process must be as objective as possible. This requires the use of a scoring system that defines the meaning of each value on a measurement scale. If a performance item is used to rate a supplier along a 10-point scale, the individual or team conducting the rating must understand what a value of a 10 versus a value of 9 means.

Objectivity means creating a quantitative scale to evaluate performance items and categories that are often subjective.

Third, the items and measurement scales must be reliable. Reliability refers to the degree of agreement among conclusions of different individuals or groups reviewing the same items and measurement scales. In other words, if two individuals evaluated the same supplier under the same conditions, a reliable item is one that results in basically the same evaluation from the two individuals. Reliable supplier evaluations require well-defined measures and well-understood items. The items and scales must be clearly written and unambiguous so the user understands exactly what each means. Perhaps, one of the best methods of obtaining objective and reliable scales is effective training of those who conduct the survey.

Fourth, a sound supplier survey is flexible. Although an organization should maintain a structure to its supplier survey, the format of the evaluation should provide some flexibility across different types of purchase requirements. The requirements for evaluating a service provider may differ substantially from those of a highly engineered subsystem purchase. The easiest way to include flexibility within the supplier evaluation process is to adjust the performance categories and weights assigned to each category. The performance categories that are most important will receive a higher weight within the total evaluation score.

Last, the supplier survey should be mathematically straightforward. The use of weights and points should be simple enough so that each individual involved in the evaluation understands the mechanics of the scoring and selection process. To ensure that a supplier survey has the right characteristics, we recommend the use of a step-by-step process when creating this tool. The following subsections discuss this framework in detail and develop a sample supplier evaluation survey.

7.7.13.1 Step 1: Identify Key Supplier Evaluation Categories

One of the first steps when developing a supplier survey is deciding which performance categories to include. Recall from an earlier section of this chapter that many possible performance evaluation categories exist. Typically, a purchaser may evaluate a supplier's cost structure, expected delivery performance, technological and process capability, quality systems, and management capability.

For illustrative purposes, assume that a purchaser selects quality, management capability, financial condition, supplier cost structure, expected delivery performance, technological capability, systems capability, and other miscellaneous performance factors as the categories to include in the evaluation. These categories would reveal the performance areas the purchaser considers most important.

7.7.13.2 Step 2: Weight Each Evaluation Category

Performance categories are usually assigned a weight that reflects the relative importance of that category. For example, if quality performance is important, a purchaser may assign a greater weight to that category. The total of the combined weights must equal 1.0.

An important characteristic of an effective evaluation system is flexibility. One way that management achieves this flexibility is by assigning different weights or by adding or deleting performance categories as required. A dynamic approach to supplier evaluation recognizes that different purchase requirements may require different performance categories or weights.

7.7.13.3 Step 3: Identify and Weight Subcategories

Step 2 specified broad performance categories included within our sample evaluation. Step 3 requires identifying performance subcategories, if they exist, within each broader performance category. For example, the quality systems category may require the identification of separate subcategories (such as those described in the Malcolm Baldrige Award criteria). If this is the case, the supplier evaluation should include any subcategories or items that make up the quality systems category. Equally important, the purchaser must decide how to weight each subcategory within the broader performance evaluation category. The sum of the subcategory weights must equal the total weight of the performance category. Furthermore, the purchaser must clearly define the scoring system used within each category. This becomes the focus of step 4.

7.7.13.4 Step 4: Define Scoring System for Categories and Subcategories

Step 4 defines each score within a performance category. If an evaluation uses a 5-point scale to assess a performance category, then a purchaser must clearly define the difference between a score of 5, 4, 3, etc. A major U.S. company scored each category and subcategory in its supplier evaluation program on a 10-point scale in which 1–2 = poor, 3–4 = weak, 5–6 = marginal, 7–8 = qualified, and 9–10 = outstanding. The scoring values did not have any further definition detailing what each means. The company has since revamped its system to include a 4-point scale that is easier to interpret and is based on the language and principles of TQM:

- *Major nonconformity (0 points earned):* The absence or a total breakdown of a system to meet a requirement or any noncompliance that would result in the probable shipment of a nonconforming product.

- *Minor nonconformity (1 point earned):* A noncompliance (though not major) that judgment and experience indicate is likely to result in the failure of the quality system or reduce its ability to ensure controlled processes or products.
- *Conformity (2 points earned):* No major or minor nonconformities were noted during the evaluation.
- *Adequacy (3 points earned):* Specific supplier performance or documentation meets or exceeds requirements, given the scope of the supplier's operations.

A clearly defined scoring system considers criteria that may be highly subjective and develops a quantitative scale for measurement. Scoring metrics are effective if different individuals interpret and score similarly the same performance categories under review. A scoring system that is too broad, ambiguous, or poorly defined increases the probability of arriving at widely different assessments or conclusions.

7.7.13.5 Step 5: Evaluate Supplier Directly

This step requires that the reviewer visit a supplier's facilities to perform the evaluation. Site visits require at least a day, and often, several days to complete. When factoring in travel time and postvisit reviews, we begin to realize that an organization must select carefully those suppliers it intends evaluating. In many cases, a cross-functional team will perform the evaluation, which allows team members with different knowledge to ask different questions.

Purchasers often notify suppliers beforehand of any documentation required to support the initial evaluation. This can save time once the evaluation begins. If a purchaser has no previous experience with a supplier, the reviewer may require a supplier to provide documentation of performance capability. For example, a supplier will have to present evidence of its process capability studies, process control systems, or delivery performance.

As shown in Figure 7.3, the company being analyzed received a total overall evaluation of 92.9 percent. A purchaser can compare objectively the scores of different suppliers competing for the same purchase contract and select one supplier over another based on the evaluation score. Based on the evaluation, it is also possible that a supplier may not qualify at this time for further consideration. Purchasers should have minimum acceptable performance requirements that suppliers must satisfy before they can become part of the supply base. In this example, the supplier performs acceptably in most major categories except service (7 out of 10

Factor	Weight	How Measured	Supplier Performance over past 12 months	Calculation	Rating
Quality	40	1% defects subtracts 5%	0.8% defective	$\frac{40\ (\ 100 - (0.8 \times 5))}{100}$	38.4
Delivery	30	1 day late subtracts 1%	Avg. 3 days late	$\frac{30\ (\ 100 - (3 \times 1))}{100}$	29.1
Price	20	lowest price paid / price charged	$46 / $50	$\frac{20\ (\ 46/50 \times 100)}{100}$	18.4
Service	10	good = 100% fair = 70% poor = 40%	fair	$\frac{10(70)}{100}$	7.0
Ttl. Points	100				92.9

Figure 7.3   Weighted point method.

possible points). The reviewer must decide if the shortcomings in this category are correctable or if the supplier simply lacks the ability to perform.

7.7.13.6 Step 6: Review Evaluation Results and Make Selection Decision

At some point the team must decide whether to recommend or reject a supplier as a source. What actually happens depends on the particular situation under review. An organization may review a supplier for consideration for expected future business and not a specific contract. Evaluating suppliers before there is an actual purchase requirement can provide a great deal of flexibility to a purchaser. Once an actual need materializes, the purchaser is in a position to move quickly because it has a prequalified supplier.

It is important to determine the seriousness of any supplier shortcomings noted during the evaluation and to assess the degree to which these shortcomings might affect performance. Evaluation scales should differentiate between various degrees of supplier shortcomings. Alcoa, for example, explicitly defines the difference between a performance problem and a deficiency. A *problem* is a discrepancy, nonconformance, or missing requirement that will have a significant negative impact on an important area of concern in an audit statement. A *deficiency* is a minor departure from an intended level of performance or a nonconformance that is easily resolved and does not materially affect the required output.

The primary output from this step is a recommendation about whether to accept a supplier for business. A purchaser may evaluate several suppliers who might be competing for a purchase contract. The initial evaluation provides an objective way to compare suppliers side by side before making a final selection decision. A purchaser may decide to use more than one supplier, based on the results of the supplier survey. The purpose of the evaluation is to qualify potential suppliers for current or expected future purchase contracts.

The authority for the final supplier selection decision varies from organization to organization. The reviewer who evaluated the supplier may have the authority to make the supplier selection decision. In other cases, the buyer or team may present or justify the supplier selection decision or findings to a committee or a manager who has final authority.

An example of a completed supplier evaluation after a visit is shown in Table 7.4.

7.8 Conclusion

At this stage in the process, the sourcing team has developed a fairly comprehensive set of insights regarding each of the potential suppliers. A lot of data has been collected, organized, filtered, and summarized in the form of supplier scoring tables. Next, the team must finalize their strategy through a supplier preferencing analysis and develop a final position paper for presentation to the sourcing council or senior executive responsible for authorizing the decision. (This is discussed in Chapter 8.) Once this has been accomplished, they are then ready to move into the next stage that is most commonly associated with purchasing: negotiation and contract development.

It is worthwhile to note that the amount of work done to reach this point in the process is significant. Performing all of the steps required to develop a comprehensive sourcing strategy based on effective SMI is laborious. In general, getting to this stage in the process may take four to eight months of full-time effort by the sourcing team if unassisted by a dedicated BI/MI function. However, the benefits delivered through this additional preparation can only be realized when the full supply market picture is scoped and researched in detail.

To conclude this discussion a checklist for performing supplier evaluation is presented followed by its results.

7.9 Checklist

- Identify key supplier evaluation criteria.
- Identify potential suppliers.
- Organize data.
- Conduct financial analysis.
- Conduct total cost/value chain assessment.
- Evaluate suppliers.

7.10 Results

- Prioritized list of key suppliers

Table 7.4 Supplier Evaluation — SureTech Company

Category	Weight	Subweight	Score (5pt scale)	Weighted Score	Comment
Quality performance	20				
Total quality commitment		5	4	4	PC week has priced the company products (reliability)
Parts per million defect performance		15	1	3	Higher ppm of the industry (10500)
Financial risk analysis	15				
Asset utilization		5	4	4	Inventory turnover problems
Capitalization		5	4	4	Good performance
Profitability		5	5	5	Best performance in the industry
Total cost analysis	10		4	8	
Delivery performance	15				
Performance to promise		5	4	4	May not meet demand; production lines may be experiencing problems; delivery record = 97 percent
Rump-up time		3	2	1.2	5 months (plus lead time, product will be ready by July)
Lead-time requirements		5	3	3	3 weeks

Criteria					Comments
Responsiveness to customer needs		2	5	2	PSC will be a high priority customer
Technical/process capability (product innovation, facility, R&D)	10		3	6	Small size, old warehouse; reputation for reliability and innovation
Management and personnel capability	5		4	4	Personnel is motivated; may lack experience, under 35 years old; manager graduated from Stanford and has IBM experience; management very interested
Service flexibility and long-term relationship potential	5		4		President meets with the team in person; willingness
Volume capacity	9		2	3.6	Extra capacity= 310,000 units
Information system capability (EDI)	2		1	0.4	N/A
Extra Risk	9				
Industry expertise/market experience		3	2	1.2	Four percent market share; one year experience in the DVD market
Exchange rate		3	5	3	
Country security risk		3	4	2.4	
Total	100			58.8	

Chapter 8

Develop Sourcing Strategy

Function	Objective	Tactical Step	Chapter/ Appendix
Supply market intelligence	Supply market research	Opportunity identification and validation	2
		Project approval	2
		Establishing the team	3
		Project plan	3
		As-is assessment	4
		Supply market research	5
		Market forecasts	5
		External and market analyses	6
	Strategy and resource commitment	Detailed supplier evaluation and research	7
		Evaluate current and alternative strategies	8
		Understand contract formation	8

Function	Objective	Tactical Step	Chapter/ Appendix
Strategic sourcing	Negotiate and select supplier	Develop relationship strategy	8
		Strategy position paper	8
		Develop requests for information (RFIs) and build negotiation strategy	9
		Negotiate	9
		Final supplier selection	9
		Form contracts	9
	Implement and promote compliance	Implement contracts	9
		Transition to relationship manager	10
Relationship management		Communicate expectations	10
	Improve supplier performance	Measure performance	10
		Resolve issues and develop supplier performance	10
Benchmarking processes and driving continuous improvement		Build an organization for supply-chain excellence	11
		Benchmark performance and drive continuous improvement	12, App. B

8.1 Chapter Outline

- Commodity analysis
- Supplier preferencing
- Evaluate strategies
- Finalize strategy
- Develop relationship strategy and bargaining position
- Develop a strategy position paper

- Obtain management approval of sourcing and negotiation strategies
- Checklist

Perception is strong and sight weak. In strategy it is important to see distant things as if they were close and to take a distant view of close things.

**— Miyamoto Musashi, 1584–1645,
legendary Japanese swordsman**

Strategy without tactics is the slowest route to victory. Tactics without strategy is the noise before defeat.

**— Sun Tzu, circa 500 B.C.,
Chinese military strategist**

After consolidating all of the information required to make a decision, the team is now ready to begin evaluating the different sourcing options and laying out a set of strategic planning alternatives. This is a process of structured brainstorming and evaluating the different possible configurations of sourcing channels. A source channel is a designated approach for internal users to source from approved suppliers. The selection of a channel also determines the approach that will be used to involve suppliers in negotiations and contract management once the decision has been made. The process is initiated by first establishing where the selected product or service fits within the context of a commodity portfolio analysis, followed by a relative positioning of the suppliers associated with the commodity. The combination of these two elements produces a logical progression toward a sourcing strategy that brings together and aligns the needs of the business with the realities of the current supply market conditions.

8.2 Commodity Analysis

A commodity analysis is a strategic planning tool that assesses a commodity or service against two criteria: one, its relative strategic impact to the business and two, the supply market challenge.

The strategic impact of a commodity is determined by several factors. The higher the total spend for a commodity, the more strategic it becomes to the business. However, classifying an element into the strategic quadrant is also a function of risk and the degree to which the commodity can impact the core business. Specifically, many companies classify the relationship with a supplier as operationally critical if loss or deterioration of the supplier's product/support or inaccurate processing/reporting would result in significant:

- Material business disruption
- Regulatory impact
- Security breaches
- Impairment or loss of intellectual property
- Customer impact
- Revenue loss
- Impact to the buying company's reputation

The second element in a commodity analysis, the supply market challenge, reflects the fact that in certain markets there may be few or many capable suppliers that can meet the company's business needs in a manner that would satisfy the product specifications and also accommodate requirements of minimum quantity and delivery timeframe. This may be a function of the fact that there is limited capacity in the market to meet the buying company's needs or that competing industries are capturing the bulk of the supplier's business. For example, the incredible growth of the economic infrastructure in China, with road building, building construction, and increased manufacturing output, is limiting the availability of critical raw materials such as steel, concrete, chemicals, and oil.

Another factor that impacts the supply market challenge is the ability to substitute alternatives for a given product. For example, the chemical additive Mill-Add used in the manufacture of plastic containers that renders the plastic "see through" is produced by only one supplier, Milliken, who has a patent on this technology. No other product available has this capability. In other cases, there may be a dearth of suppliers who can manufacture or deliver a technically complex product or service. Supply market challenge may arise because the second-tier supplier (the supplier's supplier) is highly dependent on a single-source subcontractor with no competitors. There may also be a long timeframe for obtaining the product or service or to switch suppliers, or an excessively high cost associated with switching suppliers that would require major changes across the organizational infrastructure (e.g., moving from a Macintosh to a Windows platform). Any of these situations can lead to a decision to classify the element as a high supply market challenge element.

The premise of portfolio analysis is that every purchase or family of purchases can be classified into one of four categories or quadrants: (1) nonstandard, (2) common, (3) leverage, and (4) strategic.[1] By effectively

---

[1] Monczka, R., Trent, R., and Handfield, R., *Purchasing and Supply Chain Management*, 3rd ed., Cincinnati, OH: Southwestern College Publishing, 2004.

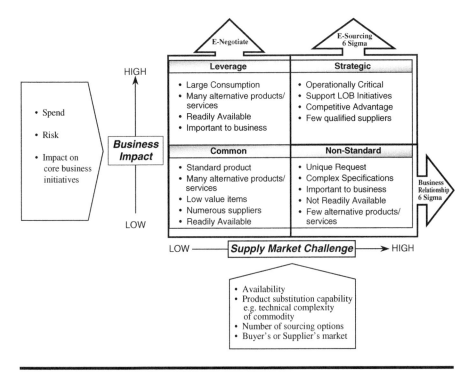

Figure 8.1   The commodity segmentation model.

classifying the goods and services being purchased into one of these categories, those responsible for proposing a strategy are able to comprehend the strategic importance of the item to the business, given the supply market conditions (see Figure 8.1).

8.2.1 Nonstandard Items

Acquisition items typically have few capable suppliers within a region and are of lower value. Many suppliers might conceivably be able to supply the item, but the cost of searching and comparing supply alternatives often outweighs the value of the item. Items that often fall into this category include office supplies; maintenance, repair, and operating (MRO) supplies; and other items users need on short notice. Despite their low value, not having these items in possession can pose a problem to the business. Generally, these items represent relatively low total dollars but may consume a disproportionate amount of time to acquire. Many nonstandard items have nonstandard quality and technology requirements, and the switching costs of moving from one supplier to another are high.

The focus when acquiring these items should be on minimizing the effort and transactions required to obtain them, through a structured process of evaluating sourcing channel alternatives. Supply management's contribution in this area is to get out of the acquisition business. In other words, the team should try to establish systems such as purchasing cards (e.g., VISA or American Express), electronic catalogs, direct ordering systems through the Internet (such as Ariba), and other automated transaction systems that eliminate unnecessary effort. This is not the quadrant purchasing on which professionals want to focus their attention. The value that purchasing contributes in this category is assuring users that they can quickly and efficiently obtain these lower-value goods and services (in other words, value = possession of the good or service).

One approach often considered under these conditions is outsourcing the management of nonstandard items to an integrator. An integrator is a third party, such as a consultant or large MRO provider, who is responsible for sourcing a purchasing organization's requirements. This may include:

- Translating a performance specification into a design specification
- Supplier selection and evaluation
- Negotiation
- Performance measurement and ongoing conflict management

In effect, integrators provide a way for the team to take the strategic sourcing process and outsource it to an expert in that particular commodity family or service. Examples of integrators include Inacom and Ingram Micro for computers and similar hardware. Integrators are also used for outsourced services such as computer programming, maintenance, and cafeteria services. The team must work closely with the integrator to establish service level agreements (SLAs) and other requirements, but it is the integrator who does a lot of the actual research, supplier evaluation, and negotiation of terms, acting on behalf of the buying company.

Advantages of using an integrator are the quick reduction of overhead (in the form of labor, time, and related procurement expenses) and the fact that the supply management organization can focus on more critical strategic products or services. Potential disadvantages are that the buying company may lose control over the product in terms of process and delivery schedules, and may also risk the loss of strategic assets or leaking of sensitive information.

8.2.2 Common Items

The value of purchases in this quadrant is still low to medium, but a greater number of suppliers are capable of providing the product or service. Examples of such items include personal computers, office furniture, steel castings and sheeting, and printers. The technology characterizing these items is usually standard and widely available. Switching costs are still relatively low, but because there are a greater number of suppliers available, purchasing should focus on price analysis as the primary tool for reducing costs. Price analysis effectively means shopping around for the best deal by sending out requests for bids or quotations to suppliers and accepting the most competitive bid. Historically, almost all items were purchased according to low price (particularly in government contracts). Bidding can be an effective strategy when conditions involve a standard item with many available sources of supply. Value in this quadrant is defined by achieving the lowest possible price (value = 1/price), assuming that delivery and quality are acceptable. Under these conditions, E-negotiation tools such as spot buys or exchanges may be applicable sourcing channels.

8.2.2.1 Spot Buys

Spot buys, otherwise known as unplanned purchases, are parts that are not included in any negotiated contract but are required to keep the factory or business unit running on a day-to-day basis. These purchases are made on the open market and tend to be awarded on the basis of lowest price. Research indicates that spot buys represent approximately 40 percent of the purchases made by an organization. Spot buys are costly because they are normally made on an individual basis and the process, which can be very time consuming, is repeated over and over again without a standard methodology. Alternatives to reduce the cost of transactions associated with spot buys include the use of desktop E-purchasing tools and procurement cards.

Clearly, all organizations are going to have some spot-buy activity, especially when the company has facilities located all over the world. For example, one major logistics company had many problems controlling convenience purchases (e.g., Joe Mechanic buys a part over the counter at the local hardware store). To combat this problem, the company now uses a monthly electronic report that provides a purchase summary showing all transactions and who authorized them. Convenience purchases are the most difficult to control, primarily because they are very easy to make. The operations side of the business may view these impulse purchases as a problem, but many inside the company value the simplicity of convenience purchases. The number of individual transactions is low, but the overall number of transactions is very high (probably 5 to 10 percent of all purchases, but 25 to 30 percent of the total number of transactions.)

Spot buys are very convenient and can be executed with a very short lead time, but the lack of long-term contracts means the supplier has little incentive to provide quality service. In addition, there is no guarantee of quality, delivery performance, exact specification matches, or long-term commitments.

8.2.3 Leverage Items

Items in this quadrant have a large number of capable suppliers and a medium-to-high annual expenditure. Steel and corrugated packaging are good examples. After analysis of the purchases in this quadrant, purchasers are often surprised to learn that items needed across the organization are often procured from many different places instead of a few select suppliers. By combining the requirements of different units, purchasing can effectively negotiate a better deal with a smaller number of approved suppliers. Consolidating purchases and reducing the supply base could yield an immediate and significant cost reduction. The remaining suppliers benefit because average fixed costs decline as these costs are allocated over larger volumes. Variable costs also decline because of improved productivity over a higher volume of product after consolidation. It is important for purchasing to ensure that the remaining suppliers have the capacity to handle additional business and that the quality of the product or service does not suffer (in fact, it should improve). Value in this quadrant is a function of the relationship between quality and price (value = quality/price).

This category is the one that really begins to challenge the supply management team. It connotes medium-to-high value commodities combined with a large number of suppliers. Proportionately, this category represents a big portion of the company's sourcing activities. The recommended sourcing strategy here is to centralize the purchasing procedures (not only sitewide, but also organizationwide), reduce the supplier base, and actively pursue volume-leveraging bargaining opportunities. This coordinated approach can yield immediate and significant cost reductions and is a key strategic sourcing opportunity.

Two E-negotiation sourcing channels often considered when a commodity falls into the category of either the common or leverage quadrants include exchanges and reverse auctions.

8.2.3.1 Exchanges

Exchanges are arranged by a group of companies (not necessarily within the same industry) for purchase of a similarly pooled set of commodities. By combining or pooling purchases, organizations benefit from leveraged purchases, allowing for economies of scale and cost savings. This sourcing option is especially attractive in commodities that do not require a high degree of specification and in which group buying power may encourage negotiations and price reductions. Group purchasing organizations for hospitals are the largest category in this sector.

Exchanges can be either public, with little or no supplier screening, or private, with prequalified and trusted suppliers. Some exchanges use reverse auctions and other tools to expedite purchasing and negotiation. Advantages of public exchanges are that both buyers and suppliers can reach more customers, whereas private exchanges can be a tool in ongoing supplier relationships. Unfortunately, many exchanges have suffered due to a lack of participation for a number of reasons. First, a fee is involved with public exchanges, and private exchanges can be expensive to set up. Partner companies may need to share their competitive business processes in exchange for gaining a shared technology platform, and in other cases, suppliers themselves may refuse to participate.

8.2.3.2 Reverse Auctions

Reverse auctions are downward price auctions in which buyers watch as suppliers lower their prices until the auction closes. A traditional auction normally involves a seller offering items for sale while potential buyers compete with each other for the purchase. The price is driven steadily up until no buyer is willing to go any higher. Reverse auction bidding continues until a preestablished bidding period ends or until no seller is willing to bid any lower, whichever comes first. Reverse auctions can be held for one specific product or service in a spot buy or for contracts to provide the products or services over the course of a year.

8.2.3.2.1 How Do Reverse Auctions Work?

The goal of reverse auctions is to bring buyers and sellers together to expose prices on a dynamic and real-time basis. A reverse auction involves suppliers' bidding on a clearly specified buyer requirement. All activity takes place online. The majority of reverse auctions are completed in 30 min or less (although some have been stretched out over 12 hr). Reverse auctions still hold much promise in terms of exploring market pricing. A recent auction carried out by a large engineering project construction firm for a large commodity group included multiple suppliers from Japan, Korea, and the United States. The pricing behaviors that were evidenced in the auction stunned the buying-company executives who witnessed them. The price paid for the commodity was well below the group's expectation of market price. One executive who participated said, "It showed us just how little we really knew about what the market was doing." Reverse auctions can provide some deep insights into true market pricing, especially in situations when there is available capacity in a supply marketplace.

A number of different technology features can be included in reverse auctions, including:

- Real-time with countdown clock and instant feedback
- Overtime or automatic extensions
- Reserve, starting, and ceiling prices
- Bid decrements
- Advanced features include multiple currencies and transformational bidding

There are clearly benefits to using reverse auctions, but some organizations have begun to apply reverse auctions to all of their purchase family spend areas. For example, one large pharmaceutical company has decided to use reverse auctions for all of its major spend items. Although this strategy succeeded the first time around, the company is discovering that they cannot squeeze any further price decreases from the same suppliers. In general, the second time around is not as productive for buyers unless there is a major shift in market dynamics. Even worse, as the process continues, returns may not cover the cost of the entire process for buyers. Performance from suppliers may also begin to slip. The pharmaceutical organization is beginning to question whether reverse auctions are a valid long-term tool in achieving their strategic purchasing objectives.

8.2.3.2.2 When Should Reverse Auctions Be Used?

Used properly and ethically, reverse auctions are extremely valuable in arriving at true market pricing for commodities and services as they are specified. However, only select items lend themselves to auctioning. Moreover, reverse auctions can identify disparities in the marketplace in terms of suppliers with excess capacity who are willing to sell their product at a lower profit margin than their competitors, which is an effective market testing tool.

An important step in using reverse auctions is to carefully define the requirement specification. Buyers who are not careful to do so may wind up in a lot of trouble. For example, in 2001, a packaging supplier bid to deliver a stretch film product to multiple locations. The buying company failed to provide detailed specifications, and although this supplier met the reserve price and beat out seven other manufacturers, one company came in lower than they did — the supplier's vendor! This vendor is a manufacturer of film, but may not understand how the original buyer is using their product. Thus, although the competitor's price beat out this supplier's bid, the buying company is now using 300 percent more product because it is not running correctly in their machines and is creating more waste. In effect, the losing supplier was not only prepared to provide the film, but also provided an invaluable service in assisting the buyer in using it properly in their machines.

A similar experience took place when the same supplier bid on a contract for paper product used in multiple locations. Again, the buyer provided incomplete specifications. The supplier met the reserve price but was not awarded the business. When they asked for the cost breakdowns provided by other suppliers, they were told the information would be forthcoming. Four months later the supplier received the requested information, but it was still unclear why they lost the contract.

8.2.3.2.3 Advantages and Disadvantages

Reverse auctions can establish real-time competition to achieve significant cost savings. They provide real-time market pricing data, which is especially useful in volatile markets. Auctions can also present automated data on pricing, products, and sellers, and can help reduce the possibility of backdoor selling and sales calls from unqualified vendors. The downside of reverse auctions is that they often do not address issues such as the total cost of ownership and can be particularly risky when involving precise specifications, tight tolerances on engineered custom parts, or other situations. They are less useful in situations when demand exceeds supply, commodities are in an up-cycle, there is reduced capacity in the industry, or suppliers are not openly competing or acting in a "cartel-like" manner.

One example of an effective reverse auction was a pharmaceutical company's bid for hotel suppliers. The company's executives travel extensively, but analysis revealed that the majority of travel takes place in 30 large cities. The sourcing analyst identified 500 major hotels located in these cities. All of the hotels were contacted electronically with request for quote (RFQ) details and asked to submit a request for information (RFI). The RFQ stipulated that each hotel should be willing to provide its best nightly rates, include a free breakfast, and collect no local phone charges. (The RFIs were sent to each individual hotel location office, not to the central hotel offices.) The auction was held with over 400 hotels participating. Reductions on the order of 15 to 20 percent were achieved through this auction, not including the other costs, and executives were informed that these hotels were now preferred providers.

8.2.4 Strategic Items

The fourth quadrant includes items that are critical to success, with few suppliers capable of supplying the good or service. This last category encompasses the biggest sourcing challenge of all: critical-path commodities that have few supplier options. These commodities are often, though not always, unique or custom made. They might involve test-phase or proprietary technology. Or they might just be very, very expensive, such as facility acquisitions, capital gains, and other types of nontraditional spend. Examples include computer microprocessors, pharmaceuticals, new chemical compounds, and aircraft engines. It is critical that major capital expenditures requiring long life-cycle maintenance agreements be managed strategically. Switching to a new supplier for anything in this group is guaranteed to be laborious owing to few supplier options and advanced product requirements. For these commodities, the sourcing strategy focus should be on developing close relationships with the suppliers to ensure adequate supply and to provide a basis for greater supply-chain collaboration. A good guideline to remember is to share the ownership of the supply process, including costs and rewards, with the supplier.

Items and services in the strategic quadrant will likely offer the greatest opportunities for collaboration with suppliers to reduce cost and add value for internal users and the end customer. As such, the majority of the sourcing team's effort and resources should be spent on these types of commodities, using E-sourcing and Six Sigma project methodologies to derive the optimum approach to collaborate and work with suppliers. However, organizations will still require lower-value, less critical items and services to operate. Steps must be taken to develop strategies to manage acquisition and multiple-type items so that resources are available for management of value-added goods and services.

Different divisions may require different types of strategic relationships with suppliers. For example, one company we met with was studying their requirements for industrial automation across multiple business units. This was the first time that a companywide sourcing strategy was being deployed. A cross-functional team from across the company was formed, and when all the players were brought together, it was discovered that the user needs for industrial controls were very fragmented and that various suppliers were viewed very differently, depending on whom the team was interviewing. The deployment was a painful but necessary process and required over eight months to complete. Some key questions asked here included:

- How do we look at vendors?
- How do they look at us?
- What do we need?

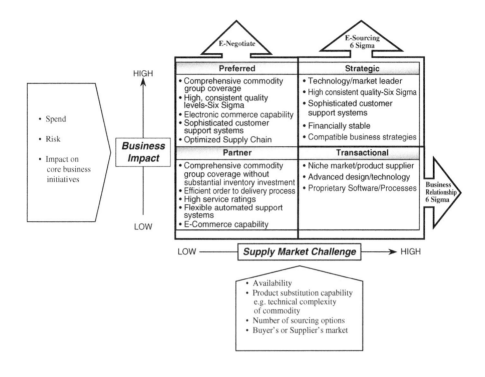

Figure 8.2   The supplier segmentation model.

8.3 Supplier Preferencing

Once a commodity has been classified into a particular commodity category, the team should consider the suppliers under evaluation in the commodity group. Suppliers can also be segmented using the same set of critieria for evaluating commodities, but the approach is slightly different (see Figure 8.2).

8.3.1 Transactional Suppliers

Transactional suppliers are characterized by having a strong market leadership position in a niche market or product that may not have a significant business impact, but which puts the buying organization at risk. A shortage of this product would potentially cause difficulties. As an example, a large computer manufacturer shut down an entire production line when a specialized $2 chip became unavailable. Transactional suppliers tend to have advanced design or technology capabilities or proprietary software that cannot be sourced elsewhere. Another example is a manufacturer of chemical slurries for the computer industry. The slurry is critical to the production process, but is a relatively low-value item. The supplier is the only manufacturer of the slurry in the world. Other examples might include special business forms, advertising, programming, and consulting services.

8.3.2 Partner Suppliers

Partner suppliers are also low value, but there may be a large number of competitors offering the same product. Why would a buying organization want to partner with this type of a supplier? One is that the ownership of this product (e.g., having it when you need it) is desired by the buying company, without the investment in the infrastructure required to manage, source, and store the product or contract the service (because of its low value). As such, the true expense of managing these products is in the transaction and inventory management costs. The ideal situation is to find a key supplier to partner with who can provide comprehensive commodity group coverage across all business units without the buying company having to make a substantial inventory investment. The supplier must be able to handle orders electronically and have efficient order-to-delivery capabilities, excellent service, and a flexible automated support system to support the buying company's needs for the product and service across multiple business units and locations. Examples include express delivery companies such as FedEx, copier maintenance services, or business relocation services.

8.3.3 Preferred Suppliers

Preferred suppliers are those that are currently serving the company and have the capability to provide comprehensive commodity group coverage. These suppliers have distinguished themselves through their supply-chain excellence and their proved ability to provide world-class levels of customer service. They have proved to have high, consistent quality levels and have established Six Sigma programs that drive continuous improvement into customer-focused processes. The buying company has been established as a preferred customer, and the supplier has gone out of its way to support the customer in difficult situations. They are capable of doing business via electronic commerce and have sophisticated customer support systems. Further, they have established optimum supply-chain systems designed to minimize cost and improve customer performance.

Clearly, these suppliers should receive preferable treatment when considering the sourcing strategy for the entire commodity group. This proven track record must be considered in light of the fact that there are many other possible untested suppliers who are also strong candidates for the business. Examples include business services, underwriting, tax appraisal services, pipes and valves, construction equipment, third-party logistics providers, commercial printers, and many others.

8.3.4 Strategic Suppliers

Strategic suppliers have many of the capabilities of preferred suppliers in that they have also proved themselves to be technology and market leaders with demonstrated quality and service performance. In addition, these suppliers have passed the scrutiny of the team in financial health evaluation. Most importantly, a strategic supplier's senior executive team has established strategically aligned plans for growth and has a common vision for creation of an integrated supply chain delivering value to the end customer. These types of suppliers are unique in their capability to deliver value and are an established strategic partner for the buying company's market growth objectives. Examples might include specialized consulting services, equipment, software licenses, personnel services, capital equipment, facility construction contractors, and other categories of major products or services.

8.4 Evaluate Strategies

Having classified commodity groups and suppliers into different buckets, the team must now consider the alignment of internal user requirements and map them against the existing set of supply relationship alternatives. There is no right or wrong answer here — in fact, a supplier in one quadrant of the matrix could end up in a different quadrant of the commodity classification matrix and vice versa. The team must evaluate the market conditions and the existing record of suppliers with the objective of minimizing risk and maximizing potential upside rewards. There are about 20 different criteria that should be considered when developing a supply strategy and evaluating a sourcing channel, some of which are discussed in the following subsections. The key to making good sourcing channel decisions is to determine which operational measures affect the efficiency and effectiveness of each channel shown in Table 8.1. These relationships represent a composite of the elements shown in the portfolio matrix and in the sourcing strategy process.

Table 8.1 Factors to Consider in Sourcing Channel Selection

	SSP	RA	EXCH	SPOT	INT
High annual spend	+	+	+	-	-
Low price as primary consideration	-	+	+	-	+
Short cycle time from need discovery to delivery	-	+	+	+	-
Supplier base highly fragmented	-	+	+	+	+
Requires detailed specifications early	-	+	+	+	-
Product is highly standardized	-	+	+	+	N/A
Minimized risk of supplier problems during service period	+	-	+	-	+
Minimized impact of supplier problems during service period	+	-	N/A	-	+
Ability to leverage product purchases exists	+	+	+	-	N/A
Frequent contract negotiation or product orders in one year	+	+	+	-	+
Easily able to switch between vendors	-	+	+	+	-
High rate of technological change	+	N/A	N/A	-	+
High market volatility (quantity/price)	-	+	+	+	+
High potential savings opportunity	+	+	+	-	+
High service requirements after purchase	+	N/A	+	-	+
Desirability of building relationship with supplier	+	+	+	-	-

Note: N/A = not applicable.

8.4.1 Annual Spend

A higher annual spend is normally associated with a leverage or strategic supplier preference. The opportunity for savings is greater under these conditions.

8.4.2 Price as Primary Consideration

If price is a very important factor in the decision-making process, spot buys are rated negative because the short lead time will prevent the company from getting the best price. Reverse auctions and exchanges are appropriate mechanisms when suppliers compete primarily on the basis of price. Integrators can also be considered as they possess a great deal of market intelligence and have information on where to get the best price.

8.4.3 Cycle Time from Discovery of Need to Delivery

If the need is to deliver the product quickly, then spot buy should be the preferred channel. This can occur in the event of a sudden breakdown requiring equipment to keep a process running. An in-depth sourcing process is not appropriate under these conditions.

8.4.4 Supply Base Highly Fragmented

If the supplier base is fragmented, using reverse auctions can create competition and positive relationships. Similarly, using exchanges and spot buys will enable the company to have a larger potential supplier pool. Integrators can also be considered as they can keep track of large numbers of suppliers and save the company the headache associated with conducting research. The strategic sourcing process requires a great deal of time and effort, so the relationship in the matrix is rated as negative.

8.4.5 Requires Detailed Specifications Early

If detailed product specifications can be provided early in the strategic sourcing process, the likelihood of using spot buys, reverse auctions, and exchanges is improved. Moreover, once the supplier has agreed to deliver the product, the company has a detailed specification that determines exact requirements. On the other hand, strategic relationships and integrators allow extensive exchange of information throughout the different stages in the process, so early specifications may not be possible. This is particularly true when a supplier is collaborating on joint product development initiatives for a technology-sharing initiative.

8.4.6 Product Is Highly Standardized

If the product is highly standardized, it will be easily available and can be easily communicated to the suppliers, so spot buys, exchanges, and reverse auctions are rated positive. Strategic sourcing takes time and effort and is not required, so it is rated negative. Integrators provide neither advantages nor disadvantages.

8.4.7 Minimized Risk of Supplier Problems during Service Period

Integrators, exchanges, and strategic sourcing provide a depth of research, analysis, and relationship opportunities that help minimize the risk of supplier problems, whereas the loose specifications typical in reverse auctions and short lead times of spot buys work against a reduced risk.

8.4.8 Minimized Impact of Supplier Problems during Service Period

If a commodity is important and will have a high impact on the company's performance, then certain channels can minimize the risk involved by providing the opportunity to develop an ongoing relationship with suppliers or with someone who can work with the suppliers. A detailed strategic sourcing process may be appropriate here. Although exchanges do provide some opportunity, even prequalified suppliers do not always have strong after-purchase service. Finally, reverse auctions and spot buys are rated negative because they have no inherent after-purchase service incentive.

8.4.9 Ability to Leverage Product Purchases

If a company has an opportunity to leverage product purchases, spot buys are definitely less favorable as they are done in isolation whenever the need arises. Strategic relationships, reverse auctions, and exchanges all offer the opportunity for cost savings through a leverage strategy.

8.4.10 Frequent Contract Negotiations or Product Orders in One Year

If the price is negotiated many times in one year, a strategic sourcing or integrator agreement using a flexible price adjustment clause may be beneficial.

8.4.11 High Switching Costs

If switching between suppliers is difficult because of proprietary technology or initial investment, then strategic or integrator relationships are appropriate. On the other hand, if switching between suppliers is easier, reverse auctions or spot buys are appropriate.

8.4.12 High Rate of Technological Change

If there is a possibility of a high rate of technological change, then the best option for the company is to utilize integrators who are field experts and up to speed with current changes. Thus, the company will be better off by not having to do the groundwork every time it has to procure an item.

8.4.13 High Market Volatility (Quantity or Price)

In a volatile market, the long lead times associated with the strategic sourcing process mean that it is not easy to respond to price changes quickly. All other channels allow the buyer to take advantage of the volatility to find the best prices, though spot buys are less useful in doing this because the extremely short lead times normally required for spot buys limit the time available for research and negotiation.

8.4.14 High Service Requirements after Purchase

After-purchase service is related to the SLAs negotiated during purchase. Strategic sourcing and integrators are all positive because the company has the opportunity to build a relationship with the supplier or someone who can work with the supplier for them, giving the supplier reasons to meet their SLAs. Spot buys are rated negative because there is no incentive to provide good service, and SLAs may not exist.

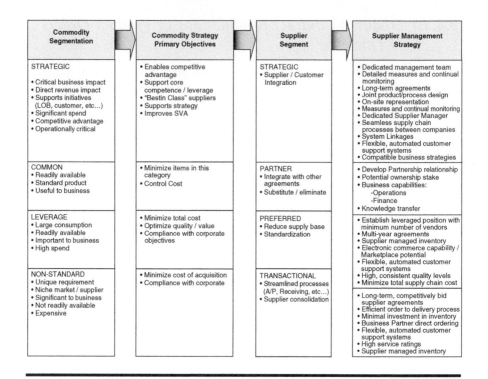

Commodity Segmentation	Commodity Strategy Primary Objectives	Supplier Segment	Supplier Management Strategy
STRATEGIC • Critical business impact • Direct revenue impact • Supports initiatives (LOB, customer, etc...) • Significant spend • Competitive advantage • Operationally critical	• Enables competitive advantage • Support core competence / leverage • "Bestin Class" suppliers • Supports strategy • Improves SVA	STRATEGIC • Supplier / Customer Integration	• Dedicated management team • Detailed measures and continual monitoring • Long-term agreements • Joint product/process design • On-site representation • Measures and continual monitoring • Dedicated Supplier Manager • Seamless supply chain processes between companies • System Linkages • Flexible, automated customer support systems • Compatible business strategies

COMMON
• Readily available
• Standard product
• Useful to business
	• Minimize items in this category
	• Control Cost
		PARTNER
		• Integrate with other agreements
		• Substitute / eliminate
			• Develop Partnership relationship
			• Potential ownership stake
			• Business capabilities:
			  -Operations
			  -Finance
			• Knowledge transfer

LEVERAGE • Large consumption • Readily available • Important to business • High spend	• Minimize total cost • Optimize quality / value • Compliance with corporate objectives	PREFERRED • Reduce supply base • Standardization	• Establish leveraged position with minimum number of vendors • Multi-year agreements • Supplier managed inventory • Electronic commerce capability / Marketplace potential • Flexible, automated customer support systems • High, consistent quality levels • Minimize total supply chain cost
NON-STANDARD • Unique requirement • Niche market / supplier • Significant to business • Not readily available • Expensive	• Minimize cost of acquisition • Compliance with corporate	TRANSACTIONAL • Streamlined processes (A/P, Receiving, etc...) • Supplier consolidation	• Long-term, competitively bid supplier agreements • Efficient order to delivery process • Minimal investment in inventory • Business Partner direct ordering • Flexible, automated customer support systems • High service ratings • Supplier managed inventory

Figure 8.3   Segmentation management strategy model.

8.4.15 *Desirability of Building Relationship with Supplier*

The extra layer that an integrator provides between a company and suppliers makes this a negative, as are spot buys owing to the one-time nature of the process. A strategic relationship is definitely preferable in these situations.

8.5 Finalize Strategy

After evaluating all of these options, several possible combinations begin to emerge as possible strategic alternatives (see Figure 8.3).

8.5.1 *Strategic Commodity–Strategic Supplier*

Generally speaking, the goals for a strategic commodity are to develop a competitive advantage, support and leverage the supplier's core competencies, develop best-in-class suppliers, support the company's overall strategy, and improve value-added services beyond a simple purchasing agreement. If the annual spend on the item is high, then it also makes sense for the company to establish a strategic supplier of choice (SOC). An SOC designation indicates that the selected supplier should receive the business under most conditions. Formally designating a supplier as strategic builds a foundation for achieving higher levels of supplier and customer integration. Opportunities for improved integration reside on a foundation of bilateral understanding regarding the ways of working in key areas such as product or process design and development, order fulfillment, service delivery, and strategic cost management.

The implication of this decision for supplier management is that the team should designate a formal supplier relationship manager to follow through with the supplier to initiate the intended process improvements to the relationship. In some cases, when a series of major projects is involved, a dedicated management team may be assigned to work closely with the supplier's team. Detailed measures and continual monitoring of the health of the relationship often govern such interactions. It is also a good idea to establish a long-term agreement specifying the general expectations and outcomes for the relationship that will govern behavior and set the baseline for performance expectations. In cases in which a high degree of interaction is required, the supplier may provide an on-site representative who resides at a customer's site to work continuously with the buying company's team.

8.5.2 Common Commodity–Partner Supplier

Another common approach is to establish a "partner" supplier relationship, given that the commodity is judged to fall into the "common" commodity classification. Because the item is a readily available standard product that is useful to the business, the goal of the team is to reduce the number of items in this category through substitution, eliminate small-volume spend, eliminate duplication of SKUs, and rationalize the number of units to control costs. A common example here is the case of a pharmaceutical company, in which the R&D group may use 50 different types of Bunsen burners and beakers simply because scientists have a particular preference that they acquired in graduate school.

In such cases, the partner supplier may be of assistance in gathering data regarding types of different products being used across business units, and in making suggestions regarding how to consolidate spending and reduce costs. This is a logical approach because the supplier has the expertise in the given commodity and is positioned to be able to suggest how best to rationalize the requirements and optimize the opportunities for cost savings. This type of savings can occur when a solid partnership relationship is established, and the partner supplier can be motivated to develop a cost savings goal that will result in additional business. It also requires a supplier who has solid business capabilities in operations and finance, understands the economics of cost savings, and provides market intelligence regarding their own supply market environment.

The partner supplier should be encouraged to develop an ongoing set of recommendations regarding cost savings opportunities and notify the buying company of potential risks and price increases in the marketplace that can provide early warning signals. This type of knowledge transfer is the optimum outcome for this type of commodity. In the words of Dave Nelson, a senior executive in supply management at Delphi Automotive: "If you develop the right relationship with your supply base, you can have 10,000 additional brains thinking about ways to improve your product and generate cost savings. And that is very powerful!"

8.5.3 Leverage Commodity–Preferred Supplier

As in the case of a common commodity, a leverage commodity also provides the opportunity for savings. These items or services have a high volume of internal consumption, are readily available, are important to the business, and represent a significant portion of spend. Because of their importance to the business, the need to maintain a high level of quality and compliance with corporate objectives is paramount. Preferred suppliers are awarded the business in these conditions with the understanding that they will be expected to significantly reduce the cost of supplying these items or services over time, in return for a significant volume of business and possible multi-year agreements. A high level of service is also expected, which may include supplier capabilities such as management of on-site inventory, E-purchasing capabilities, and the ability to quickly respond to customer requirements. In so doing, the supplier will also be expected to maintain a high level of quality and to reduce the total cost to the business of managing this commodity.

Examples of companies using this approach successfully include one company that outsourced the management of their copier systems for multiple business units to a single supplier. The supplier leased the equipment to the buying company and was responsible for managing the maintenance and service of all copiers. The agreement stipulated in SLAs was that if copiers went down, a representative had to be available to repair it within a fixed short time period, otherwise the company incurred a penalty.

8.5.4 Nonstandard Commodity–Transactional Supplier

The final combination often found in developing a sourcing strategy is for nonstandard commodities that have unique requirements or niche suppliers, yet which are significant to the business. Such items tend to be expensive owing to the exclusive market position maintained by the supplier. The goal of the team is to reduce the cost of acquisition of such items, which consists primarily of the internal labor associated with processing purchase orders and expediting requests for such products when shortages occur. In such cases, an optimum strategy is to scan the marketplace and develop an agreement with a supplier to enable a streamlined accounts payable and receivable process. If the supplier is relatively small, this may involve sending an IT team to establish this capability at the supplier's location, which may require some minimum technology investment. After a competitive bid, a detailed negotiation should take place that establishes high levels of service as critical to the business, with specific SLAs detailed. The supplier must be validated to ensure that it can deliver in a responsive manner, is capable of handling orders from multiple locations, and is responsible for managing inventory of the item. In service agreements, the supplier must be led to understand the specific requirements around providing the service.

In considering the preceding combinations, it is important to note that exceptions will always exist. That is, a company may wish to develop a strategic relationship with a supplier for a leveraged item, if other capabilities emerge that were not at first apparent. Because of the dynamic and changing nature of user requirements and supply market conditions, sourcing strategies should be revisited as conditions change. Examples here include a major consolidation of suppliers in a particular market or technology requirements that become more important than price in user requirements. Such modifications may change the entire picture associated with the commodity and supplier preferencing analysis. It is, therefore, important for the strategic sourcing team to develop a longer-term forecast for the market, which is also a function of good business and market intelligence.

8.6 Develop Relationship Strategy and Bargaining Position

As discussed earlier, the nature of the ideal relationship with the supplier should be established at this point in the process. This is an important planning requirement. Although some interaction with the supplier has occurred through the site visit, it is difficult to predict how the supplier will react when a specific proposal is put in front of it. As such, it is important to also evaluate alternative approaches to meeting the supplier and presenting the information. Ensuring that there is a champion at the supplier's end who will establish buy-in is a good idea. Identifying the appropriate way to establish the relationship strategy emerging from the sourcing process, as well as the bargaining and negotiation approach to be used with the supplier, is absolutely critical prior to jumping into negotiations. This requirement becomes even more crucial when working with international suppliers because of the cultural implications of negotiation and influence in areas such as China (see Appendix A). Some of the items that merit discussion and consideration include the following:

- Determine who will participate.
- Identify specific objectives.
- Analyze strengths and weaknesses of each party.
- Gather information.
- Recognize counterpart's needs — give-and-take.
- Identify facts and issues.
- Establish a position on each issue.
- Develop appropriate strategies and tactics.
- Brief other personnel.
- Practice the negotiation.

8.6.1 Determine Your Group's Position Relative to That of the Other Party

The relative strengths and weaknesses of each party are important to assess at this point. These considerations again rely on the accuracy and timeliness of business and market intelligence in assessing what the competition is doing, what the suppliers' competition is doing, how the market is changing, what the internal characteristics of the supplier's management issues are, and how all of this may influence the terms demanded by the supplier. Some key elements include determining the following:

- Buyer's negotiation strength (seller's weaknesses):
  - Buyer accounting for high percentage of supplier's annual sales revenues
  - Supplier/supply industry in low-capacity-utilization situation
  - High level of competition in the supplier's industry
  - Generally poor economic conditions, etc.
- Buyer's negotiation weaknesses (seller's strengths):
  - Buyer accounting for low percentage of supplier's annual sales revenues
  - Suppliers/supply industry operating at or near capacity
  - Little competition in supplier's industry
  - Favorable economic conditions

8.7 Develop a Strategy Position Paper

Upon reaching a consensus regarding the appropriate strategy, the sourcing team should summarize in a position paper the business case for their decision. This position paper should also be converted into an electronic presentation for distribution to appropriate parties, including the corporate supply council, business unit functional leaders, the executive to whom the team reports, and other parties who will be required to buy-in to the strategy and who will be impacted by the decision to proceed. The purpose of the position paper is to establish a clear and open document for input and critique that develops the rationale for the strategy based on the market intelligence, research, analysis, and assumptions used by the team in developing the strategy. It should also include a statement regarding the ideal contractual mode (long-term, short-term, multiple-source, single-source, etc.), the SLAs, the role of the relationship manager in ensuring contract compliance and continuous improvement, and the impacts on the business unit staff when the contract is implemented. There may also be a need for training in new E-purchasing technology, and this too should be clearly identified in the position paper. The paper serves as the focal point of discussion for establishing buy-in to the agreement, so there should be no hidden agenda when presenting this to the affected parties.

8.7.1 Strategy Position Paper Outline

An example of a strategy position paper outline is as follows:

Executive Summary
Part I

    1.1 Introduction
    1.2 Strategic objectives
    1.3 Spend analysis
    1.4 Value chain analysis
    1.5 Strategy (further steps)
    1.6 Sign-Off page (further steps)

Part II

    2.1 Overview
    2.2 Supply positioning and supplier preferencing
    2.3 Market analysis
    2.4 Needs analysis
    2.5 Supplier analysis

2.6 Risk analysis
2.7 Safety assessment
2.8 Sustainability
2.9 Strategies considered
2.10 Negotiation strategy and tactics
2.11 Change management

Table 8.2 describes a position paper for a strategic sourcing project for copying equipment in a large chemical company.

8.8 Obtain Management Approval of Sourcing and Negotiation Strategies

The position paper should be distributed to the appropriate parties, and the team should then schedule a formal presentation for the senior management team to present their recommendation. This is not always needed in every situation, but for especially large spend elements or for situations in which a business unit may be impacted, it is critical to do so. In rare cases, the approval team will reject the strategy. This is highly unusual, as the team should have established a rock-solid business case if they have followed all of the steps in the process up to now. It is unlikely that a senior executive will possess information that directly contradicts that of the team. If so, the team may need to validate their assumptions further and go back for another attempt at approval. However, given good business intelligence and solid decision-making rationale, most executives will clearly see the benefits delivered by the strategy to the business and will commit to support the strategy within their own business unit.

One company, FedEx, has a process for strategic sourcing outlined in Table 8.3.

8.9 Conclusion

At this stage in the process, the strategy has been finalized and, hopefully, approved by the sourcing council or senior executive staff. The team has established a clear plan for delivering benefits to the company, but has yet to complete the final step: finalizing and executing the agreement and setting the strategy in motion. It would be a mistake to think that the work is complete at this point. Too often, sourcing teams quickly lose interest once a strategy has been approved and leave the deployment to another group. On the contrary, it is absolutely critical at this point that

Table 8.2   Strategic Cost Management at a Chemical Company

In 1991, this large multinational chemical company began developing corporate-level longer-term alliance agreements with selected process equipment suppliers. The primary goal of this effort was to reduce the supplier base and future investment costs by identifying and selecting common suppliers for all 18 business units. A longer-term vision included realizing greater supplier integration in the design of new facilities and equipment.

Because this company historically accounts for less than 20 percent of a typical equipment supplier's volume, relying on fewer suppliers was expected to provide greater purchasing leverage. In addition, the company expected its alliance agreements to create benefits beyond those available from simple leveraged purchase agreements or traditional longer-term agreements. For most equipment applications, the rate of technological change is stable making longer-term agreements with fewer suppliers a realistic strategy.

Business units within this company are highly independent. The key to executing successful corporate-level sourcing agreements requires (1) including business unit participation when crafting the agreements and (2) showing how the agreements would benefit individual business units. The corporate staff helps individual buying locations to source equipment while encouraging those locations to use alliance suppliers. Currently, business units must provide justification when selecting a nonalliance supplier for an item covered by a corporate alliance agreement.

The company currently has 60 formal equipment agreements, 40 of which focus on cost reduction. For example, the company relies on one firm for all its duplicating equipment needs. This agreement features a per-page copy rate, simplified billing, and monthly preventive maintenance on each machine with no machine or service costs. Within most business units, the alliance agreements have helped promote mutually cooperative relationships with suppliers rather than adversarial relationships.

Alliance suppliers represent 40 percent of total equipment purchases. This is significant, given that 35 percent of a project's cost is engineered equipment. Furthermore, a key performance measure is the capital productivity ratio, defined as (dollars of sales)/(dollars of investment). This ratio receives attention at the highest corporate levels. Achieving the target for this measure requires efficient investment and completing projects in the most productive manner. Capital equipment supplier alliances are important because they affect the denominator of the investment ratio. These agreements are also important because the physical equipment itself may not be as important as the engineering process involved in securing the equipment. External design support is becoming increasingly important because a great deal of experienced people have left the company due to early retirements and staff reductions.

Table 8.2   Strategic Cost Management at a Chemical Company (continued)

All alliance agreements are with U.S. firms, with one third of the agreements specifying a single source. Relying on multiple sources can be the result of (1) a single supplier being unable to provide national support, (2) a single supplier's inability to provide the entire range of items within an equipment commodity, or (3) historical capacity constraints within the commodity. Some agreements, for example, have five suppliers supporting a particular equipment commodity. If an equipment item or commodity is nonstrategic, then a single supplier usually receives the contract. The company is currently reviewing and modifying each agreement to meet continuing or evolving needs.

Each negotiated agreement contains reopener clauses for poor performance. The company can reopen agreements for poor service, poor quality, or noncompetitive price or cost. Furthermore, the company uses several approaches to ensure the competitiveness of its alliance agreements. The company:

■ Identifies price trends within Standard Industrial Classification (SIC) code by tracking the producer price index (PPI) and then compares those with price trends within the alliance agreements.
■ Relies on selective market bidding to test the equipment market.
■ Uses third-party price benchmarking.
■ Develops internal cost models based on experience and price trends and compares these with the actual price behavior within the agreements.

Negotiated contracts are usually structured around a life-cycle cost. The maintenance cost of a pump, for example, may be greater than the cost of the pump. Creating total cost life-cycle models can be difficult when life-cycle data does not exist. Furthermore, price is a complex issue owing to the difficulty of comparing equipment features and options between companies. A strong internal reluctance to shift from unit price to total cost still exists because price is still the most visible indicator available.

Alliance agreements are not very structurally different from standard agreements in that (1) suppliers receive larger volumes in return for a lower price, (2) the agreements clearly establish the framework for removing costs within the relationship, and (3) the buying company usually requests preferential warranty or service. In return, the alliance agreements specify that suppliers will receive an agreed-upon portion of the buying company's total volume.

This vignette highlights the importance of carefully crafting supplier alliance agreements. These agreements are critical because *they provide the basis and foundation for pursuing early supplier design involvement and support* at this company and establishing precedence for ongoing strategic cost reductions. Ignoring the important relationship between these agreements and early supplier design involvement would result in an incomplete analysis.

Table 8.3   FedEx Sourcing Process

There is a set of reviews that takes place within the sourcing process. When the team arrives at the fifth stage (approval), one of the requirements is that they define the business case for the strategy. The team will summarize the work done in the initiative — the business case goes into an extensive review. Initially, it goes to finance and legal to ensure that the savings are valid and the assumptions used are acceptable. If the strategy is approved, it proceeds to the final step, a review by a corporate sourcing council consisting of high-level executives from each of the divisions (COO and CFO from each business unit) and chaired by the chief sourcing officer. The council will review or reject the strategy for additional work, or approve it. If they do approve it, the council has an obligation to help the sourcing team implement it. They have some strong advocates to help with the implementation and ensure compliance with the terms of the agreements.

Deals that go to the sourcing council tend to have a fairly high dollar value or an impact based on the nature of spend, on the brand image, or on other areas. Fuels and contract trucking (more than the $10 million range) go to the sourcing council. Situations such as a new supplier for FedEx boxes due to a specification change may not necessarily have a big cost impact ($2 million cost savings) but may go before the council for other reasons (to ensure the change does not affect other areas such as market image or customer preferences). This is a largely a judgment call on the part of the chief sourcing officer.

the team accomplish a successful handoff and delivery of the strategy to a dedicated relationship manager, who will establish the basis for delivering the results.

8.10   Checklist

- Carry out commodity analysis.
- Prioritize suppliers.
- Evaluate strategies.
- Select recommended strategy.
- Develop relationship strategy and bargaining position.
- Write strategy position paper.
- Obtain management approval.

8.11   Results

- Sourcing strategy developed
- Position paper written
- Management approval obtained

Chapter 9

Execute Sourcing Strategy (Nonstrategic Supplier Relationships)

Function	Objective	Tactical Step	Chapter/ Appendix
Supply market intelligence	Supply market research	Opportunity identification and validation	2
		Project approval	2
		Establishing the team	3
		Project plan	3
		As-is assessment	4
		Supply market research	5
		Market forecasts	5
		External and market analyses	6
	Strategy and resource commitment	Detailed supplier evaluation and research	7
		Evaluate current and alternative strategies	8
		Understand contract formation	8

Function	Objective	Tactical Step	Chapter/ Appendix
Strategic sourcing	Negotiate and select supplier	Develop relationship strategy	8
		Strategy position paper	8
		Develop requests for information (RFIs) and build negotiation strategy	9
		Negotiate	9
		Final supplier selection	9
		Form contracts	9
	Implement and promote compliance	Implement contracts	9
		Transition to relationship manager	10
Relationship management		Communicate expectations	10
	Improve supplier performance	Measure performance	10
		Resolve issues and develop supplier performance	10
Benchmarking processes and driving continuous improvement		Build an organization for supply-chain excellence	11
		Benchmark performance and drive continuous improvement	12, App. B

9.1 Chapter Outline

- Managing the transition to relationship management
- What type of relationship is appropriate for the commodity?
- E-procurement and the purchasing process
- Purchase approval
- Release and receive purchasing requirements

- What is the right approach to a negotiation?
- Preparing for the negotiation
- Conducting the negotiation
- Implementing the agreement
- Negotiation planning
- Power in negotiation
- Building a contract that minimizes risk

It is, indeed, not very difficult to bear that condition to which we are not condemned by necessity, but induced by observation and choice.

— Samuel Johnson: Rambler #119 (May 7, 1751)

9.2 Introduction — Managing the Transition to Relationship Management

At this stage in the process, the strategy would have been finalized and, hopefully, approved by the sourcing council or senior executive staff. The position paper would have been written and approved. An important outcome of building strategy, as we discussed in Chapter 8, is the identification of the appropriate type of supplier relationship. In particular, we identified different types of desired relationships through the supplier segmentation process. The processes for executing the sourcing strategy for supplier relationships that fall into the transactional, common, or leveraged categories are discussed in this chapter. However, it is important to recognize that strategic or supplier-of-choice situations require an entirely different approach to building a relationship and will be discussed in Chapter 10.

As shown in Figure 9.1, strategy execution and transition to relationship management are the final stages of the sourcing process. The transition is important because it is one of the most poorly performed stages of sourcing, even more so than supply market intelligence. Once the strategy is approved, many sourcing teams rush off to obtain quotes, hammer out a contract in a brutal bargaining session with typical negotiation tactics and games being played, bounce a contract back and forth a few times until they feel the suppliers' prices have been squeezed sufficiently, and then hand the contract over to the business unit with the claim that, "we saved you ten percent on your price from last year!"

This scenario is problematic for several reasons. Consider the following points of view of the individuals involved:

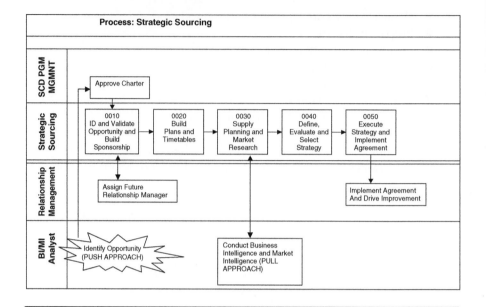

Figure 9.1   Strategic sourcing process.

- The supplier, who put forth a good faith response to provide their best price given the volume requirements, has been battered around a few times and now vows to recoup their lost margin in ways that the buying company may not realize. These may include using lower-cost materials or contract labor, compromising on quality or delivery, or extracting outrageous expediting charges on rush deliveries.
- The internal customer, who may have had nothing to do with the negotiations, now has a disenfranchised supplier to work with and has no knowledge of the terms negotiated in the contract. Further, the supplier selected may have a product or service that does not meet their needs for operations, manufacturing service delivery, or end-customer requirements. They are now forced to use this supplier or face severe penalties from corporate headquarters.
- The purchasing group feels smug in the knowledge that they have saved the company ten percent on price and holds this up to the CEO to show that they are doing a great job and adding value to the company, although the ten percent savings was never eliminated from the operating budget and the total cost of ownership for using this supplier may escalate owing to poor quality, poor delivery, extra inventory required as buffer stock, or other factors not included in the negotiation.

The point here is not that purchasing does not have the right to award the contract; an important area of control in any organization is that purchasing has the right to determine how to award purchase contracts. Purchasing should also lead or coordinate negotiations with suppliers. However, it is absolutely critical that purchasing use internal representatives from other functions to support the negotiation process, and effectively transition the ownership of the supplier's contract to a delegate who is familiar with the decision-making process. It means that purchasing retains the right to control the overall process, act as an agent to commit an organization to a legal agreement, and negotiate a purchase price. They are also responsible for transitioning to a relationship manager and ensuring a smooth handoff. It is the sourcing team's responsibility to ensure that by the time the team is dismantled, the relationship manager and the supplier are communicating effectively, understanding the value proposition, and sharing the expectations and performance measures used in evaluating the success of the relationship in moving forward.

A well-crafted position paper can address many of these issues. The position paper provides answers for the internal customer who asks:

1. How do our firm's product strategies for our end product (which contains this purchased commodity) affect the strategies and methods we use to purchase the commodity?
2. What must our organization do to ensure the efficient and effective procurement of this important commodity over the next five years?
3. How can we ensure the supply of this product or commodity and that the product received is of high quality, of low cost, delivered on time, technologically up to date, etc.?

The position paper should also define the value proposition, the desired form of relationship, and the ideal type of "buying channel" to be used for managing the supplier order. Will purchasing award a contract based on competitive bidding, negotiation, or a combination of the two approaches? If purchasing takes a competitive bidding approach, how many suppliers will it request to bid? The different types of buying channels that may be applied for procurement include the following:

■ Credit card purchase
■ Inventory goods issue
■ Emergency contractor charge collection entry
■ Non-purchase-order purchase
■ Inventory reservation
■ Materials agreement release
■ Online ordering

- Materials sole source purchase order (PO)
- Plan and inventory reservation
- Plan and materials agreement release

The overall objective of these processes is to (1) ensure that internal customers are satisfied with the right materials procured from the right supplier, delivered to the right place at the right time for the best overall value to the company; (2) improve business performance, reduce operating costs, and improve communication; (3) improve data integrity to enable more accurate tracking of costs; and (4) improve market position for sourcing and negotiating material contracts.

9.3 What Type of Relationship Is Appropriate for the Commodity?

As we noted in Chapter 8, not all relationships are strategic. Recent research suggests that there are seven major types of buyer–supplier relationships that can develop over time for any given commodity or service.[1] These relationships can be defined in terms of several different dimensions:

1. Interaction — measured through communication frequency (how often it occurred) and business volume (dollars)
2. Dependence — measured through perceived dependence (how vulnerable are we to this organization) and organizational investment in the relationship (how much have we committed to this organization)
3. Trust — measured through personal character (do I trust the agent with whom I work?) and organizational capability (do I trust the organization that this person represents?)

Each of these relationship types is described briefly, with the score on these three elements shown in Figure 9.2 to Figure 9.4.

[1] Rinehart, L., Eckert, J., Handfield, R., Page, T., and Atkin, T., An assessment of supplier-customer relationships, *Journal of Business Logistics*, 25(1), 25–62, 2003.

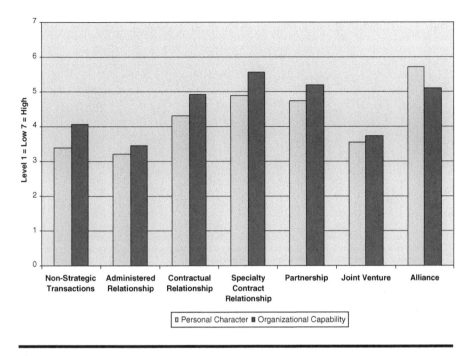

Figure 9.2   Trust.

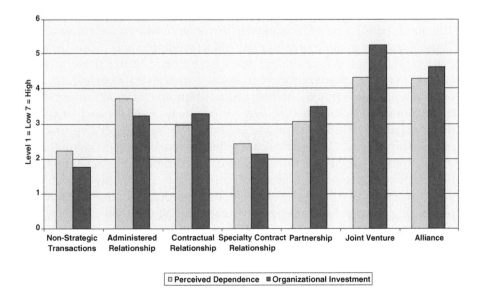

Figure 9.3   Dependence.

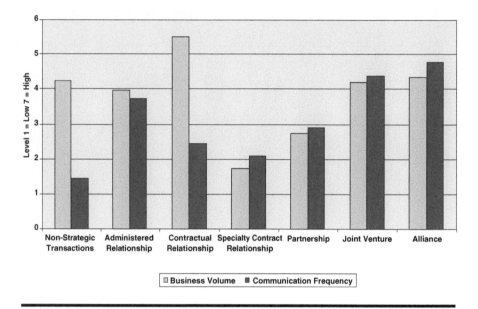

Figure 9.4   Interaction frequency.

9.3.1 Nonstrategic Transaction (16 Percent of All Relationships)

The most basic type of relationship involves nonstrategic transactions. These situations include one-time as well as multiple transactions between parties. Of the seven relationship types, nonstrategic transactions have the lowest levels of communication frequency, perceived dependence, and organizational investment in the relationship. In addition, nonstrategic transactions are below the median for personal character and organizational capability. Business volume is above the median relative to other relationship types. These situations reflect the reality of economy-based transactions in which one or both parties feel little obligation to the other because alternative sources of supply or markets are readily available. A good example of this type of relationship would be that between a purchasing manager and a supplier of standard, off-the-shelf capital equipment or commonly ordered supplies.

At the personal level, there is little on which to base a relationship. This may be partly due to the limited communication that occurs, restricting opportunities for parties to get to know one another on a personal basis. For example, in this data, 10 percent of the exchanges involved capital assets and equipment transactions. Because these situations are not everyday transactions for the customer, there is little reason for a relationship to evolve. In such cases an "arms-length" approach may dominate the negotiations for these types of purchases. Organizationally, the characteristics of these transactions reflect the underlying knowledge that the transactions that occur are based on the economic capability of the other party, such as a capital investment. Or it might involve multiple transactions between a supplier and customer in a highly competitive market, creating revenues and volumes that are substantial.

9.3.2 Administered Relationship (14 Percent)

Administered relationships are the most basic cluster that can be classified as a true "relationship." These situations also can include one-time or multiple transactions between parties, but there is a stronger emphasis on attempting to manage the relationship through nonformalized influence strategies (see Table 9.1). Relative to the other six, these relationships exhibit the lowest concern for personal character of the other party and capability of the other organization. Business volume and organizational investment are below the median score, whereas the personal dimensions of communication frequency and perceived dependence on the other party are above the median. Administered relationships include efforts related to merchandising support or business process consulting by representatives of one party with the other. A good example is a firm that helps to facilitate improved operations for the supplier or customer through supplier development programs or in distributor–retailer relationships requiring assistance with product merchandising.

In contrast to nonstrategic transactions, administered relationships have a higher percentage of transactions across multiple products and services (Table 9.1). Although there is some commonality with nonstrategic transactions, these relationships require some investment in the relationship to maintain transaction flows. However, those investments are probably for modest resources that support the relationship. For example, suppliers are increasingly providing online supplier catalogs for ease in facilitating POs of supplies. Also, firms will attempt to influence the other party's actions using supplier development meetings or distributor councils as a mechanism for getting both suppliers and customers to work together within the informal structure of the administered relationship.

9.3.3 Contractual Relationship (18 Percent)

Contractual relationships cover a broad range of activities. They are characterized by levels of communication frequency and perceived dependence that are below the median. Contractual relationships are at or above the median level relative to the other relationship types on personal

Table 9.1 Supplier–Customer Relationship Types — Relationship Characteristics

Group Names	Nonstrategic Transactions (%)	Administered Relationships (%)	Contractual Relationships (%)	Specialty Contract Relationships (%)	Partnerships (%)	Joint Ventures (%)	Alliances (%)
Type of product or service exchanged							
Materials or finished goods	72	70	78	59	81	84	72
Capital assets or equipment	10	11	9	0	10	6	7
Services	18	19	13	41	9	10	21
Total	100	100	100	100	100	100	100
Breadth of products or services exchanged							
One product or service	30	25	24	41	22	15	24
Multiple products or services with common properties	30	34	30	18	24	25	18
Multiple products or services with unique properties	40	41	46	41	54	60	58
Total	100	100	100	100	100	100	100

Contractual design, structure, and involvement							
No formal or written agreement	26	30	14	30	21	18	22
Standard form contract	31	26	43	22	43	41	28
Agreement designed by nonlegal personnel	29	22	27	37	21	21	32
Contract designed by legal personnel	7	9	9	4	10	10	4
Internal corporate policies	7	3	7	7	5	10	14
Total	100	100	100	100	100	100	100
Extent of investment or ownership between the parties							
Independent	86	80	89	96	86	73	72
Partial ownership	3	2	2	0	2	4	1
Fully owned subsidiary	1	8	2	0	3	13	12
Internal corporate units	10	10	7	4	9	10	15
Total	100	100	100	100	100	100	100

character, organizational capability, and organizational investment. Business volume scored the highest of all relationship types.

Contractual relationships reflect the need for formalized control over business activity between suppliers and customers. At the organizational level, managers recognize a strong supply or market-based need for the relationship that is based on the business volumes conducted with the other organization, without a desire to raise the level of required investment in the relationship. Contractual relationships require parties to have a higher level of personal character than in administered or nonstrategic transactions, but not as high as in other types of relationships. This may be due to the creation of a formal relationship. As the parties negotiate the contract, they get to know each other better, which can increase their perception of each other's personal character. In addition, a formal contract reduces the need for direct communication between boundary spanners and, therefore, reduces interaction frequency. For instance, a contractual relationship may exist between a manufacturer and a component part supplier to supply a wide range of parts in accordance with the terms outlined in a detailed contract.

9.3.4 Specialty Contract Relationship (6 Percent)

Specialty contract relationships involve contracts for unique products or services that are exchanged between suppliers and customers. In these situations, few alternatives exist in the supply/customer base. Specialty contract relationships are less ubiquitous but make up a large percentage of service-based situations. Another unique element of these relationships is that they seem to be less formal than other relationships (67 percent of responses indicated that there was no formal written agreement between the parties).

Specialty contract relationships score lowest on business volume and are below the median on communication frequency, perceived dependence, and organizational investment. These relationships possess above-median levels of perception of personal character of the other party and the highest level of organizational capability of all relationship types. These relationships rely on one-to-one interactions and assessments of significant organizational capability to contribute to the relationship. However, the level of business conducted between the parties is very limited relative to the other relationships.

9.3.5 Partnership (12 Percent)

The term *partnership* is used frequently in academic literature and in industry. Relative to the other relationships, partnerships demonstrate above-median levels of personal character, organizational capability, and organizational investment. Communication frequency and perceived dependence are at the median, and business volume is below the median. Partnerships span a wide range of product-oriented transactions (even though the percentage of exchange over multiple products is less than for joint ventures and alliances, which will be discussed in the following subsections). An example might be a supplier of a critical component of a manufactured product who delivers on a weekly basis.

Some partnerships also appear to reflect the need for formalized control over business activity between suppliers and customers (43 percent of the responses in this category use a standard form contract), whereas other partnerships (42 percent) indicate that less formalization in contractual design is appropriate (no written agreement or agreements designed by nonlegal personnel) (see Table 9.1). This hints at potential uncertainties that may exist in partnerships. The lack of a formal agreement may at times create confusion between the parties and could result in differences of opinion regarding performance. This could even result in legal actions taken by one party against the other.

9.3.6 Joint Venture (16 Percent)

Joint ventures are generally associated with some form of financial investment by the parties in the relationship to achieve mutual benefits. The behavioral dimensions of joint ventures are somewhat similar to contractual relationships. Relative to other relationships, joint ventures possess the highest scores on perceived dependence and organizational investment and are above the median for communication frequency. However, joint ventures are at the median for business volume and below the median for personal character and organizational capability.

Joint ventures differ from contractual relationships in the level of investment that the parties commit to the relationship. In addition, the perception of dependence by one party upon the other is greater in joint ventures than in contractual relationships. Also, joint ventures can also be associated with a slightly lower level of trust in the other party, as evidenced in the low levels of personal character and organizational capability. This causes the firms to increase investment in the relationship to ensure adequate performance and control over the relationship. In other words, the investment may occur because there is a lack of trust in the other party, and the firm uses the investment as a mechanism to maintain control over the relationship. For example, a manufacturing firm may jointly invest in capacity with another firm to produce a specialty product with which the former has little expertise, whereas the other party has the expertise but has only limited interest in expanding their capabilities.

The lack of trust by the former may cause them to invest in a joint venture to secure the commitment of the other party.

9.3.7 Alliance (18 Percent)

The final relationship type identified here are alliances. This term is used commonly in academic literature and in discussions between suppliers and customers in industry. Alliances reflect different behavioral dimensions relative to the other relationships. Alliances are above the median in perceived dependence, organizational capability, business volume, and organizational investment. In addition, alliances exhibit the highest level of personal character and communication frequency of all seven relationship types. What differentiates alliances from joint ventures is the greater level of trust in the other party based on perceptions of the personal character of the other party, and the capability of the other organization. Relative to the other relationships, alliances indicate a high level of confidence in the personal character of the other party and greater communication frequency between the parties. In addition, alliances demonstrate the second highest level of importance for dependence, business volume, and investment.

Alliances also possess the highest levels of trust, interaction frequency, and commitment. Alliances are reflective of the relational characteristics commonly discussed by academics and managers. This type of situation is reflective of a manufacturer investing in storage facilities with a "third-party logistics provider," so the third-party provider can achieve maximum efficiencies in providing either inbound or outbound logistics services for the manufacturer. Both parties recognize the joint benefits derived through the efficiencies of the new facilities. In this situation, the trust between the parties enhances the already established relationship.

In the remainder of this chapter, we will review some of the key processes around executing the sourcing strategy for suppliers that fall into the nonstrategic, administered, and contractual supplier categories (e.g., commodities that are not considered critical). Ideally, sourcing teams will put "shrink-wrapped" E-procurement processes around these types of sourcing agreements to ensure that supply management personnel are not required to spend their time managing invoices, POs, and accounts payable. It is important to note that the primary returns on investment obtained from E-purchasing tools are (1) reduction of head count in accounts payable clerks and (2) allowing supply management to focus on value-added strategic relationships (such as those we will discuss in Chapter 10). In this chapter, we will discuss some of the core elements surrounding managing nonstrategic suppliers, including E-procurement and negotiation approaches. The relationship-based approach, focused on relationships that involve specialty contracts, partnerships, joint ventures, and alliances, involves an entirely different set of processes covered in Chapter 10.

9.4 E-Procurement and the Purchasing Process

This section presents the purchasing process[2] as a cycle consisting of five major stages:

1. Identify or anticipate material or service needs.
2. Evaluate potential suppliers.
3. Select suppliers.
4. Release and receive purchase requirements.
5. Continuously measure and manage supplier performance.

These stages may vary in different organizations, depending on whether a new or repetitively purchased item is being sourced and whether there is a detailed approval process for purchases that exceed a specific dollar amount. New items require that purchasing spend much more time up front evaluating potential sources. Repeat items usually have approved sources already available. Figure 9.5 illustrates a typical purchasing process used in many enterprises with some typical contingency elements shown. This diagram also shows supplier evaluation and selection in the purchase of new items or services or during a review of existing purchase contracts. Figure 9.6 and Figure 9.7 detail the purchase requisition flow and receiving process.

A document flow accompanies the movement of orders and material throughout the purchasing process. Historically, preparing and managing the proper purchasing documents has been a time-consuming process. Most firms have streamlined the document-flow process to reduce the paperwork and handling required for each purchase. The suite of tools used to achieve efficiency in purchasing transactions is broadly defined as *E-procurement*. Companies are using E-procurement tools to manage the flow of documents by (1) automating the document generation process and (2) electronically transmitting purchase documents to suppliers. The benefits of electronically generating and transmitting purchasing-related documents include:

1. A virtual elimination of paperwork and paperwork handling.
2. A reduction in the time between need recognition and release or receipt of order.

---

[2] Monczka, R., Trent, R., and Handfield, R., *Purchasing and Supply Chain Management,* 3rd ed., Cincinnati, OH: Southwestern College Publishing, 2004.

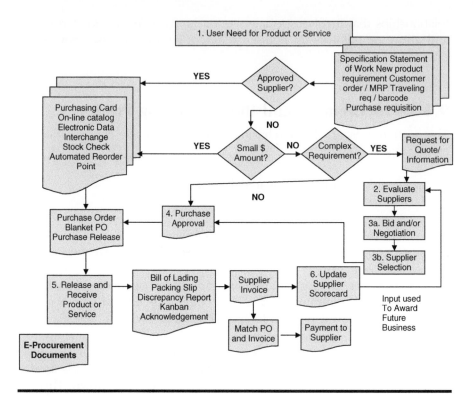

Figure 9.5   The purchasing process.

3. Improved communication within the company and with suppliers.
4. A reduction in errors.
5. Lower overhead costs in the purchasing area.
6. Purchasing personnel spend less time processing POs and invoices and more time on strategic value-added purchasing activities.

The electronic documents often used in the process are represented in Figure 9.5 by boxes with crosshatches. Elements 1, 2, and 3 (through purchase approval) were all discussed earlier in Chapter 8. So, we can assume that the approved channel for buying has been selected. In an ideal environment, what happens next?

9.5 Purchase Approval

After the supplier is selected or a requisition for a standard item is received, purchasing grants an approval to purchase the product or service. This is accomplished through several different approaches, depending on the type of system in place.

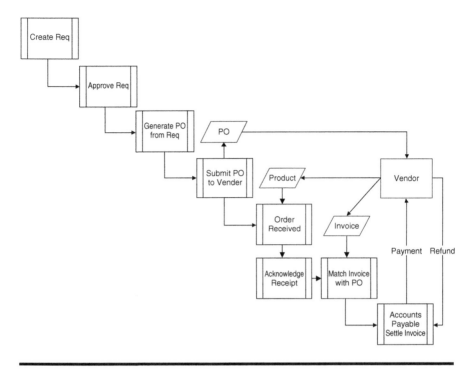

Figure 9.6 Purchase requisition flow.

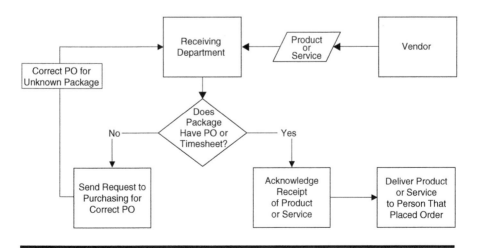

Figure 9.7 Receiving process.

9.5.1 Purchase Order

The drafting of a *purchase order* (PO), sometimes called a *purchase agreement*, takes place after supplier selection is complete. Purchasing must take great care when wording a purchase agreement because it is a legally binding document. Almost all POs include the standard legal conditions to which the order (i.e., the contract) is subject on the reverse side of the agreement. The PO details critical information about the purchase: quantity, material specification, quality requirements, price, delivery date, method of delivery, ship-to address, PO number, and order due date. This information, together with the name and address of the purchasing company, appears on the front side of the order.

Companies with an older paper system have a cumbersome process (see Figure 9.6 and Figure 9.7). Approximately seven to nine copies typically accompany the PO. In computerized environments, a file containing a copy of the PO is sent to each department's computer mailbox. The supplier receives the original copy of the PO along with a file copy. The supplier signs the original and sends it back to the buyer. This acknowledges that the supplier has received the PO and agrees with its contents. In legal terms, the transmittal of the PO constitutes a contractual offer, whereas the acknowledgment by the supplier constitutes a contractual acceptance. Offer and acceptance are two critical elements of a legally binding agreement.

Purchasing forwards (either electronically or manually) a copy of the PO to accounting (i.e., accounts payable), the requesting department, receiving, and traffic. Purchasing usually keeps several copies for its records. There are good reasons for other departments to have visibility of POs and incoming receipts:

- The accounting department gains knowledge of future accounts payable obligations. It also has an order against which to match a receipt for payment when the material arrives.
- The PO provides the requesting department with an order number to include in its records.
- The requestor can refer to the PO number if he or she needs to inquire into the status of an order.
- Receiving has a record of the order to match against the receipt of the material. Receiving also can use outstanding POs to help forecast its inbound workload.
- Traffic becomes aware of inbound delivery requirements and can make arrangements with carriers or use the company's own vehicles to schedule material delivery.

- Purchasing uses its copies of the PO for follow-up and monitoring of open orders.
- Orders remain active in all departments until the buying company acknowledges receipt of the order and that it meets quantity and quality requirements.

Firms are increasingly using computerized databases to perform these processes and are moving toward a paperless office.

9.5.2 Blanket Purchase Order

For an item or group of items ordered repetitively from a supplier, purchasing may issue a *blanket purchase order* — an open order, effective for a year, covering repeated purchases of an item or family of items. Blanket orders eliminate the need to issue a PO whenever there is a need for material. After a buyer establishes a blanket order with a supplier, the ordering of an item simply requires a routine order release. The buyer and seller have already negotiated or agreed upon the terms of the purchase contract. With a blanket PO, the release of material becomes a routine matter between the buyer and seller.

Almost all firms establish blanket POs with their suppliers. In fact, blanket orders have been the preferred method for making the purchasing process more efficient and user friendly. Buyers usually use a PO for initial purchases or a one-time purchase, which purchasing professionals may also call a *spot buy*. Blanket POs are common for production items ordered on a regular basis or for routine supplies required for operation and maintenance. A maintenance-supplies distributor, for example, may have a PO covering hundreds of items. It is not unusual for the buyer or seller to modify a PO to reflect new prices, new quantity discount schedules, or added or deleted items.

The blanket PO is similar to the PO in general content and is distributed to the same departments that receive a copy of a PO. The major difference between a PO and a blanket PO is the delivery date and the receiving department. This information on the blanket order remains open because it differs from order to order.

When negotiating a blanket PO, the buyer and supplier evaluate the anticipated demand over time for an item or family of items. The two parties agree on the terms of an agreement, including quantity discounts, required quality levels, delivery lead times, and other important terms or conditions. The blanket PO remains in effect during the time specified on the agreement. This time period is often, but not always, six months to a year. Longer-term agreements covering several years are becoming increasingly common with U.S. firms. Most buyers reserve the right to cancel the blanket order at any time, particularly in the event of poor supplier performance. This requires an "escape clause" that allows the buyer to terminate the contract in the event of persistently poor quality, delivery, etc.

9.5.3 Material Purchase Release

Buyers use *material purchase releases* to order items covered by blanket POs. Purchasing specifies the required part numbers, quantity, unit price, required receipt date, using department, ship-to address, and method of shipment. Purchasing forwards copies of this form to the supplier, accounting, receiving, and traffic. Purchasing retains several copies for its records. The copy to the supplier serves as a notification of required items. Accounting receives a copy so it can match the quantity received against the quantity ordered for payment purposes. Receiving must have visibility of incoming orders so it can compare ordered quantities with received quantities. As with other forms, this process is increasingly becoming electronic.

Different types of material releases exist. Organizations often use the material release as a means to provide visibility to the supplier about forecasted material requirements as well as actual material requirements. One U.S. automobile producer provides suppliers with an 18-month forecast for replacement parts. The first three months of the release are actual orders; the remaining months represent forecasted requirements that help the supplier plan.

9.6 Release and Receive Purchase Requirements

This phase of the purchasing cycle involves the physical transmittal of purchase requirements. This should be a fairly routine, although not necessarily the most efficient, part of the purchasing cycle. Some organizations transmit orders electronically whereas others send material releases through the mail or by fax. Purchasing or materials planning must minimize the time required to release and receive material. Electronic data interchange (EDI), which involves the electronic transfer of purchase documents between the buyer and seller, can help shorten order cycle time. EDI transactions, particularly through the Internet, will increase over the next several years. Also, better relationships with suppliers can support a just-in-time (JIT) ordering system. In some companies, once a contract is negotiated, internal end users may be directly responsible for "releasing" material orders covered under the terms of the contract, and purchasing may no longer be involved until the contract is renewed.

Purchasing or a material control group must monitor the status of open POs. There may be times when a purchaser has to expedite an order or work with a supplier to avoid a delayed shipment. A buyer can minimize order follow-up by selecting only the best suppliers and developing stable forecasting and efficient ordering systems. The receiving process should also be as efficient as possible by using bar-coding technology to receive and place supplier deliveries in inventory. The shipping and receiving processes require several other important documents (which also can be electronic), including the material packing slip, the bill of lading, and the receiving discrepancy report.

9.6.1 Material Packing Slip

The *material packing slip*, which the supplier provides, details the contents of a shipment. It contains the description and quantity of the items in a shipment. It also references a specific PO and material release number for tracking and auditing purposes. A packing slip is a critical document when receiving material at a buyer's facility. The receiving clerk compares the supplier packing slip quantity against the actual physical receipt quantity. Furthermore, the packing slip quantity should match the material release quantity. The comparison between material release quantity and packing slip quantity is critical. It identifies if suppliers have over- or undershipped.

9.6.2 Bill of Lading

Transportation carriers use a *bill of lading* to record the quantity of goods delivered to a facility. For example, the bill of lading may state that ABC carrier delivered three boxes to a buyer on a certain date. This prevents the purchaser from stating a week later that it received only two boxes. The bill of lading details only the number of boxes or containers delivered. Detailing the actual contents of each container is the supplier's responsibility; that information appears on the packing slip.

The bill of lading helps protect the carrier against wrongful allegations that the carrier somehow damaged, lost, or tampered with a shipment. This document does not necessarily protect the carrier against charges of concealed damage, however. A user may discover concealed damages after opening a shipping container. Responsibility for concealed damage is often difficult to establish. The receiving company may blame the carrier.

The carrier may blame the supplier or maintain that the damage occurred after delivery of the material. The supplier may maintain total innocence and implicate the carrier. While all this goes on, the buyer must reorder the material as a rush order. This can affect customer service or commitments.

9.6.3 Receiving Discrepancy Report

A *receiving discrepancy report* details shipping or receiving discrepancies noted by the receiving department. It is often the job of purchasing or material control to investigate and resolve material discrepancies. Material discrepancies usually result from incorrect quantity shipments. They can also result from receiving an incorrect part number or a part number incorrectly labeled.

9.6.4 JIT Purchasing

JIT purchasing and manufacturing allows firms to eliminate most receiving forms. American Honda (Marysville, Ohio) for example, assumes that if its production line has not shut down, it must have received its scheduled shipments from its suppliers. The accounts payable department makes payment unless informed otherwise. Honda's JIT system eliminates the need for packing slips and inbound material inspection. The system also eliminates the need to examine, file, and forward multiple copies of each packing slip to various departments. If a receipt does not arrive on time or is not damage free, Honda realizes this within minutes. With this system, no news implies that the shipment arrived and is ready for production.

Black and Decker employs a similar system called *backflush accounting*. In this system, suppliers are paid only for the quantity of components that are used in each week's production runs. In the event that parts are tossed aside on the production line because of defects, Black and Decker does not pay for them.

The next element, improving supplier performance and measuring performance, is discussed in Chapter 10. A best practice example is shown in Table 9.2.

9.7 What Is the Right Approach to a Negotiation?

There are many good books on negotiating tactics, styles, approaches, and processes, so these are not going to be a focus here. However, several

Table 9.2   Hotshot Best Practice: Dell's On-Demand Supply Chain

Dell implemented an inventory model that was cutting edge and that proved to be highly successful — so much so that other companies have started emulating it. Dell took "lean inventory" principles and "kicked it up a notch." They basically take a last-minute approach to inventory, so that they do not even have much inventory to speak of. Here is how they do it: they wait until a customer places an order via their customer Web site portal. Then, they in turn call their suppliers and place their orders. Their suppliers deliver the components in a few hours — standard! Once the component goods are delivered, Dell's final assembly folks assemble and test the final product, all in just a few hours. Every supplier order is thus directly tied to a customer order.

To pull off this inventory miracle, Dell builds this format into the contract agreement with each and every supplier. They do so by incorporating a performance metric into their supplier contracts that requires suppliers to carry 150 percent inventory levels for Dell components — at each of their manufacturing sites and at all times. They follow this up with another performance metric that delves even deeper: an agreement that the suppliers will hold *their* suppliers to this inventory standard as well! The result: sitting inventory = nonexistent; total turnaround = speedy; return-on-assets = very impressive; and investors = very happy.

common mistakes made by many sourcing teams during negotiations of nonstrategic commodity contracts need to be addressed.

1. Failure to prepare for the negotiation: Specifically, many supply managers do not spend time doing their homework, conducting supply market intelligence, uncovering facts, and researching, all of which are required to be effective and drive both parties to a mutually beneficial outcome.
2. Going in with the attitude that "we are going to win": Both parties must walk away with some sense of mutual satisfaction or else there will indeed be a winner and a loser. Do you really want the supplier walking away from a negotiation feeling that they have been beaten? What will this do to their commitment to providing you with the best service, technology, delivery, and quality?

This last point is critical. Strategic sourcing can indeed be an effective weapon to reduce costs, but the team must be judicious in the approach used in negotiations to be effective. For example, an anonymous manager working at General Motors during the 1990s made the following observation regarding the now famous "hard line" approach initiated by Jose Inaki

Lopez when he was brought in as chief of GM's procurement operations in North America:

> Prior to Lopez's arrival in the United States, GM was transitioning from a traditional RFQ-based strategy to a strategic sourcing relationship. And although successes were being achieved (the Northstar engine was very successful in its launch), you could see where the suppliers, because of their long history in working with GM, had heard what we were saying but did not believe it. Their pricing practices still involved "hedging their bets" with padded margins, and thus Lopez's strategy was appropriate at the time. He did save the company from bankruptcy by returning the purchasing organization to an aggressive competitive bid process.
>
> GM began taking heat because of their poor relationships, driven by a fundamental adversarial approach to supply-chain management. By 2001, the process had basically run its course, yet the pressure was still on the buyer to work on the basis of historical levels when the cost savings were no longer there! Seven years of year-to-year price decreases meant that buyers were now under pressure to continue to wring these savings, while experiencing the effects of the "law of diminishing returns." Maybe it's time for a change.
>
> Today, GM is emphasizing the importance of technology and innovation more than price in collaborating with the supply base. I do believe in my heart that GM is sincere, and that Harold Kutner [Lopez's successor] was also sincere. The reality of the situation is that there are still some fences to be mended in terms of trust. One manager recently invited suppliers to a technology fair with GM and tried to run it in a closed and confidential environment. He invited three or four suppliers to share with the organization some of their new technology and ideas. In these fairs and communications, they tried very much to send a message that GM is interested in their technology, but suppliers that showed up clearly expressed their doubts.
>
> Many suppliers during the 1990s had taken the lion's share of their new technologies to Chrysler because of the organization that Thomas Stallkamp built at Chrysler and because they trusted him. "I can remember sitting in on purchasing meetings on a weekly basis in 1993 and actually feeling sorry for Chrysler! I knew that for everything they were buying, they were paying significantly more than what GM was. But in the marketplace, Chrysler was taking market share from GM! Suppliers were willing to do anything for Chrysler but did not trust GM. When

things went wrong, the supplier would help Chrysler out, including premium transportation, engineering changes, expediting, solving start-up problems, or whatever; they would pull out all the stops to help Chrysler. They wouldn't do it for GM because they felt squeezed and wouldn't put any more into a part or process because of the additional cost. As a result, GM would have to devote resources to go out and force suppliers to perform what they were contracted to do in the first place. The costs associated with managing suppliers were many times more at GM than at Chrysler. And this money flowed directly to the bottom line. Chrysler in the end paid more for the parts they bought, but saved significant amounts by more than offsetting the cost of the higher price.

This situation illustrates the importance of building a solid business case for conducting the negotiation. (See Appendix B for additional details on how Chrysler collaborated with suppliers during this period.) An example of some specific goals or objectives that might be used to initiate a negotiation is as follows:

- Because of competitive market pressures, the cost of a key product must be reduced by fifteen percent over the next three years.
- As part of this cost reduction effort, the cost of the purchased item being negotiated, which is a major component of the end product, must be reduced by ten percent over the same three-year period.
- Your firm is willing to consolidate its purchase requirements with two suppliers of the current four and commit to the two selected suppliers under three-year contracts if the suppliers can provide the required cost reductions.

Let us discuss preparing for the negotiation and planning the strategy in more detail.

9.8 Preparing for the Negotiation

Negotiation planning[3] involves multiple steps that prepare the parties for a forthcoming negotiation. Many negotiations are relatively straightforward and require only basic preparation and planning. Other negotiations may be complex and require months of preparation. Purchasers who plan and prepare for a negotiation usually experience better outcomes than negotiators

---

[3] Monczka, R., Trent, R., and Handfield, R., *Purchasing and Supply Chain Management,* 3rd ed., 2004.

who do not. Planning is so central to effective negotiation that Section 9.11 addresses this topic in detail.

New technologies may make face-to-face negotiation, both for domestic and international requirements, less likely. This can be very attractive because more firms engage in international purchasing, which creates a host of negotiating challenges. It will also change how a buyer plans for a negotiation.

More advanced online tools that feature the ability to negotiate issues beyond price with multiple suppliers are becoming available. With these tools, E-procurement managers no longer have to spend hours in face-to-face meetings arguing over details with suppliers. A buyer simply fills out a request for quote (RFQ) template and forwards the document electronically to suppliers.[4] Suppliers can respond electronically with online proposals detailing price, payment terms, shipping methods, or any other issue relevant to the buyer. These tools enable a buyer to negotiate the process simultaneously with more than one supplier, which leads to efficiencies and lower prices due to increased competition (similar to reverse auctions).

9.9 Conducting the Negotiation

Negotiations with a supplier should occur only when a purchaser feels confident about the level of planning and preparation put forth. However, planning is not an open-ended process; buyers must usually meet deadlines that satisfy the needs of internal customers within the purchaser's firm. Thus, the buyer faces pressure to conduct the negotiation within a reasonable time. A negotiation should not begin until the negotiator:[5]

- Understands the nature and purpose of the negotiation
- Clarifies the goals and objectives sought from the negotiation
- Understands and prioritizes the important issues
- Understands the predictability of the negotiation process so that the negotiator can strategically plan how to achieve his or her goals and objectives
- Understands the personality, history, negotiating style, and important issues regarding the negotiator's counterpart
- Manages the time constraints imposed by users who require an item or service

---

[4] Waxer, C., E-negotiations are in, price-only e-auctions are out, *iSource*, 73–76, June 2001.
[5] Lewicki, R.J. and Litterer, J.A., *Negotiation*, Homewood, IL: Irwin, 1985, pp. 45–47.

Deciding where to negotiate can be an important part of the planning process. A home location can provide a great advantage to a negotiator, particularly during international negotiations. Advances in telecommunications technology now allow some negotiations to occur electronically rather than face to face. Most experts agree that the atmosphere surrounding a negotiation should be less formal whenever possible. Excessive formality can constrain the parties and restrict free exchange of ideas and solutions. It is also a good idea to summarize positions and points of agreement throughout the negotiation, which helps reduce misunderstanding while helping track progress against the negotiation agenda. It may also help to have a dedicated note taker or scribe throughout the negotiation, whose responsibility it is to record what is said, who said it, what the reaction was, and areas of agreement.

It is during the negotiation that the parties play out their strategy with tactics — the skill of employing available means to accomplish or achieve a desired end. Tactics consists of the action plans designed to help achieve a desired result.

A sequence of four phases often characterizes face-to-face negotiating sessions. The first phase consists of fact finding. This part of the process helps clarify and confirm information provided by the buyer and seller. During the second phase, the parties often take a recess after fact finding. This allows each party to reassess relative strengths and weaknesses, review and revise objectives and positions if necessary, and organize the negotiation agenda. Next, the parties meet face to face in an attempt to narrow differences on issues. Finally, the parties seek an agreement and conclusion to the negotiation.

Effective negotiators display certain behaviors or characteristics when conducting a negotiation. They are willing to compromise or revise their goals, particularly when new information challenges a negotiator's position. Effective negotiators also view issues independently without linking them in any particular sequence. Linking issues risks undermining an entire negotiation if the parties reach an impasse on a single issue. Effective negotiators also establish lower and upper ranges for each major issue, in contrast to a single, rigid position that limits the number of options available.

Effective or skilled negotiators explore twice as many options per issue as do average negotiators. Furthermore, effective negotiators make almost four times the comments about the common ground between the parties (rather than the differences) as do average negotiators. Finally, compared with average negotiators, effective or skilled negotiators make fewer irritating comments about the other party, give fewer reasons for arguments they advance (too many supporting reasons can dilute an argument), and make fewer counterproposals. Effective negotiators are willing to make counterproposals although not as many as an average negotiator. A willingness to make too many counterproposals means the negotiator is probably compromising too much or offering too many concessions.

9.10 Implementing the Agreement

Reaching an agreement is not the end of the negotiation process. Rather, an agreement represents the beginning of the contract's performance for the item, service, or activity covered by the agreement. An important part of implementing a negotiated agreement is loading the agreement into a corporate contract system so that others throughout the organization have visibility of the agreement.

During the life of an agreement, a purchaser must let a supplier know if the latter is meeting its contractual requirements. Conversely, it is a supplier's responsibility to let the buyer know if the latter is meeting its responsibilities within the negotiated agreement. Both parties should work to build on the success of a negotiation. Implementing the agreement should reaffirm the commitment of the parties to working together in the future.

9.11 Negotiation Planning

Experts on negotiation agree that planning is perhaps the most important part of the negotiation process. Unfortunately, many negotiators fail to prepare properly before entering a formal negotiation. A *plan* is a method or scheme devised for making or doing something to achieve a desired end. *Planning*, therefore, is the process of planning or devising methods to achieve a desired end. Once purchasers develop a plan, they can begin to develop the tactics to carry out that plan. Negotiators frequently fall short of their goals because they fail to commit sufficient time to the planning process, establish clear objectives with acceptable ranges, formulate convincing arguments or support for positions, or consider a counterpart's needs.[6]

At least 90 percent of the success of any negotiation is determined by effective planning. Preparing at the last minute before a negotiation is a sure recipe for disaster, especially when negotiating with someone who

[6] Lewicki, R.J. and Litterer, J.A., *Negotiation*, pp. 47–48.

is well-prepared. Being quick and clever is not enough to ensure a successful negotiating outcome. Successful negotiating planning consists of nine steps, which are discussed in the following subsections.

9.11.1 Developing Specific Objectives

The first step of the planning process involves developing the objectives sought from the negotiation. An *objective* is an aspiration or vision to work toward in the future. An obvious objective in a purchasing negotiation is to reach an agreement that covers the purchase of a good or service. A buyer or seller would not commit scarce resources if the goal were to see a negotiation fail. Before actual negotiations begin, the parties usually believe they can reach an agreement. If the parties believed otherwise, they would not put forth the time and effort to prepare for a negotiation.

An important objective during a negotiation is to reach an agreement on a fair and reasonable price between a buyer and seller. Examples of buyer objectives include achieving a unit price of $10, a four-week delivery lead time, or improving supplier quality from 500 parts per million defects to 50 parts per million defects. The buyer may also want to persuade the supplier to cooperate with the purchaser at a level higher than what other buyers receive. Not all objectives are equally important, so the purchaser must begin to identify the importance of each one. One leading company separates its objectives into "must have" and "would like to have" categories. This begins to differentiate the importance of each objective.

9.11.2 Analyzing Each Party's Strengths and Weaknesses

Experienced negotiators understand their counterpart through research and experience. This means understanding what is important to a counterpart's company along with understanding the personality and history of the negotiator. When a purchaser negotiates with a supplier for the first time, a buyer must commit additional research to understanding that supplier.

Analyzing each party requires an assessment of relative strengths and weaknesses. This process can influence the strategy and tactics adopted at the bargaining table. The buyer does not always have power or influence over the supplier. A supplier often holds a position of power over the buyer because of financial size, or perhaps the supplier does not have a great need for the contract. Section 9.12 describes various sources of power that are part of the negotiating process.

9.11.3 Gathering Relevant Information

The ability to analyze yourself and your counterpart requires information. This process is not complex if the buyer and seller have previously negotiated a purchase agreement. When this is the case, the buyer may already have the answer to a number of important questions: What happened between the parties? Are we negotiating with the same or different people? What are the important issues regarding this supplier? What were the areas of disagreement? Is there anything about the rules of the negotiation that we would like to change?

Where does a purchaser who has no experience with a supplier gather the required information? One possible source is others who have experience with that supplier. Published sources of information may also be available. These sources include trade journals, business publications, trade association data, government reports, annual reports, financial evaluations such as Dun and Bradstreet reports, commercial databases, inquiries directly to personnel at the supplier, and information through the Internet.

9.11.4 Recognizing Your Counterpart's Needs

The buyer and seller in a purchasing negotiation are, in many ways, mirror images of each other. Each side wants to reach an agreement that is favorable to longer-term success. As a buyer gathers information about a supplier, it is important to identify those issues that are particularly critical to the supplier. For example, a supplier may want to maintain market share and volume in its industry. Therefore, receiving an entire purchase contract, rather than a portion of a contract, may be an important objective to that supplier.

The issues that are most critical to a supplier may not be so critical to a buyer. When one party has an issue or requirement that is not important to the other, then the parties will likely reach agreement. For example, a supplier's production-scheduling system may require the supplier to produce a buyer's requirement late in the day with delivery during the evening. If a buyer has an evening work crew that can easily receive late deliveries, the buyer can satisfy the supplier's requirement for later deliveries. In return, the buyer may now expect the supplier to be accommodating on one or more issues that are important to the buyer. Give-and-take is essential to negotiation, and either party should not expect to prevail on all issues.

9.11.5 Identifying Facts and Issues

Negotiation planning requires differentiating between facts and issues. The two parties will want to reach an agreement early concerning what is a fact versus what is an issue. A fact is a reality or truth that the parties can easily state. In negotiation, facts are not open to debate. A buyer wants to purchase a piece of capital equipment. There is no negotiating with a supplier whether the buyer actually needs a piece of equipment (although the specific type of equipment may be an unanswered question requiring discussion).

Issues, on the other hand, are items or topics to resolve during the negotiation. Issues that might require resolution include purchase price and delivery date. The parties to a negotiation can debate many issues besides price. Part of the planning process requires identifying the critical issues that each party seeks to resolve from the negotiation.

9.11.6 Establishing a Position on Each Issue

The parties to a negotiation should establish positions that offer flexibility. Negotiators should therefore develop a range of positions — typically, a minimum acceptable position, a maximum or ideal outcome, and a most likely position. If the issue is price, a seller may have a target price at which it wants to sell a product. Of course, the seller will be willing to take a higher price if the buyer is willing to offer one. The critical part of the price range will be the seller's minimum price. This is the lowest price at which the seller is willing to sell to a buyer. The area of overlapping positions among issues, when one exists, is termed *the bargaining or settlement zone*.[7] The bargaining zone represents the heart of the negotiating process.

Figure 9.8 and Figure 9.9 demonstrate this zone for a purchase price negotiation. With example A (Figure 9.8), the parties will probably not reach an agreement unless one or both parties modify their original range or position. The minimum selling position of the seller is far above the buyer's maximum position. With example B (Figure 9.9), an overlap exists between the two positions that should lead to an agreement. The buyer is willing to pay up to $11.45 per unit. The supplier is willing to sell as low as $11.15 per unit. The two parties will likely reach an agreement somewhere between those two figures. The buyer may open with an offer to purchase at less than $11 as a tactic (i.e., start out very low). However, if the seller sticks to its original plan, the negotiation will likely conclude within the overlap range.

Several factors influence whether a party modifies, or even abandons, an original position. These include the desire for the contract, new or improved information that challenges the accuracy of an original position,

---

[7] Thompson, L., *The Mind and Heart of the Negotiator,* Upper Saddle River, NJ: Prentice Hall, 1998, pp. 19–20.

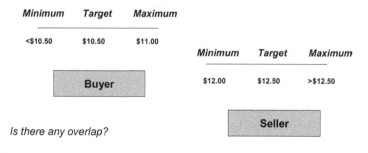

Figure 9.8   Negotiation framework (Example A).

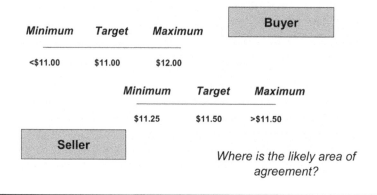

Figure 9.9   Negotiation framework (Example B).

or a major concession that leads the other party to modify its position on another issue.

9.11.7 Developing a Negotiating Strategy and Tactics

Negotiating strategy refers to the overall approach used to reach a mutually beneficial agreement with a supplier who holds different points of view from the buyer. A major part of the strategic planning process involves tactics — the art or skill of employing available means to accomplish an

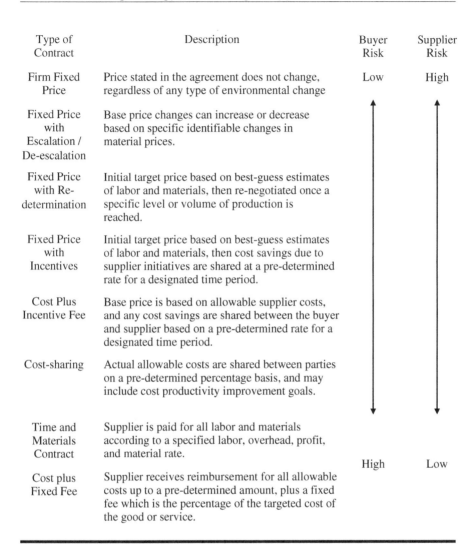

Type of Contract	Description	Buyer Risk	Supplier Risk
Firm Fixed Price	Price stated in the agreement does not change, regardless of any type of environmental change	Low	High
Fixed Price with Escalation / De-escalation	Base price changes can increase or decrease based on specific identifiable changes in material prices.		
Fixed Price with Re-determination	Initial target price based on best-guess estimates of labor and materials, then re-negotiated once a specific level or volume of production is reached.		
Fixed Price with Incentives	Initial target price based on best-guess estimates of labor and materials, then cost savings due to supplier initiatives are shared at a pre-determined rate for a designated time period.		
Cost Plus Incentive Fee	Base price is based on allowable supplier costs, and any cost savings are shared between the buyer and supplier based on a pre-determined rate for a designated time period.		
Cost-sharing	Actual allowable costs are shared between parties on a pre-determined percentage basis, and may include cost productivity improvement goals.		
Time and Materials Contract	Supplier is paid for all labor and materials according to a specified labor, overhead, profit, and material rate.	High	Low
Cost plus Fixed Fee	Supplier receives reimbursement for all allowable costs up to a pre-determined amount, plus a fixed fee which is the percentage of the targeted cost of the good or service.		

Figure 9.10 Major types of contracts.

end, objective, or strategy. They include the current set of action plans and activities adopted to achieve the negotiating objectives and strategy.

Strategic negotiating issues involve the broader questions regarding who, what, where, when, and how to negotiate. We can think of strategy and tactics as two dimensions of the negotiating process. The ideal situation is to have a well-developed negotiating strategy with tactics that support that strategy. As an analogy, think of a military battle. The best-developed strategy will fail unless a commander has the tactics and the resources to implement the strategy.

9.11.8 Briefing Other Personnel

Purchase negotiation usually affects other parties across a company. The individual or team conducting the negotiation should brief these parties to make sure they are aware of and in agreement with the objectives of the negotiation. This briefing can also address the major issues of the negotiation and positions on these issues. Briefing personnel before a negotiation helps eliminate unpleasant surprises during face-to-face negotiation.

9.11.9 Practicing the Negotiation

Experienced negotiators practice or rehearse a negotiation before commencing a formal negotiation. One way to do this is to hold a mock, or simulated, negotiation. For instance, a marketing or salesperson might represent the supplier. The counterpart in a practice negotiating session may be able to raise questions and issues that the buyer had not originally addressed or considered. When using simulation, it is important for each party to play its role as realistically as possible.

Effective planning means that a purchaser achieves an agreement that is more creative than one available to competitors. It also means managing relationships that support future negotiation.

9.12 Power in Negotiation

An important part of the negotiation process involves the power relationship between parties. *Power* is the ability to influence another person or organization. A has power over B if A can get B to do something that directly benefits A. Throughout history, we have seen both positive and negative uses of power. Within negotiation, the use of power employed by the parties can influence the outcome of a negotiation.

Individuals and organizations bring different sources of power to the negotiating table, and the use of power can be part of the negotiating strategy. Some types of power are detrimental to a continued relationship, whereas other types are the result of expertise or access to information. Negotiators must understand the advantages and disadvantages of using power. They must also understand the possible effect that using a particular source of power will have on a relationship.

The following types of power will always exist in any type of negotiation. Thus, it is important in building a negotiation strategy to recognize these power elements ahead of time and build a strategy that seeks to address them. The following subsections relate to the various types of power elements[8] and list some of the ways in which they are applied in negotiation.

9.12.1 Expert Power

An expert has accumulated and mastered vast amounts of knowledge. He or she often has credentials that testify to that mastery. Nonexperts are less likely to challenge an expert.

- The lead company in this supply-chain network is an expert in the industry.
- We respect the judgment of the lead company's representatives.
- The lead company retains business expertise that enables them to make right suggestions.

9.12.2 Referent Power

A referent has some attributes that attract another party. The nonreferent wants the referent to look upon him or her favorably.

- We really admire the way the lead company runs its business, so we try to follow its lead.
- We often do what the lead company asks because we are proud to be affiliated with it.
- We talk up the lead company to our colleagues as a great business with which to be associated.

9.12.3 Legitimate Power

The position a person holds, rather than the individual person, forms the basis of legitimate power.

- The lead company has the right to tell us what to do.
- Because the lead company is our customer, we should accept its requests and recommendations.

---

[8] Maloni, M. and Benton, W.C., Power influences in the supply chain, *Journal of Business Logistics*, 21(1), 2000.

9.12.4 Legal Legitimate Power

Perhaps the most common form of power relies on persuasion through the use of facts, data, and other information.

■ The lead company often refers to portions of an agreement to gain our compliance on a particular request.
■ The lead company makes a point to refer to any legal agreement when attempting to influence us.
■ The lead company uses sections of our sales agreement as a tool to get us to agree to their demands.

9.12.5 Reward Power

This type of power exists when one party is able to offer something of value to another party. It represents a direct effort to exert control. This is source of power only if the other party values the rewards.

■ The lead company offers incentives when we were initially reluctant to cooperate with a new program.
■ We feel that by going along with the lead company, we will be favored on other occasions.
■ The lead company offers rewards so that we will go along with its wishes.

9.12.6 Coercive Power

This power involves the ability to punish. Repeated use can damage relationships or invite retaliation. Its use is often related to the power holder's belief that the other party will comply.

■ If we do not do as asked, we will not receive very good treatment from the lead company.
■ If we do not agree to its suggestions, the lead company could make things difficult for us.
■ The lead company makes it clear that failing to comply with its requests will result in penalties against us.

9.12.7 Other Issues in Negotiation

9.12.7.1 Commitment

■ Our firm is committed to the preservation of good working relationships with the lead company.

- Our firm believes in the lead company as a partner.
- Our relationship with the lead company could be described as one of high commitment.

9.12.7.2 Conflict

- Sometimes the lead company prevents us from doing what we want to do.
- The lead company does not have our best interests at heart.
- We often disagree with the lead company.

9.12.7.3 Conflict Resolution

- The discussions we have with the lead company in areas of disagreement are usually very productive.
- Our discussions in areas of disagreement with the lead company create more problems than they solve.
- Discussions in areas of disagreement increase the strength of our relationship.

9.12.7.4 Cooperation

- Our relationship with the lead company is better described as a cooperative effort rather than an arms-length negotiation.
- Overall, our firm and the lead company perform well together in carrying out our respective tasks.
- We feel that we can count on the lead company to give us the support that other suppliers receive.

9.12.7.5 Trust

- The lead company is concerned about our welfare.
- The lead company considers how its actions will affect us.
- We trust the lead company.

9.12.7.6 Performance

- The performance of the entire supply chain has improved as a result of our relations with the lead company.

- The efficiency of our relationship with the lead company has improved the lead company's performance.
- Without the lead company, our performance would not be as good as it is with it.

9.13 Building a Contract That Minimizes Risk[9]

As it is not possible to discuss in detail all of the elements to consider in building a solid contract, a short list of key issues to consider is included.

9.13.1 Types of Contracts

Purchasing contracts can be classified into different categories based on their characteristics and purpose. Almost all purchasing contracts are based on some form of pricing mechanism and can be categorized as a variation on two basic types: fixed-price and cost-based contracts. The major types of contracts are shown in Figure 9.10.

9.13.1.1 Fixed-Price Contracts

9.13.1.1.1 Firm Fixed-Price Contract

The most basic contractual pricing mechanism is called a *firm fixed price*. In this type of purchase contract, the price stated in the agreement does not change, regardless of fluctuations in general overall economic conditions, industry competition, levels of supply, market prices, or other environmental changes. This contract price can be obtained through any number of pricing mechanisms, e.g., price quotations, supplier responses to the buying organization's requests for proposal (RFPs), negotiations, or any other method. Fixed-price contracts are the simplest and easiest for purchasing to manage because there is no need for extensive auditing or additional input from the purchasing side.

If market prices for a purchased good or service rise above the stated contract price, the seller bears the brunt of the financial loss. However, if the market price falls below the stated contract price because of outside factors such as competition, changes in technology, or raw material prices, the purchaser assumes the risk or financial loss. If there is a high level of uncertainty from the supplying organization's point of view regarding its ability to make a reasonable profit under competitive fixed-price conditions, then the supplier may add to its price to cover potential

---

[9] Monczka, R., Trent, R., and Handfield, R., *Purchasing and Supply Chain Management*, 3rd ed., Cincinnati, OH: Southwestern College Publishing, 2004.

increases in component, raw materials, or labor prices. If the supplier increases its contract price in anticipation of rising costs, and the antici-pated conditions do not occur, then the purchaser would be paying too high a price for the good or service. For this reason, it is very important for the purchasing organization to adequately understand existing market conditions prior to signing a fixed-price contract to prevent contingency pricing from adversely affecting the total cost of the purchase over the life of the contract.

9.13.1.1.2 Fixed-Price Contract with Escalation

A number of variations on the basic firm fixed-price contract exist. If the item being purchased is to be supplied over a longer time period and there is a high probability that costs will increase, then the parties may choose to negotiate an escalation clause into the basic contract, resulting in a fixed-price contract with escalation. Escalation clauses allow either increases or decreases in the base price, depending on the circumstances. A greater degree of price protection is therefore provided for the supplier while the purchaser enjoys potential price reductions. All price changes should be keyed to a third-party price index, preferably to a well-established, widely published index (such as the producer price index for a specific material).

9.13.1.1.3 Fixed-Price Contract with Redetermination

In cases in which the parties cannot accurately predict labor or material costs and quantities to be used prior to the execution of the purchase agreement (e.g., an unproven technology), a fixed-price contract with redetermination may be more appropriate. In this scenario, the buying and selling parties negotiate an initial target price based on best-guess estimates of the labor and materials to be used in manufacturing a new product. Once a contractually agreed-upon volume of production has been reached, the two parties review the production process and rede-termine a revised firm price. Depending on the circumstances surrounding the contract, the redetermined price may be applied only to production following the redetermination or to all or part of the units previously produced. Care should be taken, though, because a contract that calls for an agreement in the future is not enforceable.

9.13.1.1.4 Fixed-Price Contract with Incentives

The final type of fixed-price contract is the fixed-price contract with incentives. This contract is similar to the fixed-price contract with rede-termination except that the terms and conditions of the contract allow cost savings sharing (CSS) with the supplier. As in the redetermination contract, it is difficult for the buying and selling parties to arrive at a firm price prior to actual production.

If the supplier can demonstrate actual cost savings through production efficiencies or substitution of materials, the resulting savings from the initial price targets are shared between the supplier and the purchaser at a predetermined rate. This type of purchase contract is typically used under conditions of high unit cost and relatively long lead times. The sharing of cost savings may be 50/50 (or some other split) and is typically a negotiated part of the contract.

9.13.1.2 Cost-Based Contracts

Cost-based contracts are appropriate for situations in which there is a risk that a large contingency fee might be included when using a fixed-price contract. Cost-based contracts typically represent a lower risk level of economic loss for suppliers, but they can also result in lower overall costs to the purchaser through careful contract management. It is important for the purchaser to include contractual terms and conditions that require the supplier to carefully monitor and control costs. The two parties to the agreement must concur on what costs are to be included in the calculation of the price of the goods or services.

Cost-based contracts are generally applicable when the goods or services procured are expensive, complex, and important to the purchasing party or when there is a high degree of uncertainty regarding labor and material costs. Cost-based contracts are generally less favorable to the purchasing party because the threat of financial risk is transferred from the seller to the buyer. There is also a low incentive for the supplier to strive to improve its operations and lower costs (and hence price) to the purchaser. In fact, there is an incentive, at least in the short run, for suppliers to be inefficient in cost-based contracts because they are rewarded with higher prices.

9.13.1.2.1 Cost Plus Incentive Fee

One cost-based contract is the cost-plus-incentive-fee contract. This contract is similar to the fixed-price-plus-incentive-fee contract except that the base price depends on allowable supplier costs rather than on a fixed price.

As before, if the supplier is able to improve efficiency or material usage as compared with the initial target cost, then the buying and selling parties will share any cost savings at a predetermined rate. This type of contract is appropriate for cases in which both parties are relatively certain about the accuracy of the initial target cost estimates.

9.13.1.2.2 Cost-Sharing Contract

With pure cost-sharing contracts, allowable costs are shared between the parties on a predetermined percentage basis. The key to successful negotiation is the identification of a firm set of operating guidelines, goals, and objectives for the contract. When in doubt, the two parties to a cost-sharing contract need to spell out their expectations in as much detail as possible to avoid confusion and misunderstanding regarding their respective roles and responsibilities.

9.13.1.2.3 Time-and-Materials Contract

Another cost-based contract is the time-and-materials contract. This type of contract is generally used in plant and equipment maintenance agreements in which the supplier cannot determine accurate costs prior to the repair service. The contract should spell out the appropriate labor rate (generally computed on a per-hour basis) plus an overhead and profit percentage, resulting in a "not-to-exceed" total price. With these terms and conditions, the purchaser has little control over the estimated maximum price. Thus, labor hours spent should be carefully audited over the life of the contract.

9.13.1.2.4 Cost-Plus-Fixed-Fee Contract

In a cost-plus-fixed-fee contract, the supplier receives reimbursement for all of its allowable costs up to a predetermined amount plus a fixed fee, which typically represents a percentage of the targeted cost of the good or service being procured. Although the supplier is guaranteed at least a minimum profit above its allowable costs, there is little motivation for the supplier to dramatically improve costs over the life of the contract. The U.S. military has been severely criticized for using such contracts on a routine basis with suppliers, who are making above-normal profits on commonly used goods and services at the expense of taxpayers.

To be most effective, cost-based contracts should include cost productivity improvements to drive continuous cost reduction over the life of the contract.

9.13.1.3 Considerations When Selecting Contract Types

Among the more important factors to consider when negotiating with a supplier over contract type are the following (see Figure 9.11):

1. Component market uncertainty
2. Long-term agreements

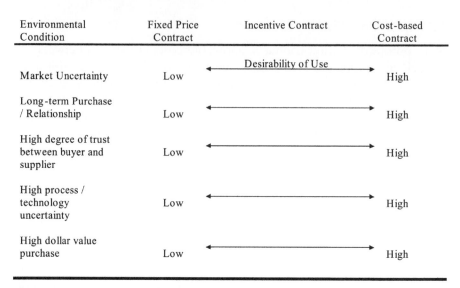

Environmental Condition	Fixed Price Contract	Incentive Contract	Cost-based Contract
Market Uncertainty	Low	← Desirability of Use →	High
Long-term Purchase / Relationship	Low	← →	High
High degree of trust between buyer and supplier	Low	← →	High
High process / technology uncertainty	Low	← →	High
High dollar value purchase	Low	← →	High

Figure 9.11   Conditions affecting choice of contract.

3. Degree of trust between buyer and seller
4. Process or technology uncertainties
5. Supplier's ability to impact costs
6. Total dollar value of the purchase

The first of these factors, component market uncertainty, refers to the volatility of pricing conditions for major elements of the product, such as raw materials, purchased components, and labor. The more unstable the underlying factor market prices, either upward or downward, the less appropriate a fixed-price contract will be for the two parties. Increasing factor market prices will place more risk on the supplying organization, whereas decreasing prices will shift the contract economic risk to the purchasing party. (This condition also applies in the case of unstable currency exchange rates in contracts with international suppliers.)

The length of the purchase agreement can also have a significant impact on the desirability of different contract types. The longer the term of the purchase agreement, the less likely it is that firm-fixed-price contracts will be acceptable to the supplier. For ongoing purchase arrangements, suppliers will generally prefer to employ fixed-price-with-escalation or any of the cost-type contracts, because they involve less economic risk for the selling party. Purchasing managers must, therefore, evaluate the economic risk of the different contract types and make a decision as to the acceptability of each type for the entire length of the agreement. For most short-term contracts and in conditions of stable component factor markets, firm-fixed-price and fixed-price-with-redetermination contracts can safely be applied. The choice of contract type is also dependent on the nature of the buyer–seller relationship.

If the relationship has been mutually beneficial in the past and has existed for a considerable period of time, a greater degree of trust may have developed between buying and selling parties. In such cases, both buyer and supplier are more likely to cooperate in the determination of allowable costs, thereby preferring cost-type purchase agreements.

For products and services characterized by high process or technological uncertainty, fixed-price contracts are less desirable for the seller. However, if the purchaser has a reasonable estimate of the supplier's cost structure, then cost-type contracts may be preferable because they allow the price to be adjusted either upward or downward depending on the efforts of the supplier. If the supplier can potentially reduce costs through continuous improvement, then an incentive-type contract may prove beneficial to both contracting parties.

As the total dollar value or unit cost of the contract increases, purchasers must spend more effort creating effective pricing mechanisms. The contracting parties must consider each of the factors in Figure 9.11 in detail, as well as the total impact of the contract over the lifetime of the agreement. It is important to remember that both parties in a contract must benefit (although not necessarily in the same proportion).

9.14 Conclusion

There are many types of buyer–supplier relationships. Clearly, selecting and developing the type of relationship is contingent on many different factors. What is important is establishing a common process for assessing the facts, utilizing the data, and planning the requirements for the strategy. The use of E-procurement tools for nonstrategic relationships should also be considered as the strategy is rolled out, with the objective of reducing non-value-added sourcing activities and allowing greater time for managing strategic relationships, which will produce the greatest value for the end customer.

Once the final contract is completed, it is time to initiate the relationship. This is discussed in the next chapter.

9.15 Checklist

- ■ Initiate RFP/RFQ/tender request.
- ■ Select qualified candidates for negotiations.
- ■ Organize negotiations.

- Build contract agreements.
- Conduct negotiation.
- Hand over and execute contract.
- Complete position paper executive summary.

9.16 Results

- Suppliers selected
- Contracts executed
- Strategy position paper complete

Chapter 10

Relationship Management (Strategic Supplier Relationships)

Function	Objective	Tactical Step	Chapter/ Appendix
Supply market intelligence	Supply market research	Opportunity identification and validation	2
		Project approval	2
		Establishing the team	3
		Project plan	3
		As-is assessment	4
		Supply market research	5
		Market forecasts	5
		External and market analyses	6
	Strategy and resource commitment	Detailed supplier evaluation and research	7
		Evaluate current and alternative strategies	8
		Understand contract formation	8

Function	Objective	Tactical Step	Chapter/ Appendix
Strategic sourcing	Negotiate and select supplier	Develop relationship strategy	8
		Strategy position paper	8
		Develop requests for information (RFIs) and build negotiation strategy	9
		Negotiate	9
		Final supplier selection	9
		Form contracts	9
	Implement and promote compliance	Implement contracts	9
		Transition to relationship manager	10
Relationship management		Communicate expectations	10
	Improve supplier performance	Measure performance	10
		Resolve issues and develop supplier performance	10
Benchmarking processes and driving continuous improvement		Build an organization for supply-chain excellence	11
		Benchmark performance and drive continuous improvement	12, App. B

10.1 Chapter Outline

■ Why relationship management? Ten reasons why you need a dedicated relationship management function
■ Making the transition from strategic sourcing to relationship management
■ Organize the relationship management team
■ The case of software development and proprietary technology
■ Define the relationship management leader, the team, and the change-management strategy

- Operate the relationship
- Manage performance, monitor relationships
- Common problems
- Strategic versus reactive approaches to supplier development
- Supplier development: a strategy for improvement
- CAPS global supplier development study
- Supplier development efforts that sometimes do not work
- Can you trust the concept of trust in supply-chain relationships?
- Dependence: too much is never a good thing

It is not the strongest of the species that survive, nor the most intelligent, but the one most responsive to change.

— **Charles Darwin**

The method of the enterprising is to plan with audacity and execute with vigor.

— **John Christian Bovee**

When performance is measured, performance improves. When performance is measured and reported back, the rate of improvement accelerates.

— **Thomas S. Monson**

Be nice to people on the way up; you're going to see them again on the way down.

— **Bob Dylan**

10.2 Introduction

Once the sourcing strategy is approved, the project closed, and the team disassembled, the member who served as the internal client department representative on the team is anointed as the strategy's relationship manager (RM). This person carries forward the approved strategy, from the plan to implementation. This is particularly important for business relationships that fall into the partnership, alliance, or joint venture categories of the relationship scale discussed in the previous chapter.

The RM is tasked with addressing any operational-level issues that arise in connection with the strategy plan. Such issues could include invoice processing, quality control measures, and follow-up; sharing market forecasts and production scheduling with suppliers; coordinating as-needed cooperative technical assistance with suppliers to resolve problems; or pursuing value-building opportunities. The RM also shares communications with relevant suppliers on emerging issues such as commodity pricing, material availability, and continuous-improvement opportunities. Finally, the RM is also tasked with maintaining a supplier scorecard that provides key information to the supplier on its performance. Many companies are also now using a two-way scorecard that allows the supplier to provide feedback on how well the customer is providing it with information, paying on time, and other key elements of bilateral performance. This ensures that there is a two-way flow of feedback regarding the terms in the contract. Ideally, a standardized scorecard can be used to allow comparison of the relationship with other similar relationships that may exist across the organization, particularly if the supplier is supporting multiple business units with a single contract.

With the recent influx of E-procurement technology into the workplace, many companies are talking about "dehumanizing" supply-chain relationships, and making them more electronic in nature. This works well for standard or non-strategic commodity items that are ordered repeatedly. However, in many situations there is a definite need for human interaction in the form of an RM. The following section argues for having a dedicated RM as opposed to "automating human relationships."

10.3 Why Relationship Management? Ten Reasons Why You Need a Dedicated Relationship Management Function

In late 2003, I received the following e-mail from Tom Linton, chief procurement officer of Agere Systems, stationed in Singapore.

> Rob, I bought your book (*Supply Chain Redesign*) this weekend and started reading it. It was in a nice display of "recommended" reading at the airport bookstore in Singapore. Having been in both IBM and E2open (supply-chain software) and now Agere Systems ... no doubt in my mind, the value is clear. Implementation is complex with competing solutions and agendas. The issue is, even in the same industry, you have too many competing solutions. I noticed CAPS has been pushing the same themes. I liked the way you put it together and got it published.
>
> I am currently focused on building a supply chain which is geographically located with the supply base. This is a huge advantage, as value chains cannot overcome the time zone–

same day impact (e.g., less communication). The core advantages of key supplier relationship management are also local and cannot be overcome by distance. If we can automate human behavior in these management systems, the value chain will really gain speed.

After reading this e-mail, I started thinking about the notion of automating human behavior. Can it be done? Is it a goal that is desirable? Is it possible? Why would we wish to do so?

At first blush, it seems ridiculous. Humans are not automatons. Yet as I thought about it, I realized that what Tom was really talking about was promoting greater understanding among different people in different geographic locations around the world; getting them to think on the same plane, as a single business, or even more important, get them to think that they are all part of the same supply chain (themes that are frequently repeated in this book). As I thought about it further, I realized how critical it is to promote alignment among people, yet how difficult it is. As Tom pointed out, there are no shortcuts in automating human behavior; you have to be "on the ground" and talking to one another. Based on my insights and discussions over the last year or two, I realized how this theme has recurred again and again. The following ten reasons provide concrete examples why human relationships cannot be automated; more important, they also provide us with some ideas regarding how we can better manage these issues.

10.3.1 A Single System Never Works

Every system requires a different approach at each location. For example, in a pilot program implementation of an information visibility solution across six different plants and 50 different suppliers, Johnson Controls, Inc. realized that "a tool is only as good as the business process execution in the plant and the standardization and acceptance of the process across plants ... one replenishment method would not work in all situations. Rather, it is better to have several different methods that are executed the same way across the organization."

10.3.2 People Need to Communicate Better

People do not "naturally" communicate. In fact, we have found in the results from roundtables with 50 different executives that the primary areas in which their people lacked skills was making presentations and communication. The next area? Ethics, information sharing, and communication!

Clearly, the new supply-chain managers of the future will need to be team leaders and be able to go in front of a group, challenge the members, and convince them of the need to change.

10.3.3 Better Be Nice to People On the Way Up; You Are Going to See Them Again on the Way Down (Bob Dylan)

Several executives have noted the importance of maintaining supplier relationships in a price-driven economy. This is particularly challenging when conditions in one's own market are forcing price reductions; it is a natural tendency to pass on the pressure to one's own supply base. This cost challenge can be particularly difficult when price pressures drive suppliers out of business. How does one manage this problem? The point is that capacity will be at a premium when the economy turns around — and will you still be a preferred customer when that happens?

10.3.4 Strong-Arm Negotiation Tactics Will Hurt You in the End

One automotive executive recently commented:

> Many suppliers over the last ten years have taken the lion's share of their new technologies to [a competitor] because they trusted him. When things went wrong, the supplier would pull out all the stops to help them — including premium transportation, engineering changes, expediting, solving start-up problems, or whatever. They would not do it for us or anyone else, because they felt squeezed, and would not add any more to a part or process because of the additional cost. This competitor in the end paid more for the parts they bought than our company, but saved significant amounts by more than offsetting the cost of the higher price.

In effect, the chief procurement officer set a precedent for managing supplier relationships that until recently was unparalleled in the automotive industry.

10.3.5 The Demise of the Reverse Auction

Many organizations have reverted to reverse auctions as a way of driving costs down. However, recent studies by the Supply Chain Research Consortium (SCRC) have shown that reverse auctions are more likely to cause harm than good, particularly in terms of supplier relationships. Further, savings down the road through second auctions are unlikely to occur.

10.3.6 Data Means Different Things to Different People

In the E-business era, software developers were selling the vision of global trade exchanges that would bring buyers and sellers together on the same platform to clear markets and drive down costs. However, they overlooked the fact that data integration is still a major challenge. In a presentation at North Carolina State University, Stephanie Miles from Bridgepoint noted that data often means very different things to different people on the ground, citing an example of a large retailer in which it took a 5-hr discussion with key stakeholders to determine the meaning of "on-time delivery" in terms of the firm's data dictionary. Thus, face-to-face conversations are almost always required to attribute meaning to data prior to automating the relationship.

10.3.7 China: Do You Have a Strategy?

China's entry into the World Trade Organization (WTO) is a reality. If you have not yet thought about what your firm's China strategy is going to be, it would be a good idea to begin thinking about it now, particularly with respect to supplier relationship management. Unless you understand the people you are dealing with and their connections to local government agencies, logistical pipeline issues are likely to occur. The theme of "being on the ground" and establishing a solid working relationship with Chinese suppliers is also discussed in greater detail in Appendix A.

10.3.8 Channel/Supply Chain Design: Ten Hats Are Better Than One

Cross-functional involvement in supply chain and channel design between internal functions, suppliers, and functional groups is critical. The most obvious example of this is the generic automotive product development process in North America; the design of the vehicle is frozen at least 24 months before start of production. This restriction is partly required because of the detailed production parts approval process mandated for safety reasons, as well as the existing sequential handoffs that occur during the process. The problem in most cases, however, is that purchasing, logistics, and order fulfillment personnel typically have no input into the design until shortly before this deadline — when the decisions have already been made. How much leverage do these people have in altering the direction of a locomotive that is speeding along at 80 mph on a track that has already been laid two years earlier?

10.3.9 People Are Strange When You Are a Stranger: Geographic Differences

Understanding geographic differences, particularly in the retail industry, can make the difference between a successful and unsuccessful merchandising strategy. Once a product is on the shelf, it is too late. These decisions must be made earlier. Channel design decisions in merchandising have dramatic impacts, but once the product is on the shelf, it is a lot harder to get rid of or sell at a discount; the decisions are a lot less costly to reverse if made earlier in the customer channel design and merchandise process. Analysis of a single product family identified gross discrepancies across price points in terms of inventory turns versus units sold. This data had to be manually extracted from the system; today, the retailer is seeking ways to allow store managers to download this data themselves, to allow them to make better merchandising decisions based on local geographic requirements.

10.3.10 Information Becomes Distorted

Remember the old game in which a word or phrase is whispered along a line of people and eventually becomes completely different when it reaches the final person in the linkage? This effect occurs with data passed through multiple organizations in a supply chain as well. In fact, a recent study by the SCRC examining forecasts developed by GM and passed backward through a textile supply chain consisting of Lear, Foamex, Textileather, and Milliken, found that although forecast error for Lear was between 5 and 20 percent, it degenerated to 22 percent at Foamex, 28 percent at Textileather, and up to 30 percent at Milliken. To overcome this issue, a shared 20-week forecast provided by GM to all parties in the supply chain was recommended.

10.4 Making the Transition from Strategic Sourcing to Relationship Management

The transition from a strategic sourcing team to a relationship management team is often a rocky road; thus, many teams will tend to avoid it directly. It is important to recognize that this transition is a formal process, which can be used to ensure that all of the different elements associated with change management, such as a new supplier or a new set of expectations, are closely monitored and that effective communication takes place throughout the process.

As shown in Figure 10.1, there are several groups associated with building and managing a buyer–seller relationship: the relationship management team, the functional sponsor, the relationship manager, the contract administrator, and the customer. The process basically falls into four major "chunks": organizing, operating, performance management, and continuous improvement. Let us review how this process takes place, and then we will delve into some of the chunks in more detail.

10.5 Organize the Relationship Management Team; Define the Vision

As shown in Figure 10.1, the transition from strategic sourcing to relationship management involves first establishing a relationship vision and a relationship team. The development of the vision and team charter should occur before the final contract negotiations and should be a direct outcome of the sourcing strategy developed in the position paper. The charter should describe the defined benefits, risks, and costs associated with the proposed relationship in light of the discovery and due-diligence findings from the supply market intelligence research. It should establish final key performance indicators (KPIs) for strategy It should also reflect the internal customer requirements discovered during the early stages of sourcing strategy development. Some of the most common of these are the following:

- Business unit and sourcing strategies for the end products or services should cover, at a minimum, business-unit-level needs in:
  - Cost/price reduction
  - Quality improvement
  - Delivery improvement
  - Product and process technology improvement
  - Reduction in concept-to-customer cycle time
  - Increased responsiveness
  - Other requirements, depending on the nature of product, commodity, or service
- It is important to review how the following requirements will be addressed for the internal customer:
  - Importance of the product to the buying firm
  - How and where the product is used by the firm
  - Price paid

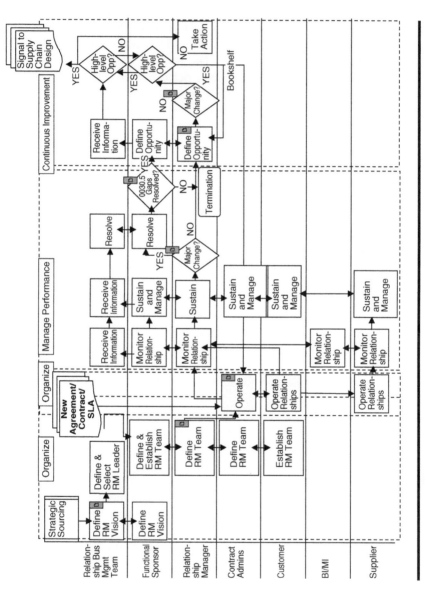

Figure 10.1 Relationship management.

- Product specifications
- Quality requirements
- Delivery requirements or scheduling information
- Packaging requirements
- Transportation requirements
- Substitution opportunities
- Standardization opportunities
- Volume requirements
- Expected design changes
- Likelihood of integration
- Other pertinent product-specific or service-specific information

Many of these issues may also come up in the form of specific contractual service-level agreements, or statements of work. It is important to explore these issues in detail and to involve the functional sponsor as well as the supplier in explicitly identifying the meaning of these elements.

In the past, performance was measured very narrowly: Were the costs reduced? Was the cycle time faster? The review was intrinsically one-dimensional. Yes, pass; no, fail. This binary analysis approach is not only overly simplistic and superficial, it rapidly deteriorates into an argument over details. Generally speaking, a team of key individuals who will be the direct recipients of the supplier's products or services should be established and involved in identifying the key metrics and elements for success. This should be done through the following approach:

- Step 1: Conduct cross-functional discussions and benchmarking to establish measures, measurement objectives, and performance targets.
- Step 2: Formalize measurement objectives into written policies and procedures.
- Step 3: Formally communicate measures and objectives to the supply base and key internal users.
- Step 4: Receive feedback from suppliers.
- Step 5: Modify, if necessary, performance measures and their objectives.
- Step 6: Implement final distribution of the measurement objective and process.
- Step 7: Collect and maintain performance data.

At one company, a core set of critical measures included the following:

Quality:
- Supplier defects in parts per million
- Internal manufacturing defects in parts per million

- Internal process capability (Cpk)
- Damage
- Number and cost of warranty claims

Price/Cost:

- Actual price versus market price comparisons
- Price/cost reductions
- Tooling cost management
- Transportation cost management

Cycle times

- New product development cycle time

Delivery and service

- Supplier on-time delivery

Inventory/Forecasting

- Total inventory dollar value over time
- Raw-material, work-in-process, and finished-goods inventory turns
- Forecast accuracy

Supplier quality performance was determined during on-site supplier visits and statistical inferences from product receipts. The frequency of calculation varies with each supplier's current quality levels. Suppliers with known quality problems or higher levels of defects are targeted for more frequent measurement.

10.6 The Case of Software Development and Proprietary Technology

Service requirements, especially in software development, may necessitate an entirely different approach. This is especially true if it involves the development of proprietary technology. If the nature of the sourcing agreement at least partially involves the development of proprietary technology, then the two companies will need to determine the respective allocations for patent ownership and funding, control over the technology, and returns on investment. The contract's confidentiality clause also assumes even greater significance in this type of scenario; be sure to include it. All of the key elements that could impact ownership of intellectual property need to be specifically communicated and discussed with the RM and the software vendor in detail prior to handoff by the strategic sourcing team. In software purchases, items that fall in the strategic/leverage quadrant typically require a high number of licenses, high maintenance, lengthy contracts, and a high degree of professional services such as consulting. Nonstandard, common contracts are typically low dollar with little maintenance, highly distributed, with shrink-wrapped terms, and few associated professional consulting services. Some of the factors considered in defining the statement of work and the contractual elements to be included are the following:

Contract execution
- Terms and conditions
- Strategies
- How much room is there for "give-and-take" in terms of defined deliverables?

Annual maintenance
- Specify exactly what the maintenance budget will be and what the exact level of support will be. This should define the labor class, availability, any added charges, etc. Do you want 8 to 5, or 24/7?
- Will annual maintenance be a professional service, and how much of it will be separated from the level of implementation support during the start-up phase.

Acceptance of work
- Revenue recognition — How and when will payments be made based on what final deliverables are provided by the vendor?
- Statement of work — Be as specific and accurate as possible. Be sure to define what is acceptable and what is not in terms of final scope of work and features to be developed.
- Scalability — Will it be an application, a utility, a desktop feature, or a data warehouse? All of these have different scope elements associated with deployment, implementation support, and postsales support.

Reviews and approvals
- How many licenses do you need? Will this software be used by a small group or across the entire organization? Is there a fee for every license or a single fee?
- Will a test product or an actual scalable product be delivered?
- What level of disaster recovery is provided by the vendor?
- What is the expected volume of work associated with delivering the product, and what are the deadlines for completion?
- Insurance, audits of performance, information security, and corporate communication channels need to be established.

Past-execution support and monitoring
- What is the intellectual property, and who owns in (including residuals)?
- Ownership of works made for hire
- Warranties and representations (beyond defined documentation)

- Term licenses versus perpetual
- Escrow
- Remedies and dispute resolution
- License fees
- Maintenance fees

10.7 Define the Relationship Management Leader, the Team, and the Change-Management Strategy

Once the charter has been defined, every agreement should have a scope that clearly defines the nature of the relationship management channels. Who is going to be the direct line of communication and the leader responsible for resolving issues as they arise? Who will define the means for managing the relationship when there are conflicts? The scope should include deliverables, deadlines, and budget. The scope should also state whether rewards and penalties will be used and if profit is going to be put at risk. It should also describe how a major scope change is to be handled. In some cases of major scope changes, the agreement can be renegotiated. The scope also needs to include nondisclosure statements to address how this situation will be handled to protect the purchasing company's interest. Finally, the scope needs to include statements as to who has control over the people once the contract is signed. Many of the issues regarding the individuals who will form the sourcing team (considered in Chapter 3) also apply to establishing the relationship management team.

One company we interviewed stated that when sourcing from a supplier they have not used previously, they develop a very detailed project scope. However, if they are using a preferred supplier, the individual project scopes will be limited. This may be due to their long-term relationships with suppliers that allow for work to be released with only a phone call.

10.7.1 Build Change-Management Strategy and Plan

Having established a scope for the relationship management team, the transition should also be carefully defined and managed. What will be the cutover policy from old suppliers to new ones? How will obsolete inventory and materials be dealt with? What is the communication plan — with suppliers, internal users, accounts payable, invoicing, etc? Think of all the people who could possibly be impacted by a change from the old supplier to a new one. In particular, communicate change orders, specifications and specific elements regarding delivery, quality, service, and other elements that are important to the end user. The devil is truly in the details on these issues; the specific requirements written in a contract may mean many different things to different people. In the earlier example in which a large retailer needed a 5-hr discussion with key stakeholders to determine what the term "on-time arrival" actually meant in the firm's data dictionary, it was found that "arrive" in various contexts meant one of the following:

- Arrive final destination — port of destination
- Received into inventory
- Arrive load port
- Arrive destination port
- Unloaded from container
- Out-gate to consignee
- Wheels down
- Portion of shipment received
- Last item of shipment received

The problem of data definition inconsistencies is one of only several major miscommunication pitfalls. Others mentioned by Miles (see Subsection 10.3.6) include:

- Location and code disparities in which different supply-chain member organizations use different sets of codes.
- Time-zone reconciliation from disparate systems (e.g., What does "ready for pick-up at 4:00 p.m." really mean?)
- The nonlinear relationships and hierarchies between supply-chain documents across different parties provide endless opportunities for error (e.g., shipment line items aligning with bills of lading, purchase orders, purchase order line items).
- Source system data quality is often poor in terms of timeliness, accuracy, and completeness.
- Data does not meet operational requirements ("I need to know the contents of specific containers on a line-item basis, but my ERP system does not provide that level of detail.")
- Data is not available when managers need it ("I need to know if my order is being shipped on time, but I do not receive the information until 48 hr after the goods have been shipped.")

The solution to many of these data problems lies in attributing meaning to data in face-to-face meetings prior to automating that aspect of the relationship. Supply-chain participants need to conduct data definition summits in which business and technology owners from all source information systems agree to common data definitions for all data exchanged. Participants need to meet and select "common denominators" for real operational events, which ultimately means translating events into consistent definitions. Once agreed upon, the participants should then publish data definition guidelines and a data dictionary. The data dictionary should be reviewed periodically to ensure that it is current and accurate. Business rules for interpreting data based on shared knowledge of trading partners' systems are also important. When data quality at the source is an issue, participants need to "scrub" the data to ensure that it is accurate and complete. When system constraints prevent data from being consistent, expectations regarding timelines and alerts for missing data need to be established. Information systems are required to effectively link supply-chain member organizations, and they will allow a level of automation in the relationship to be realized. However, the need for face-to-face discussions as well as ongoing communication to develop and implement these information systems should be understood.

The RM team should also understand the elements of change that will be required to deploy the new sourcing relationship across the business, especially the elements of communication. It may also be important to explain to people why the change is necessary. Kotter (1996) recommends the following approaches:

- Increase urgency:
  - Show examples of waste or opportunities to relevant people.
  - Describe weaknesses of the current situation, what would happen without change, and how change will create improvements and benefits.
  - Include visualization — graphs and presentations, preferably. Be as specific and detailed as possible.
- Build the guiding team:
  - Describe the guiding team and give the reasons why these people were chosen.
  - Ensure that it is a team of people with credibility, skills, connections, reputations, and formal authority.
- Get the vision right:
  - Describe the vision created by the guiding team.
  - Ensure that the guiding team creates sensible, clear, simple, and uplifting visions.
  - If necessary, use concepts and techniques to create vision.
- Communicate for buy-in:
  - Develop a communication matrix with timelines that incorporate results of adoption curve analysis to create buy-in and ensure long-term motivation.

- Recognize that the goal is to induce understanding, develop a gut-level commitment, and liberate more energy from a critical mass of people; symbols speak loudly, and repetition is the key.
■ Empower action:
  - Describe risks and obstacles, as well as measures to overcome them.
  - Understand that the issue here is removing obstacles and not giving power.
■ Create short-term wins:
  - Describe short-term wins, focus on those that have a high possibility of success.
  - Remember that wins are critical to provide credibility, resources, and momentum to the overall effort.
■ Do not let up:
  - Multiply short-term wins to create momentum; create wave after wave of change until the vision is a reality.
  - Remember, momentum builds after the first wins, and early changes are consolidated.
■ Make change stick:
  - Describe how you will make change stick (handover, sustain processes, etc.).
  - Nurture a new culture through appropriate promotions, skillful new-employee orientation, and events that engage emotions.

10.8 Operate the Relationship

Once the contract has been turned over to the relationship management team and leader, it is important to periodically assess the impact that the recommended sourcing strategy has had on operations and in meeting the project's mission. There will typically be many bumps in the road during the initial period despite the best-laid change-management plans. If the relationship management team has not taken adequate time to promote their program, communicate the changes, and define the scope of the changes, then the mission would inevitably fail, resulting in a failure spiral, as shown in Figure 10.2.

The transformation can be challenged by any number of different elements that can hit right at the roots of the change-management team, or escalate up to middle management and executive sponsors. Some of these challenges that may occur early in the relationship management process include the following:

■ Scope crisis: The nature of the changes required escalate far beyond the initial scope of the proposed changes to the new suppliers.

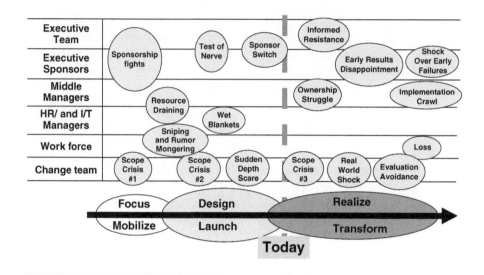

Figure 10.2   Why business transformation initiatives fail.

The changes now go beyond the impact that a single relationship management team can handle and escalate into multiple problems affecting multiple functional and business units.

- Sniping and rumor mongering: As the changes associated with scope creep and poor communication get worse, rumors start to fly, and fingers begin to be pointed in every direction.
- Resource draining: Middle managers called in to resolve these problems and mend fences find that they are being drawn into the minutiae of the conflicts and are having their time taken away from major projects on which they have been tasked to add value. HR and IT people also find themselves caught in the crossfire and become scapegoats and wet blankets for all the problems.
- Sponsorship issues: Executive sponsors may feel they are on a losing team because of the rumors and may switch their positions or even attempt to sabotage the effort.

Once the relationship management team has taken over the ownership of the supply arrangement from the strategic sourcing team, a whole set of other ugly issues may raise their heads:

- Ownership struggles: Additional scope creep occurs. Internal battles may rage over who is responsible for working with the supplier and communicating expectations and other information.
- Informed resistance: The executive team may be aware of the start-up problems and issues and may tacitly ignore them, or even

worse, deny that they exist, hoping that they will go away on their own.

■ Disappointment over results: As the early wins predicted for the program do not materialize, executives who are disappointed and at a loss to explain why they have not occurred face the wrath of the corporate council.

■ Shock over failures: These early disappointments lead to shouting and further finger-pointing. The situation becomes more tense, and the potential for a total failure of the relationship and sourcing team becomes evident.

This spiral can be avoided if many of the early elements of the relationship are established prior to the "operate" segment of the relationship. Part of the importance of designing the relationship management process lies in identifying the processes to be used when conflict occurs (as it inevitably will). This is described in the next section.

10.9 Manage Performance, Monitor Relationships

The only way to effectively manage a relationship is to monitor and measure supplier performance at regular intervals and provide feedback to your suppliers based on the performance metrics discussed during the negotiation stage. This is a two-way street, as some of the performance failures may be due to internal issues that originate from one or more individuals at the buying company. In effect, you are also asking suppliers to help your company with its developmental objectives; be willing to commit to helping them with theirs. Such aid can come in the form of colocation endeavors. Colocation involves housing some of your company's staff at the supplier's site and simultaneously housing some of the supplier's staff at your company's site to give both organizations the opportunity, at an empirical level, to learn about the issues and priorities that affect each.

Performance measurement is the first step of a new strategy called *supplier development* being deployed by many companies, which is closely related to relationship management. Supplier development is a bilateral effort by both the buying and supplying organization to jointly improve the supplier's performance or capabilities in one or more of the following areas: cost, quality, delivery, time to market, technology, managerial capability, financial viability, and environmental concern.

In employing this definition, it is important to identify the hierarchy of strategies that must be established prior to deployment of these practices. As shown in Figure 10.3, firms often begin the process of continuous

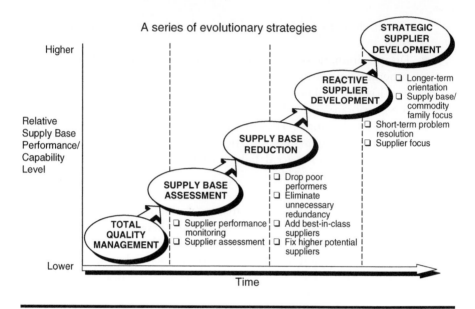

Figure 10.3   Evolution of supplier development strategies.

improvement through extensive internal programs to educate company and purchasing personnel in basic continuous-improvement principles. Quality department managers, using two- to three-day seminars, impart training on continuous improvement, customer satisfaction, basic statistics, and process capability. These initiatives later mature into a focus on the goal of assessing supplier performance. Organizations at this level realize that to improve material quality and performance, a history of supplier performance is necessary for effective decision making and sourcing strategy formulation in the future. Key measures of quality include percentage acceptable versus rejected lots, parts per million defective, warranty percentages, reliability, process capability ratios, percentage of parts rejected, and internal/external customer satisfaction. Practices also included developing a cooperative approach to setting specifications, listing of "problem" suppliers, definition of target quality levels, employing common measurement systems across strategic business units, and prequalifying suppliers.

Once assessed, companies often focus on consolidation of volumes with fewer suppliers to eliminate those suppliers incapable of meeting expectations. Supplier databases pinpoint those suppliers consistently unable to perform, resulting in fewer suppliers getting more of the business. This "first cut" of reducing the supply base is fairly easy to implement because nonperformance is identified once an assessment system is in place. Many of these practices were implemented during the 1980s and early 1990s. An evolution is outlined in Figure 10.3.

Although there are a wide array of problems that can occur in a supplier relationship, clearly establishing and measuring performance is a critical first step. Once the supplier is selected and the relationship is "kicked off," there are likely to be a series of small bumps that must be addressed on a day-to-day basis.

10.9.1 Making Changes

It is not uncommon that contract terms might need updating in light of changing circumstances. If, for example, after the contract is made, the specifications dictated by the functional sponsor change in such a way that additional costs may have to be incurred by the supplier, how should the RM handle the situation? Explore the idea of changing the contract! Talk to the supplier and explain the situation. Specifically, cite the changed circumstance and how it is impacting the scope of the contract. Explain how the contract, as it stands, no longer optimally aligns with the need. As always, be fair and equitable; do not go to the supplier every other month with a list of changes to be made to the contract. But if there are legitimate changes that were beyond anticipation, or even if there was an oversight (e.g., omitting a confidentiality clause), approach the supplier about it. Also, be sensitive to the supplier's situation, just as you would hope that he would be sensitive to yours. The supplier might not have the resources to be able to adjust the contract the way you would like. And if that is the case, sit down and brainstorm possible solutions that would work for both parties.

It is also important not to make contract changes too often (the initial contract should be well thought out in the first place). But sometimes, things do happen that are beyond our control and are not reasonably foreseeable. In these situations, it is perfectly reasonable to go back to the supplier and seek modification of the contract's terms.

If the RM asks the supplier to change deliverables, then a proposal to alleviate their concerns should also be offered. For example, if the initial order was for 1,000 widgets in exchange for $5,000, and the order increases to 2,000 widgets, then the price increases to $10,000, for example. Otherwise, the addendum order is deemed a gift and the law dictates that the seller is not obliged to perform, even if they signed the addendum. The legal rationale for this is that the supplier is simply choosing to confer a gift benefit to the buyer, and gifts are purely optional on the part of the giver; so the addendum order is not legally enforceable.

Mutually acceptable changes should be recorded in an addendum, cross-referenced to the altered term from the original contract, or specified if they are new and then described fully (keeping in mind the five mandated terms: parties, subject matter, price, quantity, and delivery).

10.9.2 Handling Problems

In any contractual relationship, some bumps are to be expected. Some are more serious than others. If a performance issue impacts the total cost of a supplier's product, the decision becomes whether to change suppliers or try to resolve the problem with the current supplier. Gauge this by assessing (1) the relationship with the supplier (How strategic are they? How compatible are they in terms of corporate culture?) and (2) the commodity's strategic value (refer to the portfolio analysis if there is some ambiguity). Performance metrics are critical in identifying the problems that need to be resolved. For instance:

> According to our computer tracking database, we have placed 17 separate service repair calls for copier breakdowns in the last month. And in the past year, we have placed a total of 221 service calls. This is a high ratio, and it causes problems at our end by having to wait for the copier to be repaired. We often have to work around the copier's functioning capability, instead of having it working around our copying needs. And we wondered if we might be able to work together in some way and assemble a team from both our companies to really address and resolve the problem.

If the supplier welcomes your recommendation, then often half the battle is won. A written action plan detailing the resolution and itemizing each party's responsibilities can become an addendum to the contract.

10.10 Common Problems

Common contract problems in supplier contracts consist of nonconforming goods and other types of nonperformance. These performance problems are collectively referred to in the legal field as breach of contract.

10.10.1 Cancellation of Orders and Breach of Contract

A good contract will protect the interests and rights of both buyer and seller. As a result, contractual obligations are equally binding upon both parties to the agreement. In some instances, however, one of the parties to a contractual arrangement may seek to cancel the agreement after it has been made. In other cases, the supplier simply fails to perform in the manner agreed upon in the contract. Under these conditions, the buyer will always go back to the original contract to determine potential remedies.

10.10.1.1 Cancellation of Orders

Contract cancellations can generally be classified into three categories: (1) cancellation for default, (2) cancellation for convenience of the purchaser (*anticipatory breach*), or (3) cancellation by mutual consent.

Cancellation for default can be defined as failure of one of the parties to live up to the terms and conditions of the contract. Supplier actions that can result in this type of breach of contract include late deliveries, failing to meet product specifications, or otherwise failing to perform in accordance with contractual provisions. The types of damages that might be awarded include production cost penalties, additional overtime, or expedited transportation costs. In actual practice, more effective settlements can be reached through negotiation with the supplier rather than through the litigation process.

Cancellation for the convenience of the purchaser, or anticipatory breach, makes the purchaser liable for any resulting injury to the supplier. A general rule here is that the supplier should not be called upon to incur any loss due to the purchaser's default. Generally speaking, purchasers should stay away from this term altogether in their purchase contracts. The term is highly interpretable in court and can result in any number of negative actions.

Cancellation by mutual consent indicates that cancellation of a previously agreed-upon contract does not automatically lead to legal action. If both parties mutually agree to terminate the agreement then they have, in effect, created another contract with the intent of nullifying the first agreement. If there is no potential loss, the supplier will often accept a purchaser's cancellation in good faith as a normal risk of doing business. Even when suppliers have purchased special components or materials in anticipation of fulfilling their responsibilities under the agreement, the parties can usually reach a mutually agreeable resolution through the process of negotiation rather than through litigation.

10.10.1.2 Breach of Contract

Under a commercial contract, the supplier is obligated to deliver the goods according to the contract's terms and conditions, and the purchaser is likewise obligated to accept and tender payment for the goods according to the terms of the agreement. A breach of contract occurs when either party fails to perform the obligations due under the contract without a valid or legal justification. A breach may entitle the offended party to certain remedies or damages.

Buyers should avoid the practice of routinely tolerating suppliers who breach purchase contracts. Doing so may result in the buyer forfeiting the right to legal action. If the purchaser has systematically accepted late deliveries from a supplier in the past and continues to accept late deliveries even though they must be expedited, then the company may have waived its right to pursue legal action for damages caused by late shipments. For example, to regain his or her legal rights, the buyer must give explicit written notice to the supplier and provide the supplier a reasonable period of time to gear up to meet the new delivery requirements. The new contract should also include the minimal lead time required for design changes, etc.

10.10.1.3 Damages

The concept of damages is based on the remedy of a party being "made whole." In other words, a purchaser who is damaged by a breach of contract must receive damages that bring the purchaser back to the position where he or she would have been if the breach had not occurred. Damages include either actual damages (which include losses that are real, known, or can reasonably be estimated), as well as punitive damages (extra money as "punishment" for the defendant's bad behavior). Normally, punitive damages are not allowed, even if such a provision is contained in the contract. There are essentially three types of damages available to the purchaser:

1. Restitution: money the plaintiff actually paid to the defendant in connection with the contract
2. Reliance: money the plaintiff lost because he or she was relying on the contract, i.e., depending on the defendant to live up to its obligations under the contract
3. Expectancy: money the plaintiff was hoping to gain from the contract

There are various methods of calculating damages. General damages are equal to the difference between the value of the purchased goods at the time of delivery and the goods' value at the time of specified delivery. Incidental damages include expenses reasonably incurred in inspection, receipt, transportation, and the care and custody of goods appropriately rejected by the purchaser. Consequential damages are those expenses incurred by the purchaser because the goods were not delivered when expected or as specified. Liquidation damages are those that result if the terms of the contract are not fulfilled and are typically defined prior to the breach under the terms of the contract.

It should be noted that attorney fees are not recoverable. Also, speculative damages and lost time of executives are not generally recoverable.

The bottom line is that a breach-of-contract lawsuit will rarely make the nonbreaching party completely whole again.

10.10.1.4 Acceptance and Rejection of Goods

The purchaser can accept part of a shipment and reject the remainder for cause, or accept or reject the entire shipment. After the point of acceptance, the supplier's rights increase and the purchaser's rights decrease. Once the purchaser accepts the goods, there is only one recourse: make a claim against the supplier. The purchaser does not have the legal right to withhold payment from the supplier once acceptance has been made. The purchaser also does not have the right at this point to send the goods back unless the supplier consents to this action.

The legal concept of acceptance is closely related to the concept of inspection. Purchasers have a legitimate right to inspect contracted goods before accepting or rejecting them, but the law is quite explicit when it states that the purchaser should accept the goods within a reasonable time whether or not the goods are physically inspected.

Obvious defects must be discovered and rejected within this reasonable timeframe, or the purchaser has no recourse against the seller. *Latent* defects are those that could not have been easily discovered during an inspection and do not fall under this rule. In certain limited situations, the purchaser is able to revoke an acceptance of delivered goods. A purchaser may revoke a prior acceptance if a problem is discovered that substantially impairs the value of the goods. Moreover, a purchaser can revoke a prior acceptance when a prior inspection could not take place for reasons not related to negligence on the part of the purchaser.

When the goods delivered by the supplier are actually rejected by the purchaser due to nonconformance, the purchaser must provide notice to the supplier within a reasonable period of time. The purchaser should be specific in notifying the supplier that it is in breach of contract. General statements about the problems at hand without stating that the supplier is considered in breach of contract are not adequate notification. The exact term "breach of contract" must be used, or the purchaser stands to lose his or her right to recourse from the supplier.

Once goods are accepted there are two obligations that the purchaser must meet to recover his or her rights. First, the purchaser must carry the burden of proof that the goods did not conform to the terms and conditions of the contract. Second, the purchaser must, within a reasonable time after the breach is discovered, notify the supplier of that breach or lose the chance for remedy.

Acceptance of the contracted goods by the purchaser means that ownership of the goods has been transferred. There are no rituals or formalities required to make the transfer of ownership. Any words or acts by the purchaser that provide an indication of the purchaser's intention to transfer ownership are enough to effect the transfer.

Even though the goods may have been formally rejected by the purchaser, actions typifying ownership may indicate that acceptance has instead been accomplished. To prevent or mitigate problems arising from the acceptance or rejection of goods, a number of steps to manage the acceptance process can be implemented by the purchaser (Hancock, 1986).

- The receiving department should stamp all receipts of goods with a statement such as, "Received subject to inspection, count, and testing."
- A thorough set of purchase order terms and conditions should indicate that all receipts from suppliers are subject to inspection, count, and testing.
- All delivered goods should be inspected as quickly as possible, ideally, immediately upon delivery.
- If goods are not inspected until they are used, it is a good idea to maintain a stock rotation system to ensure that older quantities of goods are used first.
- In some cases, purchasers may want to consider inserting language in their purchase order terms and conditions that defines the reasonable time for inspection and acceptance.
- An internal reporting system should be set up to ensure that defects encountered in the organization are reported to the purchasing department within a reasonable time so that remedies can be pursued.
- Contracts for such items as production equipment should contain a clause stating that acceptance will not be made until the equipment has been installed and run satisfactorily for a certain period of time.
- For hardware- and software-related contracts, the purchaser should carefully define the acceptance criteria and notify the supplier of the specific processes to which this equipment and software will be subjected.

10.10.1.5 Honest Mistakes

Sometimes, in spite of the best efforts of the purchaser and the supplier, honest mistakes occur when parties draw up a purchase agreement. In such instances, careful consideration of all the circumstances is necessary to determine whether the resulting contract is valid or invalid. Generally, honest mistakes by a single party to the contract will not void the contract. If the other party was truly unaware of the mistake, then the contract is still intact. Mistakes made by both parties do not necessarily affect the validity of the contract.

Parties must rely on traditional contract law to solve any dispute resulting from a mistake. "As a general rule, a party will not be given relief against a mistake induced by his or her own negligence. But the rule is not inflexible, and in many cases, relief may be granted although the mistake involved some element of negligence, particularly when the other party has been in no way prejudiced" (Hancock, The Law of Purchasing, 1986). The rules for determining whether or not a contract exists after a mistake has been made are the basic fairness rules. The judicial system will more than likely allow a supplier to be absolved from the contract owing to a mistake if the supplier gave the purchaser notification of the mistake before the purchaser relied on the bid. Buyers should therefore attempt to minimize the occurrence of contractual mistakes.

10.10.2 Dispute Resolution

Disputes can be systemically avoided or mitigated by following the good contract development practices discussed earlier and by consistently practicing good relationship skills (be clear, be fair, be considerate). But even so, parties might have disagreements over the course of the contract relationship/period. Some disagreements are relatively minor, usually due to functional and operational tensions or frustrations. Some disagreements can be nipped in the bud by holding frequent and frank discussions, and by regular, open communications. Some disagreements cannot be so easily set aside. In these cases, more severe actions might be required.

10.10.3 Collections

Another option is charge-backs, or collections for nonperformance. Consider the type of relationship with the supplier and the extent of the nonperformance. If the nature of the breach is substantial and the situation warrants switching to another supplier, instigate collections for nonperformance. If initiating collection proceedings, it might be prudent to consult with your company's legal department.

10.10.4 Continuous Improvement of the Relationship

In cases of supplier non-performance, instead of legal means, many companies are turning to a strategy known as supplier development. Results from a large-scale survey of over 500 supplier development efforts by Krause (1994) indicate that respondents found supplier development

Criteria	Before Supplier Development	After Supplier Development
Incoming defects	11.65%	5.45%
% on-time delivery	79.85%	91.02%
Cycle time (from order placement to receipt)	35.74 days	23.44 days
% orders received complete	85.47%	93.33%

Figure 10.4   Supplier development results.

results (measured as supplier performance before the development effort versus after) that included:

- Reductions in incoming defects by 6.2 percent
- Improvement in on-time delivery by 21 percent
- Reductions in order-to-delivery cycle time by 12 days
- Improvement in orders received complete by 8 percent

However, results (shown in Figure 10.4) also suggested that not all of the buyers surveyed were satisfied with the outcomes of their supplier development efforts. Moreover, some supplier development efforts actually resulted in deterioration in the level of satisfaction (Figure 10.5). This was particularly true with respect to supplier performance in product innovation and ability to reduce total cost. A supplier development manager at Chrysler noted that:

> Some suppliers do not respond after multiple interventions. Even though they are "saying the right things," nothing happens. Involvement with suppliers spans between 6 months and 1.5 years on average. During 80 percent of the time, there are significant performance improvements. In 20 percent of the cases, there are none.

So what explains these differences? In many cases, it is the approach to relationship management used to manage performance and continuously improve the relationship.

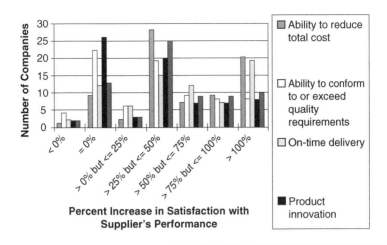

Figure 10.5   Satisfaction with supplier development results.

10.11   Strategic versus Reactive Approaches to Supplier Development

In 1996, a research effort was initiated through the Global Procurement and Supply Chain Benchmarking Initiative, focusing on supplier development best practices. This research studied written responses from 84 companies to questions regarding supplier development practices, as well as responses to a survey.

As shown in Figure 10.6, companies employed a diverse set of supplier development strategies. Moreover, these approaches can be classified into supplier-specific improvement projects or efforts to improve the capabilities of the entire supply base. Further, initiatives either focused on product-level or process-level improvements.

Companies reporting in the study were classified as belonging in one of two categories: those firms focusing on *strategic supplier development* or *reactive supplier development*. The former group of 50 companies was focused on actively concentrating efforts on improving the long-term capabilities of suppliers of the most important commodities, whereas 34 companies with reactive supplier development strategies adopted an ad hoc response to eliminating supplier deficiencies.

As can be seen in Figure 10.7, companies employing a strategic approach to supplier development often focused on improving capabilities of the entire supply base, and then "funneled" these efforts into supplier-specific improvements. On the other hand, reactive companies typically reacted to major deficiencies that arose as a result of a crisis situation (described by one manager as a "burning platform"!)

Specific techniques/tools/activities that firms employ in supplier development vary. The following framework organizes supplier development:

	PRODUCT FOCUS	PROCESS FOCUS	
Supply Base Management Activities	❏ Supplier awareness ❏ Supply base reduction ❏ Cost savings programs ❏ Supplier suggestion programs ❏ New product development information sharing ❏ Technology sharing ❏ Part level qualification databases	❏ Supplier Quality Assurance programs ❏ Supplier Councils ❏ Quality audits ❏ ISO 9000 ❏ Information system developments ❏ EDI/planning systems	**Provides for Overall Supply Base Improvement**
Supplier Development Activities	❏ New product development teams ❏ Sharing forecasts with suppliers ❏ Value analysis teams ❏ Cost savings projects ❏ Developing full service supplier capabilities ❏ Co-location	❏ Buyer-supplier alignment ❏ Process mapping ❏ Quality engineering work teams ❏ Joint cost savings sharing projects ❏ Supplier training ❏ Supplier certification ❏ Supplier continuous improvement ❏ Joint improvement efforts	**Provides for Specific Buyer/Supplier Improvement**

Figure 10.6   Approaches to supplier development.

❏ Differentiating factors: Reactive versus Strategic Supplier Development

DIFFERENTIATING FACTORS	STRATEGIC SUPPLIER DEVELOPMENT	REACTIVE SUPPLIER DEVELOPMENT
Primary Situation/Question	❏ Are resources available to develop supply base? ❏ Where should resources be allocated for best cost/benefit?	❏ What is needed to correct specific problem?
Primary Objective	❏ Continuous improvement of supply base	❏ Remedial ❏ Correction of supplier deficiency
Scope	❏ Supply base ❏ Supplier development *program* ❏ On-going	❏ Single supplier ❏ Supplier development project ❏ Ad hoc

Figure 10.7   Strategic versus reactive supplier development.

Figure 10.8 shows some of the other major differences between reactive and strategic supplier development approaches. Strategic supplier development approaches focus on allocating resources for supplier improvement with the objective of continuously improving the supply base in the long term. This process is undertaken by an executive-level assessment

❏ Differentiating factors: Reactive versus Strategic Supplier Development (cont.)

DIFFERENTIATING FACTORS	STRATEGIC SUPPLIER DEVELOPMENT	REACTIVE SUPPLIER DEVELOPMENT
Selection/Prioritization Process	❏ Portfolio analysis ❏ Pareto analysis of commodity/supplier ❏ Market driven	❏ Supplier "self selects" by being in non-conformance ❏ Problem-driven
Time Frame	❏ Long-term	❏ Short-term
Drivers of Supplier Development (examples)	❏ Supplier integration ❏ Supply chain optimization ❏ Continuous improvement ❏ Value-added collaboration ❏ Buying firm's competitive strategy ❏ Customer/market driven ❏ Competitive advantage	❏ Delivery dates missed ❏ Quality defects ❏ Negative customer feedback ❏ Competitive threat for buying firm ❏ Production disruptions ❏ Change in make/buy decision

Figure 10.8   Strategic versus reactive supplier development (cont'd).

of critical commodities and suppliers, followed by a focused improvement carried out by a commodity or development team.

Respondents were asked (using an open-ended question) to identify the five most important circumstances, events, or requirements that would be classified as drivers for supplier development. Table 10.1 shows the percentage of respondents within a specific classification (strategic or reactive) that identified the associated driver. For example, 16 of the 50 firms classified as "strategic" identified the goal of developing a strategic partnership as a key driver of their development efforts. The "Diff" column represents the difference between the two groups.

By examining the upper and lower quartiles of the differences between strategic and reactive companies' key drivers (shaded areas), the differences in the focus of their development efforts emerge. Firms employing a strategic approach to development are more likely to be driven by the proactive need for strategic partnering, technology development, and a focused effort to improve performance of high-volume critical commodities that have a major impact on the business. Reactive firms are more likely to be applying "remedial" approaches for suppliers that represent an immediate crisis or "burning platform."

Respondents also identified the total number of suppliers currently involved in development programs by choosing the category that best described their situation. Table 10.2 indicates that strategic companies

Table 10.1 Drivers for Supplier Development: Survey

Driver	Strategic (n = 50) Percentage	Reactive (n = 34) Percentage	Diff. Percentage
Strategic partnership	32	15	17
Technology	34	24	10
Amount or criticality of business	10	3	7
Standardization	4	3	1
Price/cost	64	65	−1
Lead time/delivery/process reduction	34	35	−1
Competitive advantage	2	3	−1
Minority/small-supplier development	6	9	−3
Volume/quantity/capacity	10	18	−8
Quality	62	79	−17
Supplier service/support	6	24	−18
Customer service/feedback	14	38	−24

Note: The "Diff" column indicates the difference between the two groups.

became involved in the development of a wider segment of the supply base (in a majority of cases, 50 or more suppliers). Reactive companies generally focused on a smaller group of suppliers. These summary statistics lead us to believe that reactive companies are in some cases still in the process of "rightsizing" their supply base, in eliminating poorly performing suppliers.

A manager at Chrysler noted the following:

> Supplier development has been talked about for a number of years at Chrysler, but in my opinion, this was largely lip service. Only recently has the company actually implemented development as a formal activity. Up to now, 80 to 90 percent of supplier development has been reactive in nature, and 10 to 20 percent, strategic. Chrysler's objective is to reverse this ratio, so that 60 percent is strategic and 40 percent, reactive. This can be achieved by anticipating (proactively) problems before they occur by getting involved in advanced quality processes early in the new product development cycle.

Table 10.2 Strategic Company Involvement

Number of Suppliers Currently Involved in Development Programs	Strategic (n = 47) Percentage	Reactive (n = 34) Percentage	Diff. Percentage
0–5	10.6	17.6	–7.0
6–10	8.5	8.8	–0.3
11–15	6.4	17.6	–11.2
16–20	6.4	0.0	6.4
21–25	10.6	8.8	1.8
26–30	4.3	11.9	–7.6
31–50	8.5	8.8	–0.3
>50	44.7	26.5	18.2
Total	100	100	

Note: The "Diff" column indicates the difference between the two groups.

10.12 Supplier Development: A Strategy for Improvement

Supplier development is any activity undertaken by a purchaser to improve a supplier's performance or capabilities to meet the purchaser's short- and long-term supply needs. Organizations rely on a variety of activities to improve supplier performance, including sharing technology, providing incentives to suppliers for improved performance, instigating competition among suppliers, providing capital, and direct involvement of personnel with suppliers through activities such as training (Krause and Handfield, 1999).

Direct involvement of personnel is undoubtedly the most challenging part of supplier development. Not only must internal management and employees be convinced that investing company resources in a supplier is a worthwhile risk, but the supplier must also be convinced it is in its best interest to accept direction and assistance. Even if a mutual under-standing of the importance of supplier development is reached, there is still the matter of making it happen. Effective supplier development requires the commitment of financial, capital, and human resources, skilled personnel, sharing of timely and accurate information between the purchaser and supplier, and timely performance measurement.

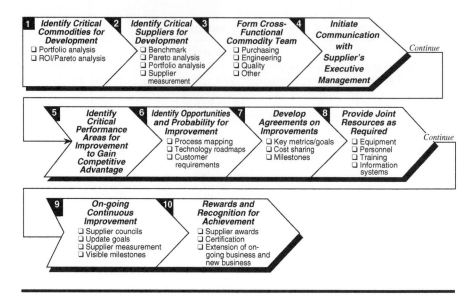

Figure 10.9   Strategic supplier development process.

10.12.1 Strategic Supplier Development Process

As noted earlier, the primary differentiator between the strategic and reactive approach is a focus on identifying critical commodities and suppliers requiring development, with the driver being a strategic intent to improve the overall performance of the supply base. The following section describes a process model developed to describe activities used by leading-edge companies in deploying a proactive, strategic approach to supplier development.

In the process shown in Figure 10.9, we differentiate between executive-level and commodity-team-level decisions. The initial steps in the process (steps 1 and 2) are typically carried out by an executive-level team and are often driven by a corporate-level procurement/supply strategic plan. The remaining steps, involving specific commodity and supplier development approaches, are typically formulated, implemented, and monitored by a cross-functional commodity team, and often involve dedicated supplier development personnel.

Once a development project has been initiated, progress must be monitored and tracked over time. Moreover, an ongoing exchange of information is needed to maintain momentum in such projects. This can be achieved by creating visible milestones for objectives, updating progress, and in turn, creating new or revised objectives based on progress to date. Project planning may require modifications to the original plan, additional resources, information, or priorities depending on events.

Table 10.3   Supplier Performance

Performance Area	Strategic (n = 50) Percentage	Reactive (n = 34) Percentage	Diff. Percentage
Order fulfillment cycle time	74	50	24
Inventory turns	66	47	19
Inventory obsolescence	50	32	18
Logistics performance	56	38	18
Process productivity	62	44	18
New product/process/service development time	64	47	17
Quality	90	76	14
Product/service cost	88	74	14
Employee satisfaction	38	24	14
On-time delivery performance	84	71	13
Total supply-chain costs	68	56	12
Customer satisfaction	64	53	11
Technology continuity	44	35	9

Note: The "Diff" column indicates the difference between the two groups.

Both strategic and reactive firms used formal supplier certification or supplier recognition programs in their development efforts. Approximately 69 percent of the strategic firms and 73 percent of the reactive firms use formal supplier certification or supplier recognition programs. However, the results in Table 10.3 show that strategic companies achieved higher performance relative to prior performance levels for their most successful development initiative, and were better able to identify suppliers requiring improvement in areas such as cycle time, quality, total cost, delivery, customer services, and responsiveness.

In all cases, strategic firms achieve a wider range of benefits more frequently than reactive firms. This may indicate that strategic firms are focusing development efforts across the supply base and are better at actively identifying, with supplier involvement, all of the issues that need to be addressed using a systematic approach.

Leading companies have successfully maintained momentum through a variety of mechanisms, including supplier participation on supplier councils, internal and external newsletters, and communication of key results via supplier performance reports.

10.13 CAPS Global Supplier Development Study

In 1997, research effort was carried out by Robert Handfield and Daniel Krause and funded by the Center for Advanced Purchasing Studies (CAPS) and the Center for International Business Education Research (CIBER). The primary thrust of this study was to compare buying firms' supplier development efforts across countries and across industries. Specifically, the research sought to compare buying firms' supplier development efforts in the United States with buying firms' supplier development efforts in the United Kingdom, Japan, and South Korea in the automotive and electronics industries. The focus of the research was on the following question: What are firms in the United States, United Kingdom, Japan, and South Korea in the automotive and electronics industries doing to effectively improve their suppliers' performance to world-class levels? These industries were chosen because they are generally characterized by high rates of competition, high rates of technological change, and high levels of reliance on suppliers. The firms participating in this research are shown in Table 10.4.

Table 10.4   Firms Participating in CAPS Research

Automotive:	*Electronics:*
BMW (United States)	Hewlett-Packard (Scotland)
Chrysler Corporation (United States)	Hitachi (Japan)
Daewoo (Korea)	IBM
Honda of America (United States)	(United States/United Kingdom)
Honda Motor Corporation (Japan)	Intel (United States)
Hyundai (Korea)	LG (Korea)
Isuzu (Japan)	NCR (United States)
Kikuchi (Japan)	NEC (Japan)
Kia (Korea)	Samsung (Korea)
Lean Enterprise Research Center	Siemens (Korea)
(United Kingdom)	Solectron
Nissan (Japan)	(United States/United Kingdom)
Plastics Engineering (United Kingdom)	Sony (Japan)
Prince Corporation (United States)	Scottish Enterprises
Rolls Royce (United Kingdom)	(United Kingdom)
Rover (United Kingdom)	Sun Microsystems
Unipart (United Kingdom)	(United Kingdom)
Varity Perkins (United Kingdom)	
Welsh Development Agency	
(United Kingdom)	

This international research was driven by the need to better understand supplier development in a global context. With the advent of this global era, the rallying cry of organizations has now become: "To compete globally, buy globally!" A common term that is used to reflect this change is *localization*. Localization refers to the capability of an organization to identify and develop a supply base in the markets in which it sells or produces. This strategy is employed for a number of reasons, such as the following:

- Cost of transportation prohibits importing from current supply base in home country.
- Government regulations in the Triad regions (NAFTA, EC, and AFTA) require higher levels of domestic content.
- Companies need to capture superior supplier capabilities in the areas of cost, quality, speed, or technology regardless of where the supplier is located.
- There is a need to configure products or services to meet local customer needs.

Whatever the reason, many organizations are seeking to develop a globally aligned world-class supply base that not only enables localization of product or service requirements, but can create a competitive advantage in terms of cost, quality, delivery, and technology.

Unfortunately, a great number of barriers lie in store for the purchasing executive seeking to deploy a global supplier development initiative. Although many of the processes for developing a local supply base are well documented, the processes required to deploy this strategy in a global environment are often not well understood.

In the CAPS report, the authors provide a process model that can aid managers in developing world-class suppliers in all corners of the world. The model is illustrated with best practices derived from case interviews and is supported with additional insights from a survey questionnaire. The model is broad enough to be applied to any industry (product or service related), yet must be interpreted and adapted to the reader's unique industry and organizational characteristics. The description of the process model is followed by three cases that provide further insights into the supplier development process. A summary of the results from this research report is provided here.

The primary purpose of this study was to investigate supplier development in terms of its use for companies that are striving to build an integrated and globally aligned network of suppliers. In doing so, the researchers sought to define the processes companies use to build a globally aligned network of suppliers. Some background questions that were used to initiate the study included:

1. Why is supplier development important? What are the drivers of these efforts? What is the ultimate goal of firms' supplier development efforts?
2. How do supplier development initiatives differ in various international regions?
3. Do supplier development efforts vary based on the goal of the effort?
4. How do buying firms and suppliers benefit from supplier development?
5. What are specific barriers to supplier development in an international context?

The focus of this research report is a model that resembles the process being followed, as a whole, by a group of case-study companies striving to build a globally aligned network of suppliers. The model is depicted in Figure 10.10. Certainly not all the case-study companies had achieved a globally aligned network of suppliers. In fact, not a single case-study company had successfully completed all of the steps in the process model across their entire supply base. Some companies had completed the process in selected regions of their supply base. Most of the interviewees noted that such a network represented the ultimate objective for their organization as they managed and sought to improve their unique set of suppliers.

Building the supplier development process model required a broad view of the case-study companies' practices and a clear idea of which companies were best at accomplishing a particular step within the model. This report incorporates descriptions of companies' best practices to illustrate the specific steps in the model. Although the researchers would remind the reader that no company had successfully negotiated every step in the model provided in Figure 10.10, many of the companies made similar statements about where their supplier development activities must culminate: a globally aligned supply base.

10.13.1 Key Findings

Before purchasing organizations become involved in supplier development, other supply base management practices such as supplier evaluation and supply base rationalization should already have been deployed. In addition, the company should be able to demonstrate effective internal processes and capabilities. Asking suppliers to adopt practices and techniques

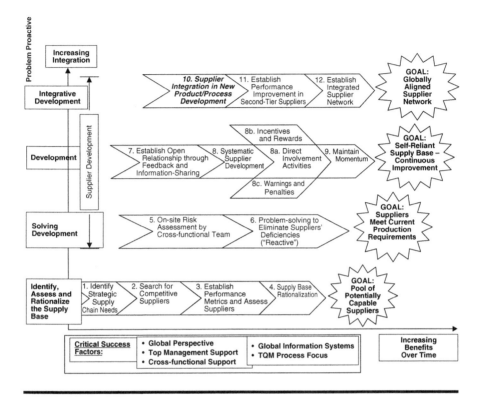

Figure 10.10   Supplier development model.

that the buying firm itself has not adopted will only result in a loss of credibility with suppliers.

The model in Figure 10.10 depicts the four major stages in developing a globally aligned supplier network. The four stages incorporate a number of intermediate steps:

10.13.1.1 Step 1: Identify Strategic Supply-Chain Needs

The first step involves the identification of a need for improved supplier performance. This need should be explicitly identified and aligned with end-customer requirements and new product development targets. Such needs are driven by customers' product-specific demands in areas such as cost, quality, delivery, technology and similar objectives, and broader needs in the areas of competitive priorities, global competition, and supply base deficiencies. It is important that cross-functional executive input occurs at this stage of the process because the objective here is to identify the overall business needs in terms of cost reduction goals, technology road maps, global market expansion plan, and so on.

10.13.1.2 Step 2: Search for Competitive Suppliers

This stage involves a worldwide search for competitive suppliers based on the criteria established in step 1. Once a targeted global region is identified, a focused search in the region of interest is carried out. This targeted search is often facilitated and carried out in conjunction with local government agencies or partners within the region.

10.13.1.3 Step 3: Establish Performance Metrics and Assess Suppliers

Companies typically established a performance measurement system to assess and track suppliers' performance over an extended period. Ideally, this should be a real-time system providing immediate feedback to the supplier.

10.13.1.4 Step 4: Rationalize the Supply Base

As a function of the search and assessment, suppliers that are clearly not capable of meeting the company's needs are eliminated and the supply base is optimized. The outcome of this strategy is a pool of suppliers that are potentially capable of meeting the purchasing organization's need for products and services.

10.13.1.5 Step 5: On-Site Risk Assessment by Cross-Functional Team

Step 5 represents the first step in a series of true "supplier development" processes. Once a pool of suppliers has been identified, performance metrics are established in the following areas: cost, quality, delivery, cycle time, product and process technology, engineering capabilities, and management skills. A detailed risk assessment of suppliers by a cross-functional team of specialists is performed. This team should spend several days with each supplier and should note suppliers' deficiencies and weaknesses as well as their strengths.

10.13.1.6 Step 6: Problem Solving to Eliminate Suppliers' Deficiencies

This step involves remedial action to correct suppliers' deficiencies. In effect, this brings suppliers' performance up to the minimum level necessary to serve the firm as a supplier. Once all immediate problems are resolved, the outcome is a supply base that is capable of meeting current requirements. In some cases, suppliers are deficient, but the deficiency does not interfere with immediate production requirements. For example, suppliers may lack effective measures or engineering capability, or they may have process inefficiencies. These problems are noted and targeted for improvement on a longer-term horizon.

10.13.1.7 Step 7: Establish Open Relationship through Feedback and Information Sharing

This step precedes proactive development of the supplier's capabilities and is initiated by establishing an open dialogue with the supplier's top management. It is here that the "future-action-required" items (from step 5) are revisited and brought to management's attention.

10.13.1.8 Step 8: Systematic Supplier Development through the Use of Direct-Involvement Activities, Incentives and Rewards, and Warnings and Penalties

Techniques for supplier improvement projects may include kaizen breakthroughs, process mapping, inventory reductions, training, total preventive maintenance, and other joint projects. These techniques are complemented by the use of award programs and increased business for the best suppliers, which serve as incentives for improved performance. Other techniques include introducing competition for the company's business and taking business away from poor performers.

At this step, a different combination of approaches may need to be adopted, depending on the specific set of circumstances with any given supplier. This is particularly true when dealing with global suppliers in different parts of the world. The same supplier may have a very different set of issues at a U.S. plant as opposed to a German or Japanese plant, requiring a completely different approach. One executive we interviewed at BMW (see Appendix B) emphasized this:

> In the case of BMW in the United States, a very different approach was required. In Germany, the plants are established, and they have a group of suppliers who have a given level of understanding with respect to what we want. Here, however, communication with domestic suppliers requires sharing and a hands-on-support attitude. We have to spend time asking them,

"What is your corrective action plan, and we will check on you from time to time." We need to suggest possible ways to put solutions in place — Which actions are more beneficial in a start-up phase?

At Honda (see Appendix B), a similar issue was noted by one manager we interviewed in Japan:

Unfortunately, there are very few cases of truly global suppliers. For instance, R&D is very efficient in Japanese suppliers, but these same suppliers may not be effective at R&D in a different location. Thus, it is very seldom that they find a supplier that can supply multiple locations, yet locating these suppliers is one of Honda's most important development strategies. Finding good suppliers to serve both the United States and Japan is not a problem; few suppliers, however, have truly global capabilities.

10.13.1.9 Step 9: Maintain Momentum

Appropriate incentives for improvement should be developed to ensure that the improvement effort is not limited to a single process. The supplier must be encouraged to maintain a momentum for improvement and to make continuous improvement a part of the company philosophy. The outcome of a successful development strategy is a self-reliant supplier who can initiate its own improvement projects based on performance feedback from the focal purchasing organization.

10.13.1.10 Step 10: Supplier Integration in New Product/Process Development

Development continues with the integration of suppliers into the purchasing organization's supply-chain network. This process may begin as the supplier provides input into the development of new products, processes, and services through mechanisms such as colocation, "guest engineers," and sharing of technology road maps.

10.13.1.11 Step 11: Establish Performance Improvement in Second-Tier Suppliers

As an ongoing dialogue between the two organizations develops, mapping of the "extended enterprise" should include an assessment and potential development of second-tier suppliers, suppliers to first-tier suppliers.

10.13.1.12 Step 12: Establish Integrated Supplier Network

Over time, the focal supplier will become part of the organization's global supplier network, may be responsible for supplying multiple global locations, and may participate in global growth opportunities. As more suppliers achieve this capability, the final objective is to achieve a globally aligned supplier network. It should be noted that even the most advanced organizations interviewed in this study were yet to achieve this level of integration. Thus, this objective remains a benchmark for organizations to strive for in the future.

This is a highly challenging goal. Some of the challenges noted by a manager at Honda include:

■ How much has Honda done to challenge the "mother" supplier to transfer technology to its "children"?

■ How to get the mother company to communicate value analysis and cost reduction ideas to their children?

■ How to enable the global network to communicate cost reduction opportunities, yet not use them exclusively to their advantage when they do so?

■ How to get Honda associates to force their local supplier to go back to the mother company and get help from a guest engineer or other form of expertise?

Some of the critical issues to consider in making this happen include:

■ Intensive negotiation and joint understanding and commitment at the top-management level in the supplier.

■ Participation by top management within Honda.

■ A common investment for multiple locations. For example, Siemens supplies air bag control units to Honda's plants in both Europe and the United States to minimize the investment in tooling. However, the control units are actually produced by the supplier's Mexican plant. Because the units are small, they can easily be shipped to both the United States and Europe.

■ Emphasizing competition. If a supplier already provides Honda with parts in, say, the United States, they certainly have a leg up over other suppliers in being considered for supplying Honda's new facility because they already know what the expectations are.

■ Honda places great value on a supplier's ability to improve. For example, if a supplier has provided defective products, but immediately takes countermeasures to prevent it from happening again, this is considered a "plus" by Honda.

We conclude with a final metaphor shared by a Japanese manager regarding the importance of supplier development in Honda's competitive strategy:

> Every new product cycle is like a 110-meter hurdle race. The hurdles are the same for all of the racers, yet some are able to master them better than others. They include factors such as quality problems, lack of trust, cycle time, FMEAs, customer requirements, new technology, etc. The finish line represents the product release. In every race, there is always a winner. The winner ultimately captures market share, profits, satisfied customers, etc. Generally, the winner is the one who is able to leap (i.e., manage) all of the hurdles and run (i.e., deploy the strategy) quickest. However, once the race is over, the racers continue to jog around the track getting ready for the next 110 meter race, which represents another chance to win. Although you did not win this time around, by the time you go around the track again next time, you may be a contender. One way of positioning supplier development is to understand what are the best practices at each of the hurdles that can turn contenders into winners. As the race continues, priorities will shift according to the nature of the hurdle.

10.13.2 Results of Supplier Development

The results of supplier development initiatives, although often difficult to identify and define, vary in scope and degree of success. Results can be largely grouped into three separate categories: improvements in suppliers' performance and capabilities, improvements to the relationship between the buying company and the supplier, and improvements in the buying firm's competence in managing suppliers. Some of the results reported by companies surveyed in the United States are shown in Table 10.5.

10.14 Supplier Development Efforts That Sometimes Do Not Work

Evidence indicates that supplier development projects work — at least some of the time. Although there is no guarantee that supplier development efforts will be equally successful, on average the development process produces worthwhile results. This does not mean that barriers to successful supplier development do not exist. In fact, other studies have found these barriers to be very real. The following subsection describes

Table 10.5   Degree of Improvement Attributable to the Firm's Supplier Development Effort

Area of Improvement	Estimated Percentage Improvement
Order cycle time (from order placement with supplier to receipt of item)	19
Quality (reduction in ppm, warranty returns, and so on)	24
On-time delivery (ability of supplier to deliver within the buying company's specified delivery window)	39
Percentage price change for this item (from this supplier)	3
Shared price reduction (cost savings shared with this supplier)	7
New product development time (from concept to volume production)	19
Access to new technologies	15

some of the techniques and tools used by leading-edge companies to address the problems or barriers that may contribute to reduced supplier development effectiveness.

10.14.1 Overcoming the Barriers to Supplier Development

The barriers to supplier development fall into three categories: (1) buyer-specific barriers, (2) barriers that focus on the interface between the purchaser and the supplier, and (3) supplier-specific barriers. Companies use a variety of approaches to overcome barriers to supplier development. In general, these approaches fall into one of three categories:

■ *Direct-involvement activities* ("hands-on"): Companies often send personnel to help suppliers. These efforts are characterized as hands-on activities in which buying-company representatives are directly involved in correcting supplier problems and increasing capabilities.

■ *Incentives and rewards* ("the carrot"): Companies also use incentives to encourage suppliers to improve, largely on their own. For example, a purchaser may increase order volumes if improvement takes place within a specific time or hold annual award ceremonies to recognize the best suppliers.

■ *Warnings and penalties* ("the stick"): In some cases, companies may withhold potential future business if a supplier's performance is poor, or a lack of improvement is evident. Purchasers may also use competition to provide a competitive threat to a poorly performing supplier.

In many cases, organizations employ a combination of these three strategies to elicit improvement as quickly as possible, applying the strategies judiciously in response to a particular supplier's needs. The following subsections address barriers that are internal, external, or interface based, and provide examples of how leading companies overcome these barriers.

10.14.1.1 Buyer-Specific Barriers

A buying company will not engage in supplier development if management does not recognize the need or the benefits from the supplier development effort. Moreover, if purchasing personnel have not consolidated purchased volumes with fewer suppliers, the size of the company's purchases with any particular supplier may not justify the investment. In addition, there is sometimes a lack of executive support for financing supplier development efforts.

10.14.1.1.1 Barrier: The Buying Company's Purchase Volume from the Supplier Does Not Justify Development Investment

10.14.1.1.1.1 Solution: Standardization and Single Sourcing — Parts standardization is a way to increase volume orders with suppliers, which may help justify a development effort. For example, IBM's Networking Hardware Division, which produces customized networking solutions for customers, is constantly striving to increase parts commonality. Currently, over 50 percent of purchased components for major hardware projects contain unique items. If IBM personnel believe customized components will provide a market advantage, they will continue to use it. However, standardization remains an important way to leverage worldwide purchases.

Concurrent with the drive to standardize parts, many purchasing managers plan to reduce their supply base, wherever possible, to achieve economies of scale. Daewoo Corporation, for example, uses single sourcing wherever possible, relying on two or more suppliers only in situations with high potential for labor disputes. Similarly, NCR, Doosan Corporation of Korea, Honda of America Manufacturing, and Rover are currently using, or are planning to move toward, single sourcing.

10.14.1.1.2 Barrier: No Immediate Benefit to Supplier Development Is Evident to the Buying Organization

10.14.1.1.2.1 Solution: Pursue Small Wins — Varity Perkins, a producer of diesel engines used in automotive and construction vehicles, found its initial supplier development efforts to be relatively unsuccessful. This resulted in lowered expectations internally and dampened enthusiasm for future efforts. However, Varity personnel realized that part of the problem was that they were trying to accomplish too much. Thus, the company focused on a smaller group of suppliers for kaizen (continuous improvement) efforts to gain a series of small wins. Varity's kaizen approach achieved incremental improvements that ultimately gained renewed commitment from internal parties.

10.14.1.1.3 Barrier: Importance of Purchased Item Does Not Justify Development Efforts

10.14.1.1.3.1 Solution: Take a Longer-Term Focus — Solectron, a contract manufacturer in the computer industry, has a competitive strategy that relies heavily on its supply-chain management competencies. The company looks beyond the price of purchased inputs and examines how its most important suppliers affect the quality and technology of its products. Solectron expects its suppliers to provide designs offering integrated solutions that their engineers can use in future product designs. Total costs and long-term strategic impact help justify investments in suppliers.

10.14.1.1.4 Barrier: Lack of Executive Support within the Buying Organization for Supplier Development

10.14.1.1.4.1 Solution: Prove the Benefits — Support for supplier development is gained when management becomes convinced that company performance can improve if supplier performance improves. For companies that spend nearly 80 percent of the cost of goods sold on purchased inputs, such an argument is easy to make; for companies with lower percentages, the argument may be more difficult. Although a specific relationship between supplier improvement and increased profits may be difficult to prove, somebody within the purchasing organization must demonstrate that outcome. Managers also note that efforts to optimize their companies' supply bases combined with part standardization can free up resources over the long term, making supplier development more acceptable. In addition, the total-cost approach to supplier performance measurement should also prove to be an effective communication tool for demonstrating the effect of poor supplier performance. Many companies view supplier development resources as additional overhead costs rather than investments in supply-chain performance.

10.14.1.2 Interface Barriers to Supplier Development

Barriers may also originate in the interface between the purchaser and supplier in areas such as communication, alignment of organizational cultures, and trust. A reluctance to share information about costs and processes is one of the more significant interface barriers to supplier development.

10.14.1.2.1 Barrier: Supplier Is Reluctant to Share Information on Costs or Processes

10.14.1.2.1.1 Solution: Create a Supplier Ombudsman Position — Honda of America (HAM) has supplier ombudsmen who deal with the "soft side of the business," primarily the human resource issues that are not associated with cost, quality, or delivery. Because an ombudsman is not involved in contract negotiations, suppliers are often much more willing to talk with the ombudsman, who often acts as a liaison between the two companies. One ombudsman emphasized that it takes time to build trust with suppliers, and this period varies with different suppliers. If a supplier approaches the ombudsman with a problem that is the result of poor communication or misunderstanding between Honda and the supplier, the ombudsman communicates the supplier's perspective within Honda while maintaining as much confidentiality as possible. Over time, suppliers have come to trust the ombudsman, and appear to be more willing to share information with the company.

10.14.1.2.2 Barrier: Confidentiality Inhibits Information Sharing

10.14.1.2.2.1 Solution: Confidentiality Agreements — Perhaps one of the biggest challenges in developing suppliers is sharing confidential information, especially when dealing with suppliers in high-technology areas. Thus, many companies require nondisclosure agreements and even exclusivity agreements (i.e., the supplier provides a specific product to only one purchaser) in development efforts, especially when dealing with technologically advanced products that contribute to the buying company's competitiveness. Nondisclosure agreements can benefit both parties.

Ethical behavior on the part of the buyer will also support the open sharing of information with suppliers.

10.14.1.2.3 Barrier: Supplier Does Not Trust the Buying Organization

10.14.1.2.3.1 Solution: Spell It Out — The driving forces behind the kaizen events at Varity Perkins indicate that the company will not run a kaizen without a signed agreement between the company and supplier. Although some procurement personnel at Varity Perkins prefer a gentleman's agreement, kaizen leaders believe the only way to gain a supplier's trust is to have the terms written and signed, especially when conducting the first few supplier development events. In one instance, it took Varity Perkins eight months to convince a supplier to consider a kaizen workshop because the supplier felt that a similar event with a different company failed to yield any improvements. The trust problem was compounded because Varity Perkins previously had a reputation for "arm's-length" relationships with suppliers, manifested by frequent switching of suppliers based on price. The company has moved aggressively to reverse this perception through a revised purchasing philosophy emphasizing cooperative relationships with suppliers.

10.14.1.2.4 Barrier: Organizational Cultures Are Poorly Aligned

10.14.1.2.4.1 Solution: Adapt New Approach to Local Conditions — When setting up production in South Carolina, Bavarian Motor Works (BMW) quickly realized it would have to change its supplier development approach to conform to North American supply conditions. BMW uses a "process-consulting" approach to supplier development in Germany, which involves analyzing suppliers' processes and telling them what is wrong. This approach works well in a mature supplier relationship, in which the supplier intuitively understands what the customer wants because the parties have worked together over a number of years. In the United States, however, a very different approach was required.

When BMW started production in the United States, suppliers had difficulty in understanding what was required of them in terms of quality and continuous improvement. This misunderstanding resulted in strained relationships. Consequently, BMW spent a great deal of time communicating its expectations with suppliers. Eventually, BMW published a supplier partnership manual that clearly delineates supplier responsibilities and expectations. The company also held supplier seminars to present their "road map to quality." These efforts have helped align expectations and create a shared culture toward improvement.

10.14.1.2.5 Barrier: Not Enough Inducements to Participate Are Provided to the Supplier

10.14.1.2.5.1 Solution: "Designed-in" Motivation — Although Solectron is now generally able to offer large order volumes to suppliers, that was not always the case. To gain supplier cooperation in the low-volume years, Solectron emphasized that a supplier could become "designed in" to its products and thus have a greater potential for future business.

10.14.1.2.5.2 Solution: Financial Incentives — Hyundai Motor Company uses financial incentives as one motivational tool for suppliers to improve. The company rates supplier performance from 1 (highest) to 4 (lowest). Class-1 suppliers receive cash, class-2 suppliers receive payment in 30 days, class-3 suppliers receive payment in 60 days, and class-4 suppliers receive no new business. Because suppliers know how Hyundai evaluates their performance, they can take the steps necessary to ensure higher levels of performance.

10.14.1.3 Supplier-Specific Barriers

Just as buyers sometimes fail to recognize the potential benefits from supplier development, a lack of recognition may also keep the supplier's top management from committing to the effort. This lack of commitment may result in a failure to implement improvement ideas or to provide the necessary technical and human resources to support the development process.

10.14.1.3.1 Barrier: Lack of Commitment on the Part of Supplier's Management

10.14.1.3.1.1 Solution: Implement after Commitment — Varity Perkins' managers state that they will not engage in a supplier development project with a supplier unless the supplier is fully committed to the process. A buyer from Varity Perkins arranges an initial contact meeting with the supplier's managing director to obtain direct involvement. To secure commitment, Perkins quality managers educate the managing director at the supplier about the impact of the improvement efforts. They explain the process then ask him or her to participate in one of the weekly internal improvement events at Perkins. If the managing director is positive about the experience, a kaizen awareness session for the supplier's senior management takes place at the supplier's facility. Varity Perkins asks the supplier to commit its workforce to the project, which typically involves eight to ten operators for one week.

10.14.1.3.2 Barrier: Supplier's Management Agrees to Improvements but Fails to Implement the Proposals

10.14.1.3.2.1 Solution: Supplier Champions — JCI Corporation, a first-tier supplier to the automotive industry, instituted a supplier champions program (SCP) designed to ensure suppliers who are proficient in areas that are important to JCI's customers. JCI initiated the program because many of the suppliers who had attended JCI's training sessions failed to implement the tools and techniques that JCI had provided. The SCP identifies what suppliers' personnel need to implement after they return from training. The program designates a supplier champion, an employee at the supplier unit who understands JCI's expectations and demonstrates a high level of competence. A certification process requires that the champion submit to JCI a number of examples of actions that the supplier has taken to improve. These actions might include process-flow mapping, failure mode effects analysis, quality control planning, best practice benchmarking, and process auditing.

10.14.1.3.3 Barrier: Supplier Lacks Engineering Resources to Implement Solutions

10.14.1.3.3.1 Solution: Direct Support — HAM has invested a significant number of resources in its supplier support infrastructure, which this chapter has highlighted in the earlier sections. Of the over 300 people in HAM's purchasing department, 50 are engineers who work exclusively with suppliers. In one case, a small supplier did not have the capacity to cope with volume, resulting in quality deterioration. HAM sent four people to the supplier for ten months at no charge, with additional services offered on an as-needed basis. The supplier improved and now is a well-established Honda supplier.

10.14.1.3.4 Barrier: Supplier Lacks Required Information Systems

10.14.1.3.4.1 Solution: Direct Electronic Data Interchange Support — At NCR Corporation, a manufacturer of ATMs, managers note that timely and accurate information is critical to decision making and, ultimately, to improved performance. An important focus of their supplier development efforts has been to get suppliers to make a commitment to electronic data interchange (EDI) with a significant amount of money committed to getting suppliers online. NCR provides direct help to suppliers producing lower-level components who do not have resources to get online. In addition, NCR provides training for suppliers and will help make recommendations on hardware and software.

10.14.1.3.5 Barrier: Suppliers Are Not Convinced Development Will Provide Benefits to Them

10.14.1.3.5.1 Solution: Let Suppliers Know Where They Stand — Varity Perkins revamped its supplier evaluation system to show suppliers where they could improve. Previously, the company sent a report to suppliers once a quarter that assessed quality, delivery, and price competitiveness performance. Varity did not use the data in any manner and suppliers did not take the assessments seriously. When revamping the system, the measures were changed to capture the impact of supplier performance on daily operations.

Varity Perkins measured delivery performance using a weekly time bucket for performance, and average on-time performance was 90 to 95 percent. With a daily time bucket, performance dropped to 26 percent on time. Since the introduction of the new measure, daily on-time delivery has improved to 90 percent. The supplier's history, its performance compared with Varity's other suppliers, and the deviation from mean performance for each performance area also appear on the modified report. The report also uses more graphics to make the data more meaningful.

This system has become the foundation for the company's supplier development program. By allowing suppliers to view their performance relative to competitors, the company expects that suppliers will see the potential benefits of participating in supplier development activities.

10.14.1.3.6 Barrier: Supplier Lacks Employee Skill Base to Implement Solutions

10.14.1.3.6.1 Solution: Establish Training Centers — JCI Corporation realized that some suppliers lacked the skills required to implement improvement ideas. With this problem in mind, JCI built a facility dedicated to providing training to internal groups, suppliers, and customers. Hyundai has also established a domestic training center that provides supplier personnel with training in areas such as specialized welding. The suppliers and Hyundai share the cost of this effort equally. The Korean government also supports these training centers by providing tax benefits for building training centers and making the training fees shared by Hyundai and suppliers tax exempt.

10.14.1.3.6.2 Solution: Provide Human Resource Support —

Hyundai Corporation recognizes that smaller suppliers with limited resources cannot consistently recruit and retain the most skilled engineers. Therefore, the majority of Hyundai's improvement efforts focus on smaller suppliers. Hyundai selects engineers from its own shops to spend time with suppliers. The engineers "live" at the suppliers, performing time and motion studies, teaching layout design, and improving productivity. Suppliers are consistently encouraged to learn, apply, and eventually teach themselves and second-tier suppliers the transferred knowledge.

10.15 Can You Trust the Concept of Trust in Supply-Chain Relationships?

One of the most misunderstood and ripe areas for research in the area of supply-chain relationships is that of trust. Trust (as well as its cousin, collaboration) seems to be the single most discussed element in making supply chains function effectively and efficiently. Barber (1983:7) notes that:

> In both serious social thought and everyday discourse, it is assumed that the meaning of trust and of its many apparent synonyms is so well known that it can be left undefined or to contextual implications.

This observation is corroborated by the evolution of trust in the fields of industrial economics, organizational behavior, marketing, and organizational theory. Of all the elements critical to managing supply chains, trust is one of the most commonly cited elements, yet one of the most difficult to measure.

A comparison of the various definitions of trust across research disciplines shows that trust can be grouped into eight conceptual paradigms (shown in Table 10.6). In paradigm one, the authors posit that trust is a cognitive predictability or reliability of another party. The second paradigm addresses the competence of a party as a component of trust. In the third paradigm, a recognition of trust as an altruistic faith or goodwill felt toward another party is proposed. The fourth paradigm relates the concept of vulnerability to trust. Paradigm number five specifies that loyalty-based trust exists when a partner consistently goes beyond the call of duty. The

Table 10.6   Theories and Definitions

Body of Theory	Definition
1. Reliability	Time and experience are critical elements in evaluating trust
2. Competence	Experience and wisdom displayed by partner
3A. Goodwill (openness)	Confidence that you can share information or problems with the other party
3B. Goodwill (benevolence)	Accepted duty to protect the rights of your partner
4. Vulnerability	Being unprotected or exposed while including an element of uncertainty or risk
5. Loyalty	A partner is not just reliable but performs well in extraordinary situations
6. Multiple forms of trust	There is more than one type of trust

sixth conceptual paradigm recognizes that multiple components of trust exist, which are defined by cognitive (reliability or task) trust and affective (altruistic) faith trust. In the following subsections, we identify each of these representative paradigms, which are drawn from the marketing, organization theory, sourcing, and organization behavior literature streams (see Table 10.6).

10.15.1 Reliability

Reliability can be broken down into several elements. Reliability is dependent on prior contact with a party, or experience. Repeated interaction over time leads to levels of confidence, consistency, and finally, trust. Reliability then leads to predictability, which is confidence in future actions. Although reliability is important, what motivates reliability is often more important. Reliability must be based on integrity or honesty to be effective. Reliability based coercion or stress eventually creates a suboptimal relationship or total breakdown.

A series of definitions define trust in terms of a firm or person's reliability or expectation of performance. One of the first definitions of trust accepted the extreme position that for trust to be present, expected loss must be greater than expected gain. Authors later extended trust as an expectation to include situations in which expected gain is greater than loss. Reliability can often be confused with predictability. Reliability primarily addresses a party's past behavior, whereas predictability actually takes past behavior and other information to address probabilities of future performance. Reliability and predictability are closely related terms, and definitions addressing either term fall into this body of theory. Firms or people who meet a threshold level of predictability can by definition be trusted. This paradigm is best described by the following definition:

> Trust is a range of observable behaviors and a cognitive state that encompasses predictability (Rossiter, Charles, and Pearch 1975).

What this means in simple terms is that trust is not something that occurs overnight, but is built up over time through repeated interactions and acts of good faith. For example, a long-term customer relationship may be based on a continuous discussion of problems that occur and are resolved over time. I recall a meeting between a senior vice president of purchasing and a senior vice president of marketing from two companies with a ten-year history of a solid business relationship. The vice president of marketing noted that the reason the relationship worked is that, "whenever there was a problem or conflict, I was able to march over to his office, shut the door, lay it out on the table, and work it out! Sometimes it took a few hours, but when I came out, we both felt better about the situation."

10.15.2 Competence

Competence is one's perception of the ability of a party to meet commitments. Competence-based trust can be broken down into three key areas. First is specific competence, which is trust in the other's function or area. Second, interpersonal competence is the ability of a person to work with people or people skills. Finally, business sense addresses a person's experience, wisdom, and common sense. A key result of this research is that to trust supply-chain partners, you have to have some confidence that they are able to do the work effectively. For a procurement manager, this might mean visiting a supplier and evaluating it to ensure that it has the facilities, people, and knowledge to carry out the contract.

10.15.3 Goodwill

Goodwill is identified with a heavy dependence on openness between people and emotional investment in the relationship. Affect-based trust could almost be confused with interpersonal or personal trust because personal issues creep into the relationship in terms of problem solving, listening, and sharing. A key distinction between cognitive and affect-based trust is that whereas cognitive-based trust may or may not exist at the interpersonal level, affect-based trust almost always exists only at the interpersonal level. The importance of interpersonal relations is recognized to be an important element of trust (McAllister 1993; Granovetter 1992).

Beyond reliability or predictability, trust can also be defined in terms of a faith in the goodwill of others. This faith recognizes the importance of interpersonal relations as an important element of trust. This new type of goodwill-based trust evolved from discussion and research on benevolence, integrity, and honesty as key ingredients to trust. For instance:

> Trust is a faith in the moral integrity or goodwill of others, which is produced through interpersonal interactions that lead to social-psychological bonds of mutual norms, sentiments and friendships in dealing with uncertainty (Ring and Van de Ven, 1994).
>
> Faith enables people to go beyond the available evidence and feel secure that a partner will continue to be responsive and caring. Feelings of faith begin with past experiences that show how much our partner cares (Rempel and Holmes, 1985).

10.15.4 Vulnerability

A key breakthrough in the use of the term *trust* is the relationship between vulnerability and trust. Vulnerability is a key issue because trust without some kind of vulnerability simply cannot exist. If a party chooses a course of action that involves no vulnerability, then the firm has simply made a rational decision. One of the first concepts was that trust involved choosing a course of action even if the probability of failure was greater than 50 percent.

Others believed that trust goes beyond expectation outcomes under uncertainty to expectation outcomes under vulnerability. Vulnerability projects a feeling of being unprotected or exposed while including an element of uncertainty or risk. If there is no uncertainty or risk, then the party is freely giving the other party something. If both firms are not exposed to risk, then they are simply making a rational decision based on probabilities.

> Trust is the mutual confidence that no party to an exchange will exploit another's vulnerabilities (Sabel, 1993:1133).
>
> Trust is a risk relationship that increases the trustor's vulnerability (Zand, 1972).

Trust is a particular level of the subjective probability with which an agent assesses that another agent or group will perform an action, both before he can monitor such an action and in a context in which it affects his won action. For trust to be present there must be the possibility of disappointment or betrayal (Gambetta, 1988: 217).

The discussion on vulnerability uncovers a key distinction that must be made between trust and trusting behavior. Trust can exist without action, but trusting behavior is the action taken based on trust in another party. Lorenz discusses how vulnerability is a key component of trusting action:

Trusting behavior consists of action that (1) increases one's vulnerability to another whose behavior is not under one's control and (2) takes place in a situation where the penalty suffered if the trust is abused would lead one to regret the action (Lorenz, 1988: 197).

A paradox was uncovered by Rempel and Holmes (1985), who wrote that to be able to trust, one must be willing to take the risk of trusting another party. To be a party to trust, one must take this risk.

10.16 Dependence: Too Much Is Never a Good Thing

Dependence has been observed two ways. First, dependence may be defined in terms of a relationship between one party (usually supplier) and another party (usually buyer). Second, the power one party has over another may be due to dependence, usually due to a high percentage of a supplier's output going to one buyer. Wal-Mart, Carrefours, The Home Depot, and other retailers come to mind. Several authors including Lascelles and Dale (1989) have addressed the issue of dependence from a volume perspective. They hypothesize that the more a buyer buys from a supplier, the more likely the buyer will be able to influence the supplier (see Table 10.7).

Dependence of a party on another means that one party will have power over another. Treleven (1987) notes that in markets with limited numbers of suppliers there is less leverage for buyers in negotiating with suppliers. Resource dependence theory also notes that when power between parties is in relative balance (high uncertainty), organizations will attempt to create negotiated environments.

Table 10.7 Dependence

Treleven (1987)	In situations with fewer suppliers, buyers have fewer opportunities to exploit suppliers
Mohr & Spekman (1994)	Interdependence is correlated with relationship performance
Emerson (1962)	Power and dependence have a reciprocal relationship
Cadotte & Stern (1979)	The power dependence relationship determines the amount of interdependence between parties
Lascelles and Dale (1989)	The volume of business with a supplier influences the ability of a buyer to impact a supplier
Frazier, Spekman and O'Neal (1988)	Coercive use of power can damage a relationship
Dwyer, Schurr and Oh (1987)	Power is a function of dependence of parties on one another
Noorweir, John and Nevin (1990)	Voluntary restraint from the use of power improves the relational exchange norms of a relationship
Williamson (1975)	Power asymmetries will always be exploited
Heide (1994)	The more dependent a supplier is, the greater the use of explicit contracts
Etgar & Valency (1983)	The greater the dependence that is present, the more vulnerable the weaker member is
Heide (1994)	The higher the degree of interdependence, the greater the commitment exhibited by both parties
Lusch & Brown (1996)	The greater the dependence of a buyer on a supplier, the more likely the buyer is to have a long-term orientation

Clearly, the interplay of trust, dependence, and power is an issue that all companies will have to manage for some time into the future. If companies are serious about deploying supply-chain management, skills in managing the interplay of relationships and forming bonds that go beyond the traditional boundaries will be key to success. One example of how this power is being wielded is Wal-Mart's request that all suppliers have RFID tags on pallets by January 2005. There are many other examples.

10.17 Conclusions: Lessons Learned about Relationship Management

A theme that underlies these examples is that many of the barriers to relationship management are related. It appears that as companies work toward solving one barrier, they make concurrent progress toward solving other barriers. We can learn several lessons from studying relationship management successes and failures:

1. Managerial attitudes are a common and difficult barrier to overcome. A purchasing executive at HAM noted that although quality problems always have a solution, the attitudes of suppliers' managers must be right before a problem is truly solved. Suppliers are sometimes not willing to accept help in the form of supplier development, perhaps because they are too proud or because they do not see the value in improving quality or delivery performance. Management attitudes significantly affect the success of supplier development efforts.

2. Realizing a competitive advantage from the supply chain requires a strategic orientation toward supply-chain management and the alignment of purchasing objectives with business unit goals. Supplier development plays a major role in helping create competitive advantage while aligning purchasing and business goals. A strong purchasing mission statement helps promote this strategic emphasis and alignment. Consider the following purchasing mission statement from an automobile parts manufacturer in the United Kingdom:

    > We are committed to procure goods and services in a way that delivers our aims and objectives of becoming the most successful auto parts business in the world.

    The company pursues this mission through (1) development of a world-class supplier base; (2) obtaining the highest-quality, most cost-effective goods and services in a timely manner; and (3) establishing long-term relationships with suppliers who strive for continuous improvement in all areas.

3. Relationship management is critical to supplier development success. Buyers can strengthen their relationships with their suppliers through supplier development activities. Besides the development of trust, the participants within a supply chain can begin to understand each other's needs and requirements. Ideally, supplier development will lead to the recognition that a codestiny exists between the buyer and seller. Successful supplier development requires a cooperative relationship between the buyer and seller.

Pursuing supplier development activities directly with suppliers is not an easy task. The objective, of course, is to transform suppliers in such a way that continuous improvement becomes an integral part of each supplier's capabilities. This is achieved only over time and only by those companies that are patient and tenacious enough to make supplier development an important part of their supplier management processes.

Relationship management and supplier development are the critical elements that take the strategic sourcing effort to its logical conclusion. As we noted earlier, strategic sourcing and market intelligence allow you to determine with whom you want to establish the relationship, as well as to fix the expectations. However, the real work occurs when it comes to managing the relationship and realizing the predicted benefits. One executive noted that the greatest improvements are made after the ink on the contract has dried. Only then can you begin to work together in a mutually beneficial fashion and drive real improvements in cost, technology, delivery, and quality through to the end customer.

10.18 Checklist

- Establish final KPIs for strategy.
- Transition project to RM and contract administrator.
- Build change-management plan.
- Add change-management section to position paper.
- Execute plans.
- Measure and manage supplier performance.

10.19 Results

Final agreement with all stakeholders
Strategy executed and communicated

References

Barber, B., *The Logic and Limits of Trust*, Rutgers University Press, New Brunswick, NJ. 1983.

Broadbent, M. and Weill, P., Management by maxim: how business and IT managers can create infrastructures, *Sloan Management Review*, 77–88, Spring 1997.

Combs, J.G. and Ketchen, D.J., Jr. Explaining interfirm cooperation and performance: toward a reconciliation of predictions from the resource-based view and organizational economics, *Strategic Management Journal*, 20, 867–888, 1999.

Dubois, F.L. and Carmel, E., Information technology and leadtime management in international manufacturing operations, in *Global Information Systems and Technology: Focus on the Organization and its Functional Areas*, P.C. Deans and K.R. Karwan, Eds., London: Idea Group Publishing, 1994, 279–293.

Dyer, J., Four Papers on Governance, Asset Specialization, and Performance: A Comparative Study of Supplier-Automaker Relationships in the U.S. and Japan, Unpublished dissertation, Los Angeles, California, University of California, February 1994.

Dyer, J., Effect interfirm collaboration: how firms minimize transaction costs and maximize transaction value, *Strategic Management Journal*, 18, 553–556, 1997.

Dyer, J. and Ouchi, W., Japanese-style partnerships: giving companies a competitive edge. *Sloan Management Review* 35, 51–63, 1993.

Gambetta, D., Mafia: the price of distrust, in Gambetta, D. (Ed.), *Trust*, Basil Blackwell, New, York, 1988, pp. 158–175.

Gambetta, D., Can we trust trust?, in Gambetta, D. (Eds.) *Trust*, Basil Blackwell, New York, 1988, pp. 213–238.

Giunipero, L. and Handfield, R., *Purchasing Education and Training Requirements for the Future*, Tempe, AZ: Center for Advanced Purchasing Studies, 2004.

Goodhue, D., Wybo, M.D., and Kirsch, L.J., The impact of data integration on the costs and benefits, *MIS Quarterly* 16, 293–321, 1992.

Goodhue, D.L., Kirsch, L.J., Quillard, J.A., and Wybo, M.D., Strategic data planning: lessons from the field, *MIS Quarterly* 16, 11–34, 1992.

Granovetter, M., Problems of explanation in economic sociology, in N. Nohria and R. Eccles (Eds.), *Networks and Organizations: Structure Form and Action*, Boston, MA: Harvard Business School Press, 1992, 25–56.

Hagedoorn, J. and Narula, R., Choosing organizational modes of strategic technology partnering: international sectoral differences. *Journal of International Business Studies* 27, 265–284, 1996.

Hancock, *The Law of Purchasing*, 2nd ed., Chesterland, OH: Business Laws, 1987.

Handfield, R. and Bechtel, C., The role of trust and relationship structure in improving supply chain responsiveness, *Industrial Marketing Management*, 31, 1–16, 2001.

Handfield, R. and Nichols, E., *Supply Chain Redesign*, Upper Saddle River, NJ: Prentice-Hall, 2002.

Handfield, R. and Nichols, E., Key issues in global supply base management, *Industrial Marketing Management*, Vol. 32, No. 8, November 2003.

Handfield, R., Straight, S., and Sterling, W., Reverse auctions: how do suppliers really feel about them?, *Inside Supply Management*, 18–24, 2002.

Holm, D.B., Eriksson, K., and Johanson, J., Creating value through mutual commitment to business network relationships, *Strategic Management Journal*, 20, 467–486, 1999.

Kogut, B., Joint ventures: theoretical and empirical perspectives, *Strategic Management Journal*, 9, 319–332, 1988.

Kotter, J.P., *Leading Change*, Cambridge, MA: HBS Press, 1996.

Lascelles, D.M. and Dale, B.G., The buyer-supplier relationship in total quality management, *Journal of Purchasing and Materials Management*, Vol. 25, No. 2, 10–19, Summer 1989.

Lorenz, E.H., Neither friends nor strangers: informal networks of subcontracting in French industry, In Gambetta, D. (Ed.), *Trust*, Basil Blackwell, New York, 1988, pp. 194–210.

Martin, J., Information Engineering, Savant Research Studies, Carnforth, Lancashire, England, 1986.

Monczka, R., Peterson, K., Handfield, R., and Ragatz, G., Determinants of successful vs. non-strategic supplier alliances, *Decision Science Journal* (special issue on "Supply Chain Linkages") 29, 553–577, 1998.

Nishiguchi, T., *Strategic Industrial Sourcing: The Japanese Advantage*, New York: Oxford University Press, 1994.

Nooteboom, B., Berger, H., and Noorderhaven, N.G., Effects of trust and governance on relational risk, *Academy of Management Journal* 40, 308–338, 1997.

Osborn, R.N. and Hagedoorn, J., The institutionalization and evolutionary dynamics of interorganizational alliances and networks, *Academy of Management Journal* 40, 261–278, 1997.

Peterson, K., Handfield, R., and Ragatz, G., A model of successful supplier integration into new product development, *Journal of Product Innovation Management* 20, 284–299, 2003.

Rempel, J.K., Holmes, J.G., and Zanna, M., Trust in close relationships, *Journal of Personality and Social Psychology*, Vol. 49, 163–168, 1985.

Ring, P.S., Fragile and resilient trust and their roles in economic exchange, *Business and Society*, Vol. 35, No. 2, 148–175, June 1996.

Ring, P.S. and Van de Ven, A.H., Structuring cooperative relationships between organizations, *Strategic Management Journal*, Vol. 49, 95–112, 1992.

Ring, P.S. and Van de Ven, A.H., Developmental processes of cooperative interorganizational relationships, *Academy of Management Review*, Vol. 19, No. 1, 90–118, January 1994.

Rossiter, C.M., Jr. and Barrett, W.P., *Communicating Personally*, New York: Bobbs-Merrill, 1975.

Sabel, C.F., Studied trust: building new forms of cooperation in a volatile economy, *Human Relations*, Vol. 46, No. 9, 1133–1170, 1993.

Saxton, T. The effects of partner and relationship characteristics on alliance outcomes, *Academy of Management Journal* 40, 443–462, 1997.

Treleven, M., Single sourcing: a management tool for the quality supplier, *Journal of Purchasing and Materials Management*, Vol. 23, No. 1, 19–24, 1987.

Williamson, O., *The Economic Institutions of Capitalism: Firms, Markets, Relational Contracting*, New York: The Free Press, 1985.

Zand, D.E., Trust and managerial problem solving, *Administrative Science Quarterly*, 17, 229–239, 1972.

Zajac, E.J. and Olsen, C.P., From transaction cost to transactional value analysis: Implications for the study of interorganizational strategies, *Journal of Management Studies* 30, 131–145, 1993.

Chapter 11

Redesigning Your Organization for Supply-Chain Intelligence and Strategic Sourcing

Function	Objective	Tactical Step	Chapter/ Appendix
Supply market intelligence	Supply market research	Opportunity identification and validation	2
		Project approval	2
		Establishing the team	3
		Project plan	3
		As-is assessment	4
		Supply market research	5
		Market forecasts	5
		External and market analyses	6
	Strategy and resource commitment	Detailed supplier evaluation and research	7
		Evaluate current and alternative strategies	8
		Understand contract formation	8

Function	Objective	Tactical Step	Chapter/ Appendix
Strategic sourcing	Negotiate and select supplier	Develop relationship strategy	8
		Strategy position paper	8
		Develop requests for information (RFIs) and build negotiation strategy	9
		Negotiate	9
		Final supplier selection	9
		Form contracts	9
	Implement and promote compliance	Implement contracts	9
		Transition to relationship manager	10
Relationship management		Communicate expectations	10
		Measure performance	10
		Resolve issues and develop supplier performance	10
Benchmarking processes and driving continuous improvement	Set a vision for change	Build an organization for supply-chain excellence	11
		Benchmark performance and drive continuous improvement	12, App. B

11.1 Chapter Outline

- Leading organizational change for supply-chain management (SCM)
- What is the required organizational structure for SCM?
- Definition of skills
- SCM knowledge definitions
- Deploying organizational change
- What is organizational modularization?

- Rollout of proposed organizational changes
- The criticality of building consensus in change management: the role of cross-functional teams
- The challenges of partnerships

No institution can possibly survive if it needs geniuses or supermen to manage it. It must be organized in such a way as to be able to get along under a leadership composed of average human beings.

— Peter F. Drucker

As organizations sought to deploy new supply-chain processes and technologies over the last decade, the promise of benefits achieved has, for the most part, fallen short of true expectations. Research suggests that much of this can be attributed to a failure to fully understand the organizational implications of SCM and only paying lip service to end-user training and executive alignment. SCM technology has evolved to a point where users' ability to fully exploit its advances lags considerably. As companies attempt to pull together supply-chain initiatives into streamlined cross-functional processes, capturing the underlying value becomes more about people and processes and less about technology.[1] High-powered systems that provide integrated business process tools, exception management policies, and closed-loop processes are only as effective as the users' systemic understanding of supply-chain cause and effect.

These observations were substantiated in an internal study conducted by a leading SCM vendor in 2000. The goal of the study was to investigate why customers failed to attain the full value potential of their SCM projects. As part of the remedy, an innovative SCM concepts education program was rolled out to a small group of stakeholders. In rolling out a novel value-based approach to deploying software applications, success was judged by the achievement of a business result rather than by the typical go-live event.

The study yielded a valuable insight: for the most part, projects achieved their business results with the implementation of a single solution within a functional silo (e.g., demand planning, transportation planning, factory planning). However, when projects involved the integration of multiple SCM modules (i.e., a cross-functional implementation), there was a significant gap between the potential value assessed before the implementation and the actual value realized afterward, leading to the conclusion that there was a need to educate users on conceptual and process

---

[1] Hameed, Sree, and Escande, Marc, *The People Factor: Accelerating Supply Chain Transformation Through Education,* working paper, 2004.

knowledge. One stakeholder noted, "We bought a Ferrari and don't know how to get it out of the garage." It was also found that other than a small minority of motivated supply-chain practitioners, participants involved in the operation of a typical supply chain lacked a systemic understanding of how supply chains work and were unable to fully exploit these tools.

Achieving organizational alignment is also difficult. Many parts of the supply chain have been operating as functional silos for a long time, and implementing a streamlined cross-functional process is extremely challenging. The study showed that resistance to change and cross-functional tensions dominate during any type of SCM initiative. Organizational alignment is achieved by ensuring that anyone who influences or is impacted by the supply-chain project understands how the business processes will work together. Not only does this help minimize resistance to change and achieve greater buy-in across all users, but with management involvement it presents an opportunity to ensure that the metrics reinforce the desired change.

The topic of supply-chain knowledge and organizational change is discussed in greater detail in this chapter. We bring together both academic research and consulting experiences in discussing these issues. All of the elements presented previously in this book will ultimately hinge on the successful management of organizational restructuring and change management.

11.2 Leading Organizational Change for SCM

Research conducted by the Supply Chain Resource Consortium (http://scrc.ncsu.edu) with a number of leading SCM organizations across a variety of industries has shown that companies that excel in the consistent application of "best-in-class" SCM processes and practices have demonstrated significantly higher financial performance than their competitors. This has not gone unnoticed by market analysts and has been amply rewarded by significant improvements in stock performance.

Poorly managed supply-chain processes, on the other hand, are recognized as a serious risk. Companies with poorly managed supply chains have experienced an average loss of 8.5 percent in their shareholder value, up to 18.5 percent when major supply-chain disruptions have occurred. In these companies, stock price recovery took 60 months or more after the organization's supply-chain problems first appeared. Analysis using best-in-class experiences of organizations that have deployed SCM strategies indicates that improvements in SCM can translate into changes of 2.5 and 2 percent in cost of goods sold (COGS) and return on capital employed (ROCE), respectively. Additional benefits not included in these estimations are improved efficiencies and productivity in manufacturing. The complete realization of these benefits is estimated to take six to eight years. The major risk to enterprises is a failure to quickly deploy the strategies and practices across business units.

Initially, a group of business unit representatives and subject matter experts from many businesses should agree on a companywide analysis and develop a vision, a mission, and key strategies for delivering the SCM "prize." Some of the typical strategies defined at this stage might include the following:

- Application of standard processes and practices, enabled with integrated technology, for the management of supply chains to ensure that business requirements are consistently met.
- Collaborative leadership of the development of supply chains across organizational boundaries to ensure they deliver exceptional value by supporting an integrated plan. Development encompasses changing the supply-chain structure (process, technology, and relationships) as well as the behaviors and culture within an enterprise and across the supply chain.
- Leveraging of corporate spend.
- Management of supply chains through the use of cross-functional teams that span organizational boundaries. These teams enable the achievement of strategic goals and provide value to stakeholders.
- Integration of key suppliers into the business. Integration allows skills, knowledge, and capabilities to be leveraged for each organization's mutual benefit.
- A disciplined focus on logistics excellence through the planning of logistics activities. Open sharing of forecasts and limitations up and down the supply chain and collaborative coordination and synchronization of logistics activities.
- Being a "customer of choice" through rapid payment and equitable and ethical treatment of suppliers.

Execution of these strategies is contingent on a supportive organizational structure.

11.3 What Is the Required Organizational Structure for SCM?

To achieve SCM benefits, a different supply-chain organizational structure is required. Contrary to what many consultants recommend, my research suggests that organizational changes are not dependent on SCM or enterprise systems being fully deployed; rather, they can begin to take effect immediately and are independent of technology-related initiatives. Benchmark studies of best-in-class SCM organization structures have been integrated into these recommendations (including results from a recent survey of 194 executives identifying best practices in supply-chain organizations).

Supply-chain improvements are achieved by organizations in which the importance of strategy is recognized at a senior level. Specifically, successful organizations are characterized by

- A senior executive responsible for SCM who reports to the CEO
- A corporate committee that is actively involved in providing direction to the implementation of SCM strategies across the enterprise
- Coordination of strategic initiatives accomplished centrally with the active involvement of business units
- Ownership of operational aspects of SCM remaining with operational business units
- The focus of SCM operational aspects moving from transaction execution to coordination and synchronization
- Common services centralized for improved efficiency and control over strategic initiatives and coordinated process planning across all business units

To drive value, the SCM organization must report to the CEO. Supply-chain transactions should become largely automated (80 percent of transactions) to allow supply-chain associates to focus their energy on value-added supply-chain strategies and processes.

In arriving at a recommended organizational design, it is also advised that workshops be used to gain support from impacted business units. For instance, at one company we worked with, three senior SCM executive teams were given the task of independently developing the "ideal" supply-chain organizational structure, based on input and lessons learned from all of the supply-chain design workshops, that would enable execution of the supply-chain design process. They were asked to deliver an ideal organizational model to present to the executive team. In the end, all three teams reached a similar consensus on the optimal structure and did so independently. The organizational model proposed as a result of these sessions is best described by Peter Drucker's management concept of "federal decentralization":

> Any organization requires both strong parts and a strong center. The term *decentralization* is actually misleading — though far too common by now to be discarded. Federal decentralization requires strong guidance from the center through the setting of

clear, meaningful, and high objectives for the whole. The objectives must demand both a high degree of business performance and a high standard of conduct throughout the enterprise[2]

Organizational capabilities and effectiveness are significantly impacted by horizontal or collaborative practices such as cross-functional teams, information sharing, and participation or involvement in decision making by customers and suppliers (including internal to the company but outside of the organization).[3] These practices increase horizontal expertise and effectiveness.

One conceptualization of an ideal SCM organizational structure might have the following characteristics:

- A senior VP of SCM reporting to the corporate CEO through regular reports on the SCM development program
- Business unit directors reporting directly to the senior SCM VP managing operational areas and interfacing directly with the managing directors
- Director of supply-chain business intelligence (evaluate) reporting to the VP, responsible for assessment of current supply-chain performance, opportunity identification and assessment, and market intelligence
- Director of supply-chain integration (sustain) responsible for tracking of payments, information, and audits
- Director of supply-chain strategy (design and implement), responsible for development of supply-chain strategy and ongoing relationship management in the supply chain

The essence of this is a decentralized business process with a strong centralized vision, capturing elements of best-in-class organizational designs identified in the research. An example of one possible variant of this structure is represented in Figure 11.1.

Deploying such an organizational structure requires significant change. Most current supply-chain organizational structures are fragmented and not aligned with senior management initiatives. A representative best-in-class organizational structure should have a senior executive of SCM reporting to the CEO, with eight directors reporting to the SCM senior executive. Responsibilities of these individuals are described in the following text.

---

[2] Drucker, P., *The Practice of Management*, 1956, p. 214.
[3] Galbraith, J.R., *Competing with Flexible Lateral Organizations*, 2nd ed., Reading, MA: Addison-Wesley, 1993, pp. 1–11.

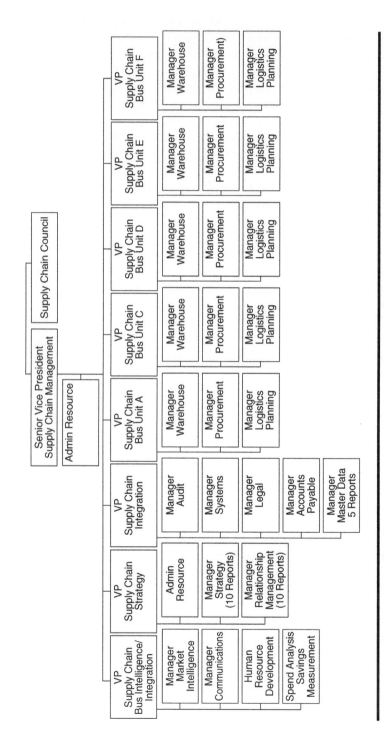

Figure 11.1 Example of a "federally decentralized" supply-chain organization.

11.3.1 Senior VP of SCM

- Reports to the CEO
- Responsible for supply-chain program management
- Resource allocation
- Setting high-level goals and objectives
- Interfacing with senior executives' business leads
- Establishing and sustaining the vision and direction of the company's supply-chain strategy

11.3.2 VP of Supply-Chain Operations at Each Business Unit

- Accountable for overseeing execution of supply-chain strategies at the site level, with feedback mechanisms to strategic groups, i.e., primarily ensures supply chains are effective and efficient.
- Accountability for human resource development at site level and coordination with central HRD manager.
- Aggregating supply-chain results and metrics through collection of stakeholder inputs on supplier performance.
- Tracking operational performance and taking corrective action.
- Resolving major conflicts that require senior leadership input from the company and suppliers over operational issues.
- Direct reports include:
  - Supply-chain managers (warehouse, procurement, accounts payable, contract administration, logistics planning, and support services) at the sites.
  - Key operational employees at sites report to these managers.

The direct reports at each business unit include the following:

Accounts payable manager
- Responsible for timely and accurate payment on all invoices to ensure accuracy and that appropriate guidelines are followed, correct coding of invoices, etc.
- Occasionally responsible for resolution of payment disputes (ombudsman role)
- Key in ensuring that the company maintains status as customer of choice

Warehouse manager, who is responsible for
- Order staging and delivery
- Reverse logistics coordination and shipping

- Maintenance of parts service
- Planning, scheduling, and dispatch of warehouse personnel and resources
- Facilities planning, rationalization, and maintenance
- Planning, scheduling, and dispatch of tools and equipment
- Stocking, picking, and counting of inventory
- Management of shipping and loading docks
- Maintenance of inventoried equipment
- Quality assurance

Manager of supplier relationships
- Supplier performance metrics
- Conflict management and resolving accounting disputes
- Quality improvement
- Ongoing communication and resolution of day-to-day conflicts and issues
- Identification of key improvement opportunities

Manager of procurement
- Responsible for the procurement of goods and services that are identified to be acquired through unstructured supply chains
- Tactical procurement not governed by sourcing strategy agreements
- Applies standard process to prequalify vendors for all business units
- Identifies and works to resolve supplier performance issues
- Collects and reports on supply-chain performance
- Ensures nonconformance to supply-chain standards is tracked and adequately resolved
- Maintains service level agreements (SLAs) with client groups and verifies conformance
- Asset management
- Manages warranty program

Manager of logistics planning
- Aggregation of demand data and future projections of demand forecasts
- Ensuring suppliers have access to and understand forecasts
- Coordination of suppliers to deliver material and services as planned
- Materials resource planning
- Ensuring supply-chain plans integrate with sales, operations, and project and maintenance planning functions
- Ensuring logistics plans are in place to support specific work
- Scheduling of logistics plan requirements and capacity planning

- Price forecasting in conjunction with the central group
- Planning of reverse logistics and disposition of scrap and waste

Manager of contract administration (separate for major projects)

- Responsible for the development and maintenance of pricing and contract terms for business units.
- Familiar with standard contractual terms and is a part of all new-contract-formation team discussions at the site
- Builds appropriate SLAs and identifies methods to measure performance
- Ensures conformance to agreements
- Ensures contracts are up to date, reflect recent changes in agreements, and resolves contractual questions and other related issues.

Manager of support services

- Responsible for mobilizing services at business units or sites
- Includes maintenance of competency profiles and qualifications of on-site suppliers.
- Ensures that supplier personnel are qualified and capable of meeting local requirements.
- Auditing and tracking of SLAs through interaction with internal customers on current supplier-provided services and development of supplier scorecards.

11.3.3 VP of Supply-Chain Business Intelligence (Performance Evaluation)

The responsibilities of this role are to:

- Develop the annual supply-chain improvement program and support the budget and forecast cycles
- Develop and maintain supply-chain models
- Maintain relationship with research and thought leaders in SCM
- Build organizational awareness and support in combination with dissemination of knowledge within supply chains
- Develop career path requirements, training, and knowledge management programs for new and existing personnel
- Track benefits realization at the program level
- Integrates data and collect information related to supply-chain performance and benchmarking
- Coordinate information requirements for the whole company that relate to SCM

- Keep up to date on competitive market intelligence across major supply markets
- Collect and validate cost savings achieved
- Complete spend analysis and opportunity analysis
- Support development of long-range planning and budgets across the company

Direct reports are described as follows:

Manager of human resource development
- Communications
- Training strategy
- Succession strategy plan
- Competency profile
- Compensation
- Leadership development
- Gap analysis (skills)
- Employee survey
- Recruitment
- Performance management and mentoring
- Coaching
- Identifying potential external hires and monitoring interest

Manager of market intelligence
- Prioritize key areas and products
- Maintain information for key areas of the business
- Feed budget processes
- Maintain communication, internal and external
- Acquire market knowledge, including competitive benchmarking intelligence on market share or positioning
- Run analytical models of supply-chain performance
- Coordinate with SCM thought leaders to identify key trends and issues

Manager of performance management
- Communications
- Evaluations
- Benchmarking, strategy development
- Metrics, measuring, and coaching

Communications manager
- Supply chain education and training (SCM University)
- Key contact notes for staff and management
- New-employee orientation
- External knowledge deployment and success stories
- Newsletters, Web-site content, etc.

11.3.4 VP of Supply-Chain Integration (Sustaining Strategy)

The responsibilities of this role are:

- Sustaining all elements of the supply-chain structures:
  - Audit
  - Data maintenance
  - Inventory control
  - Standards management
  - Integration of processes
  - Systems throughout the supply chain
  - Surveillance of contract compliance
  - Accounts payable
  - Legal
- Managing centralized services such as accounts payable (AP), E-procurement, contract management systems, and warehouse management systems
- Developing supplier ombudsman programs
- Ensuring that the standard vendor prequalification process is being applied across business units
- Coordination and management of audit process
- Integration across functional streams
- Four direct reports — information technology (IT), audit, master data, and legal managers

Direct reports are as follows:

Audit manager
- Coordinates and oversees all major audit activities to ensure that benefits established in contracts are realized at the business unit level
- Works with finance to roll up benefits to P&L and balance sheet
- Works with the spend analysis manager to identify gaps in benefits realized and goals for improvement
- Tracks maverick spending across business units and identifies key areas of noncompliance
- Highlights key suppliers requiring intervention for performance improvement

Master data manager
- Manages vendor catalog
- Ensures appropriate coding of spend data
- Handles approval process on contractor database
- Ensures standard terms and conditions

IT manager
- Responsible for customer relationship management
- Works to identify and resolve cornerstone issues and problems at the site level
- Works with user groups to identify business-level requirements, and consolidates the requirements into a statement of work for new IT systems, identifying new functionalities, etc.
- Reviews proposals for new systems that meet company's user needs and constraints
- Oversees training programs in new IT systems

Legal manager
- Dotted line reporting to legal department
- Functional expert
- Provides legal expertise to major business units on SCM and contractural issues

11.3.5 VP of Supply-Chain Strategy

The responsibilities for this role are to:

- Oversee planning and deployment of major supply-chain programs across business units
- Collaborate with director of business intelligence to prioritize list of opportunities
- Develop and implement strategic sourcing plan
- Track all programs focused on supply-chain improvements
- Manage supplier relationships, including supplier development
- Oversee direct reports, including an administrator, strategy manager, and relationship management manager

Two of the direct reports are:

Strategy manager
- Leads a team of ten to twelve people tasked with leading major supply-chain and strategic sourcing improvement initiatives across the organization — teams would effectively lead cross-functional teams, develop sourcing strategies and recommendations, and execute approved strategies
- Contributes to market intelligence
- Responsible for contract formation for strategic sourcing initiatives

Manager of relationship management
- Leads a team of relationship managers

- Contributes to performance management key performance indicators (KPIs)
- Manages the commercial relationship for the major commodity groups, ensuring that the relationship is supported with the required resources
- Responsible for supplier development to enable improved collaboration between the enterprise and improvement of key suppliers to develop a world-class supply base
- Works with suppliers to resolve variances in performance and drive continuous improvement
- Works to continuously improve relationships with critical suppliers

11.3.6 Corporate Committee

A key factor in enabling supply-chain strategy is the approval of the corporate committee to support the supply-chain redesign effort. Regular meetings with the committee will be required to approve major supply-chain mandates and decisions that will have a significant impact on operations, business requirements, and functional strategies. The committee should also participate in critical SCM sessions that impact policy and strategy. An important lesson learned from benchmarking other companies is that executive support from operational units is fundamental to the deployment of supply-chain strategies. Companies that have employed a supply-chain council include FedEx, General Motors, Honda, Toyota, and many others. A corporate committee is also believed to be a critical element of leading-edge organizational SCM design.

11.3.7 Skill Sets Required

Each of the aforementioned positions will require a new set of job descriptions, key performance (KPIs) associated with their performance, and a defined set of competencies that will qualify an individual for the position. These requirements will need to be defined prior to any major change. Every company should move to develop key skills and deploy and map them to different positions in the organization. A recent study carried out by Handfield and Giuniper[4] identified the following key skills for supply-chain managers, although not every individual in the organization would require them. Weights should be given to individuals' required skills, as shown in Table 11.1.

---

[4] Handfield, R. and Giuniper, L., *Purchasing Education and Training II,* Tempe, AZ: Center for Advanced Purchasing Studies, 2004.

Table 11.1 Weighted Skills Matrix by Position

	Category	Purchasing Assistant	Buyer Nonproduction MRO Materials	Buyer Equipment Services	Buyer Product Materials	Inventory Manager	Materials Manager
Market strategies	A	2	4	4	3	2	5
Negotiation	A	2	3	4	3	3	S
Total-cost analysis	A	2	3	4	3	3	4
Transportation	A	2	3	3	4	3	5
Supply base management	A	2	4	4	4	4	5
Ethics	A						
Supplier qualification	A						
Outsourcing	A						
Project management	B						
Inventory management and analysis	B						
Process strategies	B						
Electronic performance	B						
Supplier performance	B						

ISO 9000	B									
Supplier certification	B									
Contract administration	C									
Contract law	C									
Contract alternatives	C									
Environment and safety	C									
Communication	D									
Decision making	D									
Initiative	D									
Interpersonal skills	D									
Innovation	D									
Leadership	D									
Teamwork	D									
Problem solving	D									
Statistics	E									
Life-cycle costing	E									
Lease versus buy	E									
Forecasting	E									

Table 11.1 Weighted Skills Matrix by Position (continued)

Category	Purchasing Assistant	Buyer Nonproduction MRO Materials	Buyer Equipment Services	Buyer Product Materials	Inventory Manager	Materials Manager
Budgeting	E					
Computer skills	F					

Note: Skill-level rating key: 1 = very little, if any, use of skill in the position; 2 = has a basic understanding of the skill; 3 = working knowledge and use of skills; 4 = good understanding and use of the skill; 5 = excellent understanding and application of the skill.

Skills Weighting By Position	Purchasing Assistant	Buyer Nonproduction Materials	Buyer Equipment Services	Buyer Product Materials	Inventory Manager	Materials Manager
A = sourcing	5	30	20	35	5	20
B = asset management	5	25	25	20	40	25
C = contracts/legal	5	10	15	10	5	10
D = interpersonal	15	15	15	15	25	35
E = quantitative	15	15	20	15	20	5
F = computer skills	55	15	5	5	5	5

11.4 Definition of Skills

The definitions of various skills are as follows:

- *Ethics* — Ability to apply the Institute of Supply Management standards of ethical behavior to different purchasing and supply management situations and identify appropriate decisions and behaviors when confronted with difficult ethical situations.
- *Interpersonal communication* — Ability to effectively communicate to individuals, teams, and groups via different channels, including e-mail, one-on-one discussions, team meetings, group presentations, or Webcasts, with appropriate behavior, grammar, and language.
- *Negotiation skill* — Ability to plan for and execute negotiations with a supplier or internal customer. This includes preparation, research, developing negotiation strategy, and BATNA (best alternative to no agreement) alternatives, ability to effectively manage unethical tactics and behaviors and to reach a win–win outcome with key suppliers.
- *Strategic thinking* — Ability to understand the impact of supply management decisions on company strategic plans, customers, suppliers, and internal functions. It is also the ablity to develop commodity strategies and document white papers that support the strategy.
- *Ability to make decisions* — An individual's ability to arrive at a conclusive decision in complex situations through analysis of the situation, identification of alternatives, understanding the impact of alternatives, weighing this information, and executing the decision effectively through assignment of deliverables and actions to appropriate parties.
- *Influencing and persuading* — Ability to convince stakeholders of the value of your position through facts and logic, and the ability to understand and respond to their concerns and to identify solutions that address these concerns.
- *Cross-functional team experience* — Team leadership skills, listening to team concerns, drawing out insights from reticent team members, and defining team deliverables. It also includes effective communication skills throughout the team process and the ability to act as an intermediary in resolving team conflicts.
- *Decision making and problem solving* — Ability to apply problem-solving tools, including process mapping, root cause, cause-and-effect, and statistical analyses. It is also the ability to determine a solution to the problem and execute it in a timely manner.

■ *Leadership* — Ability to lead a team of people by personal commitment, effective organizational and project planning, communication, agenda management, mentoring, encouragement, and effective management of team concerns and problems.

■ *Ability to work in teams* — Team leadership skills, listening to team concerns, drawing out insights from reticent team members, and defining team deliverables. It also includes effective communication skills throughout the team process and the ability to act as an intermediary in resolving team conflicts.

■ *Analytical skills* — Ability to quantify uncertain and nebulous problems, apply statistical and analytical tools to solve these problems, and explain difficult analytical concepts to team members.

■ *Managing change* — Ability to identify co-workers' concerns about change, and address these concerns through effective communication of impact on individuals' ways of working. It is also the ability to openly discuss the need for change and explain it to concerned individuals.

■ *Conflict resolution* — Ability to identify the root cause associated with team member conflicts and establish a set of reasonable alternatives for resolving the conflict. It may involve individual meetings and group mediation.

■ *Interpersonal communication* — Ability to speak clearly, listen carefully, explain, mentor, and guide individuals who express concerns, ideas, or opinions.

■ *Computer literacy* — Ability to understand and explain basic elements of data structures, input, workflow, and capabilities of major application software.

■ *Assessment of ethical situations* — Ability to identify day-to-day situations and associate them with ethical guidelines and regulations for the enterprise.

■ *Managing the supply base* — Ability to effectively measure supplier performance, identify leading suppliers who demonstrate the best performance, develop sourcing strategies for major categories, and develop ongoing continuous-improvement efforts with key suppliers.

■ *Managing internal customers* — Ability to work with internal customers for specific purchase categories to understand user requirements, specific technical issues, key points of contact, delivery and logistics channel requirements, quality requirements, and software interfaces associated with internal customer requirements for the category.

■ *Managing risk* — Ability to map supply and distribution channels to identify potential sources of risk, develop probable estimate of risk potential, and create contingency plans to reduce or eliminate elements of risk in the event of a major supply-chain disruption.

■ *Listening* — Ability to understand team/supplier/user concerns and issues, and repeat them to the individual clearly. It also includes the ability to understand the context of the communication and detect hidden meanings or concerns when relevant.

■ *Planning* — Ability to take an unstructured task, develop a charter, key deliverables, milestones, schedule, and action items for team members to execute. It includes frequent monitoring and updating of plan, with changes communicated to team members.

■ *Understanding of general business conditions* — Ongoing monitoring of financial indicators, market conditions, supply conditions, global events, and other key factors that may impact the business. It also includes the ability to translate facts into specific consequences for the business.

■ *Common sense* — Ability to apply logic to difficult situations to enable team members to reach a reasonable decision and outcome.

■ *Personal learning or self-development* — Ability to acquire additional knowledge through one's own initiatives

■ *Using the Internet* — Being able to navigate the Internet to locate supplier information, new suppliers, place orders on sell-side sites, and use internal buy-side sites.

■ *Structuring supplier relationships* — Developing the appropriate type of relationship for purchase expenditures. These range from strategic to arm's-length to more contractual relationships.

■ *Customer focus* — Understanding the end customers' wants and needs and matching buying strategies in support of those needs.

■ *Project management* — Ability to lead and coordinate a major project from inception to completion while meeting company criteria for success.

■ *Being organized or time management* — Systematizing the storage and retrieval of documents, records, and contracts to facilitate the efficient and wise use of time.

■ *Tactfulness in dealing with others* — Being assertive without alienating others when interfacing on common projects.

■ *Written communication* — Ability to develop concise, well-written documents that convey the necessary information.

■ *Creativity* — Ability to conceptualize and develop new and innovative approaches to problems or situations.

■ *Financial management* — Understanding the key financial principles and statements of the corporation, e.g., income statements, balance sheets, and cash flows.

- *Contract management* — Understanding the activities required to manage a purchase after the order has been placed.
- *Motivating others* — Utilizing and molding motives, attitudes, and opinions of others to enable them to perform their required tasks effectively and efficiently.
- *Presentation skills* — Ability to verbally deliver reports, situational analyses, and purchasing department overviews to groups of people in the organization.
- *Broad-based business skills* — Ability to understand the key functions of business both quantitatively and qualitatively.
- *Process mapping* — Using flow diagrams, graphs, and illustrations to visually depict the steps in a process.
- *Inquisitive nature* — Eagerness to learn about various aspects that affect the outcome of the supply manager's job. Questioning and inquiring to develop understanding is required.
- *Innovation management* — Ability to effectively manage change in a corporate setting.
- *Salesmanship* — Ability to clearly present ideas in a manner that will gain the acceptance of others.
- *Managing others* — Leading others in an effective manner that accomplishes corporate goals.
- *Computational ability* – Ability to calculate numbers or crunch data to support decision making.
- *Economic literacy* — Ability to understand the major factors of production, distribution, and consumption that influence business activity and their impact on the supply manager's strategies.
- *Entrepreneurial behavior* — Individual behavior is action oriented: suggest, try, and experience; create and develop; take responsibility and ownership. Risks are taken but managed well.
- *Motivational principles* — Understanding human behavior, attitudes, and motives to create an environment in which people are willing to independently pursue their goals.
- *Technical ability* — Understanding the practical, industrial, or mechanical aspects of the supply manager's job.
- *Contract writing* —Awareness of the legal aspects of the purchase order dealing with the specific terms and conditions of the agreement.

11.5 SCM Knowledge Definitions

The following are some important SCM knowledge definitions:

- *Supplier relationship management* — Creating value-added relationships through effective communication, joint understanding of needs and requirements, identification of win–win alternatives, effective change management within both enterprises, and development of KPIs to guide and manage the relationship into the future with key suppliers.

- *Total-cost analysis* — Mapping of supply chains to identify cost of ownership associated with selected suppliers and distribution channels and development of cost estimates using reasonable assumptions, approximations, and actual data to develop models of cost that can assist in driving improved supply-chain performance.

- *Purchasing strategies and plans* — Planning and development of key category strategies, design of supply chains, relationship management, and performance measurement associated with improving supply-chain performance.

- *Analysis of suppliers* — Collection of primary and secondary data, filtering and assessment of data, and development of summary white papers that identify the key strengths and weaknesses of selected suppliers in a given category market.

- *Competitive market analysis* — Collection, filtering, and assessment of key elements of market intelligence as input into commodity strategies, which includes elements of current market structures, pricing, key suppliers, customer requirements, value chain elements, and SWOT analysis associated with market alternatives and risk assessment.

- *Supply-chain management* — Identification and research on primary participants, information flows, and physical flows associated with a multi-enterprise supply chain, followed by the strategic alignment of processes, technology, information, metrics, and relationships to improve performance associated with the supply chain.

- *Supplier evaluation* — Ability to perform primary and secondary research to quantitatively and qualitatively assess performance of suppliers in key areas including financial performance, technology, management structure, cost, quality, delivery, service, systems, and other relevant criteria.

- *Supplier development* — Execution of strategies to identify suppliers requiring improvement, root cause analysis of supplier deficiencies and problems, development of win–win approaches to address deficiencies, and establishment of metrics to monitor ongoing improvement of processes.

- *Price and cost analysis* — Price analysis involves monitoring of market pricing through market indices, comparison with best-in-class pricing, identification of trends, and development of appropriate techniques for reducing exposure to price increases in key markets. Cost analysis involves development of reverse price estimates to identify subcategories of cost, identification of cost drivers associated with non-value-adding activities, and strategies to reduce cost through collaborative and noncollaborative approaches.

■ *Business process improvement* — Application of process mapping to understand as-is business processes, identification of non-value-adding activities, elimination or modification of non-value-adding activities, and development of new improved processes that reduce cycle time, improve quality, reduce cost, or demonstrate other measures of improved efficiency or effectiveness.

■ *Pricing techniques* — Development of effective user requirements, RFIs, RFQs, analysis of quotes, and recommendation of sourcing strategies that reduce price-increase exposure in the longer term.

■ *Commodity expertise* — Development of subject matter expertise associated with a key commodity, which may include elements such as technical requirements, pricing, cost drivers, technology trends, key supplier capabilities, market structure, quality issues, logistics channels, and risks associated with the commodity group.

■ *E-commerce or E-purchasing* — Understanding of key elements of E-purchasing or commerce systems, including data structures, software elements, user requirements, limitations of the technology, and future trends to monitor.

■ *Early supplier involvement* — Identification of leading suppliers of a given technology; supplier technology road map assessment; evaluation of suppliers; negotiation with suppliers to integrate into group product development processes; establishing appropriate contracts to define roles in product development, process development, and sharing of intellectual property; and management of expectations and issues as a process is rolled out.

■ *Total Quality Management and Six Sigma* — Development and management of continuous-improvement project teams focused on eliminating waste, process improvement, solving problems, or other issues related to cost savings and resolution of customer- or supplier-related issues.

■ *Project management* — Ability to define project charter, develop project plan, assign deliverables and roles, estimate project activity times, update project plan over time, manage unexpected project delays, and successfully complete project by scheduled due date.

■ *Outsourcing* — Development of insourcing or outsourcing variables into a defined decision-making model for insourcing or outsourcing a particular product or process technology. Variables may include make-or-buy price or cost data, technology requirements, capacity, technology road maps, supplier capabilities, core competence of organizations, and competitive intelligence or ability to gain a competitive advantage through development of a technology.

■ *Cost of poor quality* — Factors that contribute to extra cost as a result of supplier shipping poor quality. These include lost production, extra inspection costs, replacement order costs, etc.

■ *International sourcing* — Analysis of possible places from which to purchase commodities, goods, and services and of the logistics, import, and regulatory issues.

■ *Value analysis* — Analyzing the function of an item in relation to its costs.

■ *Legal issues* — The study of Uniform Commercial Code Section 2 and the buyer's rights in contracts and purchase orders. Additional coverage of common law is often required.

■ *Cultural awareness* — Understanding the different customs, practices, and business protocols of people located in different parts of the world.

■ *Quality assurance practices* — Procedures put in place at both the buyer and seller facilities to ensure that quality products are provided and received.

■ *Value chain analysis* — Studying where the value lies in the processes that link the supply chain, which extends from the supplier to the focal firm and back to the customer.

■ *Financial evaluation of suppliers* — Understanding the key indicators and ratios that provide a picture of the supplier's financial health.

■ *Logistics or distribution strategy* — Understanding how a product gets to market and the most effective way of ensuring customer service and satisfaction.

■ *Standardization programs* — Eliminating specials by getting the organization to adopt standard items that are readily available from numerous suppliers.

■ *Service buy analysis* — Understanding how service purchases are priced and the factors that determine a fair price.

■ *Economic and market principles* — Ability to understand the major factors of production, distribution, and consumption that influence business activity and their impact on the supply manager's strategies and the markets in which they buy.

■ *Make versus buy* — Analysis of the quantitative and qualitative factors that influence the decision to source externally versus making a part in-house.

- *Capital equipment purchases* — Understanding the techniques required to successfully source large-dollar expenditures for capital requirements.
- *Managing and analyzing inventory* — Gaining insight into the practices that allow for the efficient storage and use of inventory. These techniques include ABC analysis, inventory storage systems, forecasting methods, etc.
- *Financial and accounting basics* — Understanding balance sheets, income statements, and cash flows, all of which influence profitability. Ratios and analysis of financial health are also important.
- *Cycle-time management* — Techniques required to manage and analyze the components of lead times to deliver responsive service and yet keep inventories to a minimum.
- *Understanding technical terms* — Knowledge about the terminology used by technical groups such as engineering, IT, and operations.
- *Safety issues* — Requirements for material dispensation sheets, OSHA-approved equipment, and proper disposal of hazardous wastes to ensure compliance with all state, federal, and local laws.

11.6 Deploying Organizational Change

There are three different methods that organizations can adopt in deploying organizational change:

1. *Big bang and chaos creation:* This approach involves implementing all organizational changes at one time, with everyone moving to new roles across the organization simultaneously. This is a push strategy. This approach is most likely to create the greatest degree of confusion and uncertainty. One organization we worked with has an executive team that prefers this approach, which involves creating a chaotic environment. It is likely to generate increased turnover, disgruntled associates, and the results may not turn out as expected. It is important to note that this organization had a very tight deadline in which to drive performance improvements, and the executives may not have had a stake in seeking longer-term improvements.

2. *Piecemeal, or as demanded:* This approach involves assigning people to their new roles as the opportunity arises. For example, a strategic sourcing team person might be appointed to a full-time position only when the strategy is initiated at the request of the business unit. This is a pull strategy. This approach is least likely

to cause confusion, but runs the risk of not generating results quickly enough. The organization mentioned in the first method was in this mode for quite a long time before moving to the chaos creation mode. A piecemeal approach is likely to have people thinking that change is not imminent and that the *status quo* is more than likely to return. It may also lead to individuals "sabotaging" any changes so as to discourage and build a case against disturbing the status quo.

3. *Three modular waves:* This approach involves identifying "modules" across the supply-chain organization that are self-contained and have minimal interdependencies and impacts on daily operations, and making organizational changes in three major "waves" of change. Changes are made in those modules based on some very specific criteria (defined later), which will lay the foundational elements for growth in the rest of the organization. This is a "combination" strategy. The timing of the waves is critical; organizational "digestion" or stabilization must occur before the next wave commences.

It is our position that the third approach is best suited for many companies and leads to the best long-term results. The changes are strategically targeted, the unintended impacts are minimized, and the time to stabilization and benefits realization is minimized. This approach is outlined in greater detail in the following sections.

11.7 What Is Organizational Modularization?

Modularization is related to the concept of authority and property rights. A system of property rights is defined as "a method of assigning to particular individuals the 'authority' to select, for specific goods, any use from a nonprohibited class of uses."[5] In a well-decomposed organizational design, hidden system parameters ought to be under the control of the module only and not any other part of the system. In effect, the process of defining a module of an organization is critical, and it is important to draw the boundaries so that each "property owner" has "the right to use goods (or transfer that right) in any way the owner wishes so long as the physical attributes or uses of all other people's private property is unaffected. The economic benefits of carving out a protected sphere of

---

[5] Alchian, A., Some economics of property rights, *Il Politico,* 1965.

authority result in (1) a concentration of rewards and costs more directly on each person responsible for them and (2) the comparative advantage effects of specialized applications of knowledge in control." Let us call these the incentive benefits and division-of-knowledge benefits. In addition, the systemwide suboptimization impacts due to the optimization of a specific module are minimized (unintended consequences).

The goal, then, is to develop visible design rules that are enabling, i.e., rules that encourage modular innovation and recombination, but are loose enough not to constrain the system.[6] However, it is not that simple, because there will always be elements that are shared by all modules. For example, consider the medieval open-field system that dominated agricultural systems in Europe. For some activities, such as harvesting and the periodic grazing of cattle on fallow land, rights were held in common. For other activities, however, property was held privately, and the incomes of the peasants depended on the produce of the particular parcels of land over which they held a residual claim.[7]

Following this line of thinking, then, the team should establish a set of defined organizational modules and then evaluate these modules based on whether each module (1) has a significant impact on supply-chain maturity, (2) requires a concentration of knowledge and costs, (3) has minimal interdependencies with other modules in the organization (in particular, minimal impact on business unit operations if changes are made within the module), and (4) has a shared service component, meaning that the "output" is used by many other modules and, therefore, should be centralized.

How does this translate to organizational development for SCM? In selecting different organizational modules for change, it is important to not only define modules that can stand alone and maximize incentive and division-of-knowledge benefits but also define those "shared services" that should be centralized, to ensure open access and enabling of all modules. What are the definable modules that exist in different proposed organizational structures?

11.7.1 Organizational Modules: An Example

We held workshops at one company to develop a set of proposed organizational structures, which are shown in the following text. We made

---

[6] Garud, R. and Jain, S., The embeddedness of technological systems, In J. Baum and J. Dutton (Eds.), *Advances in Strategic Management* Greenwich, CT: JAI Press, 1996, pp. 389–408.

[7] Dahlman, C.J., *The Open Field System and Beyond*, New York: Cambridge University Press, 1980.

an implicit assumption that this organizational structure was one that would enable this company's journey to supply-chain maturity. We began by defining the following organizational modules:

1. Vice president of supply chain
2. Supply-chain business intelligence
3. Supply-chain strategy
4. Division A
5. Division B
6. Division C
7. Division D
8. Division E

Next, each of these modules should be evaluated in terms of its likelihood for introducing change, based on the following criteria:

1. Impact on supply-chain maturity
2. Concentration of knowledge and specialized skills
3. Minimal impact on operations from internal module changes
4. A shared service output characteristic

A preliminary assessment of the modules and the relative criteria are shown in Table 11.2. The rationale discussed previously suggests that wave-1 changes should have a high score in criteria 1, 2, and 4, with a low score on criterion 3. On the other hand, wave-3 changes require a more in-depth phased approach that will impact operations. Wave 3 should be deployed only after other elements have been stabilized. Wave 2 is an intermediate change, which will stabilize the first set of changes and pilot-test a single functional business unit before deployment across all sites.

The assessment in Table 11.2 suggests that the appropriate actions for organizational change might be adopted in the manner described in the following section.

11.8 Rollout of Proposed Organizational Changes

11.8.1 Wave 1 — Establishing the Foundation

Wave 1 in many organizations involves establishing the foundational elements of supply-chain maturity and is anticipated to bring the organization from a stage 2 to a stage 3 level of maturity. This first stage might take six to eight months to complete and will include the establishment of the following modular changes:

Table 11.2 Proposed Changes

Wave Number	Module	Foundational to Maturity Improvement	Interdependence — Impact on Operations?	Requires Concentration of Knowledge or Cost	Shared Service?
Wave 1	1) Vice president of supply chain	5	3	5	5
	2) Supply-chain business intelligence	4	1	5	5
	3) Supply-chain strategy	5	2	5	4
	4) Supply-chain integration	5	4	3	4
Wave 3	5) Business unit 1	4	5	3	1
	6) Business unit 2	2	4	3	1
Wave 2	7) Business unit 3	2	3	3	1
Wave 3	8) Business unit 4	2	5	3	1
	9) Business unit 5	1	2	3	1

Note: 1 = Low; 5 = high.

■ Establish a VP of SCM who reports directly to the CEO, with direct authority over all property rights associated with supply-chain decisions across the business. This should also include areas of spend such as indirect spend, advertising, and areas that are currently under others. This individual will have an authorized budget, responsibility, and resources to establish new organizational modules. This individual will direct the organizational changes and is considered fundamental to the success of the SCM initiative. The VP will "own" the supply-chain design process and will have key directors keeping him or her abreast of progress in major programs underway across the enterprise.

■ Establish a supply-chain business intelligence module, which will fall under the shared-services level of responsibility. This module will consist of a director of business intelligence supported by a team of business intelligence analysts, a communications director, a human resources director (tasked with developing and deploying training across the organization), and a spend management analyst team (tasked with identifying major areas of spend that are opportunities for cost savings). This team is fundamental to the success of the SCM initiative, as it has specialized analytical skills and is self-contained, yet can provide important inputs into the strategic planning initiatives for supply-chain strategy. The business intelligence group will have an established directive to manage, summarize, and disseminate information regarding key internal business and external supply market conditions, and will focus on scanning and filtering intelligence on evolving market conditions, risks, and events. This group will develop both structured intelligence for strategic sourcing teams and unstructured information for business units to keep them abreast of changes in business conditions that will impact their business.

■ Establish a supply-chain strategy module led by a director of strategic sourcing. This individual will establish a team of "supply-chain black belts" who will lead an initial wave of five sourcing strategies across the business. The supply-chain black belts will be assigned on a six-month basis to a defined category of spend, develop a cross-functional team, and work closely with the business intelligence group to identify total spend and for background analysis of supply market conditions.

■ Establish a supply-chain integration module led by a director responsible for coordinating data management and maintenance, controlling master data, checking data elements, auditing performance, and coordinating all new contracts. Another element will be a full-time legal manager reporting to this individual who will interface directly with the legal group on all new contracts.

The elements of wave 1 will essentially build the foundational elements of supply-chain design, strategic sourcing, and operational and performance management systems. Most important among these is supply-chain design, which is the overarching program management component of organizational change and a shared service that impacts all of the organizational modules identified. An example of a short list of initiatives for year 1 of the rollout might include:

- Establishing strategic sourcing teams for three or four major spend areas across the company
- Establishing a committee to review engineering standards across all major projects to ensure standardization of requirements to enable leveraging of spend
- Establishing a team to audit current warehouse management processes that interface directly with maintenance to identify opportunities for improvement

These teams would then be assigned project leaders, who would be responsible for developing a project plan, gathering data working with the business-intelligence-and-market-intelligence team, eliciting stakeholder and supplier input, and reporting to the program committee on a timely basis with an action plan.

11.8.2 Wave 2 — Piloting Relationship Management Processes

The first round of wave-1 projects will begin coming in after six to eight months, with results hopefully exceeding expectations and the business units beginning to applaud the success of these early efforts. The next phase of change, moving the enterprise from a stage 2 to a stage 3 level of maturity, requires a two-phase process. Wave 2 will involve establishing the foundational elements of a collaborative relationship-based model of SCM. Completion of wave 2 will take another six to eight months. During this time, a second wave of strategic sourcing projects will be initiated based on the existing supply-chain business intelligence, supply-chain strategy, and supply-chain intelligence modules. However, the set of relationship-based contacts in the working business units will not yet have been fully deployed.

Wave 2 will include the establishment of a director of SCM in one division that already has a strong track record of solid customer relationships. This director should report to the VP, as well as managers in the warehouse, logistics, and procurement groups. These managers will be responsible for overseeing a team of relationship managers who will interface directly with the suppliers of choice in this division. Note that this phase of change will require high levels of training early on, followed by periodic meetings with relationship managers to understand the pitfalls, obstacles, successes, and early wins. This pilot-change module will provide invaluable information that will be used in wave 3.

11.8.3 Wave 3 — Full Deployment

In the final wave, the processes established in wave 2 for relationship-based management of the supply base will be deployed across the remaining business units. This will, in effect, bring the entire organization up to a stage-4 maturity level, and it is anticipated to take place over a nine-month period. Again, all of the other foundational modules described earlier will play a pivotal role in guiding and supporting the deployment of this strategy across business units.

11.9 The Criticality of Building Consensus in Change Management: The Role of Cross-Functional Teams

A focused performance measurement system should align supply-chain roles and career paths with a defined system of needs assessment in key knowledge and skill-set areas. Key areas of focus in terms of personnel development will include the following:

1. *Team-building skills:* Leadership, decision making, influencing, and compromising
2. *Strategic planning skills:* Project scoping, goal setting, and execution
3. *Communication skills:* Presentation, public speaking, listening, and writing
4. *Technical skills:* Web-enabled research and sourcing analysis
5. *Broader financial skills:* Cost accounting and making the business case
6. *Relationship management skills:* Ethics, facilitation, conflict resolution, and creative problem solving
7. *Legal skills:* Legal issues, contract writing, and risk mitigation

11.9.1 Roles

Success requires alignment of all personnel toward achieving SCM objectives. The standards and processes are based on the expectation that:

■ VPs and managers will ensure that supply-chain excellence is a key business objective and will promote cross-functional decision making at all levels.
■ Planners will focus on delivering future-focused executable work packages.
■ Schedulers will balance resources and maintain future-focused, challenging work schedules.
■ Supervisors will focus on assuring field personnel of safety, productivity, and compliance with quality standards.
■ Buyers will execute agreements according to plans and standards.
■ Relationship managers will work with suppliers to continuously improve processes.
■ Engineers will actively seek solutions to eliminate maintenance work.
■ Company and contract personnel deployment will be controlled centrally at the business unit to balance resources.
■ All personnel will be trained in the skills required for them to fulfill their roles or job requirements.

In addition, the following characteristics of the supply-chain organization should be developed:

1. A central SCM group should be created for governance and strategic processes, including business intelligence, to ensure that the foundational elements of the standards are established. Leadership for common spend will come from a corporate group independent of any business unit. This group needs to have enough resources to support the management of the common-spend portfolio.
2. A single A/P group should handle the A/P function for the corporation. This A/P group will report into the central SCM group. The location should be chosen to minimize one-time and ongoing costs as well as to benefit from the proximity to other groups such as treasury.
3. The procurement groups should remain within the business units. This role will transition from a transactional role to a facilitation and contract administration role and will move toward a logistics planning and scheduling role.

4. Vendor audit is a governance role that should be entrusted to a group separate from the operations areas to ensure that they provide a "cold-eye" review. This group should be centrally led to provide consistency in approach and follow-up across the enterprise and to leverage the benefits of scale. The location will be chosen to minimize one-time and ongoing costs as well as benefits associated with proximity to other SCM governance groups. Performance management should reside at both the corporate and business unit levels.

5. Spend governance should be managed according to the commonality of the spend. Strategic sourcing should be a distributed group, but the business intelligence function can be located centrally. The leads for strategic sourcing processes should be located wherever they can interact best with internal business units. A number of these individuals can be established in each business unit to support professional development in other SCM personnel, stay in touch with business unit realities, and support business-unit-specific spend requirements. However, common-spend strategic sourcing teams should be located centrally.

6. Process governance, the maintenance of the integrated standards, policies, and systems that will be built by systems, should be managed by the central SCM group. In addition, this group should monitor and support each business unit's progress toward the SCM maturity state of being optimized. Without this stewardship, the business units may be distracted by the operational realities of the business environment.

7. Business unit SCM activities should be managed to meet business unit requirements. Leadership for business unit SCM should be integrated within the business unit leadership team and needs to have organizational authority to influence the business unit management strategy.

11.10 The Challenges of Partnerships

In today's global supply-chain environment, working to create mutual benefits for partners is a key element for success. Cross-functional teams must work together to align business strategies. Teams are being asked to engage with other groups to define supply-chain strategies that can optimize price, yet ensure timely delivery and best-in-class performance from their partners. Success in today's interdependent world demands "we" leaders — people who look beyond narrow self-interest to build partnerships in pursuit of a greater good.

In a recent *Wall Street Journal* article, Jonathan Tisch (October 26, 2004, p. B2) notes that partnerships are at the heart of effective management. Because of poor experiences, the concept of partnership is not really operationalized very well. Fundamentally, it refers to the fact that whenever managers, employees, communities, shareholders, owners, and even competitors join forces in pursuit of shared goals, everybody wins.

Tisch notes that partnership is an approach to leadership that is not divisive but unifying, not competitive but collaborative, not based on a zero-sum philosophy of scarcity but on abundance — the economic, intellectual, and spiritual abundance that people can produce when their talents and energies are unleashed. Not only is it possible to "do good" and "do it well" at the same time, but you actually do better in business terms when you do good in ethical terms.

Some of the challenges identified by Tisch include the following:

■ "You can't fake partnership. Unless you're prepared to treat your partner's concerns as equal in importance to your own, you can't forge a real or lasting partnership."

■ Partnership demands creativity. It is usually easy to see how the interests of partners conflict or clash; it is not so easy to find new ways of doing business that let you transcend the conflict and meet both partners' needs.

■ Partnership requires compromise. If the idea of leaving a single dollar on the table drives you nuts, you may not be cut out for management by partnership.

■ Partnership demands commitment and consistency. When you enter a partnership, you are saying, "I will follow through on my promises; I will be here tomorrow, and the day after that, and the day after that."

■ Partnership requires flexibility. A partnership mobilizes the talents of two or more partners to benefit them all, but this cannot happen unless you are willing to let your partners unleash their talents, even if they make choices that are different from the ones you would have made.

■ Above all, a partnership requires fairness. Everyone must benefit from a partnership. If you try to use it as an opportunity to exploit or take advantage of other people or organizations, the partnership will soon collapse.

Tisch concludes with the fact that "Raising a generation of 'We' managers will require a serious ethical reorientation on the part of businesses, colleges, and universities. And managing through partnerships may be tougher than managing through manipulation. But as David Neeleman and other exceptional leaders illustrate, it can be done. It's the only way to achieve lasting success and keep American CEOs from appearing on the docket in even more courtrooms." Read the vignette in Table 11.3 for an example of partnership at work.

11.11 Conclusion

Many companies are at a critical juncture in their growth strategy. The development of a formal supply-chain organization will likely lead to the growth and development of these companies. By making a small investment in the supply-chain organization, a significant return will be realized through the effective management of capital spending and best-in-class supply management practices. The lesson learned from poorly managed supply chains is that to grow the company profitably and avoid significant waste and cost, SCM must play an integral role.

The proposals developed in this chapter are based on extensive benchmarking of industry leaders, interviews with key stakeholders across many companies, workshops identifying best practices and levels of maturity currently in existence across companies, and the integration of thought leaders' ideas in SCM. All of the benefits proposed have a high probability of realization, provided the infrastructure at your company is modified to align with these proposals. Indeed, many of these projections are conservative and may be surpassed earlier than expected if the required resources are established early. Further, these changes are not dependent on the implementation of ERP systems. Rather, we propose that changes in business processes be enabled through a formal structure. The results will be enhanced by ERP, but they could be deployed immediately without any type of ERP initiative and deliver significant cost savings and value to the business units.

11.12 Checklist

- Assess SCM organizational structure.
- Understand skills and SCM knowledge definitions.
- Deploy changes in rollout waves.

11.13 Results

- Relevant SCM organizational structure

Table 11.3   An Example of Partnership at Work

Tires. Let's face it — they are everywhere. One energy company buys them new from two suppliers who are the only producers of these tires in the world. The wear on these tires from the trucks' operations and the harsh conditions result in a short wear cycle, resulting in a stockpile of worn tires. People try to use them as guideposts, spray-paint them, and even put them up as displays in front of the visitor center. Tires are one of the biggest eyesores at many major projects. People do not know what to do with these tires.

At one company we visited, a sourcing strategy team looked at the problem of tires two years ago and came to the conclusion that the tire suppliers were very content with the current position as a duopoly. This strategy was not aligned with another strategy that had resulted in the contract for trucks alternating between two different manufacturers seven times in the last seven years. It is tough to standardize on a tire, when you have not standardized on a truck.

Consider the case of FedEx. They discovered that their truck tires had a life of approximately 30,000 mi, even though the manufacturer claimed that the life was 50,000 mi. A cross-functional team looked at the problem and discovered that the reason for the short life cycle was that tires were subjected to a great deal of sidewall stress due to FedEx employees pulling up to the curb, wearing down the sidewalls prematurely. So how did they deal with the problem?

They engaged with one of their tire manufacturers in a strategic partnership. They brought transportation engineers to the table and discussed the fundamentals of tire technology. They discussed stress factors, tire pressure, resistances, and other technical elements that went into tire design. And in the end they designed a tire that could meet the rigors and abuses of the daily schedule of a FedEx driver. They even designed different tire recommendations for rural and city drivers based on their routes, and recommended these changes to the supply management team. The team then worked on a target pricing model that would involve marginal price increases of 5 percent on these custom tires, yet would increase the life of the tire from 30,000 to 80,000 mi.

What is the total cost of ownership associated with this savings? At what level of supply planning is your organization? How aligned are your teams with the other teams working on seemingly different but interrelated strategies?

Chapter 12

Benchmarking

Function	Objective	Tactical Step	Chapter/ Appendix
Supply market intelligence	Supply market research	Opportunity identification and validation	2
		Project approval	2
		Establishing the team	3
		Project plan	3
		As-is assessment	4
		Supply market research	5
		Market forecasts	5
		External and market analyses	6
	Strategy and resource commitment	Detailed supplier evaluation and research	7
		Evaluate current and alternative strategies	8
		Understand contract formation	8

Function	Objective	Tactical Step	Chapter/ Appendix
Strategic sourcing	Negotiate and select supplier	Develop relationship strategy	8
		Strategy position paper	8
		Develop requests for information (RFIs) and build negotiation strategy	9
		Negotiate	9
		Final supplier selection	9
		Form contracts	9
	Implement and promote compliance	Implement contracts	9
		Transition to relationship manager	10
Relationship management		Communicate expectations	10
	Improve supplier performance	Measure performance	10
		Resolve issues and develop supplier performance	10
Benchmarking processes and driving continuous improvement	Set a vision for change	Build an organization for supply-chain excellence	11
		Benchmark performance and drive continuous improvement	12, App. B

12.1 Chapter Outline

- Benchmarking supply market intelligence and organizational maturity
- The supply-chain management (SCM) framework
- How will organizations progress through this framework?
- Maturity grids and guiding principles charts
- Behaviors and roles
- Conclusion — leading change in supply management

It is only by finding better practices through benchmarking and incorporating them in the work processes that the desired results will be achieved.

— **Robert C. Camp**

Benchmarking is not an exercise in imitation. It yields data, not solutions.

— **Jac Fitz-Enz**

12.2 Benchmarking Supply Market Intelligence and Organizational Maturity

A supply-chain organizational maturity model is a useful framework to develop supply-chain, sourcing, and market intelligence improvement strategies to progress from ad hoc to optimized (operational excellence) levels.

Figure 12.1 shows the relationship between organizational learning and organizational performance. Benchmarking with other major organizations in different industries shows that it is a three- to five-year journey from ad hoc to operational excellence, depending on where the particular organization or business unit begins. This is sometimes referred to as the maturity diagram and illustrates the processes and benefits associated with each level of maturity. The journey toward operational excellence shown in Figure 12.2 has to be planned and implemented carefully, as moving from one category to the next involves changing behaviors at all levels of the organization. From experience, it is not recommended to attempt to move more than one category at a time.

In the early stages of improvement, a company will deploy strategic sourcing (SS) processes that will reduce the number of suppliers. This is key; advanced strategies cannot be deployed until the number of people working with the organization is reduced. Leverage your spend to the extent possible and partner with the right group of people. Note that not every relationship will be a partnership, but we need to really understand our markets and make better decisions that reduce risk exposure. This will save money, which is the next benefit. This will impact our cost of goods sold (COGS), and we will be able to cut prices for all business units.

The majority of people working in SCM today are doing manual paperwork, that is, non-value-added work. As we become more efficient, we can grow the company without having to dedicate people to non-value-added transactional work and, instead, train our people to become more strategic in working with suppliers to find additional opportunities to improve delivery, quality, cost, technology, and ways of working. Some

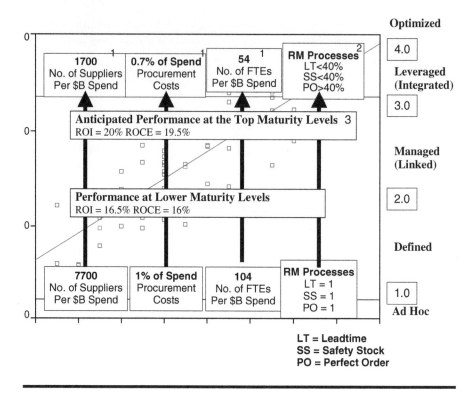

Figure 12.1   SCM maturity and associated performance.

of these benefits will accrue from enterprise systems and improved data, but the majority are a function of the new processes put in place.

Finally, the greatest opportunities occur once your company has established its supply-chain network, and it is able to deliver. In the words of one manager: "The biggest opportunity for savings occurs after the ink on the contract has dried." Moreover, by working on managing the relationship with suppliers, collaborating and sharing ideas, and innovation, we can find ways to take cost out of the supply chain in a way that mutually benefits both parties, and which would not occur otherwise. Think of it as exploiting the human capital and intellectual property that resides in our supply base and putting those ideas to work. This is the most advanced level of supply-chain maturity.

At level four, your organization can move the needle on ROI from 16.5 percent to 20 percent, and ROCE from 16 percent to 19.5 percent (depending on industry).

Organizational digestion is a big factor in building and benchmarking maturity. The organization needs to digest the changes, integrate them into the work practices and culture, stabilize, and then proceed. This must be managed and is a big leadership challenge. Leaders must:

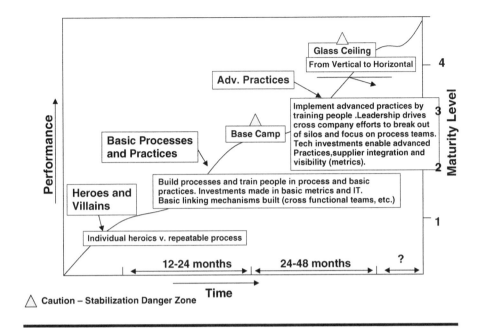

Figure 12.2   Building SCM maturity.

1. Allow enough time for each group to digest and stabilize. Each group is different, and early adaptors will want to leave late adaptors behind; this must be managed. No group can get too far behind.
2. Force the stabilization by slowing the change process enough to accomplish this without resting on your successes.
3. Get the groups restarted by overcoming inertia and leading the way on the next climb.
4. Provide the investments and resources needed to make the climb (communication, training, IT, and manpower).

There are two major caution zones on this journey — the base camp and the glass ceiling. The base camp is the first stabilization zone at about level 2.5 maturity. The organization has some basic processes and practices in place and is starting to get primary returns. This is a tough restart challenge for leadership.

The glass ceiling is the shift from functional (silo) management to horizontal management. The power and authority of the process teams are slightly greater than those of the functional leaders. Budgets are built for process teams to control. This is at about level 3.5 and is the major barrier to gaining the secondary returns, which are the major returns (see Figure 12.3).

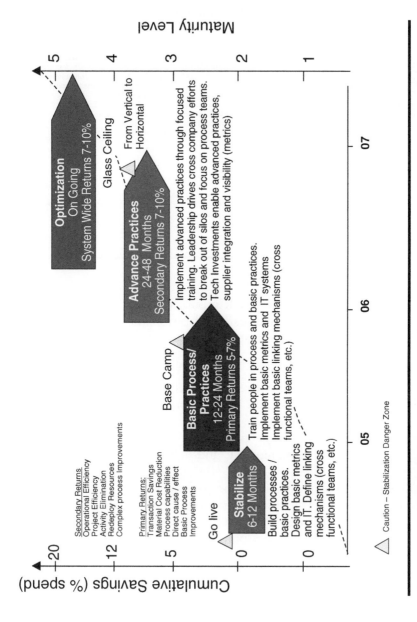

Figure 12.3 Implementation waves versus savings.

12.3 The SCM Framework

SCM is defined as the management and integration of supply-chain organizations and activities through collaborative organizational relationships, effective business processes, and high levels of information sharing.

Management of supply chains is a key element for competitive success, ensuring that organizations achieve a sustainable competitive advantage. A framework has been developed that represents the building blocks required to achieve success shown in Figure 12.4. This framework shows us the road map to operational excellence, and the key elements that an individual working for a company needs to be effective in his or her work and create value for the organization.

A useful metaphor to consider when applying this framework is that of a soldier going into battle in World War II. A soldier stepping off a gunship onto the beaches of Normandy did so knowing that behind them was an established infrastructure of solid support. They had prepared for the battle and had good training. There were established plans in place and controls to monitor the soldier's troop activity and provide guidance. Most important of all, the soldier knew that there was a solid group of leaders behind him. The soldier was confident that his generals had a clear concept of what they were trying to achieve and a clear vision of how they were going to achieve it. For every soldier achieving success on the battlefield, a lot is taking place behind him — good generals, good command and control systems, excellent supply and logistics networks, solid technology platforms, and a groundwork of detailed elements that enable success in the field.

In any given enterprise, associates, customers, suppliers, and employees go to work every day facing a new set of challenges, issues, decisions, and situations, much like the soldier getting off the gunship onto the beaches of Normandy. So, when associates go into work ready to face the situations that lie ahead, they need to know what enablers will support them as they confront these challenges. An enabler is foundational. The associate who is at the apex of the triangle knows there are four key enabling elements supporting him or her within the SCM framework:

1. Leadership — Operational excellence is built upon a foundation of solid leadership. Leadership represents the foundation of the enabler framework. Every action in the field or with the supply community takes place with the knowledge that there are strong leaders and a leadership structure committed to the success of the enterprise and its people, and a set of leaders who will support them when the going gets rough. Leaders must set clear expectations, ensure the capability and capacity to achieve them, and make

certain that the team is working collaboratively for the organization's bottom line.

2. Process control — If we do not have control over our processes, there is no way to establish consistency or improve our performance. Control provides us with the ability to clearly demonstrate the value SCM brings to the enterprise. Without an effective leadership structure, process control is at best ineffective.

3. Continuous improvement — Organizations need to continuously improve processes. When a new or modified process is designed, it is about 70 percent right, so it is critical to never be satisfied with the current level of performance. Associates are expected to continually question the status quo to get all processes to an optimal level. Note here that continuous improvement (CI) without control is futile. Without defined mechanisms to measure and control a process, improving it becomes impossible. It is only through CI that organizations can deliver functional and operational excellence.

4. Operational excellence — Once soldiers know they have leadership support, can count on the performance of well-controlled processes, and that when these processes are not working, they are aggressively improved. Through these actions, soldiers obtain *esprit de corps*, which is a well-known indicator of organizational health and a predicator of superior performance. It manifests itself as a strong desire to achieve common goals. *Esprit de corps* is a precursor to operational excellence, which is the flawless and consistent execution of integrated processes to provide superb customer service and optimal business performance.

Just as the soldier in Normandy is given orders to take an objective, enterprise associates are being told, "Here are the processes you need to complete and the method for completing them. As you execute them, you need to identify and report on methods to improve them, knowing that there is a system in place to measure the improvements and that you will have the full support of a committed leadership team. It is not acceptable to do things randomly. You are part of an integrated team working together to achieve success, and you will in turn need to act as a leader to others you work with on these processes, when that time comes."

We will now review the elements at each of these levels in greater detail and describe what the standard expectations are for all associates working in the SCM function. This framework forms the basis for the operational excellence model, which is described in greater detail later in this standards document.

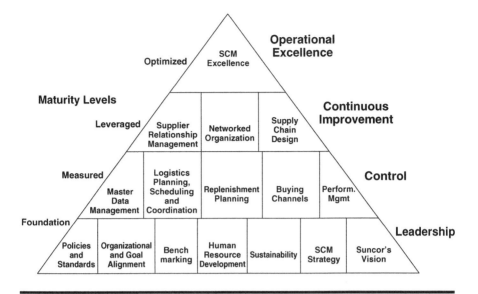

Figure 12.4   The SCM framework.

12.4   How Will Organizations Progress through This Framework?

The SCM framework (see Figure 12.4) assumes that there is a growing level of maturity that takes place as organizations build the structure from the ground up.

The SCM maturity model will be used as a framework to develop improvement strategies to progress to levels of functional excellence, leading to the peak of the operational excellence pyramid. Figure 12.4 shows the levels of SCM maturity and outlines a development path for an organization. As noted earlier, this is a three- to five-year journey from basic to advanced, depending on the starting position of the particular organization or business unit.

This maturity diagram describes the representative structure and behaviors that exist at each level of maturity. The journey toward SCM maturity has to be planned and implemented carefully because moving from one level to the next involves changing behaviors at all levels of the organization. From experience, it is not recommended to attempt to jump ahead and skip a level. Building SCM maturity is like building a house; a foundation needs to be built, and then value-added levels are laid upon the foundation. At each level, the house needs to be stabilized before proceeding to avoid collapse.

12.4.1 Foundation — Leadership

This sets the basis for all other elements. It appears that at this level of maturity, the organization is focused on putting in the foundational elements for process excellence. The focus of the organization at this level is on defining expectations. An organization that is at level two has defined roles and accountabilities against which personnel are trained. Standards of performance are captured in formal documents such as service level agreements (SLAs) and contracts. Organizational structures are defined to support the integrated processes and processes for aligning goals, and are well understood. SCM processes are documented and personnel are trained in the upstream and downstream supply-chain processes. Jobs are defined and oriented to the integrated SCM processes, and individuals have influence over their personal goals. At this level, benchmarks are identified and performance is more predictable, but functional silos still dominate thinking. The language used to describe cross-functional interactions is still in terms of "we" and "them." Remember that at this level you will see aspects of the higher levels of maturity, but the SCM group's performance is consistent in these areas.

12.4.2 Measured — Process Control

At this level of maturity, the organization is focused on establishing control, repeatability, and reliability of the processes based on a foundation of leadership. The key processes work as they were originally designed to, and they can be measured. And for the first time, they are being managed with strategic intent. As a result, there is a focus on bringing the processes under control to meet specific business value-added goals. Teams of personnel representing each function become process owners and are responsible for the total performance of an integrated process. Although the SCM function owns the primary relationship with suppliers, business unit representatives take a greater interest in the management of these relationships. Performance metrics are in place for all processes, and suppliers are regularly reviewed for progress. Nonconformances to standards are reported and mostly followed up. An internal attest process is in place, and recommendations are reviewed and responded to. Strategic relationships have two-way balanced scorecards in place that are used to maintain and defend these relationships Levels of trust increase with strategic suppliers, who now play a more active role in managing the corporate processes. Significant effort is put into ensuring that the master data is accurate, specific, universal, all encompassing, and controlled. Some CI programs are taking shape and supplier quality management (SQM) programs are beginning to be formulated.

12.4.3 Leveraged — CI

The organization begins to find the synergies in the entire system and begins to work with people across functional boundaries to continuously improve processes and operations for the greater good of the company. This level of maturity is all about improving integrated business process performance. CI programs and SQM programs are in place. Cross-functional teams include strategic suppliers who seamlessly manage integrated business processes. Cross-functional teams continuously seek a balance between SCM and business goals that will benefit the entire company. Attest recommendations and nonconformances are followed up, and corrective action is implemented. Master data is relied on heavily to coordinate the cross-functional business processes. Administrative activities have been highly automated. Forecasts, risk-based approvals, and forecast-based budgeting are an integral part of the SCM landscape. Trust levels with the supply base are increasing, resulting in self-service capabilities being extended to a significant portion of the supply base. The impacts of the supply-chain architecture are understood, and improvement programs are in place for strategically important constraints. Supply relationships are recognized as key to success, resulting in roles and organizational structures that define the nature of these relationships for the mutual benefit of both organizations.

12.4.4 Optimized — Operational Excellence

Processes have been improved to a level where general maintenance is all that is required, and the organization has reached the point of true operational excellence. The focus at this level is extending and broadening the success of integrated business processes. This is where we see that organizational boundaries are not barriers to the collaborative, effective, and efficient management of integrated business processes. Lights-out POs, supplier self-service, and suppliers managing inventory and capacity planning are the norm. Trust, mutual dependency, and *esprit de corps* are the basis for the collective success of the enterprise, its customers, and suppliers. At this point, the focus of the enterprise is on setting the structure for and managing its integrated supply network.

Proceeding through this maturity (from foundation through to optimized) is a difficult and arduous journey, but it is well worth it. It means that everyone in the organization must focus his or her full effort and energy to move to the next level of maturity. Each level of maturity represents a new hurdle. At the foundational level, leadership support and getting everyone to buy in to the vision takes a lot of communication and change management. At the next level, measurement systems support is a critical investment. For example, the systems required to support integrated processes (through cross-functional teams and shared goals linked to rewards) are critical in the leveraged level and must be built and reinforced by the leadership.

Continuously improving processes is a much more resource-intensive activity than leveraged, as people must work on improvement teams that may take them away from their regularly scheduled tasks. Once the level of operational excellence is reached, the culture for improvement is so well embedded in the organization that change is an assumed value for every individual.

But investing in the next level of maturity without also sustaining the previous level can lead to a regression to a lower level (aka the "rubber band effect"). To prevent this from occurring, leadership must reinforce and insist on the practices and discipline instituted in the lower levels to keep the foundation from cracking.

12.4.5 Elements of Leadership

12.4.5.1 Vision

Every organization must establish a leadership vision. An example might be:

- Providing the collaborative leadership that stewards our company's supply chains to create and sustain a structure of organizational relationships, business processes, information systems, logistics systems, facilities, and competencies that create value for our customers.
- Strategically managing and synchronizing our company's supply networks to deliver goods and services when and how required.

There should also be a clear relationship established between the vision and the organization's financial plan, which might, for example, include the following:

- Double shareholder value every five years.
- Achieve operational excellence.
- Environmental health and safety excellence.
- More than fifteen percent return on capital employed (ROCE).
- Twenty-five percent increase in market share in five years.

12.4.5.1.1 SCM Strategy

SCM strategy is the basis for achieving the vision and mission. SCM seeks to achieve vision and mission through the deployment of several interrelated strategies. These strategies will vary based on where the organization is in its supply-chain maturity. Examples of some strategies might include the following:

■ Application of standard processes and practices enabled with integrated technology for the management of supply chains to ensure that our company's supply chains consistently meet our business requirements.
■ Collaborative leadership of the development of supply chains across organizational boundaries to ensure they deliver exceptional value by supporting an integrated plan. Development encompasses changing the supply-chain's structure (process, technology, and relationships), as well as the behaviors and culture within our company and across the supply chain.
■ Leveraging of corporate spend for the benefit of our company.
■ Management of supply chains through use of cross-functional teams that reach across organizational boundaries. These teams will enable the achievement of our company's strategic goals and provide value to our stakeholders.
■ Integration of key suppliers into the business. Integration will allow our company's and suppliers' skills, knowledge, and capabilities to be leveraged for each organization's mutual benefit.
■ A disciplined focus on logistics excellence through the planning of logistic activities, open sharing of forecasts and limitations up and down the supply chain, and collaborative coordination and synchronization of logistics activities.
■ Being a "customer of choice" through rapid payment and equitable ethical treatment of our suppliers.

These strategies should be closely aligned with other strategies and objectives across the organization that may be held by other parties, including the following:

Shareholder
■ Process designs will provide stewardship of supply-chain assets and resources to support performance and strategy objectives.
Customer/Suppliers
■ Provide payment for services and goods when delivered rather than requiring an invoice.
■ Enable process connectivity so that information can be shared easily with supply-chain partners to drive collaborative behaviors.
■ Optimize overall business value, not functional or business segments, without disabling required business functionality.

- Reduce paperwork by shifting toward digital transactions to speed up processes and reduce costs.
- A goal not to force systems solutions on to the supplier or customer network.

Controls

- Control and approval at the lowest level. Avoid multiple controls and approval (more than one is too many).
- Design controls into process. Automated controls are preferred.
- Ensure that processes support compliance reporting.
- Avoid valueless controls.

Process

- Organize structures to enable accurate and relevant reporting and cost analysis so as to support future flexibility of business.
- Shift toward proactive planning of supply processes.
- Simplify the process as much as possible, use standard elements, eliminate non-value-added steps, and reduce delays and duplication — keep it simple.
- Maximize automation of transactions to shift focus to strategy, planning, and analysis.
- Create processes to enable both current and future requirements.
- Design standard and integrated common processes and elements to enable companywide (distributed and remote) SCM services as and when required.
- Do not hinder process design to accommodate ERP systems.
- Materials and services moving through the supply chain are only handled at points that add value.
- Single point of data entry.

In conjunction with the remaining elements of leadership they form the supporting structure for growth.

12.4.5.2 Benchmarking

This will drive improvement by:

- Providing milestones to gauge our progress in our voyage to maturity.
- Internal benchmarking to leverage organizational learning and deploy best practices across the business.
- Applying the maturity model and standards to our work, and comparing with best-in-class companies outside of the industry to bring in best practices and improve processes.

12.4.5.3 Policies and Standards

This will ensure adherence to defined ways of working, as in:

- Companywide SCM policy, including governance model for the corporate group.
- Aligned business goals and objectives.
- Long-term improvement plans (more than five years).
- Integrated and consistent processes across the value chain.
- Standardized SCM terminology.
- Documenting and assessing the standards developed and periodically auditing to ensure that CI is taking place.

Setting a standard and a set of policies is a leadership responsibility. You are not yet measuring the process, only defining and establishing a standard expectation. In other words, how can you expect people to know what to do and where they are going if they are not provided with a standard? A standard informs people what is acceptable work and what is not. If there is ever a question that comes up about an individual's actions on the job, the policy or standard is a way of gauging whether it is appropriate or not. It also ensures that everyone is pulling in the same direction.

12.4.5.4 Sustainability

This is a key element of leadership. Without it, the business is not sustainable. Sustainability is defined as:

- Respect and caring for each other's welfare.
- Ethical behaviors in combination with fair and equitable treatment of all that do business with the company.
- Respect for the value diversity brings to the company and patience to develop it.
- Engagement of communities in the benefits of business and their long-term growth.
- Environmentally conscious decisions and programs throughout supply chains.

Sustainability is operationalized through three standards:

1. Environmental policies in consideration of our communities:
   - *Redesigning* the processes to reduce environmental waste.
   - *Substituting* less polluting materials or processes, including increasing use of recycled inputs.

- *Reducing* the number and amount of materials used that contribute to waste streams.
- *Recycling* material at the end of its useful life.
- *Extending* the life cycle of inputs by selecting materials with longer useful lives.
- *Supporting* suppliers with established environmentally responsible reputations.
- *Life-cycle assessment* to better understand total costs and cradle-to-grave processes.

2. Supplier diversity — increasing the level of corporate spend going to minority, ethnic, and diverse suppliers through a focused program that emphasizes the following elements:
   - Corporate commitment to diversity.
   - A focused process to discover and identify new, diverse suppliers who are not currently in the supply base.
   - Measuring the effectiveness of diversity programs in terms of percentage of diverse spend relative to total spend.
   - Measuring diverse supplier performance and communicating this performance to suppliers on a regular basis.
   - Evaluation of diverse supplier capabilities.
   - Working with diverse suppliers to improve their performance through focused supplier development and SQM programs.

3. Ethical conduct — ensuring ethical conduct through adherence to the Institute for Supply Management code of ethics:
   - Consider, first, the interest of the company in all transactions and carry out and believe in its established policies.
   - Be receptive to competent counsel from colleagues and be guided by such counsel without compromising the dignity and responsibility of your office.
   - Buy without prejudice, seeking to obtain the maximum value for each dollar of expenditure.
   - Strive consistently for knowledge of the materials and processes of manufacturing, and establish practical methods for the management of your office.
   - Subscribe to and work for honesty and truth in buying and selling, and denounce all forms and manifestations of commercial bribery.
   - Accord a prompt and courteous reception, so far as conditions will permit, to all who call on a legitimate business mission.
   - Respect your obligations and require that obligations to you and to your concern be respected, consistent with good business practice.
   - Avoid sharp practice.

- Counsel and assist fellow supply-chain associates in the performance of their duties, whenever the occasion permits.
- Cooperate with all organizations and individuals engaged in activities designed to enhance the development and standing of SCM.

12.4.5.5 Organization and Goal Alignment

- Shared objectives aligned with our business units and internal customers.
- Defined roles and responsibilities.
- Establish clear expectations and accountabilities.
- Aligned roles throughout the organization and across organizational boundaries.
- Business process champions across the enterprise and its cross-functional teams.
- Integrated performance management (PM) and rewards.
- Maintaining *esprit de corps* and the corporate culture.

12.4.5.6 Human Resource Development

- Development and training programs.
- Succession plans within and across cross-functional teams including suppliers.
- Aligned values and beliefs.
- Focused recruiting programs to bring in talented young people who wish to have a career in SCM.
- Focused performance measurement system that aligns supply-chain roles and career paths with a defined system of needs assessment in key knowledge and skill-set areas.

12.4.6 Elements of Control

12.4.6.1 Performance Management

Monitors results through:

- Well-designed measurement systems.
- Objective, meaningful performance measures.
- Supplier scorecards assessing postcontract performance in quality, delivery, cost, flexibility, and service that are reviewed regularly with suppliers.

- Needs assessment for training and education of SCM associates.
- Companywide standardized KPIs and performance measures.
- KPIs and performance measures used for benchmarking.
- Individuals assessed against performance measures that they can influence.

12.4.6.2 Buying Channels

Define the supply structure and relationships the cross-functional teams use to:

- Support reliability methodologies used for equipment strategies (tactics).
- Support operational requirements of cross-functional teams.
- Define supply policy that will guide cross-functional team decisions and activities.
- Establish the appropriate method of supply depending on the situation in which the materials or services requirement occurs.

12.4.6.3 Logistics Planning, Scheduling, and Coordination

These are supply-chain planning and execution processes that the supply chain works cross-functionally with internal business units to ensure the company will:

- Maximize resource productivity.
- Apply standardized planning methodologies.
- Establish (at a minimum) a maximum lead time plus one-week planning horizon.
- Utilize a weekly schedule.
- Develop long-range plans and schedules to drive improved supply-chain planning.

12.4.6.4 Master Data Management

Master data management (MDM) will enable all the SCM processes to work from the "same sheet of music," through the following approaches:

- One-point data entry approach.
- Standardized materials and services.
- International standards used for classification and categorization.

- Ensuring the use of qualified suppliers with acceptable financial risk and management programs.
- Alignment with supply partners.
- Promoting environmental, health, and safety standards through control of materials and goods-entering facilities.
- Safety and respect for others through control of contract individuals entering facilities.
- Control of work and work methods being performed at facilities.
- Appropriate security measures at all facilities.
- Control of contract rates and payment terms.
- Control of community and diversity programs.
- Bill of materials (BOMs) information management systems.
- Integrated documentation.

12.4.6.5 Replenishment Planning

Replenishment planning (RP) will ensure:

- Most efficient use of staged materials and services.
- Adequate safety stock maintained for equipment, fabrication, and operational requirements.
- Optimized levels of stocked materials and staged resources.
- Optimized location for staged materials and resources.

12.4.7 Elements of Continuous Improvement (CI)

Once the processes have been established and are measured, CI of these processes becomes a priority. This occurs through the following elements.

12.4.7.1 Networked Organization

This drives collective ownership of goals and performance.

- Business cross-functional teams take ownership of the supply chain from customer to tier-two suppliers (the supplier's supplier).
- Values and beliefs are aligned irrespective of organizational orientation.
- Proactive and reliability-oriented culture is maintained.
- Information is entered by the person performing a task at point of execution.
- Interorganizational conflict is minimal and connectedness is high.

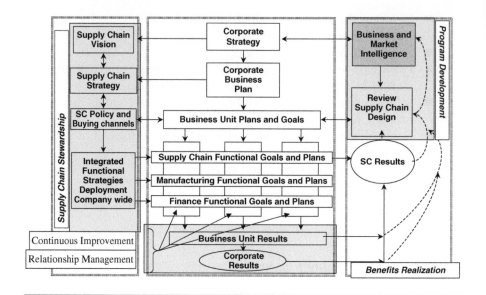

Figure 12.5   Supply-chain design.

■ SCM function is a competency center that facilitates and collaborates through cross-functional teams to achieve business goals and operational excellence.

■ Networked, multi-company *esprit de corps* defines the spirit of cross-functional teams.

12.4.7.2 Supply-Chain Design

Supply-chain design (SCD) (see Figure 12.5) establishes the supply-chain network architecture and ensures that the components are aligned with corporate and supply-chain strategy (SCS), and that our supply chains are as efficient and effective as required. The elements of SCD include:

■ Annual review of supply-chain strategies and structures.
■ Prioritization of resources to those strategies and structures that are the most beneficial.
■ Annual supply-chain improvement program approved and resourced appropriately.
■ Project management methodologies used to implement supply-chain improvements.
■ Cross-functional-team-sponsored improvement initiatives.
■ Supply-chain strategies enabled that ensure delivery reliability, responsiveness, flexibility, and efficiency.

- Forecast-based budgeting responsive to changes in supply market.
- Supply-chain performance benchmarked against marketplace.

12.4.7.3 Relationship Management

This collaboratively ensures excellent performance from strategic commercial arrangements, which:

- Align values, beliefs, processes, management programs, and goals with supply partners.
- Enable participation in cross-functional teams.
- Build trust and commitment to common goals.
- Balance performance measures (PM) that measures both suppliers' performance, as well as the company's performance as a customer of choice.
- Collaborative CI of supply-chain performance with mutual sharing of improvement rewards.
- Supplier self-service with effective controls.

12.4.8 Elements of Operational Excellence

SCM excellence is achieved, and a maturity level of "optimized" is reached in each of the standards and guiding principles defined in this chapter, including the following:

1. Organizational alignment
   a. Leadership
   b. Risk management
   c. Supply-chain strategies (SCS)
   d. Supply-chain enablers
2. Performance management
   a. Performance management (PM)
   b. Quality management (QM)
   c. Master data management (MDM)
3. Supply-chain strategies
   a. Supply-chain design (SCD)
   b. Buying channels
4. Planning, scheduling, and logistics coordination
   a. Aggregate planning (APln)
   b. Logistics planning, scheduling, and coordination
   c. Replenishment planning (RP)
5. Supply management
   a. Procurement transactions

    b. Strategic sourcing (SS)
    c. Contract management (CM)
  6. Supplier relationship management (SRM)
  7. Warehouse management (WM)
  8. Contract services management (CSM)
  9. Accounts payable (AP)
10. SCM in projects
11. Turnaround
12. Continuous improvement (CI)
13. Roles

12.5 Maturity Grids

The following maturity grids can be helpful in identifying the current level of maturity across fundamental areas of operational excellence. These are intended to provide guidelines for benchmarking and identifying areas of opportunity. They can also form the basis for training and a learning organization as the new vision and processes are deployed.

12.5.1 Guiding Principles — Leadership and Organizational Alignment (LOA)

12.5.1.1 Foundation: (Defined)

- People involved in the leadership and organizational alignment (LOA) process are aware of the process and are conversant with the process and outcomes.
- Roles and responsibilities for the various LOA components are assigned.
- Personnel assigned to perform activities in LOA are trained and knowledgeable.
- The plans for the various functions within SCM (i.e., procurement, WM, relationship management, and HR) directly tie into the SCM strategy through supporting objectives and activities.
- Input (such as strategy, goals, and objectives) from the business units is considered when developing LOA plans.
- The LOA plans clearly align with the corporate plans (line-of-sight alignment).
- LOA plans are developed using basic methods (interview methods, SWOT, risk assessment, etc.)

12.5.1.2 Basic: (Measured)

- The LOA process performance is measured (cycle time, quality, and plan versus actual) and continuously improved.
- Coordination (review meetings, checkpoints, etc.) exists between the business units, SCM functions, and SCM leadership when developing the LOA plans.
- SC business performance measures are linked to and support the LOA plans.
- LOA plans are communicated to and understood by the leaders of the business functions and CFTs.
- Suppliers and customers are asked to provide input during the LOA process.
- During the LOA process, supply market research and business intelligence (benchmarking, etc.) are used as a key input.

12.5.1.3 Advanced: (Leveraged)

- The LOA is a continuing process, not just an annual activity.
- LOA plans are frequently reviewed for adjustment.
- The LOA is integrated and coordinated with the corporate strategy and measures development activity (balanced scorecard).
- The SCM LOA plans are clearly linked to the SCM operations plans.
- Suppliers and customers are always active participants in the LOA process.
- LOA data gathering and analysis is sophisticated and looks at the entire supply network.

12.5.2 Guiding Principles — Supply Chain Strategy (SCS)

12.5.2.1 Foundation: (Defined)

- People involved in SCS are aware of the process and conversant with the process and outcomes.
- Roles and responsibilities for the various SCS components are assigned.
- Personnel assigned are trained and knowledgeable.
- The plans for the various functions within SCM (i.e., procurement, warehouse management, relationship management, and HR) directly tie in to the strategy through supporting objectives and activities.

- Input (such as strategy, goals, and objectives) from the business units is considered when developing a SC strategy.
- The SC strategy clearly aligns with the corporate strategy (line-of-sight alignment).
- SC Strategy is developed using basic methods (interview methods, SWOT, risk assessment, etc.)

12.5.2.2 Basic: (Measured)

- SCS process performance is measured and continuously improved.
- Coordination exists between the business units and SCM leadership when developing the SC strategy and plan.
- SC business performance measures are linked to and support the SC strategy.
- The detailed SCM functional plans (WM, procurement, etc.) clearly incorporate SCS goals and objectives.
- The SCS is communicated to and understood by the leaders of the functions and CFTs.
- Suppliers and customers are asked to provide input during the SCS process.
- During the SCS process, supply market research is used as a key input.

12.5.2.3 Advanced: (Leveraged)

- The SCS is a continuing "dialogue," not a backroom activity.
- SCS is frequently reviewed for adjustment.
- The SCS is integrated with the corporate strategy and measures development activity (balanced scorecard).
- The SC strategy and plans are clearly linked to the SCM operations plans.
- Suppliers and customers are always active participants in the SCS process.
- Data gathering and analysis is sophisticated and looks at the entire supply network.

12.5.3 Guiding Principles — Risk Management

12.5.3.1 Foundation: (Defined)

- Risk management processes are defined and documented.

- The impacts of risk-related events are recorded for use in risk management.
- Responsibility for risk management activities is defined and understood. People involved are aware of the process and conversant with the process and outcomes.
- Personnel assigned are trained and knowledgeable.
- Basic monitoring of predictive events is in place.

12.5.3.2 Basic: (Measured)

- Risk management processes are used across the various units of the organization.
- Risk related events are formally analyzed for lessons learned and prevention.
- Risk mitigation (prevention) activities are undertaken and measured.
- Periodic risk management reviews are conducted for process improvement.
- Suppliers are asked to input into the risk management process.

12.5.3.3 Advanced: (Leveraged)

- Fully coordinated risk management is institutionalized within the organization.
- Risk management plans are in place and communicated for most suppliers and customers.
- "Postmortems" are formally conducted when risk-related events occur.
- A cross-functional team oversees the risk management processes.

12.5.4 Guiding Principles — Enablers

12.5.4.1 Foundation: (Defined)

- Basic organizational support exists for SCM process-oriented projects.
- Leadership is generally informed of the SCM initiatives but not deeply involved ("let it happen, not make it happen").
- Jobs and organizational structures include a process aspect, but remain basically rooted in the traditional functions. The functional leaders have veto power.

- Enterprise learning management system is in place with some common nomenclature.
- Representatives from functions meet occasionally to share lessons learned and best practices but only on an informal basis.
- The IT systems support cross-functional activities, but only with modifications.
- Information needed to support decision making is frequently available, but only upon special request.

12.5.4.2 Basic: (Measured)

- Strong and active organizational support is there for SCM process-oriented projects (resource commitments, participation on projects, and strong public statements of support).
- Leadership is fully informed of the SCM initiatives but still not deeply involved ("make someone else make it happen").
- Jobs and organizational structures are built around process and function, but the functional leaders still have veto power.
- Competency models are in place to build a proficient workforce with senior-management support.
- Lessons learned and best practices are routinely gathered and made available, but knowledge sharing is on an informal basis (not included in objectives nor scheduled).
- The IT systems are focused on supporting cross-functional activities with minimal modifications.
- Information needed to support decision making is available but not in a timely manner.

12.5.4.3 Advanced: (Leveraged)

- Project leadership and participation for SCM process-oriented projects is shared and enthusiastic.
- Leadership is fully informed of SCM initiatives and deeply involved ("make it happen").
- Jobs and organizational structures are built around process primarily and supported by the functions. SCM process leaders clearly have authority.
- Business goals are aligned with work activities, and learning management systems are integrated with enterprise portal technologies.
- Lessons learned and best practices are routinely gathered and made available. Knowledge sharing is organized and measured in a virtual learning environment.

- The IT systems are built to enable cross-functional activities.
- Information needed to support decision making is easily available but only regarding internal processes.

12.5.5 Guiding Principles — Performance Management (PM)

12.5.5.1 Foundation: (Defined)

- People involved in PM are aware of the process and conversant with the process and outcomes.
- Personnel assigned are trained and knowledgeable.
- Changes to the PM processes must now go through a formal procedure.
- PM-related jobs and organizational structures are identified but remain basically focused upon traditional functional goals.
- Representatives from functions meet regularly to coordinate with each other concerning PM process activities, but only as representatives of their traditional functions and not as members of the PM team.
- Formal root cause identification, action reporting, and follow-up do not occur on a regular basis.
- There is a defined and documented process for building and managing "cockpits."
- Responsibility for cockpit development is clearly defined.

12.5.5.2 Basic: (Measured)

- Managers employ PM process management with strategic intent.
- Measures and goals clearly link to the business strategy.
- Broad PM process jobs (process owners) and structures (formal process teams) are put in place outside of traditional functions.
- Cooperation between intracompany functions, vendors, and customers takes the form of PM teams that share common process measures and goals.
- Formal root cause identification, action reporting, and follow-up occur on a regular basis.
- Incentives are clearly linked to the PM system of measures and goals.
- A cross-functional team is chartered to manage the development and deployment of cockpits.
- Metrics for measuring cockpit performance are identified and gathered.
- Best practices and lessons learned are collected and available.

12.5.5.3 Advanced: (Leveraged)

- A cross-functional PM team is operating that includes representatives from all functions.
- Formal cross-functional information sharing takes place on a regular basis.
- PM process measures and management systems are deeply embedded in the organization.
- Advanced process management practices take shape in the form of action teams that include members from different functions, suppliers, and customers.
- Proactive, predictive measures are in use.
- Cause-and-effect analysis is done using SC models before a specific change effort is executed.
- Cockpits are frequently in use across the organization.
- The use of cockpits extends to some supplier jobs.

12.5.6 Guiding Principles — Quality Management (QM)

12.5.6.1 Foundation: (Defined)

- People involved are aware of the process and are conversant with the process and outcomes.
- Personnel assigned are trained and knowledgeable.
- Testing criteria are selected based on organizational needs and are centrally documented and available.
- Standardized tests and processes are defined based on the materials or services.
- Material-testing facilities are available with qualified personnel, for example, quality control departments.
- A process is defined and documented for managing changes.
- Responsibility for change management is clearly defined.
- A policy of reporting and documenting changes is generally followed across the organization.

12.5.6.2 Basic: (Measured)

- Cross-functional teams develop metrics to evaluate testing policies based on analysis of critical measures such as defective ppm, reject ratios, criticality, and customization.
- Data regarding testing methods, measures, past tests, and problems are stored in a database that is available to everyone within the organization.

- Customers and suppliers receive information about the company's processes, facilities, and equipment, especially those to which they contribute.
- Suppliers document and adopt standards in testing. Materials are tested at the supplier's facilities.
- Change-management processes are generally followed across the organization.
- Measures for managing change are identified and gathered.
- A central repository for tracking change and version control is in place for SLAs and contracts.
- Suppliers actively participate in the change-management process.

12.5.6.3 Advanced: (Leveraged)

- Material testing is done to optimize material strategies in collaboration with suppliers.
- Suppliers provide on-site personnel to work with the organization on anticipating testing-driven design changes or problems, where appropriate.
- Suppliers manage data on testing, and this is available widely throughout the supply chain.
- Customers provide specific and explicit product and material characteristics; this information is shared with the suppliers, so that the quality is maintained.
- A fully coordinated change process is in place across the entire organization.
- Change discipline, reporting, and management are institutionalized in the organization.
- Suppliers are responsible for version control of their agreements and use the organization repository for support.
- Version control is in place for all plans within the organization.

12.5.7 Guiding Principles — Master Data Management (MDM)

12.5.7.1 Foundation: (Defined)

- The MDM processes are defined and documented for the organization.
- People involved in MDM are conversant with the process and are aware of the process and outcomes.
- Roles and responsibilities for MDM are assigned.
- Personnel assigned to MDM are trained and knowledgeable.

■ Basic DM methods (identification, storage, controls, and back ups) are identified, documented, and understood.
■ Basic critical data is stored and accessible.

12.5.7.2 Basic: (Measured)

■ MDM process measures are in place (errors, number of changes, and size).
■ Advanced MDM practices (revision tracking, auto data cleansing, conformance reporting, etc.) are being used.
■ CI processes are in place for MDM.
■ Suppliers and customers are asked for input concerning MDM efforts.
■ Data quality is reviewed on a formally scheduled basis.
■ Ownership and maintenance responsibility of data is clearly defined and distributed throughout the organization.

12.5.7.3 Advanced: (Leveraged)

■ Key suppliers' and customers' data are included in the MDM system.
■ MDM strategies are shared with suppliers and customers.
■ MDM risk management is in place.
■ MDM strategies are linked to the SC and overall business strategies.
■ MDM is used broadly across the organization.
■ An organization of MDM experts is identified (matrix or centralized).

12.5.8 Guiding Principles — Supply Chain Design (SCD)

12.5.8.1 Foundation: (Defined)

■ People involved in SCD are conversant with the process and are aware of the process and outcomes.
■ Roles and responsibilities for SCD components are assigned.
■ Personnel assigned are trained and knowledgeable.
■ The initiatives and programs within SCD are driven by the SCS through supporting goals and objectives.
■ Input (such as strategy, goals, and objectives) from the business units is considered when developing an SC improvement program.
■ SCD programs and initiatives are developed and managed using basic methods (modeling, benchmarking, risk assessment, initiative charters, etc.)

12.5.8.2 Basic: (Measured)

- SCD processes, programs, and initiatives are measured, evaluated for benefit realization, and continuously improved.
- Coordination exists between the business units and SCM leadership when developing the SCD programs and initiatives.
- SCD programs and initiatives are clearly focused on business performance measures that are important to the business unit.
- The SCD program and initiatives have clear timelines, milestones, and goals.
- SCD initiative managers are held accountable for achieving these timelines and milestones (included in salary reviews).
- The SCD program is communicated to and understood by the leaders of the functions and CFTs.
- Suppliers and customers are asked to provide input during the SCD process.
- During the SCSP process, supply market research is used as a key input.

12.5.8.3 Advanced: (Leveraged)

- The SCD is a continuing dialogue with the business units, not an isolated activity.
- SCD is frequently reviewed with the business unit leaders for adjustment.
- The SCD programs are clearly integrated with the corporate and business unit strategy and measures.
- The SC strategy and plans are clearly linked to the SCM operations plans.
- Suppliers and customers are always active participants in the SCSP process.
- Advanced data-gathering and analysis techniques (advanced models, simulation, statistics-based risk assessment, etc.) are used and examine the entire supply network, not just company activities.

12.5.9 Guiding Principles — Buying Channels' Material Requirements

12.5.9.1 Foundation: (Defined)

- Basic buying channel policies and processes exist and are defined and documented.

- Associates are familiar with buying channel policies and processes across all locations.
- Personnel assigned are trained and knowledgeable.
- Periodic meetings take place between procurement and end users to identify instances when buying channel policies are not followed, and internal users are trained as required.
- Material is delivered to the using location on time 90 percent of the time.
- Majority of materials procurement (including supplier payment) is manual, using paper.

12.5.9.2 Basic: (Measured)

- Buying channel policies and processes are consistently used across all locations by all employees.
- Noncompliance with buying channel policies is an exception, not the norm.
- Costs are correctly charged to jobs and using locations in the majority of instances.
- Instances of nonassigned costs are tracked, measured, and reported to using locations on a regular basis.
- Material is delivered to the using location on time 95 percent of the time.
- High percentage of material procurement transactions (including supplier payment) is electronic.

12.5.9.3 Advanced: (Leveraged)

- Noncompliance to buying channel policies is extremely rare.
- Spend data is consistently tracked and updated, and costs are reconciled correctly to using locations 100 percent of the time.
- Each using location receives a monthly report on material costs, vendors used, and who issued material requests.
- Suppliers, distributors, and end users have a comprehensive knowledge of buying channel policies, and self-report instances of noncompliance. Training materials are available to new associates to ensure coordination.
- The incidence of emergency, unplanned, and unstructured material requests is significantly lower.
- RF and PDA technology is deployed as appropriate across the company to ensure that data is captured in real-time as material is ordered or moved across locations.

- Spend data is routinely reviewed to monitor patterns and trends, and high-volume purchase trends on credit cards, etc., are easily spotted by SS teams for negotiation.
- Material is delivered to the using location on time 99 percent of the time.
- More than 95 percent of material procurement transactions (including supplier payment) are electronic and recorded in the enterprise system.

12.5.10 Guiding Principles — Buying Channels' Service Requirements

12.5.10.1 Foundation: (Defined)

- Basic buying channel policies and processes exist and are defined and documented.
- Associates are familiar with buying channel policies and processes across all locations.
- Periodic meetings take place between procurement and end users to identify instances when buying channel policies are not followed, and internal users are trained as required.
- Service delivery takes place at the using location 90 percent on time.
- Majority of services procurement (including supplier payment) is manual, using paper.

12.5.10.2 Basic: (Measured)

- Buying channel policies and processes are consistently used across all locations by all employees.
- Noncompliance with buying channel policies is an exception, not the norm.
- Costs are correctly charged to jobs and using locations in the majority of instances.
- Instances of nonassigned costs are tracked, measured, and reported to using locations on a regular basis.
- Service delivery to the using location is 95 percent on time.
- High percentage of material procurement transactions (including supplier payment) is electronic.

12.5.10.3 Advanced: (Leveraged)

- Noncompliance to buying channel policies is extremely rare.

- Spend data is consistently tracked and updated, and costs are reconciled correctly to using locations 100 percent of the time.
- Each using location receives a monthly report on service costs, vendors used, and who issued service requests.
- Suppliers, distributors, and end users have a comprehensive knowledge of buying channel policies, and self-report instances of noncompliance. Training materials are available to new associates to ensure coordination.
- The incidence of emergency, unplanned, and unstructured services requests is significantly lower.
- RF and PDA technology is deployed as appropriate across the company to ensure that data is captured in real-time as services are procured across locations.
- Spend data is routinely reviewed to monitor patterns and trends, and high-volume purchase trends on credit cards, etc., are easily spotted by SS teams for negotiation.
- Service delivery to the using location is 99 percent on time.
- More than 95 percent of services procurement transactions (including supplier payment) are electronic and recorded.

12.5.11 Guiding Principles — Aggregate Planning (APL)

12.5.11.1 Foundation: (Defined)

- APL processes for the organization are defined and documented.
- People involved are aware of the process and outcomes and are conversant with the process terms.
- Roles and responsibilities for the various planning components (and information submission timetables) are assigned.
- Historical data is being captured for use in future planning.
- Requirements data (BOM, etc.) is organized and available.
- Basic APL methods are in use (master planning, rough-cut capacity planning, and scheduling).

12.5.11.2 Basic: (Measured)

- APL process measures are in place (plan accuracy, fulfillment percentage, cycle times).
- Plan versus actual data is captured to be used as feedback to the process.

■ Historical data is being used with parameters for help in predicting future requirements.

■ Requirements data (BOM) is actively managed and updated.

■ Process and performance improvement areas are identified and actively pursued (inventory surplus, obsolescence, stocking levels, returns, disposals, equipment deployment, and return).

■ Suppliers and customers are asked to input into the aggregate plan and often use the plan in their processes.

■ Formal reviews are held to examine APL performance.

12.5.11.3 Advanced: (Leveraged)

■ Planning, performance, and status information for all areas is readily available, making the supply network highly visible.

■ Sophisticated planning techniques (statistical methods) are in use for predicting future requirements and changes.

■ Historical data, patterns, and trends are frequently analyzed for particular customer or commodity segments and improvement actions taken.

■ The organization has a high level of confidence in the plan.

■ Supplier and customer plans are integrated with the aggregate plan.

■ The plan is used with confidence by suppliers and customers.

12.5.12 Guiding Principles — Logistics Planning, Scheduling, and Coordination

12.5.12.1 Foundation: (Defined)

■ Logistics planning, scheduling, and coordination (LPSC) processes, policies, and strategies are defined and documented such that people are aware of them and conversant with them.

■ Roles and responsibilities for the various logistics planning and scheduling components are assigned.

■ Logistics plans and schedules are complete and issued in a timely manner.

■ Basic historical data (schedules and actuals) is being captured for reuse.

■ Logistics data (routing, shippers, costs, lead times, etc.) is organized and available.

■ Basic LPSC methods are in use (capacity planning, resource loading, and scheduling).

12.5.12.2 Basic: (Measured)

■ LPSC process measures are in place (percent ontime fulfillment, number of changes, and cycle times).
■ Schedule versus actual data is being captured to be used as feedback.
■ Historical data is being used with parameters for predicting new logistics plans and schedules.
■ Logistics data (routing, shippers, costs, lead times, etc.) is actively managed and updated.
■ LPSC improvement areas are identified and actions assigned.
■ Suppliers and customers are asked to input into the plan or schedule and use the plan or schedule in their processes.
■ Formal reviews are held to examine LPSC performance.

12.5.12.3 Advanced: (Leveraged)

■ Sophisticated scheduling techniques (statistical methods) are in use for improving the schedule.
■ Historical data, patterns, and trends are frequently analyzed for particular areas or products and used to improve plans or schedules.
■ The organization has a high level of confidence in the plan or schedule (reliable and accurate).
■ Supplier and customer performance and usage data are incorporated within the plan or schedule.
■ The plan or schedule is used with confidence by suppliers and customers.
■ The LPSC plans are continuously improved using a formal CI program.

12.5.13 Guiding Principles — Replenishment Planning (RP)

12.5.13.1 Foundation: (Defined)

■ RP processes, policies, and strategies are defined and documented such that people are aware of them and conversant with them.
■ Roles and responsibilities for the various RP and scheduling components are assigned.
■ Replenishment plans and schedules are complete and issued in a timely manner.
■ Basic historical data (schedules and actuals) is being captured for reuse.

- Replenishment data (routing, shippers, costs, lead times, etc.) is organized and available.
- Basic RP methods are in use (inventory planning, safety stock, and aging).

12.5.13.2 Basic: (Measured)

- RP process measures are in place (percentage ontime fulfillment, number of stock outs, and cycle times).
- Schedule versus actual data is being captured to be used as feedback.
- Historical data is being used with parameters for predicting new replenishment plans and schedules.
- Replenishment data (routing, shippers, costs, lead times, etc.) is actively managed and updated.
- RP improvement areas are identified and actions assigned.
- Suppliers and customers are asked to input into the plan or schedule and use the plan or schedule in their processes.
- Formal reviews are held to examine RP performance.

12.5.13.3 Advanced: (Leveraged)

- Sophisticated planning or scheduling techniques (statistical methods) are in use for improving the plan or schedule.
- Historical data, patterns, and trends are frequently analyzed for particular areas or products and used to improve plans or schedules.
- The organization has a high level of confidence in the plan or schedule (reliable and accurate).
- Supplier and customer performance and usage data are incorporated within the plan or schedule.
- The plan or schedule is used with confidence by suppliers and customers.
- The RP plans are continuously improved using a formal CI program.

12.5.14 Guiding Principles — Purchasing Transactions

12.5.14.1 Foundation: (Defined)

- Material and service PO and release processes for the organization are defined and documented.

- Roles and responsibilities for the various PO and release components are assigned.
- Basic material or service PO methods are in use.
- People involved in purchasing transactions (PT) are aware of the process and conversant with the process and outcomes.
- Personnel assigned to PT are trained and knowledgeable.
- Material items and service items are identified within a catalog.
- Pricing and basic contract terms are specified within the PO and system.
- Authorization to commit and grant of authority are separated by policy.

12.5.14.2 Basic: (Measured)

- Compliance to material or service PO and release standard processes are measured and exceptions identified.
- All material or service releases against an existing agreement are executed against that agreement, with the majority being automatically created electronically.
- Metrics for authorization such as payment cycle time and percentage of non-PO payments are defined, measured, and tracked.
- Having a PO follow contract formation for new material or service requisitions not on agreement is the exception, not the rule.
- Authorization to commit levels for buyers are uniformly established.
- Functional leaders and staff fully understand and comply with payment requirements.
- Suppliers and customers are asked to provide input into the PO and release process to improve performance.
- Material and service catalog items are defined with enough specificity to eliminate delivery errors.
- POs and releases for controlled items in the material and services catalog automatically include special risk management conditions.
- Invoicing errors relating to late pricing updates are tracked.
- Pricing and terms are made available to AP personnel.

12.5.14.3 Advanced: (Leveraged)

- Internal communications electronically notify those responsible once the materials or services are committed. Status of receipt of material and services is readily available.

- Metrics for authorization such as PO/release cycle time and percentage of errors are defined, measured, and reviewed quarterly to identify problems, with steps taken to adjust processes as required.
- Authorization metrics are tracked and used for internal purposes.
- Electronic signature systems are used and linked to receive and verification data in real-time.
- Best practices for creation of materials and services orders and releases are written and communicated within the organization and across the supply base.
- Supplier input is used for improvements in the system.
- Supplier and company systems are linked to allow for electronic payments.
- Suppliers work with company to schedule payment plans, contractor charge collection, and other options.
- Estimated receipt, pay on receipt, and pay on consumption are payment options now being evaluated.
- All materials released against a PO or release order are accurately and electronically recorded.

12.5.15 Guiding Principles — Perform Strategic Sourcing (SS)

12.5.15.1 Foundation: (Defined)

- People involved in SS are aware of the process and conversant with the process and outcomes.
- Roles and responsibilities for the various SS components are assigned.
- Personnel assigned to SS are trained and knowledgeable.
- The current contracts and major purchases are defined.
- The qualifying process and standards for suppliers are documented.
- The records of major negotiations, including the research, negotiation plan and goals, notes from meetings, and postnegotiation debriefing and analysis exist and are available to relevant personnel.

12.5.15.2 Basic: (Measured)

- Cross-functional teams analyze the qualifying process to assess the supplier measures and to set selection standards for various product and service families.

- Cross-functional teams incorporate supply base rationalization goals to determine selection goals and measures of internal adherence to the selection process, such as supply-base growth or shrinkage or spend through recurring contracts.
- Position papers exist for major product and service families.
- Negotiators are identified by role in the company or production process and receive some training in negotiation.
- Critical suppliers are assessed on their ability to be strategic partners, including their willingness to develop and implement process and technology improvements.

12.5.15.3 Advanced: (Leveraged)

- Suppliers are divided into levels based on the importance of the relationship and defined as structured, staged, or unstructured.
- Critical suppliers are assessed on measures based on the entire company, such as their breadth of product line or process efficiency.
- Negotiators are highly trained in the company's internal processes, needs, and goals.
- Negotiators are highly trained in how to negotiate in ways that build relationships as well as meet the organization's immediate goals.

12.5.16 Guiding Principles — Contract Management (CM)

12.5.16.1 Foundation: (Defined)

- Processes for managing RFxs are defined and documented, with information on any RFx choices made, the characteristic chosen (x), the reason for choosing it, how the choices support x, and the trade-offs between requests.
- The records of major negotiations exist and are available to relevant personnel.
- Pilot business units have started using the processes but often revert back to the ad hoc processes owing to lack of information.
- Periodic evaluations of successes of CM are suggested but not consistently done.
- RFx processes are done manually through mail and fax.
- A supplier scoring system has been documented but is not consistently used in selecting suppliers.
- Efforts are underway to capture supplier performance data manually.
- All measures still primarily from a purchasing perspective.

12.5.16.2 Basic: (Measured)

- Cross-functional teams are formed to follow and act upon requests from within the organization.
- Contracting and sourcing strategies are incorporated into business processes for developing and execution of contracts.
- Negotiators are identified by role in the company or production process and receive some training in negotiation.
- Periodic evaluations of the success of CM are performed.
- SCM has established metrics to determine adherence to contracts, and rewards or penalties are periodically updated based on adherence to contracts.
- Externally, processes are being developed to streamline contract development, formation, and execution with suppliers.
- Suppliers and customers are asked to provide input into CM processes to reduce cycle time and improve efficiency of the process.
- The metrics for managing RFxs are defined and measured, and suppliers are evaluated based on their fit to the specifications for x.
- There is a system in place that generates, issues, and tracks requests within the organization.
- Historical data is stored in databases and is available for use for future processes.
- Scorecard measures apply metrics that are meaningful to the entire organization, not just purchasing.
- Performance data against existing service level agreements (SLAs) is captured and recorded into electronic scorecard system database.
- Supplier measures (actual versus expected) against SLAs are shared with the suppliers on a periodic basis.

12.5.16.3 Advanced: (Leveraged)

- Any business unit within an organization is capable of obtaining any and all information about a contract using a single Web-based portal accessing a central repository of performance data (actual versus expected) for all business units.
- Periodic evaluations across organizational boundaries are regularly performed.
- The organization and its suppliers have developed processes to jointly improve the CM process.
- Negotiation of contracts with suppliers takes place through a variety of electronic tools that allow attachments, appendices, and revision controls.

- All parties are able to evaluate their contracts anytime and are able to alert the other party to potential issues, including detailed business terms such as line items, associated pricing and discounts, incentives, and rebate provisions.
- Negotiators are highly trained in the company's internal processes, needs, and goals, as well as managing supplier relationships to meet the organization's immediate goals.
- There is a seamless handoff from negotiation of contracts to relationship managers who are involved in development of contracts.
- Implementations of improved CM business processes are complete, and the organization and its suppliers are constantly looking for improvements to these processes.
- All materials released against a contract are accurately and electronically recorded to assess contract performance through global spend analysis.
- CM systems provide complete visibility and management of global contract information including bid analysis of performance to contract.
- Cross-functional teams periodically assess the information portfolio to determine what (x)s have been chosen, their effectiveness, and fit to the company strategy.
- RFx systems are linked to the supplier organization electronically, and the system generates, issues, and tracks requests throughout the supply chain. Suppliers participate in updating historical data in real-time.
- Suppliers deliver information optimized to support x, and adopt process measures and metrics in their organizations.
- External entities anticipate requests and proactively provide responses to such requests.
- Processes to assist suppliers during a downward trend in supplier performance are jointly developed with suppliers with well-defined trigger points.
- Systems to share performance data anytime with suppliers are in place and are being utilized with select suppliers, who can access its performance data whenever required via an online portal.
- Components of scorecard are adjusted periodically based on changes in conditions or customer input.

12.5.17 Guiding Principles — Relationship Management (RM)

12.5.17.1 Foundation: (Defined)

Trust	A basic working level of trust exists between key individuals rather than at company level (trust exists as a part of doing).
Behavior	Behavior is often opportunistic. However, problems are solved without formal escalation procedures.
Process	Basic RM processes (including contract administration) for the organization are defined and documented; however, they are not duplicated exactly in the supplier's organization.
Program	RM programs are defined and documented for each relationship; however, they are not duplicated exactly in the supplier's organization.
Structure	RM-related jobs and organizational structures are defined and documented; however, they are not duplicated exactly in the supplier's organization.
Management	Company and supplier relationship managers are identified and documented. Relationship managers interact on a formal basis.
Roles and responsibilities	RM personnel are assigned, trained, and are knowledgeable. Representatives from business functions or CFT meet regularly to coordinate with each other regarding RM process activities (RM business management team). Roles and responsibilities, however, are not duplicated exactly in the supplier's organization.
Quality management	Quality is managed through a formalized reactive process. However, minor problems are solved without formal escalation procedures.
Continuous Improvement	Improvement opportunities are identified through a formalized process. However, minor opportunities are captured between key personal relationships.
Communication	Information is mostly one way and transactional.
Contracts, policies, and execution	Contracts build the foundation for the relationship. The relationship performs according to contracts and SLAs. SLAs are defined and documented. There is a policy for determining when to add or delete suppliers from the RM lists.
Technologies	Partners use common technologies to perform transactions.

Investments	Technology — Few investments are made to increase efficiencies of common technologies in relationship. Investments are only undertaken if the technology is applicable in different relationships.
	Relationship — Few investments are made to improve status of relationship (e.g., training, certification, etc.). Investments are only undertaken if the improvements are applicable in different relationships.
Commitment	Commitment is considered short term and transactional in most relationships, and based on individual relationships.
Cooperation	Cooperation exists only on a transactional basis and is based on individual relationships.
Power and dependencies	Power is only one way. One relationship depends more on the other.
Organizational change and integration	The relationship has a transactional meaning for both organizations. A formal management-of-change process is in place and operating.

12.5.17.2 Basic: (Measured)

Trust	An advanced level of trust exists between key individuals. Two-way values are the norm and extend beyond the relationship into both organizations.
Behavior	Opportunistic behavior occurs only infrequently.
Process	A process for gathering input from suppliers is defined and documented. For each relationship, a balanced, two-way set of RM process measures is in place, such as timely notification, forecast availability, and on-time delivery. Performance review is on a regular and formal basis with actions and follow-ups management. SLA measurement and feedback and improvement systems are in place. RM participates early in SS processes. Supplier scorecards are documented and tracked.
Program	Existing RM programs are extended with measurements to evaluate performance status of each relationship. However, the program is not duplicated exactly in the supplier's organization.

Structure	RM-related jobs and organizational structures are defined and documented; however, they are not duplicated exactly in supplier's organization.
Management	The RM business management team is involved in resolving major disconnects or issues.
Roles and responsibilities	Contract administration performs in a proactive and constructive way. Roles and responsibilities, however, are not duplicated exactly in supplier's organization.
Quality management	Supplier scorecards are documented and tracked.
Continuous improvement	List of key products and processes for improvement are identified. Improvement activities occur with key customers and suppliers. Supplier scorecards are documented and tracked.
Communication	Information is two way but still mostly transactional.
Contracts, policies, and execution	SLAs are defined and documented. Contracts build the foundation for the relationship. The relationship performs according to contracts and SLAs. There is a policy for determining when to add or delete suppliers from the RM lists.
Technologies	Partners use common technologies to perform transactions. Key relationships are integrated in customized systems.
Investments	Technology — Few investments are made to increase efficiencies of common technologies in the relationship. Investments in customized technologies are made only for a few key relationships. Investments are undertaken by one side only and not jointly. Relationship — Few investments are made to improve status of relationship (e.g., training, certification, etc.). Investments are undertaken only if the improvements are applicable in different relationships.
Commitment	Commitment is at the organizational level in key relationships. Long-term, strategic commitment (two way) is in place for key relationships.
Cooperation	Intensified cooperation at the organizational level in key relationships.
Power and dependencies	Power is more balanced in most relationships.

Organizational change and integration	Two-way values are the norm and extend beyond the relationship into both organizations. RM participates early in SS processes. Supplier scorecards are documented and tracked.

12.5.17.3 Advanced: (Leveraged)

Trust	A high level of organizational trust exists. Two-way valuing is the norm and extends beyond the relationship into both organizations.
Behavior	A high degree of accommodation for each other exists in most relationships. Two-way valuing is the norm and extends beyond the relationship into both organizations. There is a confidence that sacrifices will be compensated in the long term. Opportunistic behavior is very rare, and negative reaction is severe.
Process	Supply-chain measures are documented, accessible, created by cross-functional teams, and focused on supporting the company strategy. Measures are reviewed at least quarterly in a face-to-face meeting with suppliers. Suppliers are formally evaluated based on measured performance, necessary actions are taken, and progress is reported. Key relationships begin to duplicate the process in own organization.
Program	Suppliers are assessed for their effectiveness in collaboration using measures such as number of suggestions made or incorporated, improved responsiveness, and reductions in NPD cycle time or cost. Key relationships begin to duplicate the program in own organization.
Structure	RM-related jobs and organizational structures are defined and documented. Key relationships begin to duplicate the structure in own organization.
Management	The RM business management team is involved in resolving major disconnects or issues.
Roles and responsibilities	Contract administration is performed in a proactive and constructive way. Key relationships begin to duplicate the roles and responsibilities in own organization.
Quality management	Supplier scorecards are documented and tracked. Key relationships perform joint quality assessments and improvements. Few key relationships develop joint improvement programs.

Continuous improvement	Performance information and improvement plans are openly shared with suppliers and internal business leads. Key relationships perform joint improvement assessments. Few key relationships develop joint improvement programs.
Communication	Information on points of contact is available and widely used to minimize extraneous contacts with customers and suppliers while maintaining clear information flows. Information is two way, openly shared and strategic, planning as well as transactional.
Contracts, policies, and execution	Cross-functional teams develop policies for establishing SLAs linked to goals, strategy, and customer segments. Suppliers and customers are frequent participants in the team to review and improve SLAs. An exit strategy exists for key relationships.
Technologies	Partners use common technologies to perform transactions. Majority of relationships are integrated in customized systems.
Investments	Technology — Key relationships share risks, and investments are considered to improve relationship over long term. Relationship — Key relationships share risks, and investments are considered to improve relationship over long term.
Commitment	Commitment is high at the organizational level, long term and strategic (two way) in the majority of relationships.
Cooperation	Cooperation is high at the organizational level, long term and strategic (two way) in the majority of relationships.
Power and dependencies	Power is balanced in most relationships and codependence is the norm.
Organizational change and integration	Suppliers participate in RM teams on a regular basis. Cross-functional RM teams review optimal rationalization measures for alignment with organization strategy and SS plans. RM process interacts with SS processes to incorporate rationalization. An exit strategy exists for key relationships.

12.5.17.4 Optimized

Trust	A high level of organizational trust exists. Two-way valuing is the norm and extends beyond the relationship into both organizations.
Behavior	A high degree of accommodation for each other exists in most relationships. Two-way valuing is the norm and extends beyond the relationship into both organizations. Opportunistic behavior is very rare and negative reaction is severe. Rewards for improvement success are mutually shared between company and suppliers.
Process	RM processes are well defined, implemented, and duplicated in most relationships. Process improvements are identified and implemented by and in most relationships. Education about the specific elements of the collaborative relationship process is included in relevant new-employee training in the organization and supplier companies.
Program	RM programs are well defined, implemented, and duplicated in most relationships. Program improvements are identified and implemented by and in most relationships. New employees are trained in RM programs and experience programs on both sides (company exchange).
Structure	RM-related jobs and organizational structures are duplicated exactly in most relationships. New employees are trained in RM processes and experience processes on both sides (company exchange). Suppliers and customers are full members of cross-functional teams.
Management	The RM business management team focuses on the improvement of relationships and the continuous identification and improvement of opportunities. RM business managers of both parties are in consistent communication and decision-making processes with the other party. RM managers participate in a company exchange program for key relationships. Open information sharing about relevant criteria, such as capacity and demand forecasting, facilitates cross-enterprise decision making.

Roles and responsibilities	Education about the specific elements of the collaborative relationship program, process, and structure is included in relevant new-employee training in the organization and supplier companies. Roles and responsibilities are duplicated exactly in the supplier's organization. Internal contacts are involved in improving the relationship through direct involvement in the supplier or RM team meetings. Supplier contacts improve the relationship by constantly seeking feedback from internal customers about the organization's current processes and products. Relationship manager is involved directly in improving key suppliers' internal processes through direct supplier development and kaizen activities. Suppliers and customers work with the RM team to determine optimal network rationalization.
Quality Management	Quality is managed through a formalized, proactive process. Internal contacts are involved in improving the relationship through direct involvement in supplier or RM team meetings. Supplier contacts improve the relationship by constantly seeking feedback from internal customers about the organization's current processes and products. Relationship manager is involved directly in improving key suppliers' internal processes through direct supplier development and kaizen activities. Clearly defined escalation process exists in all relationships. Investments to improve quality are undertaken by both parties and considered an investment in relationship. Both parties participate in quality improvement programs. Parties may participate in company exchanges. Rewards for improvement success are mutually shared between company and suppliers. Suppliers and customers work with the RM team to determine optimal network rationalization.
Continuous Improvement	All members of the supply chain scan for new technologies and processes to help with supplier assessment, communication, or potential supplier identification. Internal contacts are involved in improving the relationship through direct involvement in supplier or RM team meetings. Supplier contacts improve the relationship by constantly seeking feedback from internal customers about the organization's

	current processes and products. Relationship manager is involved directly in improving key suppliers' internal processes through direct supplier development and kaizen activities. Clearly defined process exists to communicate and capture new opportunities in all relationships. Rewards for improvement success are mutually shared between company and suppliers. Suppliers and customers work with the RM team to determine optimal network rationalization.
Communication	Information is two way, openly shared, and strategic, planning as well as transactional. Internal contacts are involved in improving the relationship through direct involvement in supplier or RM team meetings. Supplier contacts improve the relationship by constantly seeking feedback from internal customers about the organization's current processes and products. Relationship manager is involved directly in improving key suppliers' internal processes through direct supplier development and kaizen activities. Open information sharing about relevant criteria, such as capacity and demand forecasting, facilitates cross-enterprise decision making.
Contracts, policies, and execution	Cross-functional teams develop policies for establishing SLAs linked to goals, strategy, and customer segments. Suppliers and customers are frequent participants in the team to review and improve SLAs. An exit strategy for majority of relationships exists to terminate a relationship without losing the trust level.
Technologies	New technologies are jointly selected and integrated. Suppliers and customers work with the RM team to determine optimal network rationalization.
Investments	Technology — Investments in new technologies are considered investments in the relationship. Both parties share the risks. Beneficiaries of new technologies are identified by both parties (additional relationships). Multi-party investments are possible. Relationship — Both parties share the risks. Beneficiaries of new improvements are identified by both parties (additional relationships). Multi-party investments are possible.

Commitment	Commitment is high at the organizational level, long term and strategic (two way) in the majority of relationships. An exit strategy exists to terminate a relationship without losing the trust level.
Cooperation	Cooperation is high at the organizational level, long term and strategic (two way) in the majority of relationships. An exit strategy exists to terminate a relationship without losing the trust level.
Power and dependencies	Power is balanced in most relationships, and codependence is the norm. An exit strategy exists to terminate a relationship without losing the trust level.
Organizational change and integration	Supply-chain contacts have access to design documents and can make changes within existing version control processes.
	Education about the specific elements of the collaborative relationship process is included in relevant new-employee training in the organization and supplier companies.
	Internal contacts are involved in improving the relationship through direct involvement in supplier or RM team meetings.
	Supplier contacts improve the relationship by constantly seeking feedback from internal customers about the organization's current processes and products.
	The relationship manager is involved directly in improving key suppliers' internal processes through direct supplier development and kaizen activities.
	Rewards for improvement success are mutually shared between company and suppliers.
	Suppliers and customers are full members of cross-functional teams.
	Suppliers and customers work with the RM team to determine optimal network rationalization.
	Suppliers are empowered to work with each other to resolve potential problems including disaster recovery, capacity, or delivery problems.

	Open information sharing about relevant criteria, such as capacity and demand forecasting, facilitates cross-enterprise decision making.
	Review and development teams formally include supplier contacts. This may take the form of consistent meetings, electronic communications, hosting external people onsite, or locating internal personnel at external sites.

12.5.18 Guiding Principles — Warehouse Management (WM)

12.5.18.1 Foundation: (Defined)

■ Basic warehousing, material handling, and refurbishment policies and processes exist and are defined and documented.
■ Associates consistently apply policies and processes across all locations.
■ Periodic meetings take place between warehouse associates and end users to identify potential problems and areas in which performance is not satisfactory.

12.5.18.2 Basic: (Measured)

■ WM processes are measured using metrics such as inventory turns, refurbishment cycle time, percentage of user requirements met within requested window, and other relevant metrics aligned with supply-chain goals and objectives.
■ All warehouse locations are consistently using processes that are fully compliant with warehousing, material handling, and refurbishment process maps and policies.
■ Cross-functional teams of internal users and warehouse personnel work closely together to assess trade-offs in terms of location, sizing, cost and convenience, and providing higher service levels for end users.
■ Suppliers and end users are asked to provide input into WM plans.

12.5.18.3 Advanced: (Leveraged)

■ Bottlenecks and fluctuations are understood and managed to ensure that delivery times are consistently reliable and inventory levels are low.

- Warehouse data is included in the organization database systems and is available to everyone within the organization, but some discrepancies between information and physical location may still exist across sites.

- Organization works with suppliers and customers to plan warehousing requirements based on market demand, company goals, desired service levels, and risk. Vendor managed inventory (VMI) is considered in cases in which the supplier has the capability to support VMI.

- Suppliers, distributors, and end users have a comprehensive knowledge of warehousing operations and the inputs required from them at different points. Training materials available to new associates to ensure coordination.

- Cross-functional teams assess trade-offs in terms of location, sizing, cost and convenience, and providing higher service levels for key customers.

12.5.19 Guiding Principles — Contract Services Management

The standard includes the processes for overall contractor services management (CSM) process. The standard establishes the appropriate procedures when an external services requirement occurs. There are five primary processes in CSM:

1. Contractor mobilization
2. Contractor demobilization
3. Equipment deployment and return
4. Contractor charge collection
5. Contract administration

12.5.19.1 Foundation: (Defined)

Process	Standard
	A reliable workplace infrastructure is established to allow contractors to perform their assigned work.
	Legal document containing the purchasing conditions for the external service (framework or standard purchase order) is used to release external services.
	Contract worker information is captured once to reduce non-value-added work and facilitate reporting.
Mobilization	Project management, maintenance, health and safety, training, and work-site security have access to accurate and timely mobilization data for contractors.

	Documentation of individual contractor information on occupational injuries and illnesses that occur while working on a company site are recorded in a timely manner and are accessible online.
	New suppliers are required to input information into the system prior to being admitted on-site to begin work. Prejob meeting minutes are distributed to appropriate parties.
	Contractor information is captured correctly 90 percent of the time prior to work initiation.
	Training of contractors occurs in a timely manner prior to work initiation. A list of procedures and practices are explained to the contract worker.
Demobilization	The documentation of the commencement and termination of staged contract workers must be accompanied by their assignment and removal from their respective workgroup.
	Contractor mobilization and demobilization information is captured correctly 90 percent of the time prior to work initiation.
	Identification will automatically expire at the contract expiry date.
	The process includes a contract renewal or termination date for the individual contractor. This will trigger a process to extend. Without an extension, the contractor master is automatically deactivated.
	The reasons for termination are documented in the document of the contractor termination process. This information is accessed during the capture of contract individual master data and issue or reactivate company identification processes.
Equipment deployment	A common equipment deployment or return process is used across the company.
	The proper equipment is deployed (delivered and available and in proper working condition) at the proper work site, at the proper time, and returned to the supplier when it is no longer required, as per the requirements identified in job and logistics planning and scheduling.

	Documentation of equipment availability, return, location, and schedule is available in a centrally stored location.
	The documentation of commencement and termination of staged contract workers is available in a centrally stored location.
	Equipment deployment and return information is captured correctly 90 percent of the time.
Contractor charge collection	A common contractor charge collection (CCC) process is used across the company, is easy to use, and can be accessed anytime, anyplace, and anywhere.
	Contracts are available in system in 100 percent of cases to facilitate the CCC process.
	Suppliers are able to enter rates in the rate table using the system interface, which then validates, approves, and releases for execution on the system.
	Rates are captured in a condition table with various time types (OT, ST, DT, PT) for craft types per supplier and will be valid, complete, accurate, and timely 90 percent of the time; not-approved rates are rejected to supplier.
	System provides ability to build up rates (base, union, government, profit, overhead, EI, CWB, and CPP) and to perform detective analysis to ensure correct time.
	Audit trails on rates can trace all historical changes and responsibilities.
	Rate and contract information is available online.
	Contractor is paid on receipt and according to the service contract conditions.

12.5.19.2 Basic: (Measured)

Process	Standard
Mobilization	All employees consistently use contract mobilization, demobilization, equipment deployment, and CCC policies and processes across all locations.
	Changes to contractor status and individual information, including injuries, etc., are captured into an online database quickly and efficiently.

	Electronic master record facilitates security, safety, health, work assignment, recording of work completed, and the recording and validation of charges to the company resulting from work done.
	Data regarding an individual's knowledge and need for required training is captured in the database and is audited regularly to ensure accuracy.
	Contractor information is captured correctly 95 percent of the time prior to work initiation.
Demobilization	High percentages of contract services demobilized prior to payment are electronic.
	Contract extension occurs online prior to the termination of contract.
	Unsatisfactory performance or performance not in accordance with the company's practices and procedures are identified or assessed as the result of identification by other parties. If required, termination is initiated.
	The reasons for contractor dismissal are documented. An updated contractor master record will result from this process.
Equipment deployment	High percentage of equipment deployment and return transactions is electronic and performed based on advance schedule notification (as opposed to events triggered by an associate need).
	Unsatisfactory performance or performance not in accordance with company's practices and procedures are identified or assessed as the result of identification by other parties. If required, supplier termination is initiated.
Contractor charge collection	Suppliers regularly update system with information about contractor's skill set, which is electronically communicated to internal functional units.
	A single Web transactional portal exists for all data entry (LEM, lump sum, unit rates, and hourly rates), correction of rejected service sheets [entry of L (labor), E (equipment), and M (material)], or lump sum and unit rate, and these are performed within one day of work initiation.

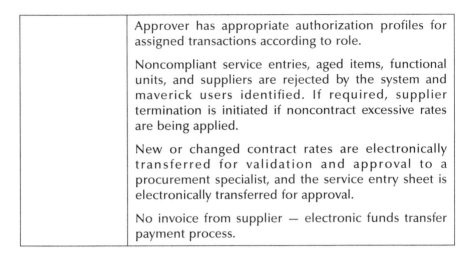

	Approver has appropriate authorization profiles for assigned transactions according to role.
	Noncompliant service entries, aged items, functional units, and suppliers are rejected by the system and maverick users identified. If required, supplier termination is initiated if noncontract excessive rates are being applied.
	New or changed contract rates are electronically transferred for validation and approval to a procurement specialist, and the service entry sheet is electronically transferred for approval.
	No invoice from supplier — electronic funds transfer payment process.

12.5.19.3 Advanced: (Leveraged)

Process	Standard
Mobilization	Mobilization, demobilization, equipment deployment, and CCC become highly integrated, seamless processes with a high degree of supplier involvement throughout the entire life cycle.
	Suppliers, distributors, and end users have a comprehensive knowledge of contract mobilization, demobilization, equipment deployment, and CCC policies, and self-report instances of noncompliance. Training materials available to new associates to ensure coordination.
	On-site suppliers are responsible for equipment inspection, repair, delivery, and maintenance, and maintain an online database of equipment status.
	RF and PDA technology is deployed as appropriate across the company to ensure that data is captured in real-time as contractors and equipment are mobilized, demobilized, ordered, or moved across locations.
	Services and equipment are mobilized to the using location 99 percent on time, work is completed 99 percent on time, and 95 percent of contract mobilization/demobilization/equipment transactions are electronic and recorded.

	Every individual's need for training status is available in the database. Online distance-training methods are utilized when appropriate to ensure all contractors are properly trained prior to arriving on-site.
	Cross-functional teams improve contract mobilization/demobilization and equipment deployment/return processes, for example, reduction of non-value-added activities such as setup times, movement and wait times, and accurate lot or batch history information for quality-tracking purposes.
	Best-performing contractors are identified through electronic supplier PM metrics and rewarded with additional business and established relationship management.
	Contractors define and document their processes to improve mobilization/demobilization performance and align with company requirements. The process is collaboratively managed with supplier interaction.
	The system is linked to supplier organization electronically for forecasting requirements, scheduling, and capacity planning before, during, and after mobilization/demobilization.
	Changes to contractor status and individual information, including injuries, etc., are captured into an online database with appropriate notifications made to all affected parties via PDA or other means.
Contractor charge collection	RF and PDA technology is deployed as appropriate across the company to ensure that data is captured in real-time via mobile devices/call center/punch phone to enter labor at field locations. Contractors enter time attendance/time on-site into company system via Web interface, card swipe, PDA, or other electronic system interface.
	Approval within one to three business days, using risk-based approval process based on business rules (e.g., tolerance limits exceptions approval).
	Spend data is consistently tracked and updated, and costs are reconciled correctly to using locations 100 percent of the time.

	Each using location receives an electronic monthly report on: ■ Spend analysis contractor services ■ Supplier (contractor company) performance ■ Transaction tracing (what, who, and when) from start to finish Audit trails on transactions can trace all historic changes and responsibilities from start to finish. Process data is available in data warehouse for operational, management, and control reporting purposes. Timely, accurate, flexible, and accessible reports available on demand for finance, procurement, maintenance, projects, environmental health and safety (EH&S).

12.5.20 Guiding Principles — Accounts Payable (AP)

12.5.20.1 Foundation: (Defined)

- AP processes for the organization are defined and documented.
- People involved in AP are aware of and conversant with the process and outcomes.
- Changes to these processes go through a formal management-of-change process.
- AP-related roles, jobs, and organizational structures are defined and documented.
- Personnel assigned are trained and knowledgeable.
- Policies are in place for determining when to pay a supplier.
- Policies are in place for resolving issues with suppliers.
- Supplier agreements (SLAs and terms and conditions) are defined and documented and AP personnel are trained on these terms and conditions.
- Electronic payment systems are available.
- Electronic invoices can be received and processed.
- Hard-copy invoices are converted to electronic format for circulation and approval.
- Invoices are directed to a location for quality review and recording of the invoice receipt date.
- Credit card expense statements are available to employees electronically for coding. Statements are printed out for attachment of

receipts and approval. Employees maintain accountability for payment of account.

■ Controls on employee expenses are after expense has occurred.
■ AP personnel are assigned responsibility for groups of suppliers for processing, invoice quality resolution, and payment status enquiries. Supplier groups are rotated among AP personnel.

12.5.20.2 Basic: (Measured)

■ AP process measures are in place such as number of suppliers on electronic payment, number of suppliers on automatic payment (pay on receipt), percentage of late payments, percentage of invoices on hold, cycle time to resolve invoices, and pay.
■ A process for gathering feedback from suppliers is defined and documented.
■ Centralized maintenance and control of supplier payment controls and approved pay points are in place across the enterprise.
■ AP performance against goals is tracked and regularly reported.
■ PO and contract details can be easily accessed.
■ Process improvement responsibility and goals are clearly defined.
■ Process improvement activities occur with key suppliers.
■ Employees can code and submit expenses electronically on a trip-by-trip basis.
■ Standards for invoices and payments are established in contracts and generally followed by suppliers.
■ Invoice processing status is tracked and performance is measured.
■ Payment discounts missed and taken are tracked.
■ Payment cycle times are tracked and communicated.
■ Payment types by buying channel are tracked and communicated.
■ A relevant percentage of credit card transactions are audited for conformance to policy and fraud.
■ Payments made against inactive contracts and obsolete terms are tracked.
■ Payment volume is tracked for each vendor.
■ Invoices are submitted electronically or directly into the system via fax. Hard-copy processing of invoices is rare.

12.5.20.3 Advanced: (Leveraged)

■ Supplier points of contact (AP related) are identified, available, and widely used to maintain clear information flows.

■ Key suppliers can access the system to track status of payments and follow up directly to resolve any issues or disputes.

■ AP measures for key suppliers are available and reviewed at least quarterly with suppliers.

■ AP process performance information and improvement plans are openly shared with suppliers and internal business leads.

■ Automated matching of invoices through electronic means is in place. Invoices that do not conform to standards are returned for resubmission.

■ PO, contract details, and receipt information are available online.

■ Pay on receipt is in place with key suppliers with monthly reconciliation statement.

■ Suppliers formally evaluate company based on measured AP performance and suggest necessary actions and report progress.

■ Suppliers participate in AP improvement teams on a regular basis.

■ Web portal exists and is used by small, regular suppliers to submit invoices. All invoices are submitted electronically.

■ AP group provides regular cash forecasts of reasonable accuracy to the treasury based on supply forecasts, contractual commitments, and historical spend patterns.

■ Payment discounts are automatically realized.

■ Payment types that do not conform to cross-functional team buying channel strategy are reported for investigation by CFT as a nonconformance incident.

■ Payments against inactive contracts and obsolete terms are identified to SCM functional management for investigation as a nonconformance incident.

■ Control of credit card expenses is against a plan submitted prior to expenses being incurred.

12.5.21 Guiding Principles — Continuous Improvement (CI)

12.5.21.1 Foundation: (Defined)

■ Customer and supplier participants are identified, documented, and trained in the application of CI process.

■ A process for gathering input from customers and suppliers is defined and documented.

■ Key commodities (both material and services) and processes for improvement are identified.

■ People involved in CI are aware of the CI process and conversant with the process and outcomes.

- Roles and responsibilities for the various CI components are assigned.
- Personnel assigned to CI are trained and knowledgeable.
- Informal development activities occur with some customers and suppliers.
- Supply-chain personnel typically initiate and lead CI initiatives.
- CI initiatives are typically event triggered and focused on customer function or company-driven issues.
- CI initiatives typically are focused on problems with interfaces between functions or organizations.
- Initiatives are started as issues occur. General performance expectations are established and understood by individuals pursuing improvement initiative.

12.5.21.2 Basic: (Measured)

- Improvement opportunities are prioritized based on company strategy and estimated value contribution.
- Cross-functional team meets regularly to review list of improvement opportunities, and members participate in execution of improvement process.
- Suppliers and customers are often asked to participate in CI efforts.
- A reward mechanism for effective development is defined and documented.
- Issues are examined systematically for root causes and actions are defined.
- Customer and supplier contact roles are defined, including primary and secondary contacts, mediators, and other functional and team-based roles.
- A method for educating contacts about the development process is defined.
- Progress on improvement opportunities is tracked with specific goals established at beginning of the improvement initiative.
- Supply-chain personnel lead CI initiatives that are identified by supply-chain network participants.
- CI lessons learned are shared with other cross-functional teams to leverage improvement benefits.
- Each function contributes equally to improvement opportunity identification.
- Initiatives are prioritized for resolution by the value contribution to the company. Initiative charters are developed to get support and buy-in from functional and business unit teams.
- CI initiatives are expanding into improvements in functional areas.

12.5.21.3 Advanced: (Leveraged)

■ Information on points of contact is available and widely used to minimize extraneous contacts with customers and suppliers while maintaining clear information flows.

■ Supply-chain measures are documented, accessible, created by cross-functional team, and reviewed at least quarterly in a face-to-face meeting with suppliers with supply-chain network participants.

■ Performance information and improvement plans are openly shared with other supply-chain network functions, suppliers, and internal business leads.

■ Suppliers are assessed for their effectiveness in collaboration using measures such as number of suggestions made or incorporated, improved responsiveness, and reductions in cycle time or cost.

■ Benefits as well as progress on finishing improvement are tracked.

■ Supply-chain personnel facilitate cross-functional team members in leading CI initiatives.

■ CI initiatives encompass all areas of supply chain including sub-suppliers (tiers 1 and 2).

■ Cross-functional team leads CI with support from SCM function. CI opportunities are continuously reviewed and implemented.

12.6 Behaviors and Roles

Success requires alignment of all personnel to achieve SCM objectives. The standard and the processes within it are based on the expectation that:

■ *VPs and managers* ensure that supply-chain excellence is a key business objective and promote cross-functional decision making at all levels.

■ *Planners* focus on delivering future-focused executable work packages.

■ *Schedulers* balance resources and maintain future-focused challenging work schedules.

■ *Supervisors* focus on assuring field personnel safety, productivity, and compliance with quality standards.

■ *Buyers* execute agreements according to plans and standards.

■ *Relationship* managers work with suppliers to continuously improve processes.

■ *Engineers* actively seek solutions to eliminate maintenance work.

■ *Company and contract personnel* deployment will be controlled centrally at business unit to balance resources.

■ *All personnel* will be trained in the skills required for them to fulfill their roles or job requirements.

In addition, the following characteristics of the supply-chain organization should be developed:

1. A central SCM group should be created for governance and strategic processes, including business intelligence, to ensure that the foundational elements of the standards are established. Leadership for common spend should come from a corporate group independent of any business unit. This group needs to have enough resources to support the management of the common-spend portfolio.
2. A single AP group should handle the AP function for the corporation. This AP group should report to the central SCM group. The location will be chosen to minimize one-time and ongoing costs as well as benefits associated with proximity to other groups such as treasury.
3. The procurement groups should remain within the business units. This role will transition from a transactional role to a facilitation and contract administration role, and will move toward a logistics planning and scheduling role.
4. Vendor audit is a governance role that should be located in a group that is separate from the operations areas to ensure that it provides a "cold-eye" review. This group should be centrally led to provide consistency in approach and follow-up across the company and leverage the benefits of scale. The location should be chosen to minimize one-time and ongoing costs as well as benefits associated with proximity to other SCM governance groups. PMs should reside at both the corporate and business unit level.
5. Spend governance should be managed according to the commonality of the spend. SS should be a distributed group, but the business intelligence function can be located centrally. The leads for SS processes should be located wherever they can interact best with internal business units. A number of these individuals will be established in each business unit to support professional development in other SCM personnel, stay in touch with business unit realities, and support business unit–specific spend requirements. However, common-spend SS teams should be located centrally.
6. Process governance, the maintenance of the integrated standards, policies, and systems should be managed by the central SCM group. In addition, this group will monitor and support each business unit's progression on their journey to SCM maturity of optimized. Without this stewardship, the business units may be distracted by the operational realities of business.
7. Business unit SCM activities should be managed to meet business unit requirements. Leadership for business unit SCM should be

integrated within the business unit leadership team and needs to have organizational authority to influence the business unit management strategy.

12.7 Conclusion — Leading Change in Supply Management

In this book, we have identified the challenges associated with driving improvement in the supply chain through strategic sourcing, supply market intelligence, management, and visionary leadership. The process requires a fundamental shift in the corporate culture involving teamwork, learning, dedication, and a major change in the typical ways of working of your associates and your team. Just as the soldier in Normandy is given orders to take an objective, your company's associates are being told, "Here are the processes you need to complete and the methods for completing them." As your company executes them, you must identify and report methods to improve them, knowing that there is a system in place to measure the improvements and that you will have the full support of a committed leadership team. It is not acceptable to do things randomly. It is up to you to take on a leadership role to lead an integrated team, working together to achieve success. And you need to act as a leader when that time comes.

Any company that has undertaken the mission of implementing an integrated SCM strategy knows that one of the greatest challenges it faces is the significant change in internal culture that is required to make the supply-chain redesign successful. It is not an easy thing to recondition people to accept change, especially in organizations in which a certain mindset has prevailed for many years. However difficult it may be to accomplish, change can be implemented successfully when directed by a strong and knowledgeable leader who understands the tools available for achieving positive change, as well as his or her role in initiating and sustaining these changes.

Change management is often very confusing for executives to deploy. With so many effective tools available, it can be difficult to determine which tools should be applied to what situations and how the tools could be used in combination. For example, benchmarking, a process that has been shown to be a valuable means of learning how one company's supply-chain performance compares with that of other organizations, has proven to be a valuable tool used in managing change in the supply chain. Through this process, companies are able to clearly identify performance gaps and, thus, focus their SCM efforts on areas most in need of improvement. Yet, this is only one example of the many mechanisms that can be used to execute supply-chain redesign.

But who is a leader of change? The answer is anyone who wishes to participate in change leadership within their organization. There are leaders at every level in a corporation. There are CEOs and board members who plot the strategy and overall direction for the organization. There are managers and supervisors who support the company's strategic plans and guide their employees to meet objectives. There are also group or team leaders who guide specific projects. The next question is: Are you ready to initiate change?

12.8 Checklist

- Identify vision, strategy, and objectives for your organization's supply-chain maturity.
- Conduct self-assessment of major supply management processes following the SCM framework.
- Establish gap and identify priority areas using maturity guides.
- Create a plan with defined metrics for improvement, and identify checkpoints to monitor progress toward a strategic improvement plan.
- Define training elements required to close gap.
- Track measurable benefits and report to senior management on a timely basis.
- Periodically reassess supply-chain maturity and identify reasons for failure to reach goals, if appropriate.

12.9 Results

A vision for the future, with a guiding mission and key performance indicators to guide your organization on its journey to supply chain maturity and industry leadership.

Appendix A

Global Sourcing in China

A.1 Low-Cost-Country Sourcing: What about China?

More and more companies are making the decision to purchase commodity goods from international sources. This decision occurs for a number of reasons, such as the search for cost or price benefits, better quality, access to superior technology, or because a foreign source is the only one available.[1] Firms may also turn to international sourcing to introduce competition to the domestic supply base and satisfy countertrade agreements, as a reaction to sourcing patterns of competitors, to establish a presence in a foreign market, or to improve supplier responsiveness.[2] The decision to seek out global sources, especially in China, should be made only after a company carefully assesses the competitive forces at work in the industry, the requirements of customers, the level of worldwide competition, and the location of suppliers for specific purchase requirements.[3] It is also critical to understand the fundamental business propositions associated with low cost–country sourcing and the challenges and opportunities that lie in developing a global sourcing model in China.

A.2 The Growth of Low-Cost-Country Sourcing

The growth of outsourcing, particularly of manufacturing to China and business process outsourcing to India, has been in the headlines regularly for the last two years. Politicians decry outsourcing and the bosses they hold responsible for perpetrating it. The same media that greeted the rise

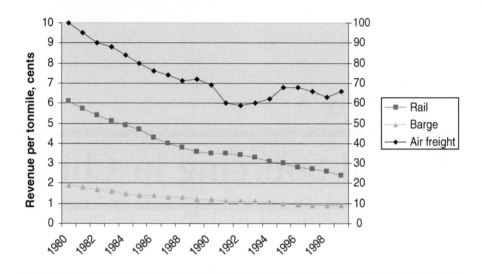

Figure A.1 Declining transportation costs. (Source: McKinsey Global Institute.)

of the new economy in the 1990s now mourn the jobs that supposedly migrate from rich countries to less developed ones. Forrester, an American research firm, has estimated these future losses down to the last detail: By 2015, America is expected to have lost 74,642 legal jobs to poorer countries and Europe will have lost 118,172 computer jobs.

Despite these sobering facts, global sourcing is an economic reality. Diana Farrell, the head of McKinsey's Global Institute, thinks that by reorganizing production intelligently, a multinational firm can hope to lower its costs by as much as 50 to 70 percent.[4] This occurs, first, thanks to the Internet and telecommunications bandwidth, whereby businesses can hand over more white-collar work to specialist outside manufacturers. Second, as transportation costs fall (see Figure A.1), globalization is beginning to separate the geography of production and consumption, with firms producing goods and services in one country and shipping them to their customers in another. Over the past ten years, countries such as Mexico, Brazil, the Czech Republic, and of course, China have emerged as important manufacturing hubs for televisions, cars, computers, and other goods for consumers in America, Japan, and Europe. Companies such as Wal-Mart and Dell lead the pack of companies who rely on this model for survival. Rich-country manufacturers have already invested hundreds of billions of dollars in building factories in China to make clothes, toys, computers, and consumer goods. In the next few years, they may invest hundreds of billions more to shift the production of cars, chemicals, plastics, medical equipment, and industrial goods.

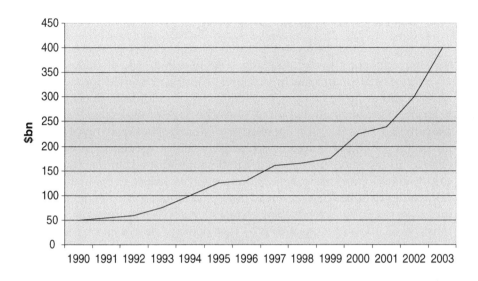

Figure A.2 Manufacturing exports have facilitated incredible growth. (Source: Thomason Datastream.)

The history of this trend is interesting. In the late 1980s and early 1990s, as transport and communications costs fell and logistics technology improved, rich-country manufacturers began moving production to cheaper nearby countries. American carmakers and consumer electronics firms started manufacturing in Mexico; European makers went to the Czech Republic, Slovakia, and Poland; and Japanese, Taiwanese, and Korean firms moved to China. By the late 1990s, European manufacturers such as Philips, Siemens, and Nokia and American ones such as GE and Motorola were moving farther, to China. American imports from China rose from $66 billion in 1997 to $163 billion last year. By one estimate, foreign companies opened 60,000 factories in China between 2000 and 2003.[5] The country's exports also rocketed (see Figure A.2).

It is important to recognize the distinction between international purchasing and global sourcing. International purchasing is a commercial transaction that occurs between a buyer and a supplier located in different countries, and is often more complex than domestic purchasing.[6] Global sourcing, on the other hand, is greater in scope and complexity and involves "proactively aggregating volumes and coordinating common items, practices, processes, designs, technologies, and suppliers across worldwide procurement, design, and operating locations."[7] Ideally, international purchasing activities will eventually become fully integrated with other supply-chain processes.

A.3 Barriers to Global Sourcing

There are a number of factors that may prevent companies from successfully implementing global sourcing. The first is a lack of understanding of international purchasing procedures; the buyer should know how to identify and evaluate foreign suppliers and what additional documentation is required for international purchases. This lack of understanding can be exacerbated by a lack of knowledge of foreign business practices, language, and cultural barriers. A firm may also experience resistance to change and loyalty to existing domestic suppliers within the purchasing organization, or an atmosphere of domestic nationalism in the marketplace. Companies experience longer lead times and lengthened material pipelines that may necessitate procedural changes. Material requirements forecasts must be as accurate as possible so that delivery delays can be managed without interrupting production.[8] Time differences between the source and purchasing companies add to the difficulties in doing business, as do poor communications and transportation infrastructure.

Companies should be aware of humanitarian and environmental issues when sourcing from less developed countries. Good workplace and environmental practices are not only a social responsibility, but can also impact business. Liz Claiborne, Inc., received negative publicity when it was discovered that some of the company's products were made in sweatshops overseas. This prompted the company to draft a detailed code of conduct for its contractors, with inputs from the same human rights groups and consumer groups that blew the whistle on them.[9] A number of other companies have followed suit, and at least three organizations exist that certify factories for compliance — the Fair Labor Association, Social Accountability International (SAI), and Worldwide Responsible Apparel Production (WRAP).[10] Companies should have some way of monitoring the workplace conditions and environmental practices of their overseas suppliers, either firsthand or through a trusted third party. Some new guidelines suggest that monitoring first-tier suppliers is not enough, but must extend below the first tier (see Table A.1).

Firms should also be aware of current sanctions that the U.S. government has in place against some countries and individual companies. These sanctions can fall under the Trading with the Enemy Act, Export Administration regulations, or the Defense Product Act, and may be in reaction to suspected nuclear weapons testing, failure to service debt to the United States, support of terrorist activity, or long-standing political tensions (e.g., Cuba and Vietnam). The U.S. government recently placed sanctions on certain computer chips manufactured by the South Korean company Hynix Semiconductor because allegations that the South Korean government had

Table A.1   The New Supply-Chain Standards: Is FTSE4Good Enough?

The New Supply-Chain Standards: FTSE4Good Enough?
By Rachelle Jackson

While we can all applaud FTSE4Good for recently launching a supply-chain labor standards requirement for indexed companies, the requirements do not currently extend far enough down the supply chain to truly mitigate brand risk.

Significantly, after recognizing that "labor standards are of greatest concern beyond the first-tier suppliers," FTSE4Good will currently limit the application of the supply-chain labor standards criteria to the first-tier suppliers only, or those with whom companies have a direct commercial relationship.

This is apparently due to the fact that even engaging the first-tier suppliers is a difficult step for many companies. In addition, companies have much greater influence with the first tier supplier and therefore can have a more immediate impact.

Yet limiting accountability to the first tier of the supply chain may not be the best means of mitigating risk to the company, which remains a primary concern of investment groups. This raises an interesting question. Just how far down the supply chain should a company go in pursuit of upholding labor standards as well as managing risk?

Beyond the first tier

The FTSE4Good criterion defines a supply chain as, "the distribution channel of a product, from its sourcing, to its delivery to the end consumer (also known as the value chain). It includes the growing of crops and acquisition of raw materials, manufacturing products, distributing finished goods to retailers and sale to the final consumer. The supply chain is typically comprised of a chain of companies, each contributing to the final product such as supplying component parts, or doing something further to the product (adding value)."

Thus, beyond the first-tier suppliers lies a network of subcontractors and component or materials suppliers, some of which engage in parts of the production process directly on branded products.

High risk supply chains

In countries as diverse as China, Japan, and Israel, it is not unheard of to find first-tier suppliers in subcontracting relationships with state prisoner rehabilitation programs, using branded production.

More frequently, first-tier suppliers subcontract production processes to home worker networks, which are notorious for labor exploitation. The most uncontrolled part of the supply chain, home worker networks frequently include child labor, unsafe work conditions, unmonitored work hours, and sub-minimum wage levels.

**Table A.1   The New Supply-Chain Standards:
Is FTSE4Good Enough? (continued)**

Even when subcontractors are one step away from the supplier-buyer relationship, they frequently have no knowledge of the buyer entity or their policy toward labor standards. First-tier suppliers may plaster their walls with buying-company codes of conduct and worker regulations, but subcontracting facilities rarely, if ever, have the same.

This lack of communication of policy expectations means that when branded goods are sent to subcontractors for processing, there is no effort on the part of the first-tier supplier to transfer knowledge of the buyer's standards farther down the supply chain. Thus, while the first-tier supplier may ensure the absence of child labor, excessive work hours, or discriminatory practices in their own establishments, the same is not to be said once the production leaves their premises for finishing, packing, or other processing activities.

Creative subcontracting

In fact, some of the more cunning first-tier suppliers will purposely set up their operations such that the practices most at risk in regards to labor and environmental practices are actually separate corporate entities.

Textiles provide an excellent example: suppliers in Pakistan frequently subcontract their washing and dye operations. Yet a visit to any dyeing facility in Lahore will reveal that the wastewater filled with colorful dyes is diverted to the local river, invariably located behind the dyeing facility. A quick walk through the backyard of the subcontractor will reveal a rainbow of colors on the riverbanks, where local wildlife feed and children play. Yet the first-tier supplier takes no responsibility for these negative environmental impacts resulting from their subcontractor's practices.

Another common practice, from New York to China, is to create separate corporate entities within the same facility. Thus, employees in the next room belong to "another company," which subcontracts work from the main entity. Look a little further and you will find that the main entity is the "showcase company," with low working hours and high wages. Meanwhile, the employees in the next room are working double shifts with no overtime pay, all the while producing your brand label.

The bottom line: If you are not including subcontractors in your risk sampling, you may fail to adequately protect your brand.

Materials and components

In addition to the risks of the subcontracting relationships themselves, some companies find there is inherent risk related to the component or raw material suppliers. Earlier this year, Human Rights Watch advocated that a major multinational should ensure corporate responsibility all the

Table A.1   The New Supply-Chain Standards: Is FTSE4Good Enough? (continued)

way down the supply chain. Their report on child labor in El Salvador's sugar fields called on the Coca-Cola Company to accept responsibility for the labor practices of farms which provide sugar to mills, who process the sugar and supply it to Coca-Cola bottling partners.

In statements published in the HRW report, Coca-Cola declined to accept responsibility beyond their first-tier suppliers. Human Rights Watch reported, "Coca-Cola's guiding principles apply only to its direct suppliers .... This omission is significant because it means that Coca-Cola's supplier mill can comply with Coca-Cola's guiding principles even though it is aware or should be aware that that the sugar it refines is harvested in part by child labor."

Human Rights Watch called on Coca-Cola to revise their supplier standards to incorporate the controversial United Nation's Norms on the Responsibilities of Transnational Corporations and Other Business Enterprises with Regard to Human Rights, which stipulate that MNCs apply the Norms "in their contracts or other arrangements and dealings with contractors, subcontractors, suppliers, licensees," etc.

NGO groups continue to advocate the adoption of the U.N. Norms, which would provide a further tool to pressure MNCs to take responsibility for their entire supply chain.

Benchmarking the supply chain

So, considering the apparent risks, who is already engaging their supply chain beyond the first tier?

As the FTSE4Good criteria specifically mentions that companies endorsing the Ethical Trading Initiative (ETI), Social Accountability 8000 (SA8000), or the Fair Labor Association (FLA) are on the right track with labor standards, this is a good place to start.

Of the three standards, only SA8000 specifically addresses subcontractors and requires suppliers to be responsible for ensuring compliance to the SA8000 standard, including through audits and the contractual relationship. The International Council of Toy Industries standard, ICTI, though not mentioned by FTSE, also requires subcontractor compliance and asks suppliers to audit their subcontractors.

As for corporate programs, companies such as Wal-Mart, The Walt Disney Company, Mattel, and McDonalds all include subcontractors in their labor standards. Some of these require first-tier suppliers to obtain written commitments from subcontractors to uphold labor standards. Others require first-tier suppliers to ensure the compliance of the subcontractor. The Nordstrom code of conduct requires approval before first-tier suppliers can even use subcontractors.

**Table A.1   The New Supply-Chain Standards:
Is FTSE4Good Enough? (continued)**

Following the chain

Of course, including subcontractors in the code of conduct is only the first step. Monitoring implementation of the standard at the subcontractor level is another step altogether.

In 2003, the India Committee of the Netherlands called on MNCs, including Advanta, Bayer, Monsanto, and Syngenta, sourcing cottonseed in India to take responsibility for the child labor employed in the cotton farms and to ensure its eradication. By 2004, only Syngenta had launched a plan to ensure acceptable working conditions for children on family farms and the removal of children from large industrial farms. In addition, Syngenta partnered with the FLA to provide monitoring of labor conditions on the cotton farms in India.

In response to the inaction of the other companies, the India Committee of the Netherlands launched a new campaign in 2004 to bring renewed attention to the issue and demand action on the part of the MNCs.

Innovative solutions

Looking beyond the simple due diligence monitoring of subcontractors to mitigate risk in the supply chain, some companies experiment with creative solutions to long-term issues, such as poverty and sustainability.

B&Q, the U.K. home improvement retailer, once reviewed working conditions in India's rug manufacturing sector. A local NGO group informed B&Q that beaters and spinners working on the rugs had a precarious financial position. B&Q determined that this group was too far down the supply chain for the company to exert sufficient influence over their working conditions. Instead of struggling to have an impact through the many agents and intermediaries, B&Q instead partnered with a local NGO to set up a micro-credit savings scheme for these workers.

Clearly, the supply chain remains a complex challenge for corporate responsibility programs and implementation of labor standards is no exception. The FTSE4Good Supply Chain criteria are a positive step that will motivate many companies to take important new actions to promote improved conditions for workers worldwide.

Yet FTSE4Good is obviously trying to ease companies into their standards by starting with the first-tier supplier requirement. In fact, FTSE4Good has already indicated the scope may be extended in the future to include more of the supply chain.

As a pure exercise in risk mitigation, however, companies should be prepared to assess the risk unique to their products, commodities, and countries of origin, and then focus their programs on prioritized parts of the supply chain.

**Table A.1   The New Supply-Chain Standards:
Is FTSE4Good Enough? (continued)**

Rachelle Jackson is the Director of Research and Development at CSCC, a corporate social responsibility service provider. rjackson@intlcompliance. com.

Source: http://www.intlcompliance.com, Jan. 3, 2005.

unfairly subsidized the company after the Asian financial crisis.[11] The United States also imposed sanctions against five Chinese companies and a North Korean company that the government believes to have assisted Iran's weapons program.[12] Information on sanctions can be found on the United States State Department Web site.

Even so, the growth of global sourcing and, particularly, the importance of China's role in the global economy are undeniable. China accounts for nearly one quarter of global economic growth, according to International Monetary Fund calculations based on "purchasing power parity," which measures output without the distortions of currency exchange rates.[13] So, when China's central bank raised interest rates on October 28, 2004, shock waves rippled out toward copper mines in Chile, carmakers' headquarters in Detroit, and oil fields in Russia. It is worth noting that in China, where the state makes 90 percent of the fixed-asset investments, getting the economy to slow requires subtle market adjustments and also not-so-subtle administrative instructions that are often the product of dubious bargains between Beijing and truculent provinces. In the words of Goldman Sachs economist Hong Linang: "It's all about making deals, making compromises."[14] In this world, family connections are also critical.

Before jumping into global sourcing, it is therefore critical that firms understand the environment in which they will be doing business. Specific capabilities and infrastructural and environmental elements should be in place. For instance, the global sourcing effort should have executive management support and the appropriate organizational structure. Coordination mechanisms should be established, such as cross-functional teams, periodic review meetings, global sourcing contracts, overseas international translators and supply base managers, and supplier performance evaluation procedures. Appropriate personnel capabilities, such as a commitment to the global integration process and a global focus on procurement, an understanding of other cultures, knowledge of global information systems, and an understanding of currency and international risk management should be developed. A worldwide information systems infrastructure needs to be built to support the level of information exchange necessary for integrated global supply-chain management.[15]

A.4 Locating Global Sources

There are a number of sources from which companies can access information on global sources of supply[16]:

- International industrial directories: These directories are organized by industry or region of the world. Some examples are:
  - Principal International Businesses: The World Marketing Directory, published by Dun and Bradstreet
  - Marconi's International Register
  - ABC Europe Production
  - Business Directory of Hong Kong
  - Japan Yellow Pages
- Trade shows: These provide the opportunity to gather information on a number of suppliers at the same time. Directories of worldwide trade shows can be found in most business libraries.
- Trading companies: Some trading companies provide a full range of services that minimize direct involvement of buyers in the global sourcing process. This may be a good starting point for small or inexperienced firms.
- External agents:
  - Independent agents: They act as purchasing representatives in foreign countries and help to locate sources of supply, evaluate the source, and handle the appropriate paperwork for a commission. They can also be a source of intelligence on trends in foreign markets. A couple of agents operating in Asia are listed in the following text:
    - William E. Connor and Associates, Ltd.
    - Li and Fung, Ltd., of Hong Kong
  - Import brokers: They help to locate foreign sources and act as intermediaries between buyer and seller.
  - Direct manufacturer's representatives: These representatives work for the selling firm in the buying firm's country.
  - International banks and financial institutions: These institutions have personnel with knowledge of foreign sources.
  - State and federal agencies: These agencies encourage and promote international trade, e.g., U.S. Department of Commerce.
- Trade consulates: Most foreign-trade consulates have trade experts interested in doing business with American companies. The following organizations are also good sources of information on international trade:
  - International Trade Association
  - World Trade Organization (WTO)
  - Organization and Economic Council for Development (OECD)

- Internal firm sources: The outsourcing firm may have foreign subsidiaries, foreign buying offices, or international joint venture partners that can provide information on global sources.
- World Wide Web: The Internet is an excellent resource for information on conducting international trade and locating suppliers. The following Web sites are good starting points:
  - http://www.ita.doc.gov/: The International Trade Association (U.S. Department of Commerce) Web site features U.S. foreign-trade highlights, market access and compliance, information on legal issues surrounding international trade, information on upcoming trade missions, as well as other pertinent information.
  - http://www.agoa.gov/tradelinks/tradelinks.html#tradeleads: This page has links to trade leads and matchmaker programs. It is part of the African Growth and Opportunity Act (AGOA) section of the Export.gov Web site, but most companies linked have a worldwide focus.

A.5 Identifying New Suppliers Globally

It is important to keep abreast of the information on new foreign suppliers as they enter the market. Trading companies and independent agents or import brokers may be the best source of information on new suppliers because they have a presence in these markets.

A.6 China's Growing Economic Strength

Not so long ago, strong American market nationalism and anticommunist sentiment made it a socially sensitive issue for U.S. companies to purchase goods from China. These days, purchasing Chinese goods may be a necessity if American companies are to survive in certain industries. Many major American companies already have a stake in Chinese-made goods, from sourcing relationships to joint ventures and direct investment in Chinese factories. China has received $600 billion in foreign investment in the last two decades, and half of China's $266.2 billion in exports in 2001 came from foreign manufacturers or their joint ventures.[17] And in the period from May to October 2002, imports to the United States from China were greater than those from Japan.[18]

Today, the bulk of outsourcing to achieve labor savings appears to be going to China. China's admission to the WTO in November 2001 has increased its appeal for outsourcing of labor by locking in lower duties for products it exports. Japanese management consultant Kenichi Ohmae compares China's emergence as a manufacturing colossus with Japan's spectacular postwar industrial boom, the rise of America's economy in

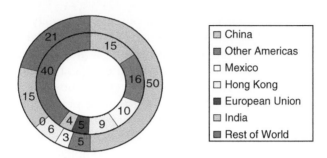

Figure A.3   U.S. clothing market share (percentage) before and after quota elimination.

the early 1900s, or even the dawn of the Industrial Revolution in Britain.[19] The new heft of China's economy is most keenly felt in Asia, where the Chinese mainland has swallowed up $321 billion, or 45 percent, of the $719 billion in foreign direct investment (FDI) flowing into the region since 1990. Companies currently producing in China include General Motors, Motorola, Solectron, Dell, Ford, DaimlerChrysler, Toshiba, Sony, Matsushita, Canon, and many others.

Competition from China has ravaged the Japanese textile industry and threatens to wipe out producers of farm goods (see Figure A.3). In addition, many Japanese electronics giants have announced plans to shed tens of thousands of workers at home. Toshiba President Tadashi Okamura notes: "We recognize that there are concerns in Japan about jobs moving to China, just as there were concerns in America 15 years ago about jobs moving to Japan. But a shift of some sort is inevitable. China is a huge market, and it offers an enormous pool of excellent workers. We have to find a way to coexist." Teizo Togawa, general manager of Japanese towel maker Ichihiro Co.'s Dalian plant also notes: "The competition for jobs is really brutal here, so people are far more serious about their work. In Japan, we have to promise workers jobs for life and pay them based on seniority. But no one even thinks about that here. Workers in China believe in merit."

The impact of China's admission to the WTO on imports to the United States will be major, especially in terms of the growth of the Chinese economy. As can be seen, China stands to grow its market share in apparel to 50 percent of the global market, which will have an enormous impact.

A.7 Labor Force

When selecting a supplier or partner in China, it is critical to be aware of the working and economic conditions. Nothing is more important than an understanding of the labor force.

The majority of these workers are known as the *liudong renkou* — the "floating population."[20] The liudong renkou consists of over 114 million migrant workers, who are, for the most part, relatively well-educated young people drawn by the promise of the big city. This group represents the growing rural elite of China and has been documented by labor historians as the largest migration in human history in terms of sheer numbers. They are younger and better educated than those who stay behind. This gap is especially wide among women. A study in the mid-1990s by the Chinese Academy of Social Sciences found that 78 percent of female migrants had a junior high school education, whereas among rural women nationwide it was only 43 percent. Remittances sent home by migrants are already the biggest source of wealth accumulation in rural China, economists say. Yet, earning money is not the only reason people migrate. In surveys, migrant workers rank "seeing the world" and "learning new skills" as important as earning cash for the family. When migrant workers speak of why they left home, their narratives often begin the same way: "There was nothing to do at home, so I came out." A survey of 700 migrant laborers conducted in the mid-1990s by a Chinese government think tank found that 87 percent left home with a work objective in mind, either a confirmed job or to find one with the help of an acquaintance in the city.

The jobs that these workers come to are often less than optimal. In many Chinese enterprises, employers pay less than the minimum wage ($50 to $70 per month on the coast), and require more than the 49 hr of work per week permitted by law.[21] Further, there are few, if any, benefits for pregnant or injured workers, and enforcement of labor laws is lax. Workers are often housed in cramped, filthy "dorms." Those who are unhappy and decide to quit may have to relinquish up to two months of pay.

This young group of workers is not happy to work under these conditions. In many large cities, "talent markets" are emerging. These are like big job fairs and are intended for technicians and managers. Many factory workers show up at these job fairs in the hope of talking their way into a better job. There are often companies seeking to find human resource workers or other clerical or knowledge-worker positions. There are commercial schools that offer programs to make up for lost education, or photo studies for professional portraits. These fairs can offer new positions as clerks, paying $100 a month plus room and board.

A.8 Centers of Growth in China

The majority of the growth that has occurred in China is in the Pearl River Delta (PRD). Transformed from a rural backwater into the world's work-shop through Deng Xiaoping's economic reforms and the proximity of

Hong Kong's capital, technology, and business skills, the PRD is centered around Guangdong province, China's richest. It is home to the world's largest suppliers of all types of goods, from television to toys. But worsening pollution, poor infrastructure, power bottlenecks, severe labor shortages, and rising wage costs are combining to take the edge off that success. The PRD is starting to lose investors to another of China's economic and political heavyweights — Shanghai and the Yangtze River Delta (YRD), which enjoys better access to China's huge domestic market. In particular, areas such as the Suzhou Industrial Park have witnessed phenomenal growth; on a recent visit I learned that the bulk of FDI goes to this area, and that an average of one plant opens each day.

The PRD has responded by announcing the creation of a "Pan-Pearl River Delta" that would extend regional cooperation in trade and investment from the south and east of the country to the center and west. Also known as the "9 + 2," it would link the nine provinces of Guangdong, Fujian, Jiangxi, Hunan, Guangxi, Hainan, Guizhou, Yunnan, and Sichuan with the two special administrative regions of Hong Kong and Macau via a new web of road, rail, and air routes.[22] Simultaneously, trade and nontariff barriers between the provinces would be eliminated to allow the PRD to develop new markets and free up the movement of labor. This area has a population of 450 million, a gross domestic product (GDP) of some $630 billion, and encompasses a fifth of China's land, and a third of its people; it produces one third of the country's exports and almost 40 percent of its economic output.

This would be a massive undertaking, given the competition from the YRD. Although Guangdong's exports have doubled in the past five years to reach $153 billion in 2003, those of the Greater Shanghai region (including Zhejian and Jiangsu) have almost quadrupled to catch up. In terms of FDI, Shanghai is already ahead, attracting $21 billion in FDI in 2003 against $7.8 billion in Guangdong. Today, there is great rivalry among provinces, towns, and local districts, which explains the duplicate investment in ports and airports in Guangdong. It has also led to unnecessary red tape and a host of trade barriers. Goods traveling across the region are routinely loaded onto different trucks at each provincial border, and tourists have to switch travel agents and guides from municipality to municipality. However, provincial officials are beginning to develop "enlightened self-interest" and are starting to see the benefits of, if not exactly cooperating, at least not competing.

By the time this book is published, this information will be obsolete. The economic and cultural aspects of China are changing so quickly that it is impossible to keep up without being actively involved in activities on the front lines. However, it does provide some insights into the types of changes that are underway.

A.8.1 Barriers to Sourcing from China

Because of China's communist government, there have been political barriers in place on both the Chinese side and the U.S. side, but the situation is improving. Since the 1970s, China has made efforts to reform its economy and liberalize trade and has set up eight special zones to draw foreign investment and trade (Shenzhen, Shanghai, Beijing, Tianjin, Guangzhou, Dalian, Xiamen, and Shatou).[23] Partially owing to the reform efforts, as well as to the potential of China in the world market, China was finally admitted to the WTO on November 11, 2001, 15 years after applying. Admission was finalized only after the Congress voted to grant China Permanent Normal Trading Rights in 2000, and President Bush certified the United States–China bilateral WTO agreement on September 10, 2001.[24]

China expects to gain several benefits from admission to the WTO.[25] The hope is that reform will continue in the national economy through restructuring and revitalization of state-owned enterprises and reform of the banking system, which is currently suffering from a tremendous amount of bad debt. The country also hopes to take advantage of the high-tech revolution, particularly through the protection of intellectual property rights. China will be seen as part of the fair-trade system, which will pave the way for increased foreign exchange to purchase imports and encourage growth by way of demand. China will also benefit from the granting of Normal Trade Relations status with the United States, and will now have a voice in the making of rules of international trade and on Taiwan's status in the WTO. There are benefits to countries wanting to do business in China as well,[26] particularly the increased transparency and predictability about the rules of doing business. Firms exporting to China will benefit from reduced tariffs in several sectors, such as agriculture, industrial products, insurance, and financial services.

Companies sourcing from China should pay particular attention to working conditions in manufacturing facilities there. Even by official Chinese government figures, the country had more deaths from work-related illness than any other country, amounting to over 386,000 deaths in 2002.[27]

A.8.2 Benefits of Sourcing from China

The main benefit to be gained from purchasing from Chinese sources is the low price, owing to China's vast and seemingly bottomless pool of cheap labor that keeps production costs low.[28] The quality of Chinese goods is also improving, although there are still problems in certain areas. For example, Ford Motor Company aimed to purchase $1 billion in auto parts from China in 2003, but now does not expect to purchase half of that amount because they have not found suppliers who produce to the necessary quality standard.[29] However, as foreign investment and trade increase, money is being put back into the production facilities to improve the quality of the output.[30] Another good reason to purchase from China is that competitors are already doing so, and they may be able to gain a competitive advantage by lowering prices or maintaining a higher profit margin. Firms will have to turn to Chinese sources to maintain a level playing field in the industry. In some cases, a Chinese source may be the only one available.

A.8.3 China as a Market

For some companies, one of the goals of global purchasing is to establish a presence in an international market, but in China this may be an elusive objective, despite the huge potential market. Many companies have built facilities in China with the hopes of selling to the local market, but have ended up exporting the goods produced because demand has failed to materialize. Usually, as industries move into a developing region and unemployment drops, real wages start to rise and demand for goods increases.[31] However, China still has a huge number of under- and unemployed people, which has kept wages low. Although this vast pool of cheap labor has continued to attract new businesses, demand in the Chinese market has been slow to develop. So, if this is one of a company's goals for global purchasing, a careful analysis of the market should be undertaken first.

A.8.4 Sources of Information on Doing Business in China

Some sources of information for those planning to do business in China are the following:

- *Integrating China into the Global Economy*, by Nicholas R. Lardy, The Brookings Institute, 2002, ISBN 0815751354, which gives an overview of China's new role in the global trading system and the new opportunities for investment in China.
- *China and the WTO: Changing China, Changing World Trade*, by Supachai Panitchpakdi and Mark L. Clifford, John Wiley and Sons, 2002, ISBN 0470820616, for an analysis of the implications for world trade because of China's accession to the WTO.
- *The China Dream: The Quest for the Last Great Untapped Resource on Earth*, by Joe Studwell, Grove Press, 2003, ISBN 0802139752, which gives a more negative view of doing business in China.

- http://www.mac.doc.gov/china/index.html, the China Gateway home page, which provides assistance with market access and compliance, links to China business guides, WTO information, and information on trade problems with China.
- http://mnistore.com/china/index.asp?source=CGJ&keyword= ChineseIndustry, the Web site for Manufacturers' News, Inc., which has available for purchase a database of Chinese manufacturers and distributors. Firms can purchase the entire database or only the portion pertaining to a particular industry.

A.9 Identifying and Negotiating with Chinese Suppliers

An interview with a U.S. expert who worked closely with Chinese businesspeople for many years reveals the unexpected difficulties that may occur when attempting to negotiate and establish a contract with a Chinese global supplier. This is surely not representative of every situation, but illustrates the potential pitfalls that may arise if one is not careful:

> In my experience, Chinese businesspeople will always want to negotiate, even after a contract is signed. Also, it would be foolish to think that many Chinese do not understand English — even if a translator is present. The translator will be used, but they understand every word. They may even look through your private papers while you are out of the room — and claim it is "intelligence." A lot of business is also done under the table in the form of payoffs. Even though I was not involved in payoffs and favors, I knew my Asian contact was doing it. We made him sign that he should not be doing these kinds of things, bearing in mind that the Foreign Corrupt Practices Act comes into play if you are working with a U.S. corporation. You could be liable. This is a big problem when dealing with government officials at all levels; they will drag their feet a lot without an incentive.
>
> One of the most useful tools I used in China was a glossary of business contracts, which contained Chinese words with English translation. I used this to go through every single one of the terms and quickly realized that I needed to use very specific words: Warranty, guarantee, and terms of payment all mean very different things. Even though there are laws to protect intellectual property, you need to have a very good American lawyer, and they are very expensive. The root cause of this practice is that people in China were "burned" by German and Russian companies earlier in the century. These companies

built plants and equipment, and then squeezed their Chinese buyers through contracts that they could not get out of. As such, Chinese businesspeople have become very careful.

Logistics and timeliness is another concern. Scheduling a shipment or business process to move product from point A to point B is a real ordeal. Simply finding and hiring a logistics carrier can take three or four or five days, and people are not in a hurry. If you wish to have a product manufactured, you need to ensure that it is commercialized. Even if you have the drawings, you may require government permissions. If it is pharmaceutical, you must connect with the commercial medicine industry. In steel, the contact is the Ministry of Metallurgy.

Finding a supplier in China is not easy. The best approach is to always get a reference. If you know of anyone who has done work in China, contact them and identify two or three potential suppliers to interview. References are critical. One of the biggest problems in sourcing from China is quality. Many manufacturers assume that they can do things their way and not necessarily follow the drawing or specification. To ensure quality, be prepared to hire someone to oversee the design and manufacture of the product at all times so that drawings are interpreted correctly. In negotiations, the manufacturers will always say "no problem" if you express concerns. Do not assume that this is the case: what matters the most is that they understand 100 percent what you are after.

A lot of U.S. companies have agents in that part of the world. They may have an agent and an office: a phone call and a cup of coffee with someone there can help you to get a reference. Before you meet, contact the agent and have them establish a set of appointments with suitable supplier candidates. It could take you a lot of time to find people on the Internet or in the phone book. During the interviews, take your time, and spend at least half a day meeting with each supplier. Ask for multiple references: who have you done work for, what are their names and numbers? Then be sure to follow up with each reference (especially the ones in the United States). Do not expect them to be perfect; if 90 percent of what they tell you is true, that is a good sign. Remember that the agent has ties with the manufacturers you are interviewing that are very tight. He is not going to upset these people for you.

It is always worthwhile to visit the facilities. The large Chinese factories will impress you, as they are absolutely incredible in size and scope. However, the smaller-sized facilities may have problems. In some factories, it was obvious that they knew what they were doing, but the working conditions were terrible. I was afraid to use the restrooms!

Do not pay a supplier just because they shipped the material. If you have an agreement that states "payment upon shipment," it is worthwhile to spend some time trying to negotiate terms for payment upon receipt, inspection, and approval of the product in the United States. You absolutely need to be tough on this. Otherwise, they have your money, and you have a product that does not work. People assume everything is okay, and it is not. In a worst-case situation, your U.S. customer receives the product and discovers a defect. For example, I bought a desk heater, and then received an e-mail from the company that they had found a faulty switch that could cause a fire, and had to do a product recall. In China this would not be viewed as a major problem.

In situations when a problem arises, have the agent explain the legal issues in detail. Ask about similar cases when there was a problem. The manufacturer can generally get out of these issues in a court of law. That is why it is very risky to write your own contract, which may not be recognized in a Chinese court of law. For that reason, you may choose to include an arbitration clause that specifies arbitration in a particular state — New York. Of course, the manufacturer will argue that it should take place in China. Stay firm on this point: "Do you want the business or not?"

When developing a new product for manufacture, ensure that the progress payments are written in stone. This is one of the biggest sources of dispute. You must have "rock-solid" performance payments or progress payments in place. The contract must have specific milestones and payments associated with each milestone. It is important to stand firm with the manufacturer early in the negotiation for these milestones, and then carefully approve each milestone one by one.

In a negotiation, if there are two Americans on your side, expect to see twenty Chinese sitting across the table. The negotiations may last for days and days — this is designed to make you tired. It is especially important to avoid making deals after a drink or dinner. If you refuse to sign an agreement or make a deal at dinner, do not worry about the Chinese taking offense — they understand that you are a businessperson who wants to do it the right way. Keep reminding them how much you appreciate them, but that you need to do it the way it is done "back home." It is also important to be respectful of the Chinese culture, but to insist that in business matters the American approach be used.

I remember one of the worst experiences I ever had occurred because I did not follow the guidelines. After 20 days in China negotiating, the other party brought in a bunch of people to ask many, many questions. We spent eight to ten hours a day going through specifications and details. We negotiated it to death. I wanted to leave, and told them that I really wanted to go home. Finally, we signed the agreement, celebrated and got a contract for $1 million. I took the next flight home. Then when I got back to the office, there was a fax saying their board needed to ratify the contract and that paragraph XX needed to be revised, even though we had signed the contract. It cost us a ton of money, and three lawyers from three countries at $1000 an hour — we made no money on that contract!

A.10 International Exchange Rate Forecasts

An *exchange rate* is the going market value of one country's money in another country. In other words, how much does currency cost? How much of one country's currency does it take to buy the requisite amount of another country's money, to buy goods and services from there? In our increasingly global economy in which buying from international suppliers should be a strategic goal for every supply-chain company, knowledge of exchange rates should become part of routine purchasing responsibilities.

Yes, even money costs money and is motored by customer demand. And because it is demand driven, it fluctuates just as stocks do. However, a country's currency usually has a baseline value relative to which the fluctuations can be measured. For example, say that one dollar normally nets 200 yen. If one day the value of the dollar drops in Japan, so that it can only buy 100 yen, then the dollar has depreciated (that is, its value has decreased; to buy the same amount of imports would require more money, in terms of dollars). On the other hand, if the dollar can bring in 300 yen, then it has appreciated (its value has increased, so that one can buy more imports with ones money).

Just how strong is the U.S. economy compared with the rest of the world, as measured by comparing the U.S. GDP with other countries' GDP? Is it stagnant, stable, or growing? If it is growing more than the economies of other countries, then this is a red flag for buying from international suppliers. When the U.S. economy is especially strong, U.S.

individual and business consumers go shopping. When demand exceeds supply, the value of the supply goes up: it will take more dollars to buy more imports, U.S. consumers sell more dollars to get foreign currency, and the value of the dollar decreases.

To find out the current exchange rate, go online. A number of Web sites offer exchange rate converters; a couple of them are www.xe.com/ucc/ and www.x-rates.com. But, if you are intrigued by formulas, here they are:

To convert foreign prices into dollars:

$$\text{Dollar price} = \text{foreign price}/\text{exchange rate}$$

To convert dollar prices into foreign prices:

$$\text{Foreign price} = \text{dollar price} \times \text{exchange rate}$$

Also, see Table A.2 for cause–effect factors that impact exchange rate analyses.

China's yuan was recently pegged to a market basket of unknown currencies, although it was pegged to the U.S. dollar for many years. Experts believe the yuan will eventually be allowed to float in the next ten years.

A.11 Conclusions

So, with all of the risks and barriers associated with low-country sourcing, is it worth the risk? Will this in the end work toward the deterioration of the American and Western European economies? Experts think not. Cheaper labor brings down production costs, keeps companies competitive, raises profits, and reduces prices as firms pass their lower costs on to their customers. Higher profits and lower prices lift demand and keep inflation in check. Customers buy more of the things they already consume or spend the money on new goods and services, stimulating innovation and creating new jobs to replace those that have gone abroad.[32] McKinsey calculates that for every dollar American firms spend on service work from India, the American economy receives $1.14 in return. This calculation depends in large part on the ability of America's economy to create new jobs for displaced workers. America's labor market is a miracle of flexibility: it creates and destroys nearly 30 million jobs a year. As global sourcing increases, the argument for free trade tends to overpower those of the protectionist politics in the West. Buying goods and services from

Table A.2 Cause–Effect Factors

No. of Factors	Target Impact	Type	Direction	Currency Effect
Single	Demand	Foreign demand for U.S. goods and services (i.e., demand for U.S. exports)	Increase	Appreciation
			Decrease	Depreciation
		Foreign demand for U.S. physical assets (e.g., plants in the United States) and financial assets (e.g., bonds and stocks)	Increase	Appreciation
			Decrease	Depreciation
	Supply	U.S. demand for foreign goods and services (i.e., demand for imports)	Increase	Depreciation
			Decrease	Appreciation
		U.S. demand for foreign physical assets and financial assets	Increase	Depreciation
			Decrease	Appreciation
Combined	Supply	U.S. price level relative to foreign price level	Increase	Depreciation
			Decrease	Appreciation
		U.S. interest rates relative to foreign interest rates	Increase	Appreciation
			Decrease	Depreciation
		U.S. growth rates relative to foreign growth rate	Increase	Depreciation
			Decrease	Appreciation

Source: Barron's Economics.

poor countries is not only hugely beneficial to the rich countries' economies, it can also provide opportunities for millions of people in poor
countries to lift themselves up and improve their lives — so everyone
can win.

Notes

1. Monczka, Trent, and Handfield, *Purchasing and Supply Chain Management,* Cincinnati: Southwestern College Publishing, 1998, pp. 370–373.
2. Ibid.
3. Ibid, pp. 379–380.
4. A world of work: a survey of outsourcing, *The Economist*, November 13, 2004, p. 4.
5. Ibid, November 13, 2004.
6. Trent and Monczka, Pursuing competitive advantage through integrated global sourcing, *Academy of Management Executive*, 16, No. 2, May 2002.
7. Ibid.
8. Monczka, Trent, and Handfield, *Purchasing and Supply Chain Management,* Cincinnati: Southwestern College Publishing, 1998, pp. 373–375.
9. Clark, Ken, Making global sourcing right, *Chain Store Age*, 78, No. 12, 122–125, December 2002.
10. Ibid.
11. Kirk, Don, U.S. Tariff on Hynix Chips Draws South Korean Protest, *The New York Times*, June 20, 2003.
12. Sanger, David E., U.S. Penalizes 6 Asian Firms for Helping Iran Arm Itself, *The New York Times*, July 4, 2003.
13. Browne, Andrew, Zhou's Theories Clash with China's Realities, *Wall Street Journal*, November 15, 2004, p. C1.
14. Ibid.
15. Monczka, Trent, and Handfield, 381–383.
16. Monczka, Trent, and Handfield, 385–387.
17. Leggett, Karby, and Wonacott, Peter, The world's factory: surge in exports from China jolts global industry — from cheap to cutting-edge, deluge of goods rewrites book on business strategy — price pressure on U.S. griddles, *Wall Street Journal*, October 10, 2002.
18. Ibid.
19. Chandler, Clay, A Factory to the World, *Washington Post Foreign Service*, November 25, 2001, p. A01.
20. Chang, Leslie, The Chinese Dream, *Wall Street Journal*, November 8, 2004, p. A1.
21. Ibid.
22. String of pearls, *The Economist*, November 20, 2004, p. 43.
23. Andreoli, Teresa, Wal-mart sees potential fortune in China debut, *Discount Store News*, 35, No. 14, pp. 1–2, July 15, 1996.
24. Prime, Penelope B., China joins the WTO: How, why, and what now?, *Business Economics*, April 2002.
25. Ibid.
26. Ibid.
27. Kahn, Joseph, Making Trinkets in China, and a Deadly Dust, *The New York Times*, June 18, 2003.

28. Leggett, Karby, and Wonacott, Peter, The world's factory: surge in exports from China jolts global industry — from cheap to cutting-edge, deluge of goods rewrites book on business strategy — price pressure on U.S. griddles, *Wall Street Journal*, October 10, 2002.
29. Newspaper article from Dr. Handfield.
30. Stundza, Tom, Pump maker lowers cost sourcing in China, *Purchasing*, 131, No. 20, 16–19, December 12, 2002.
31. Leaders: Eating your lunch?, *The Economist*, February 15, 2003.
32. *The Economist*, November 14, 2004.

Appendix B

Best Practices in Supplier Development

B.1 Three Best Practices in Supplier Development

The following cases developed from on-site interviews with automotive companies illustrate some of the key differences in approaches to supplier development used by European, U.S. and Japanese automotive companies. The three cases include BMW, Chrysler, and Honda.

B.2 Best Case 1: BMW's Approach to Supplier Development

B.2.1 Supplier Development Approaches

The primary focus at BMW in supplier development is through a program known as *Process Consulting*. This process was developed originally in Germany, but required modification before it could be adopted in North America. A senior executive at BMW shared his insights on how a new revised approach was required for North American conditions, which are substantially different from the relatively well-developed supply base conditions in Germany.

B.2.2 Major Differences between German and North American Supplier Development Approaches

The process-consulting approach used by BMW in Germany involves analyzing and telling suppliers what is wrong with their process. This works well in mature supplier environments, in which the supplier really understands what the customer wants. Because the customer and the supplier have worked together over a number of years, a type of "sixth sense" develops, wherein the supplier intuitively understands the customer's problems, which precludes the customer from having to explain their detailed expectations. (I have noted this in well-developed relationships, in which a supplier can almost predict what the customer's objections will be).

The following is a set of quotes from Richard Bourne, as best as I can recollect:

> In the case of BMW in the United States, a very different approach was required. In Germany, the plants are established and they had a group of suppliers who had a given level of understanding with respect to what we wanted. In the United States, however, communication with domestic suppliers requires sharing and a hands-on support attitude. We have to spend time asking them, "What is your corrective action plan?" And then let them know we will check on them from time to time. We need to suggest possible ways to put solutions in place. Which actions are more beneficial in a start-up phase?
>
> The state of South Carolina provided us with a good initial training program. This was a good initial round — they did screening and some initial training with respect to what it might be like to work in an automotive industry environment, but to really do it means that you need people who understand processes and who make improvements, and who also understand the consequences of mistakes (i.e., other things go wrong later in the process!)
>
> When we came here, the management teams at the new plant underestimated what support was needed and also underestimated what our quality requirements would be. As a result, we were unprepared to focus our attention on BMW's quality standards. The supply base really did not understand what would be required of them. This resulted in a number of strained relationships with our supply base. Consequently, we ended up spending a lot of time communicating and showing them what was needed. This also led to a major effort to get buy-in from these suppliers.
>
> The major difference between our approach and that used in Germany was that we could not simply act as a "prop" for their improvement, but the challenge was to get them to see it as a "two-way street." In many cases, they needed support

or needed us to make it happen — we had to make them understand that it was not simply a matter of "you need support" or "you need us to make it happen," but rather that "your problems are our problems!" "You have good products, but you have to do better, and we are here to help you!"

For example, a typical objective is to be 20 percent over the industry average, plus beat our competitors. Development is, therefore, a key impetus to make our suppliers better than the competition. One of the most important ways to achieve this is to communicate expectations. We have recently published "Supplier Partnership Manual," which clearly delineates supplier responsibilities, process maps, and all expectations. Such a manual has also been published for our logistics, quality, and engineering functions. Moreover, you must be able to clearly communicate to people what you want, before you can expect it from them. To aid in this objective, we also regularly give seminars in which we present our "Roadmap to Quality."

This is made all the more difficult because we are a relatively low-volume product (60,000 units per year). At the time that suppliers were nominated and evaluated, some of their processes were based on a low-volume approach and were not as robust as our requirements demanded. As a result of the combined effect of new people plus capital equipment problems plus low-volume processes, the result was many, many problems! To combat these problems, we worked on process capability (Cpk's), training, and capital equipment problems.

B.2.3 Capital Equipment Problems

A good example of the type of problem we encountered was a supplier's conveyor that was constantly breaking down, primarily due to poor design, and a temperature-controlled environment that was exceeding the specification level. These two issues result in (1) shutdowns and (2) product performance problems.

In the first case, the reaction was panic! Above all else, the supplier sought to keep production going, which in turn affected the second problem. We needed to fix the first problem before attacking the second problem.

B.2.4 Resource Availability

BMW does not provide financial support other than owning production tooling at the supplier's location. We have provided the services of several people over a few weeks, and we have also offered suppliers support any time they request it. For example, we have sent maintenance engineering people and procurement or logistics or quality people as needed to help suppliers.

Our current focus is that we no longer have problem-driven projects, but are Pareto-driven in the last four to five months to identify problems and prevent them from getting any worse.

B.2.5 Supplier Council

Our major suppliers have gotten together, but they are not formally represented. The council is mostly an informal affair. Our administration helps and works with them on an ad hoc basis, and we have an annual golf game, but apart from that, there is not a strong council presence.

B.2.6 Engineering Focus

BMW has traditionally maintained a very strong engineering focus in its organizational culture. This has resulted in a number of different approaches within the organization, especially with regard to the interface between supplier development and engineering personnel. We encountered a number of major obstacles within middle management that we have been able to overcome over the years.

B.2.7 Challenges — BMW

A major challenge that exists at BMW involves standardizing expectations between the United States and Munich, as well as between purchasing and quality. BMW–Spartanburg currently has 70 people in Supplier Quality Assurance. Their intention is not to have increased inspection, but they invariably require inspection for new suppliers.

An important lesson learned by BMW is that a supplier may be qualified and considered excellent in Europe, but their subsidiary in North America may not be capable of meeting the same standards. Globalization involves more than just bringing in equipment and standards from Europe. Moreover, there are often problems in enforcing expectations, and increased training is often required.

B.2.8 Communication Problems

One of the biggest problems involved the surface of bumpers and body panels, which often had scratches, etc. In setting expectations, it was important to communicate that it was not just a matter of right versus wrong, but a matter of setting objective criteria. For instance, setting the standard might involve telling the supplier to hold the part under a light, and examine it at a certain angle to look for marks. For suppliers to understand these expectations, face-to-face discussions, communication, and training are required.

(*Note:* This discrepancy was also confirmed in discussions with a BMW supplier. Engineers at a supplier we interviewed confirmed that BMW placed a strong emphasis on the physical appearance of body parts, but that such expectations were not clearly communicated in the blueprint design. Moreover physical appearances, finish, and expectations cannot be expressed on a blueprint.)

The most important task with suppliers is to set standards that everyone understands and agrees to. This is not so much a problem in electronics, but involves a huge problem in bodywork. Because BMW pays a lot of attention to detail, a big challenge is to reduce cost and reduce overdesign, with the objective of competing with the same product from the customer's perspective, even though it is built in the United States, not Germany.

B.2.9 Supplier Development in Germany (Munich)

Many supplier development efforts in Germany were established primarily with the objective of reducing cost as early as five years ago. Lately, however, the focus has been more on process optimization, as opposed to cost. Process optimization refers to the practice of stabilizing processes and reducing parts per million defective, and the methods to achieve these objectives.

B.2.10 Process Consulting

The primary tool applied in Germany is Process Consulting. Process Consulting involves having a group of BMW engineers visit a Germany facility and explain to the supplier how to improve their process (e.g., in a consulting role). Because of the cohesiveness that exists within German culture, such recommendations are easily adopted by suppliers. A senior BMW executive admits that this is an excellent set of tools, but that the manner of applying it in the United States had to be modified significantly for the U.S. supply base. Because many of the U.S. suppliers were "not mature," the process-consulting concept had to be modified significantly. In Germany, the majority of suppliers are very mature in terms of their process capabilities and so Process Consulting involved really just tweaking the supplier's processes. In addition, the cohesiveness that exists between Germans and the length of the relationship between BMW and its suppliers meant that most suppliers understood BMW's expectations very well. However, the U.S. suppliers supplying the Spartanburg, South Carolina plant have relatively new facilities and, in many cases, consist of fewer than 200 employees. The development effort has focused on helping suppliers optimize their systems. A key concept involves having suppliers understand where they are in their growth and development curve. For instance, many suppliers needed help initially just to get products out the door. In such cases, the emphasis was on solving the big problems that might lead to parts shortages, before attacking the big problems. In the first year of production, suppliers experienced severe ramp-up problems in response to the increases in production demands. In this phase of development, BMW weeded out 50 percent of the supply base. Some suppliers had gone through setup just a few months before, but because of their inability to ramp up, were shut out of the supply base.

For example, one supplier set up a paint line, but was unable to meet the different set of environmental standards imposed by BMW. They had hired a group of people who had not worked with paint processes before, and simply had no idea of cleanliness and environmental standards. In such cases, although the supplier had good methods, they required significant amounts of "massaging" before they could be used as a supplier.

B.2.11 Benchmarking Report

A benchmarking report on supplier development was recently completed, which entailed a set of detailed interviews with Toyota, Honda, Chrysler, Rover, and two other technical support organizations associated with BMW, to compare approaches. The primary question involved was: How do companies go about supplier development? This was done to augment existing benchmarking studies in this area. The focus was primarily on supplier development processes being used, as opposed to performance and strategic-level benchmarking.

B.2.11.1 Lessons Learned

- BMW — Limited time and resources are available to develop suppliers.
  - Suppliers need more hands-on help and less theoretical help in improving their processes.

- Honda — Best to work primarily with focused groups and not huge teams.
  - This is because people tend to get pulled to other activities and lose track of the project.
  - A "hit-list" approach (in which one comes up with a list of people and processes to eliminate) is devastating — one needs to listen closely to suppliers even if their concerns are not directly related to your objective.
  - Once you have a list of ideas, implement them ASAP.
  - Going in with a list of to-do's for them to implement simply does not work.
- Toyota — Spend a considerable amount of time working on the human side.
  - Adopt a very hands-on approach.
  - Emphasize spending a lot of time seeking top-management approval at the supplier, whereas others often do not see a need.
  - Supplier development operates as a separate organization.
  - Operate a "supplier support institute," which is distinct from the purchasing department. This institute is not just a cost reducer — in fact, you do not even have to be a direct supplier of Toyota to attend, as long as you are in the Kentucky region. (*Note:* BMW has an ongoing dialogue with Toyota. The attitude is "If what we do helps our competitors, that is okay, but we expect our supplier to expand their knowledge, not to train our competitor's suppliers.")
- Chrysler — Relies extensively on their Automotive Industry Association Group (AIAG) program.
  - Primary tool for development is QS 9000 that is used as a baseline to determine areas requiring more work.
  - Primary lesson learned is that development people need process experience (not theoretical experience) to command respect in working with the supply base.
- Rover — Very narrow and deep application of supplier development.
  - Use problem-solving tools to identify improvements. However, they acknowledge that this is not enough. They need to identify root causes.
  - Different levels of understanding of problem solving exist within the supply base. This is brought out especially in kaizen breakthroughs (KBs).
  - Need to follow through beyond KBs — need to ensure that process changes are standardized.

In some circles, the level of hands-on support is viewed as doing the suppliers' job for them. In reality, this level of support actually involves training the supplier to become self-sufficient. In this respect, supplier development can be very tricky. When people leave, the supplier cannot "fall apart" again. We need to come back in some cases and help them get back on their feet again.

B.2.11.2 Comparison of Supplier Development Associates

- Average number of associates is 20 to 40 senior-level people.
- By function — generally more technical or practical people, and fewer theoretical or consulting types.
- The ideal development person:
  - Is very hands-on — good technical skills.
  - Has good people skills and interaction (not just "I'm the customer — do as I say!").
  - Has ability to convince people.
  - Is a motivator — must be able to push people to exceed their perceived capabilities.
  - Has good project management skills.
- It is easy to show results, but suppliers may be forced into showing these results, and they may not continue in the long term.

B.2.11.3 Other Summary Data from Benchmark Report

- Approaches used include Score (Chrysler), BP (Honda), POZ (Process Consulting — BMW), and Toyota Production System (TPS — Toyota).
- Percentage of time spent on supplier development by associates ranges from 30 to 100 percent.
- Key measures used to assess supplier development progress include cost, ppm, and throughput time.
- Key slogan — "Powered by Honda" — phrase used for all Honda motors in 1997 appears on many different products.

B.2.11.4 Supplier Input on Approaches

- Liked BMW's approach — good communication, emphasized basics.
- Honda — good recognition as a result of their efforts. Were able to leverage with other customers.
- Ford — have not updated their tools for some time — very outdated.

B.3 Best Case 2: Supplier Development at Chrysler

(*Note:* This was written prior to Chrysler's merger with Daimler, when Purchasing was under the leadership of Thomas Stallkamp.)

B.3.1 Chrysler's Purchasing and Sourcing Strategy

Chrysler's purchasing and sourcing strategy is based on leveraging the resources and capabilities of internal organizations and external suppliers to continuously impact the quality, cost, technology, and delivery of Chrysler vehicles for our customers. The organization has evolved into one where continuous improvement has become a way of life, and suppliers are considered as integral members of the Chrysler Extended Enterprise.

SCORE (Supplier Cost Reduction Effort) is a continuous-improvement process Chrysler utilizes to increase Chrysler–supplier communications and teamwork. The SCORE approach enables Chrysler to work more closely with its suppliers in the design, development, and production of high-quality, cost-competitive products — to surpass the requirements of its vehicle customers. As a result, Chrysler has become the global benchmark for supplier relationships and cost competitiveness.

Procurement and Supply centralizes control of commodity and supplier strategies, policies, and procedures while providing focused support to Chrysler's platform teams. There are five organizations that report to the office of the executive vice president of Procurement and Supply (executive VP of P&S):

1. The P&S Process Team, which includes
   - Platform Supply
   - Supplier Management
   - Supplier Quality and Development
2. Supply
3. Special Supplier Relations
4. Operations and Strategy
5. International Procurement

B.3.2 Major Responsibilities of Each Organization

B.3.2.1 Platform Supply

- Coordinate P&S activities to meet platform-variable and investment cost objectives.
- Coordinate supplier quality activities in support of vehicle quality objectives.

- Manage vehicle supply risks.
- Manage tooling, equipment, and construction procurement.
- Communicate platform requirements to P&S and coordinate resource deployment to support requirements.

B.3.2.2 Supplier Quality and Development

- Develop and implement methods and tools to improve vehicle quality to corporate objectives.
- Manage advance quality planning and current vehicle quality problem identification and resolution.
- Measure supplier quality performance to objectives.
- Minimize quality risks on assembly tooling and equipment and production vehicle components or systems.
- Work with suppliers to improve manufacturing processes and resolve process issues.
- Work with supplier management to develop and implement supplier and commodity management strategies.

B.3.2.3 Supplier Management

- Coordinate the development and implementation of supplier and new commodity management strategies.
- Manage costs, supplier relationships, and work with engineering to introduce new technologies.
- Leverage supplier expertise across platforms.
- Encourage supplier participation in continuous-improvement initiatives.
- Manage daily supplier business transaction activities.
- Manage service and parts procurement.

B.3.2.4 Supply

- Develop and manage worldwide supply network to ensure the timely, cost-effective, and quality delivery of materials and finished vehicles to customers.
- Establish production programs and vehicle-build schedules.
- Ensure parts availability for pilot, launch, and volume production.
- In cooperation with vehicle platforms, conduct engineering development of methods and procedures for total materials management.

■ Develop and implement logistics supplier and commodity management strategies and conduct operations of Chrysler Transport, Inc.

B.3.2.5 Special Supplier Relations

■ Identify and develop qualified, ethnic minority–owned companies for Chrysler business.
■ Develop and monitor second-tier minority supplier sourcing strategy.
■ Mentor key minority suppliers.
■ Facilitate dialogue between Chrysler's senior management and key minority suppliers.
■ Participate in regional trade fairs and interview prospective suppliers.

B.3.2.6 Operations and Strategy

■ Manage procurement of nonproduction suppliers and services for Chrysler facilities.
■ Develop and implement benchmarking and training programs.
■ Develop and administer P&S policies and procedures.
■ Conduct special strategic studies to improve P&S operations.
■ Coordinate supplier special events, supplier communications, and measurement activities.
■ Coordinate P&S continuous-improvement and value-engineering efforts.
■ Coordinate Chrysler's SCORE program.

B.3.2.7 International Procurement

■ Provide procurement support to offshore assembly and manufacturing locations.
■ Identify and develop suppliers in the host country to provide for local content.
■ Facilitate the establishment of Chrysler's key North American suppliers in foreign locations.
■ Provide a liaison function between P&S international operations and the platform engineering teams.

- Provide supplier quality training and guidance to offshore Chrysler locations including certification of in-country approval laboratories.
- Assist in the resolution of parts shortage issues associated with international supply.

B.3.3 Comments from Gary — Director of Supplier Development

Gary (last name is withheld) has a total of 45 years experience working in the automotive industry. This includes 15 years of experience working with Chrysler, and 15 years prior to that working with AMC. He has been head of the Supplier Development group for one and a half years. He reports to the head of Supplier Quality, and also to the Platform Supply Group. This was effective as of March 1996 (the latest iteration of Chrysler's organization). The Supplier Quality group consists of Supplier Measurement and Feedback, Quality Process Improvement, Process Specialists, and Supplier Development and Technical Assistance.

B.3.3.1 Process Specialists

The process specialists are a group of 15 to 16 individuals who specialize in areas such as castings, machining, etc. These individuals are typically in a "reactive" mode, in that they respond to quality and delivery issues when measurement indicators signal that a problem exists. For instance, if a supplier is experiencing persistent process problems that are evident, and the normal set of contacts cannot resolve them, then the process specialists become involved. In such cases, these individuals have the requisite skill set, given that the relationship is positive (win–win), which allows them to watch the line for a while, talk to the supplier's production people, and get an idea of what the actual problem is. They then work with the supplier's technical people to determine what is wrong with the process to arrive at conclusions regarding a solution. This may take two to three days, with some repeat visits (an additional two to three times), and the isolated process incident is resolved relatively quickly. At that point, they move on to another supplier, and travel all over the world "fighting fires." This type of reactive supplier development has been used for a number of years.

B.3.3.2 Recent Applications of "Proactive" Supplier Development

Supplier development has been talked about for a number of years at Chrysler, but in Gary's opinion, this was largely "lip service." Only recently has the company actually implemented development as a formal activity. Up to now, 80 to 90 percent of supplier development has been reactive in nature, and 10 to 20 percent proactive. Chrysler's objective is to reverse this ratio, so that 60 percent is proactive and 30 percent reactive. This can be achieved by anticipating (proactively) problems before they occur by getting involved in advanced quality processes early in the new product development cycle. In this respect, the process specialists would still play a role, but would get involved in process choice decisions before they are committed to them, in advance of problems. This has started to take place. Specialists in stampings, castings, and machining are looking at process FMEAs and identifying problems in new product development on a more regular basis.

B.3.3.3 Criteria for Supplier Development Selection

On the other hand, supplier development specialists work with chronic problem suppliers with systemic issues that go beyond simple process problems. These suppliers do not just have a problem with their process, "They just don't get it!" In most cases, these suppliers:

- Choose to ignore the problem.
- Do not take the problem seriously.
- Have serious financial problems.
- Have senior managers who have the wrong philosophy.

In such cases, these suppliers are chosen for supplier development activities. Some of the other criteria that are used to involve a supplier include:

- At least $1 million business a year with Chrysler.
- Part of sourcing strategy for at least the next two years (parts for model).
- Have been identified as having a seriously poor quality track record (ppm) and a referral for assistance either from manufacturing, warranty records, or recent product launch and delivery data.
- These problems have been systemic for at least the last two years.

These type of records essentially "tell a story" regarding the supplier's history of continuous problems. The normal quality organization is unable to handle it. They may or may not have had a process specialist come in already. In such cases, these individuals have been unable to deal with the problem, or the specialist has realized that a more serious problem lies behind the supplier. In such cases, an ongoing dialogue with these suppliers has provided them with many directions for improvement, yet they have continually been unable to comply, and continue along a different path with a different agenda. In such cases, the fundamental question is: Why? When this occurs, Gary's people are called in. Although they may involve the process specialists later on in the supplier development process, this type of situation clearly demands a different approach.

B.3.3.4 Types of Suppliers Who Require Development

Interestingly enough, there is no single pattern when it comes to the types of suppliers who fit into this category. To date, Gary's group has worked with 35 different suppliers and 45 different manufacturing locations. This group has consisted of large, medium, and small suppliers. Some of them are in the top 10 in terms of volume (but problems occur in one of their facilities), top 50, as well as top 150. They also span multiple commodity groups (in fact, all of them!). There is simply no distinguishable pattern in terms of identifying which suppliers are most likely to have this problem! The only common feature linking all of these suppliers is the lack of good management.

B.3.4 Supplier Development Process

1. The supplier receives a letter signed by the commodity manager and Gary that states, "We want to help you maintain your position as a major supplier for Chrysler."
2. A meeting is held with the senior executive, top manufacturing manager, and top quality manger. At this meeting, Chrysler defines "why we're here," and emphasizes that they seek to work within a win–win environment. They want to help the supplier maintain its position with Chrysler, and then present the performance indicators ("hard facts") that explain why they are there (quality, delivery problems, etc.). In most situations, this initial meeting is welcomed with accolades, as it is an opportunity for free help! These conversations are held in extreme confidence, so no one can use them in future price negotiations, etc.

   (*Note:* Supplier development efforts in some cases still do not work. Some suppliers do not respond even after multiple interventions. Even though they are "saying the right things," nothing happens. Involvement with suppliers spans between six months and one and a half years on average. Eighty percent of the time, there are significant performance improvements. In 20 percent of the cases, there are none.)

3. In the next phase, teams of two people are dedicated to a supplier location. All of these individuals are QS 9000 trained. The same executive from Chrysler who initially met with the supplier accompanies the team to meet with the plant management group to prevent any perceptions of confrontation that may exist.

4. This is followed by a two- to three-day assessment (this is not an audit). The assessment identifies "what they do well" and where they fall short. The assessment is structured as follows:
   - Beginning with top management: "Is there a business plan? What is the operating or management philosophy?"
   - It assesses all segments of the organization, including quality, purchasing, engineering, materials handling, preventive maintenance, tooling, etc. What are the strengths and weaknesses of each area, and what is the action plan to carry out and address each of the weaknesses?
   - The assessment is held in extreme confidence. Only the top managers within the Supplier Development group are in contact with the top managers, and the information is not shared elsewhere within Chrysler. The Supplier Development people at Chrysler will not share the specifics of the supplier's problems, even with the commodity group managers at Chrysler. This is done to ensure that the supplier who shares information with the Supplier Development group can provide all required information so that they can truly help without risk of jeopardizing their position!

5. The outcome of the assessment is an action plan. This plan outlines which people in the organization are responsible for working out the problems. This typically involves a set of one- to two-day visits, once or twice per month. These visits may be to the manufacturing site or to the company's headquarters, depending on the nature of the problem. In some cases, Chrysler's intervention identifies the root cause of the problem as being the lack of communication between the plan and the engineering facility.

B.3.4.1 "Buyer Development" — Becoming a Better Customer

Chrysler is also introspective with respect to their role in supplier development, and often seeks to "look in the mirror." This is done to enhance the positive nature of the "partnership," especially in cases in which Chrysler has invested in the supplier a lot over the years and has developed significant commitment. However, in cases in which a Supplier Development project is underway with the supplier, no new volumes on new projects are committed to with the supplier. Even in situations of extensive commitment, if the intervention is unsuccessful, then Chrysler may need to switch suppliers.

B.3.4.2 Second-Tier Problems

In 40 to 60 percent of the cases that we become involved in, the problems of a first-tier supplier, when the root cause is exposed, are the second-tier supplier. What we find is that the people in the first tier are "letting it ride." In such cases, we have to ask them "why are you not developing your suppliers? Why are you not involving them in your problems?" This requires that we provide their purchasing people with training in advanced quality planning, not necessarily in supply base management!

B.3.4.3 Why Supplier Development?

In most cases, however, Chrysler is willing to invest in an ongoing supplier rather than switch. This is because "we would rather deal with a known quantity than an unknown. We have already invested lots of money with them, they understand our systems, and we understand theirs. The supplier development initiative is, in a sense, a last resort. We do not commit any incremental investment while we are involved with them. The outcome is either positive (we create new business with them) or negative (we need to find a new supplier) at the end of the process."

B.3.5 Looking in the Mirror

Chrysler also needs to take an introspective approach every now and then, and identify ways to improve communication processes. This is a form of buyer development, in that 40 to 60 percent of suppliers' problems have been contributed to by Chrysler: by changing requirements and not telling them, making design changes at the last minute, etc. The question then becomes, what can Chrysler do to help the supplier? In other cases, it is not the supplier, but their second-tier suppliers who are the root of the problem. They may be receiving poor products or later deliveries, but are letting it ride. Chrysler needs to go in and provide training in such cases on supply base management, even though they are already getting training in advanced quality planning. Suppliers must understand that they are responsible for developing their supply base to sell to Chrysler. This may involve sending the supplier to classes in Chrysler Quality Institute. Gary has a fair amount of leverage internally. His people try to correct problems within Chrysler in a nonthreatening way. The internal assessment is shared with no one else in Chrysler, so that it cannot be used in future price negotiations. At best, other Chrysler purchasing people may see an executive summary of the situation, which has been edited so that it is politically correct. In this way, Supplier Development can work with the supplier to understand what Chrysler people are doing that may be causing problems. By being approached in a reasonable manner such as this, the supplier can understand why the development team is there and why change is important.

B.3.5.1 Supplier's Top Management Is Critical

Over the last 18 months, two to three supplier interventions have failed (out of a total of 35 suppliers). Gary maintains that the key to success is top management at the supplier. If the supplier's top management is willing to listen and understand, then a major part of the problem will be eliminated, and the intervention will work. This is similar to an intervention with an alcoholic — if he or she listens and is willing to admit there is a problem, there is a chance it will work. Some of the problems may be simply that the supplier is not measuring performance internally (on cost, quality, delivery, etc). At the larger suppliers, when they talk to the people at the director level, they often find that they do not measure the right things. For instance, perhaps they are measuring the number of parts made today, but not the number of defective parts made. Generally speaking, what gets measured gets managed. This is a major insight for many directors! In some cases, the PASS reports (supplier evaluation reports) provided by Chrysler to the supplier has never been seen by the director of the supplier!

B.3.5.2 No Financial Investments

Chrysler provides almost no financial investments in suppliers, except in cases of a dire emergency. An emergency might be, for instance, a minority supplier who is facing financial distress. Some indirect financial assistance may be provided. This policy is a function of the price of entry into the auto industry as a whole: it is a capital-intensive industry, and through a process of natural selection, only those companies who can make the financial thresholds have a chance of surviving. Almost all of Chrysler's suppliers are U.S. owned and operated (nontransplant).

B.3.5.3 Human Resource Issues

In some cases, Chrysler will help suppliers with their human resource issues. For instance, at one supplier, there were too many contract people, and an excessively high turnover of salaried employees. It turned out that the pay levels for these people were too low for the region. In general, however, Chrysler does not get involved in union negotiations.

B.3.5.4 Supply Base Reduction

Chrysler has undergone a significant reduction of its supply base to date. The late 1980s and early 1990s were a period of high supply base rationalization. This is an ongoing strategy today (but at a lower rate), with the goal being to single source by part number, but with at least two suppliers per commodity. The business is then shared across platforms. However, the business for a model within a commodity group will not be shared across suppliers. This is intended to maintain and foster competition among suppliers, yet get the benefits of single sourcing.

B.3.5.5 Supplier Involvement in New Product Development

The technical people at Chrysler now understand the importance of making sure that the latest technology is being introduced into new models from the supply base. Gary is involved in ensuring that suppliers are capable of meeting Chrysler's technology requirements, and that they have the capability before they become involved in the new product development process. For example, suppose a new supplier to the automobile industry is being considered for sourcing a new technology. Gary's group will work with the supplier to help them understand how to do business with Chrysler and to shorten the learning curve. One way this is being done is through the development of a book that documents how to do business with Chrysler and covers such details as quality requirements, engineering, supply policies, etc. "We often assume that everyone knows these details, but a new supplier does not!"

B.3.5.6 International Supplier Development

This learning book will be especially useful as Chrysler begins to produce and source in Europe and South America. For instance, Chrysler will be building a jeep in Beijing, China, and is establishing assembly plants in Gratz and Stire, Austria. It also has facilities in Venezuela, Argentina, and Brazil, and is establishing a joint venture (JV) with BMW in Brazil for local assembly of six-cylinder engines. However, the involvement in supplier development to date has been 100 percent North American suppliers (including Mexico). Gradually, this will change, as the supply base is expected to move into Eastern Europe and Latin America.

B.3.5.7 Supplier Dependence

There is no formal cap on supplier volume, but for smaller suppliers, Chrysler keeps an eye on their total volume to Chrysler. If it begins to rise over 40 to 50 percent, they need to ask themselves if this is wise, as it may foster too much dependence. At this point, the supplier may be encouraged to get more business elsewhere. Gary also notes that loading up a really good supplier with too much work can cause additional problems. The supplier may lose its enthusiasm, which is something that Chrysler wants to keep in a learning organization. Chrysler also has a finance group within procurement that evaluates suppliers' financial health. It is also important to understand what the second- and third-tier suppliers are doing and what is going on. For instance, one second-tier supplier selling to a first tier was also selling directly to Chrysler. Although the quality to Chrysler was acceptable, the quality to the first tier was not, and the supplier eventually went out of business. This makes the extended enterprise all the more important.

B.3.5.8 Breadth versus Depth

In corroborating the benchmarking study, Chrysler has a wider scope of breadth than BMW, but less depth than Toyota and Honda. This is primarily because these companies have more dedicated resources in supplier development than Chrysler.

B.3.5.9 Information Systems in Supply Base

A major issue here is whether suppliers have effective measurement systems to gauge performance (especially quality), and whether they communicate effectively between their functions. This is important, because in 1998, all suppliers were required to have EDI to effectively supply Chrysler. Chrysler recently benchmarked eight to nine suppliers including two Pentastar Platinum Award suppliers. These best-in-class suppliers, in general, had the absolute essentials in place: top management was committed to excellence and the measurement systems were complete and measured all of the critical areas, including process, inventory, quality, and delivery. Further, these measures were reviewed for at least two hr every week by the entire team and were updated on a daily basis. However, they also uncovered a number of problems, even with these suppliers. The suppliers were not tracking process capability indices (Cpk's), and although they tracked SPC charts, they were not being effectively used.

Suppliers' communications with Chrysler are a big problem in information systems. Suppliers are not clearly communicating to Chrysler information on quality, purchasing, etc. Part of the problem is that Chrysler is also not clearly identifying expectations, requirements, deadlines, and late design changes. This latter issue is an especially big problem. To remedy this situation, Chrysler has instituted a new policy called "4-Ever Requirements":

- If you have a problem, call us.
- If you change your materials, call us.
- If you change a process, call us.
- If you change a manufacturing location (process location), call us.

This policy has been instituted, because even an innocuous change to a material or process can have disastrous consequences. In one case, a supplier moved an entire supplying process to a different plant, and did not tell Chrysler! At that point, they did not know who their primary contacts in engineering, purchasing, and quality were anymore!

B.3.6 Supplier Councils

This was headed by Thomas Stallkamp, executive vice president of Purchasing at Chrysler. Stallkamp meets with the supplier executive roundtable every two months. The roundtable is composed of senior executives from fifteen direct suppliers, one raw material supplier, one tooling supplier, and one indirect material supplier. Under the executive roundtable, there is also a supplier management roundtable (led by senior procurement executives), and a quality roundtable (led by supplier development and quality executives). The structure of these roundtables also mirrors the executive roundtable. Every year, one or two suppliers are rotated in and out of the roundtables. Suppliers are selected for inclusion only if they are key suppliers of key technologies, high-volume items, etc. Inclusion on the roundtable is by invitation only. Unfortunately, there is little cross-fertilization across the different roundtables. At the supplier development roundtable, Gary also runs by suppliers some of the different approaches, techniques, and tools that will be used in the future to get their feedback.

Twice a year, Chrysler also runs "supplier events," to which the top 130 suppliers are invited to get the best of them involved. At this meeting, the executive VP of Purchasing talks with suppliers on industry trends and Chrysler's needs.

B.3.7 The Formalization of Supplier Development

The impetus for a formal supplier development program at Chrysler began two years ago, which was when Gary's supplier development department was originally started. Procurement executives came to the realization that they had a lot of catching up to do in the quality area. Chrysler has significantly raised their internal and external quality benchmarks, and the company realized that suppliers were incapable of doing this on their own. This was both a top-management and a purchasing realization. "Some suppliers need a lot of help, and we don't have the time to help them! Yet we realized that if we don't do it, nobody will. Helping suppliers thus just made good business sense." This resulted in the formation of a formal Supplier Development group headed by Gary. New headcount was added — instead, several departments had to provide some of their best people, to create a vested interest. Now however, Supplier Development is in the process of adding people because of the enormous demands on it.

B.3.8 Justifying Supplier Development

To justify the formation of this group, some key measures needed to be established. Performance of the group to date has been impressive:

- Thirty-five percent of suppliers have increased quality, etc., by more than 70 percent.
- Thirty-five percent of suppliers have increased quality, etc., by 40 to 70 percent.
- Twenty percent of suppliers have increased quality, etc., by 1 to 20 percent, but
- Ten of suppliers have actually gotten worse!

In working with downstream carriers, the group has been successful in reducing damage to vehicles being transported, reducing the cycle time required to get vehicles to customers, and increasing the number of "delighted customers" at the dealerships by working to better manage diagnostics and faults. They have also worked more closely with suppliers to improve delivery of aftermarket warranty parts (this group also reports to the Supplier Management group).

B.3.9 Customer Advocate Group

This group is chartered to listen to the dealerships and bring the voice of the customer back to Chrysler (before the warranty reports start rolling in). In 1996, Chrysler established a Warranty Reduction Program that involved 14 suppliers initially, and which has 60 suppliers today. The focus of this program has changed from blaming suppliers for problems, to encouraging suppliers to take the lead in assessing warranty issues and getting them resolved. They are given warranty targets to get SCORE credit. Suppliers' leadership is incited to resolve warranty issues, and Chrysler gives these suppliers online access to warranty data. Currently, 175 suppliers have access to this data. The focus of this program is on reducing warranty costs. No finger-pointing is involved; suppliers are expected to just fix the problem.

B.3.10 Automotive Industry Action Group

This group was formed by the Big Three and its suppliers in an effort to get together and resolve issues of a common nature (such as EDI standards). Most recently, it has developed a common quality standard called QS 9000. This has also proved to be a significant supplier development technique, as it provides a common language and system for managing quality. To date, a significant portion of the supply base is registered to this standard. However, the standard represents only a base from which to begin quality improvement. The real challenge is to maintain the discipline needed after the initial QS 9000 certification and adhere to processes. QS recertification occurs every six months.

B.3.11 Work with External Parties

Chrysler has most recently been working with the Edison Welding Institute in Ohio to help provide technical assistance to suppliers. The Institute is half funded by the government, and half funded by Chrysler. The objective of the institute is to improve Chrysler's welding and joining capabilities by developing a set of procedures to follow in welding processes. So far, five suppliers have adhered to the new process, whereas a sixth supplier is not following the process, but wants to go outside of it. Gary has emphasized that the supplier must follow the process.

B.3.12 Mentoring

In some cases, suppliers have undergone mentoring by other suppliers in the supply base. This is a relatively new program that may be formalized in the future. For instance, one supplier has had problems with managing the level of torque required in their processes. This supplier has since undergone a mentoring process by another supplier, who is considered a good supplier to Chrysler, but not a competitor to the supplier experiencing the problem. The technically proficient supplier's supplier from a different commodity group has stepped in and advised them on how to manage torque, acting as a mentor.

B.4 Best Case 3: Supplier Development at Honda

Honda began in 1948 in Hamamatsu, Japan, as a manufacturer of war-surplus generators attached to bicycles, thus creating a crude form of motorcycle. The company thus began very modestly, but by 1954 had adopted the following motto:

- International viewpoint
- Products of the highest efficiency
- Reasonable price for customer satisfaction

The company was not allowed to produce cars, but early on Soichiro Honda began hounding a government official to allow him to produce cars. It first entered the automobile market in 1964, when the official finally gave him the permit after he camped out outside his office for several weeks! However, upon getting the permit, Honda found that few suppliers were willing to provide parts to the company. Thus, the few suppliers who were finally persuaded to supply the company were instrumental to its success, and Honda has maintained close relations with them. These initial suppliers are still supplying Honda today.

Currently, Honda of America (HAM) has 322 domestic suppliers, of whom 50 are raw material suppliers. The company has only separated from 12 suppliers since 1958, in cases in which the suppliers refused to improve their quality. Process and quality improvement is a major factor evaluated in supplier relations.

A supplier evaluation generally consists of a senior-level meeting, followed by visits and evaluations. The idea is to seek mutual dependability with suppliers.

Eighty percent of the value of Honda's products comes from suppliers, so purchasing holds a very strong position in the organization. The VP, Dave Nelson (now exec VP at Delphi Corporation) reports to the CEO, and two of eight members of the board of directors came from purchasing. Eighty percent of items are single sourced with one set of dies (but dual competition by platform).

An example of this strategy is as follows: Supplier A sources steering wheels for Civics, and Supplier B sources steering wheels for the Accord. Either supplier can make either part, but each is a single source by platform. When a new model is introduced, both suppliers may bid on the extra volume, with the best price and best-performing supplier likely to get the business.

The basic objective of Honda is to manufacture throughout the world: "You must build where you sell, and buy where you build." Thus, Honda seeks to develop local suppliers worldwide. Marysville is now a "mother plant" for other "children," namely the plant in Guadalajara, Mexico. The East Liberty plant produces the two-door and four-door Civic, the Acura (online in 1995, and 100 percent designed in the United States), whereas the Marysville plant produces the two-door, four-door, and station wagon Accords. Honda is today the largest exporter of cars in the United States.

The pattern of domestic supplier development for Honda is remarkable:

- 27 in 1983
- 51 in 1985
- 216 in 1990
- 322 in 1995
- 350 in 1997

In the early stages, Honda would not take on suppliers until they were ready. Today, the 96 Civic has 92 percent domestic content, and the Accord, 90 percent.

B.4.1 Honda Supplier Support

The Honda supplier support infrastructure is vast. Eleven thousand employees work in Ohio, of whom thousand work with suppliers. Currently, 310 people work in purchasing, of whom 50 are engineers who work exclusively with suppliers. Several examples illustrate the scope of this support function.

In one case, a small plastics supplier did not have the capacity to keep up with volume, resulting in quality deterioration. Honda sent four people to the supplier for ten months at no charge, with services offered on a voluntary basis. The supplier improved and is a major supplier even today.

A key part of the supplier support and development function is to ensure that everyone within the supplier organization and within Honda understands the philosophy. Tier-one suppliers are expected to be self-reliant and responsible for working with their suppliers. Top-management support is absolutely necessary within each supplier.

The premise of mutual dependability is a cornerstone of this program. Honda can be up to fifty percent of a supplier's business (maximum of three percent for steel), but in general, there is no set percentage of business that Honda wants.

B.4.2 BP Program

A major part of Honda's supplier development strategy is its BP program. BP can stand for a lot of things, including best position, best price, best productivity, best products, and best partners. In general, it signifies any type of joint improvement activity between Honda and its suppliers.

BP teams initially look at a particular model line and work with a supplier to teach them tools for continuous improvement over a three-month lead time. This serves to build a momentum and deliver some "quick hits." Goals and objectives are then set and a plan developed. If the goals are not met within the given timeframe, the development initiative is considered a failure.

In some cases, suppliers may resist development efforts. For instance, in one case a two-week situational analysis was presented to top management when a given supplier was not implementing their strategy. This presentation led to increased awareness on the part of the supplier's president, who did not realize they had so far to go! Subsequently, Honda worked closely with them over a five-month period, with three full-time people assigned to their staff. They improved quality from 700 ppm to 46 ppm per month. Best Quality is now a full-time department within this supplier.

The BP supplier development process goes through a series of stages. Phase one is a "soft program," done at the production stage, focusing on process improvements. Phase two is a more detailed strategy that occurs at the product-planning stage. This is an important difference in level of development: phase two actually involves developing suppliers for new product development prior to concept development. At this stage, the potential for reducing cost is the highest, but the cost of change is relatively low. This is in contrast to phase one, in which the cost of change is significant, with relatively minimal effect on cost reduction determined at the design stage. The supplier integration process into planning, concept, and design is shown in Figure B.1.

There is no formal supplier certification process as such, but there is certification of parts. Once a part is certified, there is no inspection, but a complete review of every operation and process associated with pro-ducing that part is conducted, which avoids the need for inspection.

An initial production part tag is used and put on any time there is a design engineering change. The line people at Honda generally use this any time they discover errors.

A supplier conference is held annually. A number of awards are presented, including awards for quality, delivery, production support, and production improvement. These awards are very hard to get, and reflect zero ppm in quality and delivery. Not many of them are given out.

The prevailing wisdom at Honda is that "It is okay to make mistakes, but you must share what you learn from your mistakes with your peers,

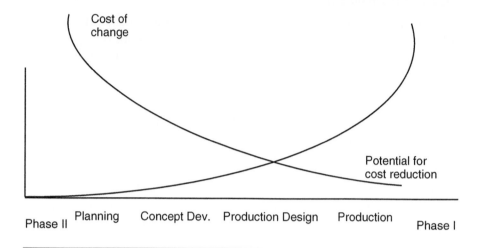

Figure B.1 Supplier integration process.

so they can learn as well." A big part of this process is supplier quality circles, which are encouraged throughout the supply base. Honda provides facilitators to help create a program that fits their environment. The company started with 700 circles in 1989 and now has 4500 circles in 2005. With each quality circle having 5 to 10 people in it, this represents over 20,000 people who are all working to make Honda's products better.

A big part of Honda's strategy is target pricing. Honda organizes Purchasing into some very nontraditional areas, including Supplier Development, Prototype, and Sales Engineering and Design. The last-named group is responsible for taking sales costs and breaking them down to the component level. It is required for suppliers to provide a detailed breakdown of price, including raw materials, labor, tooling, required packaging, delivery expenses, administrative expenses, and other expenses. The breakdown of costs is helpful in suggesting ways in which suppliers can seek to improve and thereby reduce costs, especially for mass production. Cost tables are jointly developed with suppliers and used to find differences (line item by line item) across all elements of cost. A big negotiation point, of course, is profits and overhead. A fair profit is required, but may be dependent on the level of investment. No fixed profit level is used in negotiations. Purchasing must then roll up all of the parts costs and compare them with the target costs. If total costs exceed target costs, the design department must either change the design or try to meet cost objectives in other ways.

Honda also has a "Guest Engineer" program, in which supplier's engineers involved in product development may be asked to participate and work at Honda R&D hand in hand with Honda engineers. This helps local procurement efforts and spurs the development of new technologies by both suppliers and Honda. This also helps support potential exporting of components in later models, but first the supplier must prove himself domestically with local procurement offices.

Purchasing people at Honda get over 420 hr of training over a 3- to 4-year period. Training is also offered to suppliers.

Honda routinely sends out surveys to suppliers to ask them, "How are we doing?" The results are summarized and passed out to department heads. It is also interesting that Honda uses no formal contracts with suppliers, but uses a purchases and sales agreement with boilerplate terms only. No costs, volumes, length of time, etc., are ever used.

The American plant is relatively low-volume and small, and contains only a half to one day of inventory. To facilitate JIT delivery, suppliers often have multiple deliveries per week. When they are far away, off-site storage is used to receive parts and sequence them into a "set" that is delivered multiple times per day. The parts are either put into a "marshalling line" or are received directly. Marysville gets between 50 and 100 deliveries a day. Deliveries are sequenced to their body online sequencing assembly area, which occurs after paint. A ticket on the body specifies the model, color, etc., and is printed online and also distributed to suppliers. Seats are loaded based on sequence, go onto a conveyor, and marry up to corresponding units as they arise.

A great deal of trust exists between Honda and its suppliers. Trust develops through supplier support and continuous development, and often takes a long time to build up. A good example is the case of a fire at a supplier that caused Honda to lose 29 percent of their production. Fortunately, a similar part was produced by a supplier in Japan, who was able to source it short term. However, a number of unique tools were destroyed, but because they were a key supplier, they built back their tools. The company had lawyers, engineering, and everyone involved in modifying the parts! Honda did all the repairs on the tools based on what is best, and helped them build up secondary features (as their engineers were tied up with other issues). Other suppliers in the supply base saw what was happening, which developed greater trust throughout the supply base.

Nevertheless, Honda sets very clear expectations — suppliers must meet demands, especially during new model year changeovers. Suppliers receive a monthly performance report, which uses an index system to rate performance. Production meetings are also scheduled regularly to share production plans and other detailed information. This helps supplier prepare their schedules and manage expectations regarding new models, prototypes, etc.

B.4.3 Supplier Development Process

The general sequence of events in supplier development is as follows:

1. When Honda enters a region, they have relatively little domestic content.
2. They then begin working with local suppliers in developing their quality systems. They are given a part, and asked to make it for Honda. They can then imitate the part until processes are relatively under control.
3. In the next stage, Honda works with the supplier on a single drawing and tries to find ways to make it better and reduce cost.
4. In the final stages, the supplier is involved in the concept and design work and in setting specifications and making cost and value suggestions and improvements.

When discussing particular situations in which supplier development did not go well, a major responsibility of the BP supplier development teams involves choosing the right people at the supplier to be part of the improvement team. It is important to get senior-management approval, but maybe not a good idea to get a senior person specifically involved with the team. What they have found is that when a senior person is on the team, people will go along with whatever he or she wants. Ideally, Honda wants someone who is not senior, but who will nevertheless be missed ("someone who will hurt you") when they move over to a vote on the supplier development team. The person must also be a full-time member of the team.

When discussing resources invested in suppliers, engineering support is a big factor. In some cases, they will own a percentage of the supplier for capitalization purposes, and allow them to pay back the investment over time. This is used in cases when a critical supplier requires help. They generally do not invest directly in equipment ("We are not a bank").

There was a situation in a small town when a local supplier had a welding system that drained the local power supply. All of the lights in the town went down. Honda sent a team of engineers to help them understand the step-down functions to better handle the load and avoid unhappy citizens!

In another case, Honda sent four purchasing people to a small supplier to help rebuild its infrastructure for growth. Honda was experiencing growing pains owing to increased volume from supplier, resulting in delivery and quality problems. The purchasing people spent six months with the supplier, living in temporary apartments, and solved the problem.

In another case, a small supplier was also not ready for mass production, and Honda sent 50 people (including management and support staff) to work at the supplier's location for 12 weeks. This cost millions of dollars in lost time. Today, the supplier is one of the better suppliers of Honda.

Supplier development requires tracking the "low-hanging fruit" to get the early wins and gain momentum. This is a long-term business strategy. The strategy must adopt a continuous-improvement focus; otherwise it will not be successful.

B.4.4 Honda International Purchasing Division (IPD)

At Honda, all domestic buyers are responsible for both domestic suppliers and overseas purchasing. The IPD is responsible for coordination between Honda Corporation and its overseas plant. When Honda launches a new model, the purchasing activity actually starts two years before the release of the vehicle. It is at this time that the quality, cost, and delivery criteria are evaluated. A senior executive at Honda that we interviewed (Obisan) was assigned to the United Kingdom before the plant opened and was responsible for recommending suppliers to R&D.

In developing local suppliers (no matter what country — United States, United Kingdom, or Brazil), Obisan noted that the same basic approach is used globally. This consists of using existing drawings for the models to be built at the new plant (not new drawings!), and trying to get the best among available alternatives from a domestic supplier. In approaching the new supplier with the "old blueprints," quality and engineering capability are the most important criteria to consider (although the lowest price of course plays a role). Once potential suppliers are selected, quality and R&D people visit all potential suppliers, and a final decision is reached.

When a new drawing is issued, quotes from two, three, or four suppliers may be obtained, then a final quote based on a more refined drawing is requested, followed by final supplier selection. In attracting good suppliers, it is emphasized that they also get the opportunity to buy the part from a Honda parts dealer, study it, and come to Honda and see if they can produce it. In this manner, Honda is always looking for better suppliers who can produce parts locally!

B.4.5 Single or Dual Sourcing

Honda suppliers are always subject to competition. In most cases, a parts contract will last for the life of the vehicle (four years), with each part being single sourced. The new Accord has just been launched, and the next vehicle in the pipeline is the Civic 2007 model change. Dual sourcing is used in some cases when delivery problems occur. Because orders are based on forecasts, a dual source may involve using a Japanese supplier and an overseas supplier to produce the same part. This is to avoid a potential situation in which there may not be enough capacity with a single supplier. A good example of this is the headlamp. The exterior of the headlamp is similar for the French and Japanese supplier, but the reflection mechanism is different in the interior. The French model uses a higher-grade material, so the item is dual sourced. The headlamps are essentially interchangeable, but differ slightly in their structure.

Recently, Renault came to benchmark Honda. By comparison, Renault in France has 30 suppliers with guaranteed contracts, all of whom were "preferred"! The difference, however, is that these 30 suppliers have no competition from other suppliers and are guaranteed continual contracts with Renault. In contrast, Honda's suppliers are always exposed to competition, and there is no guarantee of future business.

For almost all international sourcing, a Japanese supplier is available as a backup in case of a production problem. Dual sourcing is not preferred by Honda, but it is almost mandatory in Japan because they cannot risk delivery problems. A Honda production line in Japan must be kept running because there is no layoff system. In the United States, it is easier to shut down a line if necessary.

Recently, a Toyota brake supplier (Aicheingiki) had a fire. This was the only supplier possessing the fine machining capabilities necessary to produce the part. Their entire inventory, tooling, and machining operations were burned up. Despite the fact that it was a single source, Toyota only experienced a four-day shutdown. How? Other suppliers helped out, including one of Honda's brake suppliers. This illustrates the degree of cooperation, even between competing suppliers.

For domestic (i.e., Japanese) production, very few international suppliers supply mother plants. Almost all are Japanese suppliers. Perhaps only five percent of the parts are sourced internationally. This is partly due to the weak yen. In other cases, Honda will try to capitalize on other large automobile manufacturers' supply base. For instance, GM purchases huge quantities — can Honda capitalize on this by buying from the same suppliers? To some extent, as Honda's volumes have increased, they have become more important customers to their suppliers.

B.4.6 Suppliers' Design Capabilities

Gradually, suppliers are having greater influence on Honda designs. To some extent, this input has been limited because adding extra, unique features tends to increase the cost per unit. In the United Kingdom, Obisan fought with Honda Japan because he wished to alter the Honda specification (this is still a problem in the United States today). Today, Honda

Japan is more willing to change a specification to reduce cost or weight. For instance, engineers are now trying to use more plastic and less metal in the magnesium steering-wheel aperture core. Responsiveness of suppliers is critically important in the early stages of the product development process. Honda tries to encourage suppliers' suggestions early before finalizing drawings, particularly in the areas of cost reduction and quality improvement. This is to encourage proposals to reduce cost and machining. That is one reason top management decided that Purchasing should be at Honda R&D (this decision was made in 1991. Prior to that, Purchasing used to be in downtown Tokyo in the headquarters). Today, both R&D and Purchasing people will visit suppliers in the assessment stage of new product development. This interface between R&D and Purchasing is deemed critical. Although each party may recommend different suppliers (Purchasing emphasizing price first, then quality), a joint meeting is held to determine the final selection. This strategy was so successful that Nissan followed suit. Their Purchasing group used to be in Ginza, but is now located in their R&D center in South Tokyo. A major barrier that continues to exist is that the elderly people are well situated in terms of their housing and are reluctant to move to a new location to facilitate colocation.

B.4.7 Supplier Selection Process (New Country)

In choosing new suppliers (e.g., for Swindon, United Kingdom), the following criteria are used:

- Who are their existing customers (e.g., Nissan, VW, and Toyota)? This would indicate existing capabilities in the areas of technology and cost. Having some of these customers indicates some competency.
- What kinds of products are being supplied to these other assemblers?
- What kinds of parts are being made and what new technology is expected to be developed in two years' time that is different from existing models?

On initial visits, part-level information is collected. Obisan emphasizes that one must visit the supplier to understand them! Things to look for include:

- Evidence of continuous improvement and environmental activities.
- Kaizen activities on the shop floor.
- Machine efficiency. (For example, Canadian suppliers used very old machines and needed to invest. This resulted in fewer workers and improved productivity.)

B.4.8 Kyoryoku Kai (Cooperative Associations)

Honda is not as interested in these organizations as other major automakers in Japan and, therefore, does not utilize them. This is because they respect suppliers' independence and wish to free them from obligatory membership in an association. Unlike Toyota and Nissan, Honda wants suppliers to be free from ties. However, they do have supplier meetings at least once or twice per year, in which they present quality and cost reduction awards to suppliers.

B.4.9 Creating Competition — Core Competencies

The most important principle is to create competition in the supply base. Thus, even in-house suppliers face competition. For example, an instrument panel was traditionally produced in-house; Honda R&D designed it and Purchasing got a good quotation from an outside supplier. The in-house people could not compete with this proposal, so some portion of the business was allocated to the external supplier, and the in-house process was expected to face this competition and find ways to reduce its costs.

B.4.10 Investment

Honda invests about 20 percent of their capital in suppliers' subsidiaries. For example, Kikuchi represents a minor investment by Honda, which has a small share of the company. (Mr. Morita was the Purchasing Manager in Ohio, and is now at Kikuchi helping to manage them. This is an interesting point: Honda encourages their managers to go to work for their suppliers in some cases so they can better disseminate Honda's working philosophies.) Honda Engineering will in some cases help suppliers with robot design, tool design, welding, and injection, and may help with investments. Finally, Honda R&D may aid in product design work.

B.4.11 Honda de Mexico

Honda de Mexico has been producing motorcycles for a long time, and has only recently begun automobile production for sale in the Mexican market. This is a fairly small market, and the vehicles are not sold for export. Volumes are currently limited to fewer than 500 vehicles per month. This is a knockdown operation: parts are imported from the Marysville plant and U.S. supply base (no local suppliers) and assembled in the facility. Honda moves a lot of its old tooling that has reached its end of life from Marysville to this plant for aftermarket supply, and then may reexport the parts for the replacement market. Exchange rates continue to be a problem in this market.

B.4.12 Honda — Brazil

This facility began production of the Civic in October 1997. Many parts are exported from the Ohio plant. There are some Brazilian suppliers, including TRW, which has a plant there and is involved in some technology transfer. This is a very small market, and the peso devaluation makes it very difficult to do business. However, Honda wants to maintain a presence as this is a very big potential market.

B.4.13 Global Suppliers

A big question that arises as Honda continues to expand its operations is: Who will become the global suppliers in the United States/Japan/Europe, as well as in the future (Brazil, Mexico, etc.)? Obisan notes that different regions are competitive in different areas. An ideal global supplier is:

- Very efficient in R&D.
- Equally competitive across multiple global locations.
- Equally proficient in cost, quality, etc.

Unfortunately, there are very few cases of truly global suppliers. For instance, R&D is very efficient in Japanese suppliers, but these same suppliers may not be effective at R&D in a different location. Thus, it is very seldom that they find a supplier who can supply multiple locations, yet locating these suppliers is one of Honda's most important development strategies. Finding good suppliers to serve both the United States and Japan is not a problem: few suppliers, however, have truly global capabilities.

B.4.13.1 How to Develop Global Suppliers

Some of the critical issues involved include:

- Requiring intensive negotiation and joint understanding and commitment at the top-management level in the supplier.
- Requiring participation by top management within Honda.

■ Requiring a common investment for multiple locations. (For example, Siemens supplies air bag control units to Honda's plants in both the Europe and the United States to minimize the investment in tooling. However, the control units are actually produced by the supplier's Mexican plant! Because the units are small, they can easily be shipped to both the United States and Europe.

■ If a supplier is competitive in multiple markets, Honda will use them. This is a very rare situation.

■ Always emphasize competition. If a supplier already provides Honda with parts in, say, the United States, it certainly has a leg up over other suppliers in being considered for supplying Honda's new facility because it already knows what the expectations are.

■ A supplier's ability to improve. If a supplier provides defective products, but immediately takes countermeasures to prevent it from happening again, this is considered a plus by Honda.

B.4.14 Improving Communication across Honda in the Four Major Trade Zones

Japanese associates do the same type of liaison, and visit the United States. Toshihiko Morita was in the United States from 1990 to 1994, and was involved in the development of the Japanese car and the North America Accord, Civic, and Acura. In developing a "world car," he noted that a major challenge involved how to improve communication between the different groups across the different Honda locations in Japan, Europe, the United States, and Asia. Although Honda has an international purchasing office, its power is limited and greater communication is needed across the different production locations. The biggest challenge is how to improve communication and develop relationships across Honda in the four trade zones. This includes:

■ How to share Honda's strategy with suppliers worldwide.
■ How to transfer knowledge across Honda.
■ How to develop supplier capabilities worldwide.

B.4.14.1 The World Car — Global Planning Strategy

Each country's car is currently developed in Japan. The basic concept is the same and is then modified by local regulations. In addition, a four-region meeting is held quarterly, with representatives from Japan, the Americas, Europe, and Asia. At this meeting, planning involves a general strategy to deal with companies with which Honda intends to do business. For example, the relationship with a Japanese supplier may be "more mature" than that with the same supplier in the United States or Asia; at the meeting, executives discuss how to ensure that the "child" companies can develop to the level of the "parent" effectively and efficiently. In most cases, Japanese suppliers are well integrated and do not require development. The problem is transferring this situation to North America, Europe, and Asia.

At HAM, the BP strategy seeks to improve performance continually. The process helps develop a strategy for the next major new model (Accord) that is better than that developed for the previous new model. Although the local situation is important, the problem must be addressed at a higher level to fix major problems or to change the plan if necessary. This often requires that Honda GT (Honda R&D, which includes Purchasing, Engineering, Design, and Testing, all located in one building) become involved. Suppliers' relationships with Honda are a key factor. Purchasing should be buying from the best in the world, or must explain how and why they will not be doing so.

As Morita says: "The challenge becomes how to develop a relationship with those suppliers that we believe to be at the top. Honda places value on maintaining relationships, so we do not enter into them lightly. Because we value them, it is our responsibility to make our relationships better and ensure that things improve and mature over time. To do so, we may send people to virtually 'live' in suppliers' facilities."

On a regular basis, all of the procurement groups meet at a quarterly meeting to discuss integrated global purchasing strategy. At this meeting, the discussion focuses on opportunities for commonality and standardization, coordination with marketing's export strategy, new product planning, cost management, and technology transfer issues within the supply base.

An important part of this strategy meeting also focuses on development of a truly "global" supply base. Figure B.2 depicts how Honda establishes global supplier capabilities.

Suppose that a supplier (A) has plants or affiliations located in different regions of the globe. (This is a very common situation for first-tier automotive suppliers). For instance, suppose that A^1 is the best in terms of performance and is located in Japan. Another supplier plant, A^2, is located in North America, and a third, A^3, is located in Europe. The supplier may also be asked to start up a plant in Thailand to supply future production there. Each of these locations produces the same family of components. Through the quarterly procurement meeting, Honda can compare A's performance across different locations. Procurement managers may share insights and compare A's management styles, productivity, etc., across locations. They

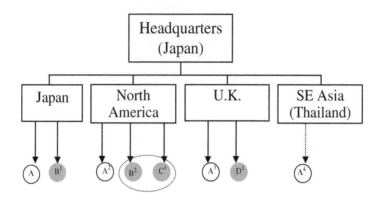

Figure B.2   Honda's global supplier capabilities.

can also openly discuss technology issues with the supplier's engineers at the A^1 location, and expect them to transfer knowledge to the different divisions abroad. For instance, Honda may deal with the supplier in developing the technology at the A^1 location, and then expect A to take their practices across A^2, A^3, and develop a new supply point at A^4! They may then transfer the technology horizontally across subsidiaries in the United States, thus spreading their cutting-edge technology globally across all of Honda's platforms. This may require that Honda be actively involved in helping the supplier to disseminate this knowledge.

A danger with this type of strategy is that Honda might become too dependent on a single supplier of a given commodity or technology. To guard against this possibility, Honda has established a network of suppliers who compete against each other globally. In the preceding diagram, suppose that supplier A is Tokyo Seat Technologies. (This Japanese supplier actually has some Honda engineers employed there, and Honda has a minority financial stake in the company.) In Japan, Tokyo Seat competes against Tachess (B^1). In the United States, Tachess has a JV with JCI (shown as B^2–C^1). In Europe, Tachess also had a JV with Bertron Fouray (20 percent ownership), which is currently dissolved. In this manner, Tokyo Seat must face competition from independent companies in each of the areas in which it operates, even though it is closely affiliated with Honda.

The relationship between Honda and Tokyo Seat is a type of *keiretsu*. Honda owns shares in Tokyo Seat. It is also common for retired Honda engineers to leave the company and go to work at Tokyo Seat, and perhaps work at any of their locations over the world. This further helps to transfer technology throughout the global supply base. However,

Honda's keiretsu's differ from other Japanese keiretsu's, because there is legitimate competition. In the words of Morita, "The supplier must earn the business — it is not automatic." Price is always the key expectation, and there is no loyalty to a competitor who can provide the same or better performance in QCDD–M (Quality, Cost, Delivery, Development, and Management).

Although this is just a single commodity example, Honda's goal is to establish an entire network of suppliers who compete against each other globally. A major driver for this objective is that at procurement meetings, designers do not wish to work with five different suppliers, but prefer to work with one and maximize the design potential across all of Honda's platforms globally. This helps to minimize the different modifications of its technology required for global diffusion, yet facilitates adaptation to local market conditions.

B.4.14.2 Global Supplier Development — The PACK Teams

Transfer of personnel also occurs to transfer supplier development practices. In one case, a senior manager from HAM went to work at HUK (Honda of the United Kingdom) to transfer supplier development expertise to its U.K. location.

The supplier development concept at Honda is defined loosely from Japanese as "a sense of performance, which is used to help suppliers improve." A major initiative involves using a technique known as PACK teams. These teams are composed of manufacturing experts who travel for extensive periods in teams, and transfer Honda know-how throughout its supply base. These individuals are hand-picked from Honda Japan, and have temporary visas that allow them to travel for five months (maximum). The team works extensively during the prototype stage to ensure that the necessary quality systems are in place within the supply base. By definition, these individuals must interact with Honda's local Supplier Development group, to find out which suppliers require immediate help. The PACK team is a major factor in ensuring that suppliers meet timing requirements in the new product development process, so that the supplier can easily slip into the mass production phase. The team also transfers knowledge from Honda's Japanese supply base to suppliers in North America and worldwide. For the most part, this team has focused on transmission parts. They also transfer knowledge to the local supplier development group, which picks up the slack when the PACK team returns back to Japan.

The mother company of the supplier is expected to transfer the technology provided by the PACK team for similar products across other locations (accounting for local variation). This is part of their responsibility as a Honda supplier. In cases in which the supplier is not global, they will send a guest engineer to Tokyo to work with Japanese designers at Honda R&D. An ongoing problem that is encountered in this process is the poor transfer of technology across the same supplier (same problem noted with BMW).

B.4.14.3 Purchasing Liaisons

An important task in managing this process is the management of the relationship between the designer and the guest engineer. To achieve this, a purchasing liaison associate is assigned to monitor the relationship over time.

The purchasing liaison is a relatively new concept. Currently, it is used only by HAM. Next year, HUK will also send a purchasing liaison.

The primary task of the liaison is to ensure that the supplier is properly prepared to work with the design team at Honda R&D. For instance, they may inform the supplier, "Don't come here and make a presentation unless you really understand and have addressed all of the following items: corrective action, FMEAs, etc." Although Honda's R&D people are prepared to treat suppliers well, it is generally a good idea to ensure that the supplier has thought through all of the relevant issues, as well as what they want to achieve, prior to meeting with the designers. The liaison ensures that the supplier is ready to present to Honda, by ensuring that supplier has done a careful self-analysis of its capabilities and has a clear goal for its presentation. This dramatically increases the success rate of the supplier and designer interface.

B.4.14.4 Performance Capabilities — QCDD–M

Honda's primary objectives are in quality, cost, delivery, development, and management. The last of these is considered critically important — it refers to the management capabilities of the supplier in terms of strategy, measurement, and planning. It is a "soft" objective, but is one of the most important. A major part of the supplier development effort involves ensuring that the supplier can hit Honda's QCDD–M targets. The PACK team helps to transfer technology worldwide before mass production. This enables long-term international global support. In December 1997, the PACK team consisted of 15 people who were on temporary assignment out of the Ohio plant for five months.

B.4.14.5 Moving Capacity Globally

To drive improvement, Honda may introduce new business to suppliers to improve them. For instance in Thailand, many of Honda's competitors have actually reduced their production because of the financial problems being experienced by many suppliers. Honda views this current crisis as an opportunity to improve the supply base, and has just begun production of the CR-V in Thailand. This makes the best of a poor situation: Thai suppliers get more business, and associated support. The timing of this move was excellent, as CR-V production in Japan was at 100 percent. To improve performance in the supply base, Honda introduced this very popular product from Japan to Thailand to force suppliers to improve their capabilities in that region of the world.

B.4.14.6 Transferring Technology Globally between Suppliers

There is very limited transfer of technology across suppliers (in contrast to the Toyota strategy). Part of this is because of Honda's wish to introduce competition within the supply base as a motivation for improvement. There is also very limited technology transfer from Japanese to non-Japanese suppliers.

In limited situations, some technology transfer occurs. For example, in welding special materials (a zinc alloy), the volume needed in the United Kingdom was not high enough for a Japanese supplier to build its own supplying plant there. Honda then requested the Japanese supplier to share limited technology transfer to a U.K. supplier. The U.K. supplier may receive assistance in developing the welding technology from the Japanese supplier, get the business from Honda, and then pay a royalty to the Japanese supplier.

In another situation in the United States, a major producer of casting products in Japan helped HAM to enter into an agreement and transfer production expertise to a U.S. supplier. HAM coordinated the transfer. HAM thus developed a local source for the casting through a royalty arrangement with the Japanese supplier. The tooling die was built in Japan and shipped to the U.S. supplier. Thus, HAM did not have to worry about the finish of the parts, because the die was sent directly to the U.S. supplier. HAM thus benefits from shorter development and delivery times, quality, etc. The Japanese supplier that effected the transfer may also benefit in ways other than the royalties, in terms of establishing a preferred relationship with Honda, which is important in gaining future business.

In rare situations, tooling in Japan is sold to a competing supplier. However, very limited help is provided in such cases.

B.4.15 Major Obstacles and Challenges in Developing a Globally Aligned Supply Base

One of the most critical challenges in deploying this strategy is getting suppliers to develop a global competence (one that is aligned with Honda's global perspective). This is not easy, as the following story illustrates.

In the preceding example (see Figure B.2) of the global supplier A, HAM has been unsuccessful in dealing with their contact at A^2. Although A^1 (the mother company) has a very close relationship with Japanese buyers at Honda Motor Company, the people working in their A^2 location may not understand A's global strategy and may not have a network in place to globally share production technology, design, expertise, etc. As a result, the buyer working at HAM may not be happy with the results of this outcome, and may not wish to source from A^2, as they may also not fully understand the role of supplier A in the Honda network. Major challenges in deploying this strategy are:

■ How much has Honda done to challenge the mother supplier to transfer technology to its children?

■ How to get the mother company to communicate value analysis and cost reduction ideas to their children?

■ How to enable the global network to communicate cost reduction opportunities, yet not use them exclusively to their advantage when they do so?

■ How to get Honda associates to force their local supplier (A^2 in this case) to go back to the mother company (A^1) and get help from a guest engineer or seek other expertise?

To some extent, these challenges will evolve as Honda continues to expand. Honda started initially in motorcycle production, which it did and still does produce in almost every country in the world. As it expanded into automobiles, it also began to expand sales country by country. Motorcycle production is not nearly as large or complicated an investment as automotive (and is largely a knockdown type of operation). However, many of the lessons learned in motorcycle production globally are being applied to Honda's automotive production expansion worldwide. Moreover, they have traveled this route before!

B.4.16 Honda's Localization Strategy

The soft area of supplier development was established because of the timing and speed of the exodus of Japanese suppliers establishing transplants in the United States. They simply needed help understanding local conditions.

Honda has established a fixed process for localization:

■ Find a local supplier (single source).
■ When volume doubles, develop a second or third source.
■ When a mismatch in the philosophies of the supplier and Honda arises, Honda must nevertheless respect the agreement or contract to do business.

When recurring problems with the supplier occur, it becomes difficult to consider them for future business unless the problems can be resolved. If the problems are basic, Honda may make less of a commitment (volumewise). If the problems are fundamental and will not go away, (e.g., an inability to even listen to Honda's proposals, and not necessarily even accept them), then Honda must consider whether they will be able to work with the supplier five years down the road. In such cases this involves a fundamental mismatch that cannot be resolved, and Honda will drop the supplier, as this is a critical stumbling block.

B.4.17 Actual Place, Actual Part, Actual Situation

A strong focus at Honda is adjusting the relationship to accommodate the local situation. For example, Japanese and U.S. buyer–supplier relationships are fundamentally different. How should Honda modify their relationships to accommodate local conditions? In another case in the United Kingdom, there was not enough volume for a Japanese supplier to enter the market, yet the U.K. suppliers employed a different engineering approach. To account for such different local situations, Honda has employed the "Gimba" or "3A" approach: actual place, actual part, actual situation. This means that the actual part produced in the supplier's location is "fitted" onto the vehicle before being approved for production to ensure that it meets Honda's requirements. This may require repetitive changes to the part over time.

Appendix C

Case Studies in Strategic Sourcing

The following case studies consider four different situations and represent several approaches used in building sourcing strategies. They cover a diverse set of commodities and services across multiple stages of the processes described in this book. The case studies are as follows:

Suncor Energy: Foothills drilling — relationship management process

Packaging Manufacturer: Building an effective request for proposal

Bank of America: Document management — supply market intelligence

FedEx: Strategic sourcing

C.1 Suncor Energy: Foothills Drilling — Relationship Management Process[1]

C.1.1 Company and Team Background

Suncor Energy, Inc., is an integrated energy company headquartered in Calgary, Alberta, focused on oil sands extraction and upgrading, as well as refining and marketing. Suncor's Natural Gas and Renewable Energy (NG and RE) business unit drills for and produces natural gas. Suncor's 2003 revenues were $6.3 billion (Canadian dollars), with 3,400 employees. NG and RE had revenues in 2003 of $512 million (Canadian dollars) and

---

[1] *Source:* Dr. Kevin McCormack, Supply-Chain Redesign, LLC, and Peter Cavanagh, Suncor Energy.

produced 34,900 barrels of oil equivalent per day (187 mmcf/day). This gas is used for production (upgrading) of oil sands and is sold in the open market. A critical function of this group is to successfully identify, drill, and produce natural gas at a cost that enables cost-effective production of oil sands.

The Foothills Asset Team lies within NG and RE and includes personnel who specialize in land acquisitions, geophysics, geology, reservoir engineering, and production engineering. This group identifies prospects for the drilling group. The typical work relationship for oil and gas companies has been for the drilling group to carry out their duties isolated from the Asset Team. In the case of the Foothills Drilling Team, the drilling personnel have been included in both the Asset Team and the Well Engineering Services Group to create a merging of issues and a shared strategy. The drilling engineers have a solid line with regards to responsibilities within the Well Engineering Services Group and a dotted line to the Asset Team. The key to the relationship has been that the Asset Team has fully recognized and supported drilling issues and the drilling group has fully supported Asset Team issues. An important part of the strategy has been to openly share ideas on drilling these complex wells.

Other key team members are the supply-chain management (SCM) procurement personnel. SCM is about more than getting supplies and services to the right place at the right time. SCM is fully integrated with the drilling group and promotes the development of longer-term business relationships with select suppliers who can work with the company to create value beyond the purchase price of material or services. SCM works with the drilling group to facilitate the development and management of the relationship with their key suppliers. Sustainability of the foothills business model has also been enhanced through strong support from the Stakeholder Relations Group within Well Engineering Services Group.

The drilling group coordinates and integrates drilling services on a per-well basis. Throughout the well-planning process, the drilling group ensures that the well objectives are feasible. The drilling group and Asset Team rationalize an optimum well design, which takes into account the potential well productivity, risks, and cost. To drill a well, materials and services are required from approximately 20 different suppliers. Of the 20 suppliers, 5 have a significant impact on the well results: (1) the directional company, (2) the drilling-fluid company, (3) the rig contractor, (4) the cementing company, and (5) the well-logging company. The first three services have personnel working at the well site for most of the drilling phase. During drilling, a representative from Well Engineering Services is on location to oversee the execution of activities, and a well-site geologist who is linked to the Foothills Asset Team is also present. Changes and optimization of the drilling parameters will occur during the drill as geological uncertainties are identified and adjusted for by the well-site team.

C.1.2 Situation or Business Drivers

As idea sharing started and the unified approach developed, team members received strong support from management. Even as the organizational structure of the company changed, management carefully ensured that the unified approach continued to grow. When the team faltered on occasion in the early stages, there was very strong support from management both from within and outside Suncor.

The Foothills Drilling Team is a small team compared with most operators. They operate only 4 rigs of the 700 in Canada. This makes their leverage in supplier relationships very small. Getting the best agreements and people was difficult using traditional approaches and getting to the top of the service providers' priority list seemed next to impossible. The dilemma they faced was how to get the best performance (in terms of both time and success rate) when they seemed to have very little leverage with suppliers to get the best agreements and the best people.

Changes in timing or design can impact each of these suppliers significantly. To overcome the preceding constraints, drilling personnel and the asset team agreed that exceptional performance could be achieved by working the rigs continuously and that they could acquire and retain the best people with this philosophy. The drilling foreman, directional drilling personnel, mudmen, and rig crews were key.

Surprises and "blindsiding" suppliers seem to be the norm in the industry, and the functional silo effect leads to difficulties in cooperation between companies and specialties. Figure C.1 illustrates the typical drilling cycle and the traditional compartmentalization of decisions and information.

The first two steps in this cycle are for the energy company to (1) select the place and the size of the effort and make the "go" decision ("go/size/place" phase) and (2) develop the cost estimates of the effort and submit a request for funding (the develop cost). As can be seen in Figure C.1, this generally took six to twelve months and traditionally only allowed for minor input from suppliers who might be involved in the effort.

The next phases of the drilling cycle are:

1. Advance Field Engineering (AFE) approval of funding
2. Finalize the scope of the well, identify suppliers, and get the well ready
3. Develop the well schedule
4. Drill the well

Figure C.1 clearly shows that suppliers are only involved after the well scope is developed; they are not involved in the scheduling but later are the main players in the drilling. All of these factors and ways of doing

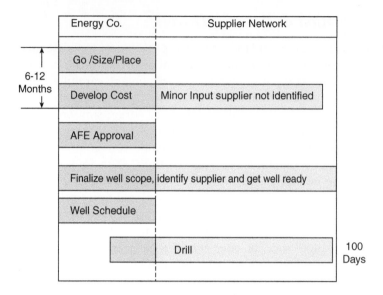

Figure C.1   The drilling cycle and traditional supplier involvement.

business had created a culture that seemed to stand in the way of effective performance of drilling teams. Service suppliers who wished to be successful in this market could not get better without a change in their philosophy and degree of cooperation. The longer the planning time, the higher the probability that personnel changes would occur and that continuity would be lost.

C.1.3 The Foothills Drilling–Asset Team Approach

Several members of the Foothills Drilling–Asset Team had worked together on other projects prior to joining the team. Their personal belief in the value of high-performance teams was a driving force in building a collaborative culture to enhance group performance. Their first step was to create a positive environment in the drilling teams at the well site. They did this by developing, communicating, and implementing some guiding principles. These are:

1. Create a continuous-work environment to stimulate operational excellence
2. Become the preferred customer through efficiency and building of high trust
3. Target the best people and empower their decision making

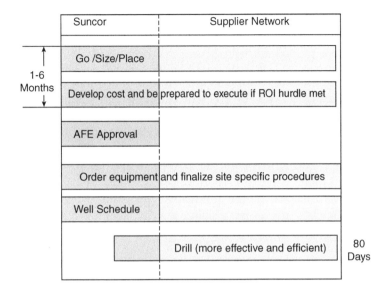

Figure C.2 The drilling cycle and the new environment.

4. Recognize what is important to the service companies and their people
5. Negotiate rather than bid; work with service companies as equals with an equal voice
6. Totally share business plans, scheduling, and problems
7. Create a shared-influence environment to help create group ownership, interest, and motivation

Figure C.2 illustrates the implementation of some of these principles. First, the deep involvement of the supplier network in the go/size/place phase and their involvement in developing the cost. In this new model, the first two phases of the drilling cycle took only one to six months as opposed to six to twelve months with the traditional approach.

After AFE approval, the "develop scope" phase has been replaced with the "order equipment and finalize site-specific procedures" phase. This new phase deeply involves the supplier network but, even more important, takes specific actions before the well schedule is actually produced. It also allows for two standardized well designs that only require minor tuning to the site-specific differences. The well design standardization was developed through a collaborative effort by the Foothills Drilling Team, which included the supplier network. The standardization of equipment compresses planning times and creates flexibility. It allows for contingency wells to be used if planning issues delay a project.

This standardization and early-action approach is made possible through several innovations developed and deployed by the team, which enable a high level of repeatability. Some are proprietary and relate to design and procedures, whereas others are cultural and relationship oriented. For example, key suppliers are selected in advance and guaranteed a level of use that allows for efficient planning and staffing. Information is also openly available to the entire network assisting in planning, which helps in minimizing blindsiding and in building trust.

The next phase of the new drilling cycle is the well schedule. This is a collaborative effort, involving all parties in the team, to develop the final, detailed plan. The team has developed several visual, collaborative-planning tools that are highly innovative. First, an overall process was built that described the entire drilling activity, including all service suppliers. In the past, contractors did their own planning, often in an information vacuum.

Then, these activities are broken down into subactivities on a Gantt chart (see Figure C.1). The development of this document by the entire team is important in that it provides an agreed-upon, standardized approach that can be used for each project. This document can now be used to quickly plan each well by just providing the timing of the activities (start and end dates) and adjusting for any location and condition changes. The plan is also reviewed after each well and continuously improved. The results are short, painless scheduling cycles and more reliable execution.

Several other visual, collaborative-planning documents are also used. An overall equipment schedule for the entire project is used, which has key commitment dates for each category of equipment and uses color coding (red, yellow, and green) to visually denote late or at-risk deliveries that need attention. A joint, visual technical-planning document that describes in detail drilling strategies and procedures was developed by the team for each specific project. These, as well as other visual collaborative-planning tools, are displayed and available to all members of the team, even if they are not directly involved.

During the drilling phase, data on progress and results are plotted on large wall maps for all to see. Joint discussions and decisions are made using this visual tool, and the open team culture generates many ideas for improvement.

As can be seen in Figure C.2, the drilling time has been reduced from 100 days to 80 days based on a 2003 drilling-cost study. The drilling-time reduction reflects mature learning in areas with a normalized oil/gas well scope. More important, almost all of the greater group objectives are being met reliably so that each group feels committed to the foothills business model.

Measurement and improvement of the team and each supplier relationship is also a key activity related to success. The performance of each group has been reviewed on a well-by-well basis. What is important is that the culture of openness and trust has created a truly cooperative discussion rather than a "trip to the woodshed." When required, suppliers can openly bring up issues on the Suncor side of the relationship that are problems. These are openly discussed and, in this new environment, responsibility is taken, not just accepted. The postwell measurement has evolved into a scorecard system that was tested for three years with one of the rig companies and is now being rolled out to all of the foothills suppliers.

C.1.4 Results

The implementation of the guiding principles in all phases of the life cycle, as well as the creation of an environment of openness, trust, and mutual success, has resulted in dramatic changes. As the Foothills Asset Team has grown, support for this integrated concept has grown. Many team members have enhanced something that started with just a few people.

Well-design standardization has been used to create a compressed planning cycle that can enable continuous work. This has then been used as a lever to enable a high-trust team environment that has reliably responded to the challenge of foothills drilling. The team is highly motivated to sustain and implement new technologies and to strive for continuous improvement.

For most of the last five years, utilization for the Suncor foothills rigs has been close to the best in the industry and has been in excess of 93 percent. Over the past year, utilization for the Suncor foothills rigs was 98 percent.

The implementation of this unified philosophy into all phases of the life cycle, as well as the creation of an environment of openness, trust, and mutual success, has resulted in substantial improvements. Based on a 2003 cost study, the team has achieved the following: (1) drilling costs reduced by 18 percent ($1.4 million/well), (2) planning times reduced by 42 percent (5 months), (3) drilling times reduced by 20 percent on average, and (4) more than 80 percent success rate on wells drilled. In addition, foothills production volumes have tripled over the past five years. These results have been accomplished against a backdrop of 5 percent inflation. Within its area of operation, the Suncor Foothills Drilling–Asset Team has become one of the preferred employers within its operating region from the service supplier perspective. This position continues to grow stronger.

Problem time, a measure of the issues encountered during drilling, has been as low as 1 to 5 percent, significantly lower than the industry average of 10 to 15 percent. The service rates paid to suppliers are preferred-customer rates in all cases. Over the past 5 years, the total recordable incident frequency on Suncor-drilled foothills wells was approximately 18 percent of the industry average. The performance standard for these teams is very high and is gradually improving with time. Over the past year the four drilling rigs used by the Foothills Drilling–Asset Team have equaled or bettered the best safety records for their respective companies. Similarly, the directional, drilling-fluid, cementing, and rig-moving company personnel have done the same. Service companies have also benefited through the strategy of openness and continuity of work. But most of all, the team has created an exciting atmosphere of success and shared rewards that provides the energy for future innovation.

C.1.5 Conclusions and Lessons Learned

A truly integrated supply network requires a high-trust environment in which to operate. A high-trust environment is also an essential part of greater group learning and improvement. Transparent failures can be corrected easily. Lack of trust results in reduced transparency and slows group learning and confidence. A highly motivated workgroup with a high degree of trust can achieve sustainable accelerated learning.

A key component of the high-trust environment is the ability of members of the group to speak with confidence on certain issues without fear of reprisal. Priorities are always changing in a dynamic world, and the ability of the group to share concerns allows for improvement areas to be identified and prioritized relative to the greater value. Knowledge shared between multidisciplinary teams can help create a value-driven organization.

Throughout the development of the Foothills Drilling–Asset Team, Suncor management strongly supported the sharing of ideas between disciplines and helped to encourage the continued growth of this unified approach. Without the strong support of a number of managers over the past five years, this unified approach may have faltered as the Foothills Drilling–Asset Team grew in size.

Finally, working in a successful high-trust and high-performance team environment can be an exciting and addictive experience. Feelings of *esprit de corps* are said to be the glue that holds a team (or a network of suppliers or customers) together and are the fuel for sustained performance.

C.2 Packaging Manufacturer — Developing an RFP

C.2.1 Internal Requirements and Opportunities

Commodity-bid requirements and potential target opportunities for improvement in the adhesives division of a packaging manufacturer were assessed by a team. Attributes were grouped into four separate categories:

- Price: This focuses on the price of materials and freight, packaging costs, and payment terms; materials price accounts for a large percentage of total manufacturing costs.
- Quality: The ability to meet technical specifications and to deliver products of uniform quality are the two most important qualifiers; certificate of analysis must be provided.
- Service: A measure of the level of responsiveness to technical issues; explores the option of consignment inventory.
- Delivery: Look for bulk shipments, when practical; must be able to provide consistent delivery in a JIT environment; must have the ability to meet packaging requirements.

C.2.2 Supplier Intelligence Process

Once the team had an understanding of the market for, and purpose of, each commodity, they were prepared to begin the process of gathering supplier intelligence. The first task was to develop an initial list of all possible suppliers for each commodity. Primary sources for creating this initial list were the Thomas Register, and the OPD Chemical Buyers Directory (both the print and online versions), and various search engines on the Internet.

The team realized that many of the suppliers on the initial list would ultimately be eliminated and filtered out of the selection process. However, the goal was to cast the net as widely as possible. Once they finalized the initial list for each commodity, they began to "sanity-check" each of the suppliers by visiting their Web sites or otherwise verifying that the supplier actually did exist and supply the commodity. The result of this sanity check was a long list for each commodity. In addition to sanity-checking each supplier, they obtained contact information for each supplier who made it to the long lists. This contact information would be needed in the next phase in which information is requested from each supplier to further shorten the lists. Figure C.3 depicts the supplier intelligence process that was used. The subsequent filters will be discussed later.

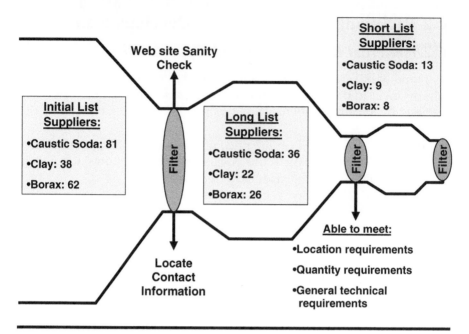

Figure C.3 Supplier intelligence process used.

C.2.3 Recommend Phase

In the Recommend Phase of the project, the team worked to develop a short list for each assigned commodity. They developed an evaluation algorithm that helped formulate what would become the official Request for Proposal (RFP) document to be distributed to the potential supply base. They also used this time to further develop negotiation strategies that would increase competition among potential bidders.

C.2.3.1 Short List Development

After passing the initial list through these filters, they were still left with a large number of suppliers. To decrease those numbers further, they ran them through another set of filters. Form letters were developed and distributed to each of the suppliers on the long list, seeking information on location, quantity, and certain technical requirements. Based on this information, suppliers were asked to indicate their interest in supplying and ability to provide these commodities. The team was able to eliminate a large number of suppliers through this filter. Suppliers were eliminated for the following reasons:

- All company locations were outside of the supplier's service area
- Supplier was unable to meet bulk shipment requirements
- Supplier was unable to meet quantity requirements
- No response to e-mail or phone calls

Once responses were received and follow-up calls were made, they were left with a short list of suppliers who would receive the RFP (see Figure C.3).

C.2.3.2 Weighted Evaluation Algorithm

As the team continued to narrow down the list and move forward in the sourcing process, they began to think about how they would ultimately evaluate the potential suppliers. They clearly needed an objective and quantitative approach to making a selection decision, and wanted to avoid going with a "gut feel" or basing a selection decision on the wrong criteria. Therefore, a weighted evaluation algorithm was created that was tailored to each commodity.

The weighted evaluation algorithm took into account the key decision categories and assigned each of them a weight based on their relative importance. The key decision categories are those elements of the product or purchase terms that the internal customer considers most important. In the case of these commodities, the internal customer emphasized the following general decision categories:

- Uniform quality
- Security of supply
- Reduced total cost (material, freight, and packaging costs)
- Adequate technical assistance
- Bulk bag shipments
- Reduced lead times
- Certificate of analysis

Therefore, the evaluation algorithm was designed to target these key areas. Although the general form and structure of the weighted algorithm was standardized across the three commodities, the categories and the weights assigned to each category varied slightly owing to the unique characteristics of each commodity. As an example, the following categories and weights were used in the weighted evaluation algorithm for a dry clay:

- 62 percent for total cost per ton
- 20 percent for package size

- 9 percent for payment terms
- 6 percent for lead time
- 3 percent for technical assistance
- Bonus for quality, on-time delivery, incumbency, innovation

Clearly, price was the most important factor (and this was true for all commodities). One characteristic of the dry clay that is unique, however, is the importance of increasing the package size from 50-lb bags to 2000-lb super sacks. The score assigned to each category could be a 10 (highest), 7, 4, or 1 (lowest). The performance required for each score was clearly defined for each category.

Bonus points were awarded for being the incumbent because staying with him or her clearly offers advantages in terms of lower risk. Bonus points were also awarded for factors such as quality, on-time delivery, and offering innovative solutions or advantages that the team had not considered.

There were other factors that were important but were not scored because they were considered order qualifiers. In other words, a supplier must have these to even be considered in the first place. Among the order qualifiers were providing a certificate of analysis with every shipment, security and reliability of supply, meeting the technical requirements, and offering adequate and uniform quality.

C.2.3.3 Strategies for Moving Forward

C.2.3.3.1 Sourcing Strategy

There were several important areas that the team began to focus on with regard to overall sourcing strategy:

- Price and quality — Price is the single most important factor in the sourcing decision. This is why, as discussed previously, total cost was given so much weight in the evaluation algorithm. In the manufacture of adhesives, the cost of materials (such as commodities) represents a large percentage of the cost. In addition, uniform quality was absolutely critical because slight variations from delivery to delivery could throw off the manufacturing process. Therefore, focusing on price reduction and assessing quality were critical.
- Multiple suppliers — It may be optimal to recommend awarding business to multiple suppliers for the same commodity for various locations. However, this decision could hurt volume discounts or package deals and would add to the complexity of the supply base.

- Innovation — Potential suppliers were encouraged to suggest new, innovative solutions. As mentioned, this was included in the evaluation algorithm as a bonus. An example of an innovative idea recommended by a supplier was the option of free pallet and bag return for dry clay.
- Freight: make or buy? — Minimizing freight cost was important. Therefore, every supplier was requested to quote their freight prices in the RFP. This was compared with the lowest possible freight the company could obtain for each supplier. This allowed the team to identify the lowest-cost carriers and examine the potential advantages of using the company's dedicated resources.
- Incumbent issues — Finally, the team had to decide how to deal with the incumbent. One issue was considering the possible impact of removing part of the business from an incumbent and awarding it to a new supplier. Clearly, this could affect the incumbent's price and possibly damage their relationship with the company. Finally, it was decided to treat incumbents in the same way as new potential suppliers. The incumbents would be given the same information and would be required to complete the same RFP. The only difference, as mentioned previously, was that the incumbent would receive a bonus in the evaluation.

C.2.3.3.2 Negotiation Strategy

The team also began to consider, at a high level, how they would approach the upcoming negotiations. The general negotiation strategy at this point was:

- As per the weighted algorithm, identify the most important items:
  - Material cost
  - Freight
  - Package size
  - Delivery
- Identify items on which the team is willing to compromise:
  - Technical assistance (minimum: via e-mail)
  - Consignment inventory
  - Payment terms (minimum: 30 days)
  - Perhaps some leeway on lead time
- Practice and work out possible scenarios
- Understand the other party's likely goals and methods:
  - Take the team's focus away from price

- – Emphasize intangible benefits
- – Secure long-term contract
- – Favorable payment terms
- – Ease of information exchange with the company (especially when ordering)
- ■ Conduct negotiations via conference call
- ■ Clarify and confirm key issues
- ■ Seek an agreement where there is a win–win situation

C.2.3.4 RFP Development

Last, as part of the Recommend Phase, the team created an RFP document for each commodity. The initial section covered such information as background on the company, an overview of the commodity and the bidding process, buyer contact information, and various quality and service requirements. There is a direct link between the weighted evaluation algorithm and the RFP, and the team wanted to be sure that the RFP specifically targeted each of the main decision categories.

Wherever possible, the team provided a table that the supplier had to complete. Such items as price, lead time, and package size were straightforward and could be entered directly into a table. Other items such as quality programs, technical assistance, and method of tracking on-time delivery were assessed via directed questions. The RFPs required that the supplier bid on each commodity and location combination individually. The supplier was also given the option of quoting a package bid — meaning the terms it would offer if awarded all of the business that it bid on.

Once completed, the RFPs were distributed via UPS both as hard copy and on a CD. All bid packages were to remain sealed until the response deadline had been reached and all returned bid packages had been received. This was to ensure that all suppliers were treated equitably.

C.2.4 Select Phase

C.2.4.1 RFP Evaluation (for Borax)

The RFP distribution list included eight participants, including the incumbent distributor and that company's supplier. At the time of evaluation, only four had responded. Despite attempts to follow up with nonresponders, who had earlier indicated a willingness to participate, the pool of participants remained at four.

Table C.1   Initial Evaluation (South Carolina Plant)

Company	Price/lb (Percent)	Lead Time	Payment Terms	Algorithm Score
Supplier A	95	1 Day	45 Days	9.1
Supplier B	80	4 Weeks	30 Days	8.3
Supplier C	93	10 Days	45 Days	7.6

Table C.2   Initial Evaluation (Indiana Plant)

Company	Price/lb (Percent)	Lead Time	Payment Terms	Algorithm Score
Supplier A	95	1 Day	45 Days	9.3
Supplier B	84	4 Weeks	30 Days	8.3
Supplier C	89	10 Days	45 Days	8.1

C.2.4.1.1 Preliminary Evaluation and Rankings

Each of these four respondents was a distributor. Details regarding the initial evaluation are in Table C.1 and Table C.2 (the top three performers are shown). The pricing on the bids is shown as a percentage of the current price to ensure confidentiality. Supplier names have also been changed for confidentiality.

C.2.4.1.2 Final Negotiation Strategies

Upon complete evaluation of the bids, there remained some questions regarding the supply chain as proposed by some of the respondents. Going into negotiations, the strategy was to clarify any concerns or questions in this area, as well as to highlight areas of weakness, to identify any potential hidden costs that had perhaps not been explicitly stated in the proposal, and finally, to lower the unit price of the product.

C.2.4.1.3 Results

Negotiations with the distributors varied greatly from one another. Although all issues were vocalized and addressed, some conversations

Table C.3   Recommendations (South Carolina Plant)

Company	Price/lb (Percent)	Lead Time	Payment Terms	Algorithm Score
Supplier B	80	4 Days	45 Days	9.5

Note: Annual cost savings = 20%.

Table C.4   Recommendations (Indiana Plant)

Company	Price/lb (Percent)	Lead Time	Payment Terms	Algorithm Score
Supplier B	84	4 Days	45 Days	9.5

Note: Annual Cost Savings = 16.08%.

veered to value-added features that are more challenging to quantify. Others were fairly straightforward, taking on each issue one at a time without impinging on other aspects of the RFP. Once all negotiations had concluded, the following were established:

- Emphasis on value-added features, such as local warehousing and product rotation
- A better understanding of the complete supply chain from supplier to end user
- The difference between proposed pricing alternatives (with or without freight included)
- Payment terms concession

C.2.4.1.4 Recommendation

Based on the information obtained through negotiations, the evaluations yielded the recommended distributors by location as seen in Table C.3 and Table C.4.

It is important to note, however, that there may be some reservations regarding the fact that supplier B sources from Turkey. The level of quality control may be called into question. Both recommendations are made with the assumption that the supplier meets or exceeds all criteria needed for qualification.

C.3 Bank of America: Document Management — Supply Market Intelligence[2]

C.3.1 In the Beginning ...

In 2002, the SCM function was initiated at the Bank of America (B of A), and the new senior vice president was tasked immediately with rationalizing and establishing a supply-chain strategy, developing a vision, and driving cost savings to the bottom line. Several immediate actions were initiated by the new senior vice president of SCM, Lance Drummond; these involved establishing a strategic plan, developing a system of supplier scorecards, reviewing and understanding total spend by commodity, and developing a crisp process and consistent approach to measuring supplier performance and sourcing products and services. The strategic Hoshin plan for the organization is shown in Figure C.4.

In 2002, the bank also began building a team of supply management professionals to develop new strategies for major commodity families, in an effort to begin to consolidate and leverage major spend items to reduce costs and improve the profitability of B of A. One of the first major commodity families analyzed was document handling. B of A's spend for document delivery was approximately $700 million ($350 million for postage) with about 7 to 8 percent going to minority-owned suppliers.

The bank chose a unique approach to documents and created a department named Document Management (DM), which was charged with oversight of the entire life cycle of documents, from conception to end-of-life functions such as archiving, recycling, and confidential destruction. This group approached the problem of reducing the end-to-end cost of documents through a methodology that began with capturing the document in a digital library that is tied to a relational database that stores the pertinent approval and manufacturing specifications of that document. Around that dual database, the DM group wrapped a disciplined change-control process that mandated review of compliance issues and a review of opportunities to reduce the end-to-end cost of delivery. They then categorized all potential delivery channels, including manufacture and distribution through warehousing, print on demand, distribute and print on demand, desktop delivery through multifunctional devices, desktop printers, reprographics networks, fax machines, and pure Web delivery.

---

[2] This case study was developed by Robert B. Handfield, Ph.D. (NC State University College of Management) and Robert Kee (Bank of America).

Draft (02/18/2003)		
Supply Chain Management		
Lance Drummond 2003-2005		

Supply Chain Management VISION		To be recognized as World Class for Supply Chain Management throughout the Financial Services Industry by 2004.
Supply Chain Management MISSION		Create a sustainable competitive advantage for the Bank by knowing the business, implementing innovative supply chain processes, executing flawlessly and working as a boundaryless high-performing team.

GOALS		Breakthrough Strategies
CUSTOMER Provider of Choice TBD% Customer/Business Partner Satisfaction	1.1	Drive suppliers to world-class performance in support of a world-class customer/client experience.
	1.2	Support the corporate commitment to our multi-cultural customers as reflected in our communities.
	1.3	Develop and implement innovative end to end supply chain processes allowing the lines of business to achieve a competitive advantage.
ASSOCIATE Employer of Choice 90% Associate Satisfaction	2.1	Create a performance driven culture, which attracts, retains, and rewards associates to drive growth.
	2.2	Provide the support and tools that Associates need to excel.
	2.3	Enable Associates to achieve professional growth balanced with personal goals.
	2.4	Reflect the diversity of the communities and customers we serve in our workforce.
SHAREHOLDER Investment of Choice Double digit year over year productivity	3.1	Focus SCM expertise and business acumen on creating SVA for our business partners.
	3.2	Leveraging Six Sigma and Kaizen Now methodologies, reduce the complexity of SCM Operations, improve quality levels, and achieve double digit year over year productivity.
	3.3	Identify key risks, and develop and execute plans to mitigate risk, while satisfying legal and regulatory requirements.
	3.4	Integrate non-U.S. SCM functions and leverage opportunities to deliver productivity.

Figure C.4   Bank of America Hoshin plan for supply chain management.

Distribution expense constituted an ever-larger percentage of the end-to-end cost, so there was an increased focus on distribution cost, freight, expedited delivery, U.S. Postal expense, interoffice mail costs, etc.

This approach had some significant implications for the work culture and how people did their jobs at branches and other business units. By digitizing all documents at origin, the bank was now shifting a good portion of the delivery of documents from the traditional print methodology to delivery at the desktop. This created a need to fully understand the cost of delivering documents at the desktop. While contrasting the cost of these channels, it became apparent that there was a huge gap in the understanding of the desktop delivery environment. Although the bank had a tight control on the cost of faxing and the cost of impressions on multifunctional devices, they discovered two disturbing elements. B of A owned one of the largest fleets of multifunctional copiers (over 5000) of any organization in the world. (A multifunctional copier is capable of not only copying, but also faxing, printing, and scanning documents.)

Although the cost per impression of running these copiers is relatively low (under 2 cents per impression, versus the Gartner Group estimate of average total cost of 4 to 12 cents per impression on regular printers), several major problems emerged in the discovery process initiated by the sourcing team.

First, only 5 percent of the copiers in use were connected to any computers or other devices; the remaining 95 percent were used solely for manual copying, and failed to exploit any of their multifunctional capabilities! Second, because there was no management of the desktop printer environment, the bank was actually pushing print from a traditional method to an even more expensive channel, the unregulated desktop printer. Finally, there were no metrics in place to understand the total cost of ownership at the desktop. The total amount spent on copying and printers was unavailable but was estimated to be in the $90 million range. To make matters worse, there was no single group responsible for managing desktop printers, no demand management, and no understanding of the total cost of ownership for these devices. The bank had no idea how many desktop printers were currently in use (best estimates put the number between 35,000 and 70,000). All of these factors made the task of managing the desktop environment or even understanding the cost of that environment almost impossible.

Faced with this situation, DM developed a program known as PrintSmart aimed at controlling the desktop environment. The team began by centralizing all responsibility for the desktop environment under one group. This organization created a demand management function to drive the cost of impressions to the lowest-cost option appropriate for the individual groups' workflow needs with a target of concentrating impressions at connected multifunctional devices. Desktop printers were required to be networked where feasible, and contracts were converted to cost-per-impression and total cost-of-ownership arrangements. A three-year technology refresh was also built into the program.

C.3.2 An End-to-End Process

Bob Kee, senior vice president of procurement responsible for DM explained the strategy in more detail:

> If you are serious about document management, you have to look at the complete end-to-end process, as the print purchase price is generally a very small piece of the total spend. The real cost of documents is the handling, freight, and waste. We realized that there was little logic other than habit that drove the selection of the channels people were using for printing.

We needed to first get our arms around all of the different elements of printing required by our users, then develop the appropriate manufacturer or channel that was the most cost-effective and efficient to meet that requirement.

DM is currently divided into six functional groups:

- Print, Digital, and Image Management
- Mail Delivery and Postage Optimization
- Desktop Print — PrintSmart
- Commercial Print
- Reprographics
- Records Management and Confidential Destruction

Each of the six areas of DM is linked under an umbrella strategy that integrates the current practices into a single integrated process. The overriding strategy is to push all documents through the following methodology:

- Change-control engine — Capture all images at creation in a single database of graphic art and specifications; immediately enforce change-control mechanisms to standardize, consolidate, and enforce policy; and direct production and distribution channels considering end-to-end process cost.
- Production — Manage all production environments in an interactive manner to lean process and minimize costs; interacting with the change-control engine and business partner to seek design opportunities to reduce cost.
- Distribution — Manage all distribution channels in an interactive manner to lean process and minimize costs; interacting with the change-control engine and business partner to seek design opportunities to reduce cost.
- End of life — Manage all end-of-life processes to lean process and minimize cost (with an emphasis on risk mitigation); interacting with the change-control engine and business partner to seek opportunities to reduce cost.
- Metadata capture — Feed all pertinent usage and cost data back into the change-control engine to update the end-to-end process view.

In addition to the multiple channels that existed throughout this process, the DM team identified a huge investment in the inventory of documents. This was generated by little use of print on demand and a focus on the cost of print — not end-to-end cost — and resulted in significant obsolescence cost and long time to market, tying up investment and causing excess warehousing expense. Three years ago, when the team first attacked the problem of warehoused documents, inventories were in the $20 to $25 million range, which have now been reduced to $5 million with better service delivery and controls.

The DM team recognized that the only way to control documents would be to create a digital library of every document used by the B of A. Only after it was in the digital library could Supply Management control how it was printed. This approach was extended further; Kee notes that:

> If it was printed or in use, we wanted it in the library! This included everything from checks, deposit tickets, magnetic integrated character recognition (MICR) documents, marketing pieces, and every other type of bank document you can image. The library had to capture, image, and upload data on the use of every document, from usage patterns that included the usual volume data, but also geographies, cost centers, lines of business, etc. This required the creation of a very large relational database.
>
> Once the digital library was established, a number of things started to happen. The team began to (1) consolidate suppliers and leverage pricing, (2) move a considerable amount of inventory to print on demand and (3) standardize and consolidate documents. The bank went from 45,000 forms to 6,000 forms through this process. The print library has effectively reduced print cost by over 20 percent year over year. This did not include the added advantages of reduced obsolescence and reduced time to market.

The current user process is shown in Figure C.5.

C.3.3 "Culture Eats Strategy For Lunch!"

This phrase is written in large bold letters on a whiteboard in Kee's office. The meaning of this phrase soon became clear:

> Our goal was to fully utilize the advantages of moving printing to the desktop, reducing the cost of freight and delivery as well as print costs. Our goal was to drive down the cost of every impression across the company to three cents or less. To do this, we had to initiate a major change in the way people work at the B of A. The barriers to driving change into the organization,

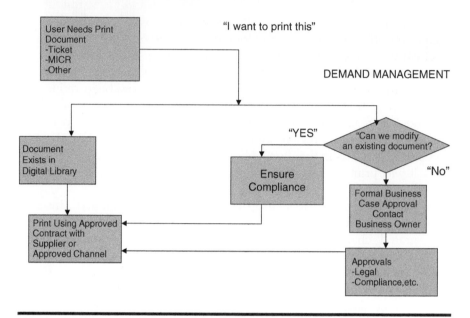

Figure C.5   DM user process.

at the time, seemed almost insurmountable. Even the best-developed strategy can fail if you are not able to change the culture of the B of A to accept the fallout and implications of the strategy — hence, the phrase "Culture Eats Strategy For Lunch"!

Looking back, Kee noted that:

> The problem we faced is that B of A grew through the acquisition of a number of different banks, which all had different systems and ways of working. In particular, people at banks are used to configuring and buying whatever printer they want for their own office. There was not a single person we talked to who felt good about standing up and walking 20 feet to a networked printer to pick up a print job, as they all wanted to keep their printers in their office. The problem is, that printing on desktop laser or inkjet printers costs an average of 8 to 12 cents per impression, or 400 to 600 percent of the cost on a multifunctional copier or printer. Part of this is due to the cost of maintenance, which can run to as much as $200 per call (even for a minor paper jam). (In our analysis, we also noted that a spike in maintenance occurred on most desktop printers at three years).

C.3.4 The Solution: PrintSmart

To control the cost of document handling and printing, the DM team initiated a strategy called PrintSmart. This was accomplished through two approaches: demand management and facility reengineering. Demand management, in the context of DM, involved having SCM redirect all requisitions for desktop printers to multifunctional devices or shared networked printers in their building. In very rare circumstances (when someone worked from home or traveled), DM would approve black-and-white stand-alone printers purchased from an approved supplier with a negotiated contract (e.g., Lexmark). Lexmark provides a total cost of ownership lease on printers (at about 3.75 cents per impression), which allows DM to monitor the network and track print copies made.

The second approach was to reengineer every facility owned by B of A across the country! (The cost of doing so was also built into the estimate of 3.75 cents per impression mentioned previously.) Early pilot program results were promising: the program reduced print cost by 15 to 20 percent. The bank has now rolled facility reengineering out to two cities or eleven buildings with an average annualized savings of $250,000 per building. To date, DM has increased connectivity for multifunctional devices from 5 percent to over 35 percent. About 70 percent of the cost is still driven by people printing from old desktop printers (about 55 percent of the total print volume).

Kee notes that

> Cut sheet volume (number of pages) per employee was esti-mated at approximately 954 sheets/month per employee. (It is interesting that even after B of A went through a significant amount of downsizing, this cut sheet volume per employee remained relatively stable.) One of the interesting trends in technology is that in spite of increasing numbers of electronic documents and the prediction of the "paperless office" by technology gurus, the ease of printing to a desktop makes it much easier to print, and associates rely on paper more than ever. The problem can thus be stated in a twofold manner:
>
> 1. How do we reduce the number of sheets used per employee?
> 2. How do we forecast usage per employee?

Kee notes that:

> Previously, we had two to three associates per print device — and in a "PrintSmarted" environment, we moved to one machine serving an average of seven employees. All of the multifunctional

copiers or printers were leased, and we paid only for the number of impressions. We are exploring an application that will allowed us to track who is making the impressions and how many per floor, allowing us to replenish paper and toner based on consumption of equipment. We could then begin to track impressions per floor versus cut sheet volumes purchased — which would allow us to do three things: (1) reduce the investment on paper held on-site, (2) improve predictive maintenance schedules, and (3) track missing paper inventory.

PrintSmart is a process that must interface with all other desktop groups within the bank, including the help desk, which is outsourced to HP. The PrintSmart solution also had to consider the impact of pushing increasing digital traffic through the bank's networks and the effects on bandwidth limitations that might exist across the bank's multiple locations. This limitation required that the document-handling team work closely with the desktop group, located within the technology and operations organization led by Richard Simpson at B of A. Prior to implementing PrintSmart, Kee ensured that the desktop technology team was 100 percent on board. The initiative required that Kee meet frequently with the Corporate Real Estate team, the Networking team, and other key facilities and technology groups that would be affected by the reengineering of facilities to accommodate PrintSmart.

Several problems soon became apparent. A typical one might be that there were an inadequate number of print servers in a given city. The team also discovered that it was simpler to centralize printer types on individual servers to enhance diagnostics. The team also set up a device-labeling methodology that mirrored the mail code system. An associate can log on to the LAN in a reengineered building, search devices by mail code, and discover the networked devices that can be accessed on that floor.

PrintSmart is a major initiative that will take over two years to implement — and will clearly entail a major culture change. The biggest change is for administrative staff, who now complain about having to walk 20 plus feet to the printer ("It ruins my workflow"). The groundswell of discontent cannot be underestimated. Kee notes that "At one point we were worried if, politically, PrintSmart could survive this onslaught of protest. A program that requires behavioral changes from almost every associate requires an unusual level of support from the higher echelons. At B of A, the executive sponsors have supported the program 1000 percent."

The DM team also made a point of implementing PrintSmart at the B of A's executive corporate offices in Charlotte first on the schedule (after the five pilot buildings). Why? "We felt that if we were going to drive change into the company, we would begin by changing Rome first. That way, people could not point to us and complain that corporate was not taking their own medicine!"

C.3.5 Demand Management

An important part of managing documents is establishing user requirements and tracking consumption of paper and services. This is essential in negotiating contracts with key suppliers, as well as for allowing suppliers to better plan their resources and capacity requirements to better serve B of A.

Since implementing this strategy, cut sheet volume per employee has remained stable at roughly 1000 sheets per associate per quarter, even though the number of employees has gone down due to reorganization during and after the merger. Thus, the strategy has not increased the number of impressions significantly, but it has cut costs because much of this volume was formerly done on desktop printers. As mentioned previously, desktop printers were often purchased for $2500 as an expensed item, but the cost of toner and maintenance was not factored in, which represents the greater cost over time. Total cost per sheet was between $0.08 to $0.12 per sheet for desktop printers versus $0.02 to $0.04 per sheet. This represents a total savings of about $0.09 per sheet, or $90 per associate per quarter. (Total savings generated by this program to date is $7.5 million with the total opportunity estimated at $30 million annually.) An application is being developed to be able to track the number of impressions made per floor and by account, which will enable the banks to replenish paper and toner based on actual consumption by individual machines (see Figure C.6).

Kee's team is also working with several new suppliers on alternative technologies to traditional lithography. Marketing pieces have very high specifications, and quality is critical. Specifically, working with NexPress (using a Kodak engine) and iGen3 (which uses a Xerox engine), the team is working to migrate commercial printing to digital color printing. Today, time to market on marketing pieces is typically 90 to 120 days based on residual inventory and large quantity requirements to offset the high cost of large press setup. The new technology will enable documents to be virtually created and distributed rationally to print shops across the country. The technology can eliminate regional variations in color and print layout, take out cost, and eliminate obsolescence and warehousing of products.

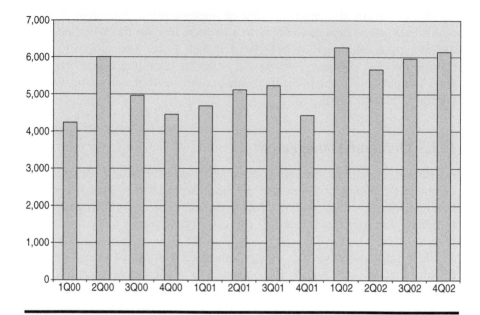

Figure C.6   Sheets consumed per associate

The key to enabling this technology is the "critical to quality" element that ensures that local printers can print the same material with the same level of quality as a high-end printer (as is done today). This is potentially a huge cultural shift, with companies quickly turning out high-quality color-stable materials for a much lower cost with huge reductions in lead time (see overview in Figure C.7).

C.4 FedEx Strategic Sourcing and Supply[3]

C.4.1 Background — FedEx

FedEx is a $20 billion market leader in transportation, information, and logistics solutions, providing strategic direction to five main operating companies. These include:

■ FedEx Express, which is the world's largest express transportation company. Leveraging its unmatched air route capabilities and

---

[3] This case was developed by Robert Handfield of NC State University based on interviews with Federal Express associates, working with Brenda Liker and Jaymie Mitchell in developing best practices in sourcing for the Bank of America.

	2000	2001	% Change Y/Y	2002	% Change Y/Y
Copy Paper	10,031.21	10,446.47	4.1%	9,759.26	-6.6%
Deposit Envelopes	773.76	755.86	-2.3%	914.06	20.9%
Envelopes	7,296.19	6,978.98	-4.3%	6,692.77	-4.1%
Forms	5,843.24	4,287.71	-26.6%	3,195.81	-25.5%
Marketing	10,672.18	9,058.67	-15.1%	19,250.21	112.5%
Statements	8,437.96	11,230.62	33.1%	8,935.55	-20.4%
Stationery	378.85	262.88	-30.6%	156.73	-40.4%
Total	43,433.39	43,021.19	-0.9%	48,904.40	13.7%

Post Consumer Recycled Content Trend Analysis

	2000	2001	% Change Y/Y	2002	% Change Y/Y
Total Recycled Tonnage	19,503.87	24,758.37	26.9%	36,589.09	47.8%
% Recycled/Total Tonnage	44.9%	57.5%	28.2%	74.8%	30.0%
Total Virgin Tonnage	23,929.52	18,262.82	-23.7%	12,315.31	-32.6%
% Virgin/Total Tonnage	55.1%	42.5%	-22.9%	25.2%	-40.7%

Associate / Account to Paper Consumption Trends

		2000	2001	% Change Y/Y	2002	% Change Y/Y
External						
Pounds		22,268,120	21,716,483	-2.5%	26,096,761	20.2%
Sheets		2,226,812,000	2,171,648,293	0.0%	2,609,676,133	20.2%
Lbs/Account		0.70	0.7	0.0%	0.9	20.2%
Sheets/Account		74.2	72.4	.0%	87.0	20.2%
Internal						
Pounds		6,687,473	6,964,313	4.1%	6,506,175	-6.6%
Sheets		668,747,333	696,431,333	0.0%	650,617,467	-6.6%
Lbs/Account		45.5	48.6	.0%	48.1	-1.0%
Sheets/Associate		4,549.34	4,857.5	.0%	4,807.2	-1.0%
Total Lbs/Account	Total	0.97	0.96	-0.95%	1.1	13.7%
Total Sheets/Account		96.52	95.60	0.00%	108.7	13.7%
Total Lbs/Associate		196.98	200.05	0.00%	240.9	20.4%
Total Sheets/Associate		19,697.68	20,004.60	0.00%	24,089.3	20.4%

Paper Recycling Trends

	2000	2001	% Change Y/Y	2002	% Change Y/Y
Total Tonnage Recycled	29,511	24,838	-15.8%	31,451	26.6%
Recycled Paper to Total Tonnage	67.9%	57.7%	-15.0%	64.3%	11.4%

Figure C.7 Product consumption by type.

extensive air and ground infrastructure, FedEx connects markets (that comprise 90 percent of the world's economic activity) within just one to two business days.

■ FedEx Ground, which is North America's second-largest ground carrier for business-to-business small-package delivery. Provider of innovative new residential delivery service — FedEx® Home Delivery — in key U.S. cities and a pioneer in applying advanced information technology to meet customer needs.

■ FedEx Freight, a $1.9 billion leading provider of next-day and second-day regional LTL freight services. FedEx Freight comprises two independent yet complementary operating companies, American Freightways and Viking Freight, known for exceptional service, reliability, and on-time performance.

■ FedEx Customer Critical, North America's largest time-specific, critical-shipment carrier provides exclusive-use, nonstop, door-to-door delivery throughout the United States and Canada and within Europe — 24 hr a day, 365 days a year.

■ FedEx Trade Networks, a full-service customs brokerage, trade consulting, and E-clearance solutions organization designed to speed shipments through by customs using advanced E-commerce programs.

■ FedEx Services, which provides customer access to the full range of FedEx transportation, logistics, E-commerce, and information services by integrating sales, marketing, and information technology.

C.4.2 FedEx Center-Led Initiative

Prior to the purchase of the ground, freight, and other non-express-based services, FedEx had reorganized all of its major indirect spend in information technology; aircraft; facilities and business services; vehicles, fuel, and ground service equipment; and supply-chain logistics groups under the Strategic Sourcing and Supply group led by Edith Kelly-Green. After the purchase of these different businesses, the supply management function was reorganized into a center-led SCM sourcing model. Over the last two years, FedEx SCM has been focusing on leveraging sourcing and contracting for all of the FedEx family of companies. For office supplies, instead of having each company run a contract, SCM has a single corporate contract for all of the negotiation effort, but allows for different transactional approaches. It has been a gradual migration getting to a centralized view of how procurement will happen. It is central for the larger spend areas, and has different policy requirements.

A major component of this model is the integration of Ariba Buyer — expanding its use to other operating companies and processing requisitions within the SCM group. Most of the best practices discussed in this case study are associated with FedEx, but are slowly being migrated across all of the operating companies (see Figure C.8).

C.4.3 The Sourcing Process

FedEx established a seven-step sourcing process (Figure C.9).

Step 1: The first step is an assessment of the category to which industry and commodity belong. The team will ensure that they are clear on the user requirements from the corporation, and try to define what that category entails. For example, on promotional items, where should the boundaries be drawn? How does the team define these? This involves doing a lot of research on the nature of the existing purchasing activity: how much, whom is it with, what are the issues with existing suppliers, how does the marketplace function, what are the drivers of competition?

Step 2: Based on this research, the team goes into the process of selecting the sourcing strategy, in essence, taking all of the information they have and deciding how they will approach that marketplace: Is a RFP appropriate? Do they need to maintain the existing relationship and revisit negotiation?

Step 3: Assuming that they are going beyond a negotiation, they do an in-depth research on suppliers in that area, including the qualification of the suppliers. Can the suppliers satisfy user requirements, service aspects, etc.? The end goal is to develop a list of to whom they would like to send RFPs. The team will conduct a supplier portfolio analysis.

Step 4: A second phase of this implementation pass is to revisit this strategy and have the team take another look at it — have they uncovered something that will cause them to change negotiation? They develop a strategy for negotiation: Do they want to use a reverse auction or a conventional RFP? What are the criteria for supplier evaluation? Is this still something they want to do?

Step 5: This is the negotiation and supplier selection. The team sends out the RFP, negotiates with suppliers, and selects suppliers.

Step 6: Once the team has made the selection, they need to do the integration. This is done by applying the Ariba tool set with the supplier and identifying integration conflicts to be solved to make the contract workable.

Step 7: Benchmark the supply market — ongoing monitoring of the suppliers through the FedEx supplier scorecard system.

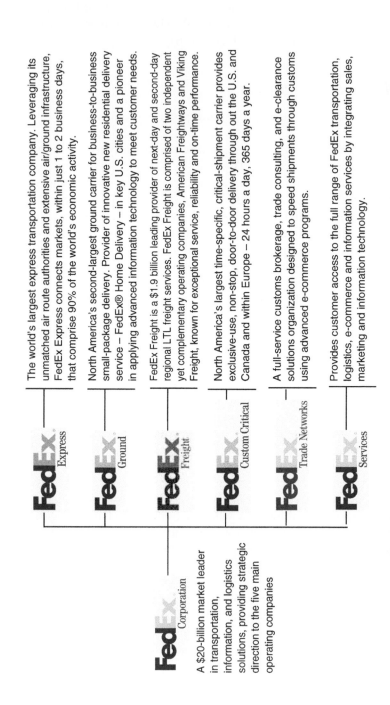

The world's largest express transportation company. Leveraging its unmatched air route authorities and extensive air/ground infrastructure, FedEx Express connects markets, within just 1 to 2 business days, that comprise 90% of the world's economic activity.

North America's second-largest ground carrier for business-to-business small-package delivery. Provider of innovative new residential delivery service – FedEx® Home Delivery – in key U.S. cities and a pioneer in applying advanced information technology to meet customer needs.

FedEx Freight is a $1.9 billion leading provider of next-day and second-day regional LTL freight services. FedEx Freight is comprised of two independent yet complementary operating companies, American Freightways and Viking Freight, known for exceptional service, reliability and on-time performance.

North America's largest time-specific, critical-shipment carrier provides exclusive-use, non-stop, door-to-door delivery through out the U.S. and Canada and within Europe – 24 hours a day, 365 days a year.

A full-service customs brokerage, trade consulting, and e-clearance solutions organization designed to speed shipments through customs using advanced e-commerce programs.

Provides customer access to the full range of FedEx transportation, logistics, e-commerce and information services by integrating sales, marketing and information technology.

A $20-billion market leader in transportation, information, and logistics solutions, providing strategic direction to the five main operating companies

Figure C.8   FedEx is much more than your typical air express carrier.

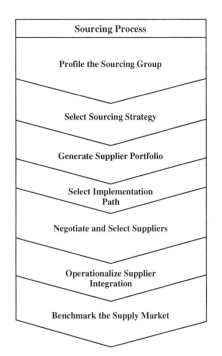

Sourcing Process	Selected Activities
Profile the Sourcing Group	• Confirm user requirements • Develop category definition • Define basic characteristics • Understand industry and supply markets
Select Sourcing Strategy	• Assess bargaining position • Evaluate alternative strategies • Select appropriate approaches and techniques
Generate Supplier Portfolio	• Identify qualified suppliers • Determine supplier value-added capabilities • Develop supplier "shortlist"
Select Implementation Path	• Verify and adjust sourcing strategy • Develop implementation plan
Negotiate and Select Suppliers	• Plan negotiation strategy • Evaluate supplier proposals • Conduct negotiations with suppliers • Recommend sourcing decision
Operationalize Supplier Integration	• Plan and implement transition to new suppliers relationships • Link key processes • Conduct joint process improvement activities
Benchmark the Supply Market	• Monitor market conditions • Assess new technology and best practices impact • Conduct benchmarking activities • Determine appropriateness for reexamining category

Figure C.9   FedEx sourcing process.

Two aspects of how the center-led sourcing process (Figure C.10) is done are important: first, a central sourcing group (a team of sourcing analysts) leads company-specific sourcing initiatives. Once they get through the process, a supply-chain associate takes over. These associates are spend category associated (e.g., aircraft components, IT contracts). Their role is to oversee the arrangement with the supplier, ensure that it is implemented, and see that it continues within that marketplace. They are responsible for completing the scorecard with the supplier to ensure that it is completed thoroughly and accurately. This handoff occurs in step 6 during integration.

There is also a set of reviews that takes place within the sourcing process. When the team arrives at the fifth stage, one of the requirements is that they define the business case for the strategy. The team will summarize the work done in the initiative — the business case goes into an extensive review. Initially, it goes to finance and legal — assertions of savings are validated, with finance ensuring that savings projections are well founded and ascertaining that the assumptions used are acceptable. If the strategy is approved, then it proceeds to the final step, which is a review by a corporate sourcing council (SC), consisting of high-level executives from each of the divisions (e.g., COO and CFO from each

1. Assessment	2. Sourcing	3. Business Case Review	4. Sourcing Council Approval	5. SMC Update	6. Implement and Manage
Functions					
• Evaluation of spend category and marketplace to determine savings opportunity (FedEx spend, supply market dynamics, FedEx specs, etc)	• Detailed market assessment • Define sourcing strategy • Identify potential suppliers • Execute sourcing strategy to exploit opportunity	• Finance, Legal, Stakeholders, CSO, and CFO review and validate Business Case assumptions and results	• Approve business Case • Authorize implementation of sourcing results based on Business Case (or) • Recommendations to SMC	• Move CSC issues beyond impasse • Support implementation • Applause	• Integrate with selected supplier (s) • Communicate new suppliers, benefits, and process changes. • Report benefits. • Continuously monitor the supplier and marketplace
Membership					
• Assessment Team of FedEx sourcing, finance, and stakeholders	• Cross-functional, cross-OpCo Sourcing Team	• Business Case Review Team	• Corporate Sourcing Council	• Strategic Management Committee	• Stakeholders and Supply Chain Management staff

Figure C.10   FedEx center-led sourcing process.

business unit), chaired by a chief sourcing officer. The council will review the strategy for additional work and reject or approve it. If they approve it, the council has an obligation to help the sourcing team implement it. They will have some strong advocates to help with the implementation and ensure compliance with the terms of the agreements.

Dollar thresholds on deals that go to the SC tend to be the larger-dollar items and when there is an impact based on the nature of spend or an impact on the brand image or other areas. Fuels and contract trucking (above the $10 million limit) go to the SC. Events such as a change in the nature of the supplier for FedEx boxes (involving a specification change) may not necessarily result in a big cost impact (e.g., $2 million cost savings) but may go before the council for other reasons (to ensure it does not affect market image or customer preferences). This is a largely a judgment call on the part of the chief sourcing officer (Edith Kelly-Green, no longer with FedEx).

FedEx does not have any service level agreements in place. They have informal agreements — each of the SC groups has a director, matrixed to the primary user vice president. The facilities director is matrixed with the VP of Properties and Facilities — dotted-line reporting relationship (see Figure C.11).

C.4.4 Supplier Scorecard

FedEx has employed a generic scorecard that pertains to most of the supply relationships; they have the capability to add some unique metrics. The SCM group determines the threshold limits for the scorecard, but most items are not part of the contract. Instead, the scorecard is viewed as a way to manage the relationship and award future business. An SCM associate will manage the performance assessment for a given supplier and convert it into a score of 1 through 5 based on available data and input from user groups. An example of the scorecard is shown in Figure C.12.

The idea behind the scorecard was to adopt a methodology that could be applied to compare "apples with apples" across the supply base. Associates tasked with managing the supplier are given the authority regarding where to draw the lines, relating percentage weights to different elements of the scorecard, and converting it to a 1-through-5 metric. The user requirements are incorporated into the contract through the statement of work. Factors that may or may not be included in a specific scorecard are: overall strategy, resources, customer service responsibility, free service, number of complaints, postsales support, knowledge of FedEx and of the product, upgrades, return time on warranty, bad-from-stock items (do not meet quality standard), certification, cost trends, discrepancy rate,

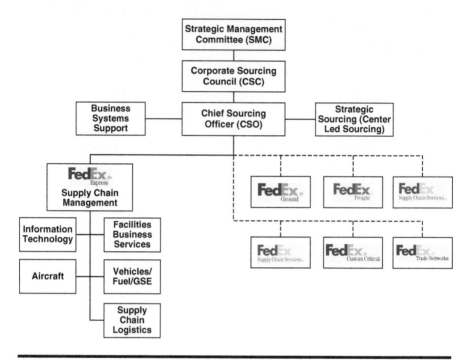

Figure C.11   FedEx reporting relationships.

financial stability, mean time between failures, on-time delivery, delivery cycle time, cycle-time improvement, their use of diverse suppliers, frequency of value of cost reductions. These items are tied into the scorecard, with the SCM associate responsible for converting raw data and input from users into a score based on the supplier's performance on that contract.

The scorecard is tied to certain business rules. If a score becomes very low, FedEx has established different stratifications for the scorecard. If it falls below 350 then the team will seriously reevaluate their supply strategy in that market. This occurs particularly at the end of certain agreements. There are no specific criteria or guidelines other than monitoring the scorecard and reevaluating it on a periodic basis as necessary. The decision tends to come in on a three-year cycle, which is when most commodity groups are reevaluated by a sourcing team. Each category has a sourcing evaluation approximately every three years, with most contracts lasting three years with an option for a three-year extension. This can vary; for example, on PCs FedEx will revisit the strategy more often because the dynamics of that market change much more frequently. The nature of PC purchases may change over the course of a single year!

Company A
Total Score: 491 (Performance
Level: Platinum)
Click here for a printer-friendly version of this card.

SUPPLIER INFORMATION		SCOREBOARD INFORMATION	
Supplier #:	**123456**	Eval Period:	**From 6/1/2002 to 11/19/2002**
Supplier:	**Company A**		
Address 1:		Eval Date:	**11/20/2002**
Address 2:		FedEx Rep:	**Joe Supplychain**
City/State/ZIP:		Manager:	**Jane Manager**
Supplier Rep:		Department:	**SFSCM, ITSCM**
FSC:		Discussed With Supplier:	**Yes**
		Reviewed by FedEx Manager:	**Yes**

Measurement	Weight	Score	Weighted Score
Strategy			
Add-ons	3	5	15
Price Competitiveness	6	5	30
Average Score for Strategy		**5.0**	
Resources			
Customer Service Responsiveness	4	5	20
Flexibility	2	5	10
Gratis Service (no)	2	5	10

Figure C.12   FedEx supplier scorecard.

Supplier management is based on the SCM teams and individuals that have been established for each role. For each supplier and contract, there is an individual who is assigned responsibility for managing the relationship. There is rarely just one supplier — but often there is only one FedEx associate responsible for all ground support, janitorial contracts, etc. His or her job is a mixture of strategic and tactical elements. For example, an associate may be responsible for catalog updates into Ariba and also for updating pricing changes. This poses a challenge to the organization: Should individuals focus on the day-to-day functioning of the contract?

Do they get involved in strategy-level work? How do they get involved in strategy-level issues? Associates are responsible for keeping track of what is happening in a particular market — so they may reinitiate a negotiation with that company and revisit what is happening and how that contract is set up. They are responsible for business process issues. They may get into specification management as well. This may not involve a lot of high-level strategic work, but may require a good deal of coordination work between the supplier and the engineering group. The challenge of how to skill or deskill associates in this area remains problematic.

C.4.5 Business Rules: Controlling Maverick Spend through E-Procurement

There are several different avenues through which purchasing occurs across FedEx. From a services perspective, there may be several different purchase methods. For a product purchase, there are currently three different methods that prevail across all of the operating companies:

1. The most simple is a convenience purchase — an individual goes into a local store and buys something using his or her FedEx badge number as an account reference, takes the invoice back to his or her manager, and it is sent in for a repayment. There is not a lot of control and the manager must give approval prior to purchase.
2. The next area (preferred) is the Ariba Buyer system. This is set up so that users have an online catalog for contracts that are in place — several thousand office supplies are established on the catalog. Requisitioners can find what they want, and once submitted, the request is bounced against a purchase approval policy.

For example, if a FedEx associate needs a PC in his area, he will select a PC online and requisition it. Depending on the threshold, he may need a supervisor's authorization and may need authorization from a higher level as well. If the spend goes into capital range, there is another set of approval rules to ensure that people who approve capital purchases also sign. The process also draws on the business rules from the IT group, which may be contradictory in some cases. Business rules can be enforced within the Ariba Buyer system, depending on the category of spend (see Figure C.13).

The value of this approach is that if FedEx supply management establishes a change in the control levels, it is easy to do. For example, if the CEO mandates a spending freeze (i.e., "No PC's without VP-level

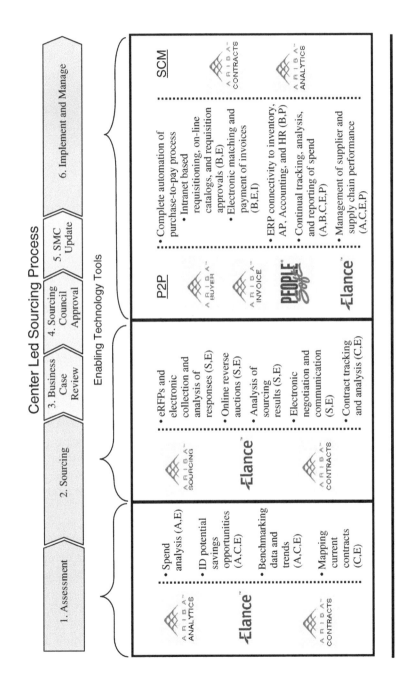

Figure C.13   FedEx technology solutions.

approval"), SCM can change the business rules on the system. (SCM does not handle travel authorization, although it has that capability. FedEx is tied in with airline agreements, so travel agreements are based on a different set of contracts.) FedEx also has another information system for temp labor or contract programmers (ELAMS). ELAMS allows online requisition for contract programmers or temp labor based on contracts that are in place. FedEx controls the rate and type of individual sent out by the supplier and can approve the invoices online. They may have issues with a temp labor contract (e.g., clerk 1 or clerk 2 at a higher rate) and can ensure that if they request a clerk 2, once the individual is sent, FedEx can come back and tell the supplier that they are only going to pay at a certain rate and for certain hours based on performance. This enables users to control the type of person that they actually pay for (in the past, they would not catch this until much later in the procure-to-pay process).

All of FedEx's spending is indirect owing to the nature of their business. A lot of their focus is on indirect materials. However, in maintenance, repair, and operating (MRO) and facility parts, they struggle to control spend. Depending on the product area, they have a greater or lesser ability to control maverick spend. The information they have about spending on indirect items tends to be based on how much they know about the company they are purchasing from and the length of the contract with them. They have a consolidated contract for paper and so have good data on this spend. On MRO, they have only done the first set of national contracts. It has been out of control and it is difficult to get a handle on the baseline spend. They need to do more in terms of understanding this, by linking into internal accounting codes and understanding details of what is being purchased under each category.

FedEx will often do an RFI before they initiate the sourcing process. One of the first things they will do is get a handle on the accounts payable information: who the largest suppliers are, and the details of the sales to FedEx with information on line items. They do that with MRO, and have contracts established with MRO suppliers.

The area in which they have had the most problems is convenience purchases (Joe Mechanic buys something over the counter at the hardware store). To control this, FedEx now uses a monthly electronic report by purchase and by avenue. If an MRO supplier such as Grainger gets 600 orders from Ariba and 100 from invoices, they have a purchase summary that shows all of them. (Convenience means that the individual has an account with that store, and it goes on their account.) FedEx does have a PCARD that has not been extensively implemented — their internal controls group still has a lot of issues to settle — even though they have convenience purchase problems.

Convenience purchases are still not well controlled. Because of the diversity and geographic dispersion of FedEx locations, convenience purchasing is still the most popular and easiest way of buying things. This has been a problem with the operations side of the business, who insist that the sheer simplicity of the process is a good reason for them to continue with the status quo. Convenience purchases have, however, become a problem that has grown and caught the attention of senior management. The individual number of transactions is low, but many, many transactions, particularly those in the MRO area, have grown to epidemic proportions. The total convenience spend is about 5 to 10 percent of all purchases, but 25 to 30 percent of all transactions.

C.4.6 Guidelines for Controlling Maverick Spend

Although FedEx has not yet established a defined spend limit for all categories, certain category limits have been deployed. In office supplies, 60 percent compliance was the initial number and a target of 80 percent was set for the first year (78 percent compliance was achieved in 2002). This was a concerted effort to go after businesses that were not complying.

One SCM associate noted that:

> If our corporate program is at Corporate Express, it is easy to see when the spend is going to Office Depot. Getting support from businesspeople was key in reducing maverick spend. It started off with having SCM people responsible for that area make some calls to purchasers who were using different suppliers. Depending on the nature of their response, different actions would follow. In many cases, the problem may have arisen due to a training issue, as people did not know how to use Ariba. In other cases, people had a competitive purchase and did not want to go through Ariba to purchase those items.

Continuing, this associate commented:

> The approach to influence business units through the Sourcing Council is less of an autocratic approach; it has been moving more toward a mandate approach. In the past this has been done on a product-by-product area basis, but the level of maturity of the program we have had in place is increasing. PCs have been on Ariba for some time, so there has not been a lot of volatility with respect to whom they buy from. It has been taken to a mandate level, whereby accounts payable can

actually agree not to pay the invoice. That mandate becomes something that affects the supplier and so they must take the risk when they send something to supply management for payment. If they have an agreement with Dell and someone buys from IBM, they are in trouble. That individual may be responsible for paying for this with his or her personal funds! (This has been announced but not yet deployed!)

Different mandates have gone out with different people. How do you determine if something is worth addressing at all, or worth putting a strategy around? There is a dollar criterion — is it worth putting a resource on this initiative? In presenting the sourcing process, there are different levels of how extensive the process should be. If FedEx has a large spend in a particular area, they will put forth more resources on doing an in-depth market assessment. For something that turns out to be a $2 million per year spend, the payback may not be worth the resources required to do it. So it becomes a minisourcing initiative done by the SCM group.

System tools can really help in this area. We need to ensure that a solid business case is put together before presenting it to the Sourcing Council. We can also ensure compliance on smaller purchases through Ariba Buyer, which is the avenue for receipts. Users must follow through on receipt of goods at many different geographic locations worldwide; yet, Ariba Buyer can ensure compliance. When an order is received, users have an obligation to enter it into the system, which generates an acknowledgement and a matching invoice in the system. If an individual does not receive it, Ariba will send e-mail reminders that will escalate eventually to senior management.

C.4.7 Moving Forward

Most of the sourcing dashboards to measure performance going forward are primarily cost-focused metrics. The group tracks the results from sourcing initiatives: cost savings, performance relative to market pricing (fuels relative to market pricing), monitoring individual, director, and corporate savings, including diverse supplier development, savings amount, and ROI based on staff and budget. These results are compared in terms of savings generated from one group relative to other directors. Another metric is sourcing timeframes — how long is it taking to implement the sourcing initiatives?

The associate concluded:

One of the biggest challenges in the center-led initiative is: how to get people involved. FedEx had an extensive communications campaign where the strategy was communicated to people, including the long-term vision on where FedEx SCM is headed in the longer term. Within the original FedEx organization, there were no dramatic changes in how things were being done. However, for each of the new operating companies acquired, we are still going through a transition period in which we are allowing people to continue doing business through localized contracts. However, this is changing, as we are slowly moving toward a homogeneous approach from an operating standpoint. Many of the newly acquired operating companies have not done this type of communication, training in core supply-chain skills, and other elements. Most of these people are totally unfamiliar with the seven-step process. Making this change is probably going to be our biggest challenge in the next five years.

Appendix D

Coding Systems

D.1 Most Commonly Used Commodity Classification and Coding Systems

D.1.1 Standard Industrial Classification Codes

Coding systems are a fundamental element in structuring the master data account for spend analysis and management, as well as controlling "maverick" spending. Standard Industrial Classification (SIC) codes are four-digit numerical codes assigned by the U.S. government to identify the primary commerce of business establishments. The classification was developed to facilitate the collection, presentation, and analysis of data, and to promote uniformity and comparability in the presentation of statistical data collected by various agencies of the federal government, state agencies, and private organizations. The classification covers all economic activities: agriculture, forestry, fishing, hunting, and trapping; mining; construction; manufacturing; transportation; communications; electric, gas, and sanitary services; wholesale trade; retail trade; finance, insurance, and real estate; personal, business, professional, repair, recreation, and other services; and public administration.

D.1.1.1 Reading an SIC Code

- The first two digits of the code identify the major industry division.
- The third digit identifies the industry group.
- The fourth digit identifies the industry.

For example:

20 — Major industry group identification: food and kindred products
209 — Industry group identification: miscellaneous food preparations and kindred products
2096 — Industry identification: potato chips, corn chips, and similar snacks

Sometimes, as per the need, it may be necessary to identify specific industries or specific products. SIC codes give companies the flexibility to expand the code to as many as seven digits. For example:

36 — Electronic and other electrical equipment and components, except computer equipment
367 — Electronic components and accessories
3674 — Semiconductors and related devices
3674125 — Random access memory circuits (specific industry/product)

D.1.2 North American Industry Classification System

The North American Industry Classification System (NAICS) is a new economic classification system that replaces the 1987 SIC system for statistical purposes. Similar to the SIC, NAICS is a system for classifying establishments by type of economic activity. Although the principles of the system are the same as for the SIC system, individual industry classification numbers are longer (six digits) and may vary considerably from the SIC codes. This new system was developed jointly by the United States, Canada, and Mexico to make international comparisons easier. Of the 1170 NAICS codes, 358 are new industries, 390 are revised from SIC, and 422 can be compared with the older SIC codes.

D.1.2.1 Reading an NAICS Code

The NAICS is arranged in a hierarchical structure similar to the SIC. The first two digits identify a major economic sector (formerly division), the third digit designates an economic subsector (formerly major group), the fourth digit designates an industry group, and the fifth digit designates the NAICS industry. For example, the NAICS number for potato chips would be:

31 — Major economic sector identification: manufacturing
311 — Economic subsector identification: food manufacturing
3119 — Industry group identification: other food manufacturing
31191 — NAICS industry identification: snack food manufacturing
311919 — Other snack food manufacturing

The internationally agreed-upon NAICS system determines only the first five digits of the code. Use of a sixth digit permits the individual countries to specify subdivisions suited to the country. Thus, five-digit codes are standardized across the three countries, but at the six-digit level, the U.S. codes may differ from those in Canada or Mexico.

D.1.3 National Institute of Governmental Purchasing Codes

The National Institute of Governmental Purchasing (NIGP) commodity classification code is a five-digit code based on the Texas commodity classification system developed in the 1950s. The first three digits of the code denote the group and the last two digits are a specific classification within that group.

D.1.3.1 Example 1

Group code 920 — Data processing, computer, and software services
  Specific classification within group code 920:

  920 21 — Data entry services
  920 22 — Data preparation and processing services

D.1.3.2 Example 2

Group code 918 — Consulting services
  Specific classification within group code 918:

  918 27 — Community development consulting
  918 29 — Computer software consulting

D.1.4 United Nations Standard Products and Services Code

The United Nations Standard Products and Services Code (UNSPSC) is a classification convention that is used to numerically identify all products and services. It is the most efficient, accurate, and flexible classification system available today for achieving companywide visibility of spend analysis, enabling procurement to deliver on cost-effectiveness demands and allowing full exploitation of E-commerce capabilities. The UNSPSC was developed jointly by the UNDP (United Nations Development Programme) and D&B (Dun & Bradstreet Corporation) in 1998.

D.1.4.1 Reading a UNSPSC Code

The UNSPSC is a hierarchical classification with five levels. These levels allow analysis by drilling down or rolling up to analyze expenditures. Each level in the hierarchy has its own unique two-digit code:

- The first level identifies the business segment.
- The second level identifies the family by grouping interrelated commodity categories.
- The third level identifies the class of the product, which groups commodities that share common characteristics.
- The fourth level identifies the commodity or service.
- The fifth level indicates the business function identifier.

An example follows:

Code: 43 20 15 01 14
Segment: 43   Information Technology Broadcasting and telecommunications Communications Devices and Accessories.
Family: 20   Components for information technology or broadcasting or telecommunications Computer Equipment and Accessories.
Class: 15   Computers Computer accessories
Commodity: 01   Computer switch boxes Docking stations
Business Function: 14   Retail

D.1.5 Harmonized Commodity Description and Coding System

The Harmonized Commodity Description and Coding System, generally referred to as "harmonized system" or simply "HS," is a multipurpose international six-digit commodity classification developed by the World Customs Organization (WCO). Individual countries have extended it to ten digits for customs purposes and to eight digits for export purposes. It comprises about 5000 commodity groups, each identified by a six-digit code, arranged in a legal and logical structure, and is supported by well-defined rules to achieve uniform classification. The system is used by more than 177 countries and economies as a basis for their customs tariffs and for the collection of international trade statistics. Over 98 percent of the merchandise in international trade is classified in terms of the HS.

In the HS, goods are classified by what they are, and not according to their stage of fabrication, use, or origin. The HS nomenclature is logically structured by economic activity or component material. For example, animals and animal products are found in one section; machinery and mechanical appliances, which are grouped by function are found in another. The nomenclature is divided into 21 sections. Each of these sections groups together goods produced in the same sector of the economy. For those goods that are grouped by raw material, a vertical structure is used in which articles are often classified according to their degree of processing. For example, one section contains items such as rough wood, wood roughly squared, and some wooden finished products such as wooden tableware. Articles may also be classified according to the use or function.

D.2 Advantages and Disadvantages

Each of the preceding commodity classification and coding systems has its pros and cons relative to maintainability, objectivity, precision, spend coverage, and ability to control "maverick" spend. Table D.1 highlights the advantages and disadvantages of several commodity classification and coding systems.

Table D.1 The Advantages and Disadvantages of Several Commodity Classification and Coding Systems

	Internal Procurement Commodity Codes	SIC	NAICS	UNSPSC
Highly objective and consistently applied	No	Yes	Yes	Yes
Comparable across companies and industries (i.e., mergers and acquisitions)	No	Yes	Yes	Yes
Ability to create comparative metrics versus peers and "best-in-class" companies	No	Yes	Yes	Yes
Industry directories widely available	No	Yes	No	No
Effective in flagging "maverick" spend	No	Yes	Yes	Yes
Estimated number of codes	300–700	11800	18000	13000
High level of granularity	No	Yes	Yes	Yes
Applies to all spend (versus just PO driven)	No	Yes	Yes	Yes
Highly customizable by procurement	Yes	Yes	Yes	Yes

The following sections give industrywise information on NAICS codes and useful Web and print resources.

D.3 Industry: Transportation

D.3.1 NAICS Code

Transportation and Warehousing

481	Air transportation
4811	Scheduled air transportation
48111	Scheduled air transportation
481111	Scheduled passenger air transportation
481112	Scheduled freight air transportation
4812	Nonscheduled air transportation
48121	Nonscheduled air transportation
481211	Nonscheduled chartered passenger air transportation
481212	Nonscheduled chartered freight air transportation
481219	Other nonscheduled air transportation
482	Rail transportation
4821	Rail transportation
48211	Rail transportation
482111	Line-haul railroads
482112	Short line railroads
483	Water transportation
4831	Deep sea, coastal, and great lakes water transportation
48311	Deep sea, coastal, and great lakes water transportation
483111	Deep sea freight transportation
483112	Deep sea passenger transportation
483113	Coastal and great lakes freight transportation
483114	Coastal and great lakes passenger transportation
4832	Inland water transportation
48321	Inland water transportation
483211	Inland water freight transportation
483212	Inland water passenger transportation
484	Truck transportation
4841	General freight trucking
48411	General freight trucking, local
484110	General freight trucking, local
48412	General freight trucking, long distance
484121	General freight trucking, long distance, truckload
484122	General freight trucking, long distance, less than truckload
4842	Specialized freight trucking
48421	Used household and office goods moving

484210	Used household and office goods moving
48422	Specialized freight (except used goods) trucking, local
484220	Specialized freight (except used goods) trucking, local
48423	Specialized freight (except used goods) trucking, long distance
484230	Specialized freight (except used goods) trucking, long distance
485	Transit and ground passenger transportation
4851	Urban transit systems
48511	Urban transit systems
485111	Mixed mode transit systems
485112	Commuter rail systems
485113	Bus and other motor vehicle transit systems
485119	Other urban transit systems
4852	Interurban and rural bus transportation
48521	Interurban and rural bus transportation
485210	Interurban and rural bus transportation
4853	Taxi and limousine service
48531	Taxi service
485310	Taxi service
48532	Limousine service
485320	Limousine service
4854	School and employee bus transportation
48541	School and employee bus transportation
485410	School and employee bus transportation
4855	Charter bus industry
48551	Charter bus industry
485510	Charter bus industry
4859	Other transit and ground passenger transportation
48599	Other transit and ground passenger transportation
485991	Special needs transportation
485999	All other transit and ground passenger transportation
488	Support activities for transportation
4881	Support activities for air transportation
48811	Airport operations
488111	Air traffic control
488119	Other airport operations
48819	Other support activities for air transportation
488190	Other support activities for air transportation
4882	Support activities for rail transportation
48821	Support activities for rail transportation
488210	Support activities for rail transportation
4883	Support activities for water transportation
48831	Port and harbor operations
488310	Port and harbor operations
48832	Marine cargo handling

<u>488320</u>	Marine cargo handling
<u>48833</u>	Navigational services to shipping
<u>488330</u>	Navigational services to shipping
<u>48839</u>	Other support activities for water transportation
<u>488390</u>	Other support activities for water transportation
<u>4884</u>	Support activities for road transportation
<u>48841</u>	Motor vehicle towing
<u>488410</u>	Motor vehicle towing
<u>48849</u>	Other support activities for road transportation
<u>488490</u>	Other support activities for road transportation
<u>4885</u>	Freight transportation arrangement
<u>48851</u>	Freight transportation arrangement
<u>488510</u>	Freight transportation arrangement
<u>4889</u>	Other support activities for transportation
<u>48899</u>	Other support activities for transportation
<u>488991</u>	Packing and crating
<u>488999</u>	All other support activities for transportation

D.3.2 Sources of Information on Supply Market Intelligence

D.3.2.1 Government Sites

Department of Transportation	www.dot.gov
Bureau of Transportation Statistics — Covers all statistics relevant to the nation's transportation systems.	http://www.bts.gov
■ Statistical economic data on individual carrier operations and the air-transportation industry, including data on financial and market/traffic.	http://www.bts.gov/oai/
■ Transportation Statistics Annual Report — Gives the extent to which the system is used and how it affects the economy and people.	http://www.bts.gov/ publications/transportation_ statistics_annual_report/
■ Commodity flow survey — Data on shipments by domestic establishments in manufacturing, wholesale, mining, and selected other industries.	http://www.bts.gov/ntda/cfs/ index.html

■ Intermodal transportation database — For databases on subjects such as safety, freight transport, passenger travel, infrastructure, social and demographic, energy used, environment, national security, and financial and economic data for all modes of transport	http://www.transtats.bts.gov/
■ Transportation indicators such as consumer price index, producer price index, components of transportation-related exports and imports, employment costs, etc.	http://www.transtats.bts.gov/ Indicators.asp?Sel_Cat=0
■ National Transportation Library	http://ntl.bts.gov/index.cfm
■ International transportation statistical programs	http://www.bts.gov/itt/
■ U.S. international travel and transportation trends	http://www.bts.gov/ publications/us_ international_travel_and_ transportation_trends/
■ Geographic information services	http://www.bts.gov/gis/
■ Laws and regulations	http://www.bts.gov/laws_and_ regulations/
■ Publications	http://www.bts.gov/ publications/journal_of_ transportation_statistics/
Federal Aviation Administration for civil aviation safety administration and enforcement	www.faa.gov
Federal Highway Administration for motor carrier safety administration and enforcement — includes freight management and operation, FHWA expertise locator, national traffic and road closure information, transportation operations, and transportation policy	http://www.fhwa.dot.gov/ fhwaweb.htm
Federal Railroad Administration for rail road transportation safety administration and enforcement	http://www.fra.dot.gov

Federal Motor Carrier Safety Administration	http://www.fmcsa.dot.gov/
■ Access to Carrier "Snapshots" — A concise electronic record of a carrier's identification, size, commodity information, safety record, safety rating, roadside out-of-service	http://www.safersys.org/about.shtml
■ Information on authorized for-hire motor carrier, freight forwarder licensing, and insurance data to the industry and public.	http://fmcsa-li.volpe.dot.gov/
■ Analysis and information online	http://ai.volpe.dot.gov/mcspa.asp
Maritime Administration for domestic and foreign waterborne commerce	http://www.marad.dot.gov
National Highway Traffic Safety Administration — Sets and enforces safety performance standards for motor vehicles and equipments	http://www.nhtsa.dot.gov
Research and Special Programs Administration — Sets rules and provides training for safe transportation and packaging of hazardous materials by all modes of transportation	http://www.rspa.dot.gov
Surface Transportation Board — Responsible for economic regulation of interstate surface transportation within the United States and ensures that safe and efficient transportation is provided to the shippers, receivers, and consumers	http://www.stb.dot.gov

D.3.3 *Supply Market Information*

Directories for suppliers in transportation, freight, trucking, fleet maintenance, and software	http://www.logisticsdirectory.com/main.htm
	http://www.logisticsworld.com/
	http://www.cargolog.com/
	http://www.freightworld.com/logistics.html
	http://www.loglink.com/
	http://www.business.smartlook.com/Business/
	    Transportation_and_Logistics/
	http://dir.jayde.com/15565.html
	http://www.azfreight.com/azworld/az-sware.htm
	http://www.logistics-sources.com/logistics-
	    sources/index.html
	http://www.business.com/directory/
	    transportation_and_logistics/
	http://www.business.com/Directory/
	    Transportation_and_Logistics/Trucking/Fleet_
	    Management/Software/
	http://www.costpermile.com/trucking%20co.html
	http://www.fleetowner.com/
	http://www.loadmatch.com/links.cfm

D.4 Industry: Energy and Utilities

D.4.1 *NAICS Code*

<u>221</u> - - Utilities

<u>2211</u> - - - Electric power generation, transmission and distribution
<u>22111</u> - - - - Electric power generation
<u>221111</u> - - - - - Hydroelectric power generation
<u>221112</u> - - - - - Fossil fuel electric power generation
<u>221113</u> - - - - - Nuclear electric power generation
<u>221119</u> - - - - - Other electric power generation
<u>22112</u> - - - - Electric power transmission, control, and distribution
<u>221121</u> - - - - - Electric bulk power transmission and control
<u>221122</u> - - - - - Electric power distribution

<u>2212</u> - - - Natural gas distribution
<u>22121</u> - - - - Natural gas distribution
<u>221210</u> - - - - - Natural gas distribution

2213 - - - Water, sewage and other systems
22131 - - - - Water supply and irrigation systems
221310 - - - - - Water supply and irrigation systems
22132 - - - - Sewage treatment facilities
221320 - - - - - Sewage treatment facilities
22133 - - - - Steam and air-conditioning supply
221330 - - - - - Steam and air-conditioning supply

33531 - - - - Electrical equipment manufacturing
335311 - - - - - Power, distribution, and specialty transformer manufacturing
335312 - - - - - Motor and generator manufacturing
335313 - - - - - Switchgear and switchboard apparatus manufacturing
335314 - - - - - Relay and industrial control manufacturing

3359 - - - Other electrical equipment and component manufacturing

486 - - Pipeline transportation
4861 - - - Pipeline transportation of crude oil
48611 - - - - Pipeline transportation of crude oil
486110 - - - - - Pipeline transportation of crude oil

4862 - - - Pipeline transportation of natural gas
48621 - - - - Pipeline transportation of natural gas
486210 - - - - - Pipeline transportation of natural gas

4869 - - - Other pipeline transportation
48691 - - - - Pipeline transportation of refined petroleum products
486910 - - - - - Pipeline transportation of refined petroleum products

48699 - - - - All other pipeline transportation
486990 - - - - - All other pipeline transportation

D.4.2 Source

http://www.rigmatch.com/ (for oil and gas industry)
http://www.enerfax.com/
http://www.retailenergy.com/links/links.htm
http://www.retailenergy.com/directories/drectory.htm

D.4.3 Supply Market Information

D.4.3.1 Macroenvironment

	Web Sites
Market dynamics	http://www.census.gov/epcd/www/97EC22.HTM
Trade ■ Imports by country and commodity ■ Imports by revenue	http://www.census.gov/foreign-trade/statistics/product/ enduse/imports/index.html http://www.eia.doe.gov/emeu/aer/txt/ptb0104.html
Demographics	http://www.census.gov/population/www/index.html
Political- United States World	http://www.odci.gov/cia/publications/factbook/ index.html
Economic	http://www.eia.doe.gov/oiaf/aeo.index.html http://www.eia.doe.gov/oiaf/aeo/assumption/ macroeconomic.html
Technology environment	
Natural Environment	

D.4.4 Industry Data

D.4.4.1 Oil and Petroleum

	Web Sites
Consumption	www.eia.doe.gov/oil_gas/petroleum/ info_glance/consumption.html
Prices	www.eia.doe.gov/oil_gas/petroleum/ info_glance/prices.html www.eia.doe.gov/emeu/steo/pub/4tab.html
Capacity utilization	www.eia.doe.gov/oil_gas/petroleum/ info_glance/refineryops.htm
Production	www.eia.doe.gov/oil_gas/petroleum/ info_glance/exploration.htm

Economies of substitution	
Forecasts and trends	www.eia.doe.gov/oiaf/aeo/aeotab_11.html
Financial information	www.eia.doe.gov/emeu/finance/indexnjava. html
Export and Import	www.eia.doe.gov/emeu/international/ petroleum.html
Buyers and their usage by industries	www.eia.doe.gov/oiaf/aeo.supplement/ supref.html
Trends and projections	www.eia.doe/oiaf/aeoref_tab.html
Competing demand — current and projected: by industry, by end-product use, and by individual firm	www.eia.doe.gov/oiaf/petgas.html
Capacity utilization situation within the industry: total capacity and capacity utilization rate	www.eia.doe.gov/emeu/cabs/opec.html
Supply origins: local, national, and worldwide	www.eia.doe.gov/geonjava.html
Overall supply and demand condition	www.eia.doe.gov/oiaf/aeo/demand.html

D.4.4.1.1 Supplier Data

	Web Sites	Print Resources
Supplier size: annual sales volume, number of employees, locations, and size of plants or distribution centers	www.hoovers.com/ company/dir/ 0,2116,6131.html	Million Dollar Directory, Corporate affiliations, Plunkett's Energy Industry Almanac
Market share information		Market Share Reporter World Market Share Reporter
Financial ratios information		

Major customers of the supplier		
Organizational ownership		
Supplier capabilities		
Capacity utilization within the firm: total capacity, capacity utilization rate, and expected additions or deletions of capacity		
Order-backlog situation: pricing history, cost structure and trends		
Length of buying firm's relationship with supplier		

D.4.5 Industry Data

D.4.5.1 Electricity

	Web Sites
Consumption	http://www.eia.doe.gov/cneaf/electricity/epm/epmt44p1.html
Prices	http://www.eia.doe.gov/cneaf/electricity/page/fact_sheets/retailprice.html
Capacity utilization	http://www.eia.doe.gov/cneaf/electricity/ipp/html1/t1p01.html
Production	http://www.eia.doe.gov/cneaf/electricity/epm/epmt02p1.html
Economies of substitution	
Forecasts and trends	http://www.eia.doe.gov/oiaf/aeo/index.html#electricity
Financial information	http://www.eia.doe.gov/cneaf/electricity/page/at_a_glance/fi_tabs.html

Export and import	http://www.eia.doe.gov/emeu/international/electric.html#IntlTrade
Buyers and their usage by industries	http://www.eia.doe.gov/emeu/consumption/index.html
Competing demand — current and projected: by industry, by end-product use, and by individual firm	http://www.eia.doe.gov/oiaf/aeo/supplement/index.html
Capacity utilization situation within the industry: total capacity and capacity utilization rate	http://www.eia.doe.gov/emeu/efficiency/ee_report_html.htm
Supply origins: local, national, and worldwide	http://www.eia.doe.gov/cneaf/electricity/page/at_a_glance/gu_tabs.html
Overall supply and demand condition	http://www.eia.doe.gov/cneaf/electricity/epm/epmt02p1.html

D.4.5.1.1 Supplier Data

	Web Sites
Manufacturing process	
Raw materials: quantity, location, and supply and demand conditions	www.eia.doe/emeu/aer/elect.html
Primary and secondary product uses	
Economics of substitution	www.fe.doe.gov/programs_coalpower.html www.eere.energy.gov/greenpower/intro.shtml
Cost structure and trends for : past, present, and future	www.eia.doe.gov/cneaf/electricity/page/at_a_glance/fue_tabs.html
Pricing trends: past, present, and future	www.eia.doe.gov/cneaf/electricity/page/at_a_glance/sales_tabs.html
Identification of key suppliers in the industry	

Type and level of competition within the industry: price, quality, delivery, and supply	www.eia.doe.gov/cneaf/electricity/epav1/wholesale.html#tab12
Availability and number of suppliers	
Technology trends	
Identification of the major buyers within the industry	
Competing demand, current and projected: by industry, by end-product use, and by individual firm	
Capacity utilization situation within the industry: total capacity and capacity utilization rate	www.eia.doe.gov/cneaf/electricity/page/capacity.html
Supply origins: local, national, and worldwide	
Overall supply and demand condition	

D.4.6 Industry Data

D.4.6.1 Coal Industry

	Web Sites
Consumption	http://www.eia.doe.gov/cneaf/coal/data/coalconsum.html
Prices	http://www.eia.doe.gov/cneaf/coal/data/coalprice.html
Capacity utilization	http://www.eia.doe.gov/cneaf/coal/data/coalenduse.html
Production	http://www.eia.doe.gov/cneaf/coal/data/coalproduct.html
Economies of substitution	

Forecasts and trends	http://www.eia.doe.gov/oiaf/aeo/forecast.html#coal
Financial information	
Export and import	http://www.eia.doe.gov/cneaf/coal/data/coalimports.html http://www.eia.doe.gov/cneaf/coal/data/coalexport.html
Buyers and their usage by industries	http://www.eia.doe.gov/cneaf/coal/data/sectors.html#all_sec
Competing demand — current and projected: by industry, by end-product use, and by individual firm	http://www.eia.doe.gov/cneaf/coal/page/coaldistrib/coaldistrib.html
Capacity utilization situation within the industry: total capacity and capacity utilization rate	http://www.eia.doe.gov/cneaf/coal/data/coalreserv.html
Supply origins: local, national, and worldwide	http://www.eia.doe.gov/cneaf/coal/data/coalproduct.html
Overall supply and demand condition	http://www.eia.doe.gov/cneaf/coal/page/coaldistrib/coaldistrib.html

D.4.6.2 Nuclear Fuel

	Web Sites
Consumption	
Prices	
Capacity utilization	http://www.eia.doe.gov/cneaf/nuclear/page/spent_fuel/radsum.html
Production	http://www.eia.doe.gov/cneaf/nuclear/page/nuc_generation/gensum.html
Economies of substitution	
Forecasts and trends	http://www.eia.doe.gov/cneaf/nuclear/page/forecast/foresum.html
Financial information	
Export and Import	

Buyers and their usage by industries	
Competing demand, current and projected: by industry, by end-product use, and by individual firm	
Capacity utilization situation within the industry: total capacity and capacity utilization rate	
Supply origins: local, national, and worldwide	http://www.eia.doe.gov/cneaf/nuclear/page/ nuc_generation/gensum.html
Overall supply and demand condition	

D.5 Industry: Information Technology

D.5.1 NAICS Code

3341 - - - Computer and peripheral equipment manufacturing
33411 - - - - Computer and peripheral equipment manufacturing
334111 - - - - - Electronic computer manufacturing
334112 - - - - - Computer storage device manufacturing
334113 - - - - - Computer terminal manufacturing
334119 - - - - - Other computer peripheral equipment manufacturing

42343 - - - - Computer and computer peripheral equipment and software merchant
    wholesalers
423430 - - - - - Computer and computer peripheral equipment and
    software merchant wholesalers

516 - - Internet publishing and broadcasting
5161 - - - Internet publishing and broadcasting
51611 - - - - Internet publishing and broadcasting
516110 - - - - - Internet publishing and broadcasting
517 - - Telecommunications
5171 - - - Wired telecommunications carriers
51711 - - - - Wired telecommunications carriers
517110 - - - - - Wired telecommunications carriers
5172 - - - Wireless telecommunications carriers (except satellite)

<u>51721</u> - - - - Wireless telecommunications carriers (except satellite)
<u>517211</u> - - - - - Paging
<u>517212</u> - - - - - Cellular and other wireless telecommunications
<u>5173</u> - - - Telecommunications resellers
<u>51731</u> - - - - Telecommunications resellers
<u>517310</u> - - - - - Telecommunications resellers
<u>5174</u> - - - Satellite telecommunications
<u>51741</u> - - - - Satellite telecommunications
<u>517410</u> - - - - - Satellite telecommunications
<u>5175</u> - - - Cable and other program distribution
<u>51751</u> - - - - Cable and other program distribution
<u>517510</u> - - - - - Cable and other program distribution
<u>5179</u> - - - Other telecommunications
<u>51791</u> - - - - Other telecommunications
<u>517910</u> - - - - - Other telecommunications
<u>518</u> - - Internet service providers, Web search portals, and data processing services
<u>5181</u> - - - Internet service providers and Web search portals
<u>51811</u> - - - - Internet service providers and Web search portals
<u>518111</u> - - - - - Internet service providers
<u>518112</u> - - - - - Web search portals
<u>5182</u> - - - Data processing, hosting, and related services
<u>51821</u> - - - - Data processing, hosting, and related services
<u>518210</u> - - - - - Data processing, hosting, and related services

<u>5415</u> - - - Computer systems design and related services
<u>54151</u> - - - - Computer systems design and related services
<u>541511</u> - - - - - Custom computer programming services
<u>541512</u> - - - - - Computer systems design services
<u>541513</u> - - - - - Computer facilities management services
<u>541519</u> - - - - - Other computer related services

D.5.2 Industry Market Information

	Web sites
Industry outlook	www.itaa.org/news
Data on computer and Internet usage	www.bls.census.gov/cps/computer/ computer.htm

International trade research by	
■ Country/regional	www.ita.doc.gov/ITI/itiHome.nsf/ cntryRegInfo?Openform
■ Industry/sector	www.ita.doc.gov/ITI/itiHome.nsf/ IndSectorInfo?Openform
■ IT reports and market briefs	www.ita.doc.gov/ITI/itiHome.nsf/ ExportITReports?Openform
■ Publications	www.ita.doc.gov/ITI/itiHome.nsf/ PublicNewsletter?Openform
Issues and policies, IT, and macroeconomy	www.itic.org/issues_policies/ www.rosettanet.org
Information on federal networking and information technology research and development	www.ccic.gov
Information Technology Laboratory of the National Institute of Standards	www.itl.nist.gov
Minority business development (size and distribution of minority-owned business in IT field)	www.mbda.gov
Research on diversity within IT industry — Recognition of companies employing women, minorities in high-tech force	www.itaa.org/workforce/studies/ diversityreport.pdf http://www.sbaonline.sba.gov/financing/ special/women.html
Statistical data	www.itic.org/isp/index.html

D.5.3 Supplier Market Data

D.5.3.1 Computer Software

	Web sites
Research and forecasts ■ by industry ■ by company	www.hoovers.com/industry/snapshot/ 0,2204,13,00.html www.hoovers.com/company/dir/ 0,2116,4798,00.html www.marcopolo.com

Pricing	www.pricewatch.com
White paper and analyst report database	www.whitepapersandreports.itworld.com/ data/rlist?t=soft_10_90 www.itpapers.zdnet.com www.computerworld.com/softwaretopics/ software
Reviews	www.reviews.cnet.com www.eopinions.com/cmsw-Software-All www.itreviews.co.uk/software/software.htm www.irt.org/software/index.htm www.webdevelopersjournal.com/software/ softlead.html
Regulations	www.bsa.org www.gigalaw.com
Company search	www.wetfeet.com/research/companies.asp

D.5.3.1.1 Link to Hoover's Directory

Computer Software & Services — Diversified Software

Computer Software & Services — Multimedia Production, Graphics & Publishing Software

Computer Software & Services — Entertainment & Games Software

Computer Software & Services — Educational Software

Computer Software & Services — Document Management Software

Computer Software & Services — Database & File Management Software

Computer Software & Services — Corporate, Professional & Financial Software

Computer Software & Services — Manufacturing & Industrial Software

Computer Software & Services — Engineering, Scientific & CAD/CAM Software

Computer Software & Services — Networking & Connectivity Software

Computer Software & Services — Communications Software

Computer Software & Services — Internet & Intranet Software & Services

Computer Software & Services — Other Application Software

Computer Software & Services — Development Tools, Operating Systems & Utility Software

Computer Software & Services — Security Software & Services

D.5.3.2 Computer Services

■ Application service providers (ASP)
  – News
    ■ www.cio.com/summaries/outsourcing/asp
    ■ www.computerworld.com/managementtopics/xsp/asp
    ■ www.vunet.com/Specials/1104943
  – Company directory
    ■ www.links.aspnews.com
    ■ www.aspstreet.com/directory
    ■ www.knowledgestorm.com
    ■ www.asp.thelist.com
    ■ www.webharbor.com
■ Consulting services
  – www.consultlink.com
  – www.iversonsoftware.com/directory.asp
  – www.supplychainredesign.com
■ Knowledge management services
■ Internet business services

	Web sites
Research and forecasts ■ by industry ■ by company	http://www.hoovers.com/industry/snapshot/0,2204,58,00.html http://www.hoovers.com/company/dir/0,2116,4798,00.html www.aberdeen.com www.amrresearch.com
Pricing	www.pricewatch.com
White paper and analyst reports	http://www.computerworld.com/services www.itpapers.zdnet.com www.supplychainredesign.com
Reviews	http://www.informationweek.com/techcenters/itservices http://www.byte.com/ http://www.bitpipe.com/
Regulations	www.bsa.org
Outsourcing	www.outsourcing.com

D.5.3.3 Mobile and Wireless Technology

- News and features
  - www.allnetdevices.com
  - www.crblaw.com
  - www.wireless.ittoolbox.com
  - www.wow-com.com/research
  - www.fcc.gov/wcb/iatd/
  - www.wirelessweek.com
  - www.itworld.com/wire/
  - http://www.bit-pipe.com/data/tlist?b=blat_wireless&src=BPHOME_BLAT_Wireless

D.5.3.4 Computer Hardware

	Web sites
Research and forecasts ■ by industry ■ by company	http://www.hoovers.com/industry/snapshot/ 0,2204,12,00.html http://www.hoovers.com/company/dir/ 0,2116,6123,00.html www.marcopolo.com
Pricing	http://shopper.cnet.com/ www.pricewatch.com
White paper and analyst report database	www.itworld.com/Comp/ www.itpapers.zdnet.com http://www.computerworld.com/ hardwaretopics/hardware
Reviews	http://reviews.cnet.com/ http://www.itreviews.co.uk/hardware/ hardware.htm www.bitpipe.com
Regulations	www.bsa.org www.gigalaw.com
Company research	www.wetfeet.com/research/companies.asp

D.5.3.5 Computer Networking

	Web sites
Research and forecasts ■ by industry ■ by company	http://www.hoovers.com/industry/snapshot/ 0,2204,12,00.html http://www.hoovers.com/company/dir/ 0,2116,6123,00.html www.marcopolo.com
Pricing	http://shopper.cnet.com/ www.pricewatch.com
White paper, news, and analyst reports	www.itworld.com/Net/ www.itpapers.zdnet.com http://www.computerworld.com/ networkingtopics/networking www.commweb.com www.commnews.com www.networking.ittoolbox.com
Reviews	http://reviews.cnet.com/ http:///www.bitpipe.com www.zdnet.com
Regulations	www.bsa.org www.gigalaw.com
Company research	www.wetfeet.com/research/companies.asp

D.6 Industry: Plastics
D.6.1 NAICS Code

Plastics and Rubber Products Manufacturing

3261   Plastics product manufacturing

32611   Plastics packaging materials and unlaminated film and sheet manufacturing

326111   Plastics bag manufacturing

326112   Plastics packaging film and sheet (including laminated) manufacturing

326113   Unlaminated plastics film and sheet (except packaging) manufacturing

32612   Plastics pipe, pipe fitting, and unlaminated profile shape manufacturing

326121   Unlaminated plastics profile shape manufacturing

326122   Plastics pipe and pipe fitting manufacturing

32613   Laminated plastics plate, sheet (except packaging), and shape manufacturing

326130   Laminated plastics plate, sheet (except packaging), and shape manufacturing

32614   Polystyrene foam product manufacturing

326140   Polystyrene foam product manufacturing

32615   Urethane and other foam product (except polystyrene) manufacturing

326150   Urethane and other foam product (except polystyrene) manufacturing

32616   Plastics bottle manufacturing

326160   Plastics bottle manufacturing

32619   Other plastics product manufacturing

326191   Plastics plumbing fixture manufacturing

326192   Resilient floor covering manufacturing

326199   All other plastics product manufacturing

Plastics and Rubber Industry Machinery Manufacturing

333220   Plastics and Rubber Industry Machinery Manufacturing

Source: http://www.census.gov/epcd/www/naics.html

Plastics industry statistics:
http://www.americanplasticscouncil.org/benefits/economic/economic.html

Economic statistics: http://www.plasticsindustry.org/industry/econstat.htm

Sources for plastics information:
http://www.plasticsindustry.org/industry/sources.htm

Plastics market forecasts and analyses:
http://www.plasticseconomics.com/outside.htm

Recycled plastics products & markets directory:

http://www.plasticsresource.com/s_plasticsresource/sec.asp?TRACKID=&CID=86&DID=127

Society of the plastics industry — buyer guide: www.spidirectory.com

Worldwide trading site for information on trade in the plastics industry: http://www.plasticx.com

Current economic analysis of the U.S. plastics industry: http://www.plasticsdatasource.org

Database of secondary plastics for sale: http://www.apexq.com/

News, information, plastics directory etc: http://www.plastics.com/

Database of suppliers of plastics materials:

http://www.plastics-ez.com/plastics/0055919_0055919_1.html

International Association of Plastics Distributors Web site, for standard product database, industry statistics, and inventory database: http://www. e-plastics.org/about.html

Some online plastics vendors:

> http://www.plasticlink.com/default.htm
> http://www.e-resin.com/index.cfm
> http://www.ask4plastic.com/
> www.plasticsrendezvous.com
> www.theplasticsexchange.com
> www.plasticscommerce.com

Service to purchasers of plastics products:

> http://www.plastic-solvers.com/default.asp?id=3

D.7 Industry: Services

D.7.1 Travel

487 -- Scenic and sightseeing transportation
4871 --- Scenic and sightseeing transportation, land
48711 ---- Scenic and sightseeing transportation, land
487110 ----- Scenic and sightseeing transportation, land
4872 --- Scenic and sightseeing transportation, water
48721 ---- Scenic and sightseeing transportation, water
487210 ----- Scenic and sightseeing transportation, water
4879 --- Scenic and sightseeing transportation, other
48799 ---- Scenic and sightseeing transportation, other
487990 ----- Scenic and sightseeing transportation, other

<u>5615</u> - - - Travel arrangement and reservation services
<u>56151</u> - - - - Travel agencies
<u>561510</u> - - - - - Travel agencies
<u>56152</u> - - - - Tour operators
<u>561520</u> - - - - - Tour operators
<u>56159</u> - - - - Other travel arrangement and reservation services
<u>561591</u> - - - - - Convention and visitors bureaus
<u>561599</u> - - - - - All other travel arrangement and reservation services

D.7.2 Security Service

<u>5616</u> - - - Investigation and security services
<u>56161</u> - - - - Investigation, guard, and armored car services
<u>561611</u> - - - - - Investigation services
<u>561612</u> - - - - - Security guards and patrol services
<u>561613</u> - - - - - Armored car services
<u>56162</u> - - - - Security systems services
<u>561621</u> - - - - - Security systems services (except locksmiths)
<u>561622</u> - - - - - Locksmiths

D.7.3 Services to Buildings and Dwellings

<u>5617</u> - - - Services to buildings and dwellings
<u>56171</u> - - - - Exterminating and pest control services
<u>561710</u> - - - - - Exterminating and pest control services

D.7.4 Janitorial Service

<u>56172</u> - - - - Janitorial services
<u>561720</u> - - - - - Janitorial services
<u>56173</u> - - - - Landscaping services
<u>561730</u> - - - - - Landscaping services
<u>56174</u> - - - - Carpet and upholstery cleaning services
<u>561740</u> - - - - - Carpet and upholstery cleaning services
<u>56179</u> - - - - Other services to buildings and dwellings
<u>561790</u> - - - - - Other services to buildings and dwellings

D.7.5 Packaging and Other Services

<u>5619</u> - - - Other support services
<u>56191</u> - - - - Packaging and labeling services
<u>561910</u> - - - - - Packaging and labeling services

<u>56192</u> - - - - Convention and trade show organizers
<u>561920</u> - - - - - Convention and trade show organizers
<u>56199</u> - - - - All other support services
<u>561990</u> - - - - - All other support services

D.7.6 Maintenance

<u>811</u> - - Repair and maintenance
<u>8111</u> - - - Automotive repair and maintenance
<u>81111</u> - - - - Automotive mechanical and electrical repair and maintenance
<u>811111</u> - - - - - General automotive repair
<u>811112</u> - - - - - Automotive exhaust system repair
<u>811113</u> - - - - - Automotive transmission repair
<u>811118</u> - - - - - Other automotive mechanical and electrical repair and maintenance
<u>81112</u> - - - - Automotive body, paint, interior, and glass repair
<u>811121</u> - - - - - Automotive body, paint, and interior repair and maintenance
<u>811122</u> - - - - - Automotive glass replacement shops
<u>81119</u> - - - - Other automotive repair and maintenance
<u>811191</u> - - - - - Automotive oil change and lubrication shops
<u>811192</u> - - - - - Car washes
<u>811198</u> - - - - - All other automotive repair and maintenance
<u>8112</u> - - - Electronic and precision equipment repair and maintenance
<u>81121</u> - - - - Electronic and precision equipment repair and maintenance
<u>811211</u> - - - - - Consumer electronics repair and maintenance
<u>811212</u> - - - - - Computer and office machine repair and maintenance
<u>811213</u> - - - - - Communication equipment repair and maintenance
<u>811219</u> - - - - - Other electronic and precision equipment repair and maintenance
<u>8113</u> - - - Commercial and industrial machinery and equipment (except automotive and electronic) repair and maintenance
<u>81131</u> - - - - Commercial and industrial machinery and equipment (except automotive and electronic) repair and maintenance
<u>811310</u> - - - - - Commercial and industrial machinery and equipment (except automotive and electronic) repair and maintenance
<u>8114</u> - - - Personal and household goods repair and maintenance
<u>81141</u> - - - - Home and garden equipment and appliance repair and maintenance
<u>811411</u> - - - - - Home and garden equipment repair and maintenance
<u>811412</u> - - - - - Appliance repair and maintenance
<u>81142</u> - - - - Reupholstery and furniture repair
<u>811420</u> - - - - - Reupholstery and furniture repair
<u>81143</u> - - - - Footwear and leather goods repair
<u>811430</u> - - - - - Footwear and leather goods repair
<u>81149</u> - - - - Other personal and household goods repair and maintenance
<u>811490</u> - - - - - Other personal and household goods repair and maintenance

Business Expenses: http://www.census.gov/prod/ec97/e97cs-8.pdf

Statistics related to services http://www.census.gov/prod/2003pubs/ 02statab/services.pdf

International statistics: http://www.census.gov/prod/2002pubs/ 01statab/intlstat.pdf

Price index: http://www.census.gov/prod/2003pubs/02statab/ prices.pdf

Revenue coefficients of ratios and year-to-year ratios: http://www. census.gov/prod/2003pubs/sas-01.pdf

Demographics: http://www.census.gov/prod/cen2000/dp1/2kh00.pdf

D.7.7 Primary Metal Manufacturing

3311 --- Iron and steel mills and ferroalloy manufacturing

33111 ---- Iron and steel mills and ferroalloy manufacturing

331111 ----- Iron and steel mills

331112 ----- Electrometallurgical ferroalloy product manufacturing

3312 --- Steel product manufacturing from purchased steel

33121 ---- Iron and steel pipe and tube manufacturing from purchased steel

331210 ----- Iron and steel pipe and tube manufacturing from purchased steel

33122 ---- Rolling and drawing of purchased steel

331221 ----- Rolled steel shape manufacturing

331222 ----- Steel wire drawing

D.8 Industry: Steel Manufacturing

D.8.1 NAICS Code for Steel Manufacturing

Source for statistical information on North American steel industry including steel production, government policy : http://www.steel.org/stats/

Steel Manufacturers Association Web site containing list of 39 North American companies and 6 international steel company, and suppliers to steel industry: http://www.steelnet.org

Statistics on steel industry price, trend analyzes and forecasts and steel industry search engine available at : http://www.steelonthenet.com

World steel information (International Iron and Steel Institute Web site): http://www.worldsteel.org/

Association of Iron and Steel Engineers (from global steel industry) Web site catering to steel manufacturing technology information, news and reports: http://www.aise.org/

Directory of iron and steel plants: http://www.steellinks.com/

International coverage of steel technology projects: http://www.
 steel-technology.com/projects/index.html

Monthly newsletter that analyzes and forecasts the economic health of
 five metal industries including steel: http://minerals.er.usgs.gov/
 minerals/pubs/mii/

Supplier news in the magazine published by Iron & Steel Society:
 http://www.iss.org/4magazine/magazine.shtml

Specialty Steel Industry of North America — A trade association of producers of specialty steel: www.ssina.com

Source: www.census.gov

D.8.2 Supplier Lists

Steel Manufacturers Association Web site containing list of 39 North
 American companies and 6 international steel companies, and
 suppliers to steel industry: http://www.steelnet.org

Internet site for buying and selling steel: http://www.metalsite.net/

Trading platform for steel buyers and suppliers: http://www.
 steelspider.com/Default.aspx

News on world steel industry, listing of world steel traders:
 www.SteelMill.com

North American Steel Producers: http://www.steelnews.org/
 companies/producers.htm

Distributors/manufacturers of stainless steel and specialty steel products
 Web sites available at: http://www.steelynx.net/

Steel quotes, prices, suppliers, distributors: http://www.procuresteel.com/

Some steel vendors:
http://www.straightline.com/straightline/welcome/index.html
www.eBigChina.com

D.9 Industry: Textiles

D.9.1 NAICS Code

313 --Textile mills
3131 ---Fiber, yarn, and thread mills
31311 ----Fiber, yarn, and thread mills
313111 -----Yarn spinning mills
313112 -----Yarn texturizing, throwing, and twisting mills
313113 -----Thread mills
3132 ---Fabric mills

31321 - - - -Broadwoven fabric mills
31322 - - - -Narrow fabric mills and schiffli machine embroidery
313221 - - - - -Narrow fabric mills
313222 - - - - -Schiffli machine embroidery
31323 - - - -Nonwoven fabric mills
31324 - - - -Knit fabric mills
313241 - - - - -Weft knit fabric mills
313249 - - - - -Other knit fabric and lace mills
3133 - - -Textile and fabric finishing and fabric coating mills
31331 - - - -Textile and fabric finishing mills
313311 - - - - -Broadwoven fabric finishing mills
313312 - - - - -Textile and fabric finishing (except broadwoven fabric) mills
31332 - - - -Fabric coating mills

Source: http://www.census.gov/epcd/www/naics.html

D.9.1.1 Fabric Coating Mills

313320 - - - - -Fabric coating mills
314 - -Textile product mills
3141 - - -Textile furnishings mills
31411 - - - -Carpet and rug mills
314110 - - - - -Carpet and rug mills
31412 - - - -Curtain and linen mills
314121 - - - - -Curtain and drapery mills
314129 - - - - -Other household textile product mills
3149 - - -Other textile product mills
31491 - - - -Textile bag and canvas mills
314911 - - - - -Textile bag mills
314912 - - - - -Canvas and related product mills
31499 - - - -All other textile product mills
314991 - - - - -Rope, cordage, and twine mills
314992 - - - - -Tire cord and tire fabric mills
314999 - - - - -All other miscellaneous textile product mills

D.9.1.2 Apparel Manufacturing

3151 - - -Apparel knitting mills
31511 - - - -Hosiery and sock mills
315111 - - - - -Sheer hosiery mills
315119 - - - - -Other hosiery and sock mills
31519 - - - -Other apparel knitting mills
315191 - - - - -Outerwear knitting mills
315192 - - - - -Underwear and nightwear knitting mills
3152 - - -Cut and sew apparel manufacturing

31521 ----Cut and sew apparel contractors
315211 -----Men's and boys' cut and sew apparel contractors
315212 -----Women's, girls', and infants' cut and sew apparel contractors
31522 ----Men's and boys' cut and sew apparel manufacturing
315221 -----Men's and boys' cut and sew underwear and nightwear
    manufacturing
315222 -----Men's and boys' cut and sew suit, coat, and overcoat manufacturing
315223 -----Men's and boys' cut and sew shirt (except work shirt) manufacturing
315224 -----Men's and boys' cut and sew trouser, slack, and jean manufacturing
315225 -----Men's and boys' cut and sew work clothing manufacturing
315228 -----Men's and boys' cut and sew other outerwear manufacturing
31523 ----Women's and girls' cut and sew apparel manufacturing
315231 -----Women's and girls' cut and sew lingerie, loungewear, and nightwear
    manufacturing
315232 -----Women's and girls' cut and sew blouse and shirt manufacturing
315233 -----Women's and girls' cut and sew dress manufacturing
315234 -----Women's and girls' cut and sew suit, coat, tailored jacket, and skirt
    manufacturing
315239 -----Women's and girls' cut and sew other outerwear manufacturing
31529 ----Other cut and sew apparel manufacturing
315291 -----Infants' cut and sew apparel manufacturing
315292 -----Fur and leather apparel manufacturing
315299 -----All other cut and sew apparel manufacturing
3159 ---Apparel accessories and other apparel manufacturing
31599 ----Apparel accessories and other apparel manufacturing
315991 -----Hat, cap, and millinery manufacturing
315992 -----Glove and mitten manufacturing
315993 -----Men's and boys' neckwear manufacturing
315999 -----Other apparel accessories and other apparel manufacturing
333292 -----Textile machinery manufacturing

D.9.2 Supply Market Information

D.9.2.1 Macroenvironment

Market dynamics	http://www.census.gov/prod/ http://www.whitehouse.gov/fsbr/prices.html
World trade	http://www.census.gov/foreign-trade/www/index.html http://www.state.gov/www/about_state/business/ com_guides/index.html http://www.tradenet.gov/
Demographics	http://www.census.gov/population/www/index.html
Political	http://www.bls.gov/blshome.htm http://www.asaenet.org/main/

Economic	http://w3.access.gpo.gov/eop/ http://econ.worldbank.org/ http://www.imf.org/
Natural environment	
Technology environment	http://www.infotechtrends.com/ http://www.informationweek.com/

D.9.2.2 Data To Be Collected

- Manufacturing process
- Raw materials: quantity, location, and supply and demand conditions
- Primary product uses; secondary product uses
- Economics of substitution
- Cost structure and trends for past, present, and future
- Pricing trends: past, present, and future
- Identification of key suppliers in the industry
- Type and level of competition found within the industry: price, quality, delivery, supply
- Availability, and number of suppliers
- Technology trends
- Identification of the major buyers within the industry
- Competing demand, current and projected: by industry, by end-product users, and by individual firms
- Capacity utilization situation within the industry: total capacity, and capacity utilization rate
- Supply origins: local, national, and worldwide
- Overall supply and demand conditions

D.9.3 Resource Directories

1. America's Textiles International — The Textile Redbook. Billion Publishing, Inc
2. Davison's Gold Book — Davison's Publishing Co.
3. Textile World Blue Book — Primedia business magazine and media
4. Davison's Textile Blue Book
5. Market Share Reporter
6. Moody's International Manual

D.9.4 Online Databases

1. World Textile, Elsevier Science, Inc.
2. Textile Technology Digest
3. Thomas Register of American Manufacturers

D.9.5 Periodicals and Newsletter

1. America's Textile International
2. International Textile Bulletin

D.9.6 Web Sites

1. http://www.business2.com/webguide
2. http://www.manufacturing.net/
3. http://www.textileweb.com
4. http://www.textileworld.com/

D.10 General Web Sites

1. http://www.statistics.com/cgi-bin/search/hyperseek.cgi
2. www.economy.com
3. www.marketshare.com
4. www.dismal.com
5. www.edgar-online.com
6. www.gartnergroup.com
7. www.ibisworld.com

D.11 Paid Services

1. www.supplierinsight.com
2. www.bizadvantage.com
3. www.dnb.telebase.com
4. www.parassolutions.com
5. www.purchasingresearchservice.com

D.12 Financial Ratios Information

D.12.1 Resource Directories

1. Quarterly financial report for manufacturing, mining, and trade corporations (published from U.S. Government Printing Office)
2. Almanac of business and industrial financial ratios
3. IRS corporate financial ratios
4. http://www.carol.co.uk/
5. http://www.lib.washington.edu/business/ratios/
6. http://www.wsrn.com/

D.13 Supplier Data To Be Collected

- Supplier size: Annual sales volume; number of employees; number, locations, and size of plants or distribution centers
- Major customers of the supplier
- Market share information
- Organizational ownership
- Supplier capabilities, regarding: management team, logistical, financial resources, R&D, work
- force composition, responsiveness, engineering, flexibility, manufacturing, and systems
- Capacity utilization situation within the firm: total capacity, capacity utilization rate, and expected additions or deletions of capacity
- Order-backlog situation; pricing history; cost structure and trends
- Length of buying firm's relationship with supplier

D.14 Purchase Order Data To Be Collected

- Quoted price
- Delivery lead time
- Transportation cost
- Duties and customs
- Insurance
- Frequency of shipment
- Tooling cost
- Ordering, inbound and quality inspection costs
- Ramp-up time

- Denomination of contract
- On-time delivery record
- Any known quality problems

D.15 Sourcing Relationship

Acquisition — Spots, buys, integration
Multiple — Exchanges
Leverage — Reverse auctions
Strategic — Sourcing process

D.16 Factors To Be Considered for Strategic Sourcing Process

- Cost/price reduction
- Quality improvements
- Delivery improvements
- Technology improvements
- Reduce cycle time in new product development
- Increase responsiveness
- Reduce the number of suppliers

Appendix E

References and Resources

Aaker, Kumar, and Day, R., *Marketing Research,* New York: John Wiley & Sons, 1998, p. 73.

Aimi, G., Cecere, L., and Souza, J., Stressed supply lines threaten christmas this year and years to come, *AMR Research,* November 18, 2004, http://www.amrresearch.com/Content/view.asp?pmillid=17766.

Alchian, A., Some economics of property rights, *Il Politico,* 1965.

Bassett, G., Searching without boundaries: the bi and enterprise search paradox, *DM Review,* September 2004, DMReview.com.

Broadbent, M. and Weill, P., Management by maxim: how business and it managers can create infrastructures, *Sloan Management Review,* 77–88, Spring 1997.

Bryan, L., Making a market in knowledge, *The McKinsey Quarterly,* No. 3, 2004.

Cabarra, J.D., Martin J., and Gabbard, J.D., What's on the books: other laws affecting purchasing and supply, *The Purchasing and Supply Yearbook,* Ed., John A. Woods, New York: McGraw-Hill, 2000, pp. 332–339.

Combs, J.G. and Ketchen, D.J., Jr., Explaining interfirm cooperation and performance: toward a reconciliation of predictions from the resource-based view and organizational economics, *Strategic Management Journal,* 20, 867–888, 1999.

Dahlman, C.J., *The Open Field System and Beyond,* New York: Cambridge University Press, 1980.

Drucker, P., *The Practice of Management,* 1956, p. 214.

Dubois, F.L. and Carmel, E., Information technology and leadtime management in international manufacturing operations, *Global Information Systems and Technology: Focus on the Organization and its Functional Areas,* P.C. Deans and K.R. Karwan, Eds., London: Idea Group Publishing, 1994, pp. 279–293.

Dyer, J., Effect interfirm collaboration: how firms minimize transaction costs and maximize transaction value, *Strategic Management Journal,* 18, 553–556, 1997.

Dyer, J., Four Papers on Governance, Asset Specialization, and Performance: A Comparative Study of Supplier-Automaker Relationships in the U.S. and Japan, Unpublished dissertation, Los Angeles, University of California, California, February, 1994.

Dyer, J. and Ouchi, W., Japanese-style partnerships: giving companies a competitive edge, *Sloan Management Review* 35, 51–63, 1993.

Galbraith, J.R., *Competing with Flexible Lateral Organizations,* 2nd ed., Reading, MA: Addison-Wesley, 1993, pp. 1–11.

Garud, R. and Jain, S., The embeddedness of technological systems, In J. Baum and J. Dutton, Eds., *Advances in Strategic Management,* Greenwich, CT: JAI Press, 1996, pp. 389–408.

Giunipero, L., and Handfield, R., *Purchasing Education and Training Requirements for the Future,* Tempe, AZ: Center for Advanced Purchasing Studies, in press.

Goodhue, D.L., Kirsch, L.J., Quillard, J.A., and Wybo, M.D., Strategic data planning: lessons from the field, *MIS Quarterly* 16, 11–34, 1992.

Goodhue, D., Wybo, M.D., and Kirsch, L.J. The impact of data integration on the costs and benefits, *MIS Quarterly* 16, 293–321, 1992.

Granovetter, M., Problems of explanation in economic sociology, N. Nohria and R. Eccles, Eds., *Networks and Organizations: Structure Form and Action,* Boston, MA: Harvard Business School Press, 1992, pp. 25–56.

Hagedoorn, J. and Narula, R., Choosing organizational modes of strategic technology partnering: international sectoral differences, *Journal of International Business Studies* 27, 265–284, 1996.

Hameed, S. and Escande, M., The People Factor: Accelerating Supply Chain Transformation through Education, working paper, 2004.

Handfield, R. and Bechtel, C., The role of trust and relationship structure in improving supply chain responsiveness, *Industrial Marketing Management,* 31, 1–16, 2001.

Handfield, R. and Giunipero, L., Purchasing and Education Training Requirements, Center for Advanced Purchasing Studies, 2004.

Handfield, R. and Giunipero, L., Purchasing Education and Training II, Center for Advanced Purchasing Studies, February, 2004.

Handfield, R. and Nichols, E., Key issues in global supply base management, *Industrial Marketing Management,* Vol. 32, No. 8, November 2003.

Handfield, R. and Nichols, E., *Supply Chain Redesign,* Upper Saddle River, NJ: Prentice-Hall, 2002.

Handfield, R. and Pannesi, R., Managing component life cycles in dynamic technological environments, *International Journal of Purchasing and Materials Management,* 20–27, Spring 1994.

Handfield, R., Straight, S., and Sterling, W., Reverse auctions: how do suppliers really feel about them? *Inside Supply Management,* 18–24, 2002.

Holm, D.B., Eriksson, K., and Johanson, J., Creating value through mutual commitment to business network relationships, *Strategic Management Journal,* 20, 467–486, 1999.

Kintner, E.W. and Lahr, J.L., *An Intellectual Property Law Primer,* New York: Macmillan, 1975, p. 6.

Kogut, B., Joint ventures: theoretical and empirical perspectives. *Strategic Management Journal* 9, 319–332, 1988.

Kotter, J.P., *Leading Change*, Cambridge, MA: HBS Press, 1996.

Krause and Handfield, Developing a World-Class Supply Base, Tempe, AZ: Center for Advanced Purchasing Studies, 1999, 7.

Lewicki, R.J. and Litterer, J.A., *Negotiation,* Homewood, IL: Irwin, 1985, pp. 45–47.

Maloni, M. and Benton, W.C., Power influences in the supply chain, *Journal of Business Logistics*, Vol. 21, No. 1, 2000.

Martin, J., Information Engineering, Savant Research Studies, Carnforth, Lancashire, England, 1986.

Menezes, S., *Purchasing Today,* January 2001, pp. 28–32.

Monczka, R., Handfield, R., Frayer, D., Ragatz, G., and Scannell, T., *New Product Development: Supplier Integration Strategies for Success*, Milwaukee, WI: ASQ Press, January 2000.

Monczka, R., Peterson, K., Handfield, R., and Ragatz, G., Determinants of successful vs. non-strategic supplier alliances, *Decision Science Journal* (special issue on "Supply Chain Linkages"), 29, 553–577, 1998.

Monczka, T. and Handfield, R., *Purchasing and Supply Chain Management*, Cincinnati, OH: South Western College Publishing, 1998, pp. 242–246.

Monczka, R., Trent, R., and Handfield, R., *Purchasing and Supply Chain Management,* 3rd ed., Cincinnati, OH: South Western College Publishing, 2004.

Nishiguchi, T., *Strategic Industrial Sourcing: The Japanese Advantage,* New York: Oxford University Press, 1994.

Nooteboom, B., Berger, H., and Noorderhaven, N.G. Effects of trust and governance on relational risk. *Academy of Management Journal* 40, 308–338, 1997.

Osborn, R.N. and Hagedoorn, J. The institutionalization and evolutionary dynamics of interorganizational alliances and networks. *Academy of Management Journal* 40, 261–278, 1997.

Peterson, K., Handfield, R., and Ragatz, G., A model of successful supplier integration into new product development, *Journal of Product Innovation Management*, 20, 284–299, 2003.

Rinehart, L., Eckert, J., Handfield, R., Page, T., and Atkin, T., An assessment of supplier-customer relationships, *Journal of Business Logistics*, Vol. 25, No. 1, 25–62, 2003.

Saxton, T., The effects of partner and relationship characteristics on alliance outcomes. *Academy of Management Journal* 40, 443–462, 1997.

Tabor, D., Strategic planning, *Parallax View*, Vol. 2, No. 8, http://www.chain-linkresearch.com/parallaxview/V2_08/home.htm.

Trent, R., Procurement and Supply Management Organizational Design Survey, Lehigh University, 2002.

Wallace, T.F., *Sales and Operations Planning — The How-To-Handbook*, Alexandria, VA: APICS, 1998.

Waxer, C., E-Negotiations are In, Price-only E-Auctions are Out, *iSource*, June 2001, 73–76.

Williamson, O., *The Economic Institutions of Capitalism: Firms, Markets, Relational Contracting*, New York: The Free Press, 1985.

Zajac, E.J. and Olsen, C.P., From transaction cost to transactional value analysis: implications for the study of interorganizational strategies. *Journal of Management Studies*, 30, 131–145, 1993.

Other Resources

A Global Study of Supply Chain Leadership and Its Impact on Business Performance, Accenture and INSEAD, White paper, 2003.

Corixa betters buy process with hosted e-procurement, *Purchasing*, June 19, 2003, pp. 36C2–36C4.

Fortune 1000 Foreign Companies (Dun and Bradstreet).

Making Business Processes Work, *The Wight Line Online Newsletter,* Issue 1, 2000.

Making Business Processes Work, *The Wight Line Online Newsletter,* Issue 2, 2000.

Paying Attention, *Traffic World*, 09-02-03.

Trade *Directories of the World* (Croner Publications).

Web sites

http://www.supplychainredesign.com

Supply Chain Resource Consortium (http://scrc.ncsu.edu)

Super Searchers on Competitive Intelligence (http://www.infotoday.com/super-searchers/ssci.htm) contains hundreds of links to good sources of information. There are free and fee-based sites for specific industries, financial data, news services, market research, university libraries, company profiles, and research tips, to name just a few.

Yahoo! Financial section (http://www.biz.yahoo.com).

Morningstar (http://www.morningstar.net).

Marketwatch (http://www.marketwatch.com).

411Stocks (http://www.411stocks.com).

The Street (http://www.thestreet.com).

Dun and Bradstreet (http://www.dnb.com).

http://www.prtm.com/pressreleases/2003/06.04.asp.

www.sec.gov/edgarhp.htm.

http://www.jeboyer.com/sandop.html.

Index

For Product Safety Concerns and Information please contact
our EU representative GPSR@taylorandfrancis.com Taylor & Francis
Verlag GmbH, Kaufingerstraße 24, 80331 München, Germany

T - #0018 - 230425 - C0 - 229/152/36 [38] - CB - 9780849327896 - Gloss Lamination